COST
ACCOUNTING

Concepts and Techniques
for Management

COST ACCOUNTING

Concepts and Techniques for Management

Larry N. Killough
Peat Marwick Professor of Accounting
Virginia Polytechnic Institute and
  State University

Wayne E. Leininger
Professor of Accounting
Virginia Polytechnic Institute and
  State University

Keith P. C. Lam

WEST PUBLISHING COMPANY
St. Paul   New York   Los Angeles   San Francisco

Copyeditor: Pat Hendricks
Composition: Parkwood Composition Service, Inc.
Artwork: Editing, Design & Production, Inc.
Cover: Delor Erickson

Library of Congress Cataloging-in-Publication Data

Killough, Larry N.
  Cost accounting.

  Includes index.
  1. Cost accounting.   I. Leininger, Wayne E.
II. Title.
HF5686.C8K488 1987   658.1'511   86-26677
ISBN 0-314-25865-5

To Irene and Dorothy

CONTENTS

CHAPTER **2**
INTRODUCTION TO COST TERMINOLOGY,
BEHAVIOR, AND ESTIMATION METHODS 20

CHAPTER **3**
THE COST-ACCOUNTING CYCLE
AND JOB-ORDER COSTING 44

CHAPTER **4**
PROCESS COSTING   82

CHAPTER **5**
ADDITIONAL PROCESS-COSTING TOPICS   112

CHAPTER **6**
SPECIAL COST-ALLOCATION PROBLEMS   144

PART II

CONCEPTS AND TECHNIQUES FOR
CONTROL   □   196

CHAPTER **7**
BUDGETING: THE KEY TO PLANNING AND
CONTROL   198

CHAPTER **8**
STANDARDS AND STANDARD COSTING   244

CHAPTER **9**
ADDITIONAL STANDARD-COSTING TOPICS   292

CHAPTER **17**
PERFORMANCE MEASUREMENT AND EVALUATION IN DIVISIONALIZED ORGANIZATIONS   576

CHAPTER **18**
TRANSFER PRICING IN DIVISIONALIZED ORGANIZATIONS   620

PREFACE

This revision is based on the authors' combined experience of thirty years in teaching cost accounting to undergraduate students. The text is designed to be used in cost accounting courses taken by accounting majors. It is assumed that students have completed one year of principles of accounting and have a basic knowledge of economics, business statistics, and mathematics.

In developing material for this book, our primary objective was to present a complete, consistent, and balanced coverage of cost accounting concepts and techniques. The reader is provided with a framework relating cost accounting to the management system. We have attempted to integrate this framework throughout the text. Strong emphasis is placed on the traditional cost accounting topics of job-order costing, processing costing, standard costing, direct costing, cost-volume-profit analysis, and budgeting. Thorough coverage is also provided in the areas of capital budgeting, linear programming, performance measurement, transfer pricing, cost allocation, and cost estimation using regression and learning curves.

Two chapters focusing attention on productivity measurement and management information systems, have been completely revised. The use of microcomputers is encouraged by providing templates for solving a wide variety of problems included in the text. The templates can be used with SuperCalc, Lotus 1-2-3, or Educate Ability, electronic spreadsheet software packages. These templates are available on diskettes from the publisher along with Educate-Ability, an integrated software package. The appendix also contains material that introduces the student to electronic spreadsheets and how they can be used to solve cost accounting problems. Those in-text problems for which we provide such computerized assistance in solving are indicated by means of a computer logo at the end of every chapter in the problem section.

All quantitative material is arranged so that it can be used to the extent desired. For those who desire to emphasize this area, advanced topics are offered either in the chapters or related appendices. Review problems are offered at the end of each chapter. An extensive glossary is also included.

The text and problems have been classroom tested. In addition, numerous additional problems are included in an instructor's guide written by Robert M. Brown. The instructor's guide also provides outlines, reading references, lecture suggestions and other supporting material. A study guide has been prepared for students' use by Professor Wallace R. Leese and Professor Karl Brugger at California State University-Chico.

The book is divided into five parts and contains sufficient material for a course or courses covering an academic year. Suggested course outlines are contained in the instructor's guide. The following is a brief overview of the material contained in each part.

Part I of the book includes six chapters and emphasizes cost accounting for cost accumulation and reporting purposes. The first chapter discusses the role of cost and management accounting in the management system and provides a rationale for material covered in the book. Chapter 2 introduces the students to cost terminology, cost behavior, and cost estimation methods.

Chapters 3 through 6 are largely concerned with product costing and cost allocation techniques. Chapter 3 covers the cost accounting cycle, cost accumulation procedures, and job order costing. Chapters 4 and 5 provide students with a sound introduction to basic process costing concepts and techniques, along with material on more difficult process costing situations. Chapter 6 contains a discussion on joint and by-product costing along with significant material on methods for solving the reciprocal service cost allocation problem. In appendix A to chapter 6, a review of matrix algebra is provided.

Part II contains four chapters devoted to control aspects of accounting. Chapter 7 introduces students to budgeting and focuses attention on significant practical and mechanical aspects of developing a master budget as well as providing material on behavioral aspects of budgeting. Responsibility accounting is also introduced at this point in the belief that a major control component of cost accounting is based on responsibility accounting, budgeting and standard costs.

Chapters 8, 9, and 10 focus attention on standard costing topics and direct (variable) costing. Standard costing is developed initially as a variation of the product costing systems covered in earlier chapters with standards implemented into the basic costing system. Then, material is presented which covers the control aspects of standard costing. While the coverage of variances is quite traditional, an attempt is made to clarify conceptual problems associated with the use of overhead variances. The direct costing chapter not only describes the basics of direct costing but also emphasizes problems associated with direct costing when actual costs are employed.

Part III includes material relating to concepts and techniques useful for planning and decision making. Chapter 11 covers cost-volume-profit relationships. Chapter 11 contains introductory material on the non-linear cost-volume-profit model and extensive analysis using the linear break-even model in different settings.

A logical extension of cost-volume-profit analysis, the scarce resource problem, is examined in Chapter 12, "The Product Mix Problem: A Linear Programming Solution." Material in the chapter demonstrates how the output from a linear programming solution can be used in preparing budgeted income statements and sensitivity analysis. An appendix to the chapter describes how the simplex algorithm is used in solving linear programming problems.

Chapter 13 contains a description of the special decision process. Examples concerning adding or dropping a product or department, make or buy decisions, and short-run pricing decisions are developed in the remainder of the chapter. Chapters 14 and 15 are capital budgeting chapters. The first of the two chapters outlines the complete capital expenditure decision framework. The balance of the chapter is devoted to capital budgeting evaluation models. Chapter 15 discusses some advanced topics in capital budgeting, including sensitivity and risk analysis.

Part IV is devoted to the general area of management control and policy. Chapter 16 highlights management information systems. A detailed description of a management information system is presented at the conclusion of this chapter. Inputs and outputs of the various systems are described in detail. Chapter 17 contains an introduction to the organizational structure of a divisionalized organization. Performance measures employed in cost, profit and investment centers are discussed and evaluated in detail. Chapter 18 presents an overview of the transfer pricing problem along with a description of the different methods of basing transfer prices.

We believe a major contribution to cost accounting education is made with the inclusion of chapter 19 on productivity measurement. This chapter contains introductory material concerning the productivity problem and how productivity is measured. The concluding sections of the chapter demonstrate how productivity measures can be developed using actual and standard labor hours.

Part V, "Quantitative Models for Cost and Profit Analysis," includes material on use of costs in inventory decisions, cost estimation by linear regression and learning curves. Chapter 20 focuses attention on the EOQ model and static inventory problems under risk. Chapter 21 provides a linear discussion of how simple regression is employed in cost estimation. An appendix contains information on multiple regression. Chapter 22 contains a description of the average-time and marginal time learning curve models. The potential impact of the learning curves on standard costs is fully developed in the chapter.

□ SIGNIFICANT CHANGES IN THIS EDITION

Several changes have been made in this edition in both content and organization. A few chapters have been completely rewritten. Several new problems have been added. Significant changes include:

1. The format used in solving process costing problems has been revised. These changes are reflected in Chapters 4 and 5.

2. A new section, "Standards and Process Costing" has been added to Chapter 8.

3. Chapter 10, "Productivity Measurement and Cost Accounting," included in the original edition has been rewritten and is now included in Chapter 19 in the revised edition.

4. The chapter on "Management Information Systems" has been revised and updated to reflect current thinking on the topic.

5. Appendix A, "Use of Electronic Spreadsheets," has been updated and the software support has been revised and expanded. Educate-Ability, an integrated software package will be provided to faculty using the book.

6. Material is included in Chapter 20 on "Just in Time Inventory Systems."

☐ **ACKNOWLEDGMENTS**

We gratefully acknowledge the kind permission of the American Institute of Certified Public Accountants to use and adopt material from CPA Examinations. We gratefully acknowledge the kind permission of the Institute of Management Accounting of the National Association of Accountants to use and adopt material from CMA Examinations.

We appreciate the efforts of Samuel A. Hicks, Jr. in the preparation of the appendix on use of electronic spreadsheets using Lotus 1-2-3, SuperCalc, and Educate-Ability. He also prepared the templates needed to solve specified problems in the book, using the different software packages.

We are indebted to numerous people for their contributions and encouragement. The following people also helped to shape this book by reviewing the manuscript prior to publication: Karl Brugger, California State University; Philip G. Cottell, Miami University; Robert P. Crum, Penn State University; Paul Sheldon Foote, New York University; Lyle Jacobsen, California State University-Hayward; Neil E. McNeill, University of Missouri-Kansas City; Fred Nordhauser, University of Texas-San Antonio; Victor Powers, California State University-Chico, Marlane K. Sanderson, Moorehead State University; Lamont Steedle, James Madison University; Jan Sweeney, CUNY-Bauch College; H. David Willis, Virginia Commonwealth University.

A special note of gratitude is expressed to Esther Craig and Dick Fenton of West Publishing Company. They have worked closely with us since the inception of the project and have made many creative suggestions that have been incorporated into the text. Their professional approach and continuous encouragement were necessary motivating forces over the life of this project. It has been a pleasure to work with them, and we hope that the final product in some way justifies their faith in our abilities. We wish to thank Bill Gabler, Production Editor, for his many valuable suggestions, patience, and encouragement. He established a realistic schedule and did a terrific job of coordinating the project.

Appreciation is extended to Bernadette Ruf for the many hours she spent typing and correcting the solutions manual. Several students helped in developing and evaluating the material for the book. David Albrecht and Mung Chiu were particularly helpful and deserve a special word of thanks.

Finally, we wish to thank our wives, Irene and Dorothy, who each in their own way allowed us to redirect time normally spent with them so that we could complete this project. Their encouragement, unselfishness, and counsel were necessary so that we could maintain a burdensome work schedule and be reminded that the revision would be completed.

L. N. K.

W. E. L.

COST ACCOUNTING

Concepts and Techniques
for Management

PART I

COST ACCOUNTING FOR COST ACCUMULATION AND REPORTING

PART OUTLINE

CHAPTER OUTLINE

THE ROLE OF ACCOUNTING IN THE MANAGEMENT SYSTEM

CHAPTER 1

☐ INTRODUCTION

Because of changes taking place in today's business environment, maintaining the ability to meet informational needs of management may well be the most important challenge facing the professional accountant in the next five to ten years. The accountant will have to consider questions such as the following: Are our standard costs acceptable for financial reporting purposes? Why are we allocating these costs to manufacturing? Of what value are these financial reports? Which of our two plywood manufacturing facilities, the one in Oregon or the one in Georgia, should be discontinued in order to consolidate company manufacturing facilities? How many of our new laser disk players must we sell to break-even? What effect will a lag in the industrywide production of compact disks have on the sale of our disk players? Do we have too much investment tied up in inventory? Are EOQ models outdated by just-in-time inventory systems? How can we establish an effective control system in our service-oriented company?

In a general way, this book is intended to improve the accountant's ability to meet the needs of various users of financial information. It focuses specifically on the concepts and techniques used by management accountants to provide product-costing information for financial reporting purposes, as well as on the concepts and techniques needed to provide information to management for planning and control decisions.

In this introductory chapter the relationships among financial, cost, and management accounting are explored. We describe a management decision-making framework, and then discuss the function of accounting within that framework in order to highlight the importance of the accountant's contribution to management. Finally, the chapter contains general information on the professional role of the management accountant.

☐ THE COMPONENTS OF ACCOUNTING

The major components of accounting might be viewed in the following manner:

3

The schematic suggests that cost accounting acts as a connection between financial and management accounting. Although this may be an oversimplification of the relationships involved, it does indicate that cost accounting encompasses a body of concepts and techniques used in both financial and management accounting.

Financial Accounting

The primary purpose of **financial accounting** is to provide information on (1) the results of company operations and (2) the company's financial position. Financial statements must conform to generally accepted accounting principles that are established by the Financial Accounting Standards Board. Information contained in the statements is in large part directed to external parties for investment, compliance, or tax-collection purposes.

Cost Accounting

Cost accounting plays a role in financial reporting because product costs are often a significant component in determining the operating results and financial position of an organization. Cost allocation is also important in financial statement preparation. Overall, cost accounting is concerned with cost estimation, cost-allocation methods, and product-cost determination.

Management Accounting

The primary focus of **management accounting** is on supplying information for management planning and control. Basically, management accounting deals with the following functions:

1. *Cost estimation.* In management accounting, the emphasis on cost estimation is for planning or control purposes rather than for financial reporting.

2. *Planning.* Planning might involve decisions on adding a product, service, or facilities; or similar decisions. Management accounting input is generally required for such decisions.

3. *Cost control.* The management accountant must monitor costs in some effective fashion so that one can determine whether costs are reasonable for the activities performed.

4. *Performance measurement.* Management-accounting information is used to evaluate managerial performance. Information is supplied to help an-

swer questions such as, Did management earn an adequate return on assets? Did management comply with regulations?

5. *Management motivation.* An important aspect of management control is concern for goal congruence. Standards, budgets, and performance-measurement methods should be developed with proper motivation in mind.

6. *Systems development.* Accounting systems that are consistent with management planning, control, and reporting needs must be developed.

While differences exist between cost and management accounting, as indicated, the two terms are used interchangeably by both academicians and practitioners. To eliminate cumbersome terminology, we have chosen to use the term *management accounting* to mean both cost and management accounting. This use is consistent with the following definition of management accounting by the National Association of Accountants:

> Management Accounting is the process of identification, measurement, accumulation, analysis, preparation, interpretation, and communication of financial information used by management to plan, evaluate, and control within an organization and to assure appropriate use of and accountability for its resources. Management accounting also comprises the preparation of financial reports for nonmanagement groups such as shareholders, creditors, regulatory agencies, and tax authorities.[1]

☐ THE MANAGEMENT DECISION-MAKING FRAMEWORK

Management accounting's orientation requires that its study be based on an understanding of the management environment and decision-making framework. Although specific uses of accounting develop from the organizational structure, complexity, and management found within a particular organization, a basic framework can be generalized.

Managers make use of goals, objectives, plans, budgets, and types of controls in carrying out their responsibilities. One way of looking at the complete system is to diagram the various components of management to show relationships. Numerous authors have focused attention on management decision making and have created terminology to describe aspects of this management function. Most authors agree that decision making is the essence of management and that managers make decisions within a basic planning and control framework.

An understanding of the decision-making framework is provided by working with its three basic components, namely, **strategic planning, management control,** and **operating control.**[2] Using these components, the de-

---

1. *Objectives of Management Accounting,* Statements on Management Accounting, Statement Number 1B, June 17, 1982, National Association of Accountants, p. 1.

2. Foundation for these concepts was provided by Robert N. Anthony, *Planning and Control Systems—A Framework for Analysis* (Boston: Division of Research, Graduate School of Business Administration, Harvard University, 1965).

FIGURE 1.1
Management
System Framework

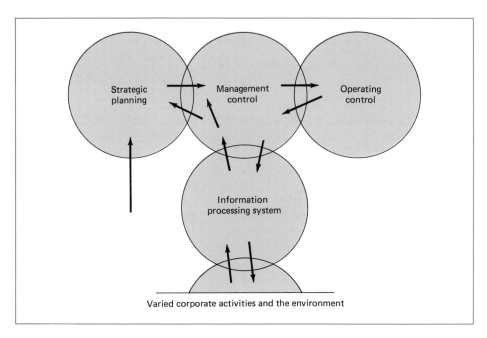

Varied corporate activities and the environment

cision-making framework can be viewed as shown in figure 1.1. These components simply take planning and control—terms that are commonly used in the business environment—and attempt to identify different levels of use or need. For instance, strategic planning (goal setting) takes place at top-level management, and continuous planning (developing programs and budgets) occurs within management control. Control also is broken down between control over people (management control) and mechanical control over specific jobs or departments (operating control). More specific comments follow about each of these areas.

Strategic Planning

Through strategic planning, basic objectives for the entity are established. Management of a business, governmental, or nonprofit entity decides at a fairly high management level what kind of product or service they intend to provide and who the beneficiaries will be. Typically, only key personnel are involved at this level, and planning is not considered to be continuous or formally structured. Although the process might be given a different name or merged with other processes, some form of strategic planning is necessary in all business activities.

Very often, accounting information is not a significant factor at the strategic level. Figure 1.1 depicts strategic planning as the initial element in the management system and indicates that guidelines for the major programs to be undertaken are a major output of strategic planning.

Assume, for instance, that the top management of Pine Fashions Company, a manufacturer of quality furniture, believes it would be in the company's best interest to expand into the home building business. Various alternatives and their expected returns are considered. A decision is reached and approved by the board of directors. Ultimately, the company acquires a prefabricated home building company.

Planning of this nature represents strategic planning. In making the decision, management probably looked at projections on home building in general and specifically at companies they may have considered acquiring. After purchasing the home building company, management establishes certain objectives and guidelines for the new segment of Pine Fashions Company.

Management Control

In figure 1.1, note that management control provides a basic structure for controlling the day-to-day activities of a firm. The management-control system encompasses all the activities involved in acquiring the various resources of a firm and insuring that they are used in an effective and efficient manner.

Implied in this phase of the management process are long- and short-range planning activities, which lead to the establishment of programs, standards, budgeting, and control activities. Annual programs are developed and operating budgets are established and communicated to all levels of management. The company acquires resources and plans their efficient use. Control systems are implemented to monitor day-to-day activities. In the management-control process, output from the accounting system provides managers with performance-measurement information as they make decisions and take actions that are expected to lead to desired results.

Continuing with the example of Pine Fashions Company, programs for the home building segment would have to be established for some reasonable time period. Depending upon the type of organizational structure, responsibility for the programs might reside with centralized management (decisions made at top-level management) or decentralized management (moving decision making to the lowest practical management level). Assuming the acquired management had expertise and knowledge of the home building business not available to top-level management at Pine Fashions Company, responsibility for the programs would probably be delegated to management of the home building company, within guidelines established by top-level management. Once programs were developed, operating budgets would be established and approved. The resulting budgets would serve as the basis for performance measurement for all levels of supervision within the home building segment of the company. Specific control techniques and measurement methods would be established to encourage managers to make decisions compatible with guidelines established by top-level management.

Operating Control

This phase of the management process provides the mechanism needed to see that individual jobs or projects are carried out within the framework of previously defined criteria. A distinction between management control and operating control is difficult to make because techniques initially used for management-control purposes may become more significant for operating-control purposes.

For instance, in the home building example, budgets and standards were established for the home building business as a result of programs accepted. Certain inventory levels would be set for some of the home building materials by using inventory-management techniques to satisfy budgetary needs. Subsequent control over these materials would then be established by decision rules predicated on economic-order quantities and reorder points.

The establishment of the budget is a management-control function; subsequent control over ordering becomes an operating-control function. At this point you should begin to realize that control techniques can be directed to different levels within an organization and to either people or processes.

☐ MANAGEMENT ACCOUNTING IN THE MANAGEMENT PROCESS

Management accounting should be viewed as an information-providing component within the management decision-making framework. An important responsibility of management accounting is to provide information needed for planning and control. In fulfilling this role, the accountant uses various techniques, beyond those required for financial reporting, to develop information for decision makers at different levels in the management structure. Figure 1.2 outlines some of the management-accounting techniques discussed in this book and where they might be used within the management decision-making framework.

FIGURE 1.2 Relation of Accounting Techniques to Management Needs

	Strategic planning	Management control	Operating control	Financial reporting
Cost-estimation methods	X	X	X	
Master budgets		X		X
Cost-allocation methods				X
Product-cost-determination systems				X
Standard costing and variance analysis		X	X	X
Cost-volume-profit analysis	X	X	X	
Capital budgeting, cost/benefit analysis	X	X		
Responsibility accounting		X	X	
Performance-evaluation methods		X	X	
Scarce-resource allocation techniques		X	X	
Inventory-management techniques		X	X	
Special decision analysis	X	X		

Although certain accounting techniques are used at the strategic-planning level, such use is extremely limited because of the nature of decision making at that level. Numerous accounting techniques are initially used at the management-control level, although most typically center around budgeting, responsibility accounting, and performance measurement. After initial use as management-control techniques, many are then used in the operating-control stage on a continuing basis. Now that we have reviewed in a general way where accounting fits within the management structure, we can examine management accounting more specifically.

☐ THE MANAGEMENT-ACCOUNTING FRAMEWORK

The environment of management accounting may be thought of as diverse sets of groups, organizations, and companies that have goals and that operate under conditions of uncertainty. Under such conditions, decision making becomes the essence of management. *The minimization of uncertainty surrounding the decision becomes the challenge of the management accountant.*

As you begin to understand management accounting and to make use of the techniques, concepts relevant to the area will become more significant. For instance, in this chapter we have already used the terms **measurement, communication, information,** and **cost** along with various other concepts in discussing management accounting. These concepts provide part of the structure needed for an understanding of management accounting. The following definitions are provided for your reference.

1. *Measurement.* Defined as a "special language which represents real world phenomena by means of numbers and relations of numbers that are predetermined within the number system."[3] In an accounting sense, it refers to the assignment of numbers to an entity's economic phenomena based on observations and according to rules.[4]

2. *Communication.* This concept identifies "the procedure by means of which one mechanism affects another mechanism," or in effect "the procedures by which one mind may affect another."[5]

3. *Information.* While the product of a management-accounting system should always be evaluated in terms of its informational content, the concepts mean different things to different people. Useful information is that which reduces uncertainty on the part of the decision maker.

---

3. Yuji Ijiri, *The Foundations of Accounting Measurement* (Englewood Cliffs, N.J.: Prentice-Hall, 1967), p. 19.

4. "Report of the Committee on Foundations of Accounting Measurement," *The Accounting Review,* Supplement to Vol. 46 (1971):3.

5. Claude E. Shannon and Warren Weaver, *The Mathematical Theory of Communication* (Urbana, Ill.: The University of Illinois Press, 1949), p. 95.

4. *Systems.* A system represents a number of objects with an identifiable relationship between the objects and the properties. Only when one understands that management accounting is contained within a structure of systems, subsystems, and smaller elements is one in a position to relate the subject matter to the other components and to recognize their interrelationship. Management-accounting systems are part of the overall information and management systems of an entity.

5. *Planning.* Planning, because of its diverse elements, is difficult to define in an operational manner. However, it may be generally thought of as the development of goals and the establishment of operational guidelines within restrictions imposed by technology and the environment.

6. *Control.* Control represents the monitored state of a system, or alternatively one might suggest that it permits the conformance of action to plans. Ideally, its components consist of criteria derived from planning, a mechanism for feedback, and some systematic output.

7. *Cost.* Cost refers to "some type of measured sacrifice evolving from an operational sequence of events and centering upon a particular activity or product."[6] More simply stated, it might represent a release of value in order to generate some benefit.

A model for management accounting is shown in figure 1.3. The structure, including the information system, has been outlined in the preceding material. Subsequent chapters of the book will develop the techniques indicated in figure 1.2 and related problem-solving applications.

☐ THE ROLE OF THE MANAGEMENT ACCOUNTANT

Now that a review of the management system and the role of accounting within the framework has been completed, some insight into the specific roles accountants may assume within organizations is necessary. As might be expected, many accountants have moved beyond basic accounting responsibilities to become top executives in industry and government. Indeed, many former accountants hold key positions in nonaccounting jobs. However, in this introduction we are primarily concerned with the titles and responsibilities held by accountants in accounting positions.

The Organizational Chart

Management uses the organizational chart to set forth key positions and to help in the definition of authority and responsibility. In your exposure to management, you will learn that many different ways exist for structuring an organization. The chart in figure 1.4 is based on a simple line-staff relationship in which line management (marketing and production)

6. Wilber E. Haseman, "An Interpretative Framework for Cost," *The Accounting Review* (October 1968):742–43.

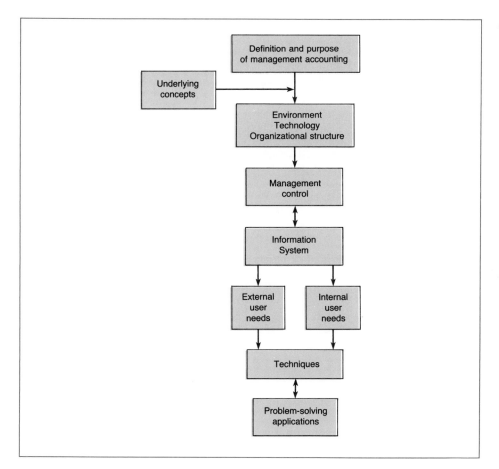

FIGURE 1.3
A Model for
Management
Accounting

makes decisions regarding production and sales, while the other groups (finance, research and development, employee relations) provide assistance or perform other necessary support functions.

Figure 1.5 shows a breakdown of functions within the financial vice-president role. Two major management categories report to the financial vice-president: treasurer and controller. While accountants may be found in both positions, accountants are more typically in the controller position, and those with a background in finance are in the treasurer position. It may be helpful to outline responsibilities associated with these two positions.

Duties of the Controller and Treasurer

The *controller* has the primary responsibility for the development and communication of financial information. As can be seen from figure 1.5, the controller typically has staff responsibility for financial, management, and tax accounting. Usually included within the controllership function is responsibility for systems, procedures, and budgeting. Even the internal audit function is sometimes included within the controllership function.

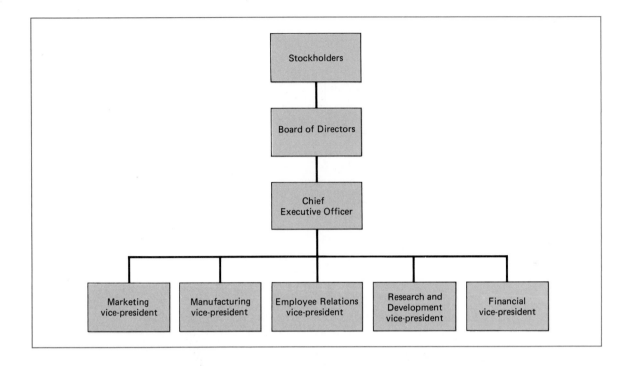

FIGURE 1.4
Sample
Organization of
Top-Management
Functions
However, internal auditors should report directly to the Board of Directors because they should, on occasion, review the actions of top management, including the controller and financial vice-president.

The *treasurer* is responsible for custody of fund flows. Responsibilities include investments, banking and credit policies, insurance, and sometimes economic analysis.

Other Accounting Positions

As management accountants move into middle and upper management, they may achieve one of the positions indicated in figure 1.5. Usually an entry-level management accountant will begin a career in one of the following (or similar) categories:

1. *Internal auditor.* Internal auditors may work in a variety of areas. They perform both financial and management audits. Internal auditors are often called upon to act as troubleshooters to develop information regarding problem areas.

2. *Cost analyst.* As the title implies, cost analysts work within the product-cost-determination systems to establish and monitor cost-accounting activities.

3. *General accountant.* The general accountant may perform a number of different jobs relating to financial accounting: accounts receivable, ac-

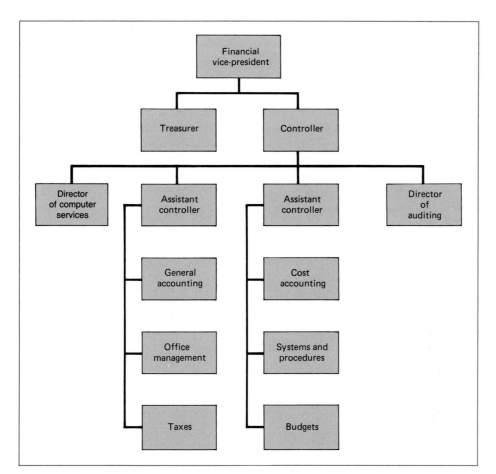

FIGURE 1.5
Sample
Organizational
Chart of Financial
Vice-President
Function

counts payable, property plant and equipment, inventory, payroll, or financial analysis.

4. *Systems analyst.* Accountants entering the field in this area usually have had a good educational background in accounting information systems and programming. They work with members of the various functional areas to provide timely reports relevant to the needs of management.

This outline of job descriptions should provide you with an understanding of the specific jobs performed by accountants within an organization. In an organizational setting, an individual is not typically labeled as a financial, cost, or management accountant. In many situations, an accountant may have some responsibility for all three functions. In other situations, job responsibilities may be much more limited. The important thing to understand is that an accountant is usually in a good position to gain an overall understanding of the operations of the business. That is why accounting and finance positions are considered "fast track" paths to middle and top management.

☐ PROFESSIONALIZATION OF MANAGEMENT ACCOUNTING

The National Association of Accountants (NAA) was founded in 1919 and has long been recognized as the primary management-accounting organization in the United States. Over the years, numerous research studies relating to the field of management accounting have been funded and published by the NAA. *Management Accounting*, one of the leading accounting journals, is published on a monthly basis by this organization.

The NAA created the Management Accounting Practices Committee (MAP) in 1969 as its primary technical committee. One of its current charges is to provide authoritative guidance to members of NAA and to the overall business community on matters relating to management-accounting concepts, policies, and practices.

A number of Statements on Management Accounting (SMAs) have been issued by MAP, beginning with initial statements on a definition of management accounting, objectives of management accounting, standards of ethical conduct, and management-accounting terminology. Subsequent to these initial statements, MAP published several others relating to problems and techniques.

In 1972, the Institute of Certified Management Accountants, formerly called the Institute of Management Accounting, was created by the NAA to develop and administer the certified management accountant program. This program is discussed in more detail in the next section. The program has been highly successful, and today several thousand accountants are CMAs. A number of major corporations prefer that their new accounting executives be certified management accountants.

As you can see, with the NAA serving as the major management-accounting organization, providing a professional examination, a code of ethics, overall standards, an official journal, and statements dealing with relevant issues, management accounting has emerged as a major partner in the accounting profession. Other professional-accounting programs are mentioned in the next section.

☐ THE MANAGEMENT ACCOUNTANT AND PROFESSIONAL EXAMINATIONS

Several different approaches to professional certification are open to people pursuing careers in management accounting. If you expect to successfully complete any of the examinations, you must develop an understanding of (1) cost terminology, behavior, and estimation; (2) product-cost-determination systems; (3) control techniques, including variance analysis within a framework of standards, budgets, and responsibility accounting; (4) internal and management control; and (5) a general understanding of quantitative techniques used by management accountants.

An individual can pursue several professional certification programs. A brief description of each follows:

Certified Management Accountant (CMA)

The CMA is offered through the Institute of Management Accounting of the National Association of Accountants. It is regarded as the primary professional designation for management accountants and financial managers. To qualify to sit for the examination, a person must hold a baccalaureate degree, or achieve a satisfactory score on either the Graduate Record Examination or Graduate Management Admissions Test, or be a Certified Public Accountant. Certificates are awarded to candidates who pass all five parts of the examination and who, within an acceptable time period, complete two years of related management-accounting experience.

Certified Public Accountant (CPA)

The CPA is offered and regulated by the individual state Boards of Accountancy. The CPA is the professional designation for people employed in the public accounting profession and is regarded by many as the trademark of all professional accountants. To qualify to take the examination, a person must generally hold a baccalaureate degree. Certificates are awarded to those who pass all four parts of the examination, which is prepared and graded by the American Institute of Certified Public Accountants, and to those who satisfy professional experience requirements administered by the individual state Boards of Accountancy.

Certified Internal Auditor (CIA)

The CIA has been offered by the Institute of Internal Auditors since 1974 and is currently being administered in several different countries. To become a CIA, a candidate must pass a four-part examination. As with the other two professional designations, candidates must have completed an undergraduate degree or its equivalent and have two years of relevant experience.

□ SUMMARY

The management process consists of strategic planning, management control, and operating control. By means of accounting, information is provided to decision makers in each component of the management structure. Accounting procedures used are derived from certain basic concepts, which include measurement, communication, and information.

In the overall relationship between accounting and management, accounting provides information through budgeting, investment analysis, and other techniques at the planning level. As specific organizational components are developed, accounting personnel may provide input on the best organizational arrangement from the standpoint of communications and control. During actual operations, accounting has the primary responsibility for accumulating data on operations and transforming it into information. Finally, accounting is responsible for providing information to be used in evaluating performance.

Within the overall organization, the financial vice-presidential function is usually the top accounting-related position. Typically, both the controller and treasurer report to the financial vice-president. The treasurer has primary responsibility for fund flows, while the controller has responsibility for the development and communication of financial information.

Graduates usually begin their accounting careers in entry-level positions such as general accountant, cost analyst, or internal auditor. A career in management accounting can be enhanced by obtaining a professional certification relevant to the field. Such designations include CMA, CPA, or CIA.

KEY TERMS

Communication	Management accounting
Cost	Management control
Cost accounting	Measurement
Financial accounting	Operating control
Information	Strategic planning

REVIEW PROBLEM

The management team at the Hooper Company is in the process of reorganizing its financial organization. They are planning to create a new position, namely, financial vice-president. Currently, the controller and treasurer report directly to the president. Included within the controller's and treasurer's organization are the following functions:

1. Internal audit manager
2. Information systems manager
3. Chief accountant
4. Purchasing director
5. Credit manager
6. Cost analyst manager
7. Budget manager
8. Tax manager
9. Personnel director
10. Financial analyst manager

Required □

1. Identify the functions that should not report to either the controller or treasurer.
2. Set up an organizational chart for the financial vice-presidential function.

Solution ☐

1. Purchasing director
Personnel director
Information systems manager
Internal audit manager

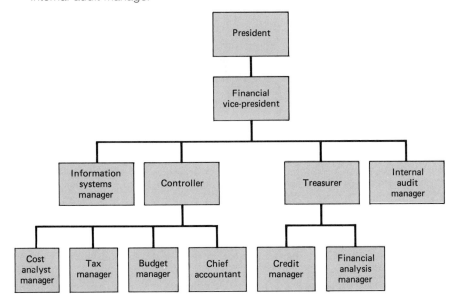

Note: Arguments could be offered for not including the internal audit manager
or the information systems manager in the Financial vice-president's organizational chart.

QUESTIONS

Q1-1. Identify and define the components of the management system.

Q1-2. In what phase of the management system does accounting play the most
important role? Why?

Q1-3. Within the management system, a number of subcomponents are required.
Identify these subcomponents.

Q1-4. Identify the basic concepts that are essential for an understanding of management accounting.

Q1-5. Why can we describe cost accounting as a link between financial accounting
and management accounting? Discuss fully.

Q1-6. Define cost accounting.

Q1-7. Define management accounting.

Q1-8. Identify some of the various accounting techniques used in management
accounting and how they might be employed to help management.

Q1-9. What is the role of accounting in the evaluation process?

Q1-10. Based on your understanding of accounting, develop an alternative to the organizational chart shown in figure 1.5. Justify your chart.

Q1-11. Describe the functions of the controller and treasurer.

Q1-12. Identify several entry-level positions for management accountants.

Q1-13. What management-level positions are available to accountants?

Q1-14. In your own words, describe the role of the management accountant.

Q1-15. You have just been employed by a major university to discuss accounting and accounting careers with new students. A new student and her parents are in your office seeking advice. After proper introductions, her father indicates he has heard people talk about financial accounting, cost accounting, and management accounting. He asks you to describe these different areas of accounting.

Required ☐ Provide a proper response to the father's request.

Q1-16. Mr. Konrad, president of Deepwater Loading, Inc., has called you regarding a significant problem facing him. He has recently been informed by the town manager that he must install a loading crane if he is to keep the franchise for the city's deepwater loading facility. The town manager revealed that another group would like to take over operations and has offered to install the crane and to increase payments to the city for the privilege of operating the facility.

Required ☐ Prepare a report for Mr. Konrad that outlines some of the significant informational needs relating to his problem.

CHAPTER OUTLINE

INTRODUCTION TO COST TERMINOLOGY, BEHAVIOR, AND ESTIMATION METHODS

CHAPTER 2

☐ INTRODUCTION

As indicated in chapter 1, managers need accounting information for planning and control, as well as for financial reporting purposes. The role of the management accountant is to provide this required information. Most often, the information called for has to do with costs of organizational activities. Costs related to recurring financial reporting practices are generally understood by the financial-report users. However, for various product-costing activities and for planning and control purposes, many types of costs exist that are classified in a variety of ways. This chapter provides a basic understanding of the various cost classifications and the ways in which they are used to meet the needs of management personnel.

☐ COST TERMINOLOGY AND BEHAVIOR

Even though **cost** is one of the more frequently used terms in management accounting, it is extremely difficult to define. A committee of the American Accounting Association wrote: "Cost is foregoing, measured in monetary terms, incurred or potentially to be incurred, to achieve a specific objective."[1] In the preceding chapter, cost was defined as "some type of measured sacrifice evolving from an operational sequence of events and centering upon a particular activity or product." From these definitions we might conclude that costs are incurred for purposes of deriving some benefits. Obviously *cost* standing alone is a difficult concept to understand, but it can be made more understandable by providing a modifier such as *variable, fixed, product, period, controllable, direct, indirect,* or some other term. These descriptions aid in identifying the reason for measuring and communicating cost information. For an example of the many variations of cost, refer to figure 2.1.

The framework indicates that cost information must be categorized according to the object being costed before the information can be used in identifying specific cost needs. While we will not attempt to define and

---

1. Report of the Committee on Cost Concepts and Standards, vol. XXVII, p. 176.

FIGURE 2.1
Framework for
Cost Terminology
Source: Adapted from
Wilber C. Haseman,
"An Interpretive
Framework For Cost,"
The Accounting
Review, *October*
1968, p. 251.

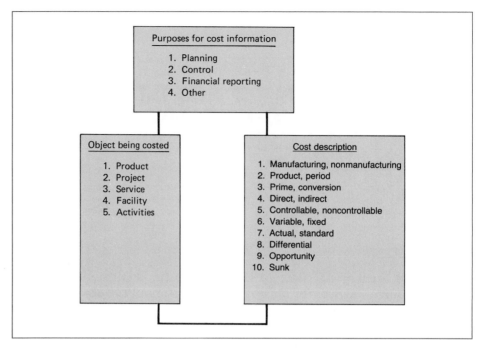

explain all the terminology at this point, some should be understood as a prerequisite for studying the next several chapters. Other terms will be discussed at the time they are introduced in chapter material.

Manufacturing Costs and Nonmanufacturing Costs

Costs are an integral part of all organizations—whether business, governmental, manufacturing, merchandising, or service oriented. The vast majority of the material in this book assumes a manufacturing environment, but most of the techniques developed are equally applicable to other types of organizations.

In the manufacturing process, basic materials are transformed into a marketable product. Three cost components—direct material, direct labor, manufacturing overhead—are involved. We usually include within the classification of **direct material** only those materials that become a significant component of the finished product and can be specifically traced to the product. For example, wood used in desks, glass in windows, and plastic in telephones are typically classified as direct materials. We can trace other items such as screws in desks, putty in glass windows, and soldering in telephones to the finished product, but only at a significant expense. Such items would likely be regarded as indirect materials and classified as part of manufacturing overhead.

Likewise, only those labor costs directly identified with manufacturing the product are considered **direct labor.** The labor costs of production line workers, carpenters, and brickmasons would be direct labor costs. Indirect labor would typically include costs of supervisory, maintenance, and janitorial personnel. The efforts of indirect personnel are essential to the manufacturing process, but they cannot be traced directly to the product. Such costs become part of manufacturing overhead.

Manufacturing overhead includes all costs other than direct material and direct labor that can be identified with the manufacturing process. We have already mentioned that indirect material and indirect labor are classified as manufacturing overhead. Examples of other overhead costs would be depreciation on manufacturing facilities, energy costs, plant taxes, insurance, maintenance, and repairs. Remember that although manufacturing overhead is included in manufacturing costs, it must be allocated to the product.

A company that produces products for sale also incurs nonmanufacturing costs. Generally, nonmanufacturing costs are classified as either marketing or administrative costs. Marketing costs are incurred in the process of selling the finished product and getting it to the customer. Advertising, promotion, commissions, travel, shipping, and depreciation of sales equipment are all examples of marketing costs. Administrative costs would generally include items not classified as manufacturing or marketing costs. Within this category we would include executive compensation, accounting and computer services, personnel, and other costs associated with overall administration.

All marketing and administrative costs are treated as **period costs;** they are recognized as expenses in the period in which they are incurred. Product costs (direct material, direct labor, and manufacturing overhead), on the other hand, are inventoried (expensed only when the product is sold).

Apply what we have just discussed about cost classification to the following situation: Lawrence Jingle decides to go into the potato chip business. He will need to acquire plant facilities (plant and manufacturing equipment), labor, and materials in order to manufacture the chips. Additionally, he will need office facilities along with office staff and marketing personnel. Retailers will have to be convinced to purchase his product. Direct materials, direct labor, and manufacturing overhead will be used to produce the potato chips. Salaries of office and marketing personnel, along with related expenses, will be incurred in operating the business and selling the potato chips. To the extent finished inventory is not sold, the finished inventory cost will represent an unexpired cost. However, when the chips are subsequently sold, their cost—along with the other expenses of operating the business—represent cost expirations. These relationships are shown in figure 2.2.

Sometimes, in cost-accounting jargon, manufacturing-cost components are classified as **prime costs** (direct material and direct labor) or **conversion costs** (direct labor and manufacturing overhead). Product costs are accumulated either on a *full (absorption) costing* (direct material, direct labor, fixed overhead, and variable overhead), or *direct (variable) costing* (direct material, direct labor, and variable overhead) basis.

Direct and Indirect Costs

A **direct cost** represents a cost incurred for a specific purpose that is uniquely traceable to that purpose. We learned earlier that material and labor that

FIGURE 2.2
Lawrence Jingle
Company
Relationship of
Product and
Period Costs to
Income
Determination

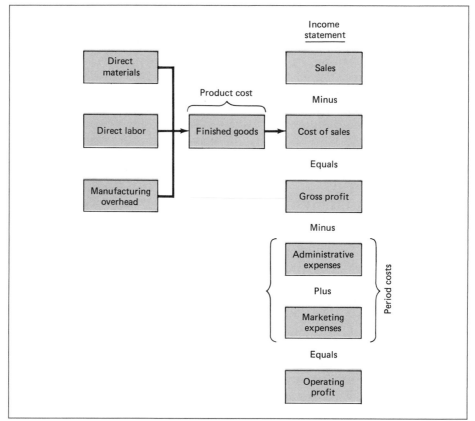

can be traced to a specific product being produced are direct costs of production. The cost of secretaries working in a controller's office is considered a direct cost of the controller's department.

The salary of the manager of a day-care center would be considered a direct cost of the center. However, if the center were broken down into departments by different age groups with a part of the manager's salary being allocated to each department, the salary would be an *indirect cost* of each of the individual departments. This is because part of the manager's salary was allocated to each of the departments on some arbitrary basis.

In many situations, service departments exist to provide some type of support or service to manufacturing departments. For reporting or product-costing purposes, costs of service departments may be allocated to the manufacturing departments. Costs allocated from service departments to the manufacturing departments are indirect costs of the manufacturing departments.

We might then define an **indirect cost** as a cost that is associated with more than one activity or product but a cost that cannot be traced specifically to any one of the activities or products.

Controllable and Noncontrollable Costs

There is some level in any organization where management has the ability to determine if costs will be incurred. All costs are controllable by someone in the organization given a sufficiently long time frame. At lower levels in the organization, costs assigned to the manager of a department may contain both controllable and noncontrollable elements.

Controllable costs are defined as those costs that can be significantly influenced by a manager. For instance, the supervisor of a producing department of a plant might exercise significant control over the cost of materials, labor, maintenance, and power within the department, but might have little or no control over the cost of taxes and insurance charged to the department. Although it is often difficult to make a clear distinction between *controllable* and *noncontrollable costs* by departments or managers, it is an important concept in developing accounting-control systems.

Variable and Fixed Costs

Whether providing information for product costing or management decision-making purposes, one of the management accountant's most important jobs is to analyze cost behavior. This kind of classification indicates how costs react or respond to changes in levels of business activity within a relevant range. The **relevant range** is the range of activity in which the cost (dependent variable) and activity relationships (independent variable) are considered valid. As activity levels change, certain costs change, while others remain constant.

In attempting to relate costs to activity, four basic cost and activity relationships are often considered. These relationships, as presented in figure 2.3, provide a classification of cost behavior that is useful for product-costing purposes as well as for planning and control.

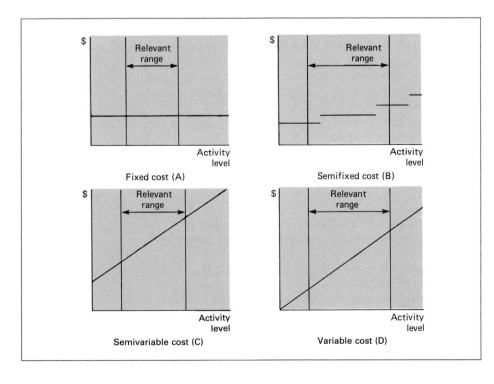

FIGURE 2.3
Cost Behavior Patterns within a Relevant Range

Fixed costs are outlined in figure 2.3(A). The figure indicates there is no change in fixed costs with changes in activity. Fixed cost levels are usually tied to time periods and capacity levels rather than to activity levels. For instance, salaries are typically fixed for a reasonable period of time. Depreciation expense is likely to be related to time periods. However, both of these costs will likely change if production is expanded beyond a certain level. Property taxes and rent expense are other examples of fixed costs.

If a cost changes directly in response to changes in the activity measure being used, it is called a **variable cost.** At zero activity there would be no variable costs. Then, as units of activity are increased, the related costs are expected to increase at some constant rate. This variable relationship is shown in figure 2.3(D). Materials, supplies, labor, and energy costs are often identified as variable costs. To illustrate, assume that sailboats are being manufactured and that each sailboat requires one sail. As sailboats are manufactured, cost of sails used will increase in direct proportion to boats manufactured.

A *semifixed* (step-fixed) cost can be described by means of a step-function as shown in figure 2.3(B). Supervisory salaries might be considered a semifixed cost, since at some level of increased activity another supervisor will be required. If, within the prescribed relevant range, a specific number of supervisors is required, the cost is considered fixed. But, if additional supervisors are called for as activity continues to increase within the relevant range of activity being considered, the cost is considered semifixed.

A *semivariable* (mixed) cost includes both fixed and variable components as shown in figure 2.3(C). For example, an electric utility might use a flat rate plus a rate-per-unit-used. Salary plus commission arrangements are often used by companies. In both cases, there is some minimum cost at zero activity, but costs increase as activity increases. Knowledge of these cost-behavior patterns is required if managers are to be successful in product costing and predicting results of various alternatives.

Other Cost Concepts

For planning and decision-making purposes several other cost concepts are of considerable importance. For the most part these concepts are used when comparing alternative courses of action. Each alternative has certain costs (often revenues also) associated with it that must be properly evaluated in order to reach a decision. Differences in costs between one alternative and another represent **differential costs.** In identifying differential costs we are focusing attention on the projected future costs that are expected to vary among the alternatives. Suppose, for instance, that in comparing costs of a new equipment proposal with those of existing equipment both require $80,000 of labor costs per year. The annual maintenance costs required to support the newer machine, however, are expected to be $20,000, while the existing equipment is likely to require $45,000. The only relevant cost in comparing the alternatives is the differential maintenance cost of $25,000.

In considering alternatives, we are not interested in sunk costs identified with the various alternatives. A **sunk cost** represents a past cost that is not relevant to alternatives currently being considered. For instance, a company may have recently purchased equipment for $100,000. Newer equipment for the same purpose has now been developed that offers considerable savings in operating costs. In order to decide if the newer equipment should be purchased, management would want to consider the outlay required for the new equipment (cost to acquire and put in operation minus any amount received from disposal of the existing equipment) and net savings in operations to be recognized from acquisition of the new equipment. The $100,000 recently paid is not relevant to the current decision because it has no effect on the current alternative being considered; it is a sunk cost. However, a cost pertaining to the existing equipment is important. The amount expected to be realized from disposing of the old equipment is crucial to the decision.

In looking at the alternatives involved in a decision, we should always consider carefully the alternatives forgone from choosing one alternative over another. The **opportunity cost** is the projected amount that is sacrificed by giving up one alternative in order to select another. For instance, the opportunity cost of selecting the newer equipment, if it proved to be the most desirable alternative, would be the forgone alternative of continuing to use the existing equipment. In a similar fashion, the opportunity cost of using a plant to produce a certain kind of product is the sacrifice of profits that could be generated by other possibilities—producing another type of product, renting the plant facilities, or possibly selling the facilities and using the funds for other investments. In attempting to quantify the opportunity cost, revenues and costs related to the next most desirable alternative are usually chosen for comparison, unless other specific information is desired.

□ COST-ESTIMATION METHODS

How much will it cost to carry out a new program, provide a service, or produce a product? What price should we bid in order to get a job? These are just a few of the problem situations in which it is necessary to identify costs by the different behavior patterns. Costs for direct material and direct labor are often based on engineering studies. Mixed overhead-cost behavior is likely determined by another type of cost-estimation study.

In **cost estimation,** an attempt is made to find predictable relationships between an activity component (independent variable) and the cost (dependent variable) so that costs can be estimated based on projections of the behavior of the independent variable. Activity components typically used include units of product, hours worked, machine hours, miles driven, patients treated, or other evidence of activity. Although one cannot determine costs at different levels with precision, a function, $f(x) = a + bx$, can usually be developed that will provide an acceptable representation of cost behavior for the purpose sought.

When using cost estimation techniques, we assume that linear functions can be used to approximate nonlinear situations and that all costs can be categorized as either fixed or variable within a relevant range. If these assumptions are found to be realistic, then reasonable approximations for costs can be developed by various methods, including (1) the engineering approach, (2) account analysis, (3) the high-low method, (4) visual curve fitting, and (5) statistical curve fitting.

Engineering Approach

The engineering approach, or time and motion study, is often used in companies in which standard costs are emphasized. When standards are employed, engineering studies are made to determine expected physical relationships between manufacturing inputs and outputs. Assume a study indicates that a process should require ten pounds of some material and two hours of direct labor for each unit of output. If estimated prices and wage rates have also been established, we can project the estimated prime cost for the product. However, because of the indirect nature of most overhead costs with respect to productive output, historical cost records are used for estimation purposes.

Account Analysis

The account analysis method involves an analysis of each overhead cost component relevant to a particular need of management. The analysis may simply involve having people familiar with cost behavior classify each account as variable, fixed, or semivariable. For example, in one company management brought together the employees they considered to be most knowledgeable in the cost area and had them classify each overhead cost account by a specific cost behavior pattern. The company's cost analysts then used this information to develop flexible budgets and related information.

After costs are classified by behavior pattern, the variable costs (dependent variable) must be related to some activity component (independent variable) for purposes of identifying the values in the cost equation.

$$f(x) = a + bx$$

where,

$f(x)$ = Estimated overhead costs
a = y intercept
b = Variable cost rate

The value for a is usually interpreted as the fixed cost component at zero output. In many cases, the y intercept lies outside the relevant range. Consequently, the value for y only establishes a level for estimating total costs within the relevant range.

Even though the account analysis method, when used alone, is considered unreliable for most purposes, certain aspects of the method are incorporated in the more sohpisticated methods. Account balances for several periods should be used in the analysis. Also, care should be taken to insure that the cost data included in the analysis result from accrual accounting, and are reflective of current conditions with respect to prices and activities.

The High-Low Method

The *high-low method* calls for identifying total overhead costs at two different activity levels, usually a representative low point and a high point within the relevant range. The specific approach can be described as follows, with an application of the approach shown in figure 2.4.

1. Select the highest representative value of the independent variable and the corresponding value of the dependent variable.

2. Select the lowest representative value of the independent variable and the corresponding value of the dependent variable.

3. Determine the difference between the dependent variables selected.

4. Determine the difference between the independent variables selected.

5. Divide the difference between the dependent variables by the difference of the independent variables. The result is the estimated slope (*b*) of the line.

6. Multiply the high or low independent variable by the slope of the line and subtract from the corresponding value of the dependent variable. The remainder represents the *y*-intercept of the line (*a*).

This method is imprecise because the two points selected may not be representative of the other points. Indeed, it may be quite difficult to select

Month	Direct-labor hours	Indirect-labor cost
January	550	$4,800
February	575	4,900
March	425	4,100
April	400	4,050
May	350	3,750
June	200	2,800
July	400	3,900
August	450	4,250

Steps
1. Highest value: Independent, 575; Dependent, $4,900
2. Lowest value: Independent, 200; Dependent, $2,800
3. $4,900 − $2,800 = $2,100
4. 575 − 200 = 375
5. $2,100 ÷ 375 = $5.60
6. $4,900 − (575 × $5.60) = $1,680
   Indirect-labor cost equation
   y = $1,680 + $5.60x

FIGURE 2.4
Use of High-Low Method for Estimating Costs

the most representative points. Consider, for example, the graph shown in figure 2.5. The two extreme points, if selected for the high and low points, would yield a linear curve somewhat different from that suggested when all points are plotted. In almost all cases, the preferred method is to plot all data to provide a visual impression of the curve. If this is done, the information should be used to fit the curve visually or statistically rather than using results from the high-low method.

Visual Curve Fitting

A more accurate way of determining the estimated variability rate of overhead than the high-low method is to plot all points of observed cost data on a graph. A line is then visually fitted to the plotted points, taking into consideration all points. Typically, the line is fitted so that approximately an equal number of points fall above and below the line. Using the example from figure 2.4, points of observed cost data are plotted on the graph shown in figure 2.6.

The graph is called a *scattergraph*, and the fitted line is the *cost line*. The variability rate can then be calculated by determining the total cost for some point on the line (in this case, $3,750 at 350 hours) and subtracting the *y*-intercept value of $1,800 to arrive at total variable costs. The variable cost is then divided by the activity level to arrive at the variable cost per unit of activity. In the example, the variable cost rate is $5.57.

In this method, rather than simply fitting a line to high and low points, all points are considered, providing a regression line based on averages. This eliminates the problem inherent in using extremes to determine the regression line.

FIGURE 2.5
Relationship of
Overhead Costs to
Activity

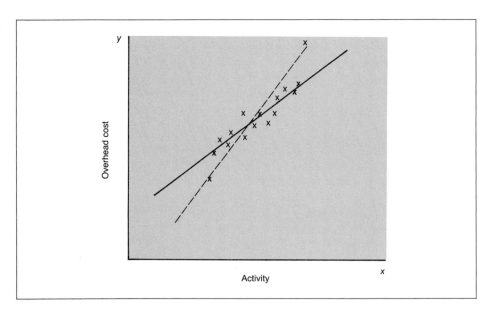

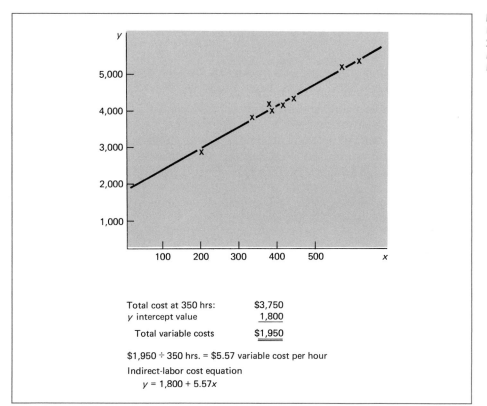

FIGURE 2.6
Use of
Scattergraph
Method for
Estimating Costs

Total cost at 350 hrs: $3,750
y intercept value   1,800
Total variable costs $1,950

$1,950 ÷ 350 hrs. = $5.57 variable cost per hour

Indirect-labor cost equation
$$y = 1,800 + 5.57x$$

Statistical Curve Fitting

Statistical curve fitting is a more sophisticated approach than the other methods discussed. It assures that we will have the best fit of a straight line drawn between the plots on a scattergraph. Indeed, statistical curve fitting, more specifically *regression analysis,* simply identifies a process by which the average amount of change in a variable that is associated with changes in one or more other variables is measured. Additionally, regression techniques provide additional data for managers' use in determining how well the equation developed describes the fit between the cost and activity used. Although coverage of the subject is too extensive to be dealt with here, an example of the *least-squares method* of regression analysis is shown in figure 2.7, which uses data from figure 2.4. (Statistical curve fitting is developed more fully in chapter 21.) Solving simultaneously the normal equations of regression analysis shown in figure 2.7, values for *a* and *b* are determined.

Regardless of the estimation method employed, the management accountant needs reliable predictions of overhead and other costs. If the cost equations developed (refer to figures 2.4–2.7) are considered reliable, they can be employed in providing cost information for reporting or decision-making purposes.

FIGURE 2.7
Use of Regression
Analysis for
Estimating Costs

n	Direct-labor hours (x)	Indirect-labor cost (y)	x^2	xy
1	550	$ 4,800	302,500	$ 2,640,000
2	575	4,900	330,625	2,817,500
3	425	4,100	180,625	1,742,500
4	400	4,050	160,000	1,620,000
5	350	3,750	122,500	1,312,500
6	200	2,800	40,000	560,000
7	400	3,900	160,000	1,560,000
8	450	4,250	202,500	1,912,500
	3,350	$32,550	1,498,750	$14,165,000

Regression Equations:
1. $\Sigma Y = na + b\Sigma x$
2. $\Sigma xy = a\Sigma x + b\Sigma x^2$

Solving simultaneously:
1. $\$32,550 = 8a + 3,350b$
2. $\underline{\$14,165,000 = 3,350a + 1,498,750b}$ Steps in solving simultaneously:
3. $\$13,630,313 = 3,350a + 1,402,813b$ 1. Multiply (1.) by 418.75 to equalize
                                                                    values of a.
2. $\underline{\$14,165,000 = 3,350a + 1,498,750b}$ 2. Subtract (3.) from (2.).

   $\$534,687 = \quad 0 + \quad 95,937b$
   $b = \$5.57$
   $a = \$1,735$
Indirect-labor cost equation:
   $y = \$1,735 + \$5.57x$

☐ SUMMARY

This chapter provides insight into the language of management accounting. More specifically, you should now be familiar with a wide variety of cost terms. Many of these terms, particularly *variable cost* and *fixed cost*, will be used throughout the book. Methods are available for separating overhead costs into fixed and variable components. Several methods were outlined in this chapter, namely, (1) the engineering approach, (2) the account analysis method, (3) the high-low method, (4) visual curve fitting (scattergraph method), and (5) statistical curve fitting (regression analysis).

Unfortunately, however, all costs cannot be conveniently classified as fixed or variable; certain assumptions must be made to make this two-way classification all-inclusive. When these assumptions are valid, they can be utilized to help management in the decision-making function.

KEY TERMS

Controllable cost	**Indirect cost**
Conversion cost	**Manufacturing overhead**
Cost	**Opportunity cost**

Cost estimation   **Period cost**
Differential cost   **Prime cost**
Direct cost   **Relevant range**
Direct labor   **Sunk cost**
Direct material   **Variable cost**
Fixed cost

REVIEW PROBLEM

On a lined sheet of paper, number the first ten lines 1 through 10. Select the graph that matches the numbered factory cost or expense data and write the letter identifying the graph on the appropriate numbered line.

1. Depreciation of equipment, where the amount of depreciation charged is computed by the machine-hours method.

2. Electricity bill, where there is a flat, fixed charge plus a variable cost after a certain number of kilowatt hours are used.

3. City water bill, which is computed as follows:
First 1,000,000 gallons or less—$1,000 flat fee
Next 10,000 gallons—.003 per gallon used
Next 10,000 gallons—.006 per gallon used
Next 10,000 gallons—.009 per gallon used
etc.

4. Cost of lubricant for machines, where cost per unit decreases with each pound of lubricant used (for example, if one pound is used, the cost is $10.00; if two pounds

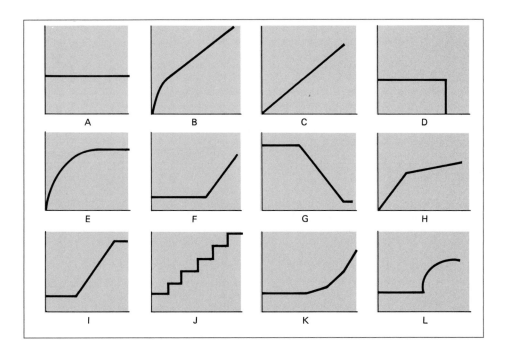

are used, the cost is $19.98; if three pounds are used, the cost is $29.94; with a minimum cost per pound of $9.25).

5. Depreciation of equipment, where the amount is computed by the straight-line method. When the depreciation rate was established, it was anticipated that the obsolescence factor would be greater than the wear-and-tear factor.

6. Rent on a factory building donated by the city, where the agreement calls for a fixed-fee payment unless 200,000 hours are worked, in which case no rent need be paid.

7. Salaries of service workers, where one worker is needed for every 1,000 hours of machine hours or less (i.e., 0 to 1,000 hours requires one worker; 1,001, to 2,000 hours requires two workers; etc.).

8. Federal unemployment compensation taxes for the year, where labor force is constant in number throughout year (average annual salary is $6,000 per worker).

9. Cost of raw material used.

10. Rent on a factory building donated by county, where agreement calls for rent of $100,000 less $1 for each direct labor hour worked in excess of 200,000 hours, but minimum rental payments of $20,000 must be paid.

(CPA)

Solutions □

1. C
2. F
3. K
4. B
5. A
6. D
7. J
8. Varies, depending on assumptions
9. C
10. G

QUESTIONS

Q2-1. Why is the term *cost* difficult to define?

Q2-2. Identify and discuss some differences between financial and management accounting in the use of the term *cost*.

Q2-3. Define the relevant range of activity. Why is this assumption made?

Q2-4. Discuss problems associated with product and period costs.

Q2-5. In decision making, why do we find estimated costs more useful than actual costs?

Q2-6. Why is it often difficult to classify costs as either variable or fixed? How are semivariable and semifixed costs handled?

Q2-7. Identify the three major components of a product cost. Identify a product and then classify the manufacturing costs that you think would be incurred in producing the product.

Q2-8. What are prime costs? What are conversion costs?

Q2-9. What are direct costs? What are indirect costs?

Q2-10. When are costs controllable?

Q2-11. Are all direct costs also variable? Explain.

Q2-12. Are all direct costs also controllable costs? Explain.

Q2-13. Why is the concept of a differential cost important?

Q2-14. Under what circumstances is a cost considered a sunk cost?

Q2-15. Identify the different methods for estimating cost behavior.

Q2-16. Is regression analysis a better method for estimating costs than the high-low method? Discuss.

Q2-17. Should the scattergraph be used in conjunction with the high-low method and regression analysis? Discuss.

PROBLEMS

P2-1. Classify the following costs as fixed, semifixed, semivariable, or variable. *Cost Behavior*

    a. Property taxes
    b. Supervisory personnel
    c. Indirect labor
    d. Direct labor
    e. Royalty payment
    f. Machinery depreciation
    g. Insurance on inventory
    h. Sales commission that guarantees a minimum amount
    i. Direct material
    j. Electric power
    k. Insurance on factory building
    l. Indirect materials
    m. Factory manager's salary
    n. Advertising

P2-2. Classify the following costs with respect to cost behavior patterns. *Cost Behavior*

    a. Gasoline costs of a traveling salesperson
    b. Energy costs associated with operating manufacturing equipment
    c. Depreciation based on units produced
    d. Royalties paid based on units sold
    e. Sales salaries
    f. Accounting fees
    g. Legal fees
    h. Advertising
    i. Computer operator's salary
    j. Equipment repair expense

Cost Behavior   **P2-3.**   The following costs are assumed to be variable. Identify the most likely activity component (independent variable) for each of the variable costs.

     a. Indirect material
     b. Sales commissions
     c. Royalties
     d. Travel expense
     e. Electric power
     f. Depreciation
     g. Sales promotion expense
     h. Medicine and drugs expense (hospital)
     i. Machinery maintenance expense

Manufacturing Costs   **P2-4.**   Classify the following factory costs incurred in manufacturing bicycles as direct materials, direct labor, or factory overhead.

     a. Factory supervision
     b. Aluminum tubing
     c. Rims
     d. Emblem
     e. Gear box
     f. Crew supervisor's salary
     g. Fenders
     h. Inventory clerk's wages
     i. Inspector's salary
     j. Handlebars
     k. Metal worker's wages
     l. Roller chain
     m. Spokes
     n. Paint

Manufacturing Costs   **P2-5.**   Classify the following factory costs incurred in manufacturing potato chips as direct materials, direct labor, or manufacturing overhead.

     a. Packaging machine operator wages
     b. Maintenance and clean-up wages
     c. Potato costs
     d. Cooking oil costs
     e. Seasoning costs
     f. Packaging material costs
     g. Packing carton costs
     h. Heating and energy costs
     i. Potato storage costs
     j. Production supervisor's salary

Controllable vs. Noncontrollable Costs   **P2-6.**   Determine which costs are controllable and which costs are noncontrollable by the production manager of the Williams Furniture Company.

     a. Heat
     b. Depreciation of the factory building
     c. Supervision
     d. Repairs on production equipment
     e. Light
     f. Damaged finished goods
     g. Scrap

    h. Shipping costs
    i. Raw materials
    j. Direct-labor wage rates
    k. Overtime wages
    l. Maintenance
    m. Insurance on the factory

P2-7. Determine which of the following costs are likely controllable by the manufacturing vice-president of Thorn Electronic Incorporated.

Controllable vs. Noncontrollable Costs

    a. Direct-labor wages
    b. Overtime wages
    c. Production manager's salary
    d. Depreciation on plant facility
    e. Allocation of corporate administrative costs
    f. Consultant fees to redesign production layout
    g. Insurance on the plant
    h. Spoilage of product (defective units)
    i. Heat, light, and power
    j. Travel costs of production staff

P2-8. Determine which of the following costs would be direct or indirect costs in the product and department where the product is manufactured.

Direct vs. Indirect Costs

Item	Product	Department	Neither
a. Material used in the product			
b. Labor used to manufacture the product			
c. Material used in installing equipment			
d. Labor used to maintain equipment			
e. Sales manager's salary			
f. President's salary			
g. Equipment depreciation			
h. Taxes on plant			
i. Departmental energy costs			
j. Repairs to departmental office			

P2-9. A group of students is considering going to Florida during the spring vacation. They will travel in a car that is owned by a member of the group. They plan to stay in motels or camp if the weather is favorable. Two members of the group own all of the camping equipment the group will need. When they camp, they will cook their meals; otherwise they will eat in restaurants.

Relevant vs. Nonrelevant Costs

Required ☐ Classify the following costs as relevant or nonrelevant to the decision concerning the trip.

    a. Cost of gas and oil for the car
    b. Cost of purchasing the car
    c. Cost of health insurance carried by each member of the group
    d. Cost of renting campsites
    e. Turnpike tolls
    f. Cost of the camping equipment

g. Cost of the car registration
h. Entertainment costs while on the trip
i. Cost of food while camping
j. Income that could be earned if they work rather than take the trip
k. Cost of meals purchased in restaurants
l. Cost of renting a motel room
m. Cost of insurance on the car

Relevant Costs   **P2-10.** A student is considering attending a six-week summer school session. If the student goes to summer school, she will be able to graduate one semester earlier than she had originally planned.

Required □ Classify the following costs as to the decision concerning summer school.

a. Cost of summer school tuition
b. Cost of housing for regular semester
c. Cost of automobile insurance
d. Cost of health fee during summer school
e. Expected income during semester if she does not attend summer school
f. Cost of air-conditioning apartment during summer session
g. Cost of yearbook
h. Cost of health fee during regular semester of school
i. Cost of regular semester tuition
j. Cost of air-conditioning and heating apartment during regular semester
k. Expected income during summer school session
l. Cost of housing during summer school session
m. Cost of books

Differential Costs   **P2-11.** The acquisition manager of Parvez International is considering the purchase of new equipment for $150,000 which should cost $20,000 a year to operate. The company recently purchased equipment for the same purpose, costing $100,000. Existing operating costs approximate $35,000 a year. The existing equipment is currently worth $60,000. Calculate the differential costs needed for a decision. What costs, if any, represent sunk costs?

Cost Description   **P2-12.** During December, XYZ Company incurred $5,000 of supplies expense. Which of the following cost descriptions can be used to identify the nature of this expense? Explain.

a. Manufacturing cost
b. Direct materials
c. Period cost
d. Controllable cost
e. Conversion cost
f. Direct cost
g. Differential cost
h. Variable cost

High-Low Method   **P2-13.** Repair and maintenance expenses of Weis Company are to be analyzed for purposes of constructing a budget. Examination of past records reveals the following costs and related activity:

	High	Low
Cost per month	$39,200	$32,000
Machine hours	24,000	15,000

Required ☐ Using the high-low method, develop values for *a* and *b* in $y = a + bx$.

P2-14. The Guamiau Company wants to calculate the fixed portion of its energy expense, as measured against direct-labor hours, for the first three months of 19X7. Information for the first three months of 19X7 is as follows:

High-Low Method

	Direct-labor hours	Energy expense
January	34,000	$610
February	31,000	585
March	34,000	610

Required ☐ Calculate the fixed portion of Guamiau's energy expense, rounded to the nearest dollars.

P2-15. Total production costs for Haley, Inc., are budgeted at $460,000 for 100,000 units of budgeted product and at $560,000 for 120,000 units of budgeted product. Because of the need for additional facilities, budgeted fixed costs for 120,000 units are 25 percent more than budgeted fixed costs for 100,000 units.

High-Low Method

Required ☐ Calculate the company's budgeted variable cost per unit of production.

P2-16. Ron Jones, controller of the Becky Corporation, has been requested by management officials to separate overhead costs of the producing department into variable and fixed-cost components. The following information is available.

High-Low Method

	Activity component units produced	Costs incurred
January	10,000	$25,000
February	12,000	28,000
March	14,000	34,000
April	16,000	37,000
May	18,000	40,000

Required ☐

1. Identify and discuss methods available for separating the cost components.

2. Using the high-low method, calculate the value for *a* and *b* in $y = a + bx$.

P2-17. Garner Company is setting up a planning system and needs to estimate costs at different levels of activity. The following schedule of maintenance costs has been developed at different levels of activity based on company records.

High-Low Method

Activity	Maintenance costs
300	$200
350	350
400	400
425	375
450	425
500	450
550	475
600	550
625	500
675	550
700	600
750	800

Using the high-low method, develop a representative cost equation for maintenance costs.

Visual Curve Fitting

P2-18. Using the information in problem P2-17, visually fit a curve to the plotted data. Evaluate the reliability of the cost equation developed in P2-17, based on an analysis of the plotted data.

Cost Estimation

P2-19. The accountants at the Alice Robinson Corporation have accumulated the following data concerning overhead costs for the last ten periods.

Period	Direct-labor hours activity level	Factory overhead costs
1	5,500	$26,700
2	5,800	27,600
3	4,700	25,300
4	6,000	28,100
5	7,300	34,800
6	6,200	28,400
7	5,750	27,100
8	7,700	43,800
9	6,400	28,900
10	6,450	29,100

Required □

1. Plot the data and sketch a line specifying the relationship between the direct-labor hours and the factory overhead cost.

2. Comment on the relevant range of the data.

3. Compute the fixed and variable costs using the high-low method.

Comprehensive Cost Estimation

P2-20. The staff of Captain, Inc., needs an estimate of what the variable portion of its supply expense, as measured against units produced, was for the first six months of 19X8. Information for the first six months of 19X8 is as follows:

	Units produced	Supply expense
January	34,000	$6,100
February	31,000	5,850
March	34,000	6,200

April	36,000	6,400
May	30,000	5,500
June	28,000	5,400

Required ☐

1. Determine the variable rate using the high-low method.

2. Estimate the variable rate using the scattergraph method.

3. Using regression analysis, calculate the variable rate.

P2-21. During your examination of the 19X9 financial statements of MacKenzie Park Co., which manufactures and sells trivets, you wish to analyze selected aspects of the company operations.   *Multiple-Choice-Regression Analysis*

Labor hours and production costs for the last four months of 19X9, which you believe are representative for the year, were as follows:

Month	Labor hours	Total production costs
September	2,500	$ 20,000
October	3,500	25,000
November	4,500	30,000
December	3,500	25,000
Total	14,000	$100,000

Required ☐ Based upon the given information and using the least-squares method of computation with the letters that follow, select the best answer for each of questions 1 through 5.

Let a = Fixed production costs per month
b = Variable production costs per labor hour
n = Number of months
x = Labor hours per month
y = Total monthly production costs
Σ = Summation

1. The equation(s) required for applying the least-squares method of computation of fixed and variable production costs could be expressed as

a. $xy = ax + bx^2$
b. $y = na + nb$
c. $\Sigma y = a + bx^2$
  $xy = na + b\Sigma x$
d. $\Sigma xy = a\Sigma x + b\Sigma x^2$
  $\Sigma y = na + b\Sigma x$

2. The cost function derived by the least-squares method

a. would be linear.
b. must be tested for minima and maxima.
c. would be parabolic.
d. would indicate maximum costs at the point of the function's point of inflection.

3. Monthly production costs could be expressed

    a. $y = ax + b$
    b. $y = a + bx$
    c. $y = b + ax$
    d. $y = a + bx$

4. Using the least-squares method of computation, the fixed monthly production cost of trivets is approximately

    a. $10,000
    b. $ 9,500
    c. $ 7,500
    d. $ 5,000

5. Using the least-squares method of computation, the variable production cost per labor hour is

    a. $6.00
    b. $5.00
    c. $3.00
    d. $2.00

(CPA)

Regression Analysis **P2-22.** Patricia Bartley, controller of the Phyllis Company, has been asked by the president to separate expenses of the shipping department into variable and fixed cost components. The following information has been provided.

	Units shipped	Expenses
January	5,000	$10,000
February	6,000	11,600
March	8,000	17,100
April	12,000	26,000
May	11,000	19,000
June	14,000	29,000
July	10,000	24,000

Required □ Using regression analysis, calculate the values for *a* and *b* in $y = a + bx$.

Product Costs **P2-23.** You have been given the following information with respect to the product cost of West Manufacturing Company:

Materials	$10.00
Labor	6.00
Overhead	6.00
	$22.00

The marketing manager has been urging the president to accept a special one-time order from East Distribution for 10,000 units of the product at a price of $200,000. The president has asked you to identify the major factors she should consider with respect to costs.

CHAPTER OUTLINE

THE COST-ACCOUNTING CYCLE AND JOB-ORDER COSTING

CHAPTER 3

☐ INTRODUCTION

Financial accounting is primarily concerned with matching expenses and revenues in order to estimate periodic income. When finished goods are purchased for resale, there are few major complicating factors to product-cost determination. However, in a manufacturing concern, the costing becomes more complex because of the cost flows related to the products manufactured.

A textile manufacturer, for example, may purchase raw material in the form of unprocessed cotton, wool, or perhaps synthetics and then convert it into yarn. The yarn is then woven into cloth and dyed. The finished cloth may, in turn, be sold as a finished product to some clothing manufacturer, who will use the cloth to manufacture clothes. The finished apparel will then be sold to retail stores, which will distribute it to the final consumer.

In the example just cited, several manufacturing companies and one merchandising company were involved in the process of converting fibers into a product to be distributed to the ultimate consumer. Different materials—fiber, yarn, and cloth—and their related costs were identified with each successive conversion process. Conversion costs, labor and overhead, were expended during each process.

Accounting procedures for a manufacturing company are designed to identify and accumulate the costs of producing the products of a company. Depending on the needs of a particular company, this is accomplished in a number of different ways, but it requires a basic understanding of the cost-accounting cycle. The first part of this chapter provides a general review of basic cost components, their flows, and manufacturing-accounting procedures. Information on a job-order costing system is then described.

☐ COST FLOWS AND RELATED ACCOUNTING PROCEDURES

Cost incurrence is necessary in order to produce and distribute products or services. When a cost ultimately results in revenue generation, its value expires and the cost becomes an expense to be subtracted from revenues.

Assume, for example, that the Johnson Company has $1,000 in cash as its sole asset. The company purchases ten tables for $100 each. All of the tables are sold for $180 each. Also assume that the sales are for cash and inventory is replaced at the same unit price. The journal entries are:

1.	Inventory	1,000	
	Cash		1,000
2.	Cost of sales	1,000	
	Inventory		1,000
3.	Cash	1,800	
	Sales		1,800
4.	Inventory	1,000	
	Cash		1,000

Transaction flows are reflected in figure 3.1. The first entry shows a cost being incurred to acquire an asset. In the second entry, the asset has been consumed in the process of producing revenues. This is reflected in the third entry. Through sales, an asset (cash) was created. Finally, the inventory was replenished in entry four.

A much more complicated set of cost flows and transformations is involved in a manufacturing operation. Material, labor, and manufacturing-overhead costs are incurred in the process of manufacturing a product for sale. These product-cost components are defined in the information that follows.

Direct Materials

All materials that are specifically identified with the finished product represent direct materials. Usually only the more significant items are classified as direct materials, since it would be too costly to trace all items to a particular product. Leather and buckles used in making luggage would be charged to direct materials, but glue and thread used in the luggage would likely be accounted for as manufacturing overhead.

Direct Labor

Labor used directly in the process of transforming various components into a finished product is considered direct labor. The labor must be phys-

FIGURE 3.1
Transaction Flows

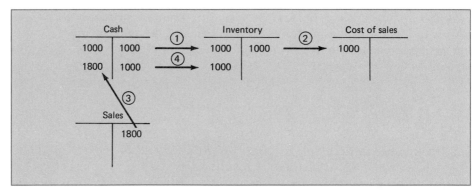

ically traceable to the finished product. Workers cutting leather frames or sewing machine operators making the luggage would be considered direct labor. However, factory supervisors, janitors, and material handlers are typically considered indirect labor, since their activities are not directly traceable to the product.

Manufacturing Overhead

All other costs considered to be associated with the manufacturing process are included in this category. These costs are subject to the discretion of management, but typically include variable and fixed costs such as indirect materials, indirect labor, factory equipment depreciation, repairs and maintenance costs, along with other indirect manufacturing costs.

In the process of producing a product, materials are purchased and used as manufacturing takes place. Labor and overhead costs are incurred not only directly but also indirectly to provide capacity for the production process. An overview of the cost-transformation process is presented in figure 3.2.

The following three inventory accounts are used in the cost-accounting cycle as shown in figure 3.2:

Raw Materials Inventory

The initial purchases of direct material and operating supplies are charged to this account.

Work-in-Process Inventory

As the manufacturing process takes place, the costs of direct materials, direct labor, and manufacturing overhead are charged to the work-in-process inventory.

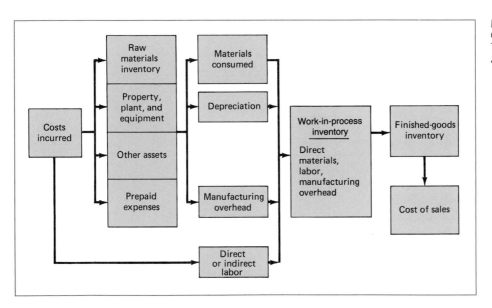

FIGURE 3.2
Cost Transformation and Flows

Finished-Goods Inventory

When products are completed, their costs are transferred from the work-in-process inventory to the finished-goods inventory.

☐ BASIC ACCOUNTING PROCEDURES

Various accounting procedures must be established to ensure that cost flows are properly recorded. A discussion of the basic procedures for recording material, labor, and overhead follows.

Direct Material

In a *periodic system* where physical inventory counts are used to update inventory balances, minimal procedures and records are needed. A general ledger account for raw materials is established. Charges are made to the account directly from approved invoices. Balances in this account are adjusted periodically by means of physical inventory counts that reflect usage of material. This process is reflected in figure 3.3.

Where *perpetual records* are maintained, it is necessary to establish a subsidiary raw materials ledger, which provides an up-to-date record of the various materials on hand. In addition to debiting the general ledger raw materials control account for purchases, one debits individual records for amounts received. The latter entry is typically made from a copy of the receiving report. In order to provide an up-to-date record, materials removed from raw materials must also be posted to both the control ac-

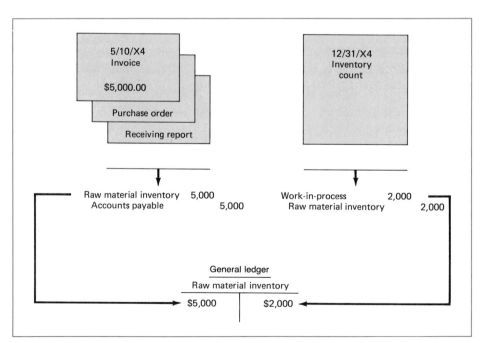

FIGURE 3.3
Periodic System
Process

count in the general ledger and the raw materials ledger. This is accomplished by posting from copies of the *store's requisitions*. The basic procedures followed are illustrated in figure 3.4.

Direct Labor

As labor is used to produce products either directly or indirectly, procedures are needed to identify the amount and kind of labor expended. Time cards are generally used to accumulate the total labor hours worked by employees. Hours may be recorded mechanically by a time clock as workers punch in and out daily, or they may be recorded manually by workers or a timekeeper. At the end of each pay period, the hours are summarized,

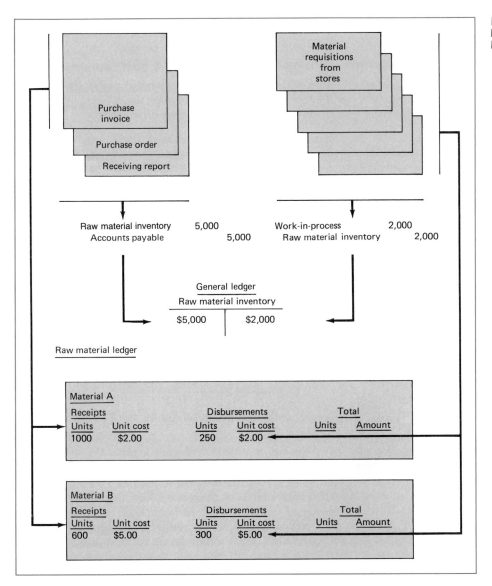

FIGURE 3.4
Procedures in
Perpetual Systems

and gross and net pay, based on payroll and withholding authorizations, are calculated for each worker.

Each worker may have worked on a number of different jobs or in several different departments during a given pay period. This work is generally evidenced by *job tickets* or other documents for each job or department. At the end of a pay period the job tickets, showing specifically where the employee worked, are accumulated and summarized. The summary indicates the jobs or departments to be charged for the employee's time and thus provides the information needed to distribute labor costs to jobs, projects, and departments by a direct and indirect classification.

This information is then used to prepare the payroll register, checks, and journal entries. The journal entries are posted to control accounts and subsidiary records. The overall process is summarized in figure 3.5.

Manufacturing Overhead

The cost of direct materials and direct labor can be measured reasonably accurately, given a basic cost-accumulation system. Because of the indirect nature of overhead costs, procedures used to assign manufacturing over-

FIGURE 3.5
Payroll Process

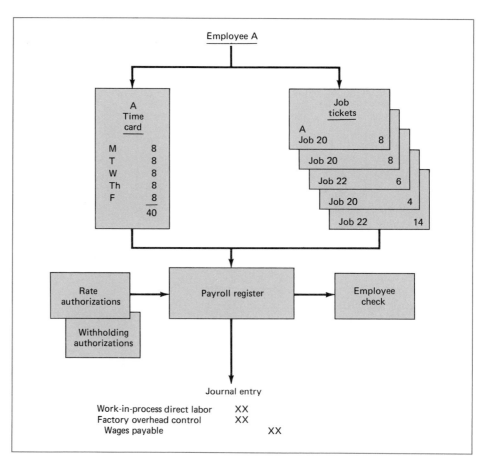

head are usually less satisfactory but nevertheless necessary. Management needs a complete costing of all products. If a company produces several units of a product, then it might be expected that the costs of material and labor directly associated with the units are properly assigned to the units.

Can the same thing be said for indirect material, indirect labor, equipment depreciation, maintenance costs of equipment, power costs used in the process, taxes paid on the plant, and other similar costs? The answer is no, since such costs cannot be traced directly to the production of the units even though they may have been incurred because the units were produced.

Manufacturing overhead can be viewed as two separate components— actual overhead costs incurred and overhead costs applied to production. Actual overhead costs incurred are typically recorded first in an overhead control account and subsidiary records, such as departmental overhead cost sheets. Sample entries to record overhead costs are shown as follows.

Repairs and maintenance	500	
Accounts payable		500
Distribution:		
Dept. A, 250		
Dept. B, 250		
Heat, light, and power	600	
Accounts payable		600
Distribution:		
Dept. A, 200		
Dept. B, 300		
Dept. C, 100		
Depreciation—Equipment	1,000	
Accumulated depreciation—Equipment		1,000
Distribution:		
Dept. A, 400		
Dept. B, 400		
Dept. C, 200		

These entries are posted to the control and subsidiary accounts as indicated in figure 3.6. This shows the process for recording actual overhead costs. However, overhead must be charged to production and eventually to products produced. This is accomplished by allocating the overhead costs to production on some reasonable basis. A relationship between manufacturing overhead costs incurred and some activity component of the production process can usually be identified, such as a relationship between manufacturing overhead and direct-labor hours. Using such a relationship, one could divide overhead costs by direct-labor hours and multiply the resulting rate by the number of hours incurred by each job or department in order to allocate overhead costs. Activity components typically used to allocate manufacturing overhead are direct-labor hours, direct-labor costs, machine hours, and units produced.

Although actual overhead costs are sometimes allocated to production on a monthly basis, allocating overhead to the final product by means of an annual averaging process based on forecasts of activity and manufacturing overhead costs is preferable. If this procedure is followed, a **pre-**

FIGURE 3.6
Manufacturing
Overhead Control
and Subsidiary
Records

Manufacturing overhead–control	
$ 500	
600	
1,000	

Overhead cost sheet–Dept. A

Indirect material	Indirect labor	Repairs	Power	Depreciation	Total
		$250	$200	$400	$850

Overhead cost sheet–Dept. B

Indirect material	Indirect labor	Repairs	Power	Depreciation	Total
		$250	$300	$400	$950

Overhead cost sheet–Dept. C

Indirect material	Indirect labor	Repairs	Power	Depreciation	Total
			$100	$200	$300

determined overhead rate is calculated by dividing expected manufacturing overhead costs by the activity base. Overhead costs can usually be applied on a more timely basis when predetermined rates are used. A more important advantage of the averaging procedure over the use of actual costs, however, is in the elimination of fluctuating overhead rates from month to month due to volume shifts. In a later section of this chapter, the basic methods for allocating overhead will be explained in more detail.

Cost of Goods Manufactured

In the absence of beginning and ending inventories of work-in-process, the basic cost-flow procedures described above provide the means for calculating the **cost of goods manufactured.** Consider the following example.

Marvick Company manufactures a single product for sale to furniture stores. During a recent accounting period, direct materials totaling $8,000 were purchased. The company had a beginning direct-material inventory of $4,000. Direct labor incurred during the period amounted to $4,000. Manufacturing overhead costs were $5,000. During the period, all units started were completed and all units were sold. There was no beginning work-in-process inventory. Ending inventory of direct materials was $5,000. Since there was no work-in-process, cost of goods manufactured consists of total costs incurred in production. The cost-of-goods-manufactured schedule appears as follows:

Direct materials used*	$ 7,000
Direct labor	4,000
Manufacturing overhead	5,000
Total	$16,000

*($4,000 + $8,000 − $5,000 = $7,000)

In the example, total manufacturing costs of $16,000 is equal to the cost of goods manufactured ($16,000) and cost of goods sold ($16,000) because of the absence of work-in-process and finished-goods inventories. When work-in-process and finished-goods inventory levels are significant, the use of a product-cost-determination system to properly accumulate costs for the different inventory categories becomes important.

☐ PRODUCT-COST DETERMINATION SYSTEMS

As greater accuracy is needed in determining cost of goods manufactured, cost of sales, and costs for work-in-process and finished goods, more sophisticated cost-accounting procedures need to be set up. Procedures are needed to calculate, accumulate, assign, and transfer production costs from one stage to another until the product has been completed. There are two basic product-cost-determination systems used for this purpose.

Job-order costing assigns costs to jobs that represent identifiable batches of product or projects. A house built for you by a contractor is substantially different from a health club built by the same contractor. The contractor would accumulate costs for each job separately because of major differences in the costs of each job. Job-order costing is designed for this kind of situation.

Process costing assigns costs to departments by time period, since large numbers of homogenous products are being manufactured on a continuous basis. For example, both the house and the health club might require the same insulation materials. Because insulation material can be manufactured in standard grades on a continuing basis for a wide variety of users, its production is the kind of process that is more suitable to process costing.

Job-order costing is outlined and explained in the balance of this chapter. Process costing is presented in chapter 4.

☐ JOB-ORDER COSTING

Job-order costing is used as a means of accumulating costs when products are made to customer specifications or when a number of identifiable units are being produced. Frequently, the production cycle extends over several months before the primary output is completed. Job-order costing is often used in furniture manufacturing, shipbuilding, heavy equipment manufacturing, building construction, and the printing industry. In fact, job-order systems are widely used by a variety of industrial, professional, and nonprofit organizations. Hospitals may use a form of job-order costing to accumulate patient costs. Governmental agencies use job-order costing in accounting for program activities. Public accounting firms use this system when they attempt to accumulate the costs of carrying out specific audit engagements.

Basic Components

The production process begins when a production order is issued to produce a product. Materials are ordered and issued; labor and overhead costs are incurred and allocated to the job. The key document in a job-order costing system is the job cost sheet (as shown in figure 3.7). Each job has a separate job cost sheet. The **job cost sheet** provides the means for accumulating material, labor, and overhead costs by specific job.

When materials are requested for a job, a direct material (stores) requisition is prepared; after proper approval, the materials are released based on the requisition. The requisition identifies the job number and serves as the basis for posting material costs to the job cost sheet (see figure 3.7). The stores requisitions, when totaled, provide the information for making entries to the direct-materials inventory and work-in-process control accounts.

As indicated earlier in the chapter (see figure 3.5), job or work tickets provide information relative to specific jobs worked on by direct-labor

FIGURE 3.7
Job-Order
Costing System

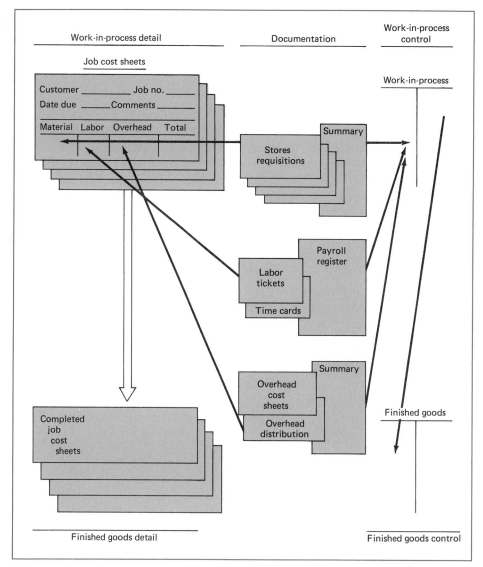

personnel. Labor tickets are sorted by job, and postings are made to the proper job cost sheets. The labor tickets and the time cards provide information needed for payroll journals. Summaries from the payroll journals are then posted to work-in-process and other control accounts.

An Illustrative Example

To illustrate more fully the assignment of costs and forms used in the job-order costing, we will use an example concerning the Ace Cabinet Company and its activities for a period of time. Ace manufactures expensive cabinets and desks to customers' specifications. Each piece is unique in terms of wood used, overall dimensions, and other particulars. Two departments produce the furniture. The cutting department cuts wood panels to specifications. The furniture department constructs the product from the previously cut material. All lumber and parts are tightly controlled by a storekeeper because of the high cost of the lumber and parts.

Florence Andersen, managing partner of a local accounting firm, places an order for an ebony wood desk with ivory handles. At the time the order is placed, a job cost sheet is set up. As shown in figure 3.8, the sheet provides basic details. The materials costing $2,000 are requisitioned from stores by the cutting department. The control entry and details are presented in figure 3.9. Normally, the entry to the control account would be a summary entry representing a series of requisitions over time.

The completed material requisition serves as the basis for entering the amount on the job cost sheet. This entry is shown in figure 3.10. When the material is received in the cutting department, it is cut into panels according to the specifications. Employees performing these tasks record their time on labor tickets as indicated in figure 3.11. At the end of a payroll period, the various labor tickets are summarized to determine the amount of direct labor and indirect labor. The time cards indicate total wages earned, and the two combined provide the information needed for an entry similar to the one shown at the bottom of figure 3.11. The direct labor of $850 applicable to job 200 is entered in the job cost sheet as shown in figure 3.12. This process continues until all direct materials, direct labor, and manufacturing overhead have been properly charged to the job by each of the departments. A completed job cost sheet is illustrated in figure 3.13.

At the time the job is completed, it is transferred to finished goods and the appropriate entry is made to the control accounts. Procedures with respect to manufacturing overhead are dealt with in the next section.

Manufacturing Overhead Allocation

In the illustrative example just cited, we did not explain how overhead was charged to the job.

The weakest link in any product-cost-determination system is the overhead-allocation component. While both the direct materials and direct labor can be specifically identified with individual jobs, it is difficult—

FIGURE 3.8
Ace Cabinet
Company
Job Cost Sheet

Job number _____   Customer name _____

Description _____   Order date _____

_____   Date needed _____

Date started _____

Date completed _____

Direct materials

Date	Requisition number	Dept.	Comments	Amount

Direct labor

Date	Labor summary number	Dept.	Comments	Amount

Overhead applied

Date	Dept.	Overhead basis	Amount

and often impossible—to identify manufacturing overhead costs with specific jobs. We must remember that manufacturing overhead costs consist of fixed and variable components. The fixed component relates to capacity decisions of management—the decision to build a certain size plant, to use certain kinds of equipment, and to employ certain levels of supervision. The variable component, while related to production activity, is tied to so many different activities—labor hours, equipment usage, and other factors—that variable overhead allocation tends to be somewhat arbitrary.

Some acceptable basis for allocating overhead costs must be found. Where multiple departments are involved, it frequently becomes necessary to allocate costs by departments on different bases. The decision must also be made whether to allocate actual costs or to use a predetermined rate based on estimated costs and activity. When actual overhead costs are allocated, the system is called an **actual job-order costing system.** When a predetermined rate that is based on estimated costs and activity is used,

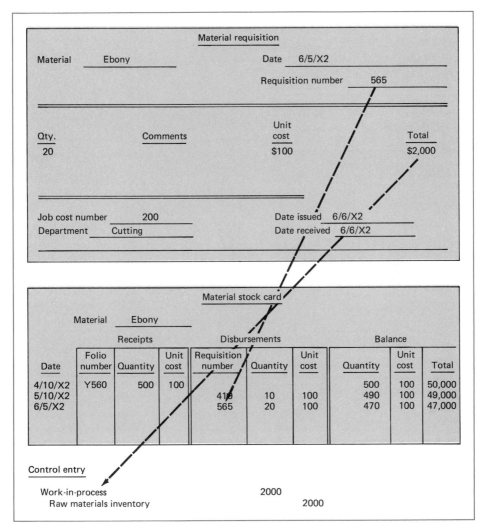

FIGURE 3.9
Ace Cabinet
Company
Material Details

the system is called a **normal job-order costing system.** Thus, **normal costing** indicates that estimated rather than actual overhead costs are allocated to production.

Actual Job-Order Costing

At this point we shall trace some hypothetical transactions through a job-order costing system. The following information is presented concerning the manufacturing activities of XYZ Company during January 19X1.

Partial Trial Balance, January 1, 19X1

Raw materials	$150,000
Work-in-process	65,000
Finished-goods inventory	20,000

FIGURE 3.10
Ace Cabinet
Company
Job Cost Sheet

Job number ___200___   Customer name ___F. Andersen___

Description ___Ebony desk___   Order date ___6/1/X2___

___w/ivory hardware___   Date needed ___8/1/X2___

Date started ___6/5/X2___

Date completed _____

Direct materials

Date	Requisition number	Dept.	Comments	Amount
6/6	565	Cutting		$2,000

Direct labor

Date	Labor summary number	Dept.	Comments	Amount

Overhead applied

Date	Dept.	Overhead basis	Amount

Transactions during the month

Purchases of raw materials	$ 60,000
Material transferred to job	
Job A	10,000
Job B	20,000
Job C	15,000
Job D	9,000
Materials used indirectly in production	10,000
Labor cost for the period	
Direct labor	
Job A	5,000
Job B	12,000
Job C	8,000
Job D	5,000
Indirect labor	10,000
Other overhead costs for the period	
Depreciation	20,000
Utilities	10,000
Supplies	5,000
Taxes	5,000

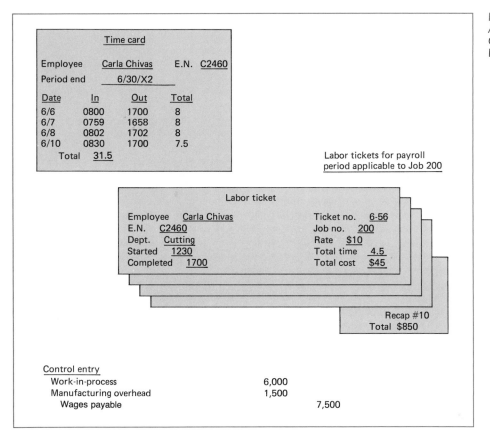

FIGURE 3.11
Ace Cabinet
Company
Labor Details

Work-in-Process January 1, 19X1

	Material	Labor	Overhead	Total
Job A	$20,000	$10,000	$5,000	$35,000
Job B	10,000	8,000	4,000	22,000
Job C	5,000	2,000	1,000	8,000

Other Information
Actual overhead costs are allocated to individual jobs using direct-labor costs as
    the activity component.
Job A was completed during the period.

Requirements
1. Prepare journal entries for the above transactions.
2. Show the balances on the job cost sheets.
3. Prepare a cost-of-goods-manufactured schedule.

Journal entries relating to the example are shown in figure 3.14. All
overhead items are charged to factory overhead control, and the total
amount of factory overhead is allocated to work-in-process.

Since overhead is allocated to jobs based on direct-labor costs, the total
overhead costs of $60,000 are divided by total direct-labor costs of $30,000
to get a rate of $2 of overhead for each direct-labor dollar. Total costs,

FIGURE 3.12
Ace Cabinet
Company
Job Cost Sheet

Job number ___200___   Customer name ___F. Andersen___

Description ___Ebony desk___   Order date ___6/1/X2___

___w/ivory hardware___   Date needed ___8/1/X2___

Date started ___6/5/X2___

Date completed _____

Direct materials

Date	Requisition number	Dept.	Comments	Amount
6/6	565	Cutting		2,000

Direct labor

Date	Labor summary number	Dept.	Comments	Amount
6/10	#10	Cutting		850

Overhead applied

Date	Dept.	Overhead basis	Amount

including beginning work-in-process costs, are shown in figure 3.15. The balance of $149,000 in the work-in-process account consists of the following incomplete jobs:

Job B	$ 78,000
Job C	47,000
Job D	24,000
	$149,000

A cost-of-goods-manufactured schedule for XYZ Company is shown in figure 3.16. This total cost of goods manufactured of $60,000 represents the amount of costs transferred from work-in-process to finished goods (that is, the cost of Job A completed).

In the work-in-process example (January 1, 19X1) shown on p. 59, you can see that for each $1 of labor incurred, $.50 of manufacturing overhead was applied. Yet the current month allocation rate was $2 per direct-labor dollar. This situation highlights one of the problems arising from an allocation of actual costs on a monthly basis. Because of shifts in production

FIGURE 3.13
Ace Cabinet
Company
Job Cost Sheet

Job number   200   Customer name   F. Andersen

Description   Ebony desk   Order date   6/1/X2

w/ivory hardware   Date needed   8/1/X2

Date started   6/5/X2

Date completed   7/20/X2

Direct materials

Date	Requisition number	Dept.	Comments	Amount
6/6	565	Cutting		2,000
7/10	610	Furniture		1,500
				3,500

Direct labor

Date	Labor summary number	Dept.	Comments	Amount
6/10	#10	Cutting		850
6/17	#20	Cutting		600
7/1	#36	Furniture		800
7/8	#45	Furniture		600
				2,850

Overhead applied

Date	Dept.	Overhead basis	Amount
6/30	Cutting	DLC	290
7/8	Furniture	DLC	560
			850
		Total	7,200

volume from month to month, higher overhead costs (due to the fixed nature of some of the costs), will be assigned to products produced in low-volume months. This happens because fixed costs remain the same from month to month while productive activity may fluctuate significantly. For instance, if costs are related to actual activity components when production varies considerably from month to month, then the fixed costs in overhead can cause significant swings in rates used to allocate overhead costs to production.

Because of management decisions, certain other costs (for instance, repairs and maintenance) may tend to be larger in months with low manufacturing activity, again causing a higher unit cost in such months. This may happen in a company that attempts to take care of most planned

FIGURE 3.14
Control Account
Journal Entries—
Actual Costing

1. Raw materials inventory	60,000	
Accounts payable		60,000
2. Work-in-process	54,000	
Raw materials inventory		54,000
3. Factory overhead control	10,000	
Raw materials inventory		10,000
4. Work-in-process	30,000	
Factory overhead control	10,000	
Wages payable		40,000
5. Factory overhead control	40,000	
Accumulated depreciation		20,000
Accounts payable (and other credits)		20,000
6. Work-in-process	60,000	
Factory overhead control		60,000
7. Finished goods	60,000	
Work-in-process		60,000

repairs and maintenance during periods of low manufacturing activity in order to minimize problems in working on equipment.

Moreover, when actual overhead costs are allocated to production, there are delays in product costing because of the need to wait until after the end of the month to determine actual overhead costs and the activity component. Most of these undesirable attributes can be eliminated by using a predetermined rate—budgeted overhead costs divided by budgeted activity.

Using Predetermined Overhead Rates

When manufacturing overhead is applied to work-in-process on a predetermined basis, the procedure is referred to as **normal costing.** Using cost-estimation methods described in the previous chapter, we can separate manufacturing overhead items into fixed and variable categories and develop a forecast of overhead costs for a year, based on an estimate of planned activity. For example, a company may develop a budget of its manufacturing overhead as shown in figure 3.17. The breakdown in costs

FIGURE 3.15
Cost
Assignment—
Actual Costs

	A	B	C	D	Total
Direct material	$30,000	$30,000	$20,000	$ 9,000	$ 89,000
Direct labor	15,000	20,000	10,000	5,000	50,000
Overhead*	15,000	28,000	17,000	10,000	70,000
	$60,000	$78,000	$47,000	$24,000	$209,000

*Overhead breakdown

	A	B	C	D	Total
Balance 1/1/X1	$ 5,000	$ 4,000	$ 1,000	$ 0	$ 10,000
Current allocation	10,000	24,000	16,000	10,000	60,000
	$15,000	$28,000	$17,000	$10,000	$ 70,000

Direct materials used	$ 54,000
Direct labor	30,000
Factory overhead	60,000
Total manufacturing costs	$144,000
Work-in-process, 1/1/X1	65,000
Total	$209,000
Work-in-process, 1/31/X1	149,000
Cost of goods manufactured	$ 60,000

FIGURE 3.16
XYZ Company—
Cost-of-Goods-
Manufactured
Schedule

represents a flexible budget, in that different rates could be calculated for different activity levels within a relevant range. We should also understand that budgets and rates might be calculated for different departments, rather than on a plantwide basis, if this results in a more accurate allocation of overhead costs.

The frequency with which rates should be adjusted is sometimes debated. If rates are adjusted too often, the results approach those achieved by applying actual overhead on a monthly basis. One of the advantages to predetermined rates, in addition to the ease with which overhead can be applied, results from the reduction of fluctuations caused by monthly volume changes. Remember, in the preceding section we discussed the problem associated with fluctuating production volume. The existence of a significant level of fixed costs may cause unit costs to change from month to month, sometimes significantly, when actual costs are applied. For this reason, we suggest annualized rates when using a normal costing system.

To see how normal costing works, we can use the XYZ Company example again. The following additional information is all that is required:

Expected factory overhead for 19X1	$600,000
Expected direct-labor costs	$400,000

Variable Costs	
Indirect materials	$ 25,000
Manufacturing supplies	45,000
Energy costs	60,000
Overtime premium	15,000
Defective unit costs	15,000
Other variable overhead	10,000
Total	$170,000
Fixed costs	
Supervision	$ 40,000
Depreciation	50,000
Taxes	10,000
Insurance	5,000
Other fixed overhead	5,000
Total	$110,000
Total manufacturing overhead projected	$280,000
Budgeted direct-labor hours	$ 70,000
Overhead rate per hour	$ 4.00

FIGURE 3.17
Manufacturing
Overhead Budget
for 19X1

Since direct-labor cost is assumed to be the activity component most closely related to overhead costs, an overhead rate of $1.50 per direct-labor dollar is obtained by dividing budgeted direct-labor costs into budgeted factory overhead. This rate is then used to allocate overhead to the various jobs. Using the same data as in the previous example, journal entries under normal costing are shown in figure 3.18.

You will note that the first five entries are the same as those shown in figure 3.14 under actual costing. However, entry six reflects overhead charges based on a predetermined rate of $1.50 per direct-labor dollar and $30,000 of direct-labor costs during the current period. Revised costs, based on normal costing are shown in figure 3.19.

In figure 3.18, you will see that work-in-process was charged for overhead and a credit was made to the account Factory Overhead Applied. Consequently, actual overhead incurred is charged to one account, Factory Overhead Control, and overhead applied to production is credited to Factory Overhead Applied.

The difference in balances between the two accounts represents **over- or under-applied overhead.** Underapplied overhead will result when actual costs exceed the applied costs. Conversely, overapplied overhead results when actual overhead costs are less than the applied costs. While the balances in the two accounts are not expected to offset one another exactly, the amount of over- or underapplied overhead is expected to be insignificant at the conclusion of an operating year.

Meeting Financial Reporting Needs

As a result of using normal costing or other estimated costs, certain financial reporting problems might exist. Generally accepted accounting principles require that product costs generated from any costing system approximate actual costs. These requirements can be met by making the following adjustments to normal costing differences.

FIGURE 3.18
Control Account Journal Entries— Normal Costing

1. Raw material inventory	60,000	
Accounts payable		60,000
2. Work-in-process	54,000	
Raw material inventory		54,000
3. Factory overhead control	10,000	
Raw material inventory		10,000
4. Work-in-process	30,000	
Factory overhead control	10,000	
Wages payable		40,000
5. Factory overhead control	40,000	
Accumulated depreciation		20,000
Accounts payable (and other credits)		20,000
6. Work-in-process	45,000	
Factory overhead applied		45,000
7. Finished goods	57,500	
Work-in-process		57,500

	A	B	C	D	Total
Direct material	$30,000	$30,000	$20,000	$ 9,000	$ 89,000
Direct labor	15,000	20,000	10,000	5,000	50,000
Overhead*	12,500	22,000	13,000	7,500	55,000
	$57,500	$72,000	$43,000	$21,500	$194,000

*Overhead breakdown

	A	B	C	D	Total
Balance 1/1/X1	$ 5,000	$ 4,000	$ 1,000	$ 0	$ 10,000
Current allocation	7,500	18,000	12,000	7,500	45,000
	$12,500	$22,000	$13,000	$ 7,500	$ 55,000

FIGURE 3.19
Cost
Assignment—
Normal Costs

1. Immaterial over- or underapplied balances can be closed to Cost of Sales.

2. Significant underapplied balances clearly resulting from abnormal operating conditions should be charged off as losses.

3. Significant estimating errors resulting in over- or underapplied overhead should be prorated to Work-in-Process, Finished Goods, and Cost of Sales.

Disposition of Differences

At the end of the operating year, any difference between over- and underapplied overhead must be disposed of in accordance with financial reporting requirements. As indicated earlier, minor and abnormal differences (losses) are charged off in the current period. However, a significant estimating difference requires an allocation of the difference between Work-in-Process, Finished Goods, and Cost of Sales. Assume that XYZ Company's year-end overhead accounts reflected underapplied overhead of $18,000 and that this difference is regarded as significant. Specific information about the End-of-Year Inventory and Cost of Sales balances is provided in figure 3.20.

Two different methods are generally available for prorating over- or underapplied factory overhead to Work-in-Process, Finished Goods, and Cost of Sales for purposes of approximating final balances under an actual costing system. Prorating by the amount of current-year factory overhead applied included in each of the various account balances is usually considered the best method because it is consistent with the manner in which overhead was allocated throughout the year. As shown in figure 3.20, the overhead-applied method requires detailed information on account balances.

The second method, which is based on balances in the accounts, will provide a reasonable basis for proration if the relative portions of material, labor, and overhead are constant from account to account. The second method is more likely to be used, since information for prorating on the basis of total balances is readily available from control accounts. Figure

FIGURE 3.20
XYZ Company—
End-of-year
Information

Balance in factory overhead control $500,000
Balance in factory overhead applied $482,000

Information on product related accounts

	Account balances at end of year			
	Work-in-process	*Finished goods*	*Cost of sales*	*Total*
Direct materials	$35,000	$30,000	$ 85,000	$150,000
Direct labor	10,000	20,000	30,000	60,000
Factory overhead applied	15,000	30,000	45,000	90,000
Total	$60,000	$80,000	$160,000	$300,000

Proration based on factory overhead applied

	Factory overhead applied included		Prorated
Work-in-process	$15,000	15/90 × 18,000 =	$ 3,000
Finished goods	30,000	30/90 × 18,000 =	6,000
Cost of sales	45,000	45/90 × 18,000 =	9,000
Total	$90,000		$18,000

Proration based on totals in accounts

	Totals		Prorated
Work-in-process	$ 60,000	60/300 × 18,000 =	$ 3,600
Finished goods	80,000	80/300 × 18,000 =	4,800
Cost of sales	160,000	160/300 × 18,000 =	9,600
Total	$300,000		$18,000

3.21 shows entries that would be required when the over- or underapplied overhead is prorated to the various account balances.

☐ SUMMARY

An understanding of cost flows and the components involved is essential to the development of product-cost-determination systems. Direct materials, direct labor, and factory overhead represent the basic cost-flow com-

FIGURE 3.21
Prorating Entries

Using factory overhead applied
    Work-in-process 3,000
    Finished goods 6,000
    Cost of sales 9,000
        Factory overhead applied 18,000

Using totals in accounts
    Work-in-process 3,600
    Finished goods 4,800
    Cost of sales 9,600
        Factory overhead applied 18,000

ponents. It is important to relate these flows to the various inventory accounts—material, work-in-process, and finished goods—and to the final objective, which is represented by sales and cost of sales.

In the simplest situation, the basic merchandising accounting system can be adapted to handle manufacturing operations. If work-in-process and finished goods can be estimated without reference to a formal system, the various costs can be accumulated by a cost-of-goods-manufactured or cost-of-goods-sold statement.

As greater accuracy is needed in determining cost of goods sold and unit costs for work-in-process and finished goods, sophisticated cost-accounting procedures must be set up to determine, accumulate, assign, and transfer production costs from one stage to another until the product has been completed. Two basic product-cost-determination systems for estimating the unit costs of manufactured products are job-order costing and process costing.

Job-order costing systems are usually used as the means of accumulating costs for products if the products are made to customer specifications or if the production cycle is particularly long so that several time periods elapse before the primary output is completed. The basic process begins with a production order being issued to produce some product or component. Costs are accumulated on a job cost sheet from the stores requisitions, the labor tickets, and the overhead applied. The overhead costs assigned are based on either an actual rate (actual costs divided by actual activity component) or a predetermined rate (budgeted overhead divided by budgeted activity component).

KEY TERMS

Actual costing　　　　　　　　　　　**Job-order costing**
Cost of goods manufactured　　　　**Normal costing**
Job cost sheet　　　　　　　　　　　**Over- or underapplied overhead**
　　　　　　　　　　　　　　　　　　　Predetermined overhead rate

REVIEW PROBLEM*

The Rich Company manufactures customized special-purpose recreational equipment. At the start of the new fiscal year, only one order was in-process. Details of the job are as follows:

	Job 5100
Direct materials	$ 5,000
Direct labor	2,800
Manufacturing overhead	5,000
	$12,800

In January of the new year, the following transactions took place:

1. Raw materials, totaling $56,000, were purchased on account.

2. Direct-material requisitions were issued for the following jobs:

Job 5100	$ 1,500
5101	3,600
5102	2,200
5103	3,400
	$10,700

3. Wages paid to manufacturing employees are related to current month manufacturing activities and total $9,000. Labor tickets indicate that direct labor should be charged to the following jobs:

Job 5100	$ 800
5101	2,200
5102	1,600
5103	1,200
	$5,800

4. Other manufacturing overhead incurred for the current month is as follows:

Depreciation	$4,000
Indirect material	1,400
Repairs	1,600
Energy expense	1,400

Jobs 5100 and 5101 were finished during the month. Job 5100 was sold to customers for $25,000. Overhead is applied to production using direct-labor cost as the activity component.

Required ☐

1. Using actual costing, prepare a cost-of-goods-manufactured schedule and prepare journal entries for all transactions.

2. Using normal costing (assume a ratio of 250 percent of direct-labor cost), prepare a cost-of-goods-manufactured schedule and prepare only those journal entries that would be different from those called for in requirement 1.

Solution ☐

1. Rich Company—Cost-of-Goods-Manufactured Schedule

Direct materials used	$10,700
Direct labor	5,800
Manufacturing overhead	11,600
Total manufacturing costs	$28,100
Beginning work-in-process	12,800
Total	$40,900
Ending work-in-process	14,000
Cost of goods manufactured	$26,900

Journal entries

Raw materials inventory	56,000	
Accounts payable		56,000

Work-in-process	10,700	
Raw materials inventory		10,700
Manufacturing overhead control	1,400	
Raw materials inventory		1,400
Work-in-process	5,800	
Manufacturing overhead control	3,200	
Wages payable		9,000
Manufacturing overhead control	7,000	
Accumulated depreciation		4,000
Other credits		3,000
Work-in-process	11,600	
Manufacturing overhead control		11,600
Finished goods	26,900	
Work-in-process		26,900
Accounts receivable	25,000	
Sales		25,000
Cost of sales	16,700	
Finished goods		16,700

2. Rich Company—Cost-of-Goods-Manufactured Schedule

Direct materials used	$10,700
Direct labor	5,800
Manufacturing overhead applied	14,500
Total manufacturing costs	$31,000
Beginning work-in-process	12,800
Total	$43,800
Ending work-in-process	15,400
Cost of goods manufactured	$28,400

Journal entries

Work-in-process	14,500	
Manufacturing overhead applied		14,500
Finished goods	28,400	
Work-in-process		28,400
Cost of sales	17,100	
Finished goods		17,100

QUESTIONS

Q3-1. Describe the basic differences between merchandising operations and manufacturing operations from the standpoint of the accounting system.

Q3-2. Discuss the basic similarities and differences between direct materials, direct labor, and factory overhead.

Q3-3. Describe the difference between a cost-of-goods-sold statement and a cost-of-goods-manufactured statement.

Q3-4. Identify source documents and essential information that might be used to provide information on material usage and labor costs.

Q3-5. Describe the purpose of the job cost sheet and the procedures for its use.

Q3-6. What does the amount for cost of goods manufactured represent? Explain.

Q3-7. Discuss the various alternatives available for assigning overhead costs to production. Which method is usually preferable? Why?

Q3-8. What type of operations generally lend themselves to job-order systems?

Q3-9. Identify some applications of job-order systems outside of manufacturing operations.

Q3-10. In an actual costing system should over- or underapplied overhead be expected? Why?

Q3-11. Does it make any difference what activity base is used for allocating overhead costs to a job? Does it matter whether the rate is set on a departmental or overall basis? Discuss fully.

Q3-12. Discuss the significance of over- or underapplied overhead and what should be done with it.

PROBLEMS

Cost of Goods Manufactured **P3-1.** A partial trial balance of XYZ Company revealed the following:

Sales	$600,000
Purchases of direct material	260,000
Indirect materials	30,000
Direct labor	48,000
Indirect labor	48,000
Plant and equipment depreciation	54,000
Heat, light, and power	22,000
Sales salaries	50,000
Administrative salaries	60,000
Beginning inventories	
Direct materials	84,000
Work-in-process	70,000
Finished goods	96,000
Ending inventories	
Direct materials	76,000
Work-in-process	69,000
Finished goods	122,000

Required □ Prepare a cost-of-goods-manufactured schedule.

Cost of Goods Manufactured **P3-2.** The Helper Corporation manufactures one product and accounts for costs by a job-order cost system. You have obtained the following information for the year ended December 31, 19X3:

a. Total manufacturing cost added during 19X3 (sometimes called cost to manufacture) was $1 million, which was based on actual direct material, actual direct labor, and applied factory overhead on actual direct-labor dollars.

b. Cost of goods manufactured was $970,000, also based on actual direct material, actual direct labor, and applied factory overhead.

c. Factory overhead was applied to work-in-process at 75 percent of direct-labor dollars. Applied factory overhead for the year was 27 percent of the total manufacturing cost.

d. Beginning work-in-process inventory, January 1, was 80 percent of ending work-in-process inventory, December 31.

Required □ Prepare a of cost-of-goods-manufactured schedule for the year ended December 31, 19X3, for Helper Corporation. Use actual direct material used, actual direct labor, and applied factory overhead. Show supporting computations in good form.

(CPA)

P3-3. The Morse Company manufactures a single product and uses a job-order cost system. The following information has been obtained from the company's records for the year ended December 31, 19X4:

Cost of Goods Manufactured

a. Direct materials purchased during 19X4 was $450,000. Total direct materials available during the year was $650,000. Ending inventory of direct materials was 150 percent of the beginning inventory.

b. Ending work-in-process inventory was 80 percent of beginning work-in-process inventory.

c. Cost of goods sold for the year ended December 31, 19X4, was $800,000. Beginning finished-goods inventory was $150,000 and ending finished-goods inventory was $200,000.

d. Direct labor was 50 percent of direct materials used in manufacturing. Direct-labor costs were 150 percent of manufacturing overhead.

Required □ Prepare a schedule of cost of goods manufactured for the year ended December 31, 19X4, for Morse Company. Show supporting computations in good form.

P3-4. The controller for XYZ Company established a predetermined rate for applying overhead in the company's job-order costing system. Using a rough projection of overhead costs for the coming year and estimated direct-labor hours, the following calculation can be developed.

Manufacturing Overhead

$$\frac{\text{Projected factory overhead}}{\text{Direct-labor hours}} = \frac{\$100,000}{10,000} = \$10$$

During the next twelve months, total direct-labor hours worked were 10,100 and actual factory overhead, broken down, was as follows:

Equipment depreciation	$25,000
Rent	20,000
Maintenance	5,000
Energy expense	8,000
Indirect materials	4,000
Taxes	6,000

Required □ What was the amount of over- or underapplied overhead? Provide some possible reasons for the difference between actual and applied overhead.

Manufacturing **P3-5.** The accountants for Blue Ribbon Company have asked for your assistance
Overhead in a decision involving use of actual overhead charges versus estimated
overhead charges in their job-order costing system. Assume they had estimated manufacturing overhead at the beginning of the year, and using
direct labor hours as a component, had calculated a rate of $5 per direct-
labor hour. However, they did not use the estimated rate.

Actual manufacturing overhead was $150,500 for the year, and 30,000 di-
rect-labor hours were incurred in manufacturing operations.

Required ☐

1. Prepare a schedule for the accountants showing the type of journal
   entries likely to be made under each system.

2. Explain the significance of the amount of over- or underapplied overhead that would have resulted had the estimated rate been used. Describe how the over- or underapplied overhead would be recognized in
   the accounting records.

3. Would you recommend that the company use an estimated overhead
   rate? Why? If you found that their manufacturing overhead costs were
   largely variable, would you change your recommendation?

Manufacturing **P3-6.** The Radford Heavy Equipment Company uses predetermined overhead
Overhead rates to apply overhead to work-in-process on an individual-department
basis. For department 1, overhead is applied based on direct-labor hours;
for department 2, it is based on machine hours.

Projected overhead for each of the two departments is as follows:

	Dept. 1	Dept. 2
Projected overhead	$250,000	$320,000
Overhead rate	$2	$4

At the conclusion of the company's operating year, overhead was underapplied by $60,000, of which 40 percent was attributable to department 1.
Actual hours in both departments equaled those used in setting the rates.

Required ☐

1. What was the amount of overhead underapplied in department 2?

2. How many direct-labor hours were used in establishing the rate for
   department 1?

3. How much overhead was applied to work-in-process in department 2?

4. What are some of the more likely causes of the underapplied overhead?

Manufacturing **P3-7.** The predetermined overhead rate was $2.50, based on a forecasted volume
Overhead of 50,000 direct-labor hours. Actual direct-labor hours for the year were
45,000 direct-labor hours. Fixed overhead included in the budget for the
year was $50,000. Assuming the actual overhead costs equal the budgeted
costs, adjusted for the difference in volume, what is the amount of over-
or underapplied overhead for the year? What caused the difference?

P3-8. The Ann Justin Company uses an actual job-order costing system. The following transactions related to a single period.

Journal Entries for Actual Job-Order Costing

a. Beginning inventory of raw materials, $40,000
b. Raw material purchases, $80,000
c. Direct-labor costs, $65,000 (Actual direct-labor hours incurred, 10,000)
d. Overhead costs, $48,000
e. Overhead applied to production on an actual basis based on actual direct-labor hours
f. Beginning inventory of work-in-process, $60,000
g. Ending inventory of raw materials $20,000 (none of the raw materials were used as indirect materials)
h. Ending inventory of work-in-process, $173,000
i. Production orders that cost $100,000 were completed and sold for $200,000.

Required ☐ Prepare journal entries for the activity just described and determine the balances of the various inventory accounts.

P3-9. The Candy Company has been using a job-order costing system for several years. However, this is the first year that the company has used normal costing. The following entries relate to transactions for the year.

Journal Entries for Normal Job-Order Costing

1. Direct materials issued to manufacturing, $250,000

2. Total manufacturing overhead for the year, $180,000

3. Direct-labor costs for the year, $200,000

4. Manufacturing overhead is applied on the basis of 85 percent of the direct-labor costs.

5. Production amounting to $600,000 was completed during the year.

6. Sales of $590,000 were made during the year. Cost of the materials sold was $350,000.

At the beginning of the year, work-in-process inventory totaled $50,000.

Required ☐ Prepare the required journal entries for the transactions.

P3-10. The Leininger Company manufactures customized special-purpose fireworks. At the beginning of the current year, only one order was in-process. Costs applicable to the job were as follows:

Actual Job-Order Costing

	Job 1050
Direct materials	$4,000
Direct labor	2,000
Factory overhead	2,500
	$8,500

During the first month of the new year, the following transactions took place:

Raw materials, totaling $60,000, were purchased on account.

Direct material requisitions for the following jobs were prepared and used:

Job 1050	$ 1,000
1051	4,000
1052	2,000
1053	2,500
1054	2,000
	$11,500

Wages paid to factory employees were related to current month activities and totaled $10,000. Labor tickets indicated direct labor should be charged to the following jobs:

Job 1050	$ 500
1051	2,500
1052	2,000
1053	2,600
1054	1,000

Depreciation applicable to production for the month was $6,000.

Indirect material charged to factory overhead was $2,000.

Miscellaneous overhead totaled $920 for the month.

Jobs 1050 and 1051 were completed during the month. Job 1050 was sold to the customers for $12,500. Overhead is applied to production on an actual basis using direct-labor cost as the activity component.

Required ☐

1. Prepare a cost-of-goods-manufactured schedule.

2. Prepare summary job cost sheets for each job.

Job-Order Costing Using Actual Costs

P3-11. The Weis Company, a custom manufacturer of furniture, uses an actual job-order costing system. At the beginning of June, three jobs were in-process:

Job	Direct material	Direct labor	Manufacturing overhead
226	2,500	1,200	900
228	800	600	450
229	950	500	375

Direct materials put into manufacturing during the month totaled $14,500. Direct-labor costs incurred were $12,000. Actual factory overhead incurred was $9,600. Overhead costs are allocated based on direct-labor costs.

During June, Jobs 230, 231, 232, 233, and 234 were started. There was no finished-goods inventory at the beginning or end of June. At the end of June, Job 234 was still in-process with costs assigned of $2,500 for direct materials and $2,000 for direct labor.

Required ☐

1. Make appropriate journal entries.

2. Prepare a cost-of-goods-manufactured schedule.

P3-12. Data relating to Job 200 produced by Quality Furniture Company have been collected.

Use of Job-Order Cost Sheet— Normal Costing

Direct materials on the job:

September 10	$2,000
September 12	1,500
September 20	1,000
September 24	500

Direct labor incurred:

	Hours	Cost
Payroll first week	400	$1,200
Payroll second week	300	900
Payroll third week	200	600
Payroll fourth week	100	300

Overhead is applied using a predetermined rate based on direct-labor hours. Expected overhead for the year is $200,000. Expected direct-labor hours are 100,000.

Required ☐ Prepare a job-order cost sheet for this job that shows the total cost of the job to date.

P3-13. Construct job-order cost sheets to accumulate the proper information from the following data:

Use of Job-Order Cost Sheet— Normal Costing

Work-in-process, beginning of period:

Job	Direct material	Direct labor	Overhead
100	$600	$400	$200
150	800	800	450
200	500	200	150

Material issued from stores:

Job	Amount
100	$200
150	300
200	400
250	450
300	500

Excess materials returned to stores from Job 100, $50. Direct-labor costs for the period:

Department	Amount
A	$2,250
B	2,600

Direct-labor hours for the period:

	Department	
Job	A	B
100	50	100
150	100	200

200	....	200	50
250	....	150	200
300	....	400	100

Overhead is charged to jobs on a normal-costing basis using direct-labor hours. The predetermined rate for Department A is $2 per hour and for Department B, $3 per hour.

Journal Entries for Job-Order Costing

P3-14. Given the information in problem 3-13 and assuming Jobs 100 and 150 were completed, prepare the various entries to record the activity for the period.

Job-Order Costing Relationships

P3-15. For each case shown in the following schedule, compute the missing values.

	Situation A	Situation B
Sales		125,000
Direct materials used	54,000	60,000
Direct labor	30,000	
Factory overhead		20,000
Finished goods 1/1/X1	30,000	10,000
Work-in-process 12/31/X1	149,000	40,000
Total manufacturing costs	104,000	
Selling expenses	10,000	6,000
Finished goods 12/31/X1		5,000
Administrative expenses	10,000	4,000
Cost of goods manufactured	60,000	80,000
Work-in-process 1/1/X1		20,000
Gross profit		
Cost of goods sold	60,000	
Operating profit	40,000	

Manufacturing Overhead— Actual vs. Normal Costing

P3-16. You have been engaged to install a cost system for the Martin Company. Your investigation of the manufacturing operations of the business discloses these facts:

a. The company makes a line of lighting fixtures and lamps. The material cost of any particular item ranges from 15 percent to 60 percent of total factory cost, depending on the kinds of metal and fabric used in making it.

b. The business is subject to wide cyclical fluctuations, since the sales volume follows new housing construction.

c. About 60 percent of the manufacturing is normally done in the first quarter of the year.

d. For the whole plant, the wages range from $1.25 to $3.75 per hour. However, within each of the eight individual departments, the spread between the high and low wage rate is less than 5 percent.

e. Each of the products made uses all eight of the manufacturing departments but not proportionately.

f. Within the individual manufacturing departments, factory overhead ranges from 30 percent to 80 percent of conversion cost.

Required ☐

1. Based on the information just given, prepare a statement for the president of the company that explains whether Martin Company should use in its cost system:

a. A normal overhead rate or an actual overhead rate
b. An overall overhead rate or a departmental overhead rate
c. A method of factory overhead distribution based on direct-labor hours, direct-labor cost, or prime cost

2. Include the reasons supporting each of your three recommendations.

(CPA)

P3-17. Rebecca Company uses a job-order costing system and applies overhead on a normal costing basis. At year-end the balance in Factory Overhead Control is $50,000 greater than the balance in Factory Overhead Applied. Information concerning relevant account balances at year-end are as follows:

Proration of Underapplied Overhead

	Work-in-process	Finished goods	Cost of sales
Direct materials	$20,000	$ 40,000	$ 60,000
Direct labor	10,000	20,000	25,000
Factory overhead applied	20,000	40,000	50,000
	$50,000	$100,000	$135,000

Required ☐

1. Using the information given, what overhead rate was likely used during the year?

2. Provide arguments to be used for deciding whether or not to prorate the underapplied overhead.

3. Assuming a decision to prorate is made, prepare the required entry using the best method for prorating.

4. Identify possible reasons for the underapplied overhead.

P3-18. Daniel Construction Company uses a job-order costing system and applies overhead based on predetermined rates. At year-end the balance in manufacturing overhead control is $10,000 less than the balance in manufacturing overhead applied. There is no beginning work-in-process. Information concerning relevant account balances at year-end are as follows:

Proration of Variances

	Work-in-process	Finished goods	Cost of sales
Direct materials	$40,000	$120,000	$200,000
Direct labor	15,000	60,000	120,000
Manufacturing overhead applied	22,500	90,000	120,000
	$77,500	$270,000	$440,000

Required ☐

1. What was the total balance in manufacturing overhead control for the year?

2. Do you think the $10,000 should be prorated? Explain.

3. Assuming a decision to prorate is made, prepare the required entry, using the best method for prorating.

4. What steps would you take to minimize the amount of under- or overapplied overhead at year-end?

Correction of Errors, Job-Order Costing

P3-19. The president of Small Corporation has requested your assistance in reconstructing a summary of factory operations during April for a job-order cost system. The records have been maintained inadequately since the bookkeeper left for another position early in the month.

The corporation's cost system includes a general ledger and a factory production ledger with reciprocal control accounts. A trial balance of the factory production ledger at April 1, 19X2, showed the following:

	Debits	Credits
Raw materials	$30,000	
Store supplies inventory	10,000	
Work-in-process	20,000	
General ledger control		$60,000
	$60,000	$60,000

After reviewing the work done up to April 1, you gathered the information presented in the following table for the month of April from the sources indicated.

| | | | | | Work-in-Process | | | |
| | | | | | Service depts. | | Producing depts. | |
Sources of information	General ledger control	Raw materials	Store supplies	Total	Power plant	General plant	Pattern foundry	Machine shop
From voucher register								
Purchases	$(27,150)	$20,000	$ 7,150					
Direct labor	(6,150)			$ 6,150	$300	$ 350	$ 2,200	$3,300
Direct-manufacturing expenses	(2,300)			2,300	50	175	730	1,345
Assets acquired	(9,400)							
Prepaid insurance	(3,000)							
From general ledger entries								
Depreciation	(1,100)			1,100	140	80	*	*
Property taxes	(250)			250	40	20	*	*
Expired insurance	(500)			500	100	25	*	*
Repairs to power plant	(320)			320	320			
From requisitions								
Raw materials		(27,000)		27,000	500	1,000	15,500	10,000
Store supplies	150		(15,150)	15,000	150	1,350	9,000	4,500
From cost-of-finished-jobs report								
Shipped to customers	45,000			(45,000)				
For company's own use	2,460			(2,460)				

Bases for distribution of costs:
   Power plant—50% to each producing department.
   General plant—store supplies issued to producing departments.
*Indirect costs of producing departments to be distributed on basis of direct-labor costs.
   Balance indicated by debit/(credit).

Required □ Prepare a summary worksheet for the month ended April 30, 19X2, to compute:

a. Direct, indirect, and total costs that should be debited to work-in-process for the month.
b. The distribution of Service department costs.
c. The April 30, 19X2, balances of the following accounts in the factory production ledger—
    (1) General ledger control
    (2) Raw materials
    (3) Store supplies
    (4) Work-in-process

(CPA)

P3-20. The Keefe Fireworks Company was a leading manufacturer of all-occasion   *Cost Flows*
fireworks. The company used a secret Chinese process in manufacturing, and its fireworks were known throughout the world for their ability to create noise.

On November 1, 19X3, the company produced its biggest bang ever when its factory blew up. Although the company was located in Churchville, Pennsylvania, people as far away as New York City heard the blast. Some scraps of accounting information were found at the scene of the blast and others were found many miles from Churchville. Your accounting instructor, Jane Hoover, and several helpful students were able to find some information relating to the Keefe cost system. Read the following information concerning these exhibits carefully and then follow the instructions at the conclusion of the problem.

a. The cost sheet for job number TO-11-19-1, for the production of 500 skyrockets ordered by the town of Churchville and Churchville Technical School to celebrate the expected Tech victory over State in Saturday's football game. This sheet, which was found to the delight of your accounting instructor, indicated that the following costs had been incurred on this particular job:

Direct material	$ 550
Direct labor	1,100
Overhead	1,375
Total	$3,025

b. A page from the accounting procedure manual stating that overapplied or underapplied factory overhead should be assigned as follows: cost of sales, 90 percent, finished goods, 10 percent. Factory overhead is to be applied as a percentage of the direct-labor cost.
c. A memo from Roman Candle, controller, to Sky Rocket, the president, explaining why factory overhead was underapplied by $1,000 for the period of January 1, 19X3, to November 1, 19X3.
d. Actual overhead detail:

Indirect material	$ 15,000
Indirect labor	20,000
Depreciation	20,000
Rent	15,000
Heat	20,000

Light	10,000
Miscellaneous	1,000
Total	$101,000

e. A copy of the Keefe annual report for the year ended December 31, 19X2, which revealed year-end inventories as follows: materials, $7,500; work-in-process, $15,000; and finished goods, $20,000.

f. A memo from John Arson, head of inventory control, to Roman Candle, controller, commenting on the inventory as of November 1, 19X3. *No adjustment had been made to the inventory figures for the over- or under-applied factory overhead.* The inventory figures were as follows: materials, $15,000, work-in-process, $20,000; and finished goods, $10,000.

g.

KEEFE FIREWORKS COMPANY
Income Statement
For eleven months ending Nov. 1, 19X3

Sales		$400,000
Cost of goods sold		
(Adjusted for overhead applied)		288.900
Gross profit		$111,100
Administrative expenses	$32,000	
Selling expenses	68,172	100,172
Net income		$ 10,928

Required □ Record the flow of cost from January 1 to November 1, 19X3, as it must have taken place. Make journal entries and post them in the T-accounts. Key your entries with letters.

Materials (Direct and indirect)	Work-in-process	Finished goods

Cost of goods sold	Factory overhead control	Factory overhead applied

Over- or under-applied overhead	Payroll

CHAPTER OUTLINE

PROCESS COSTING

CHAPTER **4**

☐ INTRODUCTION

Job-order costing systems, which were discussed in chapter 3, are not appropriate if there is continuous mass production of similar units. In such situations, a process-costing system is called for to facilitate cost accumulation and cost determination by specific periods of time.

Comprehensive material relating to process costing is presented in this chapter and the next. This chapter covers (1) the characteristics of process costing, (2) the basic procedures involved, (3) the cost-of-production report, and (4) the impact of beginning inventories. Chapter 5 covers problems related to the addition of materials in subsequent departments and assesses the impact of lost and spoiled units on process-costing systems.

☐ BASIC CHARACTERISTICS OF PROCESS COSTING

Process costing is well suited to situations in which similar products are mass produced on a more or less continuous basis. Process costing is likely to be found in the chemical, food processing, pharmaceutical, oil, textile, steel, glass, cannery, cement, mining, shoes, plastic, and paint industries. Applications of process costing may also be found in nonmanufacturing environments such as hospitals, fast-food operations and banks.

Attention is directed to processes (production departments), time periods, and unit costs. This means that during specified periods material, labor, and overhead costs are accumulated by department. When products are processed in more than one department, the work is transferred to successive departments until products are completed and ready for final disposition. The basic process is outlined in figure 4.1.

The diagram indicates that material, labor, and overhead are initially used in the Fabrication department. As units are completed in the first department, units and costs are transferred to the next department, which is Assembly. Some combination of material, labor, and overhead is used in the Assembly department (materials may or may not be added in each

FIGURE 4.1
Outline of Process
Costing Flows

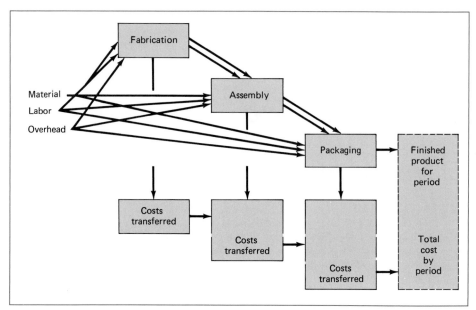

of the departments). When work is completed in Assembly, units and costs of completed units are again transferred to the next department.

Although specific procedures are likely to depend on the accounting system used, costs are summarized and transferred by means of journal entries on a periodic rather than continuous basis. Actual products are transferred continuously, as completed.

One should keep in mind that the basic procedures for accumulating costs of material, labor, and overhead discussed in chapter 3 will probably be the same whether a job-order or process-costing system is used, except for minor modifications needed because of a different product-costing system.

You should also observe that both job-order costing and process costing are averaging processes. Because job-order costing focuses attention on the manufacture of a particular product for a limited time period, units of output used in calculating unit costs tend to be smaller and are not tied to time periods.

The situation outlined in figure 4.1 might be described as sequential in that all units are assumed to flow through the indicated departments. In other production situations, work may be initiated in separate departments simultaneously, with the separate processes paralleling each other until they are merged at some point in a subsequent department. Still another production process might call for some products to run through certain departments and not others on a selective basis.

□ BASIC PROCEDURES
FOR PROCESS COSTING

Essentially, process costing is a process in which units are expressed in terms of equivalent units instead of physical units, and unit costs are developed so that costs can be assigned to current manufacturing output. Procedurally, a process-costing system should be designed to:

1. Account for the physical units in production.

2. Calculate the relevant equivalent units.

3. Accumulate the various components of cost—material, labor, and overhead—for each department.

4. Determine unit costs for each cost component.

5. Assign costs to finished goods and work in process.

As indicated earlier, the various cost components are supplied by the basic accounting system that is applicable to either job order or process costing—an inventory system with material requisitions, a payroll system with time cards and labor tickets, and various overhead records. Physical units are also accounted for through the inventory-control system, with production personnel usually estimating and assigning the percentage of completion to components of work-in-process inventories.

The management accountant's job is to gather information on the units and their costs and to assign costs to goods completed and to ending work-in-process inventories for financial reporting purposes. In addition to accounting for physical units, one of the most important initial steps is to calculate equivalent units.

Physical Units and Equivalent Units

You will likely find that your most significant hurdle in mastering process costing is learning how to handle partially completed units in ending inventory when assigning costs to current period production. To overcome this problem, information we develop concerning physical units is converted to equivalent units. Consider the following two situations:

Situation one

Units started in production	10,000
Units completed	10,000

Situation two

Units started in production	10,000
Units completed	8,000
Work-in-process, 50 percent complete	2,000
	10,000

In the first situation we encounter no problems, since we have no ending work-in-process inventory to consider. If we had information on production costs, it would be a simple matter to calculate the unit cost of products completed. Situation two is somewhat more complex because of the 2,000 units partially complete at the end of the period. In thinking about production efforts for the period, we might suggest that more than 8,000 **equivalent units** have been completed because of the efforts already devoted to the 2,000 partially completed units. If 50 percent of each cost component—material, labor, and overhead—is included in the work-in-process inventory, we logically argue that, given an equivalent amount of effort, 1,000 units should be completed (2,000 × .50). For process costing purposes, this is the justification we use to calculate output on an equivalent-unit basis so that unit costs can be developed. Continuing with situation two, we have 10,000 physical units and 9,000 equivalent units calculated as follows:

Description	Physical units	Equivalent units
Units completed	8,000	8,000
Ending work-in-process	2,000	
All components (2,000 × .50)		1,000
	10,000	9,000

Frequently, in process-costing situations, the percentages for material, labor, and overhead components will be different. In such cases, different equivalent units will have to be calculated for each of the components. How many equivalent units of output would result if all of the necessary material had been added for the 2,000 partially completed units but only fifty percent of the labor and overhead had been added? In this situation, the equivalent units would be calculated as follows:

Materials	
Units completed	8,000
Work-in-process, 100 percent complete	
for materials	2,000
Equivalent units	10,000
*Labor and Overhead**	
Units completed	8,000
Work-in-process, 50 percent complete	
for labor and overhead	1,000
Equivalent units	9,000

*When the percentage of completion is the same, labor and overhead (conversion costs) can be either combined or shown separately.

Although direct material is most often put into production at the beginning of the process, it may be entered into production at some other point or throughout the process. Labor and overhead might also vary depending on the production process.

Cost Assignment—The Goal

The goal in any product-costing system is to be able to assign the total costs of production to the units transferred to finished goods and to work-in-process inventory. In process costing, unit costs are calculated for each cost component—material, labor, and overhead—and used to assign costs to the equivalent units included in finished goods and work-in-process.

Unit costs are determined by dividing production costs for each cost component by the equivalent units for each component. Referring to our previous example in which there were 10,000 equivalent units for material and 9,000 equivalent units for labor and overhead, assume the accounting system indicated the following production costs had been incurred during the period:

Direct materials	$40,000
Direct labor	36,000
Factory overhead	18,000
Total production costs	$94,000

Given this information (available in any product-costing system), determination of the unit costs is easily accomplished.

Unit cost calculations
1. Direct materials
   $40,000 ÷ 10,000 equivalent units = $ 4.00
2. Direct labor
   $36,000 ÷ 9,000 equivalent units = 4.00
3. Factory overhead
   $18,000 ÷ 9,000 equivalent units = 2.00
   Total unit cost $10.00

Costs are then assigned to production by multiplying equivalent units in each category by their respective unit costs. For this example, costs would be assigned as follows:

Goods completed
8,000 units × $10 unit cost $80,000
Work-in-process
Materials
2,000 equivalent units × $4 unit cost 8,000
Labor and overhead
1,000 equivalent units × $6 unit cost 6,000
$14,000
Total production costs assigned $94,000

Basic Format and Control

Several steps should be followed in assigning costs in a process-costing system. The **physical flow** of production should be traced and reconciled in terms of units to be accounted for and units accounted for. Units to be accounted for include beginning inventory plus units started. Units accounted for include units completed and ending inventory. Physical flow reconciliation for the previous example is:

Physical flows
1. Units to be accounted for
   Beginning inventory 0
   Units started 10,000
   Total 10,000
2. Units accounted for
   Units completed 8,000
   Ending inventory (50 percent complete
   with respect to conversion) 2,000
   Total 10,000

Similarly, **cost flows** should be reconciled. Costs to be accounted for include all costs charged to production in the current period plus costs of beginning inventory. Costs accounted for include costs assigned to finished goods and ending work-in-process inventory. The cost-flow reconciliation for the example is:

Cost flows
1. Costs to be accounted for

Direct material	$40,000
Direct labor	36,000
Factory overhead	18,000
Total	$94,000

2. Costs accounted for

Goods completed

8,000 × $10	$80,000
Work-in-process	
Materials	
2,000 × $4	$ 8,000
Labor	
1,000 × $4	4,000
Overhead	
1,000 × $2	2,000
	$14,000
Total	$94,000

A cost-of-production report, showing complete information on the physical units and their costs, is shown in figure 4.2. The primary difference in the information shown on the cost-of-production report as compared with our preceding calculations is that direct labor and factory overhead are combined and shown as **conversion costs** in the report. Unless there is a reason to separate the two cost components, subsequent examples will combine them and use the term conversion costs. Although the basic format for a cost-of-production report varies considerably, both physical and cost flows should be included in the report. Sample journal entries related to the example are shown in figure 4.3.

Review Example

Before discussing some of the complicating factors involved in process costing, the following problem and complete solution are given so that key elements discussed in the previous material can be reviewed and better understood. Careful attention should be given to the problem and solution since the problem involves a two-department situation that is somewhat more difficult.

The Virginia Corporation manufactures one product on a continuous basis. Operations are carried on in two departments—Machining and Polishing. Materials are added at the beginning of the process in the first department. No new material is added in the Polishing department. Labor and overhead are added continuously throughout the process in each of the two departments.

Required □ For both the Machining and Polishing departments, prepare a cost-of-production report for the month of June.

FIGURE 4.2
Cost-of-Production
Report

Physical flows	Units		
	Physical	Equivalent	
		Direct materials	Conversion costs
Units to be accounted for			
Beginning work-in-process	0		
Units started	10,000		
Total	10,000		
Units accounted for			
Units completed	8,000	8,000	8,000
Ending work-in-process			
(50 percent complete)*	2,000	2,000	1,000
Total	10,000	10,000	9,000

*Materials complete; conversion costs are 50 percent complete.

Cost flows	Totals	Direct materials	Conversion costs
Costs to be accounted for			
Direct materials	$40,000	$40,000	
Conversion costs	54,000		$54,000
Total	$94,000	$40,000	$54,000
Unit cost		$4	$6
Costs accounted for			
Units completed			
(8,000 × $10)	$80,000		
Ending work-in-process			
Materials (2,000 × $4)	$8,000		
Conversion (1,000 × $6)	6,000		
Total work-in-process	$14,000		
Total	$94,000		

For the month of June, company records indicate the following physical flows:

	Machining	Polishing
Work-in-process, June 1	0	0
Units started	40,000	
Units tranferred in		30,000
Units completed	30,000	25,000
Work-in-process, June 30	10,000	5,000

Units in-process at the end of June were 80 percent complete in the Machining department and 50 percent complete in the Polishing department. Cost records indicated the following costs for the month of June:

	Machining	Polishing
Materials	$200,000	—
Labor	152,000	$165,000
Overhead	76,000	137,500

FIGURE 4.3
Sample Journal
Entries

FIGURE 4.3
Sample Journal
Entries

```
Entries relating to inputs of cost components
1. Work-in-process—materials  ............................    40,000
     Raw materials inventory  ...............................              40,000

2. Work-in-process—labor  .........................    36,000
     Wages payable  .........................................              36,000

3. Work-in-process—overhead  .........................    18,000
     Factory overhead applied  ...........................              18,000

Entries relating to assignment of costs
4. Finished-goods inventory  .............................    80,000
     Work-in-process  ......................................              80,000
```

The relationship between unit and cost figures (as highlighted in figure 4.4) should be carefully reviewed and understood before one moves on to additional examples. Total units of 40,000 to be accounted for are traced to units completed and ending work-in-process. Total costs to be accounted

FIGURE 4.4
The Virginia
Corporation Cost-
of-Production
Report—
Machining

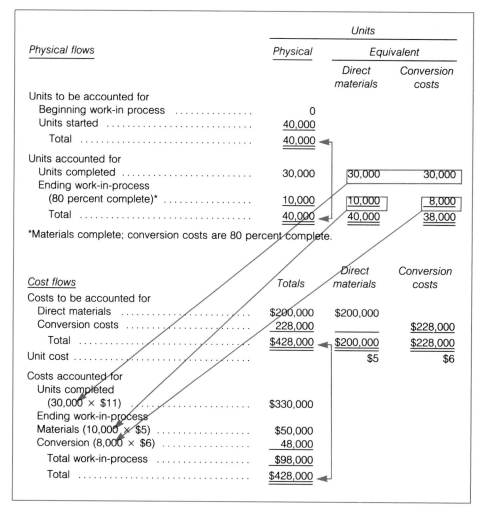

Physical flows	Units		
	Physical	Equivalent	
		Direct materials	Conversion costs
Units to be accounted for			
Beginning work-in process	0		
Units started	40,000		
Total	40,000		
Units accounted for			
Units completed	30,000	30,000	30,000
Ending work-in-process			
(80 percent complete)*	10,000	10,000	8,000
Total	40,000	40,000	38,000

*Materials complete; conversion costs are 80 percent complete.

Cost flows	Totals	Direct materials	Conversion costs
Costs to be accounted for			
Direct materials	$200,000	$200,000	
Conversion costs	228,000		$228,000
Total	$428,000	$200,000	$228,000
Unit cost		$5	$6
Costs accounted for			
Units completed			
(30,000 × $11)	$330,000		
Ending work-in-process			
Materials (10,000 × $5)	$50,000		
Conversion (8,000 × $6)	48,000		
Total work-in-process	$98,000		
Total	$428,000		

for of $428,000 are traced to cost of units completed and ending work-in-process. The 30,000 unit figure used in calculating the cost of finished goods comes directly from the equivalent unit calculations, as does the number of units used in calculating the cost for ending work-in-process. The unit cost of the finished product is $11, which includes direct-material cost of $5 and conversion costs of $6.

Information provided in the cost-of-production report for the second department—Polishing—is developed as shown in figure 4.5. This report includes one additional element: costs of units completed in Machining are transferred to the Polishing department. Costs transferred from Machining become another direct material to the second department. We usually call these **transferred-in costs** to distinguish them from other direct materials that might be introduced for the first time. Figure 4.5 highlights the impact of the transferred-in items on the cost-of-production report.

The unit cost of the finished product is $22. This cost includes $11 transferred from the Machining department plus $11 for conversion costs

FIGURE 4.5
The Virginia Corporation Cost-of-Production—Polishing

Physical flows	Physical	Equivalent	
		Transferred-in materials	Conversion costs
Units to be accounted for			
Beginning work-in-process	0		
Units transferred in	30,000		
Total	30,000		
Units accounted for			
Units completed	25,000	25,000	25,000
Ending work-in-process			
(50 percent complete)*	5,000	5,000	2,500
Total	30,000	30,000	27,500

*Materials complete; conversion costs are 50 percent complete.

Cost flows	Totals	Transferred-in materials	Conversion costs
Costs to be accounted for			
Transferred-in materials	$330,000	$330,000	
Conversion costs	302,500		$302,500
Total	$632,500	$330,000	$302,500
Unit cost		$11	$11
Costs accounted for			
Units completed			
(25,000 × $22)	$550,000		
Ending work-in-process			
Transferred in (5,000 × $11)	$55,000		
Conversion (2,500 × $11)	27,500		
Total work-in-process	$82,500		
Total	$632,500		

incurred in the Polishing department. Journal entries resulting from the work in the two departments are shown in figure 4.6. The exact nature of the entries will vary depending on the accounting system involved. It is likely that work-in-process accounts would be set up for each department, such as work-in-process—Machining.

We have completed discussion of the basic components for process costing. Material in the balance of this chapter and the next chapter will clarify some of the more complicated aspects of process costing, such as the impact of (1) beginning inventories, (2) adding materials in subsequent departments, and (3) spoilage, waste, and defective and spoiled units.

☐ BEGINNING INVENTORIES— FIFO METHOD

The examples just covered did not include beginning work-in-process inventories in order to provide an exposure to process costing under simplified conditions. Beginning inventories, as we saw with ending inventories, make the process slightly more complex because a decision must be made on how to include beginning work-in-process units and costs in current period calculations. Two methods are available, the **first-in, first-out (FIFO) method** and the **weighted-average (W/A) method.** The FIFO method will be explained first.

One of the more important things to understand about the FIFO method is that the beginning work-in-process must be separated from other units completed during the current period. We are interested in identifying equivalent units arising from current-period production in order to derive unit costs from costs incurred in the current period. For example, assume

FIGURE 4.6
Journal Entries for the Machining and Polishing Departments

Machining		
1. Work-in-process—maching	200,000	
Raw materials inventory		200,000
2. Work-in-process—maching	152,000	
Wages payable		152,000
3. Work-in-process—maching	76,000	
Factory overhead applied		76,000
Machining and Polishing		
4. Work-in-process—polishing	330,000	
Work-in-process—maching		330,000
Polishing		
5. Work-in-process—polishing	165,000	
Wages payable		165,000
6. Work-in-process—polishing	137,500	
Factory overhead applied		137,500
Polishing and Finished Goods		
7. Finished goods	550,000	
Work-in-process—polishing		550,000

SMA Company had (1) 10,000 units of beginning work-in-process, 20 percent complete, (2) 50,000 units started in the current period, (3) 40,000 units completed, and (4) 20,000 units in-process at the end of the period, 60 percent complete. Direct materials are added at the beginning of the process. Physical and equivalent units are shown in figure 4.7. As can be seen from the schedule, completed units are separated into two components, those from beginning inventory and those started and completed in the current period, in order to identify work done in the current period. Since materials are added at the beginning of the process, no new materials were added to the beginning work-in-process. On the other hand, 80 percent of the beginning inventory was incomplete at the start of current production with respect to conversion costs, so 8,000 of the 10,000 units would represent current-period efforts.

Assume also that SMA Company's manufacturing costs were as follows:

From beginning inventory	$44,000
Current costs added	
Direct materials	200,000
Conversion costs	100,000
Total	$344,000

Only the current costs would be used in calculating unit costs. Using equivalent units from figure 4.7 and the above current costs, unit costs would be:

$$\begin{array}{lll} \text{Direct materials} & \$200,000 \div 50,000 = & \$4 \\ \text{Conversion costs} & \$100,000 \div 50,000 = & \underline{2} \\ & & \underline{\underline{\$6}} \end{array}$$

Completing the process, costs are assigned to completed units and ending work-in-process as shown in figure 4.8. The assignment of costs is relatively straightforward if you remember to separate the cost of goods completed into costs related to the beginning inventory and costs of units

Physical flows	Physical	Direct materials	Conversion costs
		Units	
		Equivalent	
Units to be accounted for			
Beginning work-in-process	10,000	0	8,000
(20 percent complete)			
Units started	50,000		
Total	60,000		
Units accounted for			
From beginning inventory	10,000		
Started and completed	30,000	30,000	30,000
Ending work-in-process			
(60 percent complete)	20,000	20,000	12,000
Total	60,000	50,000	50,000

FIGURE 4.7
SMA Company Physical and Equivalent Units—FIFO Method

FIGURE 4.8
SMA Company
Total Costs
Accounted for—
FIFO Method

Costs accounted for	
Units completed	
From beginning inventory	$44,000
Required to complete:	
Conversion costs (8,000 × $2)	16,000
	$60,000
Started and completed	
(30,000 × 6)	$180,000
Cost assigned to completed units	$240,000
Ending work-in-process	
Direct material	
(20,000 × $4)	$ 80,000
Conversion costs	
(12,000 × $2)	24,000
Total work-in-process	$104,000
Total	$344,000

started and completed in the current period. All of the components just discussed are combined into a complete cost-of-production schedule shown in figure 4.9.

☐ BEGINNING INVENTORIES—
WEIGHTED-AVERAGE METHOD

The weighted-average method calls for beginning work-in-process inventory units and costs to be treated as if they were part of current-period production. Although this assumption may be somewhat more difficult to accept conceptually, it greatly simplifies calculations made under process-costing procedures, and is probably used more often in practice. Utilizing the physical units from the previous example, figure 4.10 shows the calculation of equivalent units using the weighted-average method.

When using this method, one ignores the beginning inventory in the calculation of equivalent units. One assumes that all units to be accounted for were started in the current period. Consequently, there is no need to distinguish between units started and completed from units from beginning inventory. To summarize, in the calculation of equivalent units, weighted-average equivalent units represent all units to be accounted for, whereas FIFO equivalent units represent only work performed in the current period.

In order to carry the above assumption into cost assignment, beginning inventory costs must be separated by cost component and merged with current-period costs. Continuing with data from the previous example, assume that SMA Company's beginning inventory costs of $44,000 included $40,000 of direct-material costs and $4,000 of conversion costs.

FIGURE 4.9
SMA Company
Cost-of-Production
Report—FIFO
Method

Physical flows	Units		
	Physical	Equivalent	
		Direct materials	Conversion costs
Units to be accounted for			
Beginning work-in-process			
(20 percent complete)*	10,000	0	8,000
Units started	50,000		
Total	60,000		
Units accounted for			
From beginning inventory	10,000		
Started and completed	30,000	30,000	30,000
Ending work-in-process			
(60 percent complete)*	20,000	20,000	12,000
Total	60,000	50,000	50,000

*Material complete; percentages represent conversion costs.

Cost flows	Totals	Direct materials	Conversion costs
Costs to be accounted for			
From beginning inventory	$ 44,000		
Current costs added			
Direct materials	200,000	$200,000	
Conversion costs	100,000		$100,000
Total	$344,000	$200,000	$100,000
Unit costs		$4	$2
Costs accounted for			
Units completed			
From beginning inventory	$44,000		
Required to complete:			
Conversion costs (8,000 × $2)	16,000		
	$ 60,000		
Started and completed			
(30,000 × $6)	$180,000		
Costs assigned to completed units	$240,000		
Ending work-in-process			
Direct materials (20,000 × $4)	$ 80,000		
Conversion costs (12,000 × $2)	24,000		
Total work-in-process	$104,000		
Total	$344,000		

Costs to be accounted for would be shown as:

	Total	Direct material	Conversion costs
From beginning inventory	$ 44,000	$ 40,000	$ 4,000
Current costs added			
Direct materials	200,000	200,000	
Conversion costs	100,000		100,000
Total	$344,000	$240,000	$104,000

FIGURE 4.10
SMA Company
Physical and
Equivalent Units—
W/A Method

Physical flows	Units		
	Physical	Equivalent	
		Direct materials	Conversion costs
Units to be accounted for			
Beginning work-in-process			
(20 percent complete)	10,000		
Units started	50,000		
Total	60,000		
Units accounted for			
Units completed	40,000	40,000	40,000
Ending work-in-process			
(60 percent complete)	20,000	20,000	12,000
Total	60,000	60,000	52,000

Using equivalent units calculated in figure 4.10, the unit costs would be shown as follows:

Direct materials	$240,000 ÷ 60,000 =	$4
Conversion costs	$104,000 ÷ 52,000 =	2
		$6

Finally, costs are assigned to completed units and ending work-in-process as shown in figure 4.11. The complete cost-of-production report, using the weighted-average method, is shown in figure 4.12.

At this point, we have completed the basic procedures relating to process-costing systems. These procedures sometimes require manufacturing personnel to estimate the stage of completion of work-in-process inventories. Sometimes the percentages are arbitrarily set and remain constant from period to period. In other systems, work-in-process inventories are assumed to be nonexistent, making the calculation process quire simple. In any event, you now have a good exposure to process-costing procedures for potential use in industry, public accounting, not-for-profit organizations, hospitals, and in preparing for professional examinations.

FIGURE 4.11
SMA Company
Total Costs
Accounted For—
W/A Method

Costs accounted for	
Units completed	
(40,000 × $6)	$240,000
Ending work-in-process	
Direct materials (20,000 × $4)	$ 80,000
Conversion costs (12,000 × $2)	24,000
Total work-in-process	$104,000
Total	$344,000

FIGURE 4.12
SMA Company
Cost-of-Production
Report—W/A
Method

Physical flows	Units		
	Physical	Equivalent	
		Direct materials	Conversion costs
Units to be accounted for			
Beginning work-in-process (20 percent complete)*	10,000		
Units started	50,000		
Total	60,000		
Units accounted for			
Units completed	40,000	40,000	40,000
Ending work-in-process (60 percent complete)*	20,000	20,000	12,000
Total	60,000	60,000	52,000
*Materials complete.			

Cost flows	Totals	Direct materials	Conversion costs
Costs to be accounted for			
From beginning inventory	$ 44,000	$ 40,000	$ 4,000
Current costs added			
Direct material	200,000	200,000	
Conversion costs	100,000		100,000
Total	$344,000	$240,000	$104,000
Unit costs		$4	$2
Costs accounted for			
Units completed (40,000 × $6)	$240,000		
Ending work-in-process			
Direct materials (20,000 × $4)	80,000		
Conversion costs (12,000 × $2)	24,000		
Total work-in-process	$104,000		
Total	$344,000		

☐ SUMMARY

Process costing is the product-cost-determination system likely to be used when products are mass produced on a continuous basis. In process costing, costs are accumulated by department, time period, and product. The objective is to assign costs to finished goods and ending work-in-process inventories. In order to accomplish this objective, procedures require that information on costs and units be accumulated, equivalent units be calculated by department, unit costs be determined, and proper cost assignments be made.

Although the key to successful assignment of costs is the proper calculation of equivalent units, a good format for the cost-of-production report where units and costs are reconciled is important. The existence of beginning work-in-process inventories complicates the process-costing problem because the accountant must choose between the weighted-average and FIFO methods for handling beginning inventories. Under the weighted-average method, beginning inventories units and their related costs are merged with current production and all treated as current production. Under the FIFO method, the assumption is made that units in the beginning inventory are completed before new units are started and completed.

KEY TERMS

Conversion costs
Cost flows
Equivalent units
FIFO method

Physical flows
Process costing
Transferred-in costs
Weighted-average method

REVIEW PROBLEM

The Butts Company has a two-process factory in which all cost components are placed in-process in department A throughout processing, and semifinished products are transferred to department B for completion. No additional materials are introduced in department B. The following data relate to the month of June.

Department A

Beginning inventory (50 units, 50 percent complete)
Materials $50, processing costs $50.
Raw materials put into production during the month (100 units) $102.
Conversion costs incurred during month $289.
Ending Inventory (60 units, one-third complete).

Department B

Beginning inventory (40 units, 50 percent complete)
Prior department costs $291, conversion costs from department B, $150.
Conversion costs incurred during month $540.
Ending Inventory (45 units, two-thirds complete).

Required ☐ Prepare a cost-of-production report for department A using the FIFO method and for department B using the weighted-average method.

Solution ☐

THE BUTTS COMPANY
Cost-of-Production Report—Dept. A

| | | Units | |
| | Physical | Equivalent | |
Physical Flows		Direct materials	Conversion costs
Units to be accounted for			
Beginning work-in-process			
(50 percent complete)	50	25	25
Units started	100		
Total	150		

	Totals	Direct materials	Conversion costs
Units accounted for			
From beginning inventory	50		
Started and completed	40	40	40
Ending work-in-process			
(33⅓ percent complete)	60	20	20
Total	150	85	85

Cost flows	*Totals*	*Direct materials*	*Conversion costs*
Costs to be accounted for			
From beginning inventory	$100		
Current costs added			
Direct materials	102	$102	
Conversion costs	289	____	$289
Total	$491	$102	$289
Unit costs		$1.20	$3.40
Costs accounted for			
Units completed			
From beginning inventory	$100		
Required to complete			
Materials and conversion costs (25 × $4.60)	115		
Started and completed			
(40 × $4.60)	184		
Costs assigned to completed units	$399		
Ending work-in-process			
Direct materials (20 × $1.20)	$ 24		
Conversion costs (20 × $3.40)	68		
Total work-in-process	$ 92		
Total	$491		

THE BUTTS COMPANY
Cost-of-Production Report—Dept. B

	Units		
Physical flows	*Physical*	*Equivalent*	
		Trans- ferred-in materials	*Conversion costs*
Units to be accounted for			
Beginning work-in-process			
(50 percent complete)	40		
Units transferred-in	90		
Total	130		
Units accounted for			
Units completed	85	85	85
Ending work-in-process			
(66⅔ percent complete)	45	45	30
Total	130	130	115

Cost flows	*Totals*	*Direct materials*	*Conversion costs*
Costs to be accounted for			
From beginning inventory	$ 441	$291	$150
Current costs added			
Direct materials (transferred in)	399	399	

Conversion costs	540		540
Total	$1380	$690	$690
Unit costs		$5.31*	$6.00

Costs accounted for
Units completed

(85 × $11.31)	$ 961

Ending work-in-process

Direct materials (45 × $5.31)	$239
Conversion costs (30 × $6)	180
Total work-in-process	$ 419
Total	$1,380

*Rounded to nearest cent.

QUESTIONS

Q4-1. What is the basic difference between job-order and process-costing systems?

Q4-2. Give several different examples of industries in which process costing would likely be used.

Q4-3. Would the accounting systems needed to accumulate costs of material, labor, and overhead vary depending on whether job-order or process costing were used? Explain.

Q4-4. In process costing, why are equivalent costs used as an output measure?

Q4-5. What is meant by the term *conversion costs*?

Q4-6. Describe the differences among the terms *sequential, parallel,* and *selective* as they apply to process-costing systems.

Q4-7. Outline the basic procedures required for process costing.

Q4-8. What is the basic objective in process costing?

Q4-9. What is the purpose of the cost-of-production report?

Q4-10. What is meant by unit and cost reconciliation as it applies to a cost-of-production report?

Q4-11. What is the most critical step in assigning costs in process costing? Why?

Q4-12. Describe fully the problems created by partially completed inventories and work-in-process.

Q4-13. Discuss assumptions made with respect to the weighted-average method.

Q4-14. Discuss assumptions made with respect to the FIFO method.

Q4-15. In terms of information available, under what situation would the weighted-average method not be used?

Q4-16. Will both the weighted-average and FIFO methods yield the same values for cost-assignment purposes? Discuss.

P4-1. XYZ Corporation has just completed its first month of operations. Relevant data are as follows:

Basic Process Costing

Units put into production	10,000
Units in ending inventory	3,000
Total costs	$10,000

Ending inventory is one-third complete.

Required □ Calculate cost of finished goods and work-in-process.

P4-2. The following information relates to the Polishing department for June:

Basic Process Costing

Unit information

Work-in-process, June 1	0
Units started	60,000
Completed and transferred	40,000

Cost information

Direct material	$112,000
Direct labor	208,000
Factory overhead	52,000

Direct materials are added at the start of the process. Conversion costs are added throughout the process. Work-in-process is 50 percent complete.

Required □ Calculate cost of goods completed and work-in-process.

P4-3. Information about the Melting department of XYZ Company is:

Basic Process Costing

Cost information for December

Costs transferred from Grinding	$42,000
Costs added in Melting	
Direct materials	10,000
Direct labor	31,688
Factory overhead	15,232

During December, 10,000 units were transferred in from the Grinding department and 6,000 units were completed and transferred to the Molding department. Units at the end of December were 50 percent complete with respect to materials and 20 percent complete with respect to direct labor and factory overhead.

Required □ Prepare a cost-of-production report for December.

P4-4. Greg Production Company manufactures springs for cars. Its operations are a continuing process carried on as two departments—Machining and Finishing. Materials are added in each department without increasing units produced.

Two-Department Situation

For July, company records indicated the following production results:

	Machining	Finishing
Beginning inventory, July 1	—	—
Units transferred in	—	20,000
Units started	40,000	—
Units completed	20,000	10,000
Ending inventory, July 31	20,000	10,000

Percent of units completed in-process at July 31 were Machining (materials, 100 percent; labor, 80 percent; overhead, 80 percent), Finishing (materials, 0 percent; labor, 60 percent; overhead, 40 percent).

Cost records indicated the following for July:

	Machining	Finishing
Materials	$ 80,000	$44,600
Labor	144,000	73,600
Overhead	36,000	31,920

Required □ Prepare a cost-of-production report for each of the departments.

Multiple-Choice **P4-5.**   Select the proper answers for the following multiple-choice items.
Items

1. The Wiring department is the second stage of the production cycle at the Flem Company. On May 1, the beginning work-in-process contained 25,000 units that were 60 percent complete as to conversion costs. During May, 100,000 units were transferred in from the first stage of the production cycle. On May 31, the ending work-in-process contained 20,000 units that were 80 percent complete as to conversion costs. Material costs are added at the end of the process. Using the weighted-average method, the equivalent units were:

	Transferred-in costs	Materials	Conversion costs
a.	100,000	125,000	100,000
b.	125,000	105,000	105,000
c.	125,000	105,000	121,000
d.	125,000	125,000	121,000

2. On April 1, 19X7, the Collins Company had 6,000 units of work-in-process in department B, the second and last stage of their production cycle. The costs attached to these 6,000 units were $1,200 of costs transferred in from department A, $2,500 of material costs added in department B, and $2,000 of conversion costs added in department B. Materials are added in the beginning of the process in department B. Conversion was 50 percent complete on April 1, 19X7. During April, 14,000 units were transferred in from department A at a cost of $27,000; and material costs of $3,500 and conversion costs of $3,000 were added in department B. On April 30, 19X7, department B had 5,000 units of work-in-process that was 60 percent complete as to conversion costs. The costs attached to these 5,000 units were $10,500 of costs added in department B and $800 of conversion costs added in department B.

Using the weighted-average method, what were the equivalent units for the month of April?

	Transferred in from department A	Materials	Conversion
a.	15,000	15,000	15,000
b.	19,000	19,000	20,000
c.	20,000	20,000	18,000
d.	25,000	25,000	20,000

3. The weighted-average method of process costing differs from the first-in, first-out method of process costing in that the weighted-average method

   a. Requires that ending work-in-process inventory be stated in terms of equivalent units of production.
   b. Can be used under any cost-flow assumption.
   c. Considers the ending work-in-process inventory only partially complete.
   d. Does not consider the degree of completion of beginning work-in-process inventory when computing equivalent units of production.

4. Under which of the following conditions will the first-in, first-out method of process costing produce the same cost of goods manufactured amount as the weighted-average method?

   a. When goods produced are homogeneous in nature
   b. When there is no beginning inventory
   c. When there is no ending inventory
   d. When beginning and ending inventories are each 50 percent complete

5. On November 1, 19X7, Yankee Company had 20,000 units of work-in-process in department 1 that were 100 percent complete as to material costs and 20 percent complete as to conversion costs. During November, 160,000 units were started in department 1, and 170,000 units were completed and transferred to department 2. The work-in-process on November 30, 19X7, was 100 percent complete as to material costs and 40 percent complete as to conversion costs. By what amount would the equivalent units for conversion costs for the month of November differ if the first-in, first-out method were used instead of the weighted-average method?

   a. 20,000 less
   b. 16,000 less
   c. 8,000 less
   d. 4,000 less

6. A company uses the first-in, first-out method of costing in a process-costing system. Material is added at the beginning of the process in department A and conversion costs are incurred uniformly throughout the process. Beginning work-in-process inventory on April 1 in department A consisted of 50,000 units estimated to be 30 percent complete. During April, 150,000 units were started in department A, and 160,000 units were completed and transferred to department B. Ending work-

in-process inventory on April 30 in department A was estimated to be 20 percent complete. What were the total equivalent units in department A for April for materials and conversion costs, respectively?

a. 150,000 and 133,000
b. 150,000 and 153,000
c. 200,000 and 133,000
d. 200,000 and 153,000

7. Material is added at the beginning of a process in a process-costing system. The beginning work-in-process inventory for this process this period was 30 percent complete as to conversion costs. Using the first-in, first-out method of costing, the total equivalent units for material for this process during this period are equal to the

a. Beginning inventory this period for this process.
b. Units started this period in this process.
c. Units started this period in this process plus the beginning inventory.
d. Units started this period in this process plus 70 percent of the beginning inventory this period.

8. An equivalent unit of material or conversion cost is equal to

a. The amount of material or conversion cost necessary to complete one unit of production.
b. A unit of work-in-process inventory.
c. The amount of material or conversion cost necessary to start a unit of production into work-in-process.
d. Fifty percent of the material or conversion cost of a unit of finished goods inventory (assuming a linear production pattern).

(CPA)

Equivalent **P4-6.** For each of the situations described, determine the equivalent units com-
Units—FIFO pleted using the FIFO and weighted-average method.
and Weighted-
Average

| | | Equivalent units | |
		FIFO	Weighted-Average
1. Units started in production ..	40,000		
Units transferred out	60,000		
Ending inventory (25 percent complete)	10,000		
Beginning inventory (40 percent complete)	30,000	_____	_____
2. Units started in production ..	60,000		
Units transferred out	50,000		
Beginning inventory (25 percent complete)	20,000		
Ending inventory (75 percent complete)	30,000	_____	_____
3. Units started in production ..	70,000		
Units transferred out	60,000		
Beginning inventory (33 percent complete)	30,000		
Ending inventory (50 percent complete)	40,000	_____	_____

4. Units started in production .. 40,000
    Units transferred out 30,000
    Beginning inventory
        (40 percent complete) 10,000
    Ending inventory
        (60 percent complete) .... 20,000 _____ _____

5. Units started in production .. 60,000
    Units transferred out 50,000
    Beginning inventory
        (25 percent complete) 20,000
    Ending inventory
        (60 percent complete) .... 30,000 _____ _____

P4-7. For each of the situations described, determine the equivalent units completed using FIFO and weighted-average method.

Equivalent Units—FIFO and Weighted-Average

	Equivalent units	
	FIFO	Weighted-Average

1. Units started in production .. 70,000
    Units transferred out 50,000
    Ending inventory
        (25 percent complete) 30,000
    Beginning inventory
        (40 percent complete) .... _____ _____ _____

2. Units started in production .. _____
    Units transferred out 50,000
    Ending inventory
        (60 percent complete) 30,000
    Beginning inventory
        (25 percent complete) .... 20,000 _____ _____

3. Units started in production .. 40,000
    Units transferred out .... _____
    Beginning inventory
        (40 percent complete) 10,000
    Ending inventory
        (60 percent complete) .... 20,000 _____ _____

4. Units started in production .. 70,000
    Units transferred out 60,000
    Beginning inventory
        (40 percent complete) 30,000
    Ending inventory
        (70 percent complete) .... _____ _____ _____

5. Units transferred out 80,000
    Units started in production .. _____
    Beginning inventory
        (10 percent complete) 10,000
    Ending inventory
        (80 percent complete) .... 20,000 _____ _____

P4-8. The following data are from Barb Company's production records:

Process Costing—FIFO

Units in beginning inventory, 4,000; all materials, 50 percent labor, and overhead. Cost of beginning inventory: materials, $1,992; labor, $1,074; overhead $846.

Placed in-process: 20,000 units
Cost: materials, $12,000; labor, $9,984; overhead, $9,984
Units completed and transferred: 21,000

Ending inventory: 3,000 units; all materials, 60 percent labor and overhead

Required ☐ Using the FIFO method, determine:

1. The total costs associated with the transferred units. (Break down between the beginning inventory and the started and completed units.)

2. The costs assigned to the ending work-in-process inventory.

Process Costing— Weighted-Average **P4-9.** The following data are from Link Company's manufacturing records:

Units in beginning inventory, 4,000; all materials, 50 percent labor, and overhead. Cost of beginning inventory: materials $1,992; labor $1,074; overhead $846.

Placed in-process: 20,000 units
Cost: materials, $12,408; labor, $12,606; overhead, $10,554
Units completed and transferred: 21,000

Ending inventory: 3,000 units; all materials, 60 percent labor, and overhead

Required ☐ Using the weighted-average method, determine:

1. The total costs associated with the transferred units.

2. The costs assigned to the ending work-in-process inventory.

Process Costing— Weighted-Average **P4-10.** Information concerning the Baking department of the Margaret Company is as follows:

	Units
Beginning work-in-process	5,000
Units transferred in	35,000
Total	40,000
Units completed	38,000
Ending work-in-process	2,000
Total	40,000

	Costs			
	Trans-ferred in	Materials	Conversion	Total costs
Beginning work-in-process	$ 3,500	$ —	$ 4,000	$ 7,500
Current costs	19,700	25,460	14,424	59,584
	$23,200	$25,460	$18,424	$67,084

Conversion costs were 40 percent complete as to the beginning work-in-process and 60 percent complete as to the ending work-in-process. All materials are added at the end of the process. The Margaret Company uses the weighted-average method.

Required ☐

1. The cost per equivalent unit for conversion costs.

2. The portion of the total cost of ending work-in-process attributable to transferred-in cost.

P4-11. The quantities and costs of production chargeable to department A of Kathy Products, Inc., in October, 19X3, are summarized as follows:

Process Costing—FIFO

Units-in-process, October 1	6,000
Units started in production, October	45,000
Units-in-process, October 31	5,000

All materials are added at the time the units are completed. The work-in-process on October 1 was 40 percent complete as to labor and overhead. The work-in-process on October 31 was 40 percent complete as to labor and overhead.

Costs

	Work-in-process October 1	October costs
Materials	$0	$322,000
Labor	21,600	222,000
Overhead	18,000	177,000

Required ☐ Prepare a production report for department A for October showing the calculation of equivalent units, unit costs, and cost allocation. Use the FIFO method for computing equivalent units.

P4-12. The quantities and costs of production chargeable to department A of Vaughn Products, Inc., in October, 19X3, are summarized as follows:

Process Costing— Weighted-Average

Quantities

Units in-process on October 1	6,000
Units started in production, October	45,000
Units in-process on October 31	5,000

All materials are added at the time the units are started in production. The work-in-process on October 31 was 40 percent complete as to labor and overhead.

Costs

	Work-in-process October 1	October costs
Materials	$40,800	$316,200
Labor	31,800	217,800
Overhead	27,600	193,200

Required ☐ Prepare a production report for department A for October showing the calculation of equivalent units, unit costs, and cost allocation. Use the weighted-average method for computing equivalent units.

P4-13. The Matrix Company manufactures a product for children. Materials are added at the end of the process. Conversion costs are added continuously throughout the process.

Process Costing— Weighted-Average

The following data pertain to operations for one month:

In-process, beginning 6,000 units, 40 percent complete.
Costs related to beginning inventory are:

Materials	$0
Direct labor	4,450
Overhead	2,860

During the month, 14,000 units were started in production. Costs incurred during the month included:

Materials	$27,350
Direct labor	11,200
Overhead	8,090

At the end of the month, there were 4,000 units left in process, 60 percent complete.

Required □ Prepare a cost-of-production report by the weighted-average method showing cost of goods completed and cost of ending work-in-process.

Process Costing—FIFO

P4-14. Information concerning the Cleaning department of Sponner Company is as follows:

	Units
Beginning work-in-process	8,000
Units transferred in	42,000
	50,000
Units completed	46,000
Ending work-in-process	4,000
	50,000

		Costs		
	Transferred in	*Materials*	*Conversion*	*Total costs*
From beginning inventory	$16,000	$11,200	$ 12,800	$ 40,000
Current costs	83,720	75,600	92,000	251,320
	$99,720	$86,800	$104,800	$291,320

Conversion costs were 20 percent complete with respect to beginning inventories and 40 percent complete with respect to ending inventories. All materials are added at the beginning of the process. Sponner uses the FIFO method.

Required □

1. Calculate the cost per equivalent unit for transferred-in costs.

2. Calculate the cost of units completed in the Cleaning department.

Process Costing— FIFO

P4-15. The Racquet Ball Company uses a process-cost system. Materials are added at the beginning of the process and conversion costs are incurred uniformly throughout the process. Work-in-process at the beginning is 20 percent complete and at the end is 50 percent complete.

Beginning inventory	800
Material added	10,000
Ending inventory	600
Conversion costs incurred	$20,160
Cost of materials added	$20,000
Beginning inventory costs	$ 4,200

Required ☐ Prepare a cost-of-production report by the FIFO method showing cost of goods completed and cost of ending work-in-process.

P4-16. Hill Company produces a product that must be processed through two departments. Basic information relating to the operations of a recent period is: *Process Costing—Two Departments*

	Department	
Units	Assembly	Finishing
Beginning inventory	10,000	12,000
Units started	20,000	
Units transferred	26,000	
Ending inventory	4,000	10,000
Costs		
Material costs added	$22,000	$14,000
Labor	8,000	12,000

Other Information

Beginning work-in-process in the Assembly department was one-half complete with respect to conversion costs. Material is added at the start of production. Beginning inventories include $6,000 for material and $2,000 for conversion costs. Overhead is applied at the rate of 50 percent of labor. Ending inventory was two-fifths complete.

Beginning work-in-process in the Finishing department was three-fourths complete with respect to conversion costs. Material is added at the end of the process. Beginning inventories include $10,000 for transferred costs and $10,000 for conversion costs. Overhead is applied at the rate of 100 percent of labor. Ending inventory was estimated to be one-fourth complete.

Required ☐ Calculate cost of goods transferred from each department and the cost of ending work-in-process inventories. Use the FIFO method for the first department and the weighted-average method for the second department.

P4-17. Hillford, Inc., produces cabinets that must be processed through two departments. Basic information relating to Hillford's operations is provided by the following: *Process Costing—Two Departments*

	Department	
Units	Processing	Fabricating
Beginning work-in-process	8,000	10,000
Units completed during period	18,000	20,000
Units put into production	12,000	
Ending work-in-process	2,000	8,000

Costs		
Material costs added	$20,000	$12,000
Labor	6,000	12,000
Overhead	6,000	6,000

Other Information

Beginning work-in-process in the Processing department was one-half complete with respect to conversion costs. Material is added at the start of production. Beginning inventories include $6,000 for material and $2,000 for conversion costs. Ending inventories were two-fifths complete.

Beginning work-in-process in the Fabricating department was three-fourths complete with respect to conversion costs. Material is added halfway through the process. Beginning inventories include $2,000 for material, $8,000 for transferred costs, and $9,000 for conversion costs. Ending inventory was one-fourth complete.

Required ☐ Develop a cost-of-production report for each department. Use the weighted-average method for the first department and the FIFO method for the second department.

Equivalent Units of Inventory Components

P4-18. The Felix Manufacturing Company uses a process-cost system to account for the costs of its only product known as "Nino." Production begins in the Fabrication department where units of raw material are molded into various connecting parts. After fabrication is complete, the units are transferred to the Assembly department. There is no material added in the Assembly department.

After assembly is complete, the units are transferred to the Packaging department where the units are packaged for shipment. At the completion of this process, the units are complete and they are transferred to the Shipping department.

On December 31, 19X7, the following inventory is on hand:

■ No unused raw material or packing material.

■ Fabrication department: 6,000 units, 25 percent complete as to raw material and 40 percent complete as to direct labor.

■ Assembly department: 10,000 units, 75 percent complete as to direct labor.

■ Packaging department: 3,000 units, 60 percent complete as to packing material and 75 percent complete as to direct labor.

■ Shipping department: 8,000 units.

Required ☐ Prepare schedules showing the following on December 31, 19X7:

a. The number of equivalent units of raw material in all inventories.
b. The number of equivalent units of Fabrication department direct labor in all inventories.
c. Number of equivalent units of Packaging department material and direct labor in the Packaging department inventory.

(CPA)

P4-19. Bisto Corporation manufactures valves and pumps for liquids. On December 1, 19X4, Bisto paid $25,000 to Poplen Company for the patent for its Watertite valve. Bisto planned to carry on Poplen's procedure of having the valve casing and parts cast by an independent foundry and doing the grinding and assembling in its own plant.

Inventory by FIFO Layers

Bisto also purchased Poplen's inventory of the valves at 80 percent of its costs to Poplen. The purchased inventory was comprised of the following:

	Units
Raw material (unfinished casings and parts)	1,100
Work-in-process	
Grinding (25 percent complete)	800
Assembling (40 percent complete)	600
Finished valves	900

Poplen's cost-accounting system provided the following unit costs:

	Cost per unit
Raw material (unfinished casing and parts)	$2
Grinding costs	1
Assembling costs	2

Bisto's cost-accounting system accumulated the following costs for the month of December that do not include cost of the inventory purchased from Poplen:

Raw material purchases (casings and parts for 5,000 units)	$10,500
Grinding costs	2,430
Assembling costs	5,664

Bisto's inventory of Watertite valves at December 31, 19X4, follows:

Raw material (unfinished casings and parts)	2,700
Work-in-process	
Grinding (35 percent complete)	2,000
Assembling (33⅓ percent complete)	300
Finished valves	2,250

(Bisto uses the process-costing method in its accounting system.)

Required ☐

1. Prepare a schedule to compute the equivalent units produced and costs incurred per unit for the month of December 19X4.

2. Prepare a schedule of inventories based on the FIFO method as of December 1 and December 31, 19X4, setting forth by layers the number of equivalent units of materials, grinding department costs, and assembling department costs in all inventories. Do not attempt to assign costs. Show all supporting schedules in good form.

(CPA)

CHAPTER OUTLINE

ADDITIONAL PROCESS-COSTING TOPICS

CHAPTER 5

☐ INTRODUCTION

In chapter 4, the basic process-costing system was introduced and explained in detail. In this chapter, we consider two additional problems often encountered with process costing, namely, an increase in units due to the addition of materials in subsequent departments and the problems related to spoilage and defective units. This chapter also contains information on terminology related to disappearance and scrap.

☐ INCREASED UNITS IN SUBSEQUENT DEPARTMENTS

The transfer of units to subsequent departments was discussed in chapter 4. We learned that completed units in one department become the direct material (transferred-in units and costs) of another department. Additional materials added in the subsequent department, provided additional units are not created, only results in the need for the calculation of equivalent units and unit cost for another product-cost component.

There are situations in which the addition of materials in a subsequent department also causes a change in the number of units to be accounted for. For instance, assume 10,000 gallons of some component are transferred from the Processing department at $20,000 to a Completion department, where an equal amount of cost-free water is added at the beginning of the process. Conversion costs of $5,000 are needed to transform the ingredients into a finished product. Work-in-process inventories do not exist. Figure 5.1 provides the cost-of-production report for the Completion department.

In the example, an initial unit cost of $2 for transferred-in materials is reduced to $1 because of the addition of the free material, namely, the water. Although the example is quite basic, it serves to introduce the problem created by having additional units generated in subsequent departments. In many cases, we would also expect to have additional costs

113

FIGURE 5.1
Cost-of-Production
Report—
Completion
Department

Physical flows	Physical	Transferred in	Conversion costs
Units			
		Equivalent	
Units to be accounted for			
Beginning work-in-process	0		
Gallons transferred in	10,000		
Gallons added	10,000		
Total	20,000		
Units accounted for			
Gallons completed	20,000	20,000	20,000
Ending work-in-process	0		
Total	20,000	20,000	20,000

Cost flows	Totals	Transferred in	Conversion costs
Costs to be accounted for			
Transferred in	$20,000	$20,000	
Conversion costs	5,000		$5,000
Total	$25,000	$20,000	$5,000
Unit cost		$1	$.25
Costs accounted for			
Units completed			
(20,000 × $1.25)	$25,000		

incurred as materials and additional units are introduced in a subsequent department. Consider the following example:

Marrick Company produces a chemical used in window cleaners. In the first department, Cooking, various ingredients are mixed and cooked, causing a 50 percent decrease in initial volume almost immediately. The resulting product is then transferred to a second department, Mixing, where it is combined with an equal amount of alcohol and bottled in containers for distribution to window cleaner producers.

In the first department, materials are added at the beginning of the process with conversion costs added throughout the process. In the second department, alcohol is added immediately. The final product is bottled at the conclusion of the process. Conversion costs are added only during the bottling operation in the second department. The weighted-average method is used in both departments. Information for the current month is as follows:

	Cooking	Mixing
Units (gallons)		
Beginning inventory	5,000	4,000
Started	20,000	
Completed	8,000	
Ending inventory	7,000	6,000
Costs		
Beginning inventory,		
40 percent complete (materials, $40,000; conversion,		
$4,000)	$44,000	

100 percent complete as to alcohol only. (transferred in, $40,000; alcohol, $8,000). No conversion costs.		$48,000
Materials		
Cooking	$80,000	
Mixing—alcohol		$32,000
Mixing—bottles		$56,000
Conversion costs	$19,000	$42,000
Ending inventory		
50 percent complete	—	
100 percent complete as to alcohol only. No conversion costs.		—

The calculations involved in developing a cost-of-production report for the first department are straightforward once it is understood that 50 percent of the initial volume of the material disappears almost immediately in the cooking process. The complete cost-of-production report is shown in figure 5.2.

In the first department, a 50 percent disappearance of materials was expected and rigidly controlled. Consequently, in calculating equivalent units, one must recognize that 10,000 gallons of chemicals evaporated as a normal part of the production process.

Development of costs for the second department is somewhat complicated because two different kinds of materials are added. The first, alcohol, is used to complete the solution, and it increases the gallons available in the production process. The alcohol is added at the start of the process. The second material, bottles, is used to package the solution and represents the final step in the process. Since conversion costs are directly related to the bottling operation, ending work-in-process inventories would not include conversion costs. Figure 5.3 presents the cost-of-production report for the Mixing department.

As can be seen from figure 5.3, additional complexities, which are brought on by the additional units and different classifications of materials, are easily handled by recognizing them correctly in the cost-of-production report. The additional units were built into units to be accounted for so that the initial 8,000 units transferred in were doubled. Because the materials—alcohol and bottles—were added at different points in the process, they were handled as two separate equivalent-unit calculations and unit-cost components.

Many different possibilities exist when considering the problem of additional units being created in subsequent departments. Most situations can be dealt with in a straightforward manner by documenting the details when the cost-of-production report is prepared.

☐ DISAPPEARANCE, SPOILAGE, DEFECTIVE UNITS, AND SCRAP

Accountants are likely to encounter problems of product **disappearance, spoilage, defective units,** and **scrap material** in the design and implementation of product-cost-determination systems. This section is presented so

FIGURE 5.2
Cost-of-Production
Report—Cooking
Dept.

Physical flows	Units		
	Physical	Equivalent	
		Direct materials	Conversion costs
Units to be accounted for			
Beginning work-in-process			
(40 percent complete)*	5,000		
Units started	20,000		
Total	25,000		
Units accounted for			
Transferred out	8,000	8,000	8,000
Disappearance	10,000		
Ending work-in-process			
(50 percent complete)*	7,000	7,000	3,500
Total	25,000	15,000	11,500

*Materials complete.

Cost flows	Totals	Direct materials	Conversion costs
Costs to be accounted for			
From beginning inventory	$ 44,000	$ 40,000	$ 4,000
Current costs added			
Direct materials	80,000	80,000	
Conversion costs	19,000		19,000
Total	$143,000	$120,000	$23,000
Unit costs		$8	$2
Costs accounted for			
Units completed			
(8,000 × $10)	$ 80,000		
Ending work-in-process			
Direct materials (7,000 × $8)	$ 56,000		
Conversion costs (3,500 × $2)	7,000		
Total work-in-process	$ 63,000		
Total	$143,000		

that one might distinguish between the terms and develop some understanding of record-keeping possibilities before looking at specific cost-accounting applications for control and product-costing purposes.

Terminology

While terminology in this subject area remains unsettled, the terms used in this book are defined as follows:

■ *Disappearance.* Disappearance refers to material that evaporates or disappears as an expected part of the productive process. For instance, a certain portion of liquid that runs through lines disappears; cooking pro-

FIGURE 5.3   Cost-of-Production Report—Mixing Dept.

Physical flows	Physical	Transferred in	Alcohol	Bottles	Conversion costs
Units to be accounted for					
Beginning work-in-process					
(0 percent complete)*	4,000				
Transferred in	8,000				
Resulting from material added	8,000				
Total	20,000				
Units accounted for					
Completed units	14,000	14,000	14,000	14,000	14,000
Ending work-in-process					
(0 percent complete)*	6,000	6,000	6,000	0	0
Total	20,000	20,000	20,000	14,000	14,000

*Transferred in and alcohol complete.

Cost flows	Totals	Transferred in	Alcohol	Bottles	Conversion costs
Costs to be accounted for					
From beginning inventory	$ 48,000	$40,000	$ 8,000	0	0
Current costs added					
Alcohol	32,000		32,000		
Bottles	56,000			56,000	
Transferred in	80,000	80,000			
Conversion costs	42,000				42,000
Total	$258,000	$120,000	$40,000	$56,000	$42,000
Unit costs		$6	$2	$4	$3
Costs accounted for					
Units completed					
(14,000 × $15)	$210,000				
Ending work-in-process					
Transferred in (6,000 × $6)	36,000				
Alcohol (6,000 × $2)	12,000				
Total work-in-process	$48,000				
Total	$258,000				

cesses involve some loss due to evaporation; and other uncontrollable losses take place as a normal part of the production process. Some accountants choose to refer to this form of disappearance as *waste* or shrinkage.

■ *Spoilage.* Products that do not meet production standards and cannot be reworked are called *spoiled goods.* When spoilage takes place, the goods are removed from production. Spoilage cost includes cost of production to the point of discovery less any residual value of the spoiled units.

■ *Defective products.* Products that do not meet quality-control standards but that can be reworked and sold as a final product at an acceptable return are referred to as *defective products.*

■ *Scrap material.* Scrap material is the residue remaining at the conclusion of the production process that cannot be used further in the production process. This residue often has a reasonable but relatively minor value. Items such as sawdust, wood and metal shavings, food residue, scrap lumber, or cloth remnants might be classified as scrap.

Cost-Accounting Objectives

The cost-accounting objective is to properly monitor all costs related to disappearance, spoilage, defective production, and scrap materials. As long as costs are considered normal, they are properly included as a cost of the product produced. However, information on abnormal spoilage is not only valuable to management in monitoring operations but it is also essential to product costing. Abnormal costs arising from inefficient operations or other out-of-control situations should be segregated and charged off as losses to current operations.

Defective Units

Reworking defective units requires that certain basic accounting procedures be established to account for the additional costs. As mentioned earlier, defective units are reworked because the reworked units are expected to provide an acceptable profit contribution. Otherwise, the units should be regarded as spoilage and not reworked. (Spoilage problems are discussed later.)

If defective work is expected as a normal part of the manufacturing process, estimated costs of reworking the units should be included in projected manufacturing overhead so that the costs to rework are spread over all units produced in an accounting period. Assume, for instance, that 1,000 units of some product are produced with direct-material costs of $5,000, direct-labor costs of $4,000, and overhead costs of $6,000 applied on the basis of 150 percent of direct-labor costs. One hundred of the units have to be reworked and are considered to be within existing quality-control standards. Materials of $200 and labor of $400 are required to correct defects in the 100 units. Entries required are as follows:

Initial costs of production
Work-in-process	15,000	
Raw materials		5,000
Wages payable		4,000
Factory overhead applied		6,000

Rework costs
Factory overhead control	600	
Raw materials		200
Wages payable		400

Costs of finished goods
Finished goods	15,000	
Work-in-process		15,000

Since estimated costs of reworking defective units for the year are built into the predetermined overhead rate, the actual costs of reworking the 100 units are charged to Factory Overhead Control. Finished-goods costs are then represented by the total of the original costs charged to production.

Scrap

Although accounting for scrap may be accomplished in a number of different ways, two basic procedures are typically used to handle the necessary record keeping. The first method is the simplest and probably the most widely used. Under this method, a formal accounting entry would not be made until the scrap is sold. When the scrap is sold, the following entry would be made:

```
Cash ..........................................................  XX
    Factory overhead control  .......................................     XX
```

This entry indicates that scrap sales are anticipated and built into projections of annual factory overhead costs. Consequently, projected overhead costs are reduced somewhat, which, in turn, reduces the predetermined rate used to apply overhead to production.

In some cases, where cost recovery is likely to be delayed and the monetary value is considered significant, a company might assign the net realizable value to scrap at the time it is placed in inventory. This would insure that Factory Overhead Control for the proper period would be credited for scrap recovery. Under this method, the entry to be made at the time scrap is inventoried would be:

```
Scrap inventory ................................................  XX
    Factory overhead control  .......................................     XX
```

When the scrap is sold, the entry would be:

```
Cash ..........................................................  XX
    Scrap inventory  ...............................................     XX
```

Any amount remaining in Scrap Inventory after it has been sold would be closed to Factory Overhead Control.

Spoilage

In manufacturing processes, goods in-process will be lost or spoiled as a result of management's efforts to produce a product in the most profitable manner. To this extent, disappearance and spoilage are similar. Fluids evaporate in the cooking process, impure food is canned, and bottles break. The problem for management is to establish acceptable limits for **normal spoilage** and then properly monitor and assign costs of spoilage.

Within acceptable limits, spoilage should be regarded as uncontrollable. Thus, it is considered a normal cost of producing the product. Spoilage beyond acceptable limits is considered **abnormal spoilage.** When classified as abnormal, spoilage represents a loss to be written off in the current period.

In accounting for spoilage, it is important both to provide information for control purposes and to allocate spoilage costs to current period operations (abnormal spoilage), work-in-process (normal spoilage), and finished goods (normal spoilage). Although a variety of approaches exist for handling spoilage costs, one should recognize that some approaches misstate product costs and operating results.

☐ PROCESS COSTING AND SPOILAGE

Units will often be spoiled in the production process. From an accounting point of view, a decision must be reached as to the proper treatment for spoilage costs.

One approach is to allow the costs of spoilage to be spread over good production. This can be accomplished by including only good units in equivalent-unit calculations, which automatically spreads spoilage over good units manufactured. Consider the following example:

Assume the production of the XYZ Company for the current period is as follows:

	Units
Started in production	1,500
Completed	1,000
Work-in-process (materials, 100 percent complete; conversion, 60 percent complete)	200
Normal spoilage (detected at end of process)	300
Material costs	$6,000
Conversion costs	5,041

If the cost of spoilage is to be spread over good units, then the cost of production would be developed as shown in figure 5.4.

In this example, the 300 spoiled units were ignored in the equivalent-unit calculations. The calculations and results would have been the same if only 1,200 units had been started (assuming same total costs) with no spoilage in production. This approach can be regarded as acceptable only if all units spoiled are normal and if either (1) all cost components, including spoilage costs, are incurred uniformly throughout the process or (2) work-in-process inventories do not exist. Otherwise, it is likely that ending work-in-process inventories will be charged with costs that should be charged to finished goods.

By including spoiled units in equivalent-unit calculations, not only will the potential problem of overcharging ending inventories be avoided but also the costs attributable to spoilage can be highlighted for management's use in controlling operations. The resulting costs of spoilage can then be allocated to the proper inventory accounts. Using data from the previous

FIGURE 5.4
XYZ Company
Cost-of-Production
Report

Physical flows	Units Physical	Equivalent Direct materials	Equivalent Conversion costs
Units to be accounted for			
Beginning work-in-process	0		
Units started	1,500		
Total	1,500		
Units accepted for			
Completed units	1,000	1,000	1,000
Ending work-in-process			
(60 percent complete)*	200	200	120
Spoilage	300		
Total	1,500	1,200	1,120

*Materials complete.

Cost flows	Totals	Direct materials	Conversion costs
Costs to be accounted for			
Direct materials	$ 6,000	$6,000	
Conversion costs	5,041		$5,041
Total	$11,041	$6,000	$5,041
Unit costs		$5	$4.50
Costs accounted for			
Completed units			
(1,000 × $9.50)	$ 9,500		
Work-in-process			
Direct materials (200 × $5)	$ 1,000		
Conversion costs (120 × $4.50)	540		
Total work-in-process	$ 1,540		
Total	$11,040†		

†Rounding difference of $1.

example, results of assigning costs to spoilage are given in figure 5.5 As can be seen from reviewing these results, decisions had to be made regarding the calculation of the spoilage costs and their allocation to cost of production.

When we compare results shown in figure 5.4 with those in figure 5.5, we see that $314 is overcharged to ending work-in-process when spoiled units are not included in the calculation of equivalent units.

Because the spoiled units are detected at the end of the process, they are assigned the same cost as completed units. Had they been detected halfway through the process, the spoiled units would have been assigned full material costs (300 × $4) but only one-half of the conversion costs (150 × $3.55).

To ensure that normal spoilage costs are properly allocated, after being calculated, they should be allocated to finished goods and possibly work-

FIGURE 5.5
XYZ Company
Cost-of-Production
Report

Physical flows	Units		
	Physical	Equivalent	
		Direct materials	Conversion costs
Units to be accounted for			
Beginning work-in-process	0		
Units started	1,500		
Total	1,500		
Units accounted for			
Completed units	1,000	1,000	1,000
Ending work-in-process			
(60 percent complete)*	200	200	120
Spoilage	300	300	300
Total	1,500	1,500	1,420

*Materials complete.

Cost flows	Totals	Direct materials	Conversion costs
Costs to be accounted for			
Direct materials	$ 6,000	$6,000	
Conversion costs	5,041		$5,041
Total	$11,041	$6,000	$5,041
Unit costs		$4.00	$3.55
Costs accounted for			
Completed units			
(1,000 × $7.55)	$7,550		
Allocation of spoilage			
(300 × $7.55)	2,265		
Total completed	$9,815		
Work-in-process			
Direct materials (200 × $4)	$ 800		
Conversion costs (120 × $3.55)	426		
Total work-in-process	$ 1,226		
Total	$11,041		

in-process, depending on the point at which spoilage is detected. Keep in mind that normal spoilage should be allocated only to units that have been inspected because spoilage costs relate only to those units.

If inspection takes place at the end of the production process, all normal spoilage costs should be assigned to finished goods, since units included in work-in-process have not yet passed the **inspection point.** In the event that spoilage is discovered at some other point (for example, halfway through the process) and work-in-process has progressed beyond this point, then some of the spoilage cost should be allocated to work-in-process.

In the example shown, we did not need to allocate any of the normal spoilage to ending work-in-process, since inspection took place at the end of production. What happens when work-in-process has passed the point of inspection? When this situation exists, we must determine how best to allocate spoilage costs to the cost of production. One of the more popular methods calls for the allocation of a full, proportionate amount of spoilage costs to work-in-process inventories that have been inspected. This is often interpreted to mean a ratio is developed between units in work-in-process and finished goods. Assume that inspection takes place halfway through the conversion process and work-in-process has received 70 percent of conversion costs to be charged to the process. Let us further assume that there are 20,000 units completed and 5,000 units in work-in-process. Using these units as a basis, four-fifths of the spoilage costs would be allocated to finished goods and one-fifth to work-in-process.

The possibility always exists that some or all of the spoilage will be considered abnormal. If the proper procedures have been followed in assigning costs to spoilage, costs of abnormal spoilage can be separated out and charged off as a current-period loss. If the cost of spoilage determined in figure 5.5 had all been abnormal, the journal entry required would be:

```
Loss, abnormal product spoilage  ..................................  2,265
    Work-in-process  ..............................................          2,265
```

Figure 5.6 recaps the calculations and allocation of the cost of spoilage determined in figure 5.5. The journal entry for the cost of completed units is also shown.

A Summary of Basic Procedures

In accounting for spoilage, it is a good policy first to separate spoilage costs for management-control purposes. The spoilage costs should then be separated into two components—normal and abnormal—with abnormal costs being charged off as a current-period loss. Cost of normal spoilage can then be allocated to finished goods and also to work-in-process, if the work-in-process has been inspected.

```
Calculations
  Normal spoilage  ..........................................  $2,265

  Allocated to:
    Finished goods*  ........................................  $2,265
    Work-in-process  ........................................        0
                                                              $2,265

Journal entry
  Finished goods  ....................................  9,815
    Work-in-process  ..................................          9,815

The $9,815 includes $7,550 originally charged to completed units plus the $2,265 of normal spoilage.
*Allocated to finished goods because work-in-process has not yet been inspected.
```

FIGURE 5.6
XYZ Company
Allocation of
Normal Spoilage

Comprehensive Example

The following example will provide a better understanding of how to account for spoiled units under the FIFO and weighted-average methods.

ABC Company uses a process-cost-accounting system. Materials are added at the start of the process and conversion costs are incurred evenly throughout the process. In this process, some units are spoiled. Spoilage is not detected until the end of the process. Normal spoilage represents one-fifth of the completed output. Additional information concerning current production is as follows:

Units
Beginning inventory (80 percent complete)	1,000
Units started	9,000
Units completed	6,200
Ending inventory (40 percent complete)	2,500

Costs
Beginning inventory (materials, $13,000; conversion cost, $10,900)	$23,900
Material added	$27,000
Conversion costs added	$23,100

Determine the cost of finished goods, ending work-in-process inventories, and abnormal spoilage.

Figure 5.7 presents the cost-of-production report under the FIFO method. The total spoilage cost is separated into normal and abnormal components, based on the information given that normal spoilage was expected to be one-fifth of the completed output. The total number of spoiled units is determined by comparing the difference between units to be accounted for and the sum of the completed units and ending work-in-process. Since the inspection point is at the end of the process, all normal spoilage costs are charged to cost of goods completed. The abnormal spoilage cost of $360 is charged off as a current-period loss. A minor problem exists when charging spoilage costs to completed-unit costs under the FIFO assumption. All costs assigned to spoilage are based on current-period costs. A strict interpretation of the FIFO method would suggest that this approach is correct only for units started and completed during the period. Nevertheless, the problem is considered a minor one.

Figure 5.8 presents the cost-of-production report under the weighted-average method. The solution process is essentially the same as in figure 5.7, with spoiled units and related costs developed in a similar manner.

☐ SUMMARY

Process-costing procedures become more complicated when additional units are generated as a result of adding materials in subsequent departments. However, complexities created by additional units can be handled by recognizing them in the cost-of-production report.

Accountants should expect to encounter problems of product disappearance, spoilage, defective units, and scrap residuals in the design and implementation of product-cost-determination systems. Disappearance problems take place when material evaporates or disappears as part of

FIGURE 5.7
ABC Company
Cost-of-Production
Report—FIFO
Method

Physical flows	Units		
	Physical	Equivalent	
		Direct materials	Conversion costs
Units to be accounted for			
Beginning work-in-process			
(80 percent complete)*	1,000		200
Units started	9,000		
Total	10,000		
Units accounted for			
From beginning inventory	1,000		
Started and completed	5,200	5,200	5,200
Ending work-in-process			
(40 percent complete)*	2,500	2,500	1,000
Spoilage	1,300	1,300	1,300
Total	10,000	9,000	7,700

*Materials complete.

Cost flows	Totals	Direct materials	Conversion costs
Costs to be accounted for			
From beginning inventory	$23,900		
Current costs added			
Direct materials	27,000	$27,000	
Conversion costs	23,100		$23,100
Total	$74,000	$27,000	$23,100
Unit costs		$3	$3
Costs accounted for			
Units completed			
From beginning inventory	$23,900		
Required to complete			
Conversion costs (200 × $3)	600		
	$24,500		
Started and completed			
(5,200 × $6)	31,200		
Spoilage costs			
(1,240 × $6)	7,440†		
Total completed goods	$63,140		
Ending work-in-process			
Direct materials (2,500 × $3)	$ 7,500		
Conversion costs (1,000 × $3)	3,000		
Total work-in-process	$10,500		
Abnormal spoilage (60 × $6)	$360		
Total	$74,000		

†Based on ⅕ × 6,200 = 1,240.

the production process. Spoilage results when materials fail to meet production standards and cannot be reworked. Defective products are items that initially fail to meet quality-control standards but that can be re-

FIGURE 5.8
ABC Company
Cost-of-Production
Report—W/A
Method

Physical flows	Units		
	Physical	Equivalent	
		Direct materials	Conversion costs
Units to be accounted for			
Beginning work-in-process			
(80 percent complete)*	1,000		
Units started	9,000		
Total	10,000		
Units accounted for			
Completed units	6,200	6,200	6,200
Ending work-in-process			
(40 percent complete)*	2,500	2,500	1,000
Spoilage	1,300	1,300	1,300
Total	10,000	10,000	8,500

*Materials complete.

Cost flows	Totals	Direct materials	Conversion costs
Costs to be accounted for			
From beginning inventory	$23,900	$13,000	$10,900
Current costs added			
Direct materials	27,000	27,000	
Conversion costs	23,100		23,100
Total	$74,000	$40,000	$34,000
Unit costs		$4	$4
Costs accounted for			
Units completed			
(6,200 × $8)	$49,600		
Spoilage costs (1,240 × $8)	9,920†		
Total completed units	$59,520		
Ending work-in-process			
Direct materials (2,500 × $4)	$10,000		
Conversion Costs (1,000 × $4)	4,000		
Total work-in-process	$14,000		
Abnormal spoilage (60 × $8)	$480		
Total	$74,000		

†Based on ⅕ × 6,200 = 1,240.

worked. Scrap is a residual that may have a minor value but cannot be used directly in the production process.

In manufacturing operations, some units will be spoiled. From a reporting point of view, a decision must be reached as to how the cost of these units will be handled. The basic decision becomes one of whether to implicitly or explicitly recognize the spoiled units. The explicit method will permit isolation of inefficient operations in the form of abnormal spoilage so that this loss can be removed from inventory costs.

KEY TERMS

Abnormal spoilage
Defective units
Disappearance
Inspection point

Normal spoilage
Scrap material
Spoilage

REVIEW PROBLEM

The Roget Company produces a product that is processed in one department. Basic information relating to the operations of the current period is:

Units	
Beginning inventory	10,000
Units started	20,000
Units transferred	25,000
Ending inventory	4,000
Spoilage	1,000

Costs	
Material costs added	$30,000
Labor	10,000

Beginning work-in-process was one-half complete with respect to conversion costs. Material is added at the beginning of production. Beginning inventories include $6,000 for material and $2,000 for conversion costs. Overhead is applied at the rate of 50 percent of labor. Ending inventory was three-fifths complete. All spoilage is normal and was detected at the end of the process.

Required □ Calculate cost of goods completed and work-in-process, using the weighted-average method, where:

    a. Spoilage is ignored.
    b. Spoilage is recognized.

Solution □

ROGET COMPANY
Cost-of-Production Report
(Ignoring Spoilage)

		Units	
Physical flows	Physical	Equivalent	
		Direct materials	Conversion costs
Units to be allocated			
Beginning work-in-process			
(50 percent complete)*	10,000		
Units started	20,000		
Total	30,000		
Units accounted for			
Completed units	25,000	25,000	25,000

	Physical	Direct materials	Conversion costs
Ending work-in-process (60 percent complete)*	4,000	4,000	2,400
Spoilage	1,000		
Total	30,000	29,000	27,400

*Materials complete.

Cost flows	Totals	Direct materials	Conversion costs
Costs to be accounted for			
From beginning inventory	$ 8,000	$ 6,000	$ 2,000
Current costs added			
Direct materials	30,000	30,000	
Conversion costs	15,000		15,000
Total	$53,000	$36,000	$17,000
Unit costs		$1.2414	$ .6204
Costs accounted for			
Units completed (25,000 × $1.8618)	$46,545		
Ending work-in-process			
Direct materials (4,000 × $1.2414)	$4,966		
Conversion costs (2,400 × $.6204)	1,489		
Total work-in-process	$6,455		
Total	$53,000		

ROGET COMPANY
Cost-of-Production Report
(Recognizing Spoilage)

		Units	
Physical flows	Physical	Equivalent	
		Direct materials	Conversion costs
Units to be allocated			
Beginning work-in-process (50 percent complete)*	10,000		
Units started	20,000		
Total	30,000		
Units accounted for			
Completed units	25,000	25,000	25,000
Ending work-in-process (60 percent complete)*	4,000	4,000	2,400
Spoilage	1,000	1,000	1,000
Total	30,000	30,000	28,400

*Materials complete.

Cost flows	Totals	Direct materials	Conversion costs
Costs to be accounted for			
From beginning inventory	$ 8,000	$ 6,000	$2,000
Current costs added			
Direct materials	30,000	30,000	
Conversion costs	15,000		15,000
Total	$53,000	$36,000	$17,000
Unit costs		$1.20	$.5986

Costs accounted for
  Units completed
    (25,000 × $1.7986) $44,965
  Spoilage costs (1,000 × $1.7986)   1,798
    Total completed costs $46,763

  Ending work-in-process
  Direct materials (4,000 × $1.20) .... $ 4,800
  Conversion costs (2,400 × $.5986)   1,437
    Total work-in-process .... $ 6,237
    Total $53,000

QUESTIONS

Q5-1. What problems are created by having materials added in subsequent departments?

Q5-2. Describe a situation in which additional units are likely created by the addition of materials in a subsequent department.

Q5-3. Define disappearance, spoilage, defective units, and scrap.

Q5-4. Describe entries required for defective units. Explain.

Q5-5. Discuss possible record-keeping methods used for scrap.

Q5-6. Discuss similarities and differences between disappearance and spoilage.

Q5-7. What is the difference between a defective unit and a spoiled unit?

Q5-8. Distinguish between normal and abnormal spoilage.

Q5-9. Discuss the methods for allocating spoilage costs to units produced.

Q5-10. What problems may be created by having costs of spoilage spread over good units?

Q5-11. Describe the preferred method for allocating spoilage costs to production.

Q5-12. Explain under what conditions costs of normal spoilage would be allocated to work-in-process.

PROBLEMS

P5-1. Information concerning department B of the Dextro Company is as follows: *Material Added in a Subsequent Department*

	Units	Costs
Beginning work-in-process	5,000	$ 6,300
Units transferred in	35,000	58,000
	40,000	$64,300

Units completed		37,000	
Ending work-in-process		3,000	

	Costs			
	Transferred in	Materials	Conversion	Total costs
Beginning work-in-process	$ 2,900	$ —	$ 3,400	$ 6,300
Current costs	17,500	25,500	15,000	58,000
	$20,400	$25,500	$18,400	$64,300

Conversion costs were 20 percent complete as to the beginning work-in-process and 40 percent complete as to the ending work-in-process. All materials are added at the end of the process. Dextro uses the weighted-average method.

Required □ Prepare a cost-of-production report.

Assumptions of FIFO Method

P5-2. Assume that Dextro Company uses the FIFO method and that you are working with the same information presented in problem 5-1. Describe how the cost-of-production report will differ from one prepared under the weighted-average method, and explain the basic assumption of the FIFO method. You do not need to make specific computations.

Material Added in a Subsequent Department

P5-3. At the Patsy Corporation, 20,000 gallons of liquid have been transferred from processing at a total cost of $40,000 to the Mix-Container department. In the Mix-Container department, an equal amount of oil is added at the beginning of the process at a cost of $1 per gallon of oil. Conversion costs of $10,000 are needed to transform the ingredients into a finished product. At the end of the process, the finished product is packaged in ten-gallon containers costing $5 per container. There are no work-in-process inventories.

Required □ Prepare a cost-of-production report for the Mix-Container department.

Disappearance of Material in the First Department; Material Added in Second Department

P5-4. Sarah Company produces a chemical used in melting ice. In the first department, Cooking, various ingredients are mixed and cooked, causing a 60 percent decrease in initial volume very early in the process. The resulting product is then transferred to a second department, Mixing, where it is combined with an equal amount of alcohol and bottled in containers for distribution.

In the first department, materials are added at the beginning of the process. Conversion costs are added throughout the process. In the second department, alcohol is added in the beginning of the process, and the final product is bottled at the conclusion of the process. Conversion costs are added during bottling in the second department. The FIFO method is used in both departments. Information for the current month is as follows:

	Cooking	Mixing
Units (gallons)		
Beginning inventory	6,000	4,000
Starts	20,000	
	26,000	

Completed	8,000	
Ending inventory	6,000	6,000
Evaporation	12,000	
	26,000	

Costs
Beginning inventory,
  40 percent complete $44,000
  100 percent complete as to
    alcohol only. No
    conversion costs. $48,000
Materials
  Cooking $80,000
  Mixing—alcohol $16,000
  Mixing—bottles $56,000
  Conversion costs $19,000 $46,000
  Ending inventory
    50 percent complete .... —
    100 percent complete as to alcohol
      only. No conversion costs. .... —

Required □ Prepare a cost-of-production report for each department.

P5-5. Assume that in problem 5-4 beginning inventory costs in the two departments consist of the following:

Material Added in Second Department

Cooking
  Material $42,000
  Conversion costs 2,000
                                                                 $44,000

Mixing
  Transferred in $38,000
  Direct materials 10,000
                                                                 $48,000

Required □ Prepare a cost-of-production report for each department, using the weighted-average method.

P5-6. Poole, Inc., produces a chemical compound by a unique chemical process that Poole has divided into two departments, A and B, for accounting purposes. The process functions as follows:

Material Added in Second Department; Normal Spoilage in First Department

The formula for the chemical compound requires one pound of chemical X and one pound of chemical Y. In the simplest sense, one pound of chemical X is processed in department A and transferred to department B for further processing, where one pound of chemical Y is added when the process is 50 percent complete. When the processing is complete in department B, the finished chemical compound is transferred to finished goods. The process operates continuously 24 hours a day.

Normal spoilage occurs in department A. Five percent of chemical X is lost in the first few seconds of processing.

No spoilage occurs in department B.

In department A, conversion costs are incurred uniformly throughout the process and are allocated to good pounds produced because spoilage is normal.

In department B, conversion costs are allocated equally to each equivalent pound of output.

Poole's unit of measure for work-in-process and finished-goods inventories is pounds.

The following data are available for the month of October 19X4:

	Department A	Department B
Work-in-process, October 1	8,000 pounds	10,000 pounds
Stage of completion of beginning inventory (one batch per department)	¾	³⁄₁₀
Started or transferred in	50,000 pounds	?
Transferred out	46,500 good pounds	?
Work-in-process, October 31	?	?
Stage of completion of ending inventory (one batch per department)	⅓	⅕
Total equivalent pounds of material added in departments		44,500 pounds

Required ☐ Prepare a schedule computing the equivalent unspoiled pounds of production (materials and conversion costs) for department A and for department B for the month of October 19X4. Use the first-in, first-out method for inventory costing.

(CPA)

Basic Process Costing—Lost Units with Incomplete Information

P5-7. The XYZ Corporation has now completed its second month of operations. Relevant data are as follows:

Units in beginning inventory (one-third complete)	3,000
Units put into production	12,000
Units completed	9,000
Units in ending inventory (one-half complete)	5,000
Costs in beginning inventory	$ 2,500
Costs of current period	$16,000

Required ☐

1. Using FIFO, calculate cost of finished goods and work-in-process. Assume all costs are added throughout the process.

2. Repeat requirement 1, using the weighted-average method.

3. Discuss your handling of the lost units. What additional information would you have wanted?

Basic Process Costing—Spoiled Units with Incomplete Information

P5-8. The Racquet Ball Company uses a process-cost system. Materials are added at the beginning of the process, and conversion costs are incurred uniformly throughout the process. Work-in-process at the beginning is 40 percent complete and at the end is 60 percent complete. Current data are as follows:

Beginning inventory	800
Units added	10,000
Units completed	6,000
Ending inventory	600
Conversion costs incurred	$20,160
Cost of materials added	$20,000
Beginning inventory costs (materials, $2,000; conversion costs, $2,200)	$ 4,200

Required ☐

1. Using both the FIFO and the weighted-average methods, prepare a cost-of-production report showing cost of goods completed and cost of ending work-in-process.

2. What information would be needed to assign a cost to spoilage?

P5-9. ABC Corporation has now completed its second month of operations. Relevant data are as follows:

Basic Process Costing—Spoiled Units with Information on Point of Detection

Units in beginning inventory (one-third complete)	3,000
Units put in production	12,000
Units completed	9,000
Units in ending inventory (one-half complete)	5,000
Costs in beginning inventory	$ 2,500
Costs of current period	$16,000

Spoilage, all abnormal, is detected at the end of the process.

Required ☐ Using FIFO, calculate cost of finished goods and work-in-process. Assume all costs are added throughout the process.

P5-10. In problem 5-9, assume the weighted-average method is used.

Basic Process Costing—Spoiled Units with Information on Point of Detection

Required ☐ Calculate cost of finished goods and work-in-process, assuming all costs are added throughout the process.

P5-11. The Hill Company produces a product that must be processed through two departments. Basic information relating to the operations of the recent period is:

Two Departments: Spoilage in the First Department

Units	Assembly	Finishing
	Department	
Beginning inventory	10,000	12,000
Units started	20,000	
Units transferred	25,000	
Ending inventory	4,000	10,000
Spoilage, all normal, detected at end of process	1,000	
Costs		
Material costs added	$22,000	$14,000
Labor	8,000	12,000

Other Information

Beginning work-in-process in the Assembly department was one-half complete with respect to conversion costs. Material is added at the start of production. Beginning inventories include $6,000 for material and $2,000 for conversion costs. Overhead is applied at the rate of 50 percent of labor. Ending inventory was two-fifths complete.

Beginning work-in-process in the Finishing department was three-fourths complete with respect to conversion costs. Material is added at the end of the process. Beginning inventories include $8,000 for transferred costs and

$10,000 for conversion costs. Overhead is applied at the rate of 100 percent of labor. Ending inventory was estimated to be one-fourth complete.

Required □ Calculate cost of goods transferred from each department and the cost of ending work-in-process inventories. Use the weighted-average basis for the first department and the FIFO method for the second department. Give proper recognition to spoilage.

*Process
Costing—Service
Department
Allocation, Lost
Units*

P5-12. In the course of your examination of the financial statements of the Zeus Company for the year ended December 31, 19X1, you have ascertained the following concerning its manufacturing operations.

Zeus has two production departments (Fabricating and Finishing) and a Service department. In the Fabricating department, polyplast is prepared from miracle mix and bypro. In the Finishing department, each unit of polyplast is converted into six tetraplexes and three uniplexes. The Service department provides services to both production departments.

The Fabricating and Finishing departments use process-cost-accounting systems. Actual production costs, including overhead, are allocated monthly.

Service department expenses are allocated to production departments as follows:

Expenses	Allocation base
Building maintenance	Space occupied
Timekeeping and personnel	Number of employees
Other	One-half to Fabricating, One-half to Finishing

Raw-materials inventory and work-in-process are priced on a December 19X1 FIFO basis. The following data were taken from the records of the fabricating department:

Quantities (units of polyplast):

In-process, December 1	3,000
Started in-process during month	25,000
Total units to be accounted for	28,000
Transferred to Finishing department	19,000
In-process, December 31	6,000
Lost in-process	3,000
Total units accounted for	28,000

Cost of work-in-process, December 1:

Materials	$ 13,000
Labor	17,500
Overhead	21,500
Direct-labor costs, December	$154,000
Departmental overhead, December	$132,000

Polyplast work-in-process at the beginning and end of the month was partially completed as follows:

	Materials	Labor and overhead
December 1	66⅔ percent	50 percent
December 31	100 percent	75 percent

The following data were taken from raw-materials inventory records for December:

	Miracle Mix		Bypro	
	Quantity	Amount	Quantity	Amount
Balance, December 1	62,000	$62,000	265,000	$18,550
Purchases:				
December 12	39,500	49,375		
December 20	28,500	34,200		
Fabricating department				
usage	83,200		50,000	

Service department expenses for December (not included in departmental overhead above) were:

Building maintenance	$ 45,000
Timekeeping and personnel	27,500
Other	39,000
	$111,500

Other information for December 19X1 is presented below:

	Square feet of space occupied	Number of employees
Fabricating	75,000	180
Finishing	37,500	120
	112,500	300

Required ☐

1. Compute the equivalent number of units of polyplast, with separate calculations for materials and conversion costs incurred during December.

2. Compute the following items to be included in the Fabricating department production report for December 19X1, with separate calculations for materials, direct labor, and overhead. Prepare supporting schedules and include:

   a. Total costs to be accounted for.
   b. Unit costs for equivalent units manufactured.
   c. Transfers to finishing department during December and work-in-process on December 31. Reconcile your answer to total costs to be accounted for.

(CPA)

P5-13. Crews Company produces a chemical agent for commercial use. The company accounts for production in two cost centers, Cooking and Mix-pack. In the first cost center, liquid substances are combined in large cookers and boiled; the boiling causes a normal decrease in volume from evaporation. After the batch is cooked, it is transferred to Mix-pack, the second cost center. A quantity of alcohol is added equal to the liquid measure of the batch. It is mixed and then bottled in one-gallon containers.

Normal Evaporation in the First Department; Material Added in the Second Department

Material is added at the beginning of production in each cost center, and labor is added equally during production in each cost center. Overhead is applied on the basis of 80 percent of labor cost. Lost units are ignored (i.e., all costs are allocated only to equivalent good units); the process is "in control" as long as the yield ratio for the first department is not less than 78 percent.

The FIFO method is used to cost work-in-process inventories, and transfers are made at an average unit cost; that is, the total cost transferred is divided by the total number of units transferred.

The following information is available for the month of October 19X7:

Cost information	Cooking	Mix-pack
Work-in-process, October 1, 19X7		
Materials	$ 990	$ 120
Labor	100	60
Prior department cost		426
Month of October		
Materials	39,600	15,276
Labor	10,050	16,000

Inventory and production records show that Cooking had 1,000 gallons 40 percent processed on October 1 and 800 gallons 50 percent processed on October 31; Mix-pack had 600 gallons 50 percent processed on October 1 and 1,000 gallons 30 percent processed on October 31.

Production reports for October show that Cooking started 50,000 gallons into production and completed and transferred 40,200 gallons to Mix-pack, and Mix-pack completed and transferred 80,000 one-gallon containers of the finished product to the distribution warehouse.

Required ☐ In good form, prepare a cost-of-production report for the Cooking cost center and for the Mix-pack cost center.

(CPA)

Basic Process Costing with Spoilage—FIFO

P5-14. Costs of producing the product of the Kosak Company are accumulated on a process-cost-accounting basis. Materials are added 50 percent of the way through the process, and conversion costs are added continuously throughout the process. In the process, some units are spoiled that are not detected until the end of the process. Normal spoilage represents about one-fifth of the completed output. Additional information is provided as follows:

Units	
Beginning inventory (60 percent complete)	1,000
Units started	9,000
Units completed	6,200
Ending inventory (40 percent complete)	2,400

Costs	
Beginning inventory	$24,000
Material added	22,800
Conversion costs	52,000

Required ☐ Prepare a cost-of-production report using the FIFO method that shows cost of goods completed, cost of ending work-in-process, and cost of abnormal spoilage.

P5-15. Using information given in problem 5.14 and the following additional information on beginning work-in-process, prepare a cost-of-production report, using the weighted-average method.

Basic Process Costing with Spoilage—Weighted-Average

Beginning inventory
Direct materials $18,000
Conversion costs   6,000
                                                                                                                                $24,000

P5-16. The Ferraro Company produces wheels for bicycles. Materials are put in at the beginning of the process with conversion costs distributed evenly over the process. Some units of this product are spoiled with detection taking place halfway through the process. Normal spoilage equals about one-tenth of the finished output.

Basic Process Costing with Spoilage—Weighted-Average

At the beginning of the period, the inventory of work-in-process was represented by 4,000 units, two-fifths complete ($12,000 materials and $8,600 conversion costs). During the period, 10,000 units were put into production. Material costs were $60,500. Inventory at the end of the period was 2,000 units, one-half complete. Ten thousand units were completed during the period. Conversion costs incurred were $45,000.

Required ☐ Prepare a cost-of-production report, using the weighted-average method that shows cost of goods completed, cost of ending work-in-process, and cost of abnormal spoilage.

P5-17. Four independent questions concerning a typical manufacturing company that uses a process-cost-accounting system are listed. Your response to each question should be complete, including simple examples or illustrations where appropriate.

Process-Costing Concepts—Discussion

Required ☐

1. What is the rationale supporting the use of process costing instead of job-order costing for product-costing purposes? Explain.

2. Define equivalent production (equivalent units produced). Explain the significance and use of equivalent production for product-costing purposes.

3. Define normal spoilage and abnormal spoilage. Explain how normal spoilage costs and abnormal spoilage costs should be reported for management purposes.

4. How does the first-in, first-out (FIFO) method of process costing differ from the weighted-average method of process costing? Explain.

(CPA)

P5-18. The Adept Company is a manufacturer of two products known as Prep and Pride. Incidental to the production of these two products, is the production of a scrap product known as Wilton. The manufacturing process covers two departments, Grading and Saturating.

Two Departments: Scrap, Additional Pounds Produced in Second Department

The manufacturing process begins in the Grading department when raw materials are started in-process. Upon completion of processing in the Grading department, the scrap Wilton is produced, which accounts for 20 percent of the material output. This scrap is transferred to scrap inventory.

The net realizable value of the Wilton is accounted for as a reduction of the cost of materials in the Grading department. The current selling price of Wilton is $1 per pound, and the estimated selling and delivery costs total ten cents per pound.

The remaining output is transferred to the Saturating department for the final phase of production. In the Saturating department, water is added at the beginning of the production process. This results in a 50 percent gain in weight of the materials in production.

The following information is available for the month of November 19X9:

Inventories	November 1 Quantity (pounds)	Amount	November 30 Quantity (pounds)
Work-in-process			
Grading department	None	—	None
Saturating department	1,600	$17,600	2,000
Finished goods			
Prep	600	14,520	1,600
Pride	2,400	37,110	800
Wilton	None	—	None

The work-in-process inventory (labor and overhead) in the Saturating department is estimated to be 50 percent complete both at the beginning and end of November.

Costs of production for November are as follows:

Costs of production	Materials used	Labor and overhead
Grading department	$265,680	$86,400
Saturating department	—	86,000

The material used in the Grading department weighed 36,000 pounds.

The company uses the first-in, first-out method of process costing.

Required □ Prepare a cost-of-production report for both the Grading and Saturating departments for the month of November. Show supporting computations in good form.

Your answer should include:

a. Equivalent units of production (in pounds)
b. Total manufacturing costs
c. Cost per equivalent unit (pounds)
d. Dollar amount of ending work-in-process
e. Dollar amount of inventory cost transferred out

(CPA)

P5-19. The Ranka Company manufactures high-quality leather products. Company profits have declined during the past nine months. Ranka has used unit cost data that were developed eighteen months ago in planning and controlling its operations. In an attempt to isolate the causes of poor profit performance, the management team is investigating the manufacturing operations of each of its products.

Process Costing: Normal and Abnormal Defective Units Discovered at Different Points

One of Ranka's main products is fine leather belts. The belts are produced in a single, continuous process in the Bluett plant. During the process, leather strips are sewn, punched, and dyed. Buckles are attached by rivets when the belts are 70 percent complete as to direct labor and overhead (conversion costs). The belts then enter a final finishing stage to conclude the process. Labor and overhead are applied continuously during the process.

The leather belts are inspected twice during the process: (1) right before the buckles are attached (70 percent point in the process) and (2) at the conclusion of the finishing stage (100 percent point in the process). Ranka uses the weighted-average method to calculate its unit costs.

The leather belts produced at the Bluett plant sell at a wholesale cost of $9.95. Management wants to compare the current manufacturing costs per unit with the prices that exist on the market for leather belts. Top management has asked the Bluett plant to submit data on the cost of manufacturing the leather belts for the month of October. This cost data will be used to evaluate whether modifications in the production process should be initiated or whether an increase in the selling price of the belts is justified. The cost per equivalent unit that is being used for planning and controlling purposes is $5.35 per unit.

The work-in-process inventory consisted of 400 partially completed units on October 1. The belts were 25 percent complete as to conversion costs. The costs included in the inventory on October 1 were as follows:

Leather strips	$1,000
Conversion costs	300
	$1,300

During October, 7,600 leather strips were placed in production. A total of 6,800 good leather belts were completed. A total of 300 belts were identified as spoiled at the two inspection points—100 at the first inspection point (before buckle is attached) and 200 at the final inspection point (after finishing). This quantity of spoiled belts was considered normal.

In addition, 200 belts were removed from the production line when the process was 40 percent complete as to conversion costs because they had been damaged as a result of a malfunction during the sewing operation. This malfunction was considered an unusual occurrence, and consequently the spoilage was classified as abnormal. Spoiled units are not reprocessed and have zero salvage value. The work-in-process inventory on October 31 consisted of 700 belts that were 50 percent complete as to conversion costs.

The costs charged to production during October were as follows:

Leather strips	$20,600
Buckles	4,550
Conversion costs	20,700
	$45,850

Required ☐

1. In order to provide cost data regarding the manufacture of leather belts in the Bluett plant to the top management of Ranka Company, determine for the month of October:

   a. The equivalent units for each factor of production
   b. The cost per equivalent whole unit for each factor of production
   c. The assignment of total production costs to the work-in-process inventory and to goods transferred out
   d. The average unit cost of the 6,800 good leather belts completed and transferred to finished goods

2. If Ranka Company decided to repair (rework) the 300 defective belts that were considered normal spoilage, explain how the company would account for the rework costs.

(CMA)

Two Departments: Spoilage in the Second Department **P5-20.** The Dexter Production Company manufactures a single product. Its operations are a continuing process carried on in two departments—Machining and Finishing. In the production process, materials are added to the product in each department without increasing the number of units produced.

For the month of June 19X5, the company records indicated the following production statistics for each department:

	Machining department	Finishing department
Units in-process, June 1, 19X5	0	0
Units transferred from preceding department	0	60,000
Units started in production	80,000	0
Units completed and transferred out	60,000	50,000
Units in-process, June 30, 19X5*	20,000	8,000
Units spoiled in production	0	2,000
*Percent of completion of units in-process at June 30, 19X5:		
Materials	100 percent	100 percent
Labor	50 percent	70 percent
Overhead	25 percent	70 percent

The units spoiled in production had no scrap value and were 50 percent complete as to material, labor, and overhead. Company policy is to treat the cost of spoiled units in production as a separate element of cost in the department in which the spoilage occurs.

Cost records showed the following charges for the month of June:

	Machining department	Finishing department
Materials	$240,000	$ 88,500
Labor	140,000	141,500
Overhead	65,000	25,470

Required □ For both the Machining and Finishing departments, prepare in good form a cost-of-production report for the month of June.

(CPA)

P5-21. Perry Corporation makes a standard 9′ × 12′ rug. These rugs are woven in the first department and dyed in the second department. Perry uses a process-costing system with the weighted-average system for determining unit costs.

Two Departments: Spoilage in the Second Department

The beginning inventory in the Weaving department consists of 150 rugs. They are 100 percent complete as to materials and 70 percent complete as to conversion costs. Material costs associated with the beginning inventory are $725. Conversion costs associated with the beginning inventory are $920.

During the current period, 1,150 rugs were started into production. Current materials and conversion costs are $3,500 and $5,900, respectively.

There are 100 units in the ending inventory. These rugs are 100 percent complete as to materials and 40 percent complete as to labor. No rugs are spoiled in the weaving process.

In the Dyeing department, there were 200 rugs in the beginning inventory. They were 60 percent complete as to materials and 70 percent complete as to labor. Costs associated with the beginning inventory are weaving (prior department) $2,100, materials $681, and conversion $890.

During the current period, material costs were $2,119 and conversion costs were $3,100. During the period, 50 rugs were spoiled in the dyeing process. This spoilage is not considered abnormal. The spoiled rugs were 100 percent complete as to prior department and materials costs. The spoiled rugs were 40 percent complete as to conversion. Perry Corporation expenses the spoilage costs.

The ending inventory consists of 100 units. These units are 100 percent complete as to materials and 60 percent complete as to conversion.

Required □

1. Prepare a cost-of-production report for the Weaving department. Use good form.

2. Prepare a cost-of-production report for the Dyeing department. Use good form.

P5-22. Toodept Chemical Company uses a process-cost accounting system to account for the costs of its only product, known as Quivel. Output is produced in two departments, A and B, in succession before transfer to finished-goods inventory.

Two Departments: Spoilage in Both Departments

Material is added at the beginning process of each department and conversion is added evenly throughout. Goods are inspected two-thirds of the way through the department A process, and at the end of the department B process. Accounting, cost-flow assumptions are FIFO for department A and weighted-average for department B.

The following data apply:

Conversion	Units	Department A Costs Materials	Conversion	Units	Department B Costs Materials	Conversion
Work-in-process, Jan. 1						
Dept. A (50 percent complete)	200	$ 580	$ 270			
Dept. B (60 percent complete)				1,400	$ 4,200(T/I)	$ 650
					3,500	
Units started in production	24,800			20,600		
Material costs		74,400			46,500	
Conversion costs			24,750			9,100
Units completed	20,600			18,000		
Abnormal spoilage	2,400			0		
Work in process, Dec. 31						
Dept. A (20 percent complete)	2,000					
Dept. B. (25 percent complete)				2,000		

Abnormal spoilage is separated for management control. Normal spoilage is treated separately in department A and spread over good units produced (ignored) in department B.

Required □ Prepare December 31 cost-of-production reports for departments A and B.

Comprehensive Problem with Spoilage

P5-23. Ballinger Paper Products manufactures a high-quality paper box. The Box department applies two separate operations: cutting and folding. The paper is first cut and trimmed to the dimensions of a box form by one machine group. One square foot of paper is equivalent to four box forms. The trimmings from this process have no scrap value. Box forms are then creased and folded (i.e., completed) by a second machine group. Any partially processed boxes in the department are cut-box forms that are ready for creasing and folding. These partly processed boxes are considered 50 percent complete as to labor and overhead. The Materials department maintains an inventory of paper in sufficient quantities to permit continuous processing, and transfers to the Box department are made as needed. Immediately after folding, all good boxes are transferred to the Finished Goods department.

During June 19X1, the Materials department purchased 1,210,000 square feet of unprocessed paper for $244,000. Conversion costs for the month were $226,000. A quantity equal to 30,000 boxes was spoiled during paper cutting, and 70,000 boxes were spoiled during folding. All spoilage has a zero salvage value, is considered normal, and cannot be reprocessed. All spoilage loss is allocated between the completed units and partially processed boxes. Ballinger applies the weighted-average cost method to all inventories. Inventory data for June are given below.

Inventory	Physical unit	June 30, 19X1 Units on hand	June 1, 19X1 Units on hand	Cost
Materials department:				
Paper	square feet	200,000	390,000	$76,000

Box department

Boxes cut, not folded	number	300,000	800,000	55,000*

Finished Goods department

Completed boxes on hand	number	50,000	250,000	18,000

*Materials	$35,000
Conversion cost	20,000
	$55,000

Required ☐ Prepare the following for the month of June 19X1:

a.   A report of cost of paper used for the Materials department.
b.   A schedule showing the physical flow of units (including beginning and ending inventories) in the Materials department, in the Box department, and in the Finished Goods department.
c.   A schedule showing the computation of equivalent units produced for materials and conversion costs in the Box department.
d.   A schedule showing the computation of unit costs for the Box department.
e.   A report of inventory valuation and cost of completed units for the Box department.
f.   A schedule showing the computation of unit costs for the Finished Goods department.

(CPA)

CHAPTER OUTLINE

SPECIAL COST-ALLOCATION PROBLEMS

CHAPTER 6

☐ INTRODUCTION

In previous chapters, we have considered accounting for the cost of products produced independently of each other. In these production systems, all prime inputs can be associated with a particular output. Now, we will consider accounting for the cost-of-production systems in which a single input or set of inputs yields two or more outputs. Accounting problems arise because the prime inputs cannot be associated with a single output. In cost accounting, such outputs are referred to as **joint products** or **by-products.**

One might instinctively believe that the existence of joint products or by-products is a phenomenon that is rarely encountered. Such is certainly not the case. The food processing, chemical, petrochemical, petroleum, mining, and forestry industries each have numerous production systems producing joint products and by-products. The increased emphasis on conserving resources has resulted in more production systems that produce joint products and by-products. **Cost allocations** are handled differently for joint products than for by-products.

The other special cost-allocation problem considered in this chapter concerns the allocation of service-department costs when reciprocal relationships exist between the service departments. In such cases, service departments provide services to production and other service departments. This is also a frequently encountered problem, and we shall consider several algorithms for making cost allocations when this condition is encountered.

☐ JOINT PRODUCTS AND BY-PRODUCTS

Let us consider an example using copper ore, which contains significant amounts of sulphur and trace amounts of silver and gold. Since the single input—copper ore—results in more than one output, the various elements of output are referred to as the joint products. These elements remain as joint products until they are separated at a smelter. In the smelter, which

145

is the **split-off point** in processing ore, the ore is separated into copper, sulphur, silver, and gold. All mining, transportation, and processing costs that are incurred before the elements are separated at the smelter are joint costs because they are indivisible among the copper, sulphur, silver, and gold.

Joint costs are indivisible because the products cannot be obtained separately. For example, it is not possible to mine only the portion of the ore that contains copper. All of the **joint costs** (that is, the costs incurred prior to the split-off point) must be allocated among the joint products to determine a unit cost for each output. These unit costs are dependent upon the allocation scheme employed. Any costs incurred beyond the split-off point are separable and are incurred to put one or more of the products into a saleable condition. Such separable costs are directly traceable to a particular joint product; thus, there is no need to allocate such costs to all of the joint products. In fact, allocation of separable costs would be inappropriate.

The existence of joint costs creates two problems in cost accounting. The initial problem concerns the allocation of joint costs to joint products for inventory valuation. The second problem concerns the treatment of joint costs in decision making.

For accounting purposes, two classes of joint products are considered. The term by-product is used to identify products that have a relatively small value and are produced simultaneously with products that have greater value. In our example, a ton of ore from a copper mine may yield $100 of copper, $50 of sulphur, $2 of silver, and $1 of gold. The silver and gold would be accounted for as by-products, while the copper and sulphur would be accounted for as joint, or main, products. Figure 6.1 shows the relationship between the ore and the joint and by-products.

It should not be assumed that the classification of products as main or joint or as by-products is fixed. There are numerous examples in which the relative positions of products have been reversed. For example, in refining oil, kerosene was originally a main product and gasoline a by-product. Invention of the automobile increased demand for gasoline, making it the main product, while electricity almost eliminated the use of

FIGURE 6.1
Joint Products and
By-products

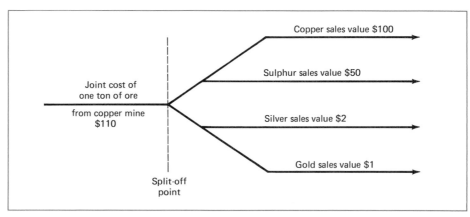

kerosene for lighting. Kerosene has regained some of its prominence as fuel for jet engines. Current fluctuations in the prices of gold and silver could result in these products being treated as main or joint products rather than by-products in some mining operations.

Recent environmental protection legislation requires manufacturers to process some types of waste before disposal. This creates an increased number of by-products in many industries and, therefore, the need to account for more by-products.

The impact on net income resulting from procedures used in accounting for joint and by-products is a question of timing because different methods result in income being recognized in different accounting periods. However, the relationships upon which the allocations are based should pass a reasonableness test. Such a reasonableness test is based on either the physical identification or the benefits associated with the system outputs. These considerations become paramount when a firm is dealing with a governmental agency or working under a cost or cost-plus contract. Under these circumstances, the accountant may be called upon to justify the reasonableness of the joint or by-product cost allocation.

☐ ACCOUNTING FOR JOINT PRODUCTS

Inventories on financial statements are valued using one of several methods based on historical cost. Cost allocation is necessary to establish inventory valuation so that income can be determined. We will consider several allocation schemes based on physical measures and market prices. Resulting from the various allocation schemes are unit costs that are employed in valuing the cost of goods sold and inventories. An example will be developed to show how the different methods result in different unit costs.

Assume joint costs of $40,000 are associated with a process that produces three products. The following relates to the output of the process:

Product identification	Unit output	Unit weight (lb)	Selling price at split-off	Additional processing costs	End product selling price
A	5,000	4	$4	$ .50	$ 6.50
B	7,500	5	$3	$1.00	$ 5.00
C	7,500	3	$5	$2.00	$10.00

Based on physical measures, the joint costs in this problem could be allocated based on units of output or weight. If the allocation is based on units of output, the joint cost to be allocated per unit is:

$$\frac{\text{Joint cost}}{\text{Units of output}} = \frac{\$40,000}{20,000} = \$2 \text{ per unit}$$

If the allocation is based on weight, the joint cost to be allocated per unit is determined as follows:

A		$5{,}000 \times 4 \text{ lb} = 20{,}000 \text{ lb}$
B		$7{,}500 \times 5 \text{ lb} = 37{,}500 \text{ lb}$
C		$7{,}500 \times 3 \text{ lb} = \underline{22{,}500} \text{ lb}$
Total weight of output		$\underline{\underline{80{,}000}} \text{ lb}$

$$\frac{\text{Joint cost}}{\text{Total weight of output}} = \frac{\$40{,}000}{80{,}000 \text{ lb}} = \$.50 \text{ per pound}$$

			Joint cost to be allocated per unit
A		$4 \text{ lb} \times \$.50 =$	$2.00
B		$5 \text{ lb} \times \$.50 =$	$2.50
C		$3 \text{ lb} \times \$.50 =$	$1.50

If the allocation is based on selling prices at split-off, the first step is to calculate the total market value at split-off as follows:

A		$5{,}000 \times \$4.00 = \$20{,}000$
B		$7{,}500 \times \$3.00 = \$22{,}500$
C		$7{,}500 \times \$5.00 = \underline{\$37{,}500}$
Total market value at split-off		$\underline{\underline{\$80{,}000}}$

The $40,000 in joint costs can now be allocated to the three products, based on sales value at split-off.

A	$\dfrac{\$20{,}000}{\$80{,}000} \times \$40{,}000 = \$10{,}000$
B	$\dfrac{\$22{,}500}{\$80{,}000} \times \$40{,}000 = \$11{,}250$
C	$\dfrac{\$37{,}500}{\$80{,}000} \times \$40{,}000 = \$18{,}750$

Thus, joint cost to be allocated per unit is:

A	$\dfrac{\$10{,}000}{5{,}000} = \$2.00 \text{ per unit}$
B	$\dfrac{\$11{,}250}{7{,}500} = \$1.50 \text{ per unit}$
C	$\dfrac{\$18{,}750}{7{,}500} = \$2.50 \text{ per unit}$

Partial product-line income statements for each joint-cost allocation scheme are shown in table 6.1. Note that when units were employed to allocate the joint costs, product B has a gross margin of $7,500. When the allocations are based on the weight, the gross margin for product B is reduced to $3,750. This points out one of the potential problems when physical measures are employed to allocate joint costs. When there is not a close relationship between the physical measure and the selling price of the products, management might be misled by the product-line information. If the joint costs were allocated using weight, management might be tempted to discontinue the sale of product B when in fact there is an advantage of $3 for every unit of B that is sold.

This problem can be overcome by using the sales value at split-off as a basis for joint-cost allocation. Note in table 6.1 that when the joint costs

TABLE 6.1 Partial Income Statements—Output Sold at Split-Off of Different Joint-Cost Allocation Assumptions

Product	A	B	C	Total
Units sold at split-off	5,000	7,500	7,500	
Joint costs allocated				
Based on units				
Sales	$20,000	$22,500	$37,500	$80,000
Cost of goods sold	10,000	15,000	15,000	40,000
Gross margin	$10,000	$ 7,500	$22,500	$40,000
Joint-cost allocated				
Based on weight				
Sales	$20,000	$22,500	$37,500	$80,000
Cost of goods sold	10,000	18,750	11,250	40,000
Gross margin	$10,000	$ 3,750	$26,250	$40,000
Joint-costs allocated				
Based on selling price				
At split-off				
Sales	$20,000	$22,500	$37,500	$80,000
Cost of goods sold	10,000	11,250	18,750	40,000
Gross margin	$10,000	$11,250	$18,750	$40,000

are allocated based on the sales value at split-off, a constant ratio between sales and the cost of goods sold is maintained for all three joint products.

Since the sales value at split-off is often not available (because the intermediate product is not marketable), the net realizable value at split-off is often employed as a basis for joint-cost allocation. This method assigns the joint cost to be allocated per unit to products in proportion to their ability to absorb them. From our example, the net realizable values of A, B, and C are:

Selling price (end product)	–	Additional processing costs	=	Net realizable value at split-off
A	$ 6.50		$ .50	$6.00
B	$ 5.00		$1.00	$4.00
C	$10.00		$2.00	$8.00

The total net realizable values at the split-off point are:

A   5,000 × $6.00 = $ 30,000
B   7,500 × $4.00 = $ 30,000
C   7,500 × $8.00 = $ 60,000
   Total $120,000

The $40,000 in joint costs can now be allocated based on the net realizable value at split-off.

A $\dfrac{\$30,000}{\$120,000} \times \$40,000 = \$10,000$

B $\dfrac{\$30,000}{\$120,000} \times \$40,000 = \$10,000$

C $\dfrac{\$60,000}{\$120,000} \times \$40,000 = \$20,000$

The unit costs at split-off are:

A .... $\dfrac{\$10,000}{5,000}$ = $2.00 per unit

B .... $\dfrac{\$10,000}{7,500}$ = $1.33 per unit

C .... $\dfrac{\$20,000}{7,500}$ = $2.67 per unit

If we assume that the three products are processed beyond the split-off point, then we can compare the different unit costs that have been determined.

	Products		
	A	B	C
Joint cost (allocation: units)	$2.00	$2.00	$2.00
Additional processing costs	.50	1.00	2.00
Unit cost end product	$2.50	$3.00	$4.00
Joint cost (allocation: weight)	$2.00	$2.50	$1.50
Additional processing costs	.50	1.00	2.00
Unit cost end product	$2.50	$3.50	$3.50
Joint costs (allocation: selling prices at split-off)	$2.00	$1.50	$2.50
Additional processing costs	.50	1.00	2.00
Unit cost end product	$2.50	$2.50	$4.50
Joint costs (allocation: net realizable values at split-off)	$2.00	$1.33	$2.67
Additional processing costs	.50	1.00	2.00
Unit cost end product	$2.50	$2.33	$4.67

Note that for product **A** each allocation method results in a unit cost of $2.50, whereas the unit cost varies for product B between $2.33 and $3.50 and for product C between $3.50 and $4.67. Other allocation procedures would certainly result in another set of unit costs.

Although allocations based on physical measures may have some economic justification, allocations based on market prices are most generally employed because they assign cost to products in proportion to their ability to absorb them. However, regardless of which allocation scheme is used, these unit costs are of extremely limited value in decision making.

☐ MULTIPLE SPLIT-OFFS

In complex manufacturing processes, multiple split-offs are frequently encountered. The allocation of joint costs can become complicated if sales values are employed as the basis for the allocation. Generally, the solution to this type of problem requires three steps. First, a diagram of the system is helpful in understanding the relationships among the departments and products. Then it is necessary to determine the sales value of final products and work backwards to determine the net realizable values at the split-off points. Finally, working forward, the joint costs are allocated among the joint products. This procedure will be demonstrated by means of an example.

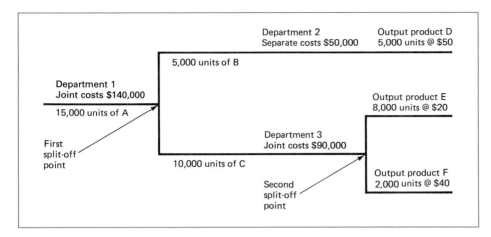

FIGURE 6.2
Diagram of
Relationships—
Multiple Split-Offs

Assume Department 1 incurs joint costs of $140,000 while processing 15,000 units of input A. Output from Department 1 consists of 5,000 units of B that are transferred to Department 2 and 10,000 units of C that are transferred to Department 3. In Department 2, $50,000 in costs are incurred in further processing the 5,000 units into D, which is sold at $50 per unit. In Department 3, $90,000 in joint costs are incurred and the output consists of 8,000 units of E and 2,000 units of F, which are sold for $20 and $40 per unit, respectively. Figure 6.2 contains a diagram of the relationships among the departments and outputs.

Table 6.2 contains the calculations that are used to determine net realizable values and to allocate joint costs. Note that the net realizable values of products E and F are determined before those of B and C. This is the backward step that was previously described. Next, one must work forward in allocating the joint costs. (B and C, then E and F). As expected, total costs of $280,000 ($140,000 plus $50,000 plus $90,000) are assigned to outputs D, E, and F.

At times, a joint product may be sold at split-off rather than processed further. If this is the case, the sales value at the split-off point is used rather than the net-realizable value for allocating the joint costs. In the problem described in figure 6.2, assume that product C could be sold for $12 a unit or processed further into products E and F. Given this new situation, the joint cost would be allocated as shown in table 6.3. Note that the sales value of product C ($120,000) rather than the net-realizable value of C ($150,000 from table 6.2) is now used in allocating the joint costs. As expected, the cost allocations to the final products are different when the sales values of the intermediate products are employed rather than the net-realizable values at split-off.

□ ACCOUNTING FOR BY-PRODUCTS

By-products, by definition, are joint products for which the market value is not material when considering the total value of the joint products. From the example in figure 6.1, the gold and silver are accounted for as by-products because their total market value of $3 ($2 silver and $1 gold)

TABLE 6.2 Allocation of Joint Costs with Multiple Split-Offs

	Computations of Net Realizable Values				
Second split	Sales value	− Separate costs =		Net realizable value	Percentage
E	8,000 × $20 = $160,000	−	$0	= $160,000	66.67
F	2,000 × $40 = $ 80,000	−	$0	= $ 80,000	33.33
First split					
B	5,000 × $50 = $250,000	−	$50,000	= $200,000	57.14
C	$160,000 + $80,000* = $240,000	−	$90,000	= $150,000	42.86

	Allocation of Joint Costs				
	Allocated joint costs	Additional joint costs	Total		Allocation
B					$140,000 × 57.14% = $ 80,000
C	$0	+ $140,000	= $140,000		$140,000 × 42.86% = $ 60,000
E					$150,000 × 66.67% = $100,000
F	$60,000	+ $ 90,000	= $150,000		$150,000 × 33.33% = $ 50,000

	Determination of Cost of Output		
	Joint costs + Separate costs = Total cost		
D	$ 80,000 +	$50,000	= $130,000
E	$100,000 +	$0	= $100,000
F	$ 50,000 +	$0	= $ 50,000
	Total assigned costs		$280,000

*The sales values of products E and F, respectively (8,000 × $20 = $160,000; 2,000 × $40 = $80,000).

is not considered material, given that the total output from a ton of ore has a market value of $153. Therefore, the joint mining costs of $110 a ton will only be allocated among the outputs classified as joint products, in this case the copper and the sulphur. Note that even though an ounce of gold or silver is worth significantly more than an ounce of copper or sulphur, the decision to treat the gold and silver as by-products is based on the yield from the ore and not the unit values of the outputs.

There are two frequently used methods of accounting for by-products. The first and most straightforward method is to ignore by-products in inventory valuation and credit Other Income or some appropriate revenue account when the by-product is sold. A sample journal entry at the time of sale of $50 of a by-product is:

Accounts receivable	50	
Other income—Sale of by-product		50

This method is frequently used for by-products that require no additional processing beyond the split-off point and for those whose value is not material. Therefore, omitting a by-product with no material value from inventory has an imperceptible effect on a firm's financial statements.

If a by-product requires additional processing beyond the split-off point, generally the net-realizable-value method of accounting is employed. The objective of this method is to reduce the joint costs of the joint products by the net-realizable value of the by-product.

TABLE 6.3 Allocation of Joint Costs—Sales Value Known at Split-Off

	Computations of Relative Values			
Second split	Sales value	− Separate costs =	Net realizable value	Percentage
E	8,000 × $20 = $160,000	− $0 =	$160,000	66.67
F	2,000 × $40 = $ 80,000	− $0 =	$ 80,000	33.33
First split				
B	5,000 × $50 = $250,000	− $50,000 =	$200,000	62.5
C	10,000 × $12 = $120,000	− $0 =	$120,000	37.5

	Allocation of Joint Costs				
	Allocated joint costs	+ Additional joint costs =	Total		Allocation
B				$140,000 × 62.5% =	$87,500
C	$0	+ $140,000 = $140,000		$140,000 × 37.5% =	$52,500
E				$142,500 × 66.67% =	$95,000
F	$52,500	+ $ 90,000 = $142,500		$142,500 × 33.33% =	$47,500

	Determination of Costs of Output		
	Joint costs + Separate costs = Total costs		
D	$87,500 +	$50,000	= $137,500
E	$95,000 +	$0	= $ 95,000
F	$47,500 +	$0	= $ 47,500
	Total assigned costs		$280,000

Assume a by-product has an estimated market value of $10 and before it can be sold additional processing costs of $4 must be incurred. The net realizable value of the by-product is $6 ($10 minus $4). Employing the net-realizable-value method, at split-off the following journal entry is made:

Inventory—By-product	6	
Work-in-process inventory		6

The effect of this entry is to reduce the joint costs allocated to the joint products by the net realizable value of the by-product.

When the additional processing of the by-product is complete, the following entry is made:

Inventory—By-product	4	
Miscellaneous credits		4

The effect of this entry is to value the by-product inventory at its expected market value.

If the by-product is sold at the expected market value, the journal entry is:

Accounts receivable	10	
Inventory—By-product		10

Employing this method, if the actual selling price is different from the expected selling price, we recognize a gain or loss. For example, if the actual selling price was $9, a loss of $1 is recognized. The following journal entry is made:

```
Accounts receivable  .........................................   9
Loss on sale of by-product  ..................................   1
    Inventory—By-product  ....................................          10
```

In summary, there are two general methods for accounting for by-products.

1. Ignore by-products in inventory valuation and recognize any revenue as other income.

2. Inventory by-products at their net realizable value.

Conceptually, the second method is preferred because some value is assigned to the by-product inventory. Additional processing beyond the split-off point is not required in order to use this method. In practice, however, when additional processing is required, this method is frequently used. The first method is used most frequently because of the insignificance of the values involved.

☐ JOINT COSTS AND DECISION MAKING

The majority of decisions concerning joint costs and joint products concern whether additional processing should be undertaken on a joint product. In making these decisions, the joint cost is not relevant and therefore should not be considered. For example, assume a production system outputs A, B, and C. Assume a market exists for A and B at the split-off, but additional processing is required before C can be sold. If the separable additional processing costs for C are $60,000, then one can analyze the problem as follows:

	A	B	C	Total
Units of output	5,000	7,500	7,500	
Selling price	$4.00	$2.00	$10.00	
Sales	$20,000	$15,000	$75,000	$110,000
Separable cost			60,000	60,000
Product contribution	$20,000	$15,000	$15,000	$ 50,000
Joint cost				40,000
Joint profit				$ 10,000

Another alternative is not to engage in the additional processing of C. In this case, the anticipated results are:

	A	B	C	Total
Units of output	5,000	7,500	—	
Selling price	$4.00	$2.00	—	

Sales	$20,000	$15,000	—	$35,000
Separable cost			—	
Product contribution	$20,000	$15,000	—	$35,000
Joint cost				40,000
Joint profit				($ 5,000)

We note that the difference between the two alternatives is the $15,000 product contribution from C with the additional processing. The meaning of this product contribution can perhaps be emphasized if the selling price of C after the additional processing is assumed to be $8. In that case, the results of our analysis are:

	A	B	C	Total
Units of output	5,000	7,500	7,500	
Selling price	$4.00	$2.00	$8.00	
Sales	$20,000	$15,000	$60,000	$95,000
Separable cost			$60,000	60,000
Product contribution	$20,000	$15,000	—	$35,000
Joint cost				40,000
Joint profit				($ 5,000)

In this case one would be indifferent as to whether C is disposed of or the additional processing is undertaken. From these examples, one could conclude that the incremental revenue and incremental cost after split-off are relevant in making this type of decision.

The joint costs are only relevant if a decision is being made concerning all of the joint products. That is, the joint costs are relevant if one is deciding whether to produce all of the joint products or not to produce any of them. In most joint-product situations, this decision concerns whether a plant should be shut down or remain in production. In this case, the joint costs are treated as incremental costs.

☐ REGULATORY REQUIREMENTS AND THE COSTING OF JOINT AND BY-PRODUCTS

Over the past decade, there has been a substantial increase in the regulatory requirements that relate to the costing of joint and by-products. The Federal Income Tax Regulations contain an overview of accepted procedures for allocating joint costs for federal tax purposes.

A taxpayer engaged in mining or manufacturing who by a single process or uniform series of processes derives a product of two or more kinds, sizes, or grades, the unit cost of which is substantially alike, and who in conformity to a recognized trade practice allocates an amount of cost to each kind, size, or grade of product, which in the aggregate will absorb the total cost of production, may, with the consent of the Commissioner, use such allocated cost as a basis for pricing inventories, provided such allocation bears a reasonable relation to the respective selling values of the different kinds, sizes, or grades of product.

From this quotation, one can infer that the Internal Revenue Service prefers joint-cost allocations that are based on market values. When a large business encounters a joint-cost-allocation problem, the IRS Commissioner must approve the method employed to allocate the joint costs.

When the Federal Power Commission is involved in establishing prices for natural gas, joint-cost-allocation problems are encountered. Natural gas and crude oil are joint products, and the joint-cost-allocation problem is encountered in attempting to determine the cost of the natural gas. Suggested solutions to the problem involve allocating the joint costs based on sales, British Thermal Unit (BTU) content of the joint products, and the relative costs. In the relative-cost-allocation method, the joint costs are allocated based on the costs incurred in situations in which single products (oil or gas) are produced.

The Securities and Exchange Commission (SEC) requires that annual reports contain information by lines of business. The Federal Trade Commission (FTC) requires that certain businesses provide accounting information by specific product categories. In addition, the Financial Accounting Standards Board (FASB)[1] requires business enterprises, except nonpublic enterprises, to report annually revenue, operating profit or loss, identifiable assets, depreciation, depletion, and capital expenditures for each significant industry segment. Generally, 10 percent of the respective amount is used to define the term *significant*. Firms also must disclose the methods used in the allocation of cost. Finally, the lower of cost- or market-inventory valuation procedures must also be employed when valuing the inventories of joint or by-products.

☐ RECIPROCAL-SERVICE COST ALLOCATION

In most organizations, service departments exist to provide services to other units within the organization. Since these departments do not participate directly in output production, the costs associated with service departments are indirect. It is necessary to allocate these costs to the production departments as part of the cost-aggregation process in determining the full cost of the final product or service. Service costs are also allocated to satisfy the external reporting requirements of the FASB and SEC. Since the transactions between departments are internal, often no market price exists for the service and the allocation is based on an index of activity.

Transportation, power, public relations, legal, industrial relations, testing, laboratory, and stores are examples of service departments in commercial organizations in which the **reciprocal-service-cost-allocation** problem may be encountered.

---

1. See *Statement of Financial Accounting Standards, No. 14,* "Financial Reporting for Segments of a Business Enterprise" (Stamford, Conn.: Financial Accounting Standards Board, 1976); *Statement of Financial Accounting Standards, No. 21,* "Suspension of the Reporting of Earnings per Share and Segment Information by Nonpublic Enterprises" (Stamford, Conn.: Financial Accounting Standards Board, 1978); and *Statement of Financial Accounting Standards, No. 18,* "Financial Reporting for Segments of a Business Enterprise—Interim Financial Statements" (Stamford, Conn.: Financial Accounting Standards Board, 1977).

In hospitals, for example, the housekeeping, maintenance, personnel, accounting, and cafeteria departments may be considered as service departments. This type of allocation problem is complicated when reciprocal relationships exist between the service departments. In a hospital, the housekeeping department may service the maintenance department. It is also possible that the maintenance department may service the housekeeping department. Proper allocation of service costs in such situations may require the solution of several algebraic expressions.

Service-department costs are allocated to production departments based on some reasonable index of economic activity. Table 6.4 contains examples of service departments and bases that can be employed in allocating costs. The reciprocal-service cost problem is frequently encountered in the health care industry. Any shift in the allocation base may result in significant changes in the reimbursement received from government agencies or insurance companies. In such cases, the cost allocation is often subject to audit. Similar situations are encountered in industry, especially when cost or cost-plus contracts are involved.

The National Association of Accountants (NAA) issues statements on management accounting principles and practices. In statement number 4B dealing with the allocation of service and administrative costs, the following criteria are suggested in selecting specific allocation base:

If the objective is to measure full costs, the preferable method of allocating service and administrative costs is based on a hierarchy of alternatives, arranged in the order of how closely they are related to the cause of the cost's incurrence:

a. To the extent feasible, elements of these costs should be allocated by measuring the amount of resources consumed by the cost center receiving the service. For example, if a division uses a measured number of hours of the corporate legal staff for a problem that relates to that division, the legal cost should be assigned on the basis of a cost per hour used.

b. If a direct measure of the amount of services provided to a cost center is not available or is not cost-effective to produce, the costs should be allocated on some basis that reflects the relative amount caused by the various cost centers.

TABLE 6.4 *Service Departments and Possible Allocation Bases*

Service department	Possible allocation bases
Receiving, Shipping, and Stores	Number of transactions, Units handled, Weight of units handled, Volume of units handled, Mode of transportation, Hours of service
Personnel	Number of employees hired and terminated, Number of employees, Labor hours
Heat, Light, and Power	Metered usage, Square footage heated, Cubic footage heated, Square footage lighted, Capacity requirement of machinery
Cafeteria	Number of employees, Number of meals served, Types and number of meals served
Cost accounting	Labor hours, Number of transactions
Housekeeping	Number of offices, Square footage occupied, Number of employees

c. If no causal connection for the amount of cost applicable to cost centers can be found, service and administrative costs should be allocated on the basis of the relative overall activity of the cost center. Activity may be measured by a single criterion, such s the total costs incurred in each cost center, or by an average of several criteria. A commonly used measure is the three-factor "Massachusetts Formula," which is a simple average of the cost center's payroll, revenue, and assets.[2]

Another set of criteria for allocating costs identified by the NAA are respectively referred to as (1) benefit, (2) cause, (3) fairness, and (4) ability to bear the costs. The benefit and cause criterion are most frequently employed. The *benefit criterion* is applied when a production department benefits from the activity of a service department. For example, a personnel department screens and hires new employees for a production department. The *cause criterion* comes into play when activities in a production department precipitate the costs incurred by a service department. For example, an unsafe production practices course includes use of the plant infirmary. The *fairness criterion* sounds attractive but is almost impossible to put into operation. *Ability to bear costs* is generally used when the allocation is being employed to determine divisional profit. Employment of this criterion can have an dysfunctional effect on management. This problem is considered in the material concerning performance measurement in chapter 17.

Frequently, questions arise concerning the allocation of variable and fixed service-department costs. In general, variable service-department costs are allocated to production departments based on an index of activity that best reflects the incurrence of the particular cost. Fixed costs present a different problem. These costs are directly related to the available capacity in the service department. This service-department capacity was obtained partially based on the expected demands of the production departments.

Two approaches are used in allocating fixed service-department costs. They can be allocated using a variable-allocation base. This method has serious problems that will be demonstrated by means of an example. Assume service department Z has annual fixed costs of $60,000 and these costs are on the basis of direct-labor hours in the production departments. The allocation for the first year was:

Year 1

Department X	....	10,000 hours @ $3 = $30,000
Department Y	....	10,000 hours @ $3 = 30,000
Total	....	$60,000

The $3 rate was determined by dividing the $60,000 fixed cost by the 20,000 total direct-labor hours.

In the second year, department X worked 5,000 hours and department Y continued to work 10,000 hours. The allocation for the second year was:

2. Statements on Management Accounting, Statement No. 4B, June 13, 1985, "Allocation of Service and Administrative Costs" (Montvale, N.J.: National Association of Accountants, 1985) pp. 4–5.

Year 2

Department X	....	5,000 hours @ $4 = $20,000
Department Y	....	10,000 hours @ $4 = <u>40,000</u>
Total	....	<u>$60,000</u>

Department Y has been penalized in the second year for maintaining the same activity level. Because of problems in department X, department Y has received an additional $10,000 in allocated fixed service-department costs. For this reason, fixed costs are often allocated in predetermined lump-sum amounts. For example, if it was determined that $30,000 of service-department fixed costs should be allocated to departments X and Y, this amount would be allocated independently from the activity levels in the department. Lump-sum amounts are determined when the decision to incur the service-department fixed costs is made. These amounts are not subject to frequent review.

Finally, should actual or budgeted costs be allocated from a service department? If actual costs are allocated, there is a decreased incentive for management personnel in the service department to control costs. Therefore, budgeted rather than actual costs are allocated from the service to production departments.

In summary, budgeted variable service-department costs should be allocated to production departments based on some reasonable and justifiable index of economic activity. Fixed costs are allocated in predetermined lump-sum amounts.

Now we will consider three methods for solving the reciprocal-service-cost problem. The method of neglect disregards the service departments in allocating the costs. The step method is a means of obtaining an approximation of the reciprocal allocation. Using algebra and related matrix techniques, we can obtain the mathematically correct allocation that considers all the relationships among the service and production departments.

We should, however, keep in mind that the allocation is only as good as the index of activity upon which it is based. While we can always allocate the costs, the important point is how well the index of activity represents the economic relationships among the departments.

☐ METHOD OF NEGLECT FOR SOLVING THE RECIPROCAL-COST-ALLOCATION PROBLEM

Assume a system has two service departments and three production departments; the relationships are summarized as follows:

Costs of	Percentage allocated to					Cost to be allocated
	S_1	S_2	P_1	P_2	P_3	
S_1	0	.6	.2	.1	.1	$480
S_2	.2	.4	.1	.1	.2	600

Each of the numbers indicates the percentage of services consumed by each department. A reciprocal relationship exists because 60 percent of the service from Service department 1 is allocated to Service department

2, and 20 percent of the service from Service department 2 is allocated to Service department 1. Our problem also has self-consumption in that 40 percent of the service from Service department 2 is allocated to Service department 2. The relationships among the service and production departments is shown in figure 6.3.

One procedure to allocate the costs from the service departments to the production departments is to completely ignore or neglect the reciprocal relationships and self-consumption. Employing this method, the service-department costs are allocated to the production departments as follows:

Service department	Cost to be allocated	Production departments		
		P_1	P_2	P_3
		(50%)	(25%)	(25%)
S_1	$480	$240	$120	$120
		(25%)	(25%)	(50%)
S_2	$600	$150	$150	$300
Total allocation		$390	$270	$420

The allocation percentages take into account only the services provided to the production departments. For example, from Service department 1, 40 percent of the output goes to the production departments. Since 20 percent is allocated to Production department 1, 50 percent of the cost (20 percent/40 percent) from the service department is allocated to Production department 1.

☐ STEP-METHOD SOLUTION TO THE RECIPROCAL-COST-ALLOCATION PROBLEM

The reciprocal relationships are taken into account to some degree in the step method. This method will be demonstrated by allocating the service-department costs in their numeric order.

FIGURE 6.3
Service-Department Allocations

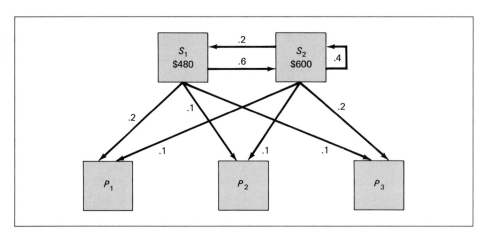

	S_1	S_2	P_1	P_2	P_3
Cost to be allocated	$480	$600	—	—	—
Allocation of S_1		(60%)	(20%)	(10%)	(10%)
	(480)	288	96	48	48
Allocation of S_2			(25%)	(25%)	(50%)
		(888)	222	222	444
Total	—	—	$318	$270	$492

It should be recognized that the results would differ if the order of allocation were changed. By reversing the order in the example, the allocated costs are:

	S_1	S_2	P_1	P_2	P_3
Cost to be allocated	$480	$600	—	—	—
Allocation of S_2	(33.3%)		(16.7%)	(16.7%)	(33.3%)
	200	(600)	100	100	200
Allocation of S_1			(50%)	(25%)	(25%)
	(680)		340	170	170
Total	—	—	$440	$270	$370

Simplicity and ease of calculation are the advantages of the step method. The disadvantage is that the different allocations are obtained by revising the order in which the service departments are considered. Dramatically different answers can be obtained by altering the order of the service departments in the step method.

☐ ALGEBRAIC SOLUTION TO THE RECIPROCAL- COST-ALLOCATION PROBLEM

The reciprocal-cost-allocation problem can be solved by determining the cost equations for the service departments. From the example, the cost equations are:

$S_1 = \$480 + .2S_2$
$S_2 = \$600 + .6S_1 + .4S_2$

By substitution, one can solve the equations.

$S_2 = \$600 + .6(\$480 + .2S_2) + .4S_2$
$S_2 = \$888 + .52S_2$
$.48S_2 = \$888$
$S_2 = \$1,850$

After solving for S_2, one can substitute and solve for S_1.

$S_1 = \$480 + .2(\$1,850)$
$S_1 = \$850$

Note that initially there was \$1,080 (\$480 + \$600) to allocate and that the sum of S_1 and S_2 was \$2,700. This discrepancy exists because S_1 and S_2 are gross activity in the accounts of the service departments. Activity in the service-department accounts exceeds the total costs to be allocated because costs could be allocated back and forth between the service departments several times before being allocated to a production department. An adjustment is necessary to obtain the costs allocated to the production departments.

From the problem, note that 20 percent of the service in S_1 and 10 percent of the service in S_2 are allocated to P_1. For the three production departments these relationships can be expressed as:

$$P_1 = .2(\$850) + .1(\$1,850) = \$355$$
$$P_2 = .1(\$850) + .1(\$1,850) = \$270$$
$$P_3 = .1(\$850) + .2(\$1,850) = \$455$$

These adjusted allocated costs total \$1,080, which is the amount to be allocated. These results take into account the reciprocal relationship between the service departments. A problem with the algebraic approach is that when a number of service departments are encountered, the number of equations expands accordingly and obtaining the solution becomes more difficult.

☐ MATRIX APPROACH TO THE RECIPROCAL-COST-ALLOCATION PROBLEM

A general solution to the reciprocal-cost-allocation problem can be derived by employing matrix algebra.[3] This solution allows us to solve problems with any number of service and production departments. Also, the matrix manipulations are the basis for a computer program that will solve the reciprocal-cost-allocation problem. In addition, it is possible to manipulate the matrices to determine the percentage of cost allocated from each service department to each production department. Therefore, a general solution to the reciprocal-cost problem based on matrix algebra will provide a means for solving all such cost-allocation problems.

From the previous example, the two cost equations were:

$$S_1 = \$480 + .2S_2$$
$$S_2 = \$600 + .6S_1 + .4S_2$$

In matrix notation, the equations can be expressed as:[4]

$$s = b + As$$

---

3. An appendix at the end of this chapter contains a brief review of matrix algebra.

4. We will represent vectors with lowercase letters and matrices with uppercase letters.

where

$$s = \begin{bmatrix} s_1 \\ s_2 \end{bmatrix} \quad b = \begin{bmatrix} \$480 \\ \$600 \end{bmatrix} \quad A = \begin{bmatrix} 0 & .2 \\ .6 & .4 \end{bmatrix}$$

Solving for the gross activity vector s, one finds:

$$s = b + As \qquad\qquad\qquad (6\text{-}1)$$
$$s - As = b$$
$$(I - A)s = b$$
$$(I - A)^{-1}(I - A)s = (I - A)^{-1}b$$
$$s = (I - A)^{-1}b$$

Substituting from the example, the result is:

$$s = \left[\begin{bmatrix} 1 & 0 \\ 0 & 1 \end{bmatrix} - \begin{bmatrix} 0 & .2 \\ .6 & .4 \end{bmatrix} \right]^{-1} \begin{bmatrix} \$480 \\ \$600 \end{bmatrix}$$

$$s = \begin{bmatrix} 1.25 & .4167 \\ 1.25 & 2.0833 \end{bmatrix} \begin{bmatrix} \$480 \\ \$600 \end{bmatrix}$$

$$s = \begin{bmatrix} \$\ 850 \\ \$1,850 \end{bmatrix}$$

To obtain the allocations from the gross activity vector s, one must solve the following expression:

$$c = Ps \qquad\qquad\qquad (6\text{-}2)$$

The P matrix is the transpose of the matrix containing the allocation coefficients from the service departments to the producing departments. Solving the example, one finds:

$$c = \begin{bmatrix} .2 & .1 \\ .1 & .1 \\ .1 & .2 \end{bmatrix} \begin{bmatrix} \$\ 850 \\ \$1850 \end{bmatrix}$$

$$c = \begin{bmatrix} \$355 \\ \$270 \\ \$455 \end{bmatrix} \begin{matrix} P_1 \\ P_2 \\ P_3 \end{matrix}$$

As expected, this is the same result as was obtained after adjustment employing the algebraic method.

Considering the P and $(I-A)^{-1}$ matrices, one can gain additional insight into the cost allocation. Let the matrix E equal:

$$E = P(I - A)^{-1} \tag{6-3}$$

In the example, E equals:

$$\begin{bmatrix} .375 & .29167 \\ .25 & .25 \\ .375 & .45833 \end{bmatrix} = \begin{bmatrix} .2 & .1 \\ .1 & .1 \\ .1 & .2 \end{bmatrix} \begin{bmatrix} 1.25 & .4167 \\ 1.25 & 2.0833 \end{bmatrix}$$

Note that the E is an effective matrix in that the sum of each column is one. Each element e_{ij} is the fraction of cost from Service department j that is allocated to Production department i. For example, 29.167 percent of the cost from Service department 2 will be allocated to the Production department 1.

It should be noted that the allocated costs can be determined directly from E where:

$$c = Eb \tag{6-4}$$

This can be shown from the example in which:

$$\begin{bmatrix} \$355 \\ \$270 \\ \$455 \end{bmatrix} = \begin{bmatrix} .375 & .29167 \\ .25 & .25 \\ .375 & .45833 \end{bmatrix} \begin{bmatrix} \$480 \\ \$600 \end{bmatrix}$$

Perhaps additional insight into the system can be gained by considering the percentage employed in the allocations and the gross-activity levels in each service department. Multiplying the gross activity for a service department by the allocation percentage one finds:

Costs from			Allocated to		
	S_1	S_2	P_1	P_2	P_3
S_1	$ 0	$ 510	$170	$ 85	$ 85
S_2	370	740	185	185	370
Subtotal	$370	$1,250	$355	$270	$455
Primary allocation	480	600	0	0	0
Total	$850	$1,850	$355	$270	$455

Note that the $510 allocated from S_1 to S_2 was obtained by multiplying .6 by $850. This same procedure was employed to obtain the other entries in the matrix.

There are several observations that can be made about the above matrix. It is clear that in gross terms $510 was allocated from S_1 to S_2. Likewise, $370 was allocated from S_2 to S_1. The self-consumption in S_2 was $740 in gross terms. Also, note that the total for S_1 of $370 plus the primary allocation of $480 equals $850. This $850 is the gross activity in S_1. In the same manner, the $1,250 from S_2 plus the $600 from the primary allocation equals the gross activity in the department of $1,850. One can conclude that the matrix is a mapping of the flows resulting from the reciprocal relationship between the departments.

In complicated service-cost-allocation problems, costs in the service departments are frequently grouped into relatively homogeneous pools.

For example, pools may be created for personnel, materials, and space related costs. Different bases are employed to allocate the cost to the production departments. For example, personnel costs such as payroll, cafeteria, and medical may be allocated based on the number of employees in the service and production departments. Whereas space-related costs such as insurance depreciation and maintenance may be allocated based on departmental square footage.

After the service-department costs are allocated to the production departments, they are generally treated as overhead costs in the production departments. These overhead costs plus the direct costs associated with the production departments are employed in costing the output of the departments. In this situation, one should always keep in mind that altering the basis upon which the cost allocation was made could result in a significant shift in the output costs of the production departments.

□ SUMMARY

In this chapter, two frequently encountered cost-allocation problems were considered. The first problem relates to the accounting for joint costs. Joint costs are indivisible because the products cannot be obtained separately. All joint costs (that is, costs incurred prior to the split-off point) are allocated among the joint products. Any costs incurred beyond the split-off point are separable and directly traceable to a particular joint product.

The difference between a joint product and a by-product is determined based on the sales value of the joint products. By-products are joint products that have a relatively small sales value and are produced simultaneously with joint products. The unit costs resulting from the allocation of joint costs are used for inventory valuation. These unit costs cannot be used for making decisions relating to any subset of the joint products.

The second cost-allocation problem considered in this chapter concerns reciprocal-service cost allocation. This problem is encountered when service departments exist within an organization. Costs in these service departments must be allocated to production departments so that the full costs of outputs can be determined.

Algorithms entitled neglect, step, algebraic, and matrix were considered as means for solving the reciprocal-service-cost-allocation problem. Using a computer program that employs the matrix algorithm is the most convenient method for solving these problems. Once again, one must keep in mind that this is a cost-allocation problem and the primary input is the index of activity used as the basis for allocating the costs.

KEY TERMS

By-products	Reciprocal-service cost allocation
Cost allocation	Service-department costs
Joint costs	Split-off point
Joint products	

REVIEW PROBLEMS

Joint and By-products

Hogan Corporation produces three final products, C, D, and E, with unit selling prices of $50, $1, and $3, respectively. During a recent period, joint costs of $30,000 were incurred in department 1, 1,000 units of A were transferred to department 2, and 31,000 units of B were transferred to department 3. Costs of $20,000 were incurred in department 2, and 1,000 units of product C were produced. In department 3, joint costs of $30,000 were incurred, and 1,000 units of product D and 30,000 units of product E were produced. There was no beginning or ending work-in-process inventory in any department. Management requests that the joint cost be allocated to the joint products, based on the net realizable values of the products.

The first step in solving this problem is to develop a diagram that specifies the relationships among the departments.

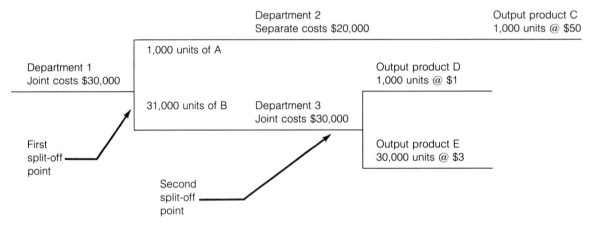

The next step is to determine if any of the products should be accounted for as by-products.

Product identification	Selling price	Unit production	Total sales	Percentage of sales
C	$50	1,000	$ 50,000	35.47%
D	$ 1	1,000	1,000	0.71
E	$ 3	30,000	90,000	63.82
			$141,000	100%

Sales value of product D is not considered material; therefore, it will be considered as a by-product. Since no additional processing is required, the by-product will be ignored in determining costs for inventory valuation.

Joint costs allocated to product E in department 3 = $30,000.
Net realizable value of product B = ($3 × 30,000) − $30,000 = $60,000
Net realizable value of product A = ($50 × 1,000) − $20,000 = $30,000

Allocation of Joint Costs from Department 1

Product

A $\dfrac{\$30,000}{\$90,000}$ × $30,000 = $10,000

B $\dfrac{\$60,000}{\$90,000}$ × $30,000 = $20,000

Determination of Costs of Outputs

	Joint costs + Separate costs	= Total costs
C	$10,000 + $20,000	= $30,000
D	$30,000 + $20,000 + $0	= $50,000
	Total costs of outputs	$80,000

Now let us change the conditions in the problem so that product D requires additional processing after the split-off. Assume product D now sells for $1.50 a unit and $500 of additional processing costs are incurred after the split-off. Now the by-product will be accounted for using the net-realizable method, and the joint costs in department 3 will be reduced by the net-realizable value of the by-product.

Joint costs allocated to product E in department 3 = $30,000 −
(1,000 × ($1.50 − $.50)) = $29,000
Net realizable value of product B = ($3 × 30,000) − $29,000 = $61,000
Net realizable value of product A = ($50 × 1,000) − $20,000 = $30,000

Allocation of Joint Costs from Department 1

Product

A $\frac{\$30,000}{\$91,000} \times \$30,000 = \$9,890$

B $\frac{\$61,000}{\$91,000} \times \$30,000 = \$20,110$

Determination of Costs of Outputs

	Joint costs + Separate costs	= Total costs
C	$ 9,890 + $20,000	= $29,890
D	$ 1,000 + $ 500	= 1,500
E	$20,110 + $29,000	= 49,110
	Total costs of outputs	= $80,500

Service-Department Cost Allocation

Hospitals frequently encounter the reciprocal-service-cost-allocation problem because much of their reimbursement from insurance companies and government agencies is based on some definition of "full cost." Of course, this is very important because much of the revenue to the hospital will be based upon these calculations.

Assume the Montgomery County Hospital has two service departments and three production departments. The service departments are Housekeeping and the Power Plant. Housekeeping takes care of all janitorial services in the hospital, and it is determined that its costs should be allocated based on square footage. The power plant generates steam to heat and cool the hospital. The steam is also used to generate the electricity consumed by the hospital. The electricity consumption is metered for each department, and the heating and cooling costs are allocated based on the cubic footage.

Medical, Pediatrics, and Surgery are the three production departments in the hospital. During the upcoming year, it is estimated that these departments will have 30,000, 6,000, and 25,000 patient-days, respectively. A patient-day is one patient for one day and is the basis for billing for hospital usage.

Based on the budgeted costs for each department and the cost allocations, the problem is to determine the "full cost" per patient-day for each of the production departments. The following data are available:

		Allocation Percentage			
	Housekeeping	Power Plant	Medical	Pediatrics	Surgery
Housekeeping	0	.1	.4	.2	.3
Power Plant	.2	.1	.3	.1	.3
Budgeted costs	$1,500,000	$2,000,000	$2,750,000	$540,000	$2,950,000
Patient-days			30,000	6,000	25,000

Using formula (6-3), the allocation percentages based on the reciprocal relationships are:

$$\begin{bmatrix} .4431818 & .4318181 \\ .2159091 & .1590910 \\ .3409091 & .4090909 \end{bmatrix} = \begin{bmatrix} .4 & .3 \\ .2 & .1 \\ .3 & .3 \end{bmatrix} \left(\begin{bmatrix} 1 & 0 \\ 0 & 1 \end{bmatrix} - \begin{bmatrix} 0 & .2 \\ .1 & .1 \end{bmatrix} \right)^{-1}$$

Then, using formula (6-4), the allocated costs are:

$$\begin{bmatrix} \$1,528,408.90 \\ \$642,045.65 \\ \$1,329,545.45 \end{bmatrix} = \begin{bmatrix} .4431818 & .4318181 \\ .2159091 & .1590910 \\ .3409091 & .4090909 \end{bmatrix} \begin{bmatrix} \$1,500,000 \\ \$2,000,000 \end{bmatrix}$$

Now, using the allocated costs, the "full costs" in each of the production departments can be found.

	Medical	Pediatrics	Surgery
Allocated cost	$1,528,408.90	$642,045.65	$1,329,545.45
Direct cost	2,750,000.00	540,000.00	2,950,000.00
Total	$4,278,408.90	$1,182,045.65	$4,279,545.45
	$4,278,408.90	$1,182,045.65	$4,279,545.45
	30,000	6,000	25,000
Cost per patient-day	$142.61	$197.01	$171.18

These patient-day costs for each department would serve as the basis for billing full-pay patients of the hospital or seeking reimbursement from insurance companies or governmental agencies.

APPENDIX: A Review of Matrix Algebra

As quantitative techniques have been increasingly employed in accounting and business, it has become necessary to manipulate large amounts of numerical data. Matrix algebra is a vehicle by which mathematical manipulation can be specified in a manner that is independent of the size of the problem. This appendix contains a review of matrix manipulations that were employed extensively throughout this chapter.

In accounting, matrix algebra is very useful because a matrix provides a means for organizing the presentation of numerical data, and the algebra permits a large number of mathematical manipulations to be condensed into a manageable set of symbols. In addition, expressing accounting manipulations in terms of matrices simplifies the transformation of an accounting system for a computer.

MATRIX ARITHMETIC

A matrix is a rectangular array of numbers arranged in rows and columns. All rows of a matrix are of equal length as are all of the columns. The matrix A with m rows and n columns follows:

$$A = \begin{bmatrix} a_{11} & a_{12} & a_{13} & \cdot & \cdot & a_{1n} \\ a_{21} & a_{22} & a_{23} & \cdot & \cdot & a_{2m} \\ \cdot & \cdot & \cdot & \cdot & \cdot & \cdot \\ \cdot & \cdot & \cdot & \cdot & \cdot & \cdot \\ a_{m1} & a_{m2} & a_{m3} & \cdot & \cdot & a_{mn} \end{bmatrix}$$

The expression m by n specifies the size of the matrix and the numbers a_{ij} are called the elements of the matrix, where i identifies the row and j the column. Although the matrix A contains m times n elements, the entire matrix should be considered as a single entity. **Matrix algebra** is a set of rules for manipulating matrices as separate entities.

A matrix containing a single column is called a *column vector*. For example,

$$c = \begin{bmatrix} 4 \\ -3 \\ 8 \\ 9 \\ 0 \end{bmatrix}$$

is a column vector with dimension five by one. Likewise, a matrix containing only one row is called a row vector.[1] The row vector r has dimension one by four.

$$r = \begin{bmatrix} -4 & -2 & 0 & 5 \end{bmatrix}$$

A single number in matrix algebra is called a *scalar*. For the sake of clarity in notation, all matrices will be uppercase letters, while lowercase letters will be used for vectors and scalars.

Assume a firm has three products and four sales regions and the cumulative unit sales (not including the current month) are contained in the matrix X.

	Region I	Region II	Region III	Region IV
Product A	30	65	53	47
$X =$ Product B	21	71	84	51
Product C	89	85	81	69

Sales for the current month are contained in the matrix Y where

$$Y = \begin{bmatrix} 10 & 12 & 11 & 6 \\ 3 & 8 & 6 & 9 \\ 10 & 4 & 7 & 9 \end{bmatrix}$$

The cumulative sales including the current month are

---

1. In some sets of notation, a prime is used to distinguish a row vector from a column vector. Therefore, r is a column vector and r' is a row vector. This feature will not be employed in this text.

$$\begin{bmatrix} 30 + 10 & 65 + 12 & 53 + 11 & 47 + 6 \\ 21 + 3 & 71 + 8 & 84 + 6 & 51 + 9 \\ 89 + 10 & 85 + 4 & 81 + 7 & 69 + 9 \end{bmatrix} = \begin{bmatrix} 40 & 77 & 64 & 53 \\ 24 & 79 & 90 & 60 \\ 99 & 89 & 88 & 78 \end{bmatrix}$$

The above is the sum of matrix X plus Y and is the updated cumulative unit sales by product and region. Addition of two matrices is the sum formed by adding the matrices element by element. The sum Z of matrices X and Y, both having m rows and n columns is given by:

$$Z_{ij} = X_{ij} + Y_{ij} \text{ (for all } i,j) \tag{A6-1}$$

It should be noted that for addition of matrices X and Y to be defined, both matrices must have the same dimensions. Consider these two examples.

$$[2 \quad 4 \quad 6] + [1 \quad 3 \quad 5] = [3 \quad 7 \quad 11]$$

$$[8 \quad 10 \quad 12] + \begin{bmatrix} 7 \\ 9 \\ 11 \end{bmatrix} = \text{undefined}.$$

In the first case, addition is defined because both vectors have the same dimensions. However, in the second example, addition is undefined because the vectors do not have the same dimension.

Matrix subtraction is performed by subtracting element by element two matrices of the same dimension. The difference X of matrices Y subtracted from Z is

$$X_{ij} = Z_{ij} - Y_{ij} \text{ (for all } i,j). \tag{A6-2}$$

For example, if the sales for the current month are subtracted from the cumulative sales, the result is the cumulative sales at the start of the month. From the example, the result of subtracting the matrices is:

$$\begin{bmatrix} 40 - 10 & 77 - 12 & 64 - 11 & 53 - 6 \\ 24 - 3 & 79 - 8 & 90 - 6 & 60 - 9 \\ 99 - 10 & 89 - 4 & 88 - 7 & 78 - 9 \end{bmatrix} = \begin{bmatrix} 30 & 65 & 53 & 47 \\ 21 & 71 & 84 & 51 \\ 89 & 85 & 81 & 69 \end{bmatrix}$$

Matrix multiplication will be introduced by first demonstrating the product of two vectors. Assume a row vector, p, that contains the selling prices of the three products for the firm in the example.

	Product A	Product B	Product C
$p =$	[$25	$50	$100]

Let the column vector f contain the unit sales for each of the three products for region 1.

$$f = \begin{bmatrix} 10 \\ 3 \\ 10 \end{bmatrix}$$

Total sales revenue in region 1 for the current month is

$$pf = [\$25 \quad \$50 \quad \$100] \begin{bmatrix} 10 \\ 3 \\ 10 \end{bmatrix}$$

$pf = (\$25)(10) + (\$50)(3) + (\$100)(10) = \$1,400.$

A general rule for multiplying a row vector by a column vector can be determined by letting

$$p = [p_1 \quad p_2 \cdots p_n]$$

and

$$f = \begin{bmatrix} f_1 \\ f_2 \\ \cdot \\ \cdot \\ f_n \end{bmatrix}$$

The product pf is defined as

$$pf = p_1f_1 + p_2f_2 + \cdots + p_nf_n \qquad \text{(A6-3)}$$

$$= \sum_{i=1}^{n} p_if_i$$

This manipulation is only defined if the number of columns in p equals the number of rows in f. It should be noted that the dimension of the answer has the number of rows in p and the number of columns in f.

The above can be illustrated by multiplying a row vector by a column vector.

$$\begin{bmatrix} 2 \\ 1 \\ 4 \end{bmatrix} [3 \quad 2 \quad 4 \quad 5] = \begin{bmatrix} 2 \times 3 & 2 \times 2 & 2 \times 4 & 2 \times 5 \\ 1 \times 3 & 1 \times 2 & 1 \times 4 & 1 \times 5 \\ 4 \times 3 & 4 \times 2 & 4 \times 4 & 4 \times 5 \end{bmatrix} = \begin{bmatrix} 6 & 4 & 8 & 10 \\ 3 & 2 & 4 & 5 \\ 12 & 8 & 16 & 20 \end{bmatrix}$$

Assuming an m element column vector c and an n element row vector r, the product is defined as:

$$cr = \begin{bmatrix} c_1r_1 & c_1r_2 & \cdot & \cdot & c_1r_n \\ c_2r_1 & c_2r_2 & \cdot & \cdot & c_2r_n \\ \cdot & \cdot & \cdot & \cdot & \cdot \\ \cdot & \cdot & \cdot & \cdot & \cdot \\ c_mr_1 & c_mr_2 & \cdot & \cdot & c_mc_n \end{bmatrix} \qquad \text{(A6-4)}$$

Once again, the manipulation is only defined if the number of columns in c equals the number of rows in r and the dimension of the answer is the number of rows in c and the number of columns in r.

Extending the original example, a vector-matrix product is the next step in considering matrix multiplication. The total sales in each region are:

		Region I	Region II	Region III	Region IV
[\$25 \$50 \$100]	$\begin{bmatrix} 10 & 12 & 11 & 6 \\ 3 & 8 & 6 & 9 \\ 10 & 4 & 7 & 9 \end{bmatrix}$ =	[\$1,400	\$1,100	\$1,275	\$1,500]

A general rule for multiplying a row vector by a matrix can be determined by letting

$$p = [\, p_1 p_2 \quad . \quad . \quad p_n \,] \tag{A6-5}$$

$$X = \begin{bmatrix} x_{11} & x_{12} & . & . & x_{1m} \\ x_{21} & x_{22} & . & . & x_{2m} \\ . & . & . & . & . \\ x_{n1} & x_{n2} & . & . & x_{nm} \end{bmatrix}$$

$$pX = \left[\, \sum_{i=1}^{n} p_i x_{ij} \quad \sum_{i=1}^{n} p_i x_{i2} \quad . \quad . \quad \sum_{i=1}^{n} p_i x_{im} \,\right]$$

Once again this manipulation is only defined if the number of columns in p equals the number of rows in X.

Multiplying a matrix by a matrix is merely an extension of the vector and matrix operations. Assume the matrix A with dimension m by n and matrix B with dimension n by z. General subscript notation for this problem is as follows:

$$A = \begin{bmatrix} a_{11} & a_{12} & . & . & a_{1n} \\ a_{21} & a_{22} & . & . & a_{2n} \\ . & . & . & . & . \\ . & . & . & . & . \\ a_{m1} & a_{m2} & . & . & a_{mn} \end{bmatrix}$$

$$B = \begin{bmatrix} b_{11} & b_{12} & . & . & b_{1z} \\ b_{21} & b_{22} & . & . & b_{2z} \\ . & . & . & . & . \\ . & . & . & . & . \\ b_{n1} & b_{n2} & . & . & b_{nz} \end{bmatrix}$$

$$AB = \begin{bmatrix} \sum_{i=1}^{n} a_{1i} b_{i1} & \sum_{i=1}^{n} a_{1i} b_{i2} & . & . & \sum_{i=1}^{n} a_{1i} b_{iz} \\ \sum_{i=1}^{n} a_{2i} b_{i1} & \sum_{i=1}^{n} a_{2i} b_{i2} & . & . & \sum_{i=1}^{n} a_{2i} b_{iz} \\ . & . & . & . & . \\ . & . & . & . & . \\ \sum_{i=1}^{n} a_{mi} b_{i1} & \sum_{i=1}^{n} a_{mi} b_{i2} & . & . & \sum_{i=1}^{n} a_{mi} b_{iz} \end{bmatrix} \tag{A6-6}$$

To demonstrate matrix multiplication, assume the following two matrices:

$$A = \begin{bmatrix} 1 & 0 & 4 & 5 \\ 3 & 1 & 2 & 3 \\ 2 & 2 & 0 & 4 \end{bmatrix}$$

$$B = \begin{bmatrix} 2 & 0 & 1 \\ 3 & 0 & 5 \\ 1 & 4 & 2 \\ 0 & 5 & 1 \end{bmatrix}$$

$$AB = \begin{bmatrix} 1 & 0 & 4 & 5 \\ 3 & 1 & 2 & 3 \\ 2 & 2 & 0 & 4 \end{bmatrix} \begin{bmatrix} 2 & 0 & 1 \\ 3 & 0 & 5 \\ 1 & 4 & 2 \\ 0 & 5 & 1 \end{bmatrix} = \begin{bmatrix} 6 & 41 & 14 \\ 11 & 23 & 15 \\ 10 & 20 & 16 \end{bmatrix}$$

The last multiplication operation concerns multiplying vectors and matrices by a scalar. Given a row vector r and a column vector c, multiplication by a scalar is defined by:

$$\lambda r = [\,\lambda r_1 \quad \lambda r_2 \quad . \quad . \quad \lambda r_n\,] \tag{A6-7}$$

$$\lambda c = \begin{bmatrix} \lambda c_1 \\ \lambda c_2 \\ . \\ . \\ \lambda c_n \end{bmatrix} \tag{A6-8}$$

Vector multiplication by a scalar is demonstrated by the following examples:

$$[.2] \quad [5 \quad 8 \quad 6 \quad 0] = [1 \quad 1.6 \quad 1.2 \quad 0]$$

$$[4] \begin{bmatrix} 3 \\ 6 \\ 8 \end{bmatrix} = \begin{bmatrix} 12 \\ 24 \\ 32 \end{bmatrix}$$

Matrix multiplication by a scalar is defined by:

$$\lambda A = \begin{bmatrix} \lambda a_{11} & \lambda a_{12} & . & . & \lambda a_{1n} \\ \lambda a_{21} & \lambda a_{22} & . & . & \lambda a_{2n} \\ . & . & . & . & . \\ . & . & . & . & . \\ \lambda a_{m1} & \lambda a_{m2} & . & . & \lambda a_{mn} \end{bmatrix} \tag{A6-9}$$

This manipulation is demonstrated by:

$$[5] \begin{bmatrix} 3 & 4 & 7 \\ 9 & 1 & 8 \\ 0 & 5 & 2 \end{bmatrix} = \begin{bmatrix} 15 & 20 & 35 \\ 45 & 5 & 40 \\ 0 & 25 & 10 \end{bmatrix}$$

THE INVERSE OF A MATRIX

The inverse of a square matrix A with dimension n is usually denoted by the symbol A^{-1} and has the property so that $AA^{-1} = I$ where I is an n dimension identity matrix.[2] Although the inverse matrix is extremely useful in all applications of matrix algebra, it is at times difficult to determine and there are square matrices that do not possess an inverse. An algebraic method for determining the inverse of a matrix with a dimension of two will first be demonstrated. This will aid in understanding some of the other methods for determining an inverse.

Let A and A^{-1} equal:

$$A = \begin{bmatrix} a & b \\ c & d \end{bmatrix}; \; A^{-1} = \begin{bmatrix} w & x \\ y & z \end{bmatrix}$$

Therefore the product of AA^{-1} can be expressed as:

$$\begin{bmatrix} a & b \\ c & d \end{bmatrix} \begin{bmatrix} w & x \\ y & z \end{bmatrix} = \begin{bmatrix} 1 & 0 \\ 0 & 1 \end{bmatrix}$$

2. An identity matrix is square and all elements along the main diagonal equal one. All other elements equal zero.

This product can be expressed in these four equations according to the law of matrix multiplication

$$
\begin{array}{ll}
(1) & aw + by = 1 \\
(2) & ax + bz = 0 \\
(3) & cw + dy = 0 \\
(4) & cx + dz = 1
\end{array}
$$

Solving for w and y by (3) and (1):

$$
\begin{array}{ll}
(3) & cw + dy = 0 \\
& y = \dfrac{-cw}{d} \\
(1) & aw + by = 1
\end{array}
$$

Now substituting from (3) into (1):

$$aw + b\left(\frac{-cw}{d}\right) = 1$$

$$w\left(a - \frac{bc}{d}\right) = 1$$

$$w\left(\frac{ad - bc}{d}\right) = 1$$

$$w(ad - bc) = d$$

$$w = \frac{d}{ad - bc}$$

Now substituting into (3) for w:

$$y = \left(\frac{-c}{d}\right)\left(\frac{d}{ad - bc}\right)$$

$$y = \frac{-c}{ad - bc}$$

In a similar manner, solving equations (2) and (4) for x and z the following results are obtained:

$$x = \frac{-b}{ad - bc} \; ; \; z = \frac{a}{ad - bc}$$

Placing the results into the A^{-1} matrix and factoring out the scalar, the following results are obtained:

$$\textbf{(A6-10)}$$

$$A^{-1} = \begin{bmatrix} \dfrac{d}{ad - bc} & \dfrac{-b}{ad - bc} \\[3mm] \dfrac{-c}{ad - bc} & \dfrac{a}{ad - bc} \end{bmatrix}$$

$$A^{-1} = \frac{1}{ad - bc} \begin{bmatrix} d & -b \\ -c & a \end{bmatrix}$$

Now, find the inverse of the matrix A where

$$A = \begin{bmatrix} 3 & 5 \\ 6 & 10 \end{bmatrix}; a = 3, b = 5, c = 6, d = 10$$

$$A^{-1} = \frac{1}{(3 \times 10) - (5 \times 6)} \begin{bmatrix} 10 & -5 \\ -6 & 3 \end{bmatrix}$$

$$A^{-1} = \frac{1}{0} \begin{bmatrix} 10 & -5 \\ -6 & 3 \end{bmatrix} \quad \text{(undefined)}$$

The inverse of this matrix does not exist because the solution involves division by zero, which is undefined.

The inverse of this matrix A employing the algebraic technique is determined as follows

$$A = \begin{bmatrix} 7 & 3 \\ 1 & 5 \end{bmatrix}; a = 7, b = 3, c = 1, d = 5$$

$$A^{-1} = \frac{1}{(7 \times 5) - (3 \times 1)} \begin{bmatrix} 5 & -3 \\ -1 & 7 \end{bmatrix}$$

$$A^{-1} = \begin{bmatrix} \dfrac{5}{32} & \dfrac{-3}{32} \\ \dfrac{-1}{32} & \dfrac{7}{32} \end{bmatrix}$$

This inverse can be checked by evaluating $AA^{-1} = I$ where:

$$\begin{bmatrix} 7 & 3 \\ 1 & 5 \end{bmatrix} \begin{bmatrix} \dfrac{5}{32} & \dfrac{-3}{32} \\ \dfrac{-1}{32} & \dfrac{7}{32} \end{bmatrix} = \begin{bmatrix} 1 & 0 \\ 0 & 1 \end{bmatrix}$$

AN ALGORITHM FOR DETERMINING A MATRIX INVERSE

Employing the determinant and matrix of cofactors in determining the inverse of a matrix is at times awkwards. Here, an algorithm for determining the inverse of a matrix is presented. The algorithm consists of a set of row operations and is sometimes referred to as inverting a matrix.

Initially, the matrix to be inverted is augmented with an identity matrix. The purpose of the row operations is to transform the original matrix into an identity matrix using the row operations. If this is possible, the resulting matrix where the original identity matrix was located is the inverse of the *original* matrix. The permissible row operations are:

1. Any pair of rows can be interchanged;

2. A row can be multiplied by a nonzero real number;

3. A nonzero real number times any row can be added to or subtracted from any other row.

This algorithm can be best understood by carefully studying the following examples.

Example (1)
$$A = \begin{bmatrix} 7 & 3 \\ 1 & 5 \end{bmatrix}$$

$$\begin{array}{cc} A & I \end{array}$$
$$\left[\begin{array}{cc|cc} 7 & 3 & 1 & 0 \\ 1 & 5 & 0 & 1 \end{array}\right]$$

Augmenting the original A matrix with the identity matrix

$$\left[\begin{array}{cc|cc} 1 & \dfrac{3}{7} & \dfrac{1}{7} & 0 \\ 1 & 5 & 0 & 1 \end{array}\right]$$

Multiplying the first row by $\dfrac{1}{7}$

$$\left[\begin{array}{cc|cc} 1 & \dfrac{3}{7} & \dfrac{1}{7} & 0 \\ 0 & \dfrac{32}{7} & \dfrac{-1}{7} & 1 \end{array}\right]$$

Multiplying the first row by -1 and adding the result to the second row

$$\left[\begin{array}{cc|cc} 1 & \dfrac{3}{7} & \dfrac{1}{7} & 0 \\ 0 & 1 & \dfrac{-1}{32} & \dfrac{7}{32} \end{array}\right]$$

Multiplying the second row by $\dfrac{7}{32}$

$$\begin{array}{cc} I & A^{-1} \end{array}$$
$$\left[\begin{array}{cc|cc} 1 & 0 & \dfrac{5}{32} & \dfrac{-3}{32} \\ 0 & 1 & \dfrac{-1}{32} & \dfrac{7}{32} \end{array}\right]$$

Multiplying the second row by $\dfrac{-3}{7}$ and adding the result to the first row

Check of results by multiplication:

$$\begin{array}{ccc} A & A^{-1} & I \end{array}$$
$$\begin{bmatrix} 7 & 3 \\ 1 & 5 \end{bmatrix} \begin{bmatrix} \dfrac{5}{32} & \dfrac{-3}{32} \\ \dfrac{-1}{32} & \dfrac{7}{32} \end{bmatrix} = \begin{bmatrix} 1 & 0 \\ 0 & 1 \end{bmatrix}$$

Example (2)

$$B = \begin{bmatrix} 2 & 1 & 3 \\ 1 & 5 & 7 \\ 3 & 1 & 8 \end{bmatrix}$$

$$\left[\begin{array}{ccc|ccc} 2 & 1 & 3 & 1 & 0 & 0 \\ 1 & 5 & 7 & 0 & 1 & 0 \\ 3 & 1 & 8 & 0 & 0 & 1 \end{array}\right]$$

Augmenting the original B matrix with the identity matrix

$$\left[\begin{array}{ccc|ccc} 1 & 5 & 7 & 0 & 1 & 0 \\ 2 & 1 & 3 & 1 & 0 & 0 \\ 3 & 1 & 8 & 0 & 0 & 1 \end{array}\right]$$

Exchanging the first and second rows

$$\left[\begin{array}{ccc|ccc} 1 & 5 & 7 & 0 & 1 & 0 \\ 0 & -9 & -11 & 1 & -2 & 0 \\ 3 & 1 & 8 & 0 & 0 & 1 \end{array}\right]$$

Multiplying the first row by -2 and adding the result to the second row

$$\left[\begin{array}{ccc|ccc} 1 & 5 & 7 & 0 & 1 & 0 \\ 0 & -9 & -11 & 1 & -2 & 0 \\ 0 & -14 & -13 & 0 & -3 & 1 \end{array}\right]$$

Multiplying the first row by -3 and adding the result to the third row

$$\left[\begin{array}{ccc|ccc} 1 & 5 & 7 & 0 & 1 & 0 \\ 0 & 1 & \frac{11}{9} & \frac{-1}{9} & \frac{2}{9} & 0 \\ 0 & -14 & -13 & 0 & -3 & 1 \end{array}\right]$$

Multiplying the second row by $\frac{-1}{9}$

$$\left[\begin{array}{ccc|ccc} 1 & 0 & \frac{8}{9} & \frac{5}{9} & \frac{-1}{9} & 0 \\ 0 & 1 & \frac{11}{9} & \frac{-1}{9} & \frac{2}{9} & 0 \\ 0 & -14 & -13 & 0 & -3 & 1 \end{array}\right]$$

Multiplying the second row by -5 and adding the result to the first row

$$\left[\begin{array}{ccc|ccc} 1 & 0 & \frac{8}{9} & \frac{5}{9} & \frac{-1}{9} & 0 \\ 0 & 1 & \frac{11}{9} & \frac{-1}{9} & \frac{2}{9} & 0 \\ 0 & 0 & \frac{37}{9} & \frac{-14}{9} & \frac{1}{9} & 1 \end{array}\right]$$

Multiplying the second row by 14 and adding the result to the third row

$$\left[\begin{array}{ccc|ccc} 1 & 0 & \frac{8}{9} & \frac{5}{9} & \frac{-1}{9} & 0 \\ 0 & 1 & \frac{11}{9} & \frac{-1}{9} & \frac{2}{9} & 0 \\ 0 & 0 & 1 & \frac{-14}{37} & \frac{1}{37} & \frac{9}{37} \end{array}\right]$$

Multiplying the third row by $\frac{9}{37}$

$$\left[\begin{array}{ccc|ccc} 1 & 0 & \frac{8}{9} & \frac{5}{9} & \frac{-1}{9} & 0 \\ 0 & 1 & 0 & \frac{13}{37} & \frac{7}{37} & \frac{-11}{37} \\ 0 & 0 & 1 & \frac{-14}{37} & \frac{1}{37} & \frac{9}{37} \end{array}\right]$$

Multiplying the third row by $\frac{-11}{9}$ and adding the result to second row

$$\begin{bmatrix} 1 & 0 & 0 \\ 0 & 1 & 0 \\ 0 & 0 & 1 \end{bmatrix} \begin{bmatrix} \dfrac{33}{37} & \dfrac{-5}{37} & \dfrac{-8}{37} \\ \dfrac{13}{37} & \dfrac{7}{37} & \dfrac{-11}{37} \\ \dfrac{-14}{37} & \dfrac{1}{37} & \dfrac{9}{37} \end{bmatrix}$$

Multiplying the third row by $\dfrac{-8}{9}$ and adding the result to the first row

Check of results by multiplication

$$\overset{B}{\begin{bmatrix} 2 & 1 & 3 \\ 1 & 5 & 7 \\ 3 & 1 & 8 \end{bmatrix}} \quad \overset{B^{-1}}{\begin{bmatrix} \dfrac{33}{37} & \dfrac{-5}{37} & \dfrac{-8}{37} \\ \dfrac{13}{37} & \dfrac{7}{37} & \dfrac{-11}{37} \\ \dfrac{-14}{37} & \dfrac{1}{37} & \dfrac{9}{37} \end{bmatrix}} \overset{=}{=} \overset{I}{\begin{bmatrix} 1 & 0 & 0 \\ 0 & 1 & 0 \\ 0 & 0 & 1 \end{bmatrix}}$$

QUESTIONS

Q6-1. The greater the advances in technology, the more joint products will be encountered. Comment.

Q6-2. Explain the differences in accounting for joint products and by-products.

Q6-3. Describe the different methods used in accounting for by-products.

Q6-4. In the future, what factors might contribute to treating a by-product as a joint product?

Q6-5. What conditions might prompt management personnel to seek to have a joint product treated as a by-product?

Q6-6. What conditions might influence a management team to seek to have a by-product treated as a joint product?

Q6-7. What arguments are used to support the relative-sales-value method of allocating joint costs?

Q6-8. The output of a college or university is a joint product. Explain.

Q6-9. Since reciprocal-service cost allocation is just another cost-allocation method, it does not matter how the costs are allocated. Comment.

Q6-10. What are some of the problems encountered in allocating fixed service-department costs to production departments?

Q6-11. Budgeted rather than actual costs should be allocated from service to production departments. Explain.

Q6-12. Identify the four criteria suggested by the NAA for use in allocating service-department costs.

P6-1. The Hokie Company is a food processing concern located in western Maryland. Three joint products are produced, and the joint costs are $25,000. *Joint and By-products*

Product identification	Units of output	Unit weight	Additional processing costs	Selling price
AB	8,000	2 lb	$ .75	$4.00
CB	9,000	3 lb	$1.00	$4.25
D	500	½ lb	$ .10	$ .40

Required □

1. Allocate the joint costs based on the net realizable value at split-off, assuming the additional process was undertaken for each product. If necessary, use the net-realizable-value method for accounting for any by-products.

2. Determine the value of the inventory, assuming the following finished-goods inventories after the additional processing:

Product	Units
AB	500
CB	1,000
D	74

P6-2. The Nipo production process at the Jones Chemical Company results in three products that can either be sold or processed further and then sold. The costs associated with the Nipo process are $60,000. *Joint and By-products*

Product identification	Units of output	Unit weight	Selling price at split-off	Additional processing costs	Selling price
X	7,500	3	$3.00	$1.00	$4.25
Y	10,000	2	$2.00	$ .50	$3.00
Z	12,500	3	$2.00	$ .75	$3.00

Required □

1. Determine if any of the products should be accounted for as by-products.

2. Allocate the joint costs based on the units of output, weight, and sales value at split-off, assuming the additional processing is undertaken. If necessary, use the net-realizable-value method in accounting for any by-product.

3. Assume all products are put through the additional processing and completed. At the end of the period, the inventories are:

Product	Units
X	500
Y	1,000
Z	1,500

Determine the values of the inventories based on answers obtained in part 2 of the problem.

Joint and **P6-3.** The Near Eastern Petro-Chemical Company has a production process that
By-products produces joint products. The joint costs associated with the process are $30,000.

Product identification	Units of output	Unit weight	Selling price at split-off	Additional processing costs	Selling price
XX	10,000	5 lb	$1.00	$ .75	$1.50
YY	20,000	3 lb	$ .50	$1.00	$3.00
BX	500	1 lb	$ .75	$ .10	$ .90

Required ☐

1. Determine if product BX should be treated as a joint product or a by-product. Allocate the joint costs based on the units produced, weight, and selling price at the split-off. If necessary, use the net-realizable-value method in accounting for any by-products.

2. Determine which products the firm should process beyond the split-off point.

Joint and **P6-4.** The Brown Manufacturing Company manufactures four final products—
By-products C, D, E, and F. During a recent month, joint costs of $11,000 were incurred
Multiple in department 1, 2,000 units of product A were transferred to department
Split-offs 2, and 3,000 units of product B were transferred to department 3. In department 2, $12,500 in joint costs were incurred, and 500 units of product C and 1,500 units of product D were produced. During the month in department 3, $10,000 in joint costs were incurred, and 1,000 units of product E and 2,000 units of product F were produced. The unit selling prices of C, D, E, and F are $20, $10, $5, and $10, respectively. There was no beginning or ending work-in-process inventory in any department.

Required ☐

1. Prepare a diagram showing the relationships among the departments.

2. Prepare a schedule determining the net realizable values, and allocate the joint costs to the joint products based on the net realizable values.

3. If the monthly output of 2,000 units of product A could have been sold for $10,000, should it have been processed further? Explain.

4. If the monthly output of 3,000 units of product B could have been sold for $16,000, should it have been processed further? Explain.

Joint and **P6-5.** Gregg Corporation produces four final products, C, D, E, and F, with unit
By-products selling prices of $10, $20, $50, and $180, respectively. During a recent
Multiple period, joint costs of $15,000 were incurred in department 1, and 400 units
Split-offs of product A were transferred to department 2, and 600 units of product B were transferred to department 3. Joint costs of $16,000 were incurred in department 2, and 800 units of product C and 1,200 units of product D

were produced. In department 3, joint costs of $14,000 were incurred, and 200 units of product E and 100 units of product F were produced. There was no beginning or ending work-in-process inventory in any department.

Required □

1. Prepare a diagram showing the relationships among the departments.

2. Prepare a schedule determining the net realizable value, and allocate the joint costs to the joint products based on the realizable values.

3. Determine the value of the finished-goods inventory if it consists of 80, 100, 10, and 20 units of products C, D, E, and F, respectively.

4. If the output of 600 units of product B could have been sold for $10,000, should it have been processed further? Explain.

5. If the output of 400 units of product A could have been sold for $18,000, should it have been processed further? Explain.

P6-6. The APS Corporation manufactures five final products, E, F, D, G, and H. *Joint and* All products are considered joint products except F, which is considered *By-products* a by-product. The by-product F sells for $1 a unit, and selling expenses *Multiple* related to the by-product are $5. In the recent period, joint costs of $16,000 *Split-offs* were incurred in department 1. Departments 2 and 3 received 6,000 units of A and 4,000 units of B, respectively, from department 1. Joint costs of $15,000 were incurred in department 2 and 5,000 units of C were transferred to department 4. One thousand units of D were transferred from department 2 to finished goods and sold at $10 per unit.

Department 4 incurred $5,000 in joint costs, and 4,000 units of E were transferred to finished goods and then sold for a total of $20,500. One thousand units of the by-product F were transferred from department 4 and then sold. Department 3 incurred joint costs of $9,000, and 3,000 units of product G were transferred to finished goods. The unit selling price of G is $5; 2,000 units were sold during the period. Product H was transferred from department 3 to finished goods. One thousand units were transferred and 500 were sold at a unit cost of $3. There were no work-in-process inventories at the beginning or end of the period.

Required □

1. Prepare a diagram showing the relationships among the departments.

2. Prepare a schedule determining the net realizable values, and allocate the joint costs to the joint products, based on the realizable values.

3. Determine the value of the finished-goods inventory.

4. Assume the joint costs for each department were 50 percent material, 30 percent labor, and 20 percent overhead. Prepare journal entries for the period for all activities affecting the work-in-process, finished-goods, and cost-of-goods-sold accounts.

P6-7. In its three departments, Amaco Chemical Company manufactures several *Joint Products* products. In department 1, the raw materials amanic acid and bonyl hydroxide are used to produce Amanyl, Bonanyl, and Am-Salt. Amanyl is sold to others who use it as a raw material in the manufacture of stimulants. Bonanyl is not saleable without further processing. Although Am-Salt is a commercial product for which there is a ready market, Amaco does not sell this product, preferring to submit it to further processing.

In department 2, Bonanyl is processed into the marketable product Bonanyl-X. The relationship between Bonanyl used and Bonanyl-X produced has remained constant for several months.

In department 3, Am-Salt and the raw material colb are used to produce Colbanyl, a liquid propellant that is in great demand. As an inevitable part of this process, Demanyl is also produced. Demanyl was discarded as scrap until discovery of its usefulness as a catalyst in the manufacture of glue; for two years Amaco has been able to sell all of its production of Demanyl.

In its financial statements, Amaco states inventory at the lower of cost (on the first-in, first-out basis) or market. Unit costs of the items most recently produced must therefore be computed. Costs allocated to Demanyl are computed so that after allowing for packaging and selling costs of $.04 per pound no profit or loss will be recognized on sales of this product.

Certain data for October 19X2 follow:

Raw materials	Pounds used	Total cost
Amanic acid	6,300	$5,670
Bonyl hydroxide	9,100	6,370
Colb	5,600	2,240

Conversion costs (labor and overhead)	Total cost
Department 1	$33,600
Department 2	3,306
Department 3	22,400

Products	Pounds produced	Inventories, Pounds September 30	October 31	Sales price per pound
Amanyl	3,600			$ 6.65
Bonanyl	2,800	210	110	
Am-Salt	7,600	400	600	6.30
Bonanyl-X	2,755			4.20
Colbanyl	1,400			43.00
Demanyl	9,800			.54

Required □

1. Prepare for October 19X2 the schedules listed. Supporting computations should be prepared in good form. Round answers to the nearest cent.

   a. Cost per pound of Amanyl, Bonanyl, and Am-Salt produced—relative-sales-value method.
   b. Cost per pound of Amanyl, Bonanyl, and Am-Salt produced—average-unit-cost method.
   c. Cost per pound of Colbanyl produced. Assume that the cost per pound of Am-Salt produced was $3.40 in September 19X2 and $3.50 in October 19X2.

(CPA)

P6-8. The Harbison Company manufactures two sizes of plate glass. They are *Joint Products* produced simultaneously in the same manufacturing process. Since the small sheets of plate glass are cut from large sheets that have flaws in them, the joint costs are allocated equally to each good sheet, large and small, produced. The difference in after split-off costs for large and small sheets is material.

In 19X6, the company decided to increase its efforts to sell the large sheets because they produced a larger gross margin than the small sheets. Accordingly, the amount of the fixed advertising budget devoted to large sheets was increased and the amount devoted to small sheets was decreased. However, no changes in sales prices were made.

By midyear, the production scheduling department had increased the monthly production of large sheets in order to stay above the minimum inventory level. However, it also had cut back the monthly production of small sheets because the inventory ceiling had been reached.

At the end of 19X6, the net result of the change in product mix was a decrease of $112,000 in gross margin. Although sales of large sheets had increased 34,500 units, sales of small sheets had decreased 40,200 units.

Required ☐

1. Distinguish between joint costs and

    a. after split-off costs
    b. fixed costs
    c. prime costs
    d. indirect costs

2. Discuss the propriety of allocating joint costs for general-purpose financial statements on the basis of

    a. physical measures, such as weights or units
    b. relative sales or market value

3. In the development of weights for allocating joint costs to joint products, why is the relative sales value of each joint product usually reduced by its after split-off costs?

4. Identify the mistake that the Harbison Company made in deciding to change its product mix, and explain why it caused a smaller gross margin for 19X6.

(CPA)

P6-9. The Harrison Corporation produces three products—Alpha, Beta, and *Joint Products* Gamma. Alpha and Gamma are joint products, while Beta is a by-product of Alpha. No joint cost is to be allocated to the by-product. The production processes for a given year are as follows:

In department 1, 110,000 pounds of raw material, Rho, are processed at a total cost of $120,000. After processing in department 1, 60 percent of the units are transferred to department 2, and 40 percent of the units (now Gamma) are transferred to department 3.

In department 2, the material is further processed at a total additional cost of $38,000. Seventy percent of the units (now Alpha) are transferred to department 4, and 30 percent emerge as Beta, the by-product, to be sold at $1.20 per pound. Selling expenses related to disposing of Beta are $8,100.

In department 3, Gamma is processed at a total additional cost of $165,000. In this department, a normal loss of units of Gamma occurs. This loss equals 10 percent of the good output of Gamma. The remaining good output of Gamma is then sold for $12 per pound.

In department 4, Alpha is processed at a total additional cost $23,660. After this processing, Alpha is ready for sale at $5 per pound.

Required □

1. Prepare a schedule showing the allocation of the $120,000 joint cost between Alpha and Gamma using the relative-sales-value approach. The net realizable value of Beta should be treated as an addition to the sales value of Alpha.

2. Independent of your answer to requirement 1, assume that $102,000 of total joint costs were appropriately allocated to Alpha. Assume also that there were 48,000 pounds of Alpha and 20,000 pounds of Beta available to sell. Prepare a statement of gross margin for Alpha using the following facts:

   a. During the year, sales of Alpha were 80 percent of the pounds available for sale. There was no beginning inventory.
   b. The net realizable value of Beta available for sale is to be deducted from the cost of producing Alpha. The ending inventory of Alpha is to be based on the net cost of production.
   c. All other cost, selling-price, and selling-expense data are those presented in the facts of the original problem.

   (CPA)

Joint and By-products **P6-10.** The McLean Processing Company produces a chemical compound Supergro that is sold for $4.60 per gallon. The manufacturing process is divided into the following departments:

1. Mixing department. The raw materials are measured and mixed in this department.

2. Cooking department. The mixed materials are cooked for a specified period in this department. In the cooking process, there is a 10 percent evaporation loss in materials.

3. Cooling department. After the cooked materials are cooled in this department, under controlled conditions the top 80 percent in the cooling tank is syphoned off and pumped to the Packing department. The 20 percent residue, which contains impurities, is sold in bulk as the by-product Groex for $2 per gallon.

4. Packing department. In this department, special one-gallon tin cans that cost $.60 each are filled with Supergro and shipped to customers.

The Research and Development department recently discovered a new use for the by-product if it is further processed in a new Boiling department. The new by-product, Fasgro, would sell in bulk for $5 per gallon.

In processing Fasgro, the top 70 percent in the cooling tank would be syphoned off as Supergro. The residue would be pumped to the Boiling department where one-half gallon of raw material, SK, would be added for each gallon of residue. In the Boiling department process, there would be a 40 percent evaporation loss. In processing Fasgro, the following additional costs would be incurred.

Material SK	$1.10 per gallon
Boiling department variable processing costs	$1.00 per gallon of input
Boiling department fixed processing costs	$2,000 per month

In recent months, because of heavy demand, the company has shipped Supergro and Groex on the same day that their processing is completed. Fasgro would probably be subject to the same heavy demand.

During the month of July 19X3, which was considered a typical month, the following raw materials were put into process in the Mixing department:

Material FE—10,000 gallons @ $.90 per gallon
Material QT—4,000 gallons @ $1.50 per gallon
July processing cost per gallon of departmental input were:

Mixing department	$.40
Cooking department	.50
Cooling department	.30
Packing department	.10

For accounting purposes, the company assigns costs to its by-products equal to their net realizable value.

Required □ Prepare a statement computing total manufacturing costs and gross profit for the month of July that compares (1) actual results for July and (2) estimated results if Fasgro had been the by-product.

(CPA)

P6-11. Miller Manufacturing Company buys zeon for $.80 a gallon. At the end of   *Joint Products*
processing in department 1, zeon splits off into products A, B, and C. Product A is sold at the split-off point, with no further processing. Products B and C require further processing before they can be sold; product B is processed in department 2 and product C is processed in department 3. A summary of costs and other related data for the year ended June 30, 19X3, follows:

	Department		
	1	2	3
Cost of zeon	$96,000	—	—
Direct labor	$14,000	$45,000	$ 65,000
Manufacturing overhead	$10,000	$21,000	$ 49,000

	Products		
	A	B	C
Gallons sold	20,000	30,000	45,000
Gallons on hand at June 30, 19X3	10,000	—	15,000
Sales in dollars	$30,000	$96,000	$141,750

There were no inventories on hand at July 1, 19X2, and there was no zeon on hand at June 30, 19X3. All gallons on hand at June 30, 19X3, were complete as to processing. There were no manufacturing overhead variances. Miller uses the net realizable value at split-off method of allocating joint costs.

Required □

1. For allocating joint costs, the net realizable sales value of product A, for the year ended June 30, 19X3, would be

    a. $30,000
    b. $45,000
    c. $21,000
    d. $ 6,000

2. The joint costs for the year ended June 30, 19X3, to be allocated are

    a. $300,000
    b. $ 95,000
    c. $120,000
    d. $ 96,000

3. The cost of product B sold for the year ended June 30, 19X3, is

    a. $90,000
    b. $66,000
    c. $88,857
    d. $96,000

4. The value of the ending inventory for product A is

    a. $24,000
    b. $12,000
    c. $ 8,000
    d. $13,333

(CPA)

Reciprocal Cost Allocation   **P6-12.** The Plate Corporation has two service departments and two production departments. The following allocation percentages and primary cost allocations have been determined.

	S_1	S_2	P_1	P_2
Primary cost allocation	$500	$600	$800	$700
S_1	0	.3	.5	.2
S_2	.5	0	.2	.3

Required □

1. Allocate the costs sequentially by allocating S_1 and then S_2.

2. Allocate the costs sequentially by allocating S_2 and then S_1.

3. Determine the total cost activity in each service department from the algebraic solution.

4. Allocate the costs using the algebraic or matrix method.

Reciprocal Cost Allocation   **P6-13.** The Hendricks Rest Home has two service departments and three production departments. The following allocation percentages and primary cost allocations have been determined.

	S_1	S_2	P_1	P_2	P_3
Primary cost allocation	$1,000	$2,000	$2,000	$5,000	$8,000
S_1	.1	.3	.2	.2	.2
S_2	.3	.2	.3	.1	.1

Required ☐

1. Allocate the costs sequentially by allocating S_1 and then S_2.

2. Allocate the costs sequentially by allocating S_2 and then S_1.

3. Determine the total cost activity in each service department from the algebraic solution.

4. Allocate the costs using the algebraic or matrix method.

P6-14. The Green Tool and Die Company has three service departments servicing three production departments. The following allocation percentages and primary cost allocations have been determined.

Reciprocal Cost Allocation

	S_1	S_2	S_3	P_1	P_2	P_3
Primary cost allocation	$30,000	$20,000	$50,000	$80,000	$30,000	$60,000
S_1	.1	0	.3	.2	.3	.1
S_2	.2	.2	.3	0	.2	.1
S_3	.1	.4	0	.2	.1	.2

Required ☐

1. Allocate the costs sequentially by allocating S_1, then S_2, and finally S_3.

2. Allocate the costs sequentially by allocating S_3, then S_2, and finally S_1.

3. Allocate the costs using the algebraic or matrix method.

P6-15. The Highway department of the town of Bluefield runs a vehicle repair facility that services all departments in the town. Any parts used in the repair operation are charged directly to the department being serviced. Labor and overhead are charged on the basis of the mechanic's time spent on a particular job. The Maintenance department performs the house-keeping functions for all departments in the town. Costs are allocated on the basis of the square feet maintained.

Reciprocal Cost Allocation

	Highway	Mainte-nance	Water	Fire	Police	Library	Adminis-tration
Highway (hours)	2,000	500	800	450	1,200	—	50
Maintenance (square feet)	400	600	760	—	1.500	40,000	2,750
Costs to be allocated	$25,000	$60,000					

Required ☐

1. Allocate the costs sequentially by allocating the highway and then maintenance.

2. Allocate the costs using the algebraic or matrix method.

3. The manager of the Water department indicates that she is the only department head who is involved in setting rates for users. She states

that the other department heads can live with arbitrary allocations, but she must know the true costs in order to establish rates. Comment.

Reciprocal Cost Allocation

P6-16. In the Rolling Hills Hospital, the Cafeteria and Housekeeping departments service the Medical, Maternity, Surgical, and Emergency Room departments of the hospital. Allocations from the Cafeteria are made on the number of meals provided. Square feet maintained is the basis of allocating the costs from the Housekeeping department.

	Cafeteria	House-keeping	Medical	Maternity	Surgical	Emergency Room
Cafeteria (meals served)	100	200	150	50	200	160
Housekeeping (square feet cleaned)	2,500	500	17,500	7,500	15,000	5,000
Costs to be allocated	$10,000	$15,000				

Required □

1. Allocate the costs sequentially by allocating the cafeteria and then housekeeping.

2. Allocate the costs sequentially by allocating housekeeping and then the cafeteria.

3. Allocate the costs using the algebraic or matrix method.

4. Assume the Rolling Hills Hospital is operated on a nonprofit basis and only seeks to recover its costs from government agencies, insurance companies, and self-pay patients. How will the service-department cost allocation influence the rate structure of the hospital?

Service Cost Allocation

P6-17. Thrift-Shops, Inc., operates a chain of three food stores in a state that recently enacted legislation permitting municipalities within the state to levy an income tax on corporations operating within their respective municipalities. The legislation establishes a uniform tax rate that the municipalities may levy and impose regulations that provide that the tax is to be computed on income derived within the taxing municipality after a reasonable and consistent allocation of general overhead expenses. General overhead expenses have not been allocated to individual stores previously and include warehouse, general office, advertising, and delivery expenses.

Each of the municipalities in which Thrift-Shops, Inc., operates a store has levied the corporate income tax as provided by state legislation, and the management team is considering two plans for allocating general overhead expenses to the stores. The 19X9 operating results before general overhead and taxes for each store were as follows.

	Ashville	Burns	Clinton	Total
Sales, net	$416,000	$353,600	$270,400	$1,040,000
Less cost of sales	215,700	183,300	140,200	539,200
Gross margin	200,300	170,300	130,200	500,800

Less local operating expenses				
Fixed	60,800	48,750	55,200	159,750
Variable	54,700	64,220	22,448	146,368
Total	115,500	112,970	77,648	306,118
Income before general overhead and taxes	$ 84,800	$ 57,330	$ 52,552	$ 194,682

General overhead expenses were as follows:

Warehousing and delivery expenses		
Warehouse depreciation	$20,000	
Warehouse operations	30,000	
Delivery expenses	40,000	$ 90,000
Central office expenses		
Advertising	18,000	
Central office salaries	37,000	
Other central office expenses	28,000	83,000
Total general overhead		$173,000

Additional information includes the following:

1. One-fifth of the warehouse space is used to house the central office, and depreciation on this space is included in other central office expenses. Warehouse operating expenses vary with quantity of merchandise sold.

2. Delivery expenses vary with distance and number of deliveries. The distances from the warehouse to each store and the number of deliveries made in 19X9 were as follows:

Store	Miles	Number of deliveries
Ashville	120	140
Burns	200	64
Clinton	100	104

3. All advertising is prepared by the central office and is distributed in the areas in which stores are located.

4. As each store was opened, the fixed portion of central office salaries increased $7,000, and other central office expenses increased $2,500. Basic fixed central office salaries amount to $10,000, and other basic fixed central office expenses amount to $12,000. The remainder of central office salaries and the remainder of other central office expenses vary with sales.

Required □

1. For each of the following plans for allocating general overhead expenses, compute the income of each store that would be subject to the municipal levy on corporation income.

■ **Plan A.** Allocate all general overhead expenses on the basis of sales volume.

■ **Plan B.** First, allocate central salaries and other central office expenses evenly to warehouse operations and each store. Second, allocate the resulting warehouse operations expenses, warehouse depreciation, and advertising to each store on the basis of sales volume. Third, allocate delivery expenses to each store on the basis of delivery miles times number of deliveries.

2. The management team has decided to expand one of the three stores to increase sales by $50,000. The expansion will increase local fixed operating expenses by $7,500 and require ten additional deliveries from the warehouse. Determine which store management should select for expansion to maximize corporate profits.

(CPA)

Service Cost   **P6-18.**   The Parker Manufacturing Company has two production departments (Fab-
Allocation rication and Assembly) and three service departments (General Factory Administration, Factory Maintenance, and Factory Cafeteria). A summary of costs and other data for each department prior to allocation of service-department costs for the year ended June 30, 19X3, appears below.

The costs of the General Factory Administration department, Factory Maintenance department, and Factory Cafeteria are allocated on the basis of direct-labor hours, square-footage occupied, and number of employees, respectively. There are no manufacturing overhead variances. Round all final calculations to the nearest dollar.

	Fabrication	Assembly	General Factory Administration	Factory Maintenance	Factory Cafeteria
Direct-labor costs	$1,950,000	$2,050,000	$90,000	$82,100	$87,000
Direct-material costs	$3,130,000	$ 950,000	—	$65,000	$91,000
Manufacturing overhead costs	$1,650,000	$1,850,000	$70,000	$56,100	$62,000
Direct-labor hours	562,500	437,500	31,000	27,000	42,000
Number of employees	280	200	12	8	20
Square footage occupied	88,000	72,000	1,750	2,000	4,800

Required ☐

1. Assuming that the management of Parker elects to distribute service-department costs directly to production departments without inter-service-department cost allocation, the amount of Factory Maintenance departments costs that would be allocated to the Fabrication department would be

   a. $0
   b. $111,760
   c. $106,091
   d. $91,440

2. Assuming the same method of allocation as in item a, the amount of General Factory Administration department costs that would be allocated to the Assembly department would be

   a. $0
   b. $63,636
   c. $70,000
   d. $90,000

3. Assuming that Parker management officials elect to distribute service-department costs to other service departments (starting with the service

department with the greatest total costs), as well as the production departments, the amount of Factory Cafeteria department costs that would be allocated to the Factory Maintenance department would be (Note: Once a service department's costs have been reallocated, no subsequent service-department costs are recirculated back to it.)

a. $0
b. $96,000
c. $3,840
d. $6,124

4. Assuming the same method of allocation as in requirement 3, the amount of Factory Maintenance department costs that would be allocated to the Factory Cafeteria would be

a. $0
b. $5,787
c. $5,856
d. $148,910

(CPA)

P6-19. The plant at a manufacturing company has two service departments (designated as S_1 and S_2) and three production departments (designated as P_1, P_2, and P_3) and wishes to allocate all factory overhead to production departments. A primary distribution of overhead to all departments has already been made and is indicated. The company makes the secondary distribution of overhead from service departments to production departments on a reciprocal basis, recognizing the fact that services of one service department are utilized by another. Data regarding costs and allocation percentages are as follows:

Service Cost Allocation

Service Department Overhead Cost Allocation
Percentages to Be Allocated to Departments

Service department	S_1	S_2	P_1	P_2	P_3
S_1	0	10	20	40	30
S_2	20	0	50	10	20

Primary Overhead to Be Allocated

$98,000 $117,600 $1,400,000 $2,100,000 $640,000

Matrix algebra is to be used in the secondary-allocation process. The amount of overhead to be allocated to the service departments is expressed in two simultaneous equations as:

$S_1 = 98,000 + .20S_2$ or $S_1 - .20S_2 = \$98,000$
$S_2 = 117,600 + .10S_1$ or $S_2 - .10S_1 = \$117,600$

Required □

1. The system of simultaneous equations above may be stated in matrix form as:

$$a. \quad \overset{A}{\begin{bmatrix} 1 & -.20 \\ -.10 & 1 \end{bmatrix}} \quad \overset{S}{\begin{bmatrix} S_1 \\ S_2 \end{bmatrix}} = \overset{b}{\begin{bmatrix} \$98,000 \\ \$117,600 \end{bmatrix}}$$

b.
$$\begin{matrix} A \\ \begin{bmatrix} 1 & \$\,98{,}000 & 1 \\ -.20 & \$117{,}600 & -.10 \end{bmatrix} \end{matrix} = \begin{matrix} S \\ \begin{bmatrix} S_1 \\ S_2 \end{bmatrix} \end{matrix} \quad \begin{matrix} b \\ \begin{bmatrix} \$\,98{,}000 \\ \$117{,}600 \end{bmatrix} \end{matrix}$$

c.
$$\begin{matrix} A \\ \begin{bmatrix} 1 & S_1 & 1 \\ -.20 & S_2 & -.10 \end{bmatrix} \end{matrix} \quad \begin{matrix} S \\ \begin{bmatrix} S_1 \\ S_2 \end{bmatrix} \end{matrix} = \begin{matrix} b \\ \begin{bmatrix} \$\,98{,}000 \\ \$117{,}600 \end{bmatrix} \end{matrix}$$

d.
$$\begin{matrix} A \\ \begin{bmatrix} 1 & 1 & S_1 \\ -.20 & -.10 & S_2 \end{bmatrix} \end{matrix} \quad \begin{matrix} S \\ \begin{bmatrix} S_1 \\ S_2 \end{bmatrix} \end{matrix} = \begin{matrix} b \\ \begin{bmatrix} \$\,98{,}000 \\ \$117{,}600 \end{bmatrix} \end{matrix}$$

2. For the correct matrix A in requirement 1, there exists a unique inverse matrix A^{-1}. Multiplication of the matrix A by the matrix A will produce

   a. the matrix A
   b. another inverse matrix
   c. the correct solution to the system
   d. an identity matrix

3. Without prejudice to your previous answers, assume that the correct matrix form in item a was:

$$\begin{matrix} A \\ \begin{bmatrix} 1 & -.20 \\ -.10 & 1 \end{bmatrix} \end{matrix} \quad \begin{matrix} S \\ \begin{bmatrix} S_1 \\ S_2 \end{bmatrix} \end{matrix} = \begin{matrix} b \\ \begin{bmatrix} \$\,98{,}000 \\ \$117{,}600 \end{bmatrix} \end{matrix}$$

Then, the correct inverse matrix A^{-1} is:

a.
$$\begin{bmatrix} \dfrac{1}{.98} & \dfrac{.20}{.98} \\[2ex] \dfrac{.10}{.98} & \dfrac{1}{.98} \end{bmatrix}$$

b.
$$\begin{bmatrix} \dfrac{1}{.98} & \dfrac{1}{.98} \\[2ex] \dfrac{.20}{.98} & \dfrac{.10}{.98} \end{bmatrix}$$

c.
$$\begin{bmatrix} \dfrac{1}{.30} & \dfrac{.20}{.30} \\[2ex] \dfrac{.10}{.30} & \dfrac{1}{.30} \end{bmatrix}$$

d.
$$\begin{bmatrix} \dfrac{1}{.98} & \dfrac{-1}{.98} \\[2ex] -\dfrac{.20}{.98} & \dfrac{.10}{.98} \end{bmatrix}$$

4. The total amount of overhead allocated to department S_1 after receiving the allocation from department S_2 is

   a. $141,779
   b. $124,000
   c. $121,520
   d. $117,600

5. The total amount of overhead allocated to department S_2 after receiving the allocation from department S_1 is

   a. $392,000
   b. $220,000
   c. $130,000
   d. $127,400

6. Without prejudice to your previous answers, assume that the answer to requirement 4 is $100,000 and to requirement 5 is $150,000; then the total amount of overhead allocated to production department P_1 would be

a. $1,508,104
b. $1,495,000
c. $1,498,800
d. $108,104

(CPA)

P6-20. The head office of Icy Bottling Company is organized into three major service departments—Personnel, General Administration and the Controller's office. The company is currently evaluating alternative approaches for allocating service-department costs to its four regional bottling plants. The costs to be allocated and the expected allocation rates are as follows:

Service Cost Allocation

	Personnel	General Administration	Controller's Office	P_1	P_2	P_3	P_4
Costs	$150,000	$400,000	$600,000				
Rates:							
Personnel	0	.03	.05	.21	.23	.18	.30
General Administration	.10	.03	.08	.21	.12	.25	.21
Controller's Office	.05	.25	.03	.12	.17	.14	.24

In order to provide comprehensive data on the impact of alternative allocation approaches, you have been assigned the task of preparing four different cost-allocation schedules along with graphic presentations of the results. The suggested approaches are:

Required ☐

1. Allocate the costs sequentially starting with the unit that contributes the smallest dollar amount of service.

2. Allocate the costs sequentially starting with the unit that provides the most dollar amount of service.

3. Allocate the costs ignoring reciprocal relationships.

4. Allocate the costs using a matrix approach.

5. Provide a brief discussion of the results.

P6-21. The Super Center is a five-outlet food chain operating in a major metropolitan area. The company is currently preparing its budget for the next year and is evaluating alternative approaches for allocating the fixed costs of four services that are centrally provided by a head office—Purchasing, General Administration, Data Processing, and Marketing. Budgeted operating data for the five outlets are as follows:

Service Cost Allocation

	Total	North	South	East	West	Central
Sales (mil.)	$125.00	$10.00	$25.75	$18.00	$40.00	$31.25
Cost of goods sold (mil.)	83.00	6.50	16.90	11.90	26.40	21.30
Number of employees	260	30	50	46	74	60

There are reciprocal relationships between the departments and estimates are as follows:

| | | Percentages | | | |
| | | | | Data | |
	Total	Purchasing	Administration	Processing	Marketing
Purchasing	7	4	1	2	0
Administration	11	2	2	3	4
Data processing	15	4	5	2	4
Marketing	8	1	5	0	2

The fixed costs to be allocated are:

Purchasing	$ 800,000
Administration	1,850,000
Data Processing	1,700,000
Marketing	900,000
Total costs to be allocated	$5,250,00

Required ☐

1. Prepare a schedule showing the rates you would recommend for allocating the fixed costs of the services provided by the head office.

2. Allocate the costs using the matrix method.

3. Allocate the costs ignoring the reciprocal relationships.

4. Display your results graphically.

5. Comment briefly on your results.

PART OUTLINE

PART II

CONCEPTS AND TECHNIQUES FOR CONTROL

CHAPTER OUTLINE

BUDGETING: THE KEY TO PLANNING AND CONTROL

CHAPTER 7

☐ INTRODUCTION

The budget, in many respects, represents the cornerstone for a company's management-control system. Budgeting utilizes goals, objectives, and forecasts in developing plans for production, revenues, costs, cash flows, and resource procurement. Budgets also become an integral part of responsibility accounting and other control systems. Yet, management is often challenged in developing a proper budgeting approach because of its potential impact on employee behavior. This chapter provides insight into the basic budgeting framework along with material on responsibility accounting and certain behaviorial implications.

☐ BUDGETING AND THE MANAGEMENT SYSTEM

Budgeting is one of the techniques used most frequently by management accountants to assist management personnel in planning and control. The basic information system can be enhanced when budgets are introduced and become part of a formal reporting system comparing actual results with budgeted performance.

In the initial stages of a company's evolution and growth, planning is frequently the domain of the owner-manager, with control being largely exercised through physical observation. The accounting system is set up to provide needed reports, such as those required by credit grantors and regulatory agencies. These financial reports are used by the owner-manager along with physical observations and expectations to evaluate the performance of the company and its employees.

As the company develops into a large, complex organization with various levels of management, more formal planning is usually required. Consequently, budgeting programs are much more common in large companies where sophisticated planning and control techniques are often used. Yet, there is substantial reason for smaller companies to make use of budgeting. For example, the management team of a small company in the soft drink industry made a decision to consolidate two bottling plants and to serve the two marketing territories from one bottling operation. Management members believed the expected results were so obvious that they did not need to quantify and evaluate their plans. However, the results were a disaster, and no one in management could explain what went wrong.

The starting point for budgeting originates in strategic planning decisions made with respect to company goals. As goals are implemented and programs developed, management personnel need information on the impact of various alternatives being considered so that they can be evaluated. When a decision is reached regarding a specific plan of action, the budget becomes the management team's master plan for a period of time. It then serves not only as a means of communicating those plans within the organization but also provides a basis for evaluating segment and management performance. The overall cycle is shown in figure 7.1.

☐ BUDGETING BASICS

In this section, we will define and discuss the purpose of budgeting, identify the different types of budgets, and outline the advantages and disadvantages of budgeting.

FIGURE 7.1
Planning and
Budgeting Cycle

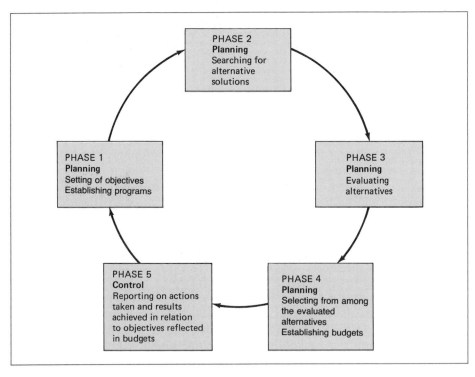

A Definition of Budgeting

A budget is a detailed written expression of an entity's expectations with respect to acquisition and use of resources for a specified period of time. In the initial planning stages, projections are made to indicate the impact of various alternatives on profitability. After decisions have been made on a course of action, budgets reflect expected profit results from decisions made. Budgets provide specific targets for sales, purchasing, production, marketing, and financing activities.

The Budgeting Time Frame

Some budgets may reflect periods of one year or less, while others—such as capital budgets—may be established for several years. Historically, the time frame for most budgeting programs has been one year, with the budget broken down by months for at least twelve months. In recent years, continuous budgets have become popular. In a continuous budget, twelve months are always projected by adding a new month in the future as a month is completed and dropped. These budgets are considered desirable because they encourage managers to continually think about the future.

Kinds of Budgets

We have already mentioned budgets as part of the master plan. There are numerous other kinds of budgets. The following types are the most prevalent:

1. *Capital budgets.* These budgets reflect long-term planning for capital expenditures. They are discussed in chapters 14 and 15.

2. *Flexible budgets.* A flexible budget is typically an overhead budget where overhead costs are established for a relevant range rather than a single level of activity. As a result, the budget can be adjusted to changes in activity levels. This budget is discussed in chapter 8.

3. *Static budgets.* Budgets prepared for specific levels of activity and not changed automatically if the levels of activity change.

4. *Special budgets.* Various special budgets are prepared as needed for special decisions. They may include certain components of a master budget, reflect breakeven analysis, or other techniques.

5. *Governmental budgets.* In governmental entities, expenditures are made based on appropriations authorized by a legislative body. In this sense, the expenditure budget establishes a ceiling on expenditures by categories. The revenue portion of the budget indicates sources of funds for the authorized expenditures.

Advantages of Budgets

Budgets are considered a significant component of management-control systems. When used properly, budgets should focus the management team's attention on planning, on improved communication, and on coordination within the organization. In addition, a properly used budget should provide a basis for performance measurement and evaluation.

Many managers believe that budgeting is not worthwhile because of the size of their company or because of significant uncertainties the company faces. Financial planning and control consultants often hear managers say, "Budgeting is too time-consuming and doesn't tell us anything we do not already know." For instance, to the management staff of one large dairy, budgeting is simply a matter of adjusting last year's operating results to next year's sales days so that actual results can be compared with last year's adjusted performance. In such environments, operations are likely to be predicated on prior year performance until management finds itself in undesirable situations that might have been anticipated and avoided by careful planning.

All managers should plan. Budgeting simply encourages a formalization of those plans. In most organizations, budgets can provide direction, help to make managers more aware of emerging problems, and aid in the development of timely solutions. Coordination of various business activities is facilitated by means of budgeting. Obviously, managers of different functional areas have different points of view on what objectives ought to be and how they can best be accomplished. To arrive at a workable plan, the desires and efforts of each segment must be considered and brought together. For example, the marketing group must recognize the restrictions placed on the production department in terms of time required for production and capacity limitations. Manufacturing personnel must schedule production based on efforts of the marketing group and qualitative requirements.

Related to coordination is the need to communicate plans that will properly motivate employees. If individual segments of the budget conform to overall company guidelines, and if they are compatible with employee goals, the budget can become an effective management communications tool.

Finally, a well-developed budgeting program should provide a proper basis for control. Unfortunately, this is an area where budgeting programs are often the least successful. In a management-control system, budgets provide the basis for performance measurement and evaluation in a responsibility-accounting system. Responsibility-accounting systems are discussed later in this chapter.

Budget Limitations

Although a sound budgeting program can provide a positive input to the management system, there are certain inherent dangers to guard against. The budget is a quantification of many subjective judgments. The budget is often allowed to become a rather inflexible tool. Unless the budgeting process is continuous, personnel are often led to think of planning as something that takes place only at certain times during a year. The failure of personnel management to give proper consideration to the behavioral aspects of budgeting may be one of the major problems of budgeting.

☐ BEHAVIORAL CONSIDERATIONS

Why are budgeting systems effective in some organizations but not in others? This question has plagued management for years. The answer, at least in part, appears to be found in the attitudes of lower-level management and other affected personnel toward the budget. If budgeting is used as a means of rigidly controlling activities, without the advance participation or consent of concerned personnel, the system is likely to fail.

If budgeting is to be successful, it should be used in a positive manner as a planning and monitoring device, with full support and participation from all levels of management. Indeed, management-control systems—of which budgeting is a significant component—are much more likely to be effective if they are developed to encourage **employee behavior** that promotes the best interests of the total organization while achieving company goals.

Traditional Behavioral Assumptions

Unfortunately, for years the budget was used as a rigid control tool to identify blame for particular problems. Undoubtedly, much of this approach stems from the work of Frederick Taylor and others identified with the scientific-management movement that took place around the turn of the century. The leaders of this movement used techniques such as time-and-motion studies to identify the most efficient ways of accomplishing jobs. Since workers were assumed to be individuals with limited capacity, who lacked initiative, and who were motivated only by financial rewards, it was believed that they required careful supervision. Acceptance of these assumptions led to the development of an authoritarian organization in which each manager's authority was accepted without question.

Even now, budgetary systems are often based on notions of authoritarian management, profit maximization, general disregard for the needs of individual employees, and mechanistic-control systems. Indeed, the early contributions of accounting in the standard costing, budgeting, and responsibility accounting areas were made in this kind of environment. As a result, employees may continue to view these techniques with a certain amount of distrust.

Recent Behavioral Assumptions

In today's business environment, top managers are concerned with multiple goals (e.g., profits, productivity, market share, product quality, employee development, and public responsibility. Yet, budgets often appear to emphasize profitability and cost control. If overall program and company objectives are not properly accepted or understood, employees may take undesirable actions to achieve different objectives (or their personal objectives). For instance, product quality may be reduced, maintenance costs may be delayed, or other shortcuts may be taken. Such actions on the part of employees suggest a lack of **goal congruence.** Goal congruence exists when the goals of each employee, to the extent possible, are consistent with overall company goals. An attempt must be made by top-management members to structure the management-control system so that these varied goals are consistent. Douglas McGregor points out:

> The essential task of management is to arrange occupational conditions and methods of operations so that people can achieve their own goals best by directing their own efforts toward organizational objectives.[1]

A number of theories on motivation have been advanced in modern times; some of them relate directly to the budgeting problem. A. H. Maslow identified certain categories of individual needs, starting with the physiological needs for food, shelter, and basic concerns. Next are needs for protection against threats and dangers, followed by concerns for acceptance and friendship. Finally, he identified the need for status, self-esteem, and respect of peers.[2] Maslow indicated that people first attempt to satisfy their basic needs; and as certain needs are satisfied, others become important.

Douglas McGregor, in developing his "Theory X" and "Theory Y," identified two extreme views of management—an authoritarian view (Theory X) and a participative view (Theory Y).[3] In his work, McGregor advanced the notion that employees are motivated to work only if the environment is conducive to work. He suggested that employees are goal-oriented and, given the proper inducement, they are capable of being creative in their work.

An assumption frequently made is that the budgeting process should involve all levels of management in the various phases of budget development and implementation and in the plan of action that identifies proposed accomplishments and costs. According to this assumption, if active participation has been accomplished, the budget should be internalized as personal goals by the participants. For instance, one behavioralist concludes that

> . . . as subordinates were given a larger influence in decisions, their performance improved, partly because of the ego involvement which participation generated. In a budgetary context, this may be interpreted to mean a greater willingness by budgeted individuals to accept the budget goal; with a difficult goal this acceptance would be likely to result in improved performance.[4]

1. Douglas McGregor, *The Human Side of Enterprise* (New York: McGraw-Hill Book Company, 1960).

2. A. H. Maslow, *Motivation and Personality* (New York: Harper & Row, 1954).

3. McGregor, *The Human Side of Enterprise.*

4. Michael Schiff and Arie Y. Lewin, eds., *Behavioral Aspects of Accounting* (Englewood Cliffs, N.J.: Prentice-Hall, Inc., 1974), p. 144.

However, other evidence indicates that the consequences associated with participation are likely to vary from situation to situation.

Another approach, referred to as expectancy theory, suggests that employees behave according to their expectations regarding outcomes from different kinds of behavior and the benefits expected from each outcome. In other words, personnel assign probabilities to outcomes and rewards, with higher probabilities generating higher motivation. Although expectancy theory has been tested with conflicting results, it can probably be used to give us a better understanding of the complexities of the budgeting process.[5]

The needed participation leading to goal congruence can be difficult to achieve. In many cases, individual goals will be in conflict with long-established company goals that focus attention on profit maximization. This may require a review and realignment of goals on the part of top-management leaders. Participation and concern for goal congruence are only part of the solution.

As efforts are expended to develop active participation and cooperation in the budgeting process, managers must be encouraged not to build abnormal slack into their projections. **Slack,** or *padding,* is defined as the difference between minimum required costs and budgeted costs proposed by a company segment. Anytime the budget is viewed as a rigid control tool, managers may attempt to build in slack as a protective device. For example, assume a manager has negotiated an $80,000 cost budget for her department even though a more realistic budget might have been $60,000. The manager now has some flexibility that can be used in avoiding any potential negative consequences from exceeding realistic costs.

☐ BUDGET ADMINISTRATION

Employee concerns about budgeting programs can be overcome with top-management support and proper administration of the budget. An effective administrative framework should be established that will encourage participation and provide the basis for successful implementation and follow-up of the budgeting program. For instance, one of the worst possible approaches is to have the accounting department charged with development and implementation of the program. However, this does happen, as indicated in the following situation:

> In the managers' meeting of Haseman Company, the new executive vice-president asked one of the divisional managers to discuss his budget proposal. The divisional manager quickly replied that he would need to call in his controller since, 'those people develop the sales forecasts and related operating schedules.'

In the case just cited, responsibility has been effectively removed from those in the division who should have contributed to the divisional budget.

---

5. J. Ronen and J. L. Livingstone, "An Expectancy Theory Approach to the Motivational Impact of Budgets," *The Accounting Review* (October 1975):671–685.

Line-management personnel should have primary responsibility for the development of individual components of the budget. Nevertheless, there is need for a technically competent individual to provide assistance and to assume responsibility for formalization of the overall budget. Consequently, a budget director is sometimes appointed to administer the total budgeting program. The director should coordinate the different phases of the program, assemble the various components of the budget, and identify and correct problems as they arise.

A budget committee is often appointed to provide advice to the director and help to coordinate the various budgeting activities. The committee typically includes senior management, or their representatives, from the various operating areas. However, the actual composition of the committee depends on the philosophy of the company with respect to the type of budgeting program desired. As a minimum, the presence of the committee, if staffed by top-level executives, lends credence to the process and indicates a strong management commitment to budgeting.

The final step in the administration of budgets is to insure that the budgets are used as a performance measurement and evaluation tool. As indicated earlier, budgets should be incorporated into the reporting system within a responsibility-accounting framework. Significant deviations from budgets need to be highlighted and explained on a timely basis.

☐ RESPONSIBILITY ACCOUNTING

Responsibility accounting is considered essential to the design of a good management system. Since many of the reports created in such a system are used by management for performance measurement, it is necessary that the information be presented with this objective in mind. Responsibility accounting views the organization as consisting of a group of responsibility centers (see chapter 17). The area of responsibility is usually defined in terms of one of the following:

1. *Cost center.* A responsibility center in which the supervisor is responsible only for costs. Controllable costs should be segregated from noncontrollable direct and allocated costs assigned to the center.

2. *Profit center.* A center in which revenues are matched against applicable expenses.

3. *Investment center.* A center in which managers have responsibility for both investments and profits.

Product-cost-determination systems were initially developed to provide manufacturing cost data for the purpose of preparing financial statements. These systems continue to be geared to determining how much of a particular manufacturing cost should be attached to a unit of output as it moves through the production process. With responsibility accounting, these systems can be upgraded for management-control purposes by employing budgets. The variances between actual and budgeted costs, by departments (cost centers), can be used by management personnel in their periodic performance measurement and evaluation of the operations.

Only those costs that are under the control of management at the responsibility center should be emphasized in a responsibility-accounting system. The objective is to associate costs with the locations within the organization where the decision to incur the cost was made. Other direct and allocated costs, if assigned to the center, should be segregated and clearly labeled. Figure 7.2 is an example of a set of responsibility reports for an organization.

In this sample report, both budgeted and actual costs are reported for the current period and the year-to-date. The same format is employed in reporting variances, which are defined as the difference between the budgeted and actual amounts. These variances enable the management team to make use of the exception principle in identifying problem areas at any

FIGURE 7.2
Responsibility Reports

President — Monthly Responsibility Report

	Budget Current Month	Budget Year-to-date	Actual Current Month	Actual Year-to-date	Variances Current Month	Variances Year-to-date
Vice-Pres. Prod.	$236,500	$ 730,000	$235,700	$ 733,500	$ 800	$ (3,500)
Vice-Pres. Market	126,000	360,000	131,000	378,000	(5,000)	(18,000)
Vice-Pres. Research	60,000	180,000	58,000	176,000	2,000	4,000
Controller	27,000	81,000	26,200	78,000	800	3,000
Total control. costs	$449,500	$1,351,000	$450,900	$1,365,500	$(1,400)	$(14,500)

Vice-President—Production — Monthly Responsibility Performance Report

	Budget Current Month	Budget Year-to-date	Actual Current Month	Actual Year-to-date	Variances Current Month	Variances Year-to-date
Foundry	$ 68,000	$210,000	$ 65,500	$202,000	2,500	$ 8,000
Machining dept.	81,500	258,000	83,400	262,500	(1,900)	(4,500)
Finishing dept.	42,000	130,000	40,000	133,000	2,000	(3,000)
Shipping dept.	27,000	78,000	27,800	83,000	(800)	(5,000)
Warehouse	18,000	54,000	19,000	53,000	(1,000)	1,000
Total control. costs	$236,500	$730,000	$235,700	$733,500	$ 800	$ (3,500)

Machining Department — Monthly Responsibility Performance Report

	Budget Current Month	Budget Year-to-date	Actual Current Month	Actual Year-to-date	Variances Current Month	Variances Year-to-date
Direct materials	$12,000	$ 36,000	$12,500	$ 38,000	$ (500)	$(2,500)
Direct labor	40,000	120,000	43,000	127,000	(3,000)	(7,000)
Lubricants	6,000	20,000	6,300	19,700	(300)	300
Set-up	8,000	31,000	7,400	29,300	600	1,700
Machine tolls	5,000	17,000	5,400	18,500	(400)	(1,500)
Rework	7,500	24,000	6,100	21,500	1,400	2,500
Other	3,000	10,000	2,700	8,500	300	1,500
Total control. costs	$81,500	$258,000	$83,400	$262,500	$(900)	$(6,000)

level within the organization. Performance measurement in these responsibility or decision centers is based on some cost, profit, or return-on-investment objective (chapter 19).

☐ FORECASTING REQUIREMENTS AND BUDGETING COMPONENTS

The sales forecast usually represents the starting point for the quantification and development of the entire budget. Responsibility for the forecast lies with marketing management personnel and marketing research personnel. Whatever approach to the forecasting process is taken, management people must first analyze all the relevant information related to past, present, and future marketing policies along with other items such as:

1. Past sales volume and trends
2. Market share and potential
3. Economic indicators
4. Product mix profitability
5. Sensitivity of market to prices and advertising
6. Quality of product and sales force
7. Sales indicators
8. Operating conditions and business environment.

In its most subjective form, sales forecasting involves asking marketing personnel to make sales projections by territories and product. Prior-year performance usually serves as the basis for this kind of projection. Input on economic indicators, advertising, and other relevant factors can then be used to adjust the data as they flow from individual sales personnel through the various marketing management levels.

A slightly more sophisticated approach might involve the use of a qualitative method such as the "Delphi method."[6] This method reflects an attempt to solicit information from a panel of experts, perhaps managers, by means of a series of questionnaires. As each questionnaire is completed, data are refined and questionnaires resubmitted until acceptable information is obtained. The "Delphi" or other similar methods might be especially appropriate if historical data are limited, if significant changes have taken place, or if new products are to be introduced.

Time-series analysis can be used for sales forecasting when historical data are available and when the relationship between sales trends and time appears to be clear and relatively stable. Examples of this type of technique are *moving average* and *exponential smoothing*. Because of the problem with changing conditions, these methods are typically used only for projections over the short term.

6. John C. Chambers, Satinder K. Mullick, and Donald D. Smith, "How to Choose the Right Forecasting Technique," *Harvard Business Review* (July-August 1971):45–74.

Other causal methods might be used where potential explanatory variable components can be found that are closely correlated with the company's or industry's sales. These methods make use of *regression analysis* and *econometrics*.[7] Explanatory variables should be sought that are useful for predicting company or industry sales. It would be of little or no use to have indicators that move exactly with sales—such as number of automobiles manufactured as a basis for predicting demand for original equipment tires—since the manufacture of each takes place at about the same time. However, the number of automobiles manufactured might provide the basis for predicting sales of replacement tires.

☐ THE BUDGETING PROCESS ILLUSTRATED

Once the sales forecast has been finalized, the production and sales budgets can be prepared. Using these budgets as a basis, other budgets, such as direct materials (purchasing), direct labor, and overhead (expense) can then be prepared. Finally, projected financial statements and cash-flow projections can be derived. This overall process is depicted for a manufacturing company in figure 7.3.

To illustrate the budgeting process, a **master budget** for the first quarter of 19X4 for the Novel Company is presented. The company manufactures two products, bottles and boxes, for sale to dealers. The following initial information is needed for preparation of the master budget:

Selling price for products manufactured

Bottles	$50
Boxes	$65

Product requirements per unit of finished product

	Bottles	Boxes
Material A	2 lb	6 lb
Material S	4 lb	2 lb
Direct labor	4 hr	6 hr

Material and labor cost data for 1/1/X4
Material A, $1 per lb
Material S, $2 per lb
Direct labor, $4 per hr

Trial balance on 12/31/X3

	Debit	Credit
Cash	$ 180,000	
Accounts receivable	373,000	
Material A (40,000 × $2)	80,000	
Material S (20,000 × $4)	80,000	
Bottles (2,000 × $44)	88,000	
Boxes (4,000 × $52)	208,000	
Land	150,000	
Building and equipment	1,000,000	
Allowance for depreciation		$ 320,000
Accounts payable		220,000

7. *Ibid.*, p. 50.

Taxes payable		40,000
Capital stock		1,000,000
Retained earnings		579,000
Total	$2,159,000	$2,159,000

FIGURE 7.3
Comprehensive
Budgeting for a
Manufacturing
Company

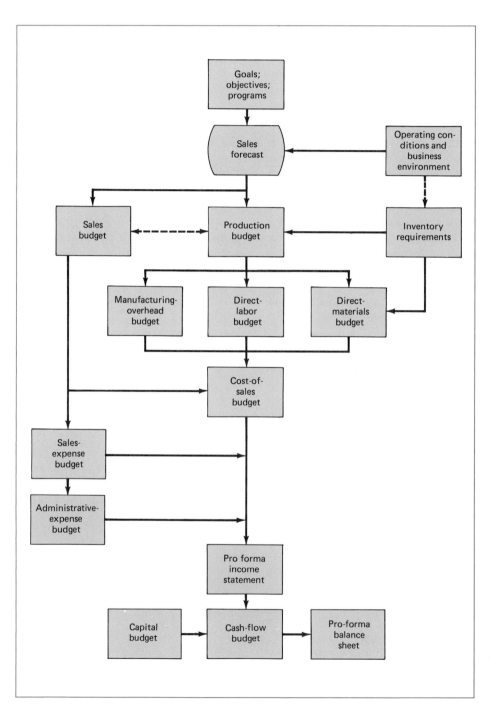

Desired inventory end of each month
The company desires to maintain inventories equal to next month's production/sales needs.

Other information
1. All sales are on account. Approximately 40 percent are collected in month of sale, 50 percent in the month after sale, and 9 percent in the second month after sale. The balance results in bad debts.
2. On January 1, 19X4, the accounts-receivable balance is broken down as follows:

From November	$ 48,500
From December	324,500
	$373,000

3. Cash-disbursement requirements
   a. Raw materials are paid in month following purchase.
   b. Direct labor is paid in month incurred.
   c. Manufacturing, selling, and administrative-expense disbursements are spread over month incurred and subsequent month, with 50 percent being paid in each month.
   d. Income taxes are assumed to be paid in the month following the end of a quarter.
4. The accounts payable on January 1, 19X4, consists of the following:

Raw-material purchases	$120,000
Various expenses	100,000
	$220,000

5. The income tax rate is 40 percent.
6. Changes have taken place in raw-material prices and raw-material requirements that cause a change in product costs. Inventories should be based on the FIFO method.

The company has appointed a budget director who operates under the direction of a budget committee. Information is sent to the committee, which acts and forwards decisions to the budget director for incorporation into the budget.

The Sales Budget

As indicated in figure 7.3, the sales forecast provides the basis for development of other segments of the budget. The sales budget should show units expected to be sold by month for the quarter. Budgeted sales for the Novel Company are shown in figure 7.4, assuming the units shown have been provided by a sales forecast.

The Production Budget

After the sales budget has been completed, the production requirements can be calculated. This budget should reflect needed production by month

Product	January Units	Revenues	February Units	Revenues	March Units	Revenues	Total Revenues
Bottles	3,000	$150,000	4,000	$200,000	5,000	$250,000	$ 600,000
Boxes	6,000	390,000	5,000	325,000	5,000	325,000	1,040,000
		$540,000		$525,000		$575,000	$1,640,000

FIGURE 7.4 Novel Company—Sales Budget by Month for First Quarter

for the quarter. Since production requirements call for a consideration of beginning and ending inventories, the process involves adding sales and ending inventory needs and then subtracting the beginning inventory. Figure 7.5 shows the Novel Company production budget for the quarter by month. For purposes of completing the budget, *assume forecasted sales for April are the same as for February.*

The Materials and Direct-Labor Budgets

From the production budget, materials and direct-labor budgets can be developed if the material and direct labor to be used in each product have previously been estimated (this information is provided in the first part of the section). Figures 7.6 and 7.7 present these two budgets.

The Manufacturing, Selling, and Administrative-Expense Budgets

The Novel Company budgets for manufacturing overhead and selling and administrative expenses are given in figures 7.8 and 7.9.

FIGURE 7.5
Novel Company—
Production Budget
for First Quarter

	Bottles		
	January	*February*	*March*
Sales requirements (see figure 7.4)	3,000	4,000	5,000
Desired ending inventory (based on sales)	4,000	5,000	4,000
Total	7,000	9,000	9,000
Beginning inventory	2,000	4,000	5,000
Production requirements	5,000	5,000	4,000

	Boxes		
	January	*February*	*March*
Sales requirements (see figure 7.4)	6,000	5,000	5,000
Desired ending inventory (based on sales)	5,000	5,000	5,000
Total	11,000	10,000	10,000
Beginning inventory	4,000	5,000	5,000
Production requirements	7,000	5,000	5,000

Recap of material production requirements

	Material		
	A	*S*	
Unit purchases requirement	130,000	100,000	(see figure 7.6)
From ending inventory	40,000	30,000	
Total	90,000	70,000	
Unit cost	$1	$2	
Total	$ 90,000	$140,000	
From beginning inventory	80,000	80,000	
Material production costs	$170,000	$220,000	

		Material A	
	January	February	March
Production requirements (from figure 7.5)			
Bottles (2 × production)	10,000	10,000	8,000
Boxes (6 × production)	42,000	30,000	30,000
Total	52,000	40,000	38,000
Desired ending inventory (based on production)	40,000	38,000	40,000
Total	92,000	78,000	78,000
Beginning inventory	40,000	40,000	38,000
Purchasing requirements	52,000	38,000	40,000
Unit cost	$1	$1	$1
Dollar requirements	$52,000	$38,000	$40,000

		Material S	
	January	February	March
Production requirements (from figure 7.5)			
Bottles (4 × production)	20,000	20,000	16,000
Boxes (2 × production)	14,000	10,000	10,000
Total	34,000	30,000	26,000
Desired ending inventory (based on production)	30,000	26,000	30,000
Total	64,000	56,000	56,000
Beginning inventory	20,000	30,000	26,000
Purchasing requirements	44,000	26,000	30,000
Unit cost	$2	$2	$2
Dollar requirements	$88,000	$52,000	$60,000

	January	February	March
Production requirements (from figure 7.5)			
Bottles (4 × production)	20,000	20,000	16,000
Boxes (6 × production)	42,000	30,000	30,000
Direct-labor hours required	62,000	50,000	46,000
Direct-labor cost per hour	$4	$4	$4
Total direct-labor costs	$248,000	$200,000	$184,000

Cash Collections and Disbursements

The Novel Company expects to finance its operations through internally generated funds. Consequently, outside financing is undertaken only when cash flows from revenues fall short of immediate needs. Collections and disbursements are shown in figures 7.10 and 7.11.

FIGURE 7.8
Novel Company—
Manufacturing-
Overhead Budget

	January	February	March	Total
Expected hours (from figure 7.7)	62,000	50,000	46,000	158,000
Expected overhead costs				
Variable ($2 per DLH)	$124,000	$100,000	$ 92,000	$316,000
Fixed*	79,000	79,000	79,000	237,000
Total	$203,000	$179,000	$171,000	$553,000

*Includes depreciation of $10,000
Fixed overhead rate: $237,000 ÷ 158,000 = $1.50

FIGURE 7.9
Novel Company—
Selling and
Administrative-
Expense Budget

	January	February	March	Total
Projected sales (from figure 7.4) ...	$540,000	$525,000	$575,000	$1,640,000
Expected expenses				
Variable (5% × sales)	$ 27,000	$ 26,250	$ 28,750	$ 82,000
Fixed*	40,000	40,000	40,000	120,000
Total	$ 67,000	$ 66,250	$ 68,750	$ 202,000

*Includes depreciation of $5,000

FIGURE 7.10
Novel Company—
Schedule of
Accounts
Receivable
Collections*

		Collections	
Month	January	February	March
From November	$ 48,500		
From December	275,000	$ 49,500	
From January	216,000	270,000	$ 48,600
From February		210,000	262,500
From March			230,000
	$539,500	$529,500	$541,100

*Bad-debt expense and accounts receivable (March 31)

From month	Bad-debt expense	Accounts receivable
January	$ 5,400	$ 0
February	5,250	47,250
March	5,750	339,250
	$16,400	$386,500

In the schedule of accounts receivable collections, the balance of $373,000 shown at December 31, 19X3, includes $48,500 from November and $324,500 from December. Since the $324,500 represents 59 percent of December sales (see other information on p. 211), February collections for December sales are $49,500 ($550,000 × .09). It is assumed that December uncollectible account expenses are recognized in month of sale.

In the schedule of cash disbursements, the accounts payable balance from December 31, 19X3, is shown as December purchases, $120,000, and December expenses, $100,000. The rest of the payments are taken directly from the indicated schedules.

FIGURE 7.11
Novel Company—
Schedule of Cash
Disbursements*

	January	Payments February	March
Raw materials			
December purchases	$120,000		
January purchases (from figure 7.6)		$140,000	
February purchases (from figure 7.6)			$ 90,000
Expenses (manufacturing, selling, and administrative)			
December	100,000		
January (from figures 7.8 and 7.9)	127,500	127,500	
February (from figures 7.8 and 7.9)		115,125	115,125
March (from figures 7.8 and 7.9)			112,375
Direct labor (from figure 7.7)	248,000	200,000	184,000
Taxes payable	40,000		
	$635,500	$582,625	$501,500

*Accounts payable on March 31

Source	Amount
Expenses (from figures 7.8 and 7.9)	$112,375
Raw materials (from figure 7.6)	100,000
	$212,375

Since the company does not attempt to maintain a minimum cash balance, the only need for external funds would arise when receipts are expected to be insufficient to cover disbursements for a quarter. The cash-flow budget is shown in figure 7.12.

The cash-flow budget does not indicate an immediate problem with respect to the company's cash position. However, management officials of the Novel Company should be concerned about the indicated reduction in future cash balances. They may have to consider temporary or long-term financing, especially if the projected level of sales is expected to continue for the balance of the year.

Financial Statements

The final step in developing a master budget is to prepare projected financial statements. Along with the cash-flow statement, these documents can be used to gain a better understanding of expectations and reasons

FIGURE 7.12
Novel Company—
Summary Cash-
Flow Budget

	January	February	March
Beginning cash	$180,000	$ 84,000	$ 30,875
Cash collections (from figure 7.10)	539,500	529,500	541,100
Total	$719,500	$613,500	$571,975
Cash disbursements (from figure 7.11)	635,500	582,625	501,500
Ending cash	$ 84,000	$ 30,875	$ 70,475

for changes that are revealed by the statements. Figure 7.13 presents the income statement and figure 7.14 shows the balance sheet.

☐ THE DECISION ASPECTS OF BUDGETING

The final budget reflects an integration of many decisions that must be coordinated and tied together. Starting with the sales estimate, decisions have to be made with respect to product mix, prices, promotional efforts, and the effect of varying economic conditions on sales. In the production area, decisions have to be made regarding effects of stock-outs and optimal inventory levels and production schedules.

Decisions also have to be made regarding the most efficient organization and operating methods; type and quality of labor that will probably be needed; fixed and variable cost relationships; credit policies; and perhaps minimum cash balances needed. Certainly, decisions have to be made regarding prospects for new capital facilities. These are only a few of the multitude of decisions that are reflected in the final budget. All too often the importance and difficulties involved in budgeting are overlooked be-

FIGURE 7.13
Novel Company—
Projected Income
Statement

Sales (from figure 7.4)			$1,640,000
Cost of sales (see below)			1,436,000
Gross profit			$ 204,000
Selling and administrative expenses (from figure 7.9)			202,000
Bad-debt expense (from figure 7.10)			16,400
Total expenses			$ 218,400
Net loss			$ 14,400

Cost-of-sales schedule
Raw materials

Beginning inventory		$160,000	
Purchases (from figure 7.6)		330,000	
Total		$490,000	
Ending inventory (from figure 7.14)		100,000	$ 390,000
Direct labor (from figure 7.7)			632,000
Manufacturing overhead (from figure 7.8)			553,000
Total manufacturing costs			$1,575,000
Beginning finished goods			296,000
Total			$1,871,000
Ending finished goods (from figure 7.14)			435,000
Cost of sales			$1,436,000

Ending finished goods unit costs

Material	Bottles	Boxes
A	$ 2	$ 6
S	8	4
Direct labor	16	24
Manufacturing overhead		
$3.50 per DLH	14	21
	$40	$55

FIGURE 7.14
Novel Company—
Projected Balance
Sheet

Current assets		
Cash (from figure 7.12)		$ 70,475
Net accounts receivable (from figure 7.10)		386,500
Inventories		
Raw materials (1)	$ 100,000	
Finished goods (2)	435,000	535,000
Property, plant, and equipment		
Land	$ 150,000	
Building and equipment	1,000,000	
Allowance for depreciation (3)	<365,000>	785,000
Total assets		$1,776,975
Current liabilities		
Accounts payable (from figure 7.11)		$ 212,375
Stockholders' equity		
Capital stock	$1,000,000	
Retained earnings (4)	564,600	1,564,600
Total liabilities and stockholders' equity		$1,776,975

(1) Beginning inventory + purchases − production = ending inventory
$160,000 + $330,000 − $390,000 = $100,000

(2) Beginning inventory + production − cost of sales = ending inventory
$296,000 + $1,575,000 − $1,436,000 = $435,000

(3) $320,000 + [(3 × $10,000) + (3 × $5,000) = $365,000

(4) $579,000 − $14,400 (net loss) = $564,600

cause of undue concentration on the mechanical aspects of assembling the many different components of the budget.

☐ SUMMARY

Budgeting is the formalization of the planning process. The budget reflects planning in the form of a detailed written expression of the management team's expectations for some future period of time. A master budget reflects total plans and an attempt to integrate planning and control.

Budgeting should help management personnel identify and pursue the more promising courses of action in light of limitations imposed by the known business environment. In effect, budgeting should aid planning and provide a means for properly communicating and coordinating plans so that personnel will be properly motivated. Control, in the sense of a monitoring device, should also be provided by budgeting.

The proper recognition of behavioral factors are essential to a successful budgeting program. Active participation on the part of relevant personnel and a high level of goal congruence are considered essential. This comes from development of a proper structure for the budgeting program and by implementing a sound, participative program.

The starting point for the budget is the sales forecast. From this, a production schedule can be developed, which in turn provides the basis for development of material, direct-labor, and manufacturing-overhead budgets. These, along with sales and administrative-expense budgets, provide necessary input for development of the cash-flow budget and projected financial statements.

KEY TERMS

Budgeting	**Master (comprehensive) budget**
Capital budget	**Responsibility accounting**
Employee behavior	**Slack**
Flexible budget	**Static budget**
Goal congruence	

REVIEW PROBLEM

The XYZ Company manufactures two products, APBs and SASs, for sale to dealers. In order to simplify the situation, it is assumed that the master budget is being prepared immediately after the close of the year 19X3. The following information is presented for XYZ Company.

Product requirements

	APB	SAS
Material A	2 lb	4 lb
Material S	4 lb	2 lb
Direct labor	4 hr	6 hr

Inventory and labor cost data
Material A, $2 per lb
Material S, $4 per lb
Direct labor, $4 per hr

Trial balance on 12/31/X3

Cash	$36,400
Accounts receivable	8,600
Material A (4,000 @ $2)	8,000
Material S (2,500 @ $4)	10,000
APB (200 × $44)	8,800
SAS (400 × $52)	20,800
Land	20,000
Building and equipment	60,000
Allowance for depreciation	<20,000>
Accounts payable	<24,000>
Taxes payable	<16,000>
Capital stock	<80,000>
Retained earnings	<32,600>

Desired inventory on 12/31/X4

Material A	5,000 units
Material B	4,000 units
APB	250 units
SAS	500 units

The company has appointed a budget director who operates under the direction of a budget committee. Information is sent to the committee, which acts on it and forwards decisions to the budget director for incorporation into the budget.

Additional information is provided on sales, manufacturing expense, selling and administrative expense, and expected cash flows as follows:

Sales budget

Product	Units	Unit price	Expected revenues
APB	3,000	$50	$150,000
SAS	6,000	65	390,000
			$540,000

Manufacturing-expense budget*

Supervision and inspection	$30,000
Factory depreciation	22,000
Taxes	3,520
Insurance	600
Repairs and maintenance	12,000
Supplies	15,000
Heat and light	2,480
Energy	12,000
	$97,600

*Actual overhead is allocated to products produced based on direct-labor hours used.

Selling and administrative-expense budget

Salaries	$42,000
Sales commissions	10,800
Advertising and promotion	12,000
Depreciation	1,200
Office supplies	500
Taxes	100
Insurance	100
Miscellaneous	200
	$66,900

The company expects to finance its operations through internally generated funds. Consequently, outside financing is undertaken only when cash flows from revenues fall short of immediate needs. Expected cash flows are shown below by quarter:

	Quarter			
	1	2	3	4
Sales collections	$120,000	$126,000	$142,000	$151,000
Expenditures				
Materials	36,050	40,000	42,000	45,400
Direct labor	46,000	50,000	49,800	49,400
Other expenses	15,200	29,520	41,000	55,580
Income taxes	16,000			

Required □ Prepare a master budget for the XYZ Company that includes a projected income statement and balance sheet.

Solution □

Sales budget
   Given in the problem.

Production budget

	Product	
	APB	SAS
Expected sales	3,000	6,000
Ending inventory planned	250	500
	3,250	6,500
Beginning inventory	200	400
Production required	3,050	6,100

Materials budget

	Material	
	A	S
Production required	30,500(1)	24,400(2)
Ending inventory planned	5,000	4,000
	35,500	28,400
Beginning inventory	4,000	2,500
Pounds of material needed	31,500	25,900
Unit cost	$2	$4
Material requirements in dollars	$63,000	$103,600

(1) (3,050 × 2) + (6,100 × 4) = 30,500
(2) (3,050 × 4) + (6,100 × 2) = 24,400

Direct-labor budget

	APB	SAS
Production requirements	3,050	6,100
Hours required per unit of product	4	6
Total hours needed for production	12,200	36,600
Labor rate per hour	$4	$4
Total labor costs required	$48,800	$146,400

Manufacturing-expense budget
   Given in the problem.

Selling and administrative-expense budget
   Given in the problem.

Cash-flow budget

	Quarter			
	1	2	3	4
Beginning cash	$ 36,400	$ 43,150	$ 49,630	$ 58,830
Receipts				
Collections	120,000	126,000	142,000	151,000
Disbursements				
Materials	36,050	40,000	42,000	45,400
Direct labor	46,000	50,000	49,800	49,400
Other expenses	15,200	29,520	41,000	55,580
Income taxes	16,000			
	$113,250	$119,520	$132,800	$150,380
Ending cash	$ 43,150	$ 49,630	$ 58,830	$ 59,450

Projected income

Sales	$540,000
Cost of sales	444,000 (1)
Gross profit	$ 96,000
Selling and admin. expenses	66,900
Net income before taxes	$ 29,100
Provision for income taxes	8,000
Net income	$ 21,100

	Product	
	APB	SAS
(1) Unit costs		
Material	20	16
Labor	16	24
Overhead ($2 per DLH)	8	12
	$44	$52
Units sold	3,000	6,000
Cost of sales by product	$132,000	$312,000

Projected balance sheet

Current assets		
Cash		$ 59,450
Accounts receivable		9,600
Inventories		
Raw materials	$26,000	
Finished goods	37,000	63,000
Property, plant, and equipment		
Land	$20,000	
Buildings and equipment	60,000	
Allowance for depreciation	<43,200>	36,800
Total assets		$168,850
Current liabilities		
Accounts payable		$ 27,150
Taxes payable		8,000
Total liabilities		$ 35,150
Stockholders' equity		
Capital stock	$80,000	
Retained earnings	53,700	
Total stockholders' equity		133,700
Total liabilities and stockholders' equity		$168,850

QUESTIONS

Q7-1.   Describe the process of budgeting.

Q7-2.   What are the purposes of budgeting?

Q7-3.   Discuss the similarities and differences between a master budget and a flexible budget.

Q7-4.   How are budgets related to control?

Q7-5.   Why is the sales forecast usually considered the starting point for budgets?

Q7-6. Identify some of the methods available for developing the sales forecast.

Q7-7. Discuss the function of the budget committee.

Q7-8. What are some of the prerequisites for a successful budgeting program?

Q7-9. Why is the notion of goal congruence and participation essential to budgeting?

Q7-10. Describe some of the decisions integrated in budgets.

Q7-11. What is responsibility accounting? Discuss.

Q7-12. How is responsibility accounting related to budgeting?

PROBLEMS

Production Schedule

P7-1. The projected sales, in units, for the ABC Company by month for the first four months were:

January	10,000
February	15,000
March	20,000
April	24,000

Inventory of finished goods on December 31 was 8,000 units. The company desires to have an ending inventory each month of one-half of next month's estimated sales.

Required □ Determine the company's production requirements for each month of the first quarter.

Production and Related Schedules

P7-2. The XYZ Company manufactures and sells two products, balls and squares. Estimated needs for a unit of each are:

	Balls	Squares
Material A	2 lb	1 lb
Material B	4 lb	4 lb
Direct labor	2 hr	2 hr

Overhead is applied on the basis of $2 per direct-labor hour.

The estimated sales by product for 19X5 are:

	Balls	Squares
Sales	42,000	24,000

The beginning inventories are expected to be as follows:

Material A	4,000 lb
Material B	6,000 lb
Balls	1,000 units
Squares	500 units

The desired inventories are one month's requirements, assuming constant sales throughout the year.

Required ☐ Prepare the following information.

a. Production schedule
b. Purchases budget
c. Direct-labor budget
d. Overhead to be charged to production

P7-3. Your company has prepared a sales forecast calling for 96,000 units to be sold in the first quarter. Information on finished-goods inventory is provided below: *Budgeted Material Purchases*

	1/1	3/31
Estimated finished goods	40,000	48,000

In manufacturing your product it takes 2 pounds of material X and 1 gallon of material Y to produce one unit of finished product. Direct material inventories are as follows:

	1/1	3/31
Estimated X	80,000	85,000
Estimated Y	40,000	38,000

Required ☐ Prepare a purchases budget for the first quarter.

P7-4. The dollar sales of the ABC Company for the first four months are expected to be: *Budgeted Cash-Flow Statement*

January	$50,000
February	60,000
March	70,000
April	80,000

The receivable balance on December 31 is $28,000. Sales are collected 50 percent in the month of sale and 25 percent in each of the next two months. Of the December balance, $10,000 related to November sales.

Expected expenditures are as follows:

	Materials	Labor	Overhead	Other
January	10,000	8,000	12,000	14,000
February	20,000	16,000	20,000	8,000
March	25,000	18,000	24,000	4,000
April	28,000	20,000	26,000	6,000

The beginning cash balance is $10,000, and the company would like to maintain this minimum cash balance at the end of each month. Assume loans, if needed, are interest-free.

Required ☐ Prepare a budgeted cash-flow statement for ABC Company for the four months.

P7-5. The December 31, 19X3, balance sheet of Margink Company is as follows: *Budgeted Cash-Flow Statement*

Cash	$ 40,000
Accounts receivable	60,000
Inventory	42,000

Fixed assets (less $40,000
    accumulated depreciation) 60,000
                                                                                 $202,000

Accounts payable	$ 68,000
Common stock	40,000
Retained earnings	94,000
	$202,000

Additional information is presented below:

■ Projected sales for first quarter

January	$120,000
February	$160,000
March	$210,000

■ Collections on sales are expected to be 60 percent in month of sales, and 20 percent each of the next two months.

■ Purchases are based on 50 percent of the next month's sales and are paid in full the month following purchase.

■ Selling and administrative expenses are $24,000 per month, including $4,000 depreciation.

■ Assume accounts receivable at December 31 will be evenly distributed over the next two months.

Required ☐ Prepare a cash-flow budget for the first quarter.

Projected Income **P7-6.** Last year's income statement for XYZ Company is presented as follows:
Statement

Sales (50,000 × $10)		$500,000
Cost of sales		
Direct materials	$200,000	
Direct labor	100,000	
Overhead	50,000	350,000
Gross profit		$150,000
Expenses		
Selling	$ 60,000	
Administrative	40,000	100,000
Net income before taxes		$ 50,000

Sales are expected to decrease by 10 percent, and material and labor costs are expected to increase by 10 percent. Overhead is applied to production based on a percentage of direct-labor costs. Ten thousand dollars of selling expenses are considered fixed. The balance varies with dollar sales. All administrative costs are fixed.

Management personnel desire to earn 5 percent on sales this year and will adjust the unit selling price, if necessary.

Required ☐ Develop a pro forma income statement for the year for XYZ Company that incorporates the indicated changes.

P7-7. The budget director of the Smooth Flow Company, Inc., plans to develop a master budget for next year. Information relating to last year is as follows:

Master Budget and Financial Statements

Trial balance

Cash		$10,000
Accounts receivable		5,000
Inventories		
Raw material A (4,000 × $2)	$ 8,000	
Finished goods (500 × $20)	10,000	18,000
Fixed assets	$50,000	
Accumulated depreciation	(10,000)	40,000
Accounts payable		(16,000)
Capital stock		(40,000)
Retained earnings		(17,000)

The company produces a single product that requires the following:

	Product
Direct material	4 lb
Direct labor	2 hr
Factory overhead	$2 per DLH

The direct-labor rate is expected to be $4 per hour, the same as last year. Material cost is not expected to change from last year's cost.

The accounts receivable at year-end are expected to be $10,000 and accounts payable $18,000. Only purchases of raw materials are involved in the accounts-payable balance. Selling and administrative expenses for the year are expected to be $20,000, of which $2,000 is for depreciation. Factory overhead for the year is assumed to equal the amount of overhead applied to production and includes $4,000 of depreciation.

The company expects to sell 2,000 units for the year. Estimated selling price is $40 per unit. A raw-materials inventory of 6,000 pounds and a finished-goods inventory of 600 units are desired.

Required ☐ Develop a master budget, including the pro forma financial statements, for Smooth Flow Company, Inc.

P7-8. The Scarborough Corporation manufactures and sells two products, Thingone and Thingtwo. In July 19X7, Budget department managers gathered the following data in order to project sales and budget requirements for 19X8.

Various Budgeting Schedules

19X8 projected sales

Product	Units	Price
Thingone	60,000	$ 70
Thingtwo	40,000	$100

19X8 inventories—In units

Product	Expected January 1, 19X8	Desired December 31, 19X8
Thingone	20,000	25,000
Thingtwo	8,000	9,000

In order to produce one unit of Thingone and Thingtwo, the following raw materials are used:

		Amount used per unit	
Raw material	Unit	Thingone	Thingtwo
A	lb	4	5
B	lb	2	3
C	each		1

Projected data for 19X8 with respect to raw materials is as follows:

Raw Material	Anticipated purchase price	Expected inventories January 1, 19X8	Desired inventories December 31, 19X8
A	$8	32,000 lb	36,000 lb
B	$5	29,000 lb	32,000 lb
C	$3	6,000 each	7,000 each

Projected direct-labor requirements for 19X8 and rates are as follows:

Product	Hours per unit	Rate per hour
Thingone	2	$3
Thingtwo	3	$4

Overhead is applied at the rate of $2 per direct-labor hour.

Required □ Based upon the above projections and budget requirements for 19X8 for Thingone and Thingtwo, prepare the following budgets for 19X8:

a. Sales budget (in dollars)
b. Production budget (in units)
c. Raw-materials purchase budget (in quantities)
d. Raw-materials purchase budget (in dollars)
e. Direct-labor budget (in dollars)
f. Budgeted finished-goods inventory on December 31, 19X8 (in dollars).

(CPA)

Multiple-Choice Items— Budgeting

P7-9. Select the best answer for the following multiple-choice items:

1. The management team at the Jasmin Corporation is preparing the master budget for the year. In developing the cash-budget portion, the following projections were made:

Projected sales for the year	$2,800,000
Gross profit expected	40 percent
Decrease in inventories	$ 70,000
Reduction in accounts payable due to inventories	$ 150,000

What is Jasmin's estimated cash disbursements required for inventories?

a. 1,200,000
b. 1,040,000

    c. 1,760,000
    d. 1,600,000

Items 2, 3, and 4 are based on the following information:

The January 31, 19X1, balance sheet of Shelpat Corporation follows:

Cash	$ 8,000
Accounts receivable (net of allowance for uncollectible accounts	
of $2,000)	38,000
Inventory	16,000
Property, plant, and equipment	
(Net of allowance for accumulated depreciation of $60,000)	40,000
	$102,000
Accounts payable	$ 82,500
Common stock	50,000
Retained earnings (deficit)	(30,500)
	$102,000

Additional information:

■ Sales are budgeted as follows:
    February $110,000
    March $120,000

■ Collections are expected to be 60 percent in the month of sale, 38 percent the next month, and 2 percent uncollectible.

■ Shelpat's gross margin is 25 percent of sales. Purchases each month are 75 percent of the next month's projected sales. The purchases are paid in full the following month.

■ Other expenses for each month, paid in cash, are expected to be $16,500. Depreciation each month is $5,000.

2. What are the budgeted cash collections for February 19X1?

    a. $63,800
    b. $66,000
    c. $101,800
    d. $104,000

3. What is the pro forma income (loss) before income taxes for February 19X1?

    a. ($3,700)
    b. ($1,500)
    c. $3,800
    d. $6,000

4. What is the projected balance in accounts payable on February 29, 19X1?

    a. $82,500
    b. $86,250
    c. $90,000
    d. $106,500

5. Betz Company's sales budget shows the following projections for the year ending December 31, 19X3:

Quarter	Units
First	60,000
Second	80,000
Third	45,000
Fourth	55,000
Total	240,000

Inventory on December 31, 19X2, was budgeted at 18,000 units. The quantity of finished-goods inventory at the end of each quarter is to equal 30 percent of the next quarter's budgeted sales of units. How much should the production budget show for units to be produced during the first quarter?

a. 24,000
b. 48,000
c. 66,000
d. 72,000

6. The budget director at the Pratt Company is preparing the cash budget for the month ending November 30, 19X2. The following information pertains to Pratt's past collection experience from its credit sales:

Current month's sales	12 percent
Prior month's sales	75 percent
Sales two months prior to current month	6 percent
Sales three months prior to current month	4 percent
Cash discounts (2/30, net 90)	2 percent
Doubtful accounts	1 percent

Credit sales	
November—estimated	$200,000
October	180,000
September	160,000
August	190,000

How much is the estimated credit to accounts receivable as a result of collections expected during November?

a. $170,200
b. $174,200
c. $176,200
d. $180,200

7. In preparing the budget for July 19X2, the management team of the Robinson Company has the following accounts receivable information available:

Accounts receivable on June 30, 19X2	$350,000
Estimated credit sales for July	400,000
Estimated collections in July for credit sales in July and prior months	320,000
Estimated write-offs in July for uncollectible credit sales	16,000
Estimated provision for doubtful accounts for credit sales in July	12,000

What is the projected balance of accounts receivable at July 31, 19X2?

a. $402,000
b. $414,000
c. $426,000
d. $430,000

8. Eriksen Company has budgeted its activity for October 19X2, based on the following information:

■ Sales are budgeted at $300,000. All sales are credit sales and a provision for doubtful accounts is made monthly at the rate of 3 percent of sales.

■ Merchandise inventory was $70,000 on September 30, 19X2, and an increase of $10,000 is planned for the month.

■ All merchandise is marked up to sell at invoice cost plus 50 percent.

■ Estimated cash disbursements for selling and administrative expenses for the month are $40,000.

■ Depreciation for the month is projected at $5,000.

Eriksen is projecting operating income for October 19X2 in the amount of

a. $96,000
b. $56,000
c. $55,000
d. $46,000

9. The management personnel of Walsh, Inc., is preparing its cash budget for the month of November. The following information is available concerning its inventories:

Inventories at beginning of November	$180,000
Estimated cost of goods sold for November	900,000
Estimated inventories at end of November	160,000
Estimated payments in November for purchases prior to November	210,000
Estimated payments in November for purchases in November	80 percent

What are the estimated cash disbursements for inventories in November?

a. $720,000
b. $914,000
c. $930,000
d. $1,042,000

10. Bert Company has projected cost of goods sold of $2,000,000, including fixed costs of $400,000 and variable costs that are expected to be 75 percent of net sales. What will be the projected net sales?

a. $2,133,333
b. $2,400,000
c. $2,666,667
d. $3,200,000

(CPA)

Cash Disbursements **P7-10.** In preparing its cash budget for September 19X4, Weisenfeld Company made the following projections related to cash disbursements:

Sales	$2,500,000
Gross margin percentage	20 percent
Decrease in inventories	$85,000
Decrease in accounts payable	$140,000

Assuming that the only transactions in accounts payable relate to the purchase of merchandise for resale, calculate the estimated cash disbursements for inventories during September.

Material Purchases Budget **P7-11.** A sales forecast for the first quarter of 19X5 is provided below for a major product line manufactured by Leslie, Inc.

Month	Units
January	12,000
February	14,500
March	16,000

The inventory of finished goods at the end of each month is expected to equal 20 percent of estimated sales for the next month. Assume April and May sales equal January sales. At December 31, there were 2,000 finished units on hand.

Two different types of materials are required to produce a finished unit. Materials and quantities are as follows:

Zinc	4 units
Iron	6 units

Materials equal to one-half of the next month's production requirements are expected in materials inventory at the end of each month. This requirement has consistently been met.

Required □ Prepare a material purchases budget for the first quarter. Show any supporting schedules needed.

Cash Receipts and Disbursements **P7-12.** Management of Ruf Company has projected the following activity for the month of June:

Revenues	$600,000
Gross margin percentage	25 percent
Increase in inventory during June	$8,000
Increase in accounts receivable during June	$20,000
Decrease in accounts payable during June	$10,000
Variable operating expenses, based on sales	10 percent
Fixed operating expenses, including depreciation	$40,000

Depreciation is $15,000. Assume expenses are paid in current month.

Required □ Estimate cash receipts and cash disbursements for June. Ignore any consideration of uncollectible account expense.

P7-13. You have been engaged to assist the management of the Stenger Corporation in making certain decisions. The Stenger Corporation has its home office in Philadelphia and leases factory buildings in Rhode Island, Georgia, and Illinois. The same single product is manufactured in all three factories. The following information is available regarding 19X4 operations:

Projected-Income Information

	Total	Rhode Island	Illinois	Georgia
Sales	$900,000	$200,000	$400,000	$300,000
Fixed costs				
Factory	180,000	50,000	55,000	75,000
Administration	59,000	16,000	21,000	22,000
Variable	500,000	100,000	220,000	180,000
Allocated home office				
expenses	63,000	14,000	28,000	21,000
Total	802,000	180,000	324,000	298,000
Net profit from				
operations	$ 98,000	$ 20,000	$ 76,000	$ 2,000

The home office expense is allocated on the basis of units sold. The sales price per unit is $10.

Management is undecided whether to renew the lease of the Georgia factory, which expires on December 31, 19X5, and will require an increase in rent of $15,000 per year if renewed. If the Georgia factory is shut down, the amount expected to be realized from the sale of the equipment is greater than its book value and would cover all termination expenses.

If the Georgia factory is shut down, the company can continue to serve customers of the Georgia factory by one of the following methods:

a. Expanding the Rhode Island factory, which would increase fixed costs by 15 percent. Additional shipping expense of $2 per unit will be incurred on the increased production.
b. Entering into a long-term contract with a competitor who will serve the Georgia factory customers and who will pay the Stenger Corporation a commission of $1.60 per unit.

The Stenger Corporation is also planning to establish a subsidiary corporation in Canada to produce the same product. Based on estimated annual Canadian sales of 40,000 units, cost studies produced the following estimates for the Canadian subsidiary:

	Total annual costs	Percent of total annual cost that is variable
Material	$193,600	100
Labor	90,000	70
Overhead	80,000	64
Administration	30,000	30

The Canadian production will be sold by manufacturer's representatives, who will receive a commission of 8 percent of the sales price. No portion of the United States home office expense will be allocated to the Canadian subsidiary.

Required □

1. Prepare a schedule computing the Stenger Corporation's estimated net profit from United States operations under each of the following procedures:

    a. Expansion of the Rhode Island factory.
    b. Negotiation of a long-term contract on a commission basis.

2. Management officials want to price the Canadian product to realize a 10 percent profit on the sales price. Compute the sales price per unit that would result in an estimated 10 percent profit on sales.

(CPA)

Not-For-Profit Budgeting— College **P7-14.** The regents of DeMars College have asked your assistance in developing the college's budget for the coming 19X1–X2 academic year. You are supplied with the following data for the current year:

	Lower division (Freshman-Sophomore)	Upper division (Junior-Senior)
Average number of students per class	25	20
Average salary of faculty members	$10,000	$10,000
Average number of credit hours carried each year per student	33	30
Enrollment including scholarship students	2,500	1,700
Average faculty teaching load in credit hours per year (ten classes of three credit hours)	30	30

For 19X1–X2, the lower-division enrollment is expected to increase by 10 percent, while the upper-division enrollment is expected to remain stable. Faculty salaries will be increased by a standard 5 percent, and additional merit increases to be awarded to individual faculty members will be $90,750 for the lower division and $85,000 for the upper division.

The current budget is $210,000 for operation and maintenance of plant and equipment; this includes $90,000 for salaries and wages. Experience of the past three months suggests that the current budget is realistic, but that expected increases for 19X1–X2 are 5 percent in salaries and wages and $9,000 in other expenditures for operation and maintenance of plant and equipment.

The budget for the remaining expenditures for 19X1–X2 is as follows:

Administrative and general	$240,000
Library	160,000
Health and recreation	75,000
Athletics	120,000
Insurance and retirement	265,000
Interest	48,000
Capital outlay	300,000

The college expects to award twenty-five tuition-free scholarships to lower-division students and fifteen to upper-division students. Tuition is $22 per credit hour, and no other fees are charged.

Budgeted revenues for 19X1–X2 are as follows:

Endowments $114,000
Net income from auxiliary services 235,000
Athletics 180,000

The college's remaining source of revenue is the annual support campaign held during the spring.

Required ☐

1. Prepare a schedule computing by division for 19X1–X2

   a. The expected enrollment
   b. The total credit hours to be carried
   c. The number of faculty members needed

2. Prepare a schedule computing the budget for faculty salaries by division for 19X1–X2.

3. Prepare a schedule computing the tuition revenue budget by division for 19X1–X2.

4. Assuming that the faculty salaries budget computed in requirement 2 was $2.4 million and that the tuition-revenue budget computed in requirement 3 was $3 million, prepare a schedule computing the amount that must be raised during the annual support campaign in order to cover the 19X1–X2 expenditures budget.

(CPA)

P7-15. Vernon Enterprises designs and manufactures toys. Past experience indicates that the product life cycle of a toy is three years. Promotional advertising produces large sales in the early years, but there is a substantial sales decline in the final year of a toy's life.

Projected Sales and Cash Flow

Consumer demand for new toy	Chance of occurring (%)	Estimated sales in Year 1	Year 2	Year 3
Above average	30	$1,200,000	$2,500,000	$600,000
Average	60	700,000	1,700,000	400,000
Below average	10	200,000	900,000	150,000

Variable costs are estimated at 30 percent of the selling price. Special machinery must be purchased at a cost of $860,000. It will be installed in an unused portion of the factory that Vernon has unsuccessfully been trying to rent to someone for several years at $50,000 per year and has no prospects for future utilization. Fixed expenses (excluding depreciation) of a cash-flow nature are estimated at $50,000 per year on the new toy. The new machinery will be depreciated by the sum-of-the-years'-digits method with an estimated salvage value of $110,000 and will be sold at the beginning of the fourth year. Advertising and promotional expenses will be incurred uniformly and will total $100,000 the first year, $150,000 the second year, and $50,000 the third year. These expenses will be deducted as incurred for income tax reporting.

Vernon believes that state and federal income taxes will total 60 percent of income in the foreseeable future and may be assumed to be paid uniformly over the year income is earned.

Required □

1. Prepare a schedule computing the probable sales of this new toy in each of the three years, taking into account the probability of above-average, average, and below-average sales occurring.

2. Assume that the probable sales computed in requirement 1 are $900,000 in the first year, $1,800,000 in the second year, and $410,000 in the third year. Prepare a schedule computing the probable net income for the new toy in each of the three years of its life.

3. Prepare a schedule of net cash flows from sales of the new toy for each of the years involved and from disposition of the machinery purchased. Use the sales data given in requirement 2.

(CPA)

Cash-Flow Projections— Mathematical Model **P7-16.** Over the past several years, the Programme Corporation has encountered difficulties estimating its cash flows. The result has been a rather strained relationship with its banker.

Programme's controller would like to develop a means by which she can forecast the *firm's monthly operating cash flows*. The following data were gathered to facilitate the development of such a forecast:

a. Sales have been and are expected to increase at .5 percent each month.
b. Thirty percent of each month's sales is for cash; the other 70 percent is on open account.
c. Of the credit sales, 80 percent is collected in the first month following the sale and the remaining 20 percent is collected in the second month. There are no bad debts.
d. Gross margin on sales averages 25 percent.
e. Programme purchases enough inventory each month to cover the following month's sales.
f. All inventory purchases are paid for in the month to cover the following month's sales.
g. Monthly expenses are: payroll, $1,500; rent, $400; depreciation, $120; other cash expenses, 1 percent of that month's sales. There are no accruals.
h. Ignore the effects of corporate income taxes, dividends, and equipment acquisitions.

Required □ Using the data just given, develop a mathematical model the controller can use for her calculations. Your model should be capable of calculating the monthly operating cash inflows and outflows for any specified month.

(CMA)

Forecasted Cash Position **P7-17.** The Barker Corporation manufactures and distributes wooden baseball bats. The bats are manufactured in Georgia at its only plant. This is a seasonal business, with a large portion of sales occurring in late winter and early spring. The production schedule for the last quarter of the year is heavy in order to build up inventory to meet expected sales volume.

The company experiences a temporary cash strain during this heavy production period. Payroll costs rise during the last quarter because overtime is scheduled to meet the increased production needs. Collections from customers are low because the fall season produces only modest sales. This year the company concern is intensified because of the rapid increases in prices during the current inflationary period. In addition, the Sales department manager forecasts sales of less than one million bats for the first time in three years. This decrease in sales appears to be caused by the popularity of aluminum bats.

The cash account builds up during the first and second quarters as sales exceed production. The excess cash is invested in U.S. Treasury bills and other commercial paper. During the last half of the year, the temporary investments are liquidated to meet the cash needs. In the early years of the company, short-term borrowing was used to supplement the funds released by selling investments, but this has not been necessary in recent years. Because costs are higher this year, the treasurer asks for a forecast for December to judge if the $40,000 in temporary investments will be adequate to carry the company through the month with a minimum balance of $10,000. Should this amount ($40,000) be insufficient, she wants to begin negotiations for a short-term loan.

The unit sales volume for the past two months and the estimate for the next four months are:

October (actual)	70,000	January (estimated)	90,000
November (actual)	50,000	February (estimated)	90,000
December (estimated)	50,000	March (estimated)	120,000

The bats are sold for $3 each. All sales are made on account. Fifty percent of the accounts are collected in the month of the sale, 40 percent are collected in the month following the sale, and the remaining 10 percent in the second month following the sale. Customers who pay in the month of the sale receive a 2 percent cash discount.

The production schedule for the six-month period beginning with October reflects the company's policy of maintaining a stable year-round work force by scheduling overtime to meet production schedules:

October (actual)	90,000	January (estimated)	90,000
November (actual)	90,000	February (estimated)	100,000
December (estimated)	90,000	March (estimated)	100,000

The bats are made from wooden blocks that cost $6 each. Ten bats can be produced from each block. The blocks are acquired one year in advance so they can be properly aged. Barker pays the supplier one-twelfth of the cost of this material each month until the obligation is retired. The monthly payment is $60,000.

The plant is normally scheduled for a forty-hour, five-day work week. During the busy production season, however, the work week may be increased to six ten-hour days. Workers can produce 7.5 bats per hour. Normal monthly output is 75,000 bats. Factory employees are paid $4 per hour (up $.50 from last year) for regular time and time-and-one-half for overtime.

Other manufacturing costs include variable overhead of $.30 per unit and annual fixed overhead of $280,000. Depreciation charges totalling $40,000 are included among the fixed overhead. Selling expenses include variable costs of $.20 per unit and annual fixed costs of $60,000. Fixed administrative costs are $120,000 annually. All fixed costs are incurred uniformly throughout the year.

The controller has accumulated the following additional information:

1. The balances of selected accounts as of November 30, 19X4, are as follows:

Cash	$ 12,000
Marketable securities (cost and market are the same)	40,000
Accounts receivable	96,000
Prepaid expenses	4,800
Account payable (arising from raw-material purchase)	300,000
Accrued vacation pay	9,500
Equipment note payable	102,000
Accrued income taxes payable	50,000

2. Interest to be received from the company's temporary investments is estimated at $500 for December.

3. Prepaid expenses of $3,600 will expire during December, and the balance of the prepaid account is estimated at $4,200 for the end of December.

4. Barker purchased new machinery in 19X4 as part of a plant-modernization program. The machinery was financed by a twenty-four-month note of $144,000. The terms call for equal principal payments over the next twenty-four months with interest paid at the rate of 1 percent per month on the unpaid balance at the first of the month. The first payment was made May 1, 19X4.

5. Old equipment, which has a book value of $8,000, is to be sold during December for $7,500.

6. Each month the company accrues $1,700 for vacation pay by charging Vacation Pay Expense and crediting Accrued Vacation Pay. The plant closes for two weeks in June when all plant employees take a vacation.

7. Quarterly dividends of $.20 per share will be paid on December 15 to stockholders of record. Barker Corporation has authorized 10,000 shares. The company has issued 7,500 shares, and 500 of these are classified as treasury stock.

8. The quarterly income taxes payment of $50,000 is due on December 15, 19X4.

Required □

1. Prepare a schedule that forecasts the cash position on December 31, 19X4. What action, if any, will be required to maintain a $10,000 cash balance?

2. Without prejudice to your answer in requirement 1, assume Barker regularly needs to arrange short-term loans during the November to February period. What changes in its methods of doing business might

Barker consider to reduce or eliminate the need for short-term borrowing?

(CMA)

Cash-Flow Statement

P7-18. The Pantex Corporation has gone through a period of rapid expansion to reach its present size of seven divisions. The expansion program has placed strains on its cash resources. Therefore, the need for better cash planning at the corporate level has become very important.

Currently, each division is responsible for the collection of receivables and the disbursement for all operating expenses and approved capital projects. The corporation does exercise control over division activities and has attempted to coordinate the cash needs of the divisions and the corporation. However, it has not yet developed effective division cash reports from which it can determine the needs and availability of cash in the next budgetary year. As a result of inadequate information, the corporation permitted some divisions to make expenditures for goods and services that need not have been made or that could have been postponed until a later time while other divisions had to delay expenditures that should have had a greater priority.

The 19X8 cash receipts and disbursements plan prepared by the Tapon Division for submission to the corporate office is presented below.

TAPON DIVISION
Budgeted Cash Receipts and Disbursements
For the year ended December 31, 19X8
(in thousands)

Receipts
Collections on accounts	$9,320
Miscellaneous	36
	$9,356

Disbursements
Production	
Raw materials	$2,240
Labor and fringe benefits	2,076
Overhead	2,100
Sales	
Commissions	395
Travel and entertainment	600
Other	200
Administrative	
Accounting	80
Personnel	110
General management	350
Capital expenditures	1,240
	$9,391
Excess of receipts over (under) disbursements	$ (35)

The following additional information was used by the Tapon Division to develop the cash receipts and disbursements budget.

1. Receipts—Miscellaneous receipts are estimated proceeds from the sales of unneeded equipment.

2. Sales—Travel and entertainment represents the costs required to produce the sales volume projected for the year. The other sales costs consist of $50,000 for training new sales personnel, $25,000 for attendance by sales personnel at association meetings (not sales shows), and $125,000 for sales management salaries.

3. Administration—The personnel costs include $50,000 for salary and department operating costs, $20,000 for training new personnel, and $40,000 for management training courses for current employees. The general management costs include salaries and office costs for the division management, $310,000, plus $10,000 for officials' travel to Pantex Corporation meetings, and $30,000 for industry and association conferences.

4. Capital expenditures—Planned expenditures for capital items during 19X8 are as follows:

Capital programs approved by the corporation:

Items ordered for delivery in 19X8 .... $300,000
Items to be ordered in 19X8 for
  delivery in 19X8 .... $700,000
New programs to be submitted to
  corporation during 19X8 .... $240,000

Required ☐ Present a revised Budgeted Cash Receipts and Disbursement Statement for the Tapon Division. Design the format of the revised statement to include adequate detail so as to improve the ability of the corporation to judge the urgency of the cash needs. Such a statement would be submitted by all divisions to provide the basis for overall corporation cash planning.

(CMA)

Annual Operating Plan **P7-19.** Western Company recently acquired Papion Men's Clothing Company, which now operates as a western subsidiary. Papion offers dress, casual, and sports clothing and related incidental accessories. The clothing is manufactured at several plants throughout the United States. The company's different lines are sold through company-owned stores and other retailers.

Western exercises close control over its subsidiaries. Western's management expects the subsidiaries' reports to present the proposed operating plans and to evaluate past performance in order to provide a foundation for this degree of control. However, Western's controller failed to provide Papion management with complete specifications regarding the format and the content of the reports because he had been devoting all of his energies to the final details of the acquisition.

The Papion Annual Operating Plan Report that follows is the first report prepared and submitted to Western since the acquisition. Papion's management developed its own format for the report. The report includes the proposed budget for 19X8 and related remarks regarding past and future operations.

Required ☐

1. Would the proposed budget and accompanying remarks included in Papion Men's Clothing Company's Annual Operating Plan Report fulfill

the needs of Western Company's management to exercise close control? Explain your answer.

2. Irrespective of your answer to requirement 1, what changes would you recommend in this report to improve its effectiveness for communicating the 19X8 plans of Papion Men's Clothing Company?

19X8 Annual Operating Plan Report
PAPION MEN'S CLOTHING CO.

The Papion Men's Clothing Company expects the operating results for 19X8 to be better than last year. Several actions have been taken that will improve sales and solve problems that affected operations last year. Sales should increase substantially due to the introduction of a new line of women's sportswear to be distributed through company-owned stores. Progress also was made last year in attracting other retailers to handle Papion's lines. Additional sales increases can be expected this year if negotiations to induce a major chain to distribute Papion lines are successful. The budget includes the sales expected to be made through this large chain retailer.

Operating costs should be lower this year. A new production facility should be completed in February to replace an older plant. This older plant has caused production shortages due to frequent equipment breakdowns. Also, labor problems that existed at the Midwest Plant have been resolved. Thus, the lower output and higher costs of the Midwest Plant should be corrected.

Original Budget for 19X7
Forecast of Actual Operations for 19X7
Proposed Budget for 19X8
(in thousands)

	19X7 Budget	19X7 Forecast actual	19X8 Budget
Sales	$10,000	$8,500	$12,000
Cost of goods sold			
Material	$ 1,050	$ 975	$ 1,260
Labor	1,400	1,400	1,680
Factory overhead	1,750	1,600	1,800
Selling expenses			
Sales force	500	425	600
Advertising and promotion	600	500	950
Company stores	1,000	950	1,100
General			
Administration	750	755	825
Total expenses	$ 7,050	$6,605	$ 8,215
Net income before taxes	$ 2,950	$1,895	$ 3,785

Prepared and submitted: October 19X7

(CMA)

P7-20. United Business Education, Inc., (UBE) is a nonprofit organization that sponsors a wide variety of management seminars throughout the United States. In addition, it is heavily involved in research into improved methods

Cash-Flow Budget

of educating and motivating business executives. The seminar activity is largely supported by fees and the research program from member dues.

UBE operates on a calendar-year basis and is in the process of finalizing the budget for 19X9. The following information has been taken from approved plans that are still tentative at this time.

Seminar Program □

Revenue—The scheduled number of programs should produce $12 million of revenue for the year. Each program is budgeted to produce the same amount of revenue. The revenue is collected during the month the program is offered. The programs are scheduled so that 12 percent of the revenue is collected in each of the first five months of the year. The remaining programs, accounting for the remaining 40 percent of the revenue, are distributed evenly through the months of September, October, and November. No programs are offered in the other four months of the year.

Direct Expenses—The seminar expenses are made up of three segments:

■ Instructors' fees are paid at the rate of 70 percent of the seminar revenue in the month following the seminar. The instructors are considered independent contractors and are not eligible for UBE employee benefits.

■ Facilities fees total $5.6 million for the year. They are the same for each program and are paid in the month the program is given.

■ Annual promotional costs of $1 million are spent equally in all months except June and July when there is no promotional effort.

Research Program □

Research Grants—The research program has a large number of projects nearing completion. The other main research activity this year includes the feasibility studies for new projects to be started in 19Y0. As a result, the total grant expense of $3 million for 19X9 is expected to be paid out at the rate of $500,000 per month during the first six months of the year.

Salaries and Other UBE Expenses □

Office Lease—Annual amount of $240,000 paid monthly at the beginning of each month.

General Administrative Expenses (telephone, supplies, postage, etc.)—$1.5 million annually or $125,000 a month.

Depreciation Expense—$240,000 a year.

General UBE Promotion—Annual cost of $600,000, paid monthly.

Salaries and Benefits—

Number of employees	Annual salary paid monthly	Total annual salaries
1	$50,000	$ 50,000
3	40,000	120,000
4	30,000	120,000
15	25,000	375,000
5	15,000	75,000
22	10,000	220,000
50		$960,000

Employee benefits amount to $240,000 or 25 percent of annual salaries. Except for the pension contribution, the benefits are paid as salaries are paid. The annual pension payment of $24,000, based on 2.5 percent of salaries (included in the total benefits and the 25 percent rate), is due April 15, 19X9.

Other Information □

Membership Income—UBE has 100,000 members, each of whom pays an annual fee of $100. The fee for the calendar year is invoiced in late June. The collection schedule is as follows:

July	60 percent
August	30 percent
September	5 percent
October	5 percent
	100 percent

Capital Expenditures—The capital-exenditures program calls for a total of $510,000 in cash payments to be spread evenly over the first five months of 19X9.

Cash and Temporary Investments at January 1, 19X9, are estimated at $750,000.

Required □

1. Prepare a budget of the annual cash receipts and disbursements for UBE, Inc., for 19X9.

2. Prepare a cash budget for UBE, Inc., for January 19X9.

3. Using the information you developed in requirements 1 and 2, identify important operating problems of UBE, Inc.

(CMA)

P7-21. Springfield Corporation operates on a calendar-year basis. It begins the annual budgeting process in late August when the president establishes targets for the total dollar sales and net income before taxes for the next year.

Analysis of Budgeting Process

The sales target is given to the Marketing department, where the Marketing manager formulates a sales budget by product line in both units and dollars. From this budget, sales quotas by product line in units and dollars are established for each of the corporation's sales districts.

The Marketing manager also estimates the cost of the marketing activities required to support the target sales volume, and prepares a tentative marketing-expense budget.

The executive vice-president uses the sales and profit targets, the sales budget by product line, and the tentative marketing-expense budget to determine the dollar amounts that can be devoted to manufacturing and corporate office expense. The executive vice-president prepares the budget for corporate expenses and then forwards to the Production department the product-line sales budget in units and the total dollar amount that can be devoted to manufacturing.

The Production manager meets with the factory managers to develop a manufacturing plan that will produce the required units when needed within the cost constraints set by the executive vice-president. The budgeting process usually comes to a halt at this point because the Production department does not consider the financial resources allocated to be adequate.

When this standstill occurs, the vice-president of Finance, the executive vice-president, the Marketing manager, and the Production manager meet together to determine the final budgets for each of the areas. This normally results in a modest increase in the total amount available for manufacturing costs, while the marketing expense and corporate office expense budgets are cut. The total sales and net income figures proposed by the president are seldom changed. Although the participants are seldom pleased with the compromise, these budgets are final. Each executive then develops a new detailed budget for the operations in his or her area.

None of the areas has achieved its budget in recent years. Sales often run below the target. When budgeted sales are not achieved, each area is expected to cut costs so that the president's profit target can still be met. However, the profit target is seldom met because costs are not cut enough. In fact, costs often run above the original budget in all functional areas. The president is disturbed that Springfield has not been able to meet the sales and profit targets. He hired a consultant with considerable experience with companies in Springfield's industry. The consultant reviewed the budgets for the past four years. She concluded that the product line sales budgets were reasonable and that the cost and expense budgets were adequate for the budgeted sales and production levels.

Required □

1. Discuss how the budgeting process as employed by Springfield Corporation contributes to the failure to achieve the president's sales and profit targets.

2. Suggest how Springfield Corporation's budgeting process could be revised to correct the problems.

3. Should the functional areas be expected to cut their costs when sales volume falls below target? Explain your answer.

(CMA)

CHAPTER OUTLINE

STANDARDS AND STANDARD COSTING

CHAPTER **8**

☐ INTRODUCTION

Standard costing provides a means for including control aspects within the more traditional product-cost-accounting system. Job-order and process-accounting systems, as discussed in chapters 3–5, are product-cost-determination systems that provide costs for valuing inventory and cost of sales. In a standard-costing system, historical costs are replaced by predetermined costs. These costs, if they are reasonable approximations of actual costs, can be used not only for financial accounting purposes but also in responsibility-accounting systems for measurement and performance-evaluation purposes.

To properly develop standards for use in product costing and responsibility accounting, it is important to specify the type of standards to be developed, how the standards are to be handled in the accounting system, and how variances are to be reported and used for controlling operations. This chapter provides an orientation to the development of an effective standard-costing system by discussing the nature of the system; by giving the procedural aspects of such systems; and by citing information on the development, use, and disposition of variances provided by standard-cost-accounting systems.

☐ THE NATURE OF STANDARD-COSTING SYSTEMS

Standard costs have been defined in a number of different ways. For instance, a standard cost might be defined as a reflection of the lowest cost that can be expected under current conditions with available management. Another possibility would be to define a standard cost as a predetermined cost that reflects ideal conditions (i.e., those unattainable in a practical sense). In both cases, a standard cost is what the cost should be for a product or service under specified conditions. Consequently, before an operational definition can be developed, the nature of the standards should be understood, and the purposes for which the standards are to be developed must be identified.

Standards and Budgets

We know that standards represent predetermined or estimated costs derived for some purpose. For instance, standard costs might be expected to be used in cost-volume-profit analysis and for other types of planning decisions. Consequently, standards are typically incorporated in various budgets and are used in responsibility accounting and other control systems. It is probably true that standards are often looked upon in terms of a single unit of product or some other type of individual unit, while budgets reflect a total concept. In practice, the terms *standards*, *estimates*, and *budgets* are sometimes used interchangeably.

Kinds of Standard Costs

In some cases, companies and nonprofit organizations have developed standards to give management a gauge by which they can compare actual results. They may have no plans to incorporate the standards into the financial accounting system, and the comparison may not result in subsequent revisions. These standards are often referred to as basic or historical standards. After a period of years, such standards can only be used to indicate performance trends of actual operations from the original standards.

At the other extreme are ideal or theoretical standards. These standards represent the lowest costs that could be attained under the best possible operating conditions. For instance, the management team might have determined that in making a carton of potato chips, five pounds of potatoes and one-half pound of vegetable oil are required. From this mix, management personnel might conclude that they should expect five and one-half pounds of marketable potato chips to result from the process. Even under the most favorable circumstances, five pounds of potatoes and one-half pound of oil will yield something less than five and one-half pounds of potato chips because of the normal evaporation process that takes place. Since these ideal standards are not reasonable approximations of actual costs, they cannot be used for financial accounting purposes. It is also doubtful that they can be used effectively in a management-control system, since employees would probably react negatively to having impossible standards imposed upon them.

If standards are to be useful for both financial accounting and management-control purposes, they should reflect currently attainable conditions. Even attainable standards can be established with varying degrees of tightness. But if they are to be used for both financial accounting and control purposes, standards must reflect a good approximation of costs expected by the company under current conditions. This means that normal disappearance and expected levels of nonproductive labor should be built into the standard cost of the products being produced. Referring back to the potato chip example, if the management staff found that potatoes should yield 25 percent of their initial weight in potato chips and that 60 percent of the oil put into production should be absorbed into finished chips, then an attainable standard for 5.5 pounds of input might produce 1.5 to 1.6 pounds of finished chips.

As one moves from an ideal standard to a standard reflecting current conditions, differences between actual and standard costs might be expected to change from very large to fairly small unfavorable differences (i.e., actual costs being larger than standard costs), with the possibility of some favorable differences occurring from time to time. For purposes of this chapter, standard costs are defined as the lowest costs that can be expected under current operating conditions with reasonably competent management.

Advantages of Standard Costing

Companies often adopt standard-costing systems in order to eliminate the time and cost involved in valuing inventories on the FIFO, LIFO, or other methods. Once standards have been set for the various items in inventory, assuming they reflect reasonable approximations of actual costs, all items in inventory and cost of sales can be valued based on the developed standards. Such standards need to be adjusted periodically so that they continue to reflect a reasonable approximation of actual costs.

Although advantages offered by standards for product-costing purposes may be worthwhile, potential control advantages are even more important. Management has an obligation to monitor the production process in order to insure efficient and effective operations. Standard costs provide a means for monitoring the process. When reported by cost centers and various cost components, they provide the means by which results can be measured and evaluated. Other benefits such as the following might also be realized:

1. Because the establishment of a standard-costing system requires a thorough analysis of existing systems, deficiencies in current systems are likely to be identified.

2. Essential to the process of setting meaningful standards is a plan for efficient and economical operations. This plan should be developed for all aspects of operations.

3. The need to establish clearly defined lines of responsibility and authority as a basis for developing a control system will be highlighted. This will focus attention on responsibility systems and management-by-exception.

4. Standard costs should serve as an aid to management personnel in highlighting acceptable performance in all aspects of operations.

5. Faster reporting of operating data may result from the system, along with somewhat simplified costing procedures.

6. Standard costs should promote the implementation of an effective system of budgetary control.

Although all of the above benefits may not be realized by companies, those methods centering attention on control must be sought if the standard-costing system is to be worthwhile. Indeed, if the system is to be effective, standards must be set that represent a proper motivational device for managers (i.e., managers believe them to be a fair and reasonable goal), and it must be possible for managers to significantly influence the performance variables involved.

☐ DEVELOPMENT OF A STANDARD-PRODUCT COST

Based on the definition of standard costs provided earlier in the chapter, it is assumed that standards developed should be attainable—based on current conditions and designed to fit the existing capabilities of management and employees. This means that unavoidable (normal) spoilage, scrap, and disappearance will be incorporated into the standards established. Some allowance for avoidable inefficiencies will also likely be built into the standards. So, although a product could conceivably be manufactured using ten pounds of material and four hours of direct labor, the standards, as defined, will call for something more than ten pounds and something longer than four hours to allow for normal inefficiencies.

Assume that Jackson Products Company produces Energy, a new health food. For a fifty-pound batch, the standard-cost formula reflects the following:

Energy, Fifty-Pound Batch

	Quantity	Standard Cost per unit	Total cost
Materials			
Wheat	25 lb	$ .20	$ 5.00
Barley	25 lb	.10	2.50
Corn	12 lb	.05	.60
Total			$ 8.10
Labor			
Mixing and blending	6 hr	4.00	24.00
Overhead			
Variable	6 hr	2.00	12.00
Fixed	6 hr	1.00	6.00
Total			$18.00
Total cost			$50.10

A number of different decisions were made in developing standard costs for Energy. Use of the fifty-pound batch as a common unit of measure probably reflects the quantity normally packaged by the company. Decisions had to be reached on the tightness of the standards and, as can be seen from the formula, sixty-two pounds of material input are needed to net fifty pounds of finished product. It was determined that six hours of direct labor are needed for one batch of finished product. From the earlier chapters on cost behavior and cost estimation, it should be apparent that a number of decisions had to be made regarding manufacturing overhead before these costs could be incorporated into the standards. For instance, a distinction between manufacturing and nonmanufacturing overhead costs was needed, and some capacity level had to be identified before a fixed overhead rate could be established. We will discuss this more in a subsequent section.

The development of standard costs requires the efforts of a number of different decision-making groups, with accounting playing a rather modest role in the initial development of standards. The major contribution of the accounting staff takes place at the time a decision is made to incorporate the standards into the reporting system, and the role continues with the decision to provide an effective means of control through the utilization of the standards.

☐ STANDARDS FOR MATERIALS

As indicated by the formula for Energy, the standard-material cost consists of a price standard and a quantity standard. The price standard, which is set by the Purchasing group, reflects direct materials prices expected to be incurred per unit during manufacture of the product. The quantity standard reflects the amount of material required per unit, based on industrial engineering studies of Energy production.

Setting Price and Quantity Standards

Prices reflected in the final standards indicate efforts by production and purchasing personnel to forecast quantities required and prices that might be expected, depending on expected production requirements and purchasing policies. Price standards are then established after decisions are made on purchase quantities. The standards should also include a consideration of freight costs as well as price and quantity discounts.

Quantities used in the standard cost of a product should result from studies indicating how the product is to be produced. This should include a consideration of the quality of product desired, the quality of materials to be used, any trade-offs between material quality and labor performance, and the capabilities of the existing manufacturing process.

Material Variances

Previous comments emphasized the fact that operational standards should reflect a reasonable approximation of actual costs so that they can be used for reporting purposes. The standards should also provide a basis for control. If the first objective is met, one should normally expect differences between actual costs incurred and standard costs to be insignificant. To insure that the second objective is met, the accounting system must provide for a monitoring process that compares actual costs with standard costs by responsibility center (cost center for each phase of manufacturing) so that variances can be properly identified, responsibility determined, and exceptions evaluated.

Direct-material variances generally result from a combination of purchasing decisions and manufacturing results. Basically, the computations for variances are outlined as follows:

1. *Material-price variance.* The price variance results from differences between prices paid for materials and prices that were expected to be paid based on standards established. Although the variance arises because of purchasing decisions, it is sometimes recognized based on manufacturing activity.

2. *Material quantity (efficiency, usage) variance.* The quantity variance results from the difference between inputs of material (such as units, pounds, or gallons) actually used in manufacturing and inputs that should have been used, based on equivalent units of product completed.

More information on these two variances is presented below.

Material-Price Variance

Because direct material are purchased in advance of their use in manufacturing, some choice is available as to when to recognize the **material-price variance**—at the time of purchase or at the time the direct materials are used in manufacturing. Consider the following example based on the Energy product standards.

Jackson Products Company purchased 10,000 pounds of wheat for $2,500. During the current period, 3,000 pounds of the recently purchased wheat were used in the manufacture of 100 batches of Energy.

As indicated earlier, a decision must be reached as to when the variance should be recognized. In such cases, one should choose the alternative that best incorporates control aspects of the standard-costing system. One possibility, already mentioned, is to recognize the material-price variance at the time of purchase. Using this approach, the price variance is calculated as follows:

Material-price variance = Actual quantity of material purchased (AQ) multiplied by actual price (AP), minus actual quantity of materials purchased multiplied by standard price (SP), or

Material-price variance = The difference between actual and standard price multiplied by actual quantity purchased

Material-price variance = $(AP - SP) \times AQ$

Material-price variance = $(\$.25 - \$.20) \times 10,000 = \$500$ unfavorable (debit)

Calculated as indicated, a $500 unfavorable material-price variance is recognized—unfavorable because the actual price is greater than the standard price. A typical entry, to record the activity, would be

Direct-material inventory	2,000	
Material-price variance	500	
Accounts payable		2,500

This method of calculating the variance gives recognition to the deviation at the earliest point that a determination can be made—the best time for control purposes.

Another possibility is to recognize the variance as material is used in manufacturing. In order to recognize the variance at the production stage, multiply the price difference by the quantity of direct materials used in manufacturing ($.05 × 3,000). The entries required for giving recognition to the variance would be as follows:

Direct-material inventory	2,500	
Accounts payable		2,500
Work-in-process, materials	600	
Material-price variance	150	
Direct-material inventory		750

In these two entries, only that portion of the price variance related to materials committed to manufacturing is recognized. Although this method of recognizing the price variance might have some slight advantages from the standpoint of financial reporting—direct-materials inventories reflect actual prices paid—the price variance may be required too late to be of use for control purposes.

To summarize, from a control point of view, the material-price variance should be developed at the earliest point at which the variance can be determined with a reasonable degree of accuracy. Developed in this manner, the following explanations might result from an analysis of the material-price variance.

1. Price deviations were caused by poor purchasing decisions on the part of Purchasing department personnel.

2. Clerical errors were made in recording direct-material purchases.

3. The price for the material changed substantially because of economic conditions.

4. Material of a higher or lower quality than called for in the standards was purchased, resulting in a higher or lower price than expected.

5. Unexpected changes in manufacturing resulted in purchasing decisions at higher or lower prices than planned.

Material-Quantity Variance

Refer again to the Energy production example in which 3,000 pounds of wheat were used in the production of 100 batches of Energy. Remember that barley and corn also had to be used, but focus attention for the time being only on the wheat. How many pounds of wheat should have been used to produce the 100 batches?

In the Energy product standard, one batch of product calls for the use of 25 pounds of wheat. The production of 100 batches should require 2,500 pounds (100 × 25). We perform this operation to restate output in terms of the comparable unit that we are trying to measure—in this case, pounds of wheat. This calculation is a key component in developing standard-costing efficiency variances. It measures standard quantity allowed for a manufacturing level achieved. The material-quantity (efficiency, usage) variance is developed as follows:

Material-quantity variance = Actual quantity of material (AQ) multiplied by standard price (SP), minus standard quantity of material allowed (SQ) multiplied by standard price, or

Material-quantity variance = The difference between actual quantity of material used and the standard quantity allowed, multiplied by the standard price

Quantity variance = (AQ − SQ) × SP

Quantity variance = (3,000 − 2,500) × \$.20 = \$100 unfavorable (debit)

The following information might result from an analysis of the material-quantity variance:

1. Operations for the period were more or less efficient than expected.

2. Uncontrollable fluctuations caused the variance.

3. Clerical errors were made in processing the production data.

4. Standards used were incorrect and should be revised.

5. The quality of materials used was different from that used in setting standards.

☐ STANDARDS FOR LABOR

The standard formula for Energy indicates that the standard labor cost also consists of two basic components—a rate (price) standard and a time (quantity) standard. The rate standards, which are set by members of the Labor Relations or Personnel departments, indicate the labor rates that are expected to be in effect for some time period. These are generally negotiated and formalized through union contracts. The time standard, which is set by the Industrial Engineering department staff, indicates the amount of direct labor that should be used in producing one batch of product.

Setting Rate and Time Standards

Rates reflected in the final standards depend on a number of factors. Overall, labor rates frequently are derived as a result of contract negotiations and are set for a fixed period. Specific rates are then broken down by skill levels and seniority. Rates used in the standards are a reflection of the expectations of management concerning skill level and experience required in a particular production process or department. The result will be a weighted average of the expected hours and cost per wage classification to be generated by product and by cost center.

Hours used in standards for a product should result, as was the case for material quantities, from studies indicating how the product is to be produced. Consequently, a time standard is needed for each separate labor operation the product must go through in being produced. If a product passes through four separate departments involving direct labor, standards would be established for each department, and the final standard cost would reflect rates and time set for each department. We should understand that subsequent variances resulting from the production of the product would be computed for each department, not by product. In setting the standards, factors such as the sophistication of the production process, capabilities of workers and equipment, kind of process, estimated downtime, working conditions, and learning effect would have to be considered.

Labor Variances

Direct-labor variances are related directly to production. The total variance is derived by comparing actual direct-labor costs with the standard costs charged to production for direct labor. Direct-labor variances are typically broken down into two components.

1. *Rate differences.* The rate variance is caused because of differences between actual and standard weighted averages of contract rates established for standard-cost purposes.

2. *Efficiency (quantity, time) differences.* The efficiency variance results from differences between actual direct-labor hours incurred and **standard hours allowed,** based on units produced.

Consider the following situation from the earlier Energy example:

Jackson Products Company, in producing 100 batches of Energy, incurred direct-labor costs of $3,150, with 700 direct-labor hours being required.

The total direct-labor variance can be determined as follows:

Total direct-labor variance = Actual direct-labor costs minus standard hours allowed times the standard direct-labor rate, or

Total direct-labor variance = $3,150 − (600 × $4) = $750 unfavorable (debit)

Standard hours allowed is determined by multiplying output by standard hours required for each unit (100 × 6 = 600).

The Direct-Labor Rate Variance

From the above example, the direct-**labor rate variance** can be easily determined. It is calculated as follows:

Direct-labor rate variance = Actual hours (*AH*) times actual rate (*AR*), minus actual hours times the standard rate (*SR*), or

Direct-labor rate variance = The difference between the actual and standard rates times actual hours

Direct-labor rate variance = $(AR - SR) \times AH$

Direct-labor rate variance = ($4.50 - $4.00) \times 700 = $350 unfavorable (debit)

The following additional information might be available from an analysis of the direct-labor rate variance:

1. Workers were higher-skilled than those called for, resulting in an unfavorable rate variance.

2. Clerical errors were made in payroll record keeping.

3. Permanent changes in labor rates have not been reflected in the standards.

The Direct-Labor Efficiency Variance

The efficiency variance is calculated in the same manner the material-quantity variance is calculated. As indicated, if the company produced 100 batches of Energy, and the standard calls for six hours per batch, then the company should have used 600 direct-labor hours for the output achieved. The efficiency variance is then developed as follows:

Direct-labor efficiency variance = Actual direct-labor hours (*AH*) multiplied by the standard rate (*SR*), minus standard hours (*SH*) allowed multiplied by standard rate, or

Direct-labor efficiency variance = The difference between actual and standard hours allowed times the standard rate

Direct-labor efficiency variance = $(AH - SH) \times SR$

Direct-labor efficiency variance = $(700 - 600) \times $4 = $400 unfavorable (debit)

An analysis of the direct-labor efficiency variance should provide information such as the following:

1. Uncontrollable fluctuations caused the difference.

2. Labor productivity improved with experience. Standards may need to be revised to reflect the learning curve effect.

3. Clerical errors were made in processing the production data.

4. Labor skill level was higher than called for, resulting in improved efficiency.

5. Manufacturing operations were more or less efficient than they should have been.

A Consolidating Example

Consider the following example relating to material and labor variances:

Spafford Manufacturing Company uses a standard costing system. It manufactures one product, whose standard cost is as follows:

Materials	20 yards at $.90 per yard = $18
Direct labor	4 hours at $6.00 per hour = 24

Actual activity for the month of October was as follows:

Materials purchased	18,000 yards at $.92 per yard
Materials used	9,500 yards
Direct labor	2,100 hours at $6.10 per hour
Units produced for the period	500

Required □ Compute the following variances for the month of October.

1. Material-price variance.

2. Material-quantity variance.

3. Labor-rate variance.

4. Labor-efficiency variance.

Assuming that the price variance is to be developed on the basis of purchases, the following answers could be developed using the formulas identified earlier.

1. Material-price variance
($.92 − $.90) × 18,000 = $360 unfavorable   (debit)

2. Material-quantity variance
(9,500 − 10,000) × $.90 = $450 favorable   (credit)

3. Labor-rate variance
($6.10 − $6.00) × 2,100 = $210 unfavorable   (debit)

4. Labor-efficiency variance
(2,100 − 2,000) × $6.00 = $600 unfavorable   (debit)

In order to calculate the material-quantity variance, the standard yards allowed (500 × 20 = 10,000) had to be determined. For the labor-efficiency variance, the standard hours allowed (500 × 4 = 2,000) were required.

□ JOURNAL ENTRIES FOR MATERIAL AND LABOR

Journal entries for material and labor transactions are made periodically throughout the accounting period—weekly or monthly—based on purchase invoices, materials requisitions, payroll records, and production results. Entries made in actual situations will depend on information available and the system used. Nevertheless, in the example that follows, the orientation needed to understand the basic flows involved is provided. This example provides a comprehensive exposure to the type of material and labor entries that might be required in a standard-cost accounting system. Data available is generally similar to that in the preceding examples.

On January 5, 19X5, the raw material inventory of the Robyn O'Dell Company was completely replenished as 100,000 pounds of Crispy Rice were ordered and received. Total cost for the shipment was $500,000. During the operating period, 52,000 pounds were used in the production of 1,000 units of Crunch. Payroll for the period was $61,200, all of which represented direct labor. Direct-labor costs average $5.10 per hour.

The standard costs for Crunch are:

	Standard cost per unit of Crunch
Crispy Rice	50 lb @ $4.50 = $225.00
Direct labor	10 hr @ $5.00 = 50.00
Overhead	10 hr @ $1.00 = 10.00
	$285.00

Entries, along with explanations, relating to O'Dell Company activities are:

(A) To record purchase of raw material:

Raw-materials inventory	450,000	
Material-price variance	50,000	
Accounts payable		500,000

The price variance represents the difference between the actual price paid and the standard price. The per unit price actually paid was $.50 more than the standard, and with 100,000 pounds purchased, the total difference is $50,000.

(B) To record materials placed in production:

Work-in-process	225,000	
Material-quantity variance	9,000	
Raw-materials inventory		234,000

The entry to work-in-process is based on materials allowed (equivalent units completed times standard pounds allowed per unit) times the standard cost. The credit entry records actual pounds of material used (52,000 pounds) at the standard cost of $4.50 per pound. The quantity variance is developed based on the difference between actual materials used and materials allowed for the production level attained ([52,000 − 50,000] × $4.50).

(C) To record payroll for operating period:

Work-in-process	50,000	
Labor-rate variance	1,200	
Labor-efficiency variance	10,000	
Wages payable		61,200

Work-in-process is charged for the standard amount of direct labor called for in producing 1,000 equivalent units. The labor-rate variance is calculated by subtracting $60,000 ($5 × 12,000) from $61,200. The labor-efficiency variance is the difference between actual and allowed hours (2,000) multiplied by the standard labor rate.

(D) To record completion of the units:

Finished goods	275,000	
Work-in-process		275,000

This entry simply transfers standard costs of completed units to finished goods.

☐ DEVELOPMENT OF OVERHEAD STANDARDS

Although direct-material and direct-labor standards are often set with a reasonable degree of precision because of the use of industrial engineering methods, overhead standards are much more difficult to establish with any degree of reliability. From chapter 2 we learned that various estimation methods are used to separate mixed overhead costs into fixed and variable components. In this section, we will see how the results of those procedures are used, along with flexible budgets, to develop overhead standards.

Use of Flexible Budgets

In chapter 7, an overhead budget was included in the comprehensive budget developed. The overhead budget shown was static in that it was established only for one level of activity. For instance, a budget might be established at an expected output level of 20,000 units, yet actual output could be 30,000 units. Figure 8.1 indicates the results derived from comparing actual performance with the static budget under such conditions. The variances between actual and budgeted amounts appear to be significant, but it is not clear what caused them. We know that the production manager failed to meet the output level used in setting the static budget, but we have no information related to his success in controlling costs.

	Actual	Budget	Variance
Unit production	30,000	20,000	10,000
Indirect material	$ 56,000	$ 37,000	$ 19,000 U
Repairs and maintenance	220,500	146,500	74,000 U
Utilities	90,500	60,500	30,000 U
Depreciation	44,000	44,000	0
Taxes	12,000	12,000	0
Total	$423,000	$300,000	$123,000 U

FIGURE 8.1
Jackson Products Company—Production Performance Report—Static Budget

One of the primary reasons why we attempt to separate overhead costs into fixed and variable components is so that estimated overhead costs can be projected at different levels of activity within a relevant range. This type of budget is often referred to as a **flexible budget.** Using flexible budgeting procedures, we can prepare a performance report that indicates what overhead costs should have been at the actual level of output. Given this introductory information, we will outline typical steps taken in developing a flexible budget and overhead standards.

Generally, the starting point in the development of a flexible budget is to acquire past records on overhead costs and adjust them so that they are representative of future conditions. Consider the following data used in developing overhead standards for the Energy standard costs shown on page 248.

Direct-labor hours required	60,000	120,000	240,000
Production in units	10,000	20,000	40,000
Overhead costs			
Indirect material	$ 19,000	$ 37,000	$ 73,000
Repairs and maintenance	74,500	146,500	290,500
Utilities	30,500	60,500	120,500
Depreciation	44,000	44,000	44,000
Taxes	12,000	12,000	12,000
Total	$180,000	$300,000	$540,000

The overhead cost data indicate that most of the expenditures are mixed costs, with some fixed costs also included. The next step would be to separate the mixed cost items into fixed and variable components. Assume that we decide to use regression analysis, with direct-labor hours serving as the independent variable, for this purpose. The results are shown as follows:

Indirect material	$= \$\ 1,000 + \$\ .30x$	(where x = direct labor hours)
Repairs and maintenance	$=\quad 2,500 +\quad 1.20x$	
Utilities	$=\quad\quad 500 +\quad .50x$	
Depreciation	$=\quad 44,000$	
Taxes	$=\quad 12,000$	
Total cost	$= \$60,000 + \$2.00x$	

When we are satisfied that the regression results are satisfactory, a flexible budget can be developed for different levels of activity as the need arises. Returning to our earlier performance report example shown in figure 8.1, we can now adjust the budget to reflect an output level of 30,000 units. The revised performance report, using flexible budgeting, is shown in figure 8.2. Results indicate that the production manager has performed well in controlling his overhead costs.

	Actual	Budget	Variance
Unit production	30,000	30,000	0
Indirect material	$ 56,000	$ 55,000	$1,000 U
Repairs and maintenance	220,500	218,500	2,000 U
Utilities	90,500	90,500	0
Depreciation	44,000	44,000	0
Taxes	12,000	12,000	0
Total	$423,000	$420,000	$3,000 U

FIGURE 8.2
Jackson Products Company— Production Performance Report—Flexible Budget

Overhead Standards

To develop overhead standards for the Energy product, we use the information provided in developing the flexible budget along with information regarding the **budgeted activity level** planned (also referred to as *normal volume*, *standard volume*, or *capacity*), stated in terms of the independent variable used in the regression equation. The budgeted activity level is used as the denominator in calculating a fixed-overhead rate for the product. The fixed-overhead rate is required in allocating total overhead costs to the product, based on the activity level achieved.

Management has indicated that 60,000 direct-labor hours (10,000 units) are to be used as the budgeted activity level. The fixed-overhead rate is then calculated by dividing projected fixed costs by the budgeted direct-labor hours. The variable-overhead rate is already given by the total cost equation derived earlier. The resulting standard-overhead rate is shown as follows:

Per direct-labor hour

Fixed-overhead rate = $60,000 ÷ 60,000	$1.00
Variable-overhead rate	2.00
Overhead rate per direct-labor hour	$3.00

Now that the overhead rate is known, overhead can be applied to the production of Energy based on direct hours allowed for the output level achieved.

Overhead Variances

As we begin a detailed examination of manufacturing overhead variances, the meaning and significance of flexible budgets must be kept in mind. For instance, one of the more important overhead variances, typically referred to as a **spending variance,** is derived by comparing actual overhead costs incurred with the flexible budget at some level of output achieved. If output is expressed in terms of completed equivalent units, and if the effect of fixed-overhead costs can be ignored for the time being, the spending variance represents the sole cause of the difference between actual variable overhead and the flexible budget. This difference can be further broken down between price changes and shifts in quantities of overhead items used.

For example, assume Garner Company incurs $52,500 of actual variable-overhead costs. The company's flexible budget consists of a varible-overhead rate of $10 per equivalent unit completed. During the most recent manufacturing period, 5,000 equivalent units were completed. The spending variance is calculated as follows:

$$\$52,500 - (\$10 \times 5,000) = \$2,500 \text{ unfavorable}$$

The ($10 × 5,000) represents the flexible budget since there are no fixed-overhead costs. If Garner Company's output is expressed in terms of standard hours allowed for output achieved, an **efficiency variance**—comparable to the direct-labor efficiency variance—can be derived, reflecting the difference between actual hours worked and standard hours allowed for the level of output achieved. This variance simply measures the efficiency in the use of an activity base such as direct labor or machine hours.

Assume Garner Company's standards call for two direct-labor hours for each completed unit, and that overhead is applied based on hours rather than units. During the most recent period 10,100 direct-labor hours were used in the production of the 5,000 units. The applicable overhead variances can now be calculated as follows:

Spending variance
$$\$52,500 - (\$5 \times 10,100) = \$2,000 \text{ unfavorable}$$

Efficiency variance
$$\$5 \times (10,100 - 10,000) = \$500 \text{ unfavorable}$$

As shown, the spending variance, now incorporating actual hours used, represents price differences. The efficiency variance highlights the impact of labor inefficiencies on overhead costs.

The above discussion and examples assumes a situation with only variable-overhead costs. However, in almost all manufacturing situations, actual fixed-overhead costs represent a significant component of manufacturing overhead and should also be expected to differ somewhat from budgeted fixed overhead (*BFO*) included in the flexible budget. Any difference between actual fixed overhead and budgeted fixed overhead represents another spending variance—referred to as a fixed-spending *variance* to differentiate it from the variable-spending variance.

The inclusion of a fixed-overhead rate in the standard cost of a product creates still another special type of variance appropriately called a **volume variance.** Anytime the actual output level varies from the level used as a denominator in determining the fixed-overhead rate, a volume variance is created because fixed overhead applied to manufacturing is greater or less than the amount of budgeted fixed overhead. Consequently, the volume variance is always explained by the level of activity. To summarize our discussion to this point, overhead variances should identify the following kinds of differences:

1. *Spending differences.* This variance reflects differences between actual overhead costs and overhead that should have been incurred at a given level of activity.

2. *Efficiency differences.* The efficiency variance identifies the effect on overhead costs of using more or less hours (assuming overhead is applied based on hours) than the hours allowed for a given level of output.

3. *Volume differences.* Volume differences result from (1) using a fixed-overhead rate and (2) operating at some activity level other than the level used as a denominator in establishing the fixed-overhead rate.

From the above discussions on overhead variances you might be led to believe that actual variable- and fixed-overhead costs are recorded separately in the accounting records of the typical company. Before continuing with our discussion of overhead variances, we should briefly review the nature of actual overhead cots and the recording process. Manufacturing overhead typically includes costs that are significantly influenced by current manufacturing activity (variable) and costs that result from providing the capacity to manufacture a product (fixed). Typically, no attempt is made to separate these costs in the accounting records by their variable- and fixed-cost components because of the difficulties involved. When actual overhead costs are recorded in the accounts without attempting to separate them by cost-behavior patterns, they are referred to as **mixed costs.** Overhead-variance analysis is generally built around this particular method of classification.

Conceptually, separating the actual overhead costs in the accounting records by their fixed and variable components would be preferable. If this could be done, spending differences would then be broken down by their variable-spending and fixed-budget components. Both approaches to variance analysis will be explained in subsequent sections of this chapter.

☐ OVERHEAD VARIANCES WITH MIXED COSTS

Where actual overhead costs have not been separated into their fixed and variable components, one finds that either a **three-way** or **two-way analysis** for overhead variances is usually used. Consider the graph shown in figure 8.3, reflecting a three-way analysis.

As indicated from the graph, the total overhead variance is calculated by subtracting from actual overhead costs the overhead applied during the period (standard overhead rate times direct-labor hours allowed). The graph also indicates that the following three kinds of information sought from overhead variances is available:

1. *Spending variance.* The variance is calculated by subtracting from actual overhead costs (*AOC*) the flexible budget at actual hours ([*BFO* + (*VOR* × *AH*)]).

FIGURE 8.3
Mixed Costs and
Variance Analysis

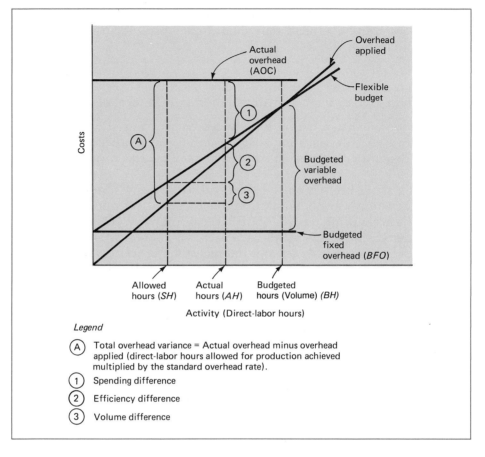

2. *Efficiency variance.* The efficiency variance represents the difference between the flexible budget at actual hours and the flexible budget at standard hours ($[BFO + (VOR \times SH)]$).

3. *Volume variance.* The volume variance is calculated by subtracting from the flexible budget at allowed hours, the overhead applied ($SOR \times SH$).

Consider the following example:

Jackson Products Company processes a single compound known as Energy and uses standard costing. The following information is available relative to overhead costs:

1. The standard cost card for a 50-pound batch shows the following standards for overhead:

Overhead	Quantity	Cost Per unit	Total
Variable	6 hr	$2	$12
Fixed	6 hr	1	6

2. During the month, 550 batches of 50 pounds each were produced, requiring 3,400 direct-labor hours.
3. Actual overhead costs incurred were $12,500.
4. The overhead standards were established for an expected volume of 5,000 direct-labor hours. At this level of production, the flexible budget is $15,000 ($5,000 budgeted fixed overhead plus $10,000 variable overhead).

Required □ Calculate the difference between actual overhead and overhead applied, analyzing the following:

a. Spending differences
b. Efficiency differences
c. Volume differences

The total overhead variance is determined as follows:

Total overhead variance = Actual overhead minus standard hours allowed times the standard overhead rate, or

Total overhead variance = $AOC - (SOR \times SH)$

Total overhead variance = $\$12,500 - (\$3 \times 3,300) = \$2,600$ unfavorable

Once again, standard hours allowed is determined by multiplying output by standard hours required for each unit (550×6).

Spending Variance

For the example just cited, the spending variance is calculated as follows:

Overhead spending variance = Actual overhead minus the flexible budget at actual hours, or

Overhead spending variance = $AOC - [BFO + (VOR \times AH)]$

Overhead spending variance = $\$12,500 - [\$5,000 + (\$2 \times 3,400)] = \$700$ unfavorable

Because we are dealing with mixed costs, the spending variance cannot be separated into variable and fixed components.

Efficiency Variance

The efficiency variance is calculated in the following manner:

Overhead efficiency variance = Flexible budget at actual hours minus flexible budget at allowed hours, or

Overhead efficiency variance =
   $[BFO + (VOR \times AH)] - [BFO + (VOR \times SH)]$

Overhead efficiency variance =
   $[\$5,000 + (\$2 \times 3,400)] - [\$5,000 + (\$2 \times 3,300)] = \$200$ unfavorable

Since the budgeted fixed overhead does not change, the efficiency variance could be calculated by determining the difference between actual and allowed hours and multiplying the result by the variable overhead rate:

$\$2 (3,400 - 3,300) = \$200$ unfavorable

Volume Variance

The volume variance is determined by calculating the difference between the flexible budget at allowed hours and overhead applied as follows:

Overhead-volume variance = $[BFO + (VOR \times SH)] - (SOR \times SH)$

Overhead-volume variance =
  [5,000 + ($2 × 3,300)] − ($3 × 3,300) = $1,700 unfavorable

As a means of reflecting the true impact of volume, this variance can also be calculated by determining the difference between fixed costs that are a lump-sum amount ($BFO = BH \times FOR$) and not expected to vary within the relevant range, and fixed overhead applied. Specific calculation is as follows:

Overhead-volume variance = $(BH - SH) \times FOR$

Overhead-volume variance = (5,000 − 3,300) × $1 = $1,700 unfavorable

Two-Way Analysis

Although the three-way analysis satisfies the requirements for information under mixed-cost conditions, the two-way analysis has been popular for years and continues to receive a lot of attention. A major reason for its use is that overhead is often related to production output in units of product. When this is done, the efficiency variance is no longer calculated and thus becomes a part of the spending (controllable) variance. Specifically, the two-way analysis provides the following breakdown:

1. *Spending variance.* The variance represents the difference between actual overhead costs and the flexible budget, based on equivalent units manufactured. The spending and efficiency variances are simply combined into one variance.

2. *Volume variance.* The volume variance is calculated, as before, by subtracting from the flexible budget, the overhead applied ($SOR \times$ units produced).

The same results will be obtained if a company applies overhead to production based on allowed hours and, in calculating the controllable variance, the flexible budget is based on allowed hours. Consider the following example:

The Katherine Rich Company uses a standard-costing system in its manufacture of pipes. Standard overhead rates are $2 for variable costs and $4 for fixed costs, based on an expected volume of 12,000 pipes per year.

During July, 1,200 pipes were manufactured with actual overhead costs of $9,000.

Required ☐ Calculate the difference between actual overhead and overhead applied, analyzing the difference to the extent possible.

The total overhead variance is determined in the following manner:

Total overhead variance = $AOC - (SOR \times$ equivalent units produced)

Total overhead variance = $9,000 − ($6 × 1,200) = $1,800 unfavorable

Spending Variance

The spending variance is calculated as follows:

Overhead-spending variance = Actual overhead minus the flexible budget based on units produced, or

Overhead-spending variance = $AOC - [BFO + (VOR \times units)]$

Overhead-spending variance = $9,000 - [$4,000 + ($2 \times 1,200)] = $2,600$ unfavorable

Volume Variance

The volume variance is determined in the same manner as explained earlier, except that units are substituted for allowed hours (result will be the same, since allowed hours are derived from units of output).

Overhead-volume variance =
  $[$4,000 + ($2 \times 1,200)] - ($6 \times 1,200) = 800 favorable

☐ OVERHEAD VARIANCES
WITH SEPARATE COSTS

In some cases, actual overhead costs may be separated in the accounts into fixed and variable components. In such cases, it becomes logical to initially separate overhead variances into two components: a variable-overhead variance and a fixed-overhead variance. Each of these can then be split into two additional variances. Consider the diagram in figure 8.4.

Although overhead-variance analysis with **separate costs** has not received as much attention in practice as the more traditional analysis discussed, one should be aware of its potential value. It provides more information than three-way analysis because the spending variance is broken down into the variable and fixed components mentioned previously.

Consider the following comprehensive example:

XYZ Company has a standard overhead rate of $5 per hour for use in its standard-costing system. Expected volume of 10,000 hours (5,000 units) was used for purposes of developing the rate. The budget at that level consisted of $30,000 and $20,000 of variable and fixed costs, respectively. The actual level of operations was 9,000 hours and 4,600 units of production. Actual overhead was $45,000, consisting of $19,000 of fixed costs and $26,000 of variable costs.

Required ☐ Develop relevant variances for analysis.

With the given data, it should be possible to develop variances by (1) a two-way analysis, (2) a three-way analysis, and (3) a breakdown by variable and fixed components. The solution follows:

Total overhead variance
  Actual overhead . . . . = $45,000
  Overhead applied (9,200 × $5) . . . . = 46,000
    Favorable overhead variance . . . . $ 1,000

FIGURE 8.4
Variable-and
Fixed-Overhead
Analyses

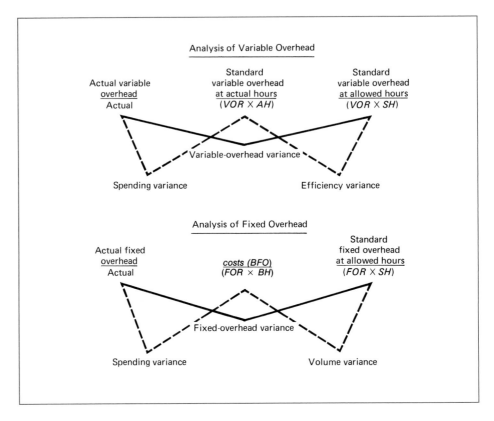

Two-way analysis

Actual overhead	=	$45,000
Budgeted overhead at allowed hours		
[$20,000 + ($3 × 9,200)]	=	47,600
Favorable controllable variance		$ 2,600
Budgeted overhead (computed above)	=	$47,600
Overhead applied	=	46,000
Unfavorable volume variance		$ (1,600)

Three-way analysis

Actual overhead	=	$45,000
Budgeted overhead at actual hours		
[20,000 + ($3 × 9,000)]	=	47,000
Favorable spending variance		$ 2,000
Variable-overhead at actual hours ($3 × 9,000)	=	$27,000
Variable overhead at allowed hours ($3 × 9,200)	=	27,600
Favorable efficiency variance		$ 600
Budgeted fixed overhead	=	$20,000
Fixed overhead applied ($2 × 9,200)	=	18,400
Unfavorable volume variance		$ (1,600)

Variable and fixed-component analysis

Actual variable overhead	=	$26,000
Variable-overhead rate × actual hours ($3 × 9,000)	=	27,000
Favorable variable-spending variance		$ 1,000

Variable-overhead rate × actual hours	=	$27,000
Variable-overhead rate × allowed hours ($3 × 9,200)	=	27,600
Favorable efficiency variance		$ 600
Actual fixed overhead	=	$19,000
Budgeted fixed overhead	=	20,000
Favorable fixed-spending variance		$ 1,000
Budgeted fixed overhead	=	$20,000
Fixed overhead applied ($2 × 9,200)	=	18,400
Unfavorable volume variance		$ (1,600)

Note that the volume variance is the same for all analyses. The sum of the spending and efficiency variances in the last analysis equals the spending variance of the two-way analysis. The sum of the spending variances of the last analysis equals the spending variance in the three-way analysis.

☐ JOURNAL ENTRIES FOR OVERHEAD

Journal entries for actual overhead are made as the costs are incurred throughout the accounting period, based on purchase invoices, material requisitions, payable records, end-of-period adjustments, as well as from other sources. The following example serves to show that two basic overhead accounts exist whenever predetermined overhead rates are used. Data from the immediately preceding example are used as the basis for the following:

During the period just completed, the XYZ Company incurred $45,000 of overhead costs. The costs included $20,000 for equipment depreciation, $5,000 of indirect material, and $10,000 of indirect labor. During the period, overhead of $46,000 was applied to production. All production started was completed. The company uses the three-way analysis for analyzing variances.

Entries relating to XYZ Company's activities are:

(A) To record overhead costs incurred:		
Manufacturing overhead control	45,000	
Accumulated depreciation—equipment		20,000
Raw-material inventory		5,000
Wages payable		10,000
Other credits		10,000
(B) To record overhead applied:		
Work-in-process	46,000	
Manufacturing overhead applied		46,000
(C) To close the factory overhead accounts:		
Manufacturing overhead applied	46,000	
Overhead variance		1,000
Manufacturing overhead control		45,000
(D) To transfer overhead to finished goods:		
Finished goods	46,000	
Work-in-process		46,000

In an actual situation, these entries would typically be combined with ones for material and labor and shown as one entry to finished goods. Individual overhead variances do not need to be journalized. They would be reported separately by cost center on performance reports. Some final disposition would also have to be made of the material, labor, and overhead variances. This topic is discussed next.

☐ DISPOSITION OF VARIANCES

Depending on the circumstances, variances are disposed of in several different ways. What is the theoretical justification for each of the following methods of accounting for the net amount of all standard-cost variances for year-end financial reporting?

1. Presenting the net variances as an income or expense item on the income statement.

2. Allocating the net variance among inventories and cost of goods sold.

3. Presenting the net variance as an adjustment to cost of goods sold.

Requirements such as the three listed focus attention on the interpretive aspects of variances, along with the continued problem of historical versus standard costs. If variances are interpreted to reflect inefficiencies as opposed to adjustments from historical costs, they can be written off in the period recognized. If historical cost reporting continues to dominate the interpretation, then a partial capitalization is probably justified. Consider, then, the following theoretical justification for each of the described methods of accounting for the annual net amount of standard-cost variance:

1. Presenting the net variance as a charge or credit on the income statement indicates that it is regarded as an appropriate charge or credit in the period in which it arises, because it is considered to be the result of favorable or unfavorable departures from expected (standard) conditions. The variance should be disclosed separately from cost of goods sold at standard and, thus, provide management with unobscured information, permitting immediate corrective action. Inventory valuations and cost of goods sold should not be distorted by variances that represent abnormal efficiencies or inefficiencies. Standard cost represents the amount that is reasonably necessary to produce finished products and, therefore, should be considered the best measure of cost of goods manufactured and inventory valuation, as long as the underlying operating conditions remain unchanged.

2. Accountants who advocate allocation of net variance among inventories and cost of goods sold regard standard costs as a useful tool for purposes of management control, not as substitutes for actual historical costs in the financial statements. They also believe that only actual historical costs should be used for financial reporting, even if they are greater or less than standard costs and regardless of the reasons for their differences from standard costs. Standard-cost variances are neither gains nor losses but cost of goods manufactured (or reductions therein) and, as such, should be allocated among inventories and cost of goods sold; to treat them otherwise distorts both the inventory and gross profit. This distortion is even greater if the standards have been carelessly determined and are lacking in accuracy or reliability. Furthermore, to substitute standard costs for actual historical costs in the financial statements is an unwarranted sacrifice of objectivity.

3. Presenting the net variance as an adjustment to cost of goods sold indicates that the charge or credit should be included in the period during which it occurs and that it should be identified with manufacturing costs instead of with other operating costs. This presentation is appropriate only if the variance is not material in relation to the total cost of goods manufactured.

☐ STANDARDS AND PROCESS COSTING

As you may have guessed from our discussions, standards are ideally suited to repetitive manufacturing situations in which the same or similar products are mass-produced on a continuing basis. When standards are integrated with a process-costing system, one of the major problems of process costing—the FIFO, weighted-average decision—is eliminated. The standard-costing system, like the FIFO method under process costing, recognizes work done only in the current period as the basis for calculating equivalent units. But, the problem of calculating unit costs is eliminated, along with the problem associated with inventory layers when standards are used. These advantages have made standard costing increasingly important in process-costing systems. To see more specifically how standards tend to simplify the process-costing situation, consider the following example:

The Koh Corporation has developed a standard process-costing system for its major manufacturing operations. The standard cost per unit of product is

Direct material	1 lb at $4 per lb
Direct labor	2 hr at $4 per hr
Manufacturing overhead	2 hr at $1 per hr

The company's flexible budget for the current period, based on standard hours allowed, is $23,000. Information on units is as follows:

Beginning work-in-process	2,500 (60 percent complete)
Started	10,000
Completed	10,500
Ending work-in-process	2,000 (50 percent complete)

Direct materials are added to the beginning of production. The percentages shown relate to conversion costs only. Beginning inventory costs totaled $25,000. In the current month, the following standard costs were applied in production:

Direct materials	$40,000
Direct labor	80,000
Manufacturing overhead	20,000

The actual costs, related to manufacturing, are as follows:

Direct materials (10,500 pounds)	$42,000
Direct labor (21,000 actual hours)	86,750
Manufacturing overhead	23,100

The material price variance is recognized at the time the direct materials are purchased. Equivalent units would be calculated in the same way they were done on the FIFO basis to give recognition to work done in the current period. Physical and equivalent units would appear as follows:

	Units		
		Equivalent	
Physical flows	Physical	Direct materials	Conversion costs
Units to be accounted for			
Beginning work-in-process			
(60 percent complete)	2,500		
Units started	10,000		
Total	12,500		
Units accounted for			
From beginning inventory	2,500		1,000
Started and completed	8,000	8,000	8,000
Ending work-in-process			
(50 percent complete)	2,000	2,000	1,000
Total	12,500	10,000	10,000

Since standards are being used, we do not need to calculate unit costs; they are available from the standard cost sheet. To assign costs to finished units and ending work-in-process, simply multiply the various components by the appropriate standard cost. Again, as in the FIFO method, we assume that beginning inventory is completed first. However, when applying standard costing, remember to price beginning inventory at the current standards. As a result, costs can be developed in layers or simply on a units-completed basis. The two calculations are shown below.

Costs accounted for
Units completed
From beginning inventory .... $ 25,000
Required to complete
Conversion costs (1,000 × $10) 10,000
Started and completed   or,
(8,000 × $14) 112,000   Completed units
Total completed units .... $147,000   (10,500 × $14) ... $147,000

Ending work-in-process
Direct materials
(2,000 × $4) .... $ 8,000
Conversion costs
(1,000 × $10) 10,000
Ending work-in-process .... $ 18,000
Total $165,000

The complete cost-of-production report is shwon in figure 8.5. What about the variances arising from the manufacturing process? The variances for Koh Corporation should be calculated and shown in a performance report format similar to that shown in figure 8.6.

FIGURE 8.5
Koh Corporation
Cost-of-Production
report

	Physical	Units Equivalent	
		Direct materials	Conversion costs
Physical flows			
Units to be accounted for			
Beginning work-in-process			
(60 percent complete)	2,500		
Units started	10,000		
Total	12,500		
Units accounted for			
From beginning inventory	2,500		1,000
Started and completed	8,000	8,000	8,000
Ending work-in-process			
(50 percent complete)	2,000	2,000	1,000
Total	12,500	10,000	10,000
Cost flows (at standard)			
Costs to be accounted for			
From beginning inventory	$ 25,000		
Current costs added			
Direct materials	40,000		
Conversion costs	100,000		
Total	$165,000		

Costs accounted for	or,	
Units complete	Completed units	
From beginning inventory	$25,000	$(10,500 × 14) = $147,000
Required to complete		
Conversion costs		
(1,000 × $10)	10,000	
Started and completed		
(8,000 × $14)	112,000	
Completed units	$147,000	
Ending work-in-process		
Direct materials		
(2,000 × $4)	$ 8,000	
Conversion costs		
(1,000 × $10)	10,000	
Total work-in-process	$ 18,000	
Total	$165,000	

Material variances
  Material-quantity variance
    Actual materials (10,500 × $4) $42,000
    Standard materials (10,000 × $4) 40,000
      Unfavorable .... $ 2,000

Labor variances
  Labor-rate variance
    Actual labor costs $86,750
    Actual hours at standard rate (21,000 × $4) 84,000
      Unfavorable .... $ 2,750
  Labor-efficiency variance
    Actual hours at standard rate $84,000
    Allowed hours at standard rate (20,000 × $4) 80,000
      Unfavorable .... $ 4,000

Overhead variances
  Spending variance
    Actual overhead costs $23,100
    Flexible budget 23,000
      Unfavorable .... $ 100
  Volume variance
    Flexible budget $23,000
    Allowed overhead 20,000
      Unfavorable .... $ 3,000

☐ SUMMARY

Standard costing is defined in a number of ways. Operationally, standard costs are the best obtainable costs under current conditions with reasonably competent management. Utilization of standards should provide company officials with a mechanism for controlling costs and should place emphasis on clearly defined lines of responsibility.

Under a fully integrated standard-costing system, the record keeping process may be simplified somewhat by incorporating standards into the system, thereby yielding finished goods at the standard cost. Differences between actual costs and standards are shown as variances that, when properly analyzed, provide the basis for control.

Material variances are usually broken down into price and quantity components. Labor variances are typically separated into rate and efficiency differences. Overhead variances may be reflected by means of a mixed-cost two-way or three-way analysis or by means of a variable-cost two-way and fixed-cost two-way analysis.

Variances can be accounted for in year-end financial reporting by (1) presenting the net variances as an income or expense item on the income statement, (2) allocating the net variance among inventories and cost of goods sold, or (3) presenting the net variance as an adjustment to cost of goods sold.

Budgeted activity level
Efficiency variance
Flexible budget
Labor-rate variance
Material-price variance
Material-quantity variance

Mixed costs
Separate costs
Spending variance
Standard costs
Standard hours allowed
Volume variance

REVIEW PROBLEM

Tokoya, Inc., uses a standard-costing system in the manufacture of stereo parts. The standard price for plastic used as direct material was $5 per unit. Standards called for four units in each finished part. The standard direct-hour rate was $10 per hour.

The standard allowance was two hours per finished part. The standard overhead rate was $6 per hour. In developing this rate, a normal capacity of 120,000 direct-labor hours was used. At that level, the flexible budget included $240,000 of fixed costs.

During the month just ended, 9,000 parts were manufactured. Actual direct-labor costs were $220,000 for 20,000 hours of labor. Actual manufacturing overhead was $116,000. Plastic costing $240,000 (40,000 units) was purchased, and 38,000 pieces were used in current month production.

Required □

1. Develop relevant material variances.
2. Develop relevant labor variances.
3. Develop overhead variances under each of the following methods:

   a. Two-way analysis
   b. Three-way analysis

Solution □

1. Material variances

Price variance ($6 − $5) × 40,000	=	$40,000 U
Quantity variance (38,000 − 36,000) × $5	=	10,000 U
Total		$50,000 U

2. Labor variances

Rate variance ($11 − $10) × 20,000	=	$20,000 U
Efficiency variance (20,000 − 18,000) × $10	=	20,000 U
Total		$40,000 U

3. Overhead variances

Two-way analysis
Spending variance
$116,000 − [$20,000 + ($4 × 18,000)] .... = $24,000 U

Volume variance
$[\$20,000 + (\$4 \times 18,000)] - (\$6 \times 18,000)$ .... = <u>16,000 F</u>

   Total .... <u>$ 8,000 U</u>

Three-way analysis
Spending variance
$\$116,000 - [\$20,000 + (\$4 \times 20,000)]$ .... = $16,000 U

Efficiency variance
$\$4(20,000 - 18,000)$ .... = 8,000 U

Volume
$\$2(10,000 - 18,000)$ .... = <u>16,000 F</u>

   Total .... <u>$ 8,000 U</u>

QUESTIONS

Q8-1. What is standard costing? Justify your answer.

Q8-2. Discuss the difference between theoretical and attainable standards.

Q8-3. Can standards be used for both job-order and process costing?

Q8-4. What is a flexible budget? Identify the basic concepts involved.

Q8-5. Identify and discuss the various methods for treating standard-cost variances for financial reporting purposes.

Q8-6. What benefits should be sought from a standard-costing system?

Q8-7. Identify the variances available for material and labor.

Q8-8. Describe the prerequisites for a meaningful standard-costing system.

Q8-9. What is the difference between the spending variance of the two-way analysis and the spending variance of the three-way analysis? Under what circumstance might this result in the same variance?

Q8-10. What kind of information for control purposes should be provided by the variable spending, efficiency, fixed-budget, and volume variance?

Q8-11. Which variance is likely to yield the least information for control purposes? Why?

PROBLEMS

Development of
Basic Standards

P8-1. Winston-Salem Furniture Company uses a standard-costing system. Managers have decided to add a table to their product line. Material A, costing $5 per foot, will be used as the basic material. Under ideal conditions, it should take ten feet of material A per unit of product. At the present time, 20 percent of the material used will be lost in the process due to cutting and shaping problems. Under the most favorable conditions (i.e., when avoidable losses are not present), it should take eight direct-labor hours at $5 per hour to complete one unit of the product. Unfortunately, because of present technology, labor operates only at 50 percent efficiency. The standard overhead rate per direct-labor hour is $2.

Required ☐ Develop the standard cost for one unit.

P8-2. Joboor Company has the following results for the most recent period:

Journal Entries Under Standard Costing

Purchase of materials used directly in production at standard cost	$500,000
Price variance	60,000
Sales	800,000
Marketing expense	40,000
Materials (direct) put into production	200,000
Material-quantity variance	60,000
Administrative expense	150,000
Direct labor charged to work-in-process	90,000
Labor-rate variance	5,000
Other income	10,000
Labor-efficiency variance	40,000

Required ☐ Journalize the data relating to standard costs in original transaction format, assuming that all variances are unfavorable.

Material and Labor Variances

P8-3. The XYZ Corporation develops variances in their standard-costing system at the earliest practical time. Assume that work-in-process inventories are not relevant. The standards call for three pounds of direct material at $2 per pound and one hour at $4 per hour of direct labor per finished unit.

	Actual usage	Standard allowed
Direct material	10,000 lb	$24,000
Direct labor	5,000 hr	16,000

Actual direct-labor costs were $21,000. Direct materials were purchased at $2.50 per pound at a total cost of $50,000.

Required ☐ Calculate the applicable material and labor variances.

P8-4. Standards are used by many concerns to generate data relevant to the acquisition and utilization of the component cost elements in a manufacturing process. The three basic types of standards that may be employed are (1) fixed (basic), (2) ideal, and (3) attainable.

Types of Standards

Required ☐

1. Define the three types of standards.

2. What do standards and related variances attempt to disclose with respect to acquisition and utilization within a manufacturing process? Limit the discussion to the two general categories: variable costs and fixed factory overhead. Identify specific variances, but do not discuss their computations.

3. How do standards relate to cost-accumulation procedures?

P8-5. At June 30, 19X9, the end of the current fiscal year, a partial trial balance revealed the following for Crowley Corporation:

Analysis of Material and Labor Variances

	Debits	Credits
Material-price variance		$25,000
Material-quantity variance	$ 9,000	
Labor-rate variance	30,000	
Labor-efficiency variance	7,500	

Required ☐ What conclusions, without making assumptions, can be drawn from each of the four variances shown in Crowley's trial balance? Be specific.

(CPA)

Calculation of Material and Labor Variances

P8-6. The Bronson Company manufactures a fuel additive that has a stable selling price of $40 per drum. Since losing a government contract, the company has been producing and selling 80,000 drums per month, which is 50 percent of normal capacity. Management officials expect to increase production to 140,000 drums in the coming year.

In connection with your examination of the financial statements of the Bronson Company for the year ended September 30, 19X0, you have been asked to review some computations made by the company's cost accountant. Your working papers disclose the following about company operations:

(A) Standard costs per drum of product manufactured:

Materials	
8 gallons of Miracle Mix	$15
1 empty drum	1
	$16
Direct labor—1 hr	$ 5
Factory overhead	$ 6

(B) Costs and expenses during September 19X0:

Miracle Mix
500,000 gallons purchased
at cost of $950,000; 650,000
gallons used
Empty drums
94,000 purchased at cost of
$94,000; 80,000 used
Direct labor
82,000 hours worked at cost
of $414,000

(C) None of the September 19X0 cost variances are expected to occur proportionally in future months. For the next fiscal year, the manager of the Cost Standards department expects the same standard usage of materials and direct-labor hours. The average prices expected are: $2.10 per gallon of Miracle Mix, $1.00 per empty drum, and $5.70 per direct-labor hour. The current flexible budget of factory overhead costs is considered applicable to future periods without revision.

Required ☐ Prepare a schedule computing the following variances for September 19X0: (1) materials-price variance, (2) materials-quantity variance, (3) labor-rate variance, and (4) labor-efficiency variance.

(CPA)

P8-7. A summary of Brown's flexible budget is shown below.

Variance Analysis with Flexible Budgets

	Activity level		
Direct labor hours	6,000	8,000	10,000
Variable overhead	$ 7,200	$ 9,600	$12,000
Fixed overhead	24,000	24,000	24,000
	$31,200	$33,600	$36,000

The following additional information is available:

1. For 19X4 an activity base of 8,000 budgeted direct-labor hours is selected. For 8,000 allowed direct-labor hours, the company should be able to produce 4,000 finished units.

2. During 19X4, company operations produce the following results:

a.	Units produced	4,200
b.	Direct-labor hours used	8,600
c.	Actual overhead	$34,200

Required □

1. Calculate the standard hours allowed for the output of 19X4.

2. Calculate the overhead variances, using the three-way analysis.

P8-8. Peggy Craft Company's standard cost sheet for its only product, **SHIRTS**, is as follows:

Standard Cost Sheet and Variance Analysis

Standard Cost Sheet—per SHIRT

Direct materials, 4 yards @ $4	$16.00
Direct labor, 1 hour @ $5	5.00
Overhead, 1 hour @ $2 ($1 VOR)	2.00
Total standard cost per SHIRT	$23.00

During the period, 6,000 shirts were produced, and 6,400 direct-labor hours were used. Actual overhead costs incurred were $14,800. The volume variance was $2,000 unfavorable.

Required □

1. Calculate the overhead variances, using the two-way analysis.

2. How much budgeted fixed overhead was included in the flexible budget?

P8-9.* Eastern Company manufactures special electrical equipment and parts. Eastern employs a standard cost accounting system with separate standards established for each product. A special transformer is manufactured in the Transformer Department. Production volume is measured by direct-labor hours in this department, and a flexible budget system is used to plan and control department overhead.

Calculation of Variances— Multiple Choice

Standard costs for the special transformer are determined annually in September for the coming year. The standard cost of a transformer for 19X7 was computed at $67, as shown below.

Direct materials		
Iron	5 sheets @ $2	$10
Copper	3 spools @ $3	9
Direct labor	4 hours @ $7	28
Variable overhead	4 hours @ $3	12
Fixed overhead	4 hours @ $2	8
Total		$67

Overhead rates were based on normal and expected monthly capacity for 19X7, both of which were 4,000 direct-labor hours. Practical capacity for this department is 5,000 direct-labor hours per month. Variable overhead costs are expected to vary with the number of direct-labor hours actually used.

During October 19X7, 800 transformers were produced. This was below expectations because a work stoppage occurred during contract negotiations with the labor force. Once the contract was settled, the department scheduled overtime in an attempt to catch up to expected production levels.

The following costs were incurred in October 19X7:

Direct material	Direct-materials purchased	Materials used
Iron	5,000 sheets @ $2.00 per sheet	3,900 sheets
Copper	2,200 spools @ $3.10 per spool	2,600 spools

Direct labor	
Regular time	2,000 hours @ $7.00
	1,400 hours @ $7.20
Overtime	600 of the 1,400 hours were subject to overtime premium. The total overtime premium of $2,160 is included in variable overhead in accordance with company accounting practices.
Variable overhead	$10,000
Fixed overhead	$ 8,800

Required □ Select the best answer for each of the following eight items.

1. The most appropriate time to record any variation of actual material prices from standard is

   a. At the year-end, when all variations will be known
   b. At the time of purchase
   c. At the time of material usage
   d. As needed to evaluate the performance of the Purchasing manager
   e. Some time other than those shown is appropriate

2. The total material quantity variance is

   a. $200 favorable
   b. $400 favorable
   c. $600 favorable
   d. $400 unfavorable
   e. Some amount other than those shown

3. The labor-rate (price) variation is

   a. $280 unfavorable
   b. $340 unfavorable
   c. $1,680 unfavorable
   d. $2,440 unfavorable
   e. None of the above responses is correct.

4. The variable-overhead spending variation is

   a. $200 favorable
   b. $400 unfavorable
   c. $600 unfavorable
   d. $1,600 unfavorable
   e. Some amount other than those shown

5. The efficiency variation in variable overhead is the standard variable-overhead rate times the difference between standard-labor hours of output and

   a. 2,000 hours
   b. 2,600 hours
   c. 2,800 hours
   d. 3,400 hours
   e. Some amount other than those shown

6. The fixed spending variation for fixed overhead is

   a. $2,400 unfavorable
   b. $0
   c. $800 unfavorable
   d. Not calculable from the problem
   e. Some amount other than those shown

7. The fixed-overhead volume variation is

   a. $400 unfavorable
   b. $2,200 unfavorable
   c. $2,400 unfavorable
   d. $1,600 unfavorable
   e. Some amount other than those shown

8. An unfavorable fixed-overhead-volume variation is most often caused by

   a. Actual fixed overhead incurred exceeding budgeted fixed overhead
   b. An overapplication of fixed overhead to production
   c. A decrease in the level of the finished inventory of transformers
   d. Production levels exceeding sales levels
   e. Normal capacity exceeding actual production levels

   (CMA)

P8-10. The controller for XYZ Company has calculated the company's overhead variances for the period just ended. They are as follows:

Multiple-Choice Items—Standard Costing

Variable-spending variance	$ 500 U
Efficiency variance	1,000 F

Fixed-spending variance .... 400 F
Volume variance .... 600 U

Variable overhead applied for the period was $22,000, and fixed overhead applied was $20,000.

Required □ Answer requirements 1 through 5 using the previous information.

1. Spending variance, under the two-way analysis using combined costs, would be

   a. $500 F
   b. $900 F
   c. $100 U
   d. $500 U

2. Efficiency variance, under the three-way analysis using combined costs, would be

   a. $1,400 F
   b. $500 F
   c. $900 F
   d. $1,000 F

3. The flexible budget based on standard hours allowed for actual units produced would be

   a. $42,600
   b. $41,700
   c. $41,200
   d. $41,100

4. The budgeted fixed overhead for XYZ Company would be

   a. $20,000
   b. $20,600
   c. $21,500
   d. $19,800

5. Assuming standard hours allowed for actual units were 10,000, the variable overhead rate would be

   a. $2.00
   b. $2.20
   c. $2.15
   d. $2.25

Overhead Variances   **P8-11.** The Atlanta Carpet Mills uses a standard-costing system with a standard overhead rate of $6 per unit. In developing this rate, a normal capacity of 10,000 units was used. At that level, the flexible budget included $20,000 of fixed costs. In the current period, 8,000 units were completed. Actual overhead costs for the period were $54,000.

Required □ Calculate the relevant overhead variances.

Overhead Costs and Variances   **P8-12.** The XYZ Corporation produces calendars for sale by their marketing personnel. In developing standard costs for the product, an overhead rate of

$2.80 per unit was developed. Historical records, considered reliable, had indicated that overhead was $15,000 at a 5,000 unit output and $20,000 at a 7,500 unit output. Actual overhead was $20,000 with 7,000 units of actual production.

Required □ Calculate the following:

a. Total overhead variance
b. Standard volume
c. Formula for budgeted overhead costs
d. Spending variance
e. Volume variance

P8-13. At the end of the current month's production, the following information was available:

Overhead Costs and Variances

Flexible budget based on allowed hours: $5,000 + ($2 × 1,000 DLH)
Spending variance: $200 U
Total standard overhead applied to production based on allowed hours: $4,000
Each unit produced requires: .5 DLH

Required □ Calculate the following:

a. Actual overhead costs incurred
b. Budgeted volume
c. Volume variance
d. Budgeted fixed costs
e. Number of units produced

P8-14. The ABC Company has developed a standard-overhead costing system based on a normal capacity of 10,000 hours (2,500 units). The flexible budget at that level includes $30,000 of variable costs and $20,000 of fixed costs. Actual operations required resulted in 2,300 completed units. Actual overhead was $53,000. Actual hours worked were 9,400.

Overhead Variances— Three-Way Analysis

Required □ Calculate the spending, efficiency, and volume variances.

P8-15. The XYZ Company has a standard overhead rate of $5 per hour for use in its standard-costing system. Normal capacity of 10,000 hours (5,000 units) was used for purposes of developing the rate. The budget at that level consisted of $30,000 and $20,000 of variable and fixed costs, respectively. Actual level of operations was 9,000 hours and 4,600 units of production. Actual overhead was $45,000, consisting of $19,000 of fixed costs and $26,000 of variable costs.

Overhead Variances— Variable and Fixed

Required □ Calculate the applicable variable- and fixed-cost variances.

P8-16. Select the best answer for each of the following multiple-choice questions relating to standard-costing systems.

Multiple-Choice Items—Overhead Variances

1. If the actual amount of materials used equals the standard amount of materials that should have been used, then the difference between the standard cost and actual cost of materials is called the

   a. Quantity variance
   b. Cost variance

    c.   Rate variance

    d.   Price variance

2. At the end of the fiscal year, substantial variances from standard variable manufacturing cost should be allocated to inventories and cost of sales if they were due to

    a.   Additional costs of raw material acquired under a speculative-purchase contract

    b.   Increased labor rates won by the union as a result of a strike during the year

    c.   A breakdown of equipment

    d.   Overestimates of production volume for the period resulting from failure to predict an unusual decline in the market for the company's product

3. In analysis of standard-cost variances, the item that receives the most diverse treatment in accounting is

    a.   Direct-labor cost

    b.   Manufacturing-overhead cost

    c.   Direct-material cost

    d.   Fixed costs

4. Differences in product costs resulting from the application of actual overhead rates rather than predetermined overhead rates could be immaterial if

    a.   Production is not stable

    b.   Fixed factory overhead is a significant cost

    c.   Several products are produced simultaneously

    d.   Overhead is composed only of variable costs

5. A company employing very tight (high) standards in a standard-cost system should expect that

    a.   Costs will be controlled better than if lower standards were used

    b.   Employees will be strongly motivated to attain the standards

    c.   No incentive bonus will be paid

    d.   Most variances will be unfavorable

6. Standard costing will produce the same results as actual or conventional costing when standard-cost variances are distributed to

    a.   Cost of goods sold

    b.   An income or expense account

    c.   Cost of goods sold and inventories

    d.   A balance sheet account

7. A spending variance for overhead is the difference between actual overhead cost and overhead cost that should have been incurred for the actual hours worked and results from

    a.   Price differences for overhead costs

    b.   Quantity differences for overhead costs

    c.   Price and quantity differences for overhead costs

    d.   Differences caused by production volume variation

8. The concept of "the ideal capacity of a plant" as used in cost accounting is its

   a. Theoretical maximum capacity
   b. Best capacity for normal production
   c. Capacity used for standard costing
   d. Capacity below which production should not fall

P8-17. Ross Shirts, Inc., manufactures short- and long-sleeved men's shirts for large stores. Ross produces a single-quality shirt in lots to each customer's order and attaches the store's label to each. The standard costs for a dozen long-sleeved shirts are: *Comprehensive Standard-Costing Problem*

Direct materials	24 yd $ .55	$13.20
Direct labor	3 hr $2.45	7.35
Manufacturing overhead	3 hr $2.00	6.00
Standard cost per dozen		$26.55

During October 19X9, Ross worked on three orders for long-sleeved shirts. Job-cost records for the month disclose the following:

Lot	Units in lot	Materials used	Hours worked
30	1,000 doz.	24,100 yd	2,980
31	1,700 doz.	40,440 yd	5,130
32	1,200 doz.	28,825 yd	2,890

The following information is also available:

   a. Ross purchased 95,000 yards of material during the month at a cost of $53,200. The materials-price variance is recorded when goods are purchased and all inventories are carried at standard cost.
   b. Direct labor incurred amounted to $27,500 during October. According to payroll records, production employees were paid $2.50 per hour.
   c. Overhead is applied on the basis of direct-labor hours. Manufacturing overhead totaling $22,800 was incurred during October.
   d. A total of $288,000 was budgeted for overhead for the year 19X9 based on estimated production at the plant's normal capacity of 48,000 dozen shirts per year. Overhead is 40 percent fixed and 60 percent variable at this level of production.
   e. There was no work-in-process at October 1. During October, lots 30 and 31 were completed, all material was issued for lot 32, and it was 80 percent completed as to labor.

Required ☐

1. Prepare a schedule computing the standard cost for October 19X9, of lots 30, 31, and 32.

2. Prepare a schedule computing the material-price variance for October 19X9, and indicate whether the variance is favorable or unfavorable.

3. Prepare schedules computing variances (and indicating whether the variances are favorable or unfavorable) for each lot produced during October 19X9. Include

  a. The material-quantity variance in yards
  b. The labor-efficiency variance in hours
  c. The labor-rate variance in dollars

4. Prepare a schedule computing the total spending and volume manufacturing-overhead variances for October 19X9, and indicate whether the variances are favorable or unfavorable.

(CPA)

Comprehensive Standard-Costing Problem

P8-18. The Conti Pharmaceutical Company processes a single compound-product known as NULAX and uses a standard-cost accounting system. The process requires preparation and blending of three materials in large batches with a variation from the standard mixture sometimes necessary to maintain quality. The company's cost accountant became ill at the end of October 19X8, and you were engaged to determine standard costs of October production and explain any differences between actual and standard costs for the month. The following information is available for the Blending department:

(A) The standard cost card for a 500-pound batch shows the following standard costs:

	Quantity	Price	Total	Cost
Materials				
Mucilloid	250 lb	$ .14	$35	
Dextrose	200 lb	.09	18	
Ingredients	50 lb	.08	4	
Total per batch	500 lb			$ 57
Labor				
Preparation and blending	10 hr	$3.00		30
Overhead				
Variable	10 hr	$1.00	$10	
Fixed	10 hr	.30	3	13
Total standard cost per				
500-pound batch				$100

(B) During October, 410 batches of 500 pounds each of the finished compound were completed and transferred to the Packaging department.

(C) Blending department inventories totaled 6,000 pounds at the beginning of the month and 9,000 pounds at the end of the month (assume both inventories were completely processed but not transferred and consisted of materials in their standard proportions).

(D) During the month of October, the following materials were purchased and put into production:

	Pounds	Price	Total cost
Mucilloid	114,400	$.17	$19,448
Dextrose	85,800	.11	9,438
Ingredients	19,800	.07	1,386
Totals	220,000		$30,272

(E) Wages paid for 4,212 hours of direct labor at $3.25 per hour amounted to $13,689.

(F) Actual overhead costs for the month totaled $5,519.

(G) The standards were established for a normal production volume of 200,000 pounds (400 batches) of NULAX per month. At this level of production, variable factory overhead was budgeted at $4,000, and fixed factory overhead was budgeted at $1,200.

Required ☐

1. Prepare a schedule presenting the computation for the Blending department of:

    a. October production in both pounds and batches.
    b. The standard cost of October production itemized by components of materials, labor, and overhead.

2. Prepare schedules computing the differences between actual and standard costs and analyzing the differences as:

    a. Material variances (for each material) caused by
        1. Price differences
        2. Quantity differences
    b. Labor variances caused by
        1. Rate difference
        2. Efficiency difference
    c. Overhead variances caused by
        1. Spending factors
        2. Volume factors

(CPA)

P8-19. The standard formula used by the Memphis Products Company is as follows:

Comprehensive Standard-Costing Problem

Product Y (per dozen)

Direct materials			
Material A	10 lb @ $ .50	$ 5.00	
Material B	5 lb @ 1.00	5.00	$10.00
Direct labor			
Process 1	5 hr @ $4.00	$20.00	
Process 2	4 hr @ 6.00	24.00	44.00
Overhead			
$4 per direct-labor hour*			36.00
			$90.00

*($2 VOR. Fixed costs estimated at $10,000)

Beginning inventory of materials A and B was 1,000 pounds and 500 pounds, respectively. During the period, 5,000 pounds of A were acquired at a cost of $2,800. A special price of $.80 per pound was offered on Material B so 4,000 pounds were acquired. At the end of the period, 2,000 pounds of A and 2,400 pounds of B remained in inventory.

Process 1 used 2,200 hours of labor during the period. Process 2 used 1,900 hours. Labor costs were $8,900 for Process 1 and $11,000 for Process 2.

During the period, 450 dozen units were produced. Actual overhead costs incurred during the period amounted to $18,000.

Required ☐

1. Prepare appropriate journal entries for materials purchased; material, labor, and overhead charged to production; finished goods.

2. Calculate the applicable material variances.

3. Calculate the applicable labor variances.

4. Compute the overhead variance by the three-way analysis method.

Standard Costing— Missing Numbers

P8-20. On May 1, 19X5, Bovar Company began the manufacture of a new mechanical device known as Dandy. The company installed a standard-cost system in accounting for manufacturing costs. The standard costs for a unit of Dandy are as follows:

Raw materials	6 lb at $1 per lb	$ 6.00
Direct labor	1 hr at $4 per hr	4.00
Overhead	75 percent of direct-labor costs	3.00
		$13.00

The following data were obtained from Bovar's records for the month of May:

	Units
Actual production of Dandy	4,000
Units sold of Dandy	2,500

	Debit	Credit
Sales		$50,000
Purchases (26,000 pounds)	$27,300	
Material-price variance	1,300	
Material-quantity variance	1,000	
Ditect-labor-rate variance	760	
Direct-labor-efficiency variance		800
Manufacturing-overhead-total variance	500	

The amount shown for material-price variance is applicable to raw material purchased during May.

Required ☐ Compute each of the following items for Bovar for the month of May. Show computations in good form.

a. Standard quantity of raw materials allowed (in pounds)
b. Actual quantity of raw materials used (in pounds)
c. Standard hours allowed
d. Actual hours worked
e. Actual direct-labor rate
f. Actual total overhead

(CPA)

Comprehensive Standard-Costing Problem

P8-21. The Milner Manufacturing Company uses a job-order costing system and standard costs. It manufactures one product, which has standard costs as follows:

Materials	20 yd at $ .90 per yd	$18
Direct labor	4 hr at $6.00 per hr	24

Total factory overhead	Applied at five-sixths of direct labor (the ratio of variable costs to fixed costs is 3 to 1)	20
Variable selling, general, and administrative expenses		12
Fixed selling, general, and administrative expenses		7
Total unit cost		$81

The standards are set based on normal activity of 2,400 direct-labor hours.

Actual activity for the month of October 19X5, was as follows:

Materials purchased	18,000 yd at $.92 per yd	$16,560
Materials used	9,500 yd	
Direct labor	2,100 hr at $6.10 per hr	12,810
Total factory overhead	500 units actually produced	11,100

Required □

1. Based on the standard costs, a certain selling price per unit and number of units will yield an operating profit of $5,200. Increasing this selling price by 4 percent will increase the operating profit to $6,800. All costs and the number of units remain unchanged. Compute the selling price per unit and the number of units to yield an operating profit of $5,200.

2. Compute the variable factory-overhead rate per direct-labor hour and the total fixed factory overhead based on "normal" activity.

3. Prepare a schedule computing the following variances for the month of October 19X5. Indicate whether each variance is favorable or unfavorable.

   a. Materials-price variance
   b. Materials-quantity variance
   c. Labor-rate variance
   d. Labor-efficiency variance
   e. Spending-overhead variance
   f. Volume-overhead variance

(CPA)

P8-22. The Terry Company manufactures a commercial solvent that is used for industrial maintenance. This solvent is sold by the drum and generally has a stable selling price. Due to a decrease in demand for this product, Terry produced and sold 60,000 drums in December 19X6, which is 50 percent of normal capacity.

Comprehensive Standard-Costing Problem

The following information is available regarding operations for the month of December 19X6.

(A) Standard costs per drum of product manufactured were as follows.

Materials		
10 gal of raw material	$20	
1 empty drum	1	
Total materials	$21	
Direct labor		
1 hr	$ 7	

Factory overhead (fixed)
  Per direct-labor hour .... $ 4

Factory overhead (variable)
  Per direct-labor hour .... $ 6

(B) Costs incurred during December 19X6, were as follows:

Raw materials
  600,000 gal were purchased at a
    cost of $1,150,000
  700,000 gal were used

Empty drums
  85,000 drums were purchased at a
    cost of $85,000
  60,000 drums were used

Direct labor
  65,000 hours were worked at a
    cost of $470,000

Factory overhead
  Depreciation of building and
    machinery (fixed) $230,000
  Supervision and indirect labor
    (semivariable) 360,000
  Other factory overhead
    (variable) 76,500
      Total factory overhead $666,500

(C) The fixed overhead budget for the December level of production was
    $276,000.
(D) In November 19X6, at normal capacity of 120,000 drums, supervision
    and indirect-labor costs were $680,000. All cost functions are linear.

Required □ Prepare a schedule computing the following variances for the
month of December 19X6. Indicate whether each variance was favorable
or unfavorable.

  a.   Materials-price variance (computed at time of purchase)
  b.   Materials-quantity variance
  c.   Labor-rate variance
  d.   Labor-usage (efficiency) variance
  e.   Factory overhead using the four-variance method.

(CPA)

Comprehensive   **P8-23.** At the beginning of 19X4, Beal Company adopted the following standards:
Standard Costing

	Input	Total
Direct materials	3 lb @ $2.50 per lb	$ 7.50
Direct labor	5 hr @ $7.50 per hr	37.50
Factory overhead:		
Variable	$3.00 per direct-labor hour	15.00
Fixed	$4.00 per direct-labor hour	20.00
Standard cost per unit		$80.00

Normal (budgeted) volume per month is 40,000 standard labor hours. Beal's January 19X4 budget was based on normal volume. During January Beal produced 7,800 units, with records indicating the following:

Direct materials purchased	25,000 lb @ $2.60
Direct materials used	23,100 lb
Direct labor	40,100 hr @ $7.30
Factory overhead	$300,000

Required □

1. Prepare a schedule of budgeted production costs for January 19X4, based on actual production of 7,800 units.

2. For the month of January 19X4, compute the following variances, indicating whether each is favorable or unfavorable:

   a. Direct-materials-price variance, based on purchases
   b. Direct-materials quantity variance
   c. Direct-labor-rate variance
   d. Direct-labor-efficiency variance
   e. Factory-overhead-spending variance
   f. Factory-overhead-efficiency variance
   g. Factory-overhead-volume variance

(CPA)

P8-24. Lon Company uses standard costs with its process-costing system. Standard costs for the molding process are as follows:

Standards and Process Costing

Materials	$ 4.00
Direct labor	4.00
Overhead	2.00
	$10.00

All direct materials are added at the beginning of the process. Conversion costs are added throughout the process. Operating results for the month were as follows:

Beginning work-in-process inventories	4,000 units (60 percent complete)
Ending work-in-process inventories	6,000 units (40 percent complete)
Units started during the month	20,000
Units completed during the month	?
Actual costs incurred for the month	
Direct materials	$60,000
Direct labor	58,000
Overhead	26,000

Required □

1. Calculate the cost of goods completed and in ending work-in-process.

2. Calculate variances to the extent possible.

P8-25. Melody Corporation is a manufacturing company that produces a single product known as Jupiter. Melody uses the first-in, first-out (FIFO) process-

Standards and Process Costing

costing method for both financial-statement and internal-management reporting.

In analyzing production results, standard costs are used, whereas actual costs are used for financial-statement reporting. The standards, which are based upon equivalent units of production, are as follows:

Raw material per unit	1 lb at $10 per pound
Direct labor per unit	2 hr at $4 per hour
Factory overhead per unit	2 hr at $1.25 per hour

Budgeted factory overhead for standard hours allowed for April production is $30,000.

Data for the month of April 19X7 are presented below:

(A) The beginning inventory consisted of 2,500 units that were 100 percent complete as to raw material and 40 percent complete as to direct labor and factory overhead.

(B) An additional 10,000 units were started during the month.

(C) The ending inventory consisted of 2,000 units that were 100 percent complete as to raw material and 40 percent complete as to direct labor and factory overhead.

(D) Costs applicable to April production are as follows:

	Actual cost	Standard cost
Raw material used (11,000 pounds)	$121,000	$100,000
Direct labor (25,000 hours actually worked)	105,575	82,400
Factory overhead	31,930	25,750

Required □

1. For each element of production for April (raw material, direct labor, and factory overhead) compute the following:

   a. Equivalent units of production
   b. Cost per equivalent unit of production at actual and at standard

Show supporting computations in good form.

2. Prepare a schedule analyzing for April production the following variances as either favorable or unfavorable:

   a. Total materials
   b. Materials price
   c. Materials quantity
   d. Total labor
   e. Labor rate
   f. Labor efficiency
   g. Total factory overhead
   h. Factory overhead volume
   i. Factory overhead spending

(CPA)

P8-26. The quantities and costs of production chargeable to Department A of Cathy Products, Inc., in October 19X4 are summarized as follows: *Standards and Process Costing*

Units in process, October 1	6,000
Units started in production, October	45,000
Units in-process, October 31	5,000

All materials are added at the time the units are started. The work-in-process on October 1 was 40 percent complete as to conversion costs. The work-in-process on October 31 was 40 percent complete as to conversion costs.

Costs

	Work-in-process (Standard) October 1	October costs (Actual)
Direct material (92,000 pounds)	$24,000	$184,000
Direct labor (45,800 hours)	14,400	279,380
Manufacturing overhead	9,600	182,400

Standard Cost Sheet

Direct material	2 pounds @ $2	$ 4
Direct labor	1 hour @ $6	6
Manufacturing overhead	$4 per unit	4
		$14

Required □

1. Prepare a cost-of-production report for October.

2. Prepare a performance report showing variances for the different cost components.

CHAPTER OUTLINE

ADDITIONAL STANDARD-COSTING TOPICS

CHAPTER 9

☐ INTRODUCTION

In chapter 8, the basic standard-cost-accounting system was introduced. The procedural aspects of the system were discussed and variance analysis was described. In this chapter, we will continue the discussion of variances by expanding the material-quantity variance, which was developed in chapter 8, into mix and yield variances. Two statistical methods that are often discussed in connection with determining variance significance will be presented.

☐ MIX AND YIELD VARIANCES

Quite often, in production processes, more than one raw material will be required to produce a unit of product. Although a standard may be established calling for a certain amount of each material to be used in the production of the product, the ratio of materials actually used will sometimes vary from the formula. This may happen because management officials vary the mix in an attempt to improve yield or in response to changes in material costs.

For instance, in the manufacture of potato chips, managers might have a choice of using either new potatoes or older, stored potatoes in the production process. The quantity of finished potato chips per pound of potatoes will vary depending on the moisture content of the potatoes used. The potato yield would in turn affect the amount of cooking oil utilized in the manufacture of the finished chips. As can be seen in this example, a measure of the differences in mix and yield could be valuable input to management in making a decision as to which kind of raw material to use.

In the last chapter, the variance developed to discern usage differences for raw materials was called the material-quantity variance. Deviations from the *formula* in the mix of raw materials actually used and corresponding changes in the yield tend to decrease potential information contained in the material-quantity variance. To provide management with

293

more information, it may be necessary to separate the quantity variance into mix and yield components.

The Mix Variance

The **mix variance** results from mixing raw materials in a ratio different from the standard material formula. In other words, the variance is derived by determining the difference, by components, between the materials actually used and the total quantity used adjusted to the ratio called for by the standard formula.

In many situations, it is possible to vary the material mix and end up with the same amount of product. For instance, quantities of fibers in varying mixes may sometimes be used to produce the same quantity and quality of yarn. However, in other cases, varying the mix will affect the yield. Consider the following simple example set up to indicate how the mix variance is derived:

The Wong Company uses two different components in the production of its product. The standard formula calls for the following mix per unit of finished product:

Material A	2 lb @ $5 per lb	$10
Material B	2 lb @ $4 per lb	8
Total material cost		$18

During the period 5,000 units were produced with the following material used:

	Pounds	Cost
Material A	5,000	$25,000
Material B	15,000	60,000

The material-quantity variance would be calculated in the following manner:

Material A	(5,000 − 10,000) × $5 =	$25,000
Material B	(15,000 − 10,000) × $4 =	(20,000)
Favorable quantity variance		$ 5,000

Even though the above variance is referred to as a quantity (usage) variance, the variance was caused by deviating from the mix called for in the formula. The formula called for a 1:1 ratio in the use of A and B. The ratio actually used was 1:3. To determine the effect of this change, the accountant could recast the actual quantity used into the standard ratio and compare the result with the actual ratio used.

Formula		*Ratio*
Material A	2 lb	1/2
Material B	2 lb	1/2
Total	4	2/2

	Actual quantity adjusted to
Actual quantity	*reflect standard ratio*
5,000	(1/2 × 20,000) = 10,000
15,000	(1/2 × 20,000) = 10,000
20,000	20,000

Mix variance = (Actual quantity − Actual quantity adjusted) × Standard price

Material A	(5,000 − 10,000) × $5 = $25,000
Material B	(15,000 − 10,000) × $4 = (20,000)
Favorable mix variance	$ 5,000*

*Unfavorable or debit variances are enclosed by parentheses in this and following examples.

Alternate calculation using weighted-average cost of materials.

Weighted-average cost using actual mix:

Material A	$5 × 5,000 = $25,000
Material B	$4 × 15,000 = 60,000
Total	$85,000

$85,000 ÷ 20,000 = $4.25 weighted-average cost

Weighted-average cost using standard mix:

Material A	2 × 5,000 × $5 = $50,000
Material B	2 × 5,000 × $4 = 40,000
Total	$90,000

$90,000 ÷ 20,000 = $4.50 weighted-average cost

Mix variance:

$$\left(\begin{array}{c}\text{Average unit cost} \\ \text{using actual mix}\end{array} - \begin{array}{c}\text{Average unit cost} \\ \text{using standard mix}\end{array}\right) \times \text{Actual units} = \text{Mix variance}$$

($4.25 − $4.50) × 20,000 = $5,000 favorable

Thus, in this case, the change in mix caused the total variance, but the yield was unaffected. As indicated earlier, in other cases, altering the mix might cause changes in the yield.

The Yield Variance

Yield is a measure of the output obtained from a given amount of input. A **yield variance** results when a quantity different from the quantity expected based on input is obtained. In the manufacture of potato chips, the management team might expect a certain yield such as 25 percent, or 25 pounds of chips from 100 pounds of potatoes. If this kind of standard is established, it is usually important to know whether or not it is being met. Consequently, a variance should be developed to provide a measure of the difference between quantities actually used and the standard amounts called for, based on the established formula. This sounds like the definition for a quantity variance, and indeed it is, except for the fact that in the yield-variance calculation, actual quantities are actual quantities adjusted to conform to the standard ratio indicated by the formula.

Yield variance = (Actual quantity adjusted − Standard quantity) × Standard price

Now, using the formula from the previous example, assume that 5,000 units were produced with the following material used:

	Pounds	Cost
Material A	6,000	$ 30,000
Material B	18,000	72,000
	24,000	$102,000

Quantity variance

Material A	(6,000 − 10,000) × $5 =	$20,000
Material B	(18,000 − 10,000) × $4 =	(32,000)
Unfavorable quantity variance		($12,000)

The next step is to analyze the reason for the $12,000 unfavorable quantity variance by computing mix and yield variances. If a total of 24,000 pounds of material are used in production, the standard ratio would call for 12,000 pounds of A and 12,000 pounds of B.

Mix variance

Material A	(6,000 − 12,000) × $5 =	$30,000
Material B	(18,000 − 12,000) × $4 =	(24,000)
Favorable mix variance		$ 6,000

Yield variance

Material A	(12,000 − 10,000) × $5 =	($10,000)
Material B	(12,000 − 10,000) × $4 =	(8,000)
Unfavorable yield variance		($18,000)

Alternate calculation using the weighted-average cost of materials:

Weighted-average cost using actual mix:

Material A	$5 × 6,000 =	$ 30,000
Material B	$4 × 18,000 =	72,000
		$102,000

$102,000 ÷ 24,000 = $4.25 weighted-average cost

Weighted-average cost using standard mix:

From previous example, $4.50

Mix variance:

($4.25 − $4.50) × 24,000 = $6,000 favorable

Yield variance:

$$\frac{\text{Average unit cost}}{\text{using standard mix}} \times (\text{Actual pounds} - \text{Standard pounds}) = \text{Yield variance}$$

$4.50 × (24,000 − 20,000) = ($18,000) unfavorable

The example just cited indicates that the quantity variance does not provide enough information concerning the difference. To obtain a better understanding, the difference should be separated into two components—a mix and a yield variance. Using the two variances, it can be seen that although the company had a $6,000 favorable mix variance, there was an unfavorable yield variance of $18,000. Because of the additional information provided, the management team should be in a better position to make a proper decision regarding the mix of materials used.

A Consolidating Example

The Conti Pharmaceutical Company processes a single product known as NULAX and uses a standard-cost-accounting system.[1] The process requires a preparation and blending of three materials into large batches with a variation from the standard mixture sometimes necessary to maintain the quality. The following information on materials is available for the Blending department.

1. The standard-cost card for a 500-pound batch shows the following standard costs.

Materials	Quantity	Price	Total cost
Mucilloid	250	.14	$35.00
Dextrose	200	.09	18.00
Ingredients	50	.08	4.00
			$57.00

2. During October, 410 batches of 500 pounds each of the finished compound were completed and transferred to the Packaging department.

3. Blending department inventories totaled 6,000 pounds at the beginning of the month and 9,000 pounds at the end of the month. (Assume both inventories were completely processed but not transferred and consisted of materials in their standard proportions.)

4. Inventories are carried in the accounts at standard-cost prices.

5. During the month of October, the following materials were purchased and put into production.

	Pounds	Price	Total cost
Mucilloid	114,400	$.17	$19,448
Dextrose	85,800	.11	9,438
Ingredients	19,800	.07	1,386
Total			$30,272

You are to prepare the material quantity, mix and yield variances for each material. To solve this problem, the production for the period must first be determined. Production is determined as follows:

Production			
Ending inventory	9,000	lb	(18 batches)
Beginning inventory	6,000		(12 batches)
Net increase	3,000	lb	(6 batches)
Completed and transferred	205,000		(410 batches)
Total production	208,000		(416 batches)

Using this information, we can calculate the variances.

1. Adapted from a CPA examination problem.

Quantity variances

Mucilloid	$(114,400 - 104,000) \times \$.14 = (\$1,456)$
Dextrose	$(\ 85,800 - \ 83,200) \times .09 = (\ 234)$
Ingredients	$(\ 19,800 - \ 20,800) \times .08 = \ \underline{\ \ \ \ 80}$
Net unfavorable quantity variances	$(\$1,610)$

Mix variance

Formula		Ratio
Mucilloid	250	25/50
Dextrose	200	20/50
Ingredients	50	5/50
Total	500	50/50

	Actual quantity	Actual quantity adjusted*
Mucilloid	114,400	110,000
Dextrose	85,800	88,000
Ingredients	19,800	22,000
Total	220,000	220,000

Mix variance

Mucilloid	$(114,400 - 110,000) \times .14 = (\$616)$
Dextrose	$(\ 85,800 - \ 88,000) \times .09 = \ \ 198$
Ingredients	$(\ 19,800 - \ 22,000) \times .08 = \ \underline{\ \ 176}$
Net unfavorable mix variance	$(\$242)$

*Determined by multiplying 220,000 by 25/50, 20/50, and 5/50.

Yield variance

Mucilloid	$(110,000 - 104,000) \times .14 = (\$\ \ 840)$
Dextrose	$(\ 88,000 - \ 83,200) \times .09 = (\ \ 432)$
Ingredients	$(\ 22,000 - \ 20,800) \times .08 = (\ \underline{\ \ \ 96})$
Net unfavorable yield variance	$(\$1,368)$

A Sales-Analysis Extension

Discussions in this and the preceding chapter have focused on variance analysis as it relates to the manufacturing process. Various types of similar analyses might be performed to provide additional insight into other aspects of operating performance. One example relates to the operating statement and specifically to changes in gross profit. Often, management desires a comparison of gross profit results between the current and preceding periods. In such cases, the preceding period serves as the standard (budget). In gross-profit analysis, changes in sales and cost of sales can be analyzed separately, or an analysis can be made of gross profit only. Product-mix changes are calculated in the same way mix changes were earlier calculated. Quantity differences call for the same calculation used in computing yield variances. In addition, price differences are typically part of gross-profit analysis. Consider the following example:

The Wong Company had sales, cost of sales, and gross profit for 19X1 and 19X2 as shown in the following schedules:

	Quantity	19X1 sales	19X1 Cost of sales	19X1 Gross profit
Product A	10,000	$100,000	$50,000	$50,000
Product B	6,000	48,000	36,000	12,000

	Quantity	19X2 sales	19X2 Cost of sales	19X2 Gross profit
Product A	14,000	$126,000	$84,000	$42,000
Product B	18,000	108,000	90,000	18,000

Management officials compared performance during 19X2 with 19X1 performance and discovered that, in spite of a doubling of unit volume, gross profits declined by about $2,000. They have asked the company controller to provide them with an explanation. There is no beginning and ending inventory. The results for 19X1 will be used as the standard for analysis purposes.

From a brief review of the situation, it can be seen that sales prices were reduced, possibly in an attempt to increase sales volume. Unit costs also changed in 19X2. The controller decided to prepare an analysis that would show the effects of changes in volume, prices, and product mix. Although she realized that some of the data would be interrelated, she decided to show the effect of these changes separately for sales and cost of sales. The controller hoped that her analysis would help the management team to identify responsibility for the differences. Results of the controller's analysis are shown as follows:

Analysis of change in sales

	19X2	19X1	Difference
Product A	$126.000	$100,000	$26,000
Product B	108,000	48,000	60,000
Total	$234,000	$148,000	
Net favorable change			$86,000

Caused by:

Price differences

A	($9 − $10) × 14,000 = ($14,000)	
B	($6 − $ 8) × 18,000 = (36,000)	
Unfavorable price variance		($50,000)

Product-mix differences

A	(14,000 − 20,000*) × $10 = ($60,000)	
B	(18,000 − 12,000†) × $ 8 = 48,000	
Unfavorable product-mix variance		($12,000)

Quantity differences

A	(20,000 − 10,000) × $10 = $100,000	
B	(12,000 − 6,000) × $ 8 = 48,000	
Favorable quantity variance		$148,000
Net favorable change		$ 86,000

*32,000 × 10/16 = 20,000
†32,000 × 6/16 = 12,000
The 32,000 represents total unit sales for 19X2. The ratios are developed by using total unit sales for 19X1 (16,000) as the denominator and individual product sales as the numerator.

Analysis of changes in cost of sales

	19X2	19X1	Difference
Product A	$ 84,000	$50,000	($34,000)
Product B	90,000	36,000	(54,000)
	$174,000	$86,000	
Net unfavorable change			($88,000)

Caused by:

Cost differences

A ....   ($6 − $5) × 14,000 = ($14,000)
B ....   ($5 − $6) × 18,000 =   18,000
   Favorable cost variance .... $ 4,000

Product-mix differences

A ....   (14,000 − 20,000) × $5 = $30,000
B ....   (18,000 − 12,000) × $6 = (36,000)
   Unfavorable product-mix variance ....   ($ 6,000)

Quantity differences

A ....   (20,000 − 10,000) × $5 = ($50,000)
B ....   (12,000 − 6,000) × $6 = (36,000)
   Unfavorable quantity variance ....   ($86,000)
   Net unfavorable change ....   ($88,000)

Summary of causes for change

Unfavorable change in gross profit ....   ($2,000)

Caused by
   Unfavorable price variance ....   ($50,000)
   Favorable cost variance   4,000
   Net unfavorable product-mix variance ....   (18,000)
   Net favorable quantity variance   62,000
   Unfavorable variance ....   ($2,000)

The above analysis should provide management with a better understanding of the cause for the decline in gross profits. This or some other similar analysis would be needed before management officials could pinpoint responsibility.

So far, a number of different methods for developing variances have been presented. The next section attempts to provide some insight into how the significance of variances might be evaluated.

☐ VARIANCE SIGNIFICANCE

As indicated in this and the previous chapter, a number of variances are available for providing information on differences between actual and planned results. Typically, these variances are reported to management so that corrective action can be initiated in necessary situations. How is this determination made? The determination must be based on a judgment by management, but often the decision appears to be based on size of the variance. Indeed, this kind of situation probably exists in many companies where a standard-costing system is used—a variance report is sent to a manager and the manager requires that action be taken on certain of the larger variances.

Should the decision to investigate a variance be based on its size? Before the question can be answered, the nature of the variance problem should be given consideration. To provide some initial insight into the nature of the problem, consider the following actual situation:

The manager of a branch production center had been told that his material-quantity variance was significantly unfavorable. The production manager took considerable time to investigate in order to take corrective action. He could not determine a cause for the variance. Subsequently, corporate auditors examined the entries made to the variance account and found that most of the variance could be attributed to errors made in the cost-accounting department.

This example is presented simply to suggest that variances may result for a variety of reasons and that a good understanding of the possible causes is needed in order to optimize the decision-making process.

It is important for the decision maker to recognize that the variances may result from random or nonrandom causes. This initial breakdown is shown in figure 9.1. As indicated in the figure, random variances, if known, would probably not be investigated, although management officials might want to consider changing the process to reduce the magnitude of the differences.

Should the nonrandom differences be investigated? An approach to making this type of decision will be discussed later, but one should understand possible causes for the nonrandom differences first.

Even in the more unsophisticated situations, personnel dealing with variances are generally aware that reported variances may result from accounting errors (recording and calculation errors), improper standards, and operating differences. Consequently, it is imperative that insight into the nature of the nonrandom differences be gained before a decision to undertake corrective action is made. Efforts to improve performance might prove to be futile if improperly established standards or certain measurement errors caused the differences. Indeed, measurement errors and poor standards are only examples of the types of differences, outside the operating area, that might be causing variances. An awareness of the possible causes will enhance the ability of management personnel to deal with the reported variances.

Although causes are not easily isolated, the person given the responsibility for the investigation must be aware of the possibilities, develop a

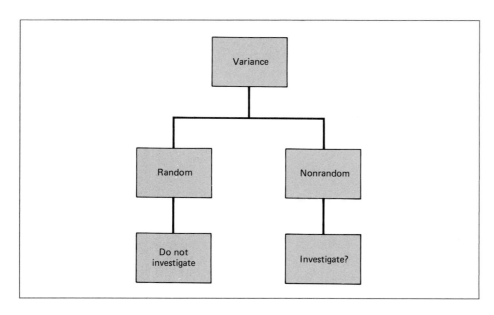

FIGURE 9.1
Variance
Composition

logical approach to the investigation, and select the proper techniques. Based on the information just given, a logical expansion of figure 9.1 might appear as shown in figure 9.2.

Following the approach indicated in figure 9.2, the investigator would need to determine how to separate random from nonrandom causes and then attempt to determine whether or not to investigate the nonrandom differences. Certain statistical methods appear to offer insights to management personnel as they attempt to evaluate the significance of variances.

Statistical Quality Control

Variances developed in the typical cost system usually cannot be identified as to type. In effect, the variance is only a measure of a difference. As indicated by figures 9.1 and 9.2, a useful first step might be to attempt to isolate the random deviations from the nonrandom deviations. A model from classical statistics can be useful for this purpose and has frequently been applied in quality-control situations.

Within a production setting, some type of control is usually established over the manufacturing and inspection process to determine acceptability

FIGURE 9.2
Variance
Composition

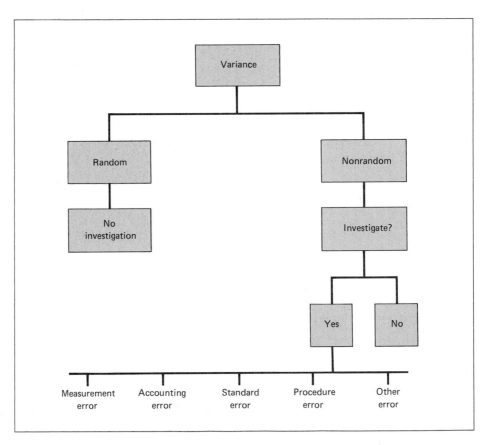

of the manufactured product. However, variations are sometimes disregarded until they become significantly large or until other trouble develops because of the difficulties in identifying problems during the process.

Statistical quality control eliminates part of the problem by providing a systematic means for monitoring ongoing operations and permits the separation of differences into two components—random and nonrandom variations. As indicated earlier, the random variation is usually not controllable within the existing process and can only be altered by a change in the production process. The nonrandom or assignable variation is of concern to the management team. These differences should be identified as early as possible so that corrective measures, if applicable, can be taken.

For statistical quality control to be applied in the standard-costing area, standards should be thought of in terms of units and ranges, rather than in terms of dollars and single-point estimates. Indeed, when a standard is set calling for eight pounds of material to be used in the production of a unit of product, something more or less than eight pounds will likely be used. The statistical quality-control technique provides a way of determining whether a process is operating in control or out of control. The process is considered in control when the variability of outputs is limited to random variations.

The basic concept of statistical quality control is indicated in figure 9.3. Some standard (or average) is set with an acceptable range, bounded by upper and lower limits. As samples are taken, they are plotted on the chart and those falling within the range are considered acceptable. Samples falling outside the range are then considered out of control and become the concern of management officials. It should be noted that the chart simply provides a signal that a problem exists. It does not indicate what kind of action is to be taken.

Control Charts

Although figure 9.3 provides an introduction to the use of **control charts**, it does not provide the information needed to develop and use control charts. In practice, two types of control charts are typically used, namely, the $\overline{X}$ chart and the R chart.

The $\overline{X}$ chart shows variations in the arithmetic mean of the characteristic being measured. The R chart tends to show the variations in ranges

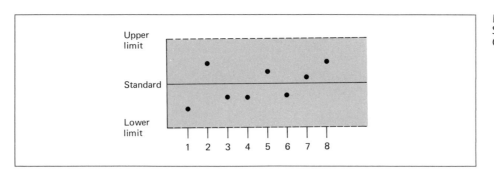

FIGURE 9.3
Statistical Quality
Control

of the samples. When something such as the diameter of a can or resistance of a spring is to be measured, the mean can be used as a basis for a decision concerning the process. However, this measure is not sufficient by itself as a test of quality. For example, two samples each of an *item* might be drawn with results as:

	Sample	
	1	*2*
	2.00	2.00
	2.20	1.90
	2.25	2.40
	2.22	2.38
$\overline{X}$ =	2.17	2.17

Even though both samples yielded the same mean, perhaps indicating an in-control situation, the range for Sample 2 is much larger, indicating that the individual items may be either too large or too small. Thus, the control chart for variability (*R* chart) should be used in conjunction with the control chart for the mean ($\overline{X}$ chart).

In establishing a control chart, twenty or more samples with a sample size of four to five are usually drawn. A mean ($\overline{X}$) and range (*R*) for each sample are determined and then a grand mean (($\overline{\overline{X}}$), ($\overline{R}$)) for each is determined. Consider the following:

Jim Rizzi has recently been put in charge of a production department. He has taken samples of time required to assemble a final component four times a day for the last twenty days to determine if his labor performance tended toward being stable or reflected significant change. Using the control-chart technique, the days were regarded as samples, with times for each of the four observations being included in the sample. Results are shown in the following schedule:

Sample number	Time required each observation				Mean ($\overline{X}$)	Range (R)
1	10	9	11	11	10.25	2
2	9	10	11	10	10.00	2
3	10	10	11	10	10.25	1
4	9	9	10	12	10.00	3
5	11	9	10	9	9.75	2
6	9	9	10	10	9.50	1
7	10	9	9	9	9.25	1
8	9	10	9	9	9.25	1
9	9	11	9	9	9.50	2
10	9	9	9	9	9.00	0
11	9	9	10	10	9.50	1
12	10	10	9	9	9.50	1
13	8	9	9	10	9.00	2
14	9	9	8	8	8.50	1
15	9	8	9	9	8.75	1
16	8	8	9	9	8.50	1
17	9	9	8	8	8.50	1
18	8	8	8	9	8.25	1
19	8	8	8	9	8.25	1
20	7	10	8	8	8.25	3
					183.75	28
				Grand mean $\overline{\overline{X}}$	9.19	$\overline{R}$ 1.4

Number of observations in subgroup	Factor for X chart	Factors for R chart		
		Lower-control limit		Upper-control limit
n	A_2	D_3		D_4
2	1.88	0		3.27
3	1.02	0		2.57
4	0.73	0		2.28
5	0.58	0		2.11
6	0.48	0		2.00
7	0.42	0.08		1.92
8	0.37	0.14		1.86
9	0.34	0.18		1.82
10	0.31	0.22		1.78
11	0.29	0.26		1.74
12	0.27	0.28		1.72
13	0.25	0.31		1.69
14	0.24	0.33		1.67
15	0.22	0.35		1.65
16	0.21	0.36		1.64
17	0.20	0.38		1.62
18	0.19	0.39		1.61
19	0.19	0.40		1.60
20	0.18	0.41		1.59

FIGURE 9.4
Factors for Determining from $\overline{R}$ the 3-Sigma Control Limits for $\overline{X}$ and R Charts

Source: Eugene Grant, *Statistical Quality Control*, 3d ed. (New York: McGraw-Hill Book Company, 1964), p. 563.

In setting up the control chart, the central line $(\overline{\overline{X}})$ represents the process average and the upper- and lower-control limits are set at three sigmas. Although the use of three-sigma limits tends to be fairly common in practice, other limits could be used. It is assumed that by using the three-sigma levels, one can minimize costs associated with **Type I** and **Type II errors**. If investigations are made only when observations fall outside of the control limits, the manager will run an increased risk of not investigating out-of-control situations (Type II error) as control limits are widened. As the limits are reduced, there is an increased risk of investigating in-control situations (Type I error). At $\overline{\overline{X}} \pm 3$ sigmas, for a process that is in-control, 99.73 percent of the observations will fall within the upper and lower limits. By using a statistical table, such as is shown in figure 9.4, control limits can be set.

Continuing then with the example of the manager of the production department, the following formulas are used to establish the limits for control charts:

For X
Control limit $= \overline{\overline{X}} \pm A_2\overline{R}$

For R
Upper-control
  limit $= D_4\overline{R}$

                $= 2.28(1.4) = 3.19$

Upper-control
  limit $= 9.19 + .73(1.4)$
           $= 10.21$

Lower-control limit	= 9.19 − .73(1.4)	Lower-control limit	$= D_3\bar{R}$
	= 8.17		= 0(1.4) = 0

The control charts would appear as follows:

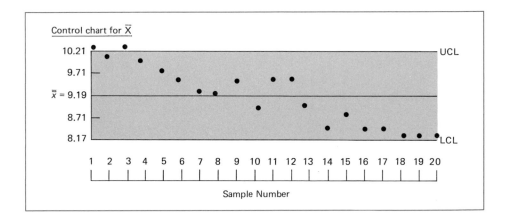

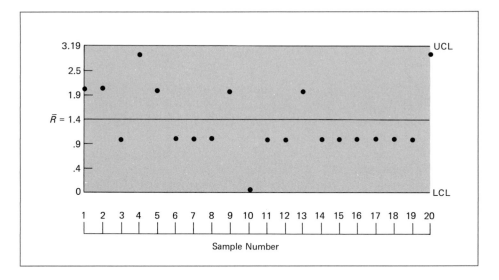

In the example situation, Jim Rizzi might be pleased with the results indicated in both charts. It appears that productivity has improved over time, and the differences in times per day tend to be getting smaller (even though some exceptions are noted). However, should the management team be pleased with the results if this represented a process being controlled? The answer would be no because the samples were taken during a period when the process was not in a stable situation. Although the $\bar{X}$ chart shows only two items (Samples 1 and 3) outside the control limits, a trend was indicated when sample items consistently fell above the line and then consistently below the line. The need for an investigation is indicated as a result of the trend. Consequently, management officials would want to draw additional samples and construct new charts for quality-control purposes since the above charts would not be acceptable for the continued monitoring process.

Management, in using control charts, should look for items to fall within control limits. Items falling outside the limits, as indicated, usually signal the need for some type of follow-up investigation. In addition, indicated trends or several successive samples falling above or below the mean also suggest out-of-control situations.

Even though control charts provide some insights into the complexities of the variance-investigation problem, it is difficult to see how they can be incorporated directly into reporting and control requirements of a standard-costing system. It would require that an item such as the material-quantity variance be sampled daily and plotted. This might be done, as indicated in the earlier example, for purposes of controlling productivity by production personnel, but these results would not be applicable for weekly or monthly reporting of standard-costing variances. Moreover, the control chart does not indicate what is wrong, only that some appropriate action may need to be taken. How can management decide whether or not to take action? This problem is discussed in the next section on cost-benefit analysis.

Concern for Cost Benefit

Assuming that the control-chart model or some similar model is to be used for identifying random and nonrandom causes, it must be recognized that some risk of incorrect action does exist. In effect, the control-chart decision process suggests that if the samples fall within control limits, the process should be left alone. If samples fall outside the control limits, investigate. The decision process can then be represented as follows:

Actions	Random	Nonrandom
Investigate	Incorrect	Correct
Do not investigate	Correct	Incorrect

Management personnel must realize that costs are involved whenever a decision is made to investigate an assumed out-of-control situation. Although savings may result from taking corrective action, managers must attempt to evaluate the costs incurred in relation to the benefits received. The probability of a process being in-control must be based on the experience and observations of the management team. Given an estimate of the probability, managers should then think in terms of the expected value of the cost-benefit decison. Consider the following example:

The Knight Company uses various statistical models in its system of quality control. The company officials have established that the probability of the process being in-control is .90 and the probability of an out-of-control situation is .10. The costs of an investigation average about $4,000 and the cost of making corrections tends to approximate $6,000. The present value of benefits are expected to be about $12,000. Management officials want to know whether or not to investigate out-of-control situations.

The expected value of the decision to investigate and the decision not to investigate should be calculated and compared. Calculations associated with each case are developed as follows:

P_1 = Probability the process is in-control
P_2 = Probability the process is out-of-control
CI = Cost of investigation
CC = Cost of correction
B = Cost of allowing process to operate in an out-of-control situation

Situation

Action	Random (P_1 = .90)	Nonrandom (P_2 = .10)
Investigate	CI = \$4,000	$CI + CC$ = (\$4,000 + \$6,000)
Do not investigate	0	B = \$12,000

$$\text{Investigate} = P_1\,(CI) + P_2\,(CI + CC)$$
$$\text{Do not investigate} = P_1\,(0) + P_2\,(B)$$

Using the equations, an indifference probability (P^*) can be calculated at which the expected costs of investigation plus correction are equal to the expected costs of allowing the process to operate in an out-of-control situation. Once this is done, the manager needs only to compare the probability of being out-of-control with the indifference probability. If $P_2 > P^*$, then investigate. Calculations are as follows:

$$P_1\,(CI) + P_2\,(CI + CC) = P_1\,(0) + P_2\,(B)$$
$$\text{Let } P_1 = (1 - P_2)$$
$$(1 - P_2)CI + P_2\,(CI + CC) = P_2\,(B)$$
$$CI - P_2 CI + P_2 CI + P_2 CC = P_2\,(B)$$
$$CI + P_2 CC = P_2 B$$
$$P_2 B - P_2 CC = CI$$
$$P_2 = \frac{CI}{B - CC} = P^*$$

The indifference probability for the example is calculated as follows:

$$P^* = \frac{\$4,000}{\$12,000 - \$6,000} = .6667$$

Since the probability of being out-of-control (.10) is less than the indifference probability, management personnel would not investigate. This decision can be checked by calculating the relevant costs.

If an investigation is made, the cost is:

$$\$4,000\,(.90) + (\$4,000 + \$6,000)(.10) = \$4,600$$

If an investigation is not made, the cost is:

$$\$12,000\,(.10) = \$1,200$$

The management staff would probably not want to make an investigation in this case. Although costs and benefits—and perhaps the probabilities—in this kind of model are highly subjective, managers should attempt to develop this kind of information for decision-making purposes. At least an attempt should be made to approach the problem with this type of framework in mind.

□ SUMMARY

In a number of cases, the material quantity variance should be separated into mix and yield components in order to provide the management team with the information needed for decision-making purposes. The mix variance represents the difference between the actual mix of quantities used and the standard mix in total quantity used. The yield variance attempts to measure the difference between quantities actually used in the standard ratio and the standard amounts called for based on the established formula.

The mix and yield variance can be used in the analysis of changes in gross profit. The mix variance is called a product-mix variance in the analysis, and the yield variance is typically referred to as a quantity variance. In addition to those two variances, a price-and-cost variance are also usually developed. Extensions of variance analysis beyond the production area into sales and other areas might be performed to provide managers with additional information.

The nature of the variance problem should be fully considered before a decision is made to investigate variances. Variances may result from random causes or nonrandom causes. If the variances result from nonrandom causes, additional consideration should be given to isolating the reason for the difference. Differences may result from accounting and measurement errors, errors in setting up the standards, and any number of other reasons.

Statistical quality-control techniques can be used to isolate random and nonrandom differences. Two types of control charts are typically used in the technique, an $\overline{X}$ chart and an R chart. The $\overline{X}$ chart shows variations in the arithmetic mean of the characteristic being measured. The R chart shows the variations in ranges of the sample. In both cases, upper and lower limits are established and items falling within the limits are considered to be in-control. Items falling outside the limits reflect out-of-control situations. Control charts simply isolate out-of-control situations. They do not indicate what is wrong.

Because of the probabilities attached to control charts, it is also possible that some random situations may be investigated and some nonrandom situations ignored. In addition, management should consider the costs and benefits involved in any decision to investigate or decision not to investigate. Consequently, an attempt should be made to calculate the expected value of investigating and the expected value of not investigating so that managers might be better informed for decision-making purposes.

KEY TERMS

Control charts	**Type I error**
Mix variance	**Type II error**
Statistical quality control	**Yield variance**

REVIEW PROBLEM

The Divers' Manufacturing Company uses a standard-costing system to accumulate, report, and analyze manufacturing costs. The standard-material cost for its major product is shown as follows:

Material	Pounds	Standard price per pound	Amount
Plastic	4	$5	$20
Rubber	6	2	12
			$32

Assume that 500 units of the major product are produced using the following materials:

Material	Total pounds
Plastic	2,600
Rubber	2,800

Required □
Calculate the quantity variance, and break it down between mix and yield components.

Solution □

Quantity variance
Plastic . . . . $(2,600 - 2,000) \times \$5 = <\$3,000>$
Rubber . . . . $(2,800 - 3,000) \times \$2 = \underline{400}$
Unfavorable quantity variance . . . . $<\$2,600>$

Mix variance
Plastic . . . . $(2,600 - 2,160) \times \$5 = <\$2,200>$
Rubber . . . . $(2,800 - 3,240) \times \$2 = \underline{880}$
Unfavorable mix variance . . . . $<\$1,320>$

Yield variance
Plastic . . . . $(2,160 - 2,000) \times \$5 = <\$\ 800>$
Rubber . . . . $(3,240 - 3,000) \times \$2 = <\underline{480}>$
Unfavorable yield variance . . . . $<\$1,280>$

Total . . . . $<\$2,600>$

QUESTIONS

Q9-1. Discuss the significance of the mix variance.

Q9-2. Discuss the significance of the yield variance.

Q9-3. If normal loss is built into the standards, should there be a yield variance? Discuss.

Q9-4. How is the product-mix variance calculated in a gross-profit analysis? Discuss.

Q9-5. In the use of control charts, why are both the $\overline{X}$ and the R charts needed?

Q9-6. Explain how control charts are set up and used.

Q9-7. When a process is in a state of statistical quality control, can the process be improved?

Q9-8. Identify the kinds of out-of-control situations indicated by control charts.

Q9-9. Discuss the various causes of variances.

Q9-10. If a process is determined to be out-of-control, discuss the approach to be used in determining whether or not to investigate.

PROBLEMS

P9-1. The Hampton Company uses two materials in the production of a box of product. The standard formula calls for the following mix per box:

Basic Material-Quantity Variance Calculation

Material A	10 pounds at $ 6 per pound
Material B	5 pounds at $10 per pound

Production for the last period was 5,000 boxes. Approximately 45,000 pounds of material A and 30,000 pounds of material B were used in the process.

Required □ Calculate the applicable material-quantity variances.

P9-2. Rick Company uses two ingredients in the production of a bottle of product. The standard formula calls for the following mix per bottle:

Basic Material-Quantity Variance Calculation

Ingredient A	10 pounds @ $5 per pound
Ingredient B	4 pounds @ $8 per pound

Production for last period was 5,000 bottles. In the process, 40,000 pounds of ingredient A and 4,800 pounds of ingredient B were used.

Required □ Calculate the variances needed for analysis.

P9-3. Assume in P9-2 that Rick paid $20 per pound for ingredient B and the standard price for ingredient A. Also, assume ingredients used represent the amounts purchased during the period.

Material Price, Mix, and Yield Variances

Required □ Calculate material price, mix, and yield variances.

P9-4. Spike, Inc., has been using a standard-costing system for product-cost determination and control. Material standards for its major product, a cannister, are as follows:

Material Mix and Yield Variances

Material	Pounds	Standard price per pound	Amount
Metal	60	$1.00	$60
Plastic	40	.50	20
			$80

During the most recent month, 1,000 cannisters were manufactured using the following materials:

Material	Total pounds
Metal	56,000
Plastic	38,000

Required ☐ Calculate the quantity variance and then separate the resulting variance into mix and yield components.

Analysis of Change in Gross Profit

P9-5.* Last year's operating results indicated the following for Armor Company:

Sales	$650,000
Cost of sales	400,000
Gross profit	$250,000

During the next year, management officials expect to sell 120,000 units at a price of $6 per unit. Last year's product cost of $4 per unit is not expected to change.

Required ☐ Prepare an analysis of the expected change in gross profit.

Mix and Yield Variance

P9-6. The standard mix for a product called for one pound of A and one pound of B for every finished unit produced. During the last operating period, four pounds of A were used for every one of B. About 100,000 pounds of material were used in producing the product, with 40,000 finished units completed. Cost for one pound of A was $5 per unit, and $640,000 of material were used. Assume that two pounds of raw material in different mixes will result in one finished unit.

Required ☐ Calculate the mix and yield variance.

Analysis of Change in Gross Profit

P9-7. Actual and budgeted sales and cost data for the Handball Company are:

	Product 1	Product 2
Actual sales—units	120,000	60,000
—dollars	$120,000	$108,000
Actual cost of sales	$ 72,000	$ 84,000
Budgeted sales—units	100,000	40,000
—dollars	$120,000	$ 80,000
Budgeted cost of sales	$ 80,000	$ 40,000

Required ☐ Calculate applicable variances for sales and cost of sales in a gross-profit analysis.

Material-Mix and Yield Variances

P9-8. The standard formula for material used by the Memphis Products Company in the production of a dozen of product Y are as follows:

	Quantity	Unit price	Total
Material A	10 pounds	.80	$ 8.00
Material B	10 pounds	1.00	10.00

During the period, 200 dozen of product Y were produced. Material used was as follows:

	Pounds
Material A	2,400
Material B	1,800

Required □ Calculate the applicable variances for material.

P9-9. The Town Company, a producer of a component part for various television sets, suffered a decline in gross profits from last year. Members of the management team have asked you to prepare an analysis showing reasons for the change in gross profits. Data for the two periods are:

Analysis of Change in Gross Profit

	Last year	This year
Sales	$500,000	$600,000
Cost of sales*	$290,000	$420,000

*Includes the volume variance, if applicable.

Normal capacity is 100,000 units, and fixed costs are about $50,000. The beginning inventory applicable to start of last year's operations was 40,000 units. The ending inventory last year was 60,000 units. This year's ending inventory was 10,000 units. Both years' selling price was $5 per unit.

Required □ Prepare an analysis of the change in gross profit, using last year as the standard.

P9-10. Jackson Products produces NOTAM, a new health food. For a 50-pound batch, the standard cost for material is shown as follows:

Material Mix and Yield Variances

	Quantity	Unit price	Total
Wheat	25 lb	$.20	$5.00
Barley	25 lb	.10	2.50
Corn	10 lb	.05	.50

During the month of June, the following materials were put into production:

	Pounds
Wheat	18,000
Barley	14,000
Corn	10,000

Production for the period was 600 batches of NOTAM.

Required □ Calculate the mix and yield variances.

P9-11. The XYZ Company employs a budget and compares actual results with the budget at the end of each operating period. The company's actual and budgeted data for gross profit of last period are:

Analysis of Change in Gross Profit

		Budget	Actual
Unit sales—Product A		12,000	10,000
Product B		8,000	15,000
Dollar sales—Product A		$96,000	$80,000
Product B		48,000	75,000
Cost of sales—Product A		$48,000	$60,000
Product B		32,000	60,000

Required □ Prepare an analysis for management, identifying reasons for the difference in gross profit.

Quality-Control Chart

P9-12. Barb Jones, foreman of the assembly department, has been working on improving time required to assemble the department's main unit. She requested the assistance of quality control with her problem. The supervisor of the Quality Control department, Tom Smith, suggested that she take about twenty samples of four observations each and perform an analysis based on the samples. Results of the samples are as follows:

Sample		Observations		
1	160	148	152	169
2	139	159	168	168
3	145	160	149	169
4	155	180	164	160
5	178	144	148	158
6	162	165	164	161
7	182	136	145	150
8	178	169	160	180
9	145	165	140	180
10	178	169	160	150
11	168	138	182	155
12	180	198	138	148
13	166	168	170	174
14	142	144	160	164
15	152	160	150	165
16	144	151	146	154
17	170	160	172	168
18	140	150	184	162
19	155	172	160	162
20	160	140	162	142

Required □ Using statistical quality-control techniques as a basis for the analysis, advise Barb Jones.

Quality-Control Chart

P9-13. The president at the XYZ Company has hired you as a consultant to establish statistical quality control for the company's production process. You have drawn twenty samples with five observations in each sample for purposes of setting up the control charts. The $\overline{X}$ chart is shown.

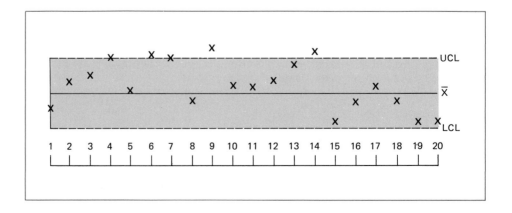

Required □ Write a memo to the president that expresses your understanding of the control charts, their potential value to the company, and your views on the specific chart.

P9-14. The manager of a production department determines that the costs involved in investigating variances are $400 and the potential costs to correct them are approximately $200. If the production process continues to operate out-of-control, then additional costs are about $6,000. The manager believes that there is about a 6 percent chance of the process being out-of-control. *Assessing the Significance of Variances*

Required □

1. Calculate the indifference probability.

2. Calculate the relevant costs of investigating and not investigating.

P9-15. The manager of a manufacturing process has estimated that the probability of the production process being in-control is 90 percent. Costs of investigation are $800 and the costs of correcting are $200. *Assessing the Significance of Variances*

Required □ What do the cost savings have to be to justify an investigation?

P9-16. The Build Company has estimated that the probability of their process being in a controlled state is 86 percent and the probability of an out-of-control situation is 14 percent. Investigating the out-of-control situations generally results in a savings of about $10,000 a year for four years. Costs of investigation averages about $6,000, and costs to correct situations approximate $6,000. The company's required cost of capital has been established at 16 percent. *Assessing the Significance of Variances*

Required □ Determine whether or not the company should investigate any out-of-control situations.

P9-17. The manager of the Book Company has found that when the probability of the process being in-control approximates 80 percent, he is indifferent as to whether or not to investigate. Assume costs of investigation are about $8,000 and the cost of correcting out-of-control situations approximates $6,000. The present probability of the process being in-control appears to be about 86 percent. *Assessing the Significance of Variances*

Required □ Calculate the current differential between the cost of investigating and the costs of not investigating the indicated out-of-control situations.

CHAPTER OUTLINE

DIRECT (VARIABLE) COSTING

CHAPTER **10**

□ INTRODUCTION

In previous chapters, various absorption-costing (full) accounting systems were discussed. In addition to material and labor costs, variable and fixed factory overhead were charged to production on the assumption that costs of production should include all costs associated with producing the product. An alternative known as **direct**, or **variable, costing** assumes that only those manufacturing costs that are variable with respect to manufacturing activity should be treated as product costs. Consequently, all other manufacturing-related costs are classified—along with administrative and marketing costs—as expenses of the period. Specifically, fixed manufacturing costs are treated as period expenses under direct costing.

Because direct costing focuses primary attention on variable-production costs, some accountants choose to refer to the method as variable costing. This chapter contains an explanation of the impact of direct costing on accounting reports and discusses possible suggestions for improving information provided to management personnel for decision-making purposes.

□ FULL vs. DIRECT COSTING—DIFFERENCES

Both full and direct costing have a place in decision making. Accountants and decision makers need to understand the applications and limitations of the two techniques within the context of past, current, and future-oriented cost information. More importantly, an attempt should be made to develop the information (i.e., the proper set of costs) for each specific problem situation. Because of the different decision-making tasks that users of cost information must perform, they are concerned not only with past costs but also with present and future costs. Historical costs are matched with revenue to measure income; current costs are compared with standards as a means of providing control; and future-oriented costs are developed for planning purposes.

Cost accounting, in early developmental stages, focused attention on income determination, with primary attention being devoted to identifying total product costs. As a result of this concern, various methods were devised for allocating fixed manufacturing costs to the product. However, the allocation of fixed manufacturing costs gives rise to certain problems: over- or underapplied overhead (largely a volume-variance problem) and differences between units produced and units sold. Consider the following example:

The Hellman Company has been in operation for three years. The following data relate to operations for each of the three years. Capacity for purposes of establishing a fixed-overhead rate has been set at 5,000 units. The accountant prepares condensed statements on a full-costing basis.

Production, Sales, and Cost Data

		Year	
	1	*2*	*3*
Production (units)	5,000	5,000	0
Sales (units)	2,000	3,000	5,000
Unit selling price	$12		
Unit manufacturing costs			
Materials	$ 4		
Labor	2		
Variable overhead	2		
Fixed overhead ($10,000 ÷ 5,000)	2		
Administrative expense per year (all fixed)	$4,000		

As indicated in the following summary, the company appears to have broken even in the first year with 2,000 units sold and to have earned a $2,000 profit in the second year on sales of 3,000 units. In the third year, the company operated at a loss even though sales increased to 5,000 units.

Summary Income Data

		Period	
	1	*2*	*3*
Sales	$24,000	$36,000	$60,000
Cost of sales	20,000	30,000	50,000
Underapplied overhead	0	0	10,000
Adjusted cost of sales	$20,000	$30,000	$60,000
Gross margin	$ 4,000	$ 6,000	$ 0
Administrative expense	4,000	4,000	4,000
Operating profit (loss)	$ 0	$ 2,000	($ 4,000)

The owner of the company, especially after results of the third year, would have to wonder about the reliability of the accounting reports. He has been given summary data that indicates that, despite increased sales, he can no longer operate at a profit. Notice in particular that the adjusted cost of sales reported in the third period has risen to $60,000 (cost of sales plus underapplied overhead). In the prior two years, $10,000 of fixed costs were deferred in inventories ($6,000 in year one and $4,000 in year two) because of the excess production over sales in each of the first two periods. Since production in year three is zero, all $10,000 in fixed costs for year three would be charged to operations, thus adding $10,000 to the cost of sales for the current period. This gives rise to two questions:

1. What would the results have been in the fourth year had the company sold 6,000 units?

2. With sales increasing each year and no basic change in the cost structure, why should operating profit first increase and then decrease?

Under absorption costing, the answer to the first question would depend on how many units were produced during the period. In other words, under absorption costing, profits may be affected by production. This can be seen by presenting alternative fourth-period results in which production first equals sales, then varies from sales. Consider the following possibilities:

	Fourth Period		
	Assumption 1	Assumption 2	Assumption 3
Production (units)	6,000	8,000	10,000
Sales (units)	6,000	6,000	6,000
Sales	$72,000	$72,000	$72,000
Cost of sales	60,000	60,000	60,000
Overapplied overhead*	(2,000)	(6,000)	(10,000)
Adjusted cost of sales	$58,000	$54,000	$50,000
Gross margin	$14,000	$18,000	$22,000
Administrative expense	$ 4,000	$ 4,000	$ 4,000
Operating profit	$10,000	$14,000	$18,000

*Capacity continues to be based on 5,000 units.

As you can readily see, profit improves as production increases (sales are held constant at 6,000 units).

The second question can be answered when it is realized that profits under absorption costing are partially tied to the level of production. Although the company owner properly expected sales to be a significant determinant, production was also a factor because of the allocation of fixed-overhead costs to products. The use of direct costing eliminates the influence of the level of production. The impact of direct costing can be illustrated by restating the original example under a direct-costing assumption.

Summary Operating Profit Data

	Period		
	1	2	3
Sales	$24,000	$36,000	$60,000
Cost of sales	16,000	24,000	40,000
Contribution margin	$ 8,000	$12,000	$20,000
Period expenses			
Administrative expense	4,000	4,000	4,000
Fixed manufacturing overhead	10,000	10,000	10,000
Operating profit (loss)	($ 6,000)	($ 2,000)	$ 6,000

Under direct costing, profitability follows sales, as the owner might have expected. By performing a simple break-even analysis, the break-even point should be reached at 3,500 units ($14,000 fixed costs ÷ [$12 − $8] contribution margin). The fact that production does not affect direct-costing profit is further emphasized by returning to the previous assumptions for the fourth period and developing operating results for each assumption.

| | Fourth Period | | |
| | Assumption | | |
	1	2	3
Production (units)	6,000	8,000	10,000
Sales (units)	6,000	6,000	6,000
Sales	$72,000	$72,000	$72,000
Cost of sales	48,000	48,000	48,000
Contribution margin	$24,000	$24,000	$24,000
Period expenses			
Administrative expense	4,000	4,000	4,000
Fixed manufacturing overhead	10,000	10,000	10,000
Operating profit	$10,000	$10,000	$10,000

Profit remains the same under all assumptions, since profit is related to sales rather than production.

Comparisons such as these have led some people to conclude that direct costing is superior to absorption costing for decision-making purposes. With this basic structure in mind, in the next section we take a closer look at the differences between direct costing and absorption costing.

☐ THE PROFIT EFFECTS OF THE TWO METHODS—STANDARD COSTING

By way of a brief review, the basic difference between the absorption and direct-costing methods lies in the treatment of fixed manufacturing overhead. Under absorption costing, fixed manufacturing overhead is allocated to the cost of the product. Under direct costing, this overhead is regarded as a cost that expires with time and, thus, becomes a period expense.

Under both methods, it is assumed that cost-estimation methods permit the proper separation and identification of variable- and fixed-cost components of manufacturing overhead. It is further assumed that manufacturing overhead costs can properly be distinguished from other costs. Estimation errors are likely to take place in both cases, but they are not generally regarded as being significant enough to minimize the usefulness of either absorption or direct costing. With this background in mind, consider the following example:

The ABC Company produces racquet balls. In the current period, 10,000 were sold at a price of $1 per ball. There was no beginning inventory. Inventory at the end of the period amounted to 4,000 balls. Product costs at standard were:

Direct materials	$4,000
Factory depreciation	2,000
Factory energy	500
Factory inspection	800
Indirect material	460
Sales commissions	660
Sales manager salary	1,000
Office salaries	600
Direct labor	1,200

An income statement prepared on an absorption-costing basis might appear as follows:

Sales (10,000 × $1)			$10,000
Cost of sales			
Raw materials		$4,000	
Direct labor		1,200	
Manufacturing overhead			
Depreciation	$2,000		
Energy	500		
Inspection	800		
Indirect material	460	3,760	
		$8,960	
Ending inventory			
(4,000 × $.64)*		2,560	6,400
Gross profit			$ 3,600
Operating expenses			
Sales commissions	$ 660		
Sales manager salary	1,000		
Office salaries	600		2,260
Operating profit			$ 1,340

*Production costs $8,960
Units produced   14,000 units
Cost per unit $8,960 ÷ 14,000 = $.64

Under direct costing, the income statement would appear as follows:

Sales		$10,000
Cost of sales		
Raw materials	$4,000	
Direct labor	1,200	
Manufacturing overhead		
Energy	500	
Indirect material	460	
	$6,160	
Ending inventory		
(4,000 × $.44)*	1,760	4,400
Manufacturing margin		$ 5,600
Sales commissions		660
Contribution margin		$ 4,940
Period expenses		
Factory depreciation	$2,000	
Factory inspection	800	
Sales manager salary	1,000	
Office salaries	600	4,400
Operating profit		$ 540

*Production costs $6,160
Units produced 14,000
Cost per unit $6,160 ÷ 14,000 = $.44

In developing the income statements, certain decisions had to be made with respect to the costs. An assumption was made that factory energy costs and indirect materials were the only variable overhead costs related to production. Consequently, all other indirect costs were either considered fixed or not related to production. It should also be noted that sales commissions (a variable cost) were deducted in order to arrive at the **contribution margin** under the direct-costing format.

The difference in profits between the two income statements is $800 ($1,340 − $540), with the larger profit being reported on the absorption-costing basis. This suggests that $800 of fixed costs were capitalized in inventory using absorption costing. To verify this, consider the following:

```
Fixed costs = $2,000 + $800 = $2,800
Production in units, 14,000
$2,800/14,000 = $.20 Fixed cost per unit
Ending inventory in units, 4,000
4,000 × $.20 = $800 Fixed costs in inventory
```

Note also that the absorption production cost-per-unit was $.64, and the variable production cost-per-unit was $.44. The $.20-per-unit difference is consistent with the verification of fixed-cost capitalization (absorption).

When standard costs are used (i.e., no change in unit prices for inventories between periods with variances being charged off as period expenses), the difference between variable and absorption costing can be calculated in the manner just cited. Furthermore, under standard costing, the following general statements can be made concerning profit differences between the two methods:

1. If production is greater than sales, absorption-costing profits will be greater than variable-costing profits.

2. If production is less than sales, absorption-costing profits will be less than variable-costing profits.

3. If production equals sales, profits under the two methods will be the same.

Example Data

Standard cost of product per unit

Direct materials	$2.00
Direct labor	1.50
Variable production costs	.40
Fixed production costs (120,000 ÷ 200,000 unit capacity)	.60
Sales price per unit	6.00

Production and inventory data

	Period 1	Period 2	Period 3
Beginning inventory	—	50,000	30,000
Production	200,000	180,000	210,000
Sales	150,000	200,000	210,000
Ending inventory	50,000	30,000	30,000

Administrative and selling expenses
   Variable selling expense per unit $.50
   Fixed administrative and selling expense $150,000

Income statements under absorption- and direct-costing methods follow:

	Period		
Absorption costing	*1*	*2*	*3*
Sales	$900,000	$1,200,000	$1,260,000
Cost of sales	675,000	900,000	945,000
Under(over)applied overhead	—	12,000	< 6,000>
Adjusted cost of sales	$675,000	$ 912,000	$ 939,000
Gross profit	$225,000	$ 288,000	$ 321,000
Operating expenses			
Selling and administrative expense	225,000	250,000	255,000
Operating profit	$ 0	$ 38,000	$ 66,000

	Period		
Direct costing	*1*	*2*	*3*
Sales	$900,000	$1,200,000	$1,260,000
Cost of sales	585,000	780,000	819,000
Manufacturing margin	$315,000	$ 420,000	$ 441,000
Variable sales expenses	75,000	100,000	105,000
Contribution margin	$240,000	$ 320,000	$ 336,000
Period Expenses			
Manufacturing overhead	120,000	120,000	120,000
Selling and administrative expense	150,000	150,000	150,000
Operating profit	$ (30,000)	$ 50,000	$ 66,000

As indicated, when using standard costing for unit costs, the differences between the methods can be reconciled by multiplying change in inventory by the fixed-overhead rate. Also, the method that will yield the more favorable results can be identified by comparing production and sales activities. For example:

Period 1
Change in inventory (50,000) × fixed-cost rate ($.60) = $30,000.

Period 2
Change in inventory (20,000) × fixed-cost rate ($.60) = $12,000.

Period 3
Change in inventory (0) × fixed-cost rate ($.60) = $0.

If the company terminated operations in the fourth period after selling all inventory with no change in costs or prices, the cumulative profits under the two methods would have been equal. This follows from earlier comments, since cumulative production would equal cumulative sales; therefore, profits under the two methods should be equal.

Summarizing, period income follows sales volume under the direct-costing method and is not affected by fluctuations in inventory from period to period. The statements made in this section regarding the pattern of differences and reconciliation methods are, of course, valid only when standard costs are used and changes have not been made to the standards.

☐ THE PROFIT EFFECTS OF THE TWO METHODS— THE IMPACT OF ACTUAL COSTS

Using an actual-costing system with different cost-flow assumptions—for instance, FIFO or LIFO—will produce different results, depending on assumptions made regarding changes in costs that take place from period to period. Nevertheless, differences between direct costing and absorption costing continue to result from the total amount of fixed overhead carried in beginning inventory versus the total amount of fixed overhead carried in ending inventory.

FIFO

To gain a better understanding of the actual-costing basis, consider a situation, using FIFO inventory flow, in which fixed manufacturing overhead increases from one period to the next. All other inventory assumptions remain the same.

The Jones Company is in its second period of operations. There is a beginning inventory of 8,000 units. Variable manufacturing costs for both periods were $50 per unit. However, fixed manufacturing costs per unit *increased* during the second period by $5 per unit, that is, from $15 to $20. During the second period, 10,000 units were produced and 8,000 units were sold at $100 per

FIGURE 10.1
Direct vs. Absorption Costing—FIFO Increasing Fixed Costs

Direct Costing			
Sales (8,000 × $100)			$800,000
Cost of sales (8,000 × $50)			400,000
Manufacturing margin			$400,000
Sales commissions (8,000 × $5)			40,000
Contribution margin			$360,000
Selling and administrative expense			120,000
Fixed manufacturing overhead			200,000
Operating profit			$ 40,000
Absorption Costing			
Sales (8,000 × $100)			$800,000
Cost of sales			
Beginning inventory	(8,000 × $65) =	$ 520,000	
Current production	(10,000 × $70) =	700,000	
Goods available		$1,220,000	
Ending inventory	(10,000 × $70) =	700,000	520,000
Gross margin			$280,000
Selling and administrative expense			160,000
Operating profit			$120,000
Reconciliation of difference			
Fixed costs in beginning inventory			
8,000 × $15		=	$120,000
Fixed costs in ending inventory			
10,000 × $20		=	200,000
Difference			$ 80,000

unit. Sales commissions were $5 per unit, and other selling and administrative costs were $120,000. Assume actual production represented normal capacity.

Figure 10.1 shows operating results for the second year under both direct and absorption costing. General results shown were as expected. With an increase in the inventory from 8,000 to 10,000 units, additional fixed costs were capitalized, causing absorption-costing profits to be higher than direct-costing profits. Because of the increased fixed-cost rate and the FIFO assumption, the difference was even more pronounced. As shown by the reconciliation, the total difference of $80,000 was caused because of the difference in fixed manufacturing costs capitalized in beginning and ending inventories.

Figure 10.2 reflects results assuming fixed costs *decreased* from $20 to $15 over the two periods. All other aspects of the situation are the same as before. Notice that results presented in figure 10.2 are not as easy to predict. Even though production was greater than sales, direct-costing profits were greater than absorption-costing profits by $10,000 because of the impact of the decrease in the fixed-cost rate.

LIFO

The LIFO assumption also complicates matters when one attempts to predict and evaluate differences between direct- and absorption-costing

FIGURE 10.2 Direct vs. Absorption Costing—FIFO Decreasing Fixed Costs

Direct Costing

Sales (8,000 × $100)	$800,000
Cost of sales (8,000 × $50)	400,000
Manufacturing margin	$400,000
Sales commissions (8,000 × $5)	40,000
Contribution margin	$360,000
Selling and administrative expense	120,000
Fixed manufacturing overhead	150,000
Operating profit	$ 90,000

Absorption Costing

Sales (8,000 × $100)		$800,000
Cost of sales		
Beginning inventory	(8,000 × $70) = $ 560,000	
Current production	(10,000 × $65) = 650,000	
Goods available	$1,210,000	
Ending inventory	(10,000 × $65) = 650,000	560,000
Gross margin		$240,000
Selling and administrative expense		160,000
Operating profit		$ 80,000

Reconciliation of differences

Fixed costs in beginning inventory		
8,000 × $20	=	$160,000
Fixed costs in ending inventory		
10,000 × $15	=	150,000
Difference		$ 10,000

profits. Working with the same basic data used in generating figures 10.1 and 10.2, operating profits are adjusted to reflect the use of the LIFO assumption in figures 10.3 and 10.4. As you can see, by using LIFO the magnitude of the profit differential shown in figure 10.1 has been reduced. In the second situation, with a reduction in fixed overhead costs from one period to the next, the use of LIFO increases the margin of profit in favor of direct costing. In both examples, the total difference is calculated by multiplying the difference between ending and beginning inventories by the fixed overhead unit cost for the current period production. However, this latter calculation is valid only in the situation in which production is greater than sales.

If sales are greater than production, the difference in ending and beginning inventories must be multiplied by the average per unit fixed cost for beginning inventories (total fixed cost included in beginning inventory divided by total units in beginning inventory). Consider the facts included in figure 10.3, except that 11,000 units are sold and 10,000 units are produced. The results are shown in figure 10.5.

In all cases, the differences between direct- and absorption-costing profits are attributable to the difference between fixed costs capitalized in beginning and ending inventories. Furthermore, such differences are affected by the choice of inventory-valuation method as well as the changes in fixed costs and the relationship of production to sales.

FIGURE 10.3
Direct vs. Absorption Costing—LIFO Increasing Fixed Costs

Direct Costing

Sales (8,000 × $100)	$800,000
Cost of sales (8,000 × $50)	400,000
Manufacturing margin	$400,000
Sales commissions (8,000 × $5)	40,000
Contribution margin	$360,000
Selling and administrative expense	120,000
Fixed manufacturing overhead	200,000
Operating profit	$ 40,000

Absorption Costing

Sales (8,000 × $100)			$800,000
Beginning inventory	(8,000 × $65) =	$ 520,000	
Current production	(10,000 × $70) =	700,000	
Goods available		$1,220,000	
Ending inventory (8,000 × $65 / 2,000 × $70)		660,000	560,000
Gross margin			$240,000
Selling and administrative expense			160,000
Operating profit			$ 80,000

Reconciliation of differences

Beginning inventory	8,000 × $15 =	$120,000
Ending inventory	8,000 × $15 =	120,000
	2,000 × $20 =	40,000
		$160,000
Difference		$ 40,000

FIGURE 10.4
Direct vs.
Absorption
Costing—LIFO
Decreasing Fixed
Costs

Direct Costing

Sales (8,000 × $100)	$800,000
Cost of sales (8,000 × $50)	400,000
Manufacturing margin	$400,000
Sales commission (8,000 × $5)	40,000
Contribution margin	$360,000
Selling and administrative expense	120,000
Fixed manufacturing overhead	150,000
Operating profit	$ 90,000

Absorption Costing

Sales (8,000 × $100)		$800,000
Cost of sales		
Beginning inventory	(8,000 × $70) = $ 560,000	
Current production	(10,000 × $65) = 650,000	
Goods available	$1,210,000	
Ending inventory $\left(\begin{array}{c}8,000 × \$70\\ 2,000 × \$65\end{array}\right)$	690,000	520,000
Gross margin		$280,000
Selling and administrative expense		160,000
Operating profit		$120,000

Reconciliation of differences

Beginning inventory	8,000 × $20 =	$160,000
Ending inventory	8,000 × $20 =	$160,000
	2,000 × $15 =	30,000
		$190,000
Difference		$ 30,000

☐ DIRECT COSTING FOR INTERNAL REPORTING

From the preceding discussion on differences between direct and absorption costing, you should now understand the impact of production on absorption-costing profits. As a result, you are in a better position to provide management personnel with internal information. Reporting with direct costing can be further enhanced by giving more attention to the separation of the various fixed-overhead components included in the operating statements. At various times, operating statements are needed for segments of a business—by division or by product line, for instance. In these cases, it is often useful to separate fixed costs into **traceable costs** and allocated cost components. Within the traceable cost category, it is usually worthwhile to subdivide the expenses into **managed** and **committed cost** categories.

By separating the period cost components into traceable managed, traceable committed and allocated costs, one can provide additional relevant information. As a result, managers are in a better position to understand the contribution of revenues to the segment as well as company overhead and profits. The management team is also more likely to identify

FIGURE 10.5
Direct vs.
Absorption
Costing—LIFO
Sales >
Production

Direct Costing

Sales (11,000 × $100)	$1,100,000
Cost of sales (11,000 × $50)	550,000
Manufacturing margin	$ 550,000
Sales commissions (11,000 × $5)	55,000
Contribution margin	$ 495,000
Selling and administrative expense	120,000
Fixed manufacturing overhead	200,000
Operating profit	$ 175,000

Absorption Costing

Sales (11,000 × $100)		$1,100,000
Cost of sales		
Beginning inventory	(8,000 × $65) = $ 520,000	
Current production	(10,000 × $70) = 700,000	
Goods available	$1,220,000	
Ending inventory	(7,000 × $65) = 455,000	765,000
Gross margin		$ 335,000
Selling and administrative expense		175,000
Operating profit		$ 160,000

Reconciliation of differences

Beginning inventory	8,000 × $15 =	$ 120,000
Ending inventory	7,000 × $15 =	105,000
Difference		$ 15,000

those costs that might be controllable in the short term. Figure 10.6 presents a hypothetical income statement showing various cost breakdowns.

Generally speaking, direct costing may be thought of as a formalization of cost-volume-profit analysis in report form (see chapter 11). Indeed, the same basic assumptions prevail—ability to separate cost components; linear cost functions over the relevant range; constant selling price; and constant unit variable costs; with the contribution margin representing amount available for coverage of fixed costs and profits.

Consequently, the principal usefulness of direct costing arises from its application "in forecasting and reporting income in a manner which clearly shows the relationships between cost, volume, and profit."[1] As such, advocates of direct costing usually suggest that the arrangement of income statement components in a direct-costing manner is a major advantage to be derived from direct costing.[2]

Reporting on a direct-costing basis accomplishes the following:

1. Results in better communication with an improved understanding of cost-volume-profit relationships by management.

1. NAA Research Report 37, "Current Application of Direct Costing," p. 68.

2. Ibid., p. 77.

Sales	$1,140,000
Cost of sales	610,000
Manufacturing margin	$ 530,000
Variable nonmanufacturing expense	180,000
Contribution to period costs	$ 350,000
Managed expenses	15,000
Committed expenses	90,000
Contribution to general costs and profits	$ 245,000
Allocated overhead	180,000
Divisional operating profit	$ 65,000

FIGURE 10.6
Jones Company—
Wholesale
Division Income
Statement

2. Provides more useful operating results for individual segments of a business, since management personnel are in a better position to evaluate profit performance of the individual segments.

3. Permits deduction from contribution margin those period costs that relate to the individual segment so that contributions made to corporate costs and profits can be better measured.

4. Enables period costs to be brought together so that management can clearly see the amount and impact of these costs on profits.

5. Provides information for pricing and special decisions (special orders).[3]

In summary, the advantages of direct costing accrue from the advantages of cost-volume-profit analysis. It can be used initially as a means of making operating results more understandable to the management team, and then its use can be extended to short-term planning decisions affecting operating segments and the company as a whole. Specifically, its uses should be found in product-mix, make or buy, sell or process further, and possibly pricing decisions. Because of some of these suggested advantages, in the past, proponents have suggested that direct costing should also be used in external reporting.

☐ DIRECT COSTING IN EXTERNAL REPORTING

While the advantages cited for direct costing in internal reporting are widely accepted, attempts to include direct costing in reports to external users have been met with significant resistance for many years. The earliest position of the American Institute of Certified Public Accountants (AICPA) is reflected in Accounting Research Bulletin 43. This bulletin indicates that a primary goal in establishing values for inventories is to properly match costs and revenues. Included in the bulletin is a statement indicating that the exclusion of overhead from inventory prevents the method from being acceptable.

3. Ibid., pp. 77–81.

Although the position of Research Bulletin 43 might not specifically exclude direct costing, most accountants agree that direct costing does not constitute an accepted accounting procedure. In 1957, the Committee on Concepts and Standards Underlying Corporate Financial Statements of the American Accounting Association (AAA) was more direct in stating:

> The cost of a manufactured product is the sum of acquisition costs reasonably traceable to that product and should include both direct and indirect factors. The omission of any element of manufacturing costs is not acceptable.[4]

Perhaps following from these positions, both the Securities Exchange Commission and the Internal Revenue Service have failed to give consent to financial statements using the direct-costing basis. As a result, where companies have attempted to use direct costing for external purposes, some adjustment for period costs has been required.

Even so, the major question is not whether direct costing is acceptable as a method for external reporting purposes but whether there is justification for using it in reporting to stockholders, creditors, and regulatory agencies.

The argument should focus attention on which method provides the most useful information. Frequently, however, the argument focuses attention on which method does the best job of deferring costs for purposes of subsequent matching of costs with revenues. Proponents of absorption costing have primarily argued that fixed factory overhead is essential to production and, therefore, should be included in the product cost. Others have supported this position by arguing that since inventory is built up in anticipation of needs, an opportunity-cost exists that, while not the same thing, might be represented by the amount of the fixed costs capitalized. Proponents of direct costing have, in some cases, simply countered that fixed manufacturing overhead is a period cost and as such should not be charged to product costs. In other cases, they have argued that the only costs properly chargeable to inventory should be those that would be avoided if inventories were not produced.

In spite of the various arguments offered, the ultimate answer must lie in the usefulness of such information to decision makers. If the decision makers' predictions are improved by use of direct costing, then it would appear logical to support the direct-costing format even though adjustments would be required to comply with regulatory agencies. Adjustments might be made as indicated in the following example, which is adapted from NAA Research Report 37:

> The XYZ Company has recently converted to direct costing for both internal and external reporting purposes. To comply with requirements of regulatory agencies, an amount equal to the amount of fixed manufacturing costs that should have been capitalized in ending inventories is set up in deferred overhead and carried until an adjustment is again required at year-end.

---

4. Committee on Accounting Concepts and Standards, "Accounting and Reporting Standards for Corporation Financial Statements: 1957 Revision," *The Accounting Review*, vol. XXXII (October 1957), p. 541.

If the year's output has exceeded normal or standard capacity, the year's fixed manufacturing costs are divided by production to develop a rate to be applied to units on hand at the end of the period. For example, if normal capacity is 3 million units and production was 3.5 million, actual production would then be divided into fixed costs of $5 million to arrive at a per-unit rate of $1.43. Assuming 500,000 units remained in ending inventory, deferred overhead would be charged for $715,000. This has the effect of adjusting ending inventory by the applicable portion of any volume variance.

On the other hand, if the year's output has been less than normal (assuming actual production of 2.4 million units), the rate is calculated as follows:

$$\frac{\text{Actual volume} \quad 2,400,000}{\text{Normal volume} \quad 3,000,000} = 80\%$$

Fixed manufacturing expenses during year	$5,000,000
Fixed manufacturing expenses applicable to production ($5,000,000 × .80) =	4,000,000
Amount applicable to idle facilities	$1,000,000

The fixed expense of $1,000,000 applicable to idle facilities is then charged off as underabsorbed overhead as might be done in an absorption-costing system.

The fixed expense of $4,000,000 applicable to production would be divided by actual volume to determine the unit rate for charging closing inventories with fixed expense as follows:

$$\frac{\text{Expenses applicable to production} \quad \$4,000,000}{\text{Actual production} \quad 2,400,000} = \$1.67$$

The amount charged to deferred overhead would then be $835,000 (500,000 × $1.67).[5]

According to the report, another company simply divided the total manufacturing cost for a period by actual production to arrive at a unit cost for pricing inventories. Still other companies came up with adjustment procedures suited to their particular situation.

□ SUMMARY

Direct costing is a product-costing method in which fixed manufacturing costs are regarded as period expenses and charged against revenue of the period. Such a procedure reduces the unit cost of inventory and generally causes certain differences in reported income when compared with the absorption-costing basis.

Using standard costing, if production is greater than sales, then absorption-costing profits will be greater than direct-costing profits. If production is less than sales, then absorption-costing profits will be less; and if production equals sales, profits under the two methods will be the same. These differences in income are caused by the effects of fixed costs capitalized in inventory.

Under actual-costing conditions differences between absorption and direct costing are less easily reconciled because of different assumptions made regarding inventory valuation and because of opposite movements that can take place between inventory and cost changes. In any event, the differences can be determined by subtracting the total fixed manufacturing

5. Ibid., pp. 94–95.

cost in the beginning inventory from the total fixed manufacturing cost in the ending inventory.

Direct costing is really nothing more than cost-volume-profit analysis in report form. Consequently, when using direct costing, assumptions of linearity, relevant range, constant product mix, and ability to separate costs are made.

Direct costing is a valuable tool for internal management personnel to use in the area of short-range profit planning. However, the application of direct costing to external reporting has been less successful. The position of the AICPA, and to a lesser extent the AAA, has created a reluctance on the part of regulatory agencies to approve its use. Consequently, direct costing has not been generally used for external-reporting purposes. Nevertheless, proponents have argued strongly for its use, with one of the more prevalent arguments suggesting that only costs that are avoided when production ceases should be charged to inventory. In the final analysis, the reporting method adopted should be the one that provides the most relevant information to persons responsible for making decisions.

KEY TERMS

Committed costs   **Managed costs**
Contribution margin   **Traceable costs**
Direct (variable) costing

REVIEW PROBLEM

The Ross Company has been reporting inventory on an absorption-costing basis. Management has recently heard of direct costing and would like to see the difference direct costing would have made on reported profits for the last several years. Data for the last three years of operations are as follows. (Capacity was set at 10,000 units.)

	Year 1	Year 2	Year 3
Absorption-costing profits	$50,000	$80,000	$140,000
Units produced	8,000	10,000	12,000
Units sold	6,000	9,000	14,000
Fixed manufacturing costs	$60,000	$60,000	$ 60,000

Required ☐ Calculate the direct-costing profit for each of the three years.

Solution ☐

	Year 1	Year 2	Year 3
Absorption-costing profits	$50,000	$80,000	$140,000
Difference between production and sales	2,000	1,000	<2,000>
Fixed-overhead rate	× $6	× $6	× $6
Difference between absorption- and direct-costing profits	$12,000	$ 6,000	<$ 12,000>
Direct-costing profit	$38,000	$74,000	$152,000

Q10-1. Distinguish between direct costs and direct costing.

Q10-2. Distinguish between direct costing and absorption costing.

Q10-3. What is meant by period costs?

Q10-4. Why is the notion of normal capacity often involved in a discussion of direct versus absorption costing?

Q10-5. What are the arguments for and against charging fixed costs to inventories?

Q10-6. Discuss the AICPA (FASB) and AAA positions on direct costing.

Q10-7. In general, explain how differences between direct and absorption costing operating results can be reconciled.

Q10-8. Discuss the effect of actual-costing methods on the attempt to compare direct costing with absorption costing.

Q10-9. What changes might be anticipated in a company's accounting system when a shift is made from absorption to direct costing?

Q10-10. Discuss the relationships between direct costing and cost-volume-profit analysis.

Q10-11. Discuss the use of direct-indirect and managed-committed costs in connection with reporting under direct costing.

Q10-12. Describe how a direct-costing structure facilitates calculation of the contribution margin and the break-even point.

P10-1. The ABC Company is considering the possibility of switching to direct costing. In an effort to better understand the significance of the possible change, the management team has asked that ending inventories be priced on both an absorption- and direct-costing basis. Production for the year was 200,000 units, of which 25,000 units remained in ending inventory. Additional information concerning production is as follows:

Comparison of Absorption and Direct Costing

Direct-material costs	$600,000
Direct-labor costs	450,000
Manufacturing overhead costs	600,000

Factory overhead has not been separated into fixed and variable components, but it is expected that the fixed-overhead rate would approximate $1.50 per direct-labor hour. The current direct-labor rate is $4 per hour.

Required □ Calculate the total costs to be assigned to ending inventory under both the absorption-costing and the variable-costing methods.

P10-2. The Cosmos Company incurred the following costs for their most recent operating period:

Comparison of Absorption vs. Direct Costing

Direct materials and direct labor	$850,000
Variable factory overhead	90,000

Other costs (all straight-line depreciation)
Manufacturing equipment   40,000
Plant facilities   60,000

Required □ Determine the inventoriable costs under

a. Absorption costing
b. Direct costing

Income Statement— Absorption vs. Direct Costing   **P10-3.**   The XYZ Company uses a standard-costing system, and variances have always been minimal. At the beginning of the year, 10,000 units were in inventory. During the current period 80,000 units were produced, and sales of 60,000 units were made at $10 per unit. The following costs applied to this period's operations:

Direct materials $160,000
Factory depreciation   20,000
Taxes on factory building   5,000
Inspection wages   6,000
Factory superintendent salary   10,000
Factory supervision   9,000
Direct labor   80,000
Factory power costs   20,000
Sales commissions   30,000
Advertising   20,000
Administrative costs   10,000

Required □ Estimate inventory costs based on the above information, and prepare an income statement on the absorption costing and direct-costing basis. Assume standards have not required adjustment for two years.

Direct Costing Using Actual Costs   **P10-4.**   Using the same information as given in problem 10-3, except that the company used actual costs, assume that the value of the beginning inventory on an absorption-costing basis was $36,000 and on a direct-costing basis was $20,000.

Required □ Prepare income statements on the absorption-costing and direct-costing bases and indicate what assumptions, if any, were made.

Comparison of Absorption Costing vs. Direct Costing Over Time   **P10-5.**   The following is information about operations at the ABC Company:

Standard cost of product per unit
Direct materials . . . . $ 4.50
Direct labor 2.00
Variable production costs 60

Fixed production costs
($200,000 ÷ 400,000 units
normal volume) 50
                                                                                                      $ 7.60

Selling price per unit $11.00
Other expenses
Variable selling expense per unit . . . . $ .60
Other fixed expenses $200,000.00

Production and sales data

	Period			
	1	*2*	*3*	*4*
Production	360,000	400,000	420,000	400,000
Sales	300,000	410,000	420,000	450,000

Required ☐ Prepare income statements under absorption-costing and direct-costing methods for the four periods.

P10-6. During the past year, Weisenfeld Garments, Inc., produced 200,000 units of product and sold 90 percent of everything produced. There was no beginning inventory of finished units. Production costs consisted of $400,000 direct materials, $600,000 direct labor, $100,000 variable manufacturing overhead, and $160,000 fixed manufacturing overhead. Normal capacity for the plant is 200,000 units. Selling price was $8.

Comparison of Absorption vs. Direct Costing

Required: ☐ Compare profit results under direct and absorption costing.

Impact of Fixed Overhead Rate

P10-7. Using direct costing, a company had income of $50,000 for a given period. Beginning and ending inventories for that period were 13,000 units and 18,000 units, respectively.

Required ☐ If the fixed overhead application rate was $2.00 per unit, what was the income using absorption costing?

(CPA)

P10-8. Smith, Inc., produces a film processor that sells for $500 per unit. Information on current year operations is:

Effect of Capacity on Results

Standard cost of product	Unit
Direct materials	$100
Direct labor	80
Variable manufacturing costs	40
Fixed manufacturing costs	20

Other expenses	
Variable selling expenses	$10 per unit
Other fixed expenses	$250,000 per year

Normal volume used to establish the fixed overhead rate was 10,000 units. Cost data given are expected to be relevant in a range of 4,000 to 10,000 units. Costs were the same in the preceding period.

Other operating data	
Beginning inventory	4,000
Production	8,000
Sales	2,000

Required ☐

1. Calculate income under absorption and direct costing. Reconcile the difference.

2. Assume that, instead of a 10,000 normal capacity, 8,000 was used both years. Discuss the impact of this change.

P10-9. Select the best answer to the following multiple-choice items:

1. What costs are treated as product costs under direct costing?

   a. Only direct costs
   b. Only variable production costs
   c. All variable costs
   d. All variable and fixed manufacturing costs

2. Operating earnings computed using direct costing would exceed operating earnings computed using absorption costing if

   a. Units sold exceed units produced
   b. Units sold are less than units produced
   c. Units sold equal units produced
   d. The unit fixed cost is zero

3. In 19X5, Fleet, Inc., manufactured 700 units of Product A, a new product. Variable and fixed manufacturing costs per unit for product A were $6 and $2 respectively. The inventory of product A on December 31, 19X5, consisted of 100 units. There had been no inventory of product A on January 1, 19X5. What would be the change in the dollar amount of inventory on December 31, 19X5, if the direct-costing method were used instead of the absorption-costing method?

   a. $800 decrease
   b. $200 decrease
   c. $0
   d. $200 increase

4. The Relay Corporation manufactures batons. Relay can manufacture 300,000 batons a year at a variable cost of $750,000 and a fixed cost of $450,000. Based on accountants' predictions, 240,000 batons will be sold at the regular price of $5.00 each. In addition, a special order was placed for 60,000 batons to be sold at a 40 percent discount off the regular price. By what amount would before-tax income be increased or decreased as a result of the special order?

   a. $60,000 decrease
   b. $30,000 increase
   c. $36,000 increase
   d. $180,000 increase

5. If net earnings were higher using standard direct costing than using standard absorption costing, what can be said about sales during the period if inventory is priced using the LIFO method?

   a. Sales increased
   b. Sales exceeded production
   c. Sales were less than production
   d. Sales decreased

6. The basic assumption made in a direct costing system with respect to fixed costs is that fixed costs are

   a. A sunk cost
   b. A product cost
   c. Fixed as to the total cost
   d. A period cost

7. When using a direct-costing system, the contribution margin discloses the excess of

    a. Revenues over fixed costs
    b. Projected revenues over the break-even point
    c.. Revenues over variable costs
    d. Variable costs over fixed costs

8. Net earnings determined using full-absorption costing can be reconciled to net earnings determined using direct costing by computing the difference between

    a. Inventoried fixed costs in the beginning and ending inventories and any deferred over or underapplied fixed factory overhead
    b. Inventoried discretionary costs in the beginning and ending inventories
    c. Gross margin (absorption-costing method) and contribution margin (direct-costing method)
    d. Sales as recorded under the direct-costing method and sales as recorded under the absorption-costing method

9. What will be the difference in net earnings computed using direct costing as opposed to absorption costing if the ending inventory increases with respect to the beginning inventory in terms of units?

    a. There will be no difference in net earnings
    b. Net earnings computed using direct costing will be higher
    c. The difference in net earnings cannot be determined from the information given
    d. Net earnings computed using direct costing will be lower

10. A basic tenet of direct costing is that period costs should be currently expensed. What is the basic rationale behind this procedure?

    a. Period costs are uncontrollable and should not be charged to a specific product
    b. Period costs are generally immaterial in amount, and the cost of assigning the amounts to specific products would outweigh the benefits
    c. Allocation of period costs is arbitrary at best and could lead to erroneous decisions by management
    d. Period costs will occur whether or not production occurs and so it is improper to allocate these costs to production and defer a current cost of doing business

Items 11 and 12 are based on the following information:

The JV Company began its operations on January 1, 19X7. The company produces a single product that sells for $7 per unit. Standard capacity is 100,000 units per year. In 19X7, 100,000 units were produced and 80,000 units were sold.

Manufacturing costs and selling and administrative expenses were as follows.

	Fixed costs	Variable costs
Raw materials	—	$1.50 per unit produced
Direct labor	—	1.00 per unit produced
Factory overhead	$150,000	.50 per unit produced
Selling and administrative expense	80,000	.50 per unit sold

There were no variances from the standard variable costs. Any over- or underapplied overhead is written off directly at year-end as an adjustment to cost of goods sold.

11. In presenting inventory on the balance sheet on December 31, 19X7, the unit cost under absorption costing is

    a. $2.50
    b. $3.00
    c. $3.50
    d. $4.50

12. What is the net income in 19X7 under direct costing?

    a. $ 50,000
    b. $ 80,000
    c. $ 90,000
    d. $120,000

13. Why is direct costing *not* in accordance with generally accepted accounting principles?

    a. Fixed manufacturing costs are assumed to be period costs
    b. Direct-costing procedures are not well known in industry
    c. Net earnings are always overstated when using direct-costing procedures
    d. Direct costing ignores the concept of lower-of-cost-or-market when valuing inventory

14. Which of the following must be known about a production process in order to institute a direct-costing system?

    a. The variable and fixed components of all costs related to production
    b. The controllable and noncontrollable components of all costs related to production
    c. Standard production rates and times for all elements of production
    d. Contribution margin and break-even point for all goods in production

(CPA)

Effect of Variances on Results **P10-10.** Leslie's Fashion Clothes, Inc., is in the process of comparing its absorption-costing procedures with direct-costing procedures used by a competitor. The company's controller has developed the following information in connection with the comparative study:

Maximum plant capacity	50,000
Normal (standard) capacity	40,000
Fixed manufacturing overhead	$80,000
Other fixed expenses	$25,000
Selling price per unit of product	$ 14
Variable manufacturing expenses per unit	$ 6
Other variable expenses per unit	$ 2

The following additional information is available relating to the current year's operations:

Units completed	38,000
Sales (units)	35,000

Finished goods beginning inventory (units)	2,000
Unfavorable variable spending and	
efficiency variances	$1,200
Favorable fixed spending variance	$ 600

Required ☐

1. Prepare an absorption-costing income statement.

2. Prepare a direct-costing income statement.

3. Evaluate the difference in profit related in the two income statements.

P10-11. The Brown Company has the following cost structure for the stereo component it produces:

Direct Costing— FIFO and LIFO

Variable manufacturing costs	*Per unit*
Direct materials	$25
Direct labor	26
Variable manufacturing overhead	5
Variable selling and administrative costs	3

Fixed costs	*Per year*
Manufacturing overhead	$135,000
Selling and administrative expense	220,000

The selling price for the components is $100 per unit. The basic cost structure remains constant within a range of 10,000 to 18,000 units produced. Last year, 10,000 units were used as normal capacity. This year, 20,000 units are being used. Other information concerning the current year is as follows:

Beginning inventory	5,000
Production	18,000
Sales	20,000
Ending inventory	3,000

Required ☐

1. Prepare income statements for the current year, using FIFO and LIFO, under each of the following methods:

   a. Absorption costing
   b. Direct costing

2. Reconcile any differences between absorption- and direct-costing income.

P10-12. The Ruthann Company is in its second year of operations. Variable manufacturing costs of $60 a unit have remained the same for both years. Variable selling and administrative expenses were $10 per unit in both years. Other selling and administrative expenses were $26,000. The selling price per unit of $120 has not changed. In the second period there is a beginning inventory of 10,000 units.

Direct Costing— FIFO

Required ☐

1. Assume fixed production costs increased during the second period by $6 per unit to $22 and that 10,000 units were produced and 8,000 were

sold. Prepare income statements for the second year (using FIFO) on direct-costing and absorption-costing bases showing a reconciliation of profit differences.

2. Assume fixed production costs increased during the second period by $5 per unit to $20 and that 9,000 units were produced and 11,000 were sold. Prepare income statements for the second year (using FIFO) on direct-costing and absorption-costing bases showing a reconciliation of profit differences.

Direct Costing—
LIFO

P10-13. The Neil Company is in its fourth year of operations. Variable manufacturing costs of $50 a unit have remained the same for all four years. Variable selling and administrative expenses were $5 per year for the first two years, but have increased to $10 per year for the last two years. Other selling and administrative expenses of $20,000 have not changed during the period of operations. Selling prices have increased by $10 to $110 during the last two years. The schedule of production, sales, and fixed production costs are:

| | Year | | | |
	1	*2*	*3*	*4*
Production	6,000	8,000	9,000	10,000
Sales	5,000	6,000	7,000	8,000
Fixed cost per unit	$15	$16	$18	$20

Required □ Using the LIFO assumption, prepare income statements for the fourth year on direct- and absorption-costing bases showing a reconciliation of profit difference.

Direct-Costing—
FIFO

P10-14. Carole Enterprises is in its third year of operations. Variable manufacturing costs of $80 a unit remained the same for the first two years, but increased to $90 in the third year. Variable selling and administrative expenses were $10 per unit in the first year and $15 per unit during the last two years. Fixed selling and administrative expenses were $26,000 in each of the three years. The selling price of $150 per unit has not changed. In each of the last two periods, there was a beginning inventory of 10,000 units. Assume that fixed manufacturing overhead increased during the second period by $6 per unit to $20 per unit and that 20,000 units were produced. During the third period, fixed manufacturing overhead increased by another $5 per unit. During the third year, 10,000 units were produced. There was no ending inventory of finished goods at the end of the third year. Carole Enterprises uses an actual costing system.

Required □ Prepare income statements for the second and third years (using FIFO) on direct-costing and absorption-costing bases showing a reconciliation of profit differences.

Reconciliation of
Differences—
Absorption vs.
Direct Costing

P10-15. Thermos, Inc., has been recording inventory on an absorption-costing basis. There are plans to convert, for internal-reporting purposes, to a direct-costing basis. In order to get an impression of its overall impact, the management team would like to see the effect on the company's profit figures since its inception, three years ago. Data for the last three years of Thermos' operations are as follows:

	Year		
	1	*2*	*3*
Absorption-costing profits	$80,000	$110,000	$200,000
Units produced	5,000	6,000	7,000
Units sold	4,000	5,000	7,000
Fixed manufacturing costs	$50,000	$ 54,000	$ 70,000

Required ☐ Calculate the direct-costing profit for each of the three years. Assume the fixed manufacturing overhead rate is based on actual units produced. Use FIFO if necessary.

P10-16. The Paul Manufacturing Company uses a job-order costing system and standard costs. It manufactures one product with standard costs as follows: *Comprehensive Direct-Costing Problem*

Materials (20 yd at $.90 per yd)	$18
Direct labor (4 hr at $6.00 per hr)	24
Total factory overhead (applied at five-sixths of direct labor [the ratio of variable costs to fixed costs is 3 to 1])	20
Variable selling, general, and administrative expenses	12
Fixed selling, general, and administrative expenses	7
Total unit cost	$81

The standards are set based on normal activity of 2,400 direct-labor hours.

Required ☐

1. Based on the standard costs, compute the inventoriable unit cost for internal reporting purposes under direct (variable) costing.

2. Based on the information just cited, a certain selling price per unit and number of units will yield an operating profit of $5,200. Increasing this selling price by 4 percent will increase the operating profit to $6,800. All costs and the number of units remain unchanged. Compute the selling price per unit and the number of units to yield an operating profit of $5,200.

3. Assume the company manufactured 800 units and sold 600 units. Calculate the profit under absorption and direct costing. The selling price was $100 per unit.

(CPA)

P10-17. The Blacksburg Corporation plans to change its method of inventory valuation from absorption costing to direct costing and has requested that you determine the effect of the proposed change on the 19X8 financial statements. The corporation produces a product called Valvet, which sells for $20 per unit. Material is added at the beginning; as processing starts, labor and overhead are added evenly throughout the process. Production capacity is set at 110,000 units per year. Standard costs per unit of Valvet are as follows: *Comprehensive Direct-Costing Problem*

Material, 2 lb	$ 3.00
Direct labor	6.00
Variable manufacturing overhead	1.00
Fixed manufacturing overhead	1.00
	$11.00

Inventory data for 19X8 follow:

	January 1	December 31
Material (pounds)	50,000	40,000
Work-in-process		
⅖ processed	10,000	
⅓ processed		15,000
Finished goods	20,000	12,000

During 19X8, 220,000 pounds of material were purchased. Also, 110,000 units of Valvet were transferred to finished goods. Actual fixed manufacturing overhead during the year was $121,000. There were no variances between standard and actual variable costs during the year.

Required □ Prepare a comparative statement of cost of sales using standard direct costing and standard absorption costing. The format is provided.

Cost-of-sales statement	Direct	Absorption
Materials		
Beginning inventory	$	$
Purchases Available	_____	_____
Ending inventory	_____	_____
Materials used	$	$
Direct labor		
Factory overhead	_____	_____
Total production costs	$	$
Beginning work-in-process		
Ending work-in-process	_____	_____
Difference	$_____	$_____
Cost-of-goods-manufactured	$	$
Beginning finished goods		
Ending finished goods	_____	_____
Difference	$_____	$_____
Cost of sales	$══════	$══════

All Variable-Cost Situation

P10-18. In Henry County, Virginia, a firm called the Dust Log Company manufactures fireplace logs. This firm is unusual in that all of its costs are variable. Sawdust and glue are combined to make the logs; all labor and sales are done on a piecework basis. The logs are manufactured in an open field by filling molds with the sawdust and glue. These molds serve as the outside wrapping for the log and are also burned with the log.

The following data relate to the operations of the Dust Log Company:

	19X3	19X4
Sales	5,000 logs	5,000 logs
Production	7,500 logs	2,500 logs
Beginning inventory	0	2,500 logs
Ending inventory	2,500 logs	0
Selling price	$10 per log	$10 per log
Costs (all variable) production	$15,000	$5,000

Selling and administrative expense	$ 5,000	$5,000
Normal production*	5,000 logs	5,000 logs

*Any capacity variance is charged to cost of goods sold in the current period.

Required ☐

1. Determine the net income for each year, using absorption and variable costing.

	19X3	19X4
Net income		
Absorption costing	$ _____	$ _____
Variable costing	$ _____	$ _____

2. Determine the values of the beginning and ending inventories for each year, using absorption and variable costing.

	19X3	19X4
Absorption costing		
Beginning inventory	$ _____	$ _____
Ending inventory	$ _____	$ _____
Variable costing		
Beginning inventory	$ _____	$ _____
Ending inventory	$ _____	$ _____

3. What is the break-even point in units under absorption costing and variable costing?

Break-even point		
Absorption costing	_____	logs
Variable costing	_____	logs

P10-19. The George Corporation of Richboro, Pennsylvania, is known throughout the accounting world because all of its costs are fixed. It manufactures fireplace logs made from coal dust that is taken from the atmosphere in Bucks County. All employees are salaried and hired on an annual basis. Output from the plant can be increased or decreased by adjusting the speed of the in-take fan that draws in air to remove the coal dust. Some of the free coal dust is burned to generate power to supply power, light, and heat.

All Fixed-Cost Situation

The following data relate to the operations of the George Corporation:

	19X3	19X4
Sales	5,000 logs	5,000 logs
Production	7,500 logs	2,500 logs
Beginning inventory	0	2,500 logs
Ending inventory	2,500 logs	0
Selling price	$10 per log	$10 per log
Costs (all fixed) production	$15,000	$15,000
Selling and administrative expense	$ 5,000	$ 5,000
Normal production*	5,000 logs	5,000 logs

*Any capacity variance is charged to cost of goods sold in the current period.

Required □

1. Determine the net income for each year, using absorption and variable costing.

	19X3	19X4
Net income		
Absorption costing	$ _____	$ _____
Variable costing	$ _____	$ _____

2. Determine the values of the beginning and ending inventories for each year, using absorption and variable costing.

	19X3	19X4
Absorption costing		
Beginning inventory	$ _____	$ _____
Ending inventory	$ _____	$ _____
Variable costing		
Beginning inventory	$ _____	$ _____
Ending inventory	$ _____	$ _____

3. What is the break-even point in units under absorption costing and variable costing?

Break-even point		
Absorption costing	_____	logs
Variable costing	_____	logs

Comprehensive Direct-Costing Problem

P10-20. The Vice President for Sales of Huber Corporation has received the Income Statement for November 19X9. The statement has been prepared on the direct-costing basis and is reproduced below. The firm has just adopted a direct-costing system for internal reporting purposes.

HUBER CORPORATION
Income Statement
For the Month of November 19X9
(in thousands)

Sales		$2,400
Less: Variable standard cost		
of goods sold		1,200
Manufacturing margin		$1,200
Less: Fixed manufacturing costs		
at budget	$600	
Fixed manufacturing costs		
spending variance	0	600
Gross margin		$ 600
Less: Fixed selling & administrative		
costs		400
Net income before taxes		$ 200

The controller attached the following notes to the statements:
■ The unit sales price for November averaged $24.
■ The standard unit manufacturing costs for the month were:

Variable cost	$12
Fixed cost	4
Total cost	$16

The unit rate for fixed manufacturing costs is a predetermined rate based upon a normal monthly production of 150,000 units.
■ Production for November was 45,000 units in excess of sales.
■ The inventory at November 30 consisted of 80,000 units.

Required ☐

1. The Vice President for Sales is not comfortable with the direct-costing basis and wonders what the net income would have been under the prior, absorption-cost basis.

   a. Present the November Income Statement on an absorption-cost basis.
   b. Reconcile and explain the difference between the direct-costing and the absorption-costing net income figures.

2. Explain the features associated with direct-costing income measurement that should be attractive to the Vice President for Sales.

(CMA)

PART OUTLINE

PART III

CONCEPTS AND TECHNIQUES FOR PLANNING

CHAPTER OUTLINE

INTRODUCTION

THE NONLINEAR MODEL

LINEAR APPROXIMATIONS AND THE
  RELEVANT RANGE

COST-VOLUME-PROFIT ANALYSIS
  WITH LINEAR FUNCTIONS

COST-VOLUME-PROFIT ANALYSIS
  WITH MULTIPLE PRODUCTS

COST-VOLUME-PROFIT ANALYSIS
  USING THE CONTRIBUTION-
  MARGIN RATIO

ASSUMPTIONS UNDERLYING THE
  LINEAR BREAK-EVEN MODEL

ANALYSIS EMPLOYING THE LINEAR
  BREAK-EVEN MODEL
Shifts In Unit-Contribution Margin
Shifts In Total Fixed Cost
Shifts In Expected Volume
Operating Leverage

SUMMARY

KEY TERMS

REVIEW PROBLEM

QUESTIONS

PROBLEMS

COST-VOLUME-PROFIT RELATIONSHIPS

CHAPTER **11**

☐ INTRODUCTION

Decision making, profit planning, and cost control by management personnel all require an understanding of revenue and cost behavior at different levels of activity. While the techniques employed in this chapter do not predict with certainty cost and revenue behavior, they do provide reasonable representation and are, therefore, useful in decision making.

Cost-volume-profit analysis is relevant to almost all areas of decision making by managers. It is useful in decisions related to pricing, make or buy, product selection, production-method selection, and capital budgeting. It allows management team members to evaluate "what if" types of questions with respect to profit concerning shifts in selling price, *variable* and *fixed costs*, and *sales volume*. This analysis is based on many of the same assumptions that are made when flexible budgets are prepared.

In this chapter, we will begin by considering a **nonlinear model** of cost-volume-profit relationships. Then, we will develop the linear break-even model and view cost-volume-profit relationships as they relate to this model.

☐ THE NONLINEAR MODEL

The economist's short-run model of a single-product firm assumes nonlinear total cost and revenue functions. These functions are mathematical expressions that permit one to determine the total revenue and cost when the sales volume is specified. This model permits the determination of the optimal short-run output for the firm. To maximize profits in the short-run, the firm should expand output to that point at which the marginal revenue equals the marginal cost. Assume a firm with total revenue (R) and total cost (C) functions as follows:

$$R = 84x - 4x^2 \qquad\qquad\qquad\qquad \textbf{(11-1)}$$

$$C = \frac{x^3}{3} - 4x^2 + 20x + 183 \qquad\qquad \textbf{(11-2)}$$

where x represents the units of output. The two functions are shown in figure 11.1.

Since *marginal revenue* equals the rate of change in revenue with respect to a change in volume, the marginal revenue (MR) function can be found by differentiating the total revenue function with respect to the output.[1]

$$MR = \frac{dR}{dx} = 84 - 8x \qquad (11\text{-}3)$$

This expression gives the rate of change in the revenue with respect to a rate of change in the volume. Likewise, the *marginal cost* equals the rate of change in cost with respect to a change in volume and can be found by differentiating the total cost function with respect to the output.[2]

1. $R = 84x^1 - 4x^2$

$$\frac{dR}{dx} = 1(84x^{1-1}) - 2(4x^{2-1})$$

$$\frac{dR}{dx} = 84 - 8x$$

2. $C = \frac{x^3}{3} - 4x^2 + 20x^1 + 183$

$$\frac{dC}{dx} = 3\left(\frac{x^{3-1}}{3}\right) - 2(4x^{2-1}) + 1(20x^{1-1})$$

$$\frac{dC}{dx} = x^2 - 8x + 20$$

FIGURE 11.1
Total Revenue and
Cost Functions

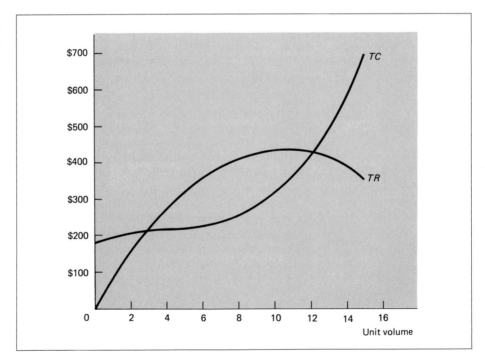

$$MC = \frac{dC}{dx} = x^2 - 8x + 20 \tag{11-4}$$

Setting the marginal revenue equal to the marginal cost and solving for x, one finds the output that results in maximum profit.

$$MR = MC \tag{11-5}$$
$$84 - 8x = x^2 - 8x + 20$$
$$x = \pm 8$$

Since negative production is not possible, the firm should produce eight units of output to maximize profits. By (11-3) and (11-4), one can see that the marginal revenue and cost both equal $20 at an output of eight units.

These results can be verified by determining the profit function of the firm. In the example, the profit function is $P = R - C$ or

$$P = \frac{-x^3}{3} + 64x - 183 \tag{11-6}$$

This profit function is shown in figure 11.2. The output that maximizes profit can be found by differentiating the profit function with respect to output x, setting the derivative equal to zero, and checking for a maximum. This is done because the slope of the profit function equals zero at the maximum and minimum points.[3]

$$\frac{dP}{dx} = -x^2 + 64 \tag{11-7}$$
$$0 = -x^2 + 64$$
$$x = \pm 8$$

As expected, the maximum profit results when the output equals eight units. With an output of eight units, the profit equals $158.33.[4] The profits at other levels of output are contained in table 11.1.[5]

The **break-even point** is that level of output at which the total revenue equals the total cost.[6] From figure 11.1, it should be noted that our example

3. $P = \frac{-x^3}{3} + 64x^1 - 183$

$\frac{dP}{dx} = 3\left(\frac{-x^{3-1}}{3}\right) + 1(64x^{1-1})$

$\frac{dp}{dx} = -x^2 + 64$

4. By taking the second derivative and the function of checking for a maximum or minimum, one finds that +8 is the maximum point of inflection.

5. It should be noted that both the revenue and cost functions are continuous. Therefore, the slightest deviation from an output of eight units will result in decreased profit.

6. Another approach to finding the break-even point is to set the profit function equal to zero and solve for x.

FIGURE 11.2
Profit Function

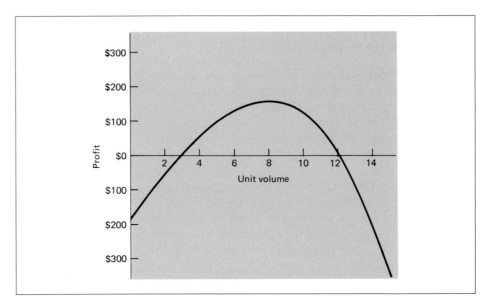

of an economic model will yield two break-even points. In solving for these points, let

$$R = C$$
$$84x - 4x^2 = \frac{x^3}{3} - 4x^2 + 20x + 183$$

Solving for x, one finds positive outputs of 3 and 12.11 units result in zero profit.

This simple, short-run economic model of a single-product firm is based on the assumption that the firm's resources, revenue, and cost functions

TABLE 11.1 Profits at Various Outputs

X	R	C	Profit	Average cost	Average selling price
0	$ 0	$183.00	$ −183.00	—	—
1	80	199.33	−119.33	$199.33	$80
2	152	209.67	− 57.67	104.84	76
3	216	216.00	0	72.00	72
4	272	220.33	51.67	55.08	68
5	320	224.67	95.33	44.93	64
6	360	231.00	129.00	38.50	60
7	392	241.33	150.67	34.48	56
8	416	257.67	158.33	32.21	52
9	432	282.00	150.00	31.33	48
10	440	316.33	123.67	31.63	44
11	440	362.67	77.33	32.97	40
12	432	423.00	9.00	35.25	36
13	416	499.33	− 83.33	38.41	32
14	392	593.67	−201.67	42.40	28
15	360	708.00	−348.00	47.20	24

are all stable. In a relatively stable economy, it would be difficult and costly for management personnel to determine an equilibrium solution. In a dynamic economy, such a task becomes almost impossible. However, by making several simplifying assumptions about a firm's revenue and cost functions, one can develop a model that is elegant in its simplicity. The accountant's cost-volume-profit model employs linear functions and highlights the relationships between profit, cost, and volume.

☐ LINEAR APPROXIMATIONS AND THE RELEVANT RANGE

From past experience, the management team of a firm is generally able to determine cost-volume relationships over a range of prior levels of output. Based on these past cost-volume relationships, a linear estimate of the total cost function is obtained.[7] There is a limited range, often referred to as the *relevant range*, over which the cost-volume relationship as specified by the linear cost function is assumed to be valid.

Price-volume relationships are determined from past experience or market analysis. This information is used to select a selling price to be used in determining a linear estimate of the total revenue function. Of course, there are limits to the range over which price-volume relationships are valid, and these must be taken into consideration when determining the relevant range for this type of analysis.

In figure 11.3, the relationship between the actual nonlinear total revenue and total cost functions and the linear estimates is shown. Figure 11.4 shows the conventional break-even diagram with both functions ex-

7. Many of the techniques discussed in chapter 21 concerning cost estimation would be employed in determining the linear estimate of the cost function.

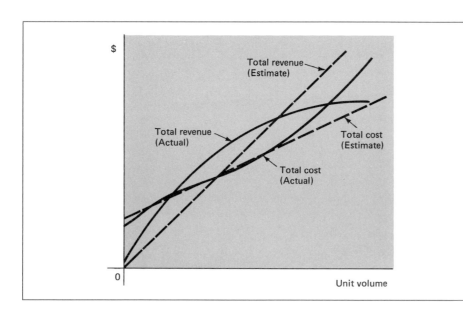

FIGURE 11.3
Actual and Estimated Revenue and Cost Functions

FIGURE 11.4
Traditional Break-
Even Diagram

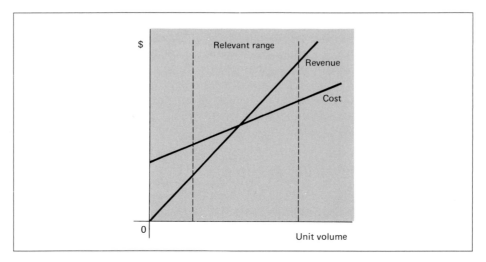

tended to the *y* axis. Figure 11.5 is a modified break-even diagram that shows both functions only within the relevant range to emphasize the limited range over which the functions are assumed to be valid.

☐ COST-VOLUME-PROFIT ANALYSIS WITH LINEAR FUNCTIONS

If it is assumed that over a relevant range of activity the total cost function is linear and the selling price is constant, then the break-even model of the accountant can be employed for profit planning. Before making use of the break-even model, it is necessary to estimate the selling price, unit variable cost, and total fixed costs. This model emphasizes how quantity of units sold, selling prices, unit variable costs, total fixed costs, and combinations of these factors affect profits.

FIGURE 11.5
Modified Break-
Even Diagram

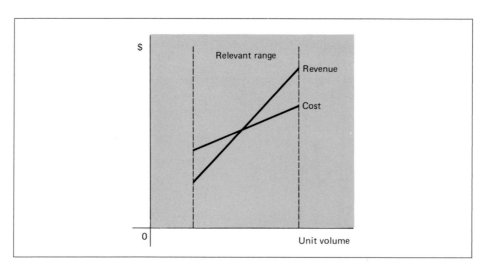

Let total sales revenue (r) and total cost (c), respectively, equal:

$$r = sx \qquad \textbf{(11-8)}$$
$$c = a + bx \qquad \textbf{(11-9)}$$

From (11-8) and (11-9) one can see that profit (p) equals:

$$p = r - c$$
$$p = sx - a - bx \qquad \textbf{(11-10)}$$

where:

s = Unit selling price
x = Sales volume in units
a = Total fixed costs
b = Unit variable costs

Figure 11.6 shows the general relationships among the revenue, cost, and profit functions.

The point at which there is no profit or loss is designated as break-even. Total sales revenue equals fixed costs plus total variable costs at break-even and one solves for the *break-even unit volume* as follows:

$$sx = a + bx$$
$$sx - bx = a$$
$$(s - b)x = a$$
$$x = \frac{a}{(s - b)} \qquad \textbf{(11-11)}$$

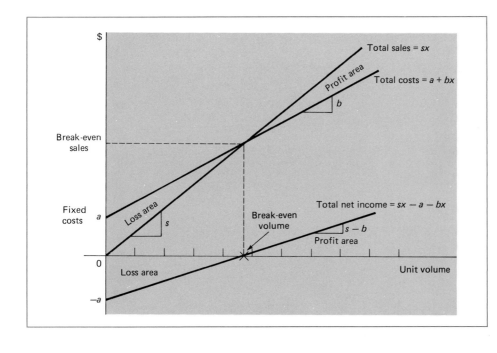

FIGURE 11.6
Break-Even
Chart

Therefore, the break-even unit volume equals the total fixed costs (a) divided by the **unit-contribution margin** $(s-b)$.[8]

The unit-contribution margin serves as a basis for many business decisions. Some examples are pricing, make or buy, and product selection decisions. In the classification and allocation of product costs, one should keep in mind the implications of decisions that may be based on the unit-contribution margin. Assume a firm manufactures and sells a single product and has supplied the following data:

Unit selling price (s)	$ 10
Unit variable cost (b)	6
Unit contribution margin ($s-b$)	$ 4
Total fixed costs (a)	$100

By substituting into (11-11), one finds the break-even unit volume to equal twenty-five units. Checking the results, one finds:

Sales (sx = $10 × 25)	$250
Less: Variable costs (bx = $6 × 25)	150
Contribution margin	$100
Less: Fixed costs (a)	100
Profit	$ 0

The relationship between profit and unit volume for the firm is shown in figure 11.7.

The analysis can be extended to include a profit goal in determining the desired unit volume. Assume a profit goal of g; then total revenue equals fixed costs plus total variable cost plus the profit goal. This relationship can be expressed as:

$$sx = a + bx + g \tag{11-12}$$

and the necessary unit volume equals:

$$x = \frac{a + g}{(s - b)} \tag{11-13}$$

If the firm in the example desired a profit of $60, from (11-13) one can determine the necessary unit volume to equal forty units. Checking the results, one finds:

8. Another approach to finding the break-even sales volume is:

$$p = sx - a - bx$$
$$p = 0$$
$$0 = sx - a - bx$$
$$a = x(s-b)$$
$$x = \frac{a}{(s - b)}$$

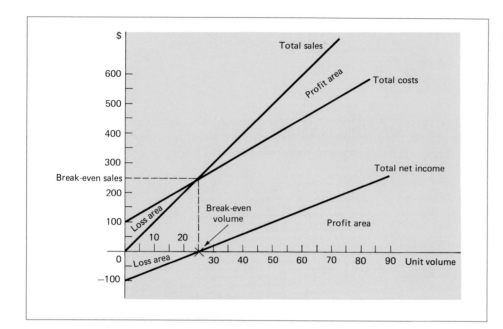

FIGURE 11.7
Break-Even Chart

Sales ($sx = \$10 \times 40$)	$400
Less: Variable costs ($bx = \$6 \times 40$)	240
Contribution margin	$160
Less: Fixed costs (a)	100
Profit (g)	$ 60

The **margin of safety** is the difference between budgeted sales and the break-even sales and is expressed as a percentage of budgeted sales. It is a measure of the risk associated with a particular sales goal. The margin of safety equals:

$$\text{Margin of safety} = \frac{\text{Budgeted sales } - \text{ Break-even sales}}{\text{Budgeted sales}} \times 100\% \quad \textbf{(11-14)}$$

In the example with a profit goal of $60, the margin of safety is:

$$\text{Margin of safety} = \frac{\$400 - \$250}{\$400} \times 100\% = 37.5\%$$

This means that if the actual sales volume is 37.5% less than the budgeted sales volume, the firm will still break-even.

Taxes can also be considered in this type of analysis. If one assumes a tax rate of t and an after-tax profit of g, then $g/(1-t)$ equals the net income before taxes. In this situation, total revenue equals fixed costs plus total variable costs plus the after-tax profit goal. This relationship can be expressed as:

$$sx = a + bx + \frac{g}{(1 - t)} \quad \textbf{(11-15)}$$

and the necessary unit volume is:

$$x = \frac{a + \dfrac{g}{(1 - t)}}{(s - b)} \tag{11-16}$$

If a tax rate of 40 percent is assumed and the firm desires an after-tax profit of $60, then from (11-16) one can see that the necessary unit volume equals fifty units. Reviewing the results, one finds:

Sales ($sx = \$10 \times 50$)	$500
Less: Variable costs ($bx = \$6 \times 50$)	300
Contribution margin	$200
Less: Fixed costs (a)	100
Profit before taxes ($g/(l-t)$)	$100
Taxes—40%	40
Profit after taxes (g)	$ 60

The margin of safety in this case is 50 percent.

☐ COST-VOLUME-PROFIT ANALYSIS WITH MULTIPLE PRODUCTS

To this point, our analysis has dealt with a single-product firm. Break-even analysis becomes more complex when the firm has more than one product. In a case in which a firm has multiple products, a constant **sales mix** is assumed. This means that the ratio of the sales among the various products remains constant. Assume the following for a firm that produces two products.

Product	A	B
Unit selling price	$6	$4
Unit variable cost	4	3
Unit-contribution margin	$2	$1
Total fixed cost	$400	

Assuming a sales mix of 1 to 2 for products A and B, the break-even unit volume can be calculated by first determining the contribution margin for one unit of A and two units of B. This is done as follows:

Sales mix	1	2		
Product	A	B	Total	Percentage
Selling price	1 × $6 = $6	2 × $4 = $8	$14	100
Variable cost	1 × $4 = 4	2 × $3 = 6	10	71.4
Unit-contribution margin	$2	$2	$ 4	28.6

By using formula (11-11), the break-even unit volume is:

$$x = \frac{\$400}{\$14 - \$10} = 100 \text{ units}$$

The question now is, what do these 100 units represent? Each unit represents one unit of product A and two units of product B. Checking the results, one finds:

Sales mix	1	2	
Product	A	B	Total
Sales	1 × 100 × $6 = $600	2 × 100 × $4 = $800	$1,400
Variable costs	1 × 100 × $4 = 400	2 × 100 × $3 = 600	1,000
Contribution margin	$200	$200	$ 400
Fixed Costs			400
Profit			$ 0

However, if the sales mix is changed, the break-even unit volume will change. For example, assume the new ratio is 2 to 1 for products A and B. The new break-even volume is:

Sales mix	2	1		
Product	A	B	Total	Percentage
Selling price	2 × $6 = $12	1 × $4 = $4	$16	100
Variable cost	2 × $4 = 8	1 × $3 = 3	11	68.75
Unit-contribution margin	$ 4	$1	$ 5	31.25

By using formula (11-11), the break-even unit volume is:

$$x = \frac{\$400}{\$16 - \$11} = 80 \text{ units}$$

Checking the results, one finds:

Sales mix	2	1	
Product	A	B	Total
Sales	2 × 80 × $6 = $960	1 × 80 × $4 = $320	$1,280
Variable costs	2 × 80 × $4 = 640	1 × 80 × $3 = 240	880
Contribution margin	$320	$ 80	$ 400
Fixed cost			400
Profit			$ 0

Therefore, one can conclude that in any multiple-product situation, a change in the sales mix will result in a change in the break-even unit volume.

☐ COST-VOLUME-PROFIT ANALYSIS USING THE CONTRIBUTION-MARGIN RATIO

To this point, our efforts have been directed towards determining the break-even volume in terms of units. The percentage of contribution margin in each dollar of sales is called the **contribution-margin ratio**. It is determined as follows:

$$\text{Contribution-margin ratio} = \frac{(s - b)}{s} \qquad \textbf{(11-17)}$$

This ratio can be used to directly determine the break-even volume in terms of sales revenue rather than units of output. The formula for determining the break-even sales revenue is:

$$\text{Break-even sales revenue} = \frac{\text{Fixed costs}}{\text{Contribution-margin ratio}} \qquad \textbf{(11-18)}$$

In the original example in this chapter, the fixed costs were $100, and the unit selling price and unit variable costs were $10 and $6, respectively. The contribution-margin ratio of 40 percent and break-even sales revenue of $250 are determined as follows, using (11-17) and (11-18):

$$\text{Contribution-margin ratio} = \frac{\$10 - \$6}{\$10} = 0.40$$

$$\text{Break-even sales revenue} = \frac{\$100}{0.40} = \$250$$

This is the same break-even sales revenue as was determined when the break-even units were determined.

This same approach can be employed in the multiple-product problem. In the first multiple-product example in which the contribution-margin ratio was 28.6 percent, the break-even sales revenue using (11-18) is $1,400.

□ASSUMPTIONS UNDERLYING THE LINEAR BREAK-EVEN MODEL

Models are abstractions from reality, and in the process of building a model, an individual makes certain assumptions concerning the real world. In constructing the linear break-even model, a series of explicit and implicit assumptions have been made. Careful consideration of these assumptions will aid in understanding the model. The following assumptions underlie the linear break-even model:

1. *Revenue behavior.* The revenue function is assumed to be linear over the relevant range of activity. From this, one can infer that selling prices and the sales mix remain constant.

2. *Cost behavior.* The cost function is assumed to be linear over the relevant range of activity. From this, one can infer that all costs can be resolved into variable and fixed components. Variable costs change proportionally with volume; fixed costs remain constant within the relevant range.

3. *Price behavior.* The dollars in revenue and costs have the same purchasing power. From this, one can infer that all financial data are comparable.

4. *Inventory behavior.* There are no significant shifts in the beginning and ending inventory levels. From this, one can infer that there will be equality in sales and production volume. For example, if a firm used LIFO for inventory valuation, and some base-stock inventory was sold, then the units sold from the inventory would most likely have a different unit cost

than the units produced and sold during the period. A similar situation would develop if base-stock raw materials were placed into production.

5. *Technological change.* Since it is assumed that selling prices and resource costs are fixed, it is also assumed that there will be no change in technology in the period under consideration. Any technological improvement would lower costs, thereby resulting in lower selling prices in a competitive market.

Recognition of the assumptions underlying the linear break-even model should minimize misuse when the assumptions are violated. Consideration of the assumptions should also make potential users recognize that the model does not pretend to represent all of the variations possible in the real world. The relevant-range assumption is the one assumption that should be kept in mind at all times when employing the model.

☐ANALYSIS EMPLOYING THE LINEAR BREAK-EVEN MODEL

One of the purposes of formulating a model is so that a decision maker can answer "what if" types of questions. Questions concerning shifts in unit selling price, unit variable cost, total fixed cost, expected sales volume, and the impact of these factors on expected profit can be evaluated by employing the break-even model. In any analysis of this type, one must keep in mind the assumptions that underlie the break-even model.

One can gain valuable insight into the relationships in the linear break-even model by observing how the shifts discussed earlier change a break-even diagram. In this section, we will discuss several situations. It would be wise for you to diagram the various situations. Then, as the situations are changed, you can note how the slope of the revenue and cost functions shift. You should also note how shifting the intersection of the cost function influences the break-even volume and the profit function.

Shifts In Unit-Contribution Margin

Shifts in the unit-contribution margin (unit selling price less unit variable cost) are caused by changes in the unit selling price, unit variable cost, or a combination of both. The result of any of these changes is to increase or decrease the unit-contribution margin.[9] If the unit-contribution margin is increased, then the break-even volume is decreased and the expected net income is increased. For example, assume the following:

Unit selling price	$3
Unit variable cost	$2
Total fixed cost	$100
Expected volume	200 units

9. If both the unit selling price and unit variable cost were changed so that the unit contribution did not change, then there would be no change in the break-even point or expected profit.

In this case, the break-even volume is 100 units and the expected net income is $100. If the unit selling price is increased to $4, then the unit contribution margin would be $2. The break-even volume is now only 50 units and the expected before-tax net income is $300.

When the unit-contribution margin is decreased, the break-even volume is increased and the expected net income is decreased. From the example just given, if the unit variable cost increased to $2.25, then the unit contribution margin would be $.75. The new break-even volume is 133.33 units and the expected before-tax net income is $50.

Shifts In Total Fixed Cost

Break-even volume and expected net income will move in opposite directions with a shift in the total fixed cost. From the original example, if the total fixed cost was increased from $100 to $150, then the new break-even volume would be 150 units (as compared to 100 units). The new expected net income would be $50 (as compared to $100).

Shifts In Expected Volume

Any shift in the expected volume will cause the expected before-tax net income to shift in the same direction. The break-even volume will not be changed. From the original example, if the expected volume increased from 200 to 250 units, then the expected before-tax net income would also increase from $100 to $150. On the other hand, if the expected volume decreased from 200 to 175 units, then the expected before-tax net income also decreased from $100 to $75. It should be noted that any shift in the expected net income equals the unit-contribution margin times the change in the volume.

The consideration of possible changes involving the linear break-even model has been limited to those situations about which generalizations can be made. It should be recognized that, in a real-life situation, the possible changes most likely would not lend themselves to a convenient classification, and each situation would require a new solution.

Operating Leverage

Operating leverage is a measure of how a firm can increase profits in a relationship to increases in sales volume. It is related to a firm's cost structure in that a firm with high fixed costs and low unit variable costs will have high operating leverage. On the other hand, firms that have low fixed costs and high unit variable costs have low operating leverage. The greater the percentage of a firm's costs that are fixed, the higher the firm's operating leverage. This works to a firm's advantage when sales are increasing and to its disadvantage when sales are decreasing.

Consider firms A and B with budgeted sales of $2,000 as shown in table 11.2. At the budgeted sales, both firms have budgeted profits of $500. As shown in table 11.2, if both firms have a 20 percent increase in sales, firm A's profit increases by $300 ($800 − $500), while firm B's profit only in-

TABLE 11.2 Operating Leverage and Break-Even Analysis

Budgeted sales

Firm	A			B	
Sales	100 × $20 = $2,000	100%		100 × $20 = $2,000	100%
Less: Variable costs	100 × $5 = 500	25%		100 × $10 = 1,000	50%
Contribution margin		$1,500	75%		$1,000	50%
Less: Fixed costs		1,000			500	
Profit		$ 500			$ 500	

Twenty Percent Increase in Sales

Firm	A			B	
Sales	120 × $20 = $2,400	100%		120 × $20 = $2,400	100%
Less: Variable costs	120 × $5 = 600	25%		120 × $10 = 1,200	50%
Contribution margin		$1,800	75%		$1,200	50%
Less: Fixed costs		1,000			500	
Profit		$ 800			$ 700	

Twenty Percent Decrease in Sales

Firm	A			B	
Sales	80 × $20 = $1,600	100%		80 × $20 = $1,600	100%
Less: Variable costs	80 × $5 = 400	25%		80 × $10 = 800	50%
Contribution margin		$1,200	75%		$ 800	50%
Less: Fixed costs		1,000			500	
Profit		$ 200			$ 300	

creases by $200 ($700 − $500). This difference occurs because firm A has a relatively high fixed costs and low unit variable costs, while firm B has relatively high unit variable costs and low fixed costs. Firm A has greater operating leverage than firm B.

One can develop a measure of the relative operating leverage of a firm at a given level of sales. This measure equals:

$$\text{Relative operating leverage} = \frac{\text{Contribution margin}}{\text{Net income}} \qquad \textbf{(11-19)}$$

For firms A and B, the relative operating leverage equals:

Firm A   *Firm B*

$$\frac{\$1,500}{\$500} = 3 \qquad\qquad \frac{\$1,000}{\$500} = 2$$

These relative numbers are interpreted as follows. For firm A, a 20 percent increase in sales resulted in a 60 percent ($300/$500 = 60 percent) increase in profit. The profit increased three times more than the increase in sales. Likewise, for firm B, the 20 percent increase in sales resulted in a 40 percent ($200/$500 = 40 percent) increase in profit. A similar interpretation can be made of the results when both firms realized a 20 percent decrease in sales.

Operating leverage is useful in evaluating the potential profitability of different firms. It is based on the cost structure of a firm and specifies the relationship between changes in sales volume and profit.

□ SUMMARY

The chapter began with a consideration of nonlinear cost-volume-profit relationships. It was demonstrated how this model could be used to determine the sales volume that will maximize profits. However, this model is used infrequently because of the excessive costs associated with obtaining the data necessary to construct the cost and revenue functions. However, linear approximations of these functions can be used to gain considerable insight into the cost-volume-profit relationships of a firm.

The linear model was developed to determine the break-even unit volume of a firm. This model was then elaborated on to incorporate a profit goal and taxes. The key parameters or constants in this model are unit selling price, unit variable cost, and fixed costs. The model was modified using the contribution-margin ratio so that the break-even sales volume could be determined. Multiple-product problems can be solved using this model if a constant sales mix is assumed.

The impact of shifts in selling price, unit variable costs, and fixed costs on the profit of a firm can be analyzed using the break-even model. However, whenever the break-even model is employed, attention must be given to the assumptions concerning revenue, cost, price, and inventory behavior and the assumption concerning no technological change.

KEY TERMS

Break-even point
Contribution-margin ratio
Cost-volume-profit analysis
Margin of safety

Nonlinear model
Operating leverage
Sales mix
Unit-contribution margin

REVIEW PROBLEM

The Hellier Corporation manufactures surf boards that sell for $300 each. Unit variable costs are $150, and total annual fixed costs are $300,000. The firm has an after-tax profit goal of $90,000 and an effective tax rate of 40 percent.

Required □

1. Determine the break-even unit volume for the firm.

2. Determine the necessary unit volume for the firm to reach its after-tax profit goal.

3. Determine the margin of safety for the firm if it reaches its budgeted unit volume.

Solution □

1. $X = \dfrac{\$300,000}{\$300 - \$150} = 2,000$ units   **(11-11)**

2. $X = \dfrac{\$300,000 + \dfrac{\$90,000}{1 - .40}}{\$300 - \$150} = 3,000$ units **(11-16)**

3. $\dfrac{3,000\ (\$300) - 2,000\ (\$300)}{3,000\ (\$300)} \times 100\% = 33\frac{1}{3}\%$ **(11-14)**

Now further assume that the Hellier Corporation is considering manufacturing sailboards. These boards will sell for $1,000 each, and the estimated unit variable costs are $650. If the firm elects to manufacture the sailboards, additional fixed costs of $100,000 are anticipated. The marketing department expects to sell three surfboards for every sailboard.

Required □

1. Determine the new break-even unit volume for the firm.

2. Determine the necessary unit volume for the firm to reach an after-tax profit goal of $120,000.

Solution □

1.

Product	Surfboard	Sailboard	Total
Sales mix	3	1	
Selling price	3 × $300 = $900	1 × $1,000 = $1,000	$1,900
Variable costs	3 × $150 = 450	1 × $ 650 = 650	1,100
Unit = Contribution margin	$450	$ 350	$ 800

$x = \dfrac{\$400,000}{\$1,900 - \$1,100} = 500$ units **(11-11)**

Sales mix	1,500 Surfboards		500 Sailboards	
Product	Surfboard		Sailboard	Total
Sales Mix	3		1	
Sales	3 × 500 × $300 = $450,000		1 × 500 × $1,000 =	$950,000
Variable costs	3 × 500 × $150 = 225,000		1 × 500 × $ 650 = $500,000	550,000
Contribution margin	$225,000		325,000	$400,000
Fixed costs			$175,000	400,000
Profit				$ 0

2.

$x = \dfrac{\$400,000 + \dfrac{120,000}{1 - .40}}{\$1,900 - \$1,100} = 750$ units **(11-16)**

Sales mix	2,250 Surfboards		750 Sailboards	
Product	Surboard		Sailboard	Total
Sales mix	3		1	
Sales	3 × 750 × $300 = $675,000		1 × 750 × $1,000 = $750,000	$1,425,000
Variable costs	3 × 750 × $150 = 337,500		1 × 750 × $ 650 = 487,500	825,000
Contribution margin	$337,500		$262,500	$ 600,000
Fixed costs				400,000
Profit before taxes				$ 200,000
Taxes (40 percent)				80,000
Profit after taxes				120,000

QUESTIONS

Q11-1. Draw a break-even chart and then consider the following questions:

  a. How will an increase in the unit selling price change the total revenue and profit functions?

  b. How will an increase in the unit selling price change the break-even volume?

  c. How will an increase in the unit variable cost change the total revenue and profit functions?

  d. How will an increase in the unit variable cost change the total cost function?

  e. How will an increase in the unit variable cost change the break-even volume?

  f. How will an increase in the total fixed cost change the total cost function?

  g. How will an increase in the total fixed cost change the break-even volume?

  h. How would your answers to questions a and b change if the unit selling price were decreased?

  i. How would your answers to questions c, d, and e change if the unit variable cost were decreased?

  j. How would your answers to questions f and g change if the total fixed cost decreased?

Q11-2. In the auto industry, unions have been demanding a guaranteed annual income for production workers. How would a guaranteed annual income influence the break-even point of an auto firm?

Q11-3. Since we know that total revenue and cost functions are not linear, what is to be gained by considering linear approximations of these functions? Discuss.

Q11-4. In the linear break-even model, what are the marginal revenue and the marginal cost? Under what condition would they be equal? Does the linear break-even model indicate the level of output that maximizes profit?

Q11-5. As technology advances and production processes become increasingly automated, how would such technological improvement influence the break-even point of a firm?

Q11-6. What costs would be taken into consideration by a university administrator in determining the break-even number of students required for a course to be offered?

Q11-7. In a particular firm, the manager of each product line is provided break-even information. The president of the firm asks why you are not providing him the same type of information. How would you answer?

Q11-8. The linear break-even model is static rather than dynamic. Explain.

Q11-9. In the airline industry, a flight is generally considered to break-even when it is 50 percent full. Why would an airline schedule a flight if the expected number of passengers did not exceed 50 percent?

Q11-10. Discuss some of the merits of having a relatively low unit-contribution margin and low total fixed costs as opposed to a relatively high unit-contribution margin and high total fixed costs.

Q11-11. Management should strive to keep all costs variable and minimize total fixed costs. Discuss.

Q11-12. What is operating leverage and how is it used?

Q11-13. What is the relationship between a firm's fixed costs and its operating leverage?

Q11-14. What is the relationship between a firm's unit variable cost and its operating leverage?

PROBLEMS

P11-1. The president of a large automotive firm was asked to a congressional hearing to specify the break-even point for his firm in either units or sales dollars. The president of the firm replied that this was not possible because of the many variables that had to be taken into consideration in determining a break-even point. The congressional investigator replied that the president was being evasive and expressed doubt that the stockholders of the firm were being adequately served by a management team that did not even know the break-even point of the firm.   *Break-even Concepts*

Required ☐

1. What are some of the variables that the president of the firm had in mind?

2. How could the congressional investigator reach the stated conclusion about the management team of the firm?

P11-2. Assume the following revenue and cost functions: *Nonlinear Break-even Problem*

$R = 82x - 3x^2$
$C = x^3/3 - 3x^2 + 18x + 180$

Required ☐

1. Determine the expression for the marginal revenue.

2. Determine the expression for the marginal cost.

3. Determine the outputs for a situation in which the marginal revenue equals the marginal cost. What situation is created if the firm produces at one of these outputs?

4. Determine the profit function for the firm, and determine the output that will maximize profits.

5. Graph the functions, and determine the approximate break-even points.

6. Explain why firms do not use this type of cost-volume-profit analysis.

P11-3. In each of the following situations, compute the number of units that must be sold if a company is going to break-even.   *Basic Break-even Problem*

a. Total fixed costs are $80,000, and the unit contibution margin is $5.

b. Unit selling price is $8, and unit variable cost is $5. Total fixed costs are $36,000.
c. Unit selling price is $10, and the contribution margin is 30 percent of revenue. Total fixed costs are $27,000.
d. Unit variable cost is 75 percent of the unit selling price, and total fixed costs are $45,000. The unit selling price is $12.
e. Unit variable cost is $5 and unit-contribution margin is $3. Total fixed costs are $57,000. What is the total sales at the break-even volume?

Basic Break-even Problem   **P11-4.**   Compute the number of units that must be sold and the total sales in each of the following situations:

a. Total fixed costs are $80,000, and the unit-contribution margin is $5. The firm has a profit goal of $40,000, and the unit selling price is $8.
b. Unit variable cost is $6, and unit-contribution margin is $4. Total fixed costs are $40,000, and the company has a profit goal of $25,000 after taxes. The tax rate is 40 percent.
c. Unit variable cost is 70 percent of the unit selling price, and total fixed costs are $60,000. The unit selling price is $10, and the after-tax profit goal is $54,000. The tax rate is 40 percent.
d. Unit-contribution margin is $3, and unit variable cost is 70 percent of the unit selling price. Total fixed costs are $60,000, and the after-tax profit goal is $30,000. The tax rate is 50 percent.
e. Unit variable cost is $9, and unit-contribution margin is 25 percent of the unit selling price. Total fixed costs are $25,000, and the after-tax profit goal is $40,000. The tax rate is 50 percent.

C-V-P Analysis with Various Levels of Activity   **P11-5.**   A large diversified corporation is considering the acquisition of two firms that manufacture electric razors. Firm A has a variable unit cost of $11, and total fixed costs of $2,500,000. Firm B has a variable unit cost of $14, and total fixed costs of $500,000. The wholesale price for the electric razors is $16, and each firm has a capacity of 800,000 razors a year.

Required □ Which firm would you recommend the corporation acquire if the estimated demand for electric razors is:

a. 400,000 units per year? What is the margin of safety?
b. 600,000 units per year? What is the margin of safety?
c. 800,000 units per year? What is the margin of safety?

C-V-P Analysis with Various Production Options   **P11-6.**   The Blacksburg Tool and Die Company is considering acquiring new equipment to set up a production line to produce a newly designed locking wrench. Demand for this new wrench is estimated at 100,000 units a year, and the selling price is to be $10. One of the production lines under consideration employs considerable labor. The estimated unit variable cost is $7, and the total fixed cost is $150,000.

The other production line is more automated. The variable unit cost is $3, and the total fixed costs are estimated to be $630,000.

Required □

1. Which production line would you recommend the firm set up? What is the margin of safety for each production line?

2. If the demand were estimated to be 120,000 units, would your recommendation change?

3. If the demand were estimated to be 150,000 units, would your recommendation change?

4. Assume the firm has an after-tax profit goal of $60,000. If the tax rate is 40 percent and estimated demand is 100,000 units, what would the selling price have to equal for both production lines?

P11-7. The Woodcock Automobile Company manufactures two basic types of cars that it sells wholesale to its dealers throughout the country. The compact car is sold to the dealers at an average price of $2,000 per unit, and the variable manufacturing costs are $1,800 per unit. The standard-size car is sold to dealers for $3,500 per unit on the average, and variable manufacturing costs average $3,000 per unit. Total fixed costs are estimated to be $360 million per year.

C-V-P Analysis with Changes in Sales Mix

Required ☐

1. Determine the break-even volume for the company if the expected sales mix is 33 percent compact cars and 67 percent standard cars.

2. Because of a gasoline shortage, the management team expects the sales mix to shift to 50 percent compact cars and 50 percent standard cars. Determine the break-even volume based on the new sales mix, and explain why your answer differs from the one you gave in requirement 1.

3. If the firm should produce more than 50 percent compact cars, fixed costs are expected to increase by $65 million. Determine the break-even volume based on a sales mix of 60 percent compact cars and 40 percent standard cars.

P11-8. The General Automobile Company manufactures three types of cars. All cars manufactured by General are sold at wholesale to dealers throughout the world. Compact models manufactured by General sell at an average price of $2,200, and the variable cost per unit totals $1,900. Standard-size General cars sell at an average price of $3,700, and variable costs per unit on the average equal $3,000. Luxury models manufactured by General sell for an average price of $6,000, and the average variable cost is $5,000. Fixed costs for the company are estimated to equal $1,080,000,000.

C-V-P Analysis with Changes in Sales Mix

Required ☐

1. The Marketing department of the company estimates the sales mix for the next year to be 30 percent, 50 percent, and 20 percent, respectively, for each type of car. What is the break-even point in units and sales for the firm?

2. If the company has an after-tax profit goal of $1 billion and the tax rate is estimated to equal 50 percent, determine the number of units of each type of car that must be sold for the goal to be reached.

3. Assume the sales mix shifted to 50 percent, 40 percent, and 10 percent, respectively. How would your answer to requirement 2 change?

4. If the company sold more luxury cars and fewer compact cars, how would your answers to requirements 1 and 2 change?

C-V-P Analysis   **P11-9.** The Far Eastern Motorcycle Company sells bikes for an average price of $1,000. The average variable cost per bike is $600. At the present time, the company sells 12,500 bikes a year, and its fixed costs are $4 million. An advertising program costing $1 million is being planned. It is estimated that the advertising program will increase sales by 15 percent in the year of the program.

Required □

1. What is the break-even volume for Far Eastern?

2. Should the company undertake the advertising program?

3. How much would volume have to be increased before the firm would consider the advertising program?

4. How would your answer to requirement 3 change if a tax rate of 40 percent is assumed?

5. At its present sales volume, determine the relative operating leverage for the firm.

C-V-P Analysis with Various Levels of Activity   **P11-10.** The business manager of a college newspaper is preparing the newspaper's annual request for the subsidy from student fees. She receives the following cost estimates for thirty issues of the paper from a local printer:

4-page paper	$500 per issue
6-page paper	685 per issue
8-page paper	800 per issue

She determines that all other expenses associated with the paper average $6,000 for an academic year. A page of advertising in the newspaper can be billed at $312.50, and she expects to collect 80 percent of all billings.

The manager does not believe that she should have more than 33 percent advertising in the paper. In addition, she expects that at least 12.5 percent of the paper will be advertising.

Required □ Assuming that only full pages of advertising are considered and that the printer's rates are for thirty issues of one size of the paper, prepare a request for the subsidy for each of the options available to the manager.

C-V-P Analysis with Different Cost Structures   **P11-11.** Two local firms manufacture slip rings and you are considering acquiring one of them. One firm, VPI, employs a considerable amount of labor in its manufacturing processes, and its salespeople all work on commission. The other firm, TECH, employs the latest technology in its manufacturing operations, and the sales personnel are salaried.

You have obtained the following financial information concerning the two firms:

	VPI		TECH	
	19X4	19X5	19X4	19X5
Sales	$100,000	$160,000	$100,000	$140,000
Costs and expenses including taxes	88,000	137,200	88,000	111,200
Net income	$ 12,000	$ 22,800	$ 12,000	$ 28,800

The tax rate for both firms is 40 percent, and after examining cost data, you determine the fixed costs to equal:

VPI	$10,000
TECH	50,000

Required ☐

1. Determine the break-even sales volume for each of the firms in years 19X4 and 19X5.

2. Determine the relative operating leverage for each firm in years 19X4 and 19X5.

3. If you could acquire either firm for $200,000, and you want an after-tax return of 12 percent on your investment, determine the sales necessary for each firm for you to reach your goal.

4. If the demand for slip rings fluctuates widely, comment on the relative positions of each firm.

P11-12. The Community Church plans to open a child-care center in the near future. The center will operate five days a week and fifty weeks each year and charge $25 per week for each child. It has been determined that $20,000 must be spent to upgrade facilities in the church to meet state standards. These facilities have an estimated life of five years.

C-V-P Analysis with Different Levels of Activity

Supplies for each child are estimated to cost $.50 per day, and food is estimated to cost $.75 per day. Each year $1,000 must be spent on new equipment for the center. For every ten children, one paraprofessional must be included on the staff. For every twenty children, there must be one professional on the staff. For the school to operate, there must be at least one professional on the staff. Salaries for professionals and paraprofessionals are $9,000 and $4,000 respectively.

Space limitations in the church limit the center to accepting sixty children. This would require a staff of three professionals and six paraprofessionals.

Required ☐

1. Prepare a schedule showing the financial results of operating the center with twenty, forty, and sixty children, respectively.

2. Discuss some of the problems of employing break-even analysis in this type of problem.

P11-13. Required ☐

1. Identify the numbered components of the break-even chart.

Break-even Chart

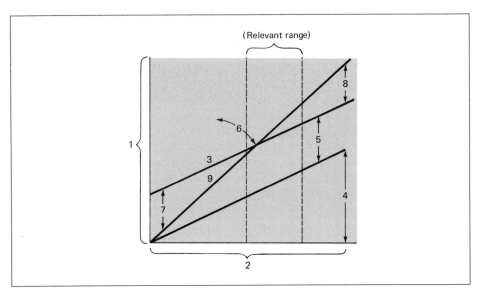

2. Discuss the significance of the concept of the relevant range to break-even analyses.

(CPA)

C-V-P Analysis Definitions and Calculations

P11-14. Cost-volume-earnings analysis (break-even analysis) is used to determine and express the interrelationships of different volumes of activity (sales), costs, sales prices, and sales mix to earnings. More specifically, the analysis is concerned with what will be the effect on earnings of changes in sales volume, sales prices, sales mix, and costs.

Required □

1. Certain terms are fundamental to cost-volume-earnings analysis. Explain the meaning of each of the following terms:

  a. Fixed costs
  b. Variable costs
  c. Relevant range
  d. Break-even point
  e. Margin of safety
  f. Sales mix

2. Several assumptions are implicit in cost-volume-earnings analysis. What are these assumptions?

In a recent period, Zero Company had the following experience:

		Fixed	Variable	
Sales (10,000 units @ $200)				$2,000,000
Costs				
Direct material		$ —	$ 200,000	
Direct labor		—	400,000	
Factory overhead		160,000	600,000	
Administrative expenses		180,000	80,000	
Other expenses		200,000	120,000	
Total costs		$540,000	$1,400,000	1,940,000
Profit				$ 60,000

Each of the following is independent:

3. Calculate the break-even point for Zero in terms of units and sales dollars. Show your calculations.

4. What is the break-even point if the management team makes a decision that increases fixed costs by $18,000? Show your calculations.

(CPA)

P11-15. The All-Day Candy Company is a wholesale distributor of candy. The company services grocery, convenience, and drug stores in a large metropolitan area.

C-V-P Analysis with Cost Increases

Small but steady growth in sales has been achieved by the All-Day Candy Company over the past few years while candy prices have been increasing. The company is formulating its plans for the coming fiscal year. Presented below are the data used to project the current year's after-tax net income of $110,400.

Average selling price	$4.00 per box
Average variable costs	
Costs of candy	$2.00 per box
Selling expenses	.40 per box
Total	$2.40 per box
Annual fixed costs	
Selling	$160,000
Administrative	280,000
Total	$440,000
Expected annual sales volume (390,000) boxes	$1,560,000
Tax rate	40%

Manufacturers of candy, including the All-Day Candy Company, have announced that they will increase prices of their products an average of 15 percent in the coming year due to increases in raw material (sugar, cocoa, peanuts, etc.) and labor costs. The All-Day Candy Company expects that all other costs will remain at the same rates or levels as the current year.

Required □

1. What is the All-Day Candy Company's break-even point in boxes of candy for the current year?

2. What selling price per box must the All-Day Candy Company charge to cover the 15 percent increase in the cost of candy and still maintain the current contribution-margin ratio?

3. What volume of sales in dollars must the All-Day Candy Company achieve in the coming year to maintain the same net income after taxes as projected for the current year if the selling price of candy remains at $4 per box and the cost of candy increases 15 percent?

(CMA)

P11-16. The president of the Beth Corporation, which manufactures tape decks and sells them to producers of sound-reproduction systems, anticipates a 10 percent wage increase on January 1 of next year to the manufacturing

C-V-P Analysis with Cost Increases

employees (variable labor). He expects no other changes in costs. Overhead will not change as a result of the wage increase. The president has asked you to assist him in developing the information he needs to formulate a reasonable product strategy for next year.

You are satisfied by regression analysis that volume is the primary factor affecting costs and have separated the semivariable costs into their fixed and variable segments by means of the least-squares criterion. You also observe that the beginning and ending inventories are never materially different.

The following current-year data are assembled for your analysis:

Current selling prices per unit	$ 80
Variable cost per unit	
Material	30
Labor	12
Overhead	6
Total	$ 48
Annual volume of sales	5,000 units
Fixed costs	$51,000

Required □ Provide the following information for the president, using cost-volume-profit analysis:

1. What increase in the selling price is necessary to cover the 10 percent wage increase and still maintain the current profit-volume-cost ratio?

2. How many tape decks must be sold to maintain the current net income if the sales price remains at $80 and the 10 percent wage increase goes into effect?

3. The president believes that an additional $19,000 of machinery (to be depreciated at 10 percent annually) will increase present capacity (5,300 units) by 30 percent. If all tape decks produced can be sold at the present price and the wage increase goes into effect, how would the estimated net income before capacity is increased compare with the estimated net income after capacity is increased? Prepare computations of estimated net income before and after the expansion.

(CPA)

C-V-P Analysis with Product Elimination   **P11-17.** The president of the Eastern Company wants guidance on the advisability of eliminating product C, one of the company's three similar products, or investing in new machinery to reduce the cost of product C in the hope of reversing product C's operating loss sustained in 19X6. The three similar products are manufactured in a single plant in about the same amount of floor space, and the markets in which they are sold are very competitive.

Below is the condensed statement of operating income for the company and for product C for the year ended October 31, 19X6.

EASTERN COMPANY
Statement of Operating Income
For the year ended October 31, 19X6

	All three products	Product C
Sales	$2,800,150	$350,000

Cost of sales		
Raw materials	565,000	80,000
Labor		
Direct	1,250,000	150,000
Indirect	55,000	18,000
Fringe benefits (15 percent of labor)	195,750	25,200
Royalties (1 percent of product C sales)	3,500	3,500
Maintenance and repairs	6,000	2,000
Factory supplies	15,000	2,100
Depreciation (straight-line)	25,200	7,100
Electrical power	25,000	3,000
Scrap and spoilage	4,300	600
Total cost of sales	2,144,750	291,500
Gross profit	655,400	58,500
Selling, general, and administrative expenses		
Sales commissions	120,000	15,000
Officers' salaries	32,000	10,500
Other wages and salaries	14,000	5,300
Fringe benefits (15 percent of wages, salaries,		
and commissions)	24,900	4,620
Delivery expense	79,500	10,000
Advertising expense	195,100	26,000
Miscellaneous fixed expenses	31,900	10,630
Total selling, general, and administrative		
expenses	497,400	82,050
Operating income (loss)	$ 158,000	$ (23,550)

Required ☐ (Disregard income taxes)

1. Prepare a schedule showing the contribution of product C to the re-covery of fixed costs and expenses (marginal income) for the year ended October 31, 19X6. Assume that each element of cost and expense is entirely fixed or variable within the relevant range and that the change in inventory levels has been negligible.

2. Assume that in fiscal 19X6 the variable costs and expenses of product C totaled $297,500 and that its fixed costs and expenses amounted to $75,100. Prepare a schedule computing the break-even point of product C in terms of annual dollar sales volume. Sales for 19X6 amounted to $350,000.

3. Based on part 2, assume the direct-labor costs of product C could have been reduced by $75,000 and the indirect-labor costs by $4,000 by in-vesting an additional $340,000 (financed with 5 percent bonds) in ma-chinery with a ten-year life and an estimated salvage value of $30,000 at the end of the period. However, the company would have been liable for total severance pay costs of $18,000 (to be amortized over a five-year period), and electrical power costs would have increased $500 annually.

   Assuming the information given in requirement 2, prepare a schedule computing the break-even point of product C in terms of annual dollar sales volume if the additional machinery had been purchased and installed at the beginning of the year.

(CPA)

P11-18. The Pralina Products Company is a regional firm that has three major product lines—cereals, breakfast bars, and dog food. The income state-ment for the year ended April 30, 19X8, is shown; the statement was

C-V-P Analysis with Multiple Products

prepared by product line using absorption (full) costing. Explanatory data related to the items presented in the income statement appear in the adjoining column.

PRALINA PRODUCTS COMPANY
Income Statement
For the Year Ended April 30, 19X8
(in thousands)

	Cereals	Breakfast bars	Dog food	Total
Sales in pounds	2,000	500	500	3,000
Revenue from sales	$1,000	$400	$200	$1,600
Cost of sales				
Raw materials	$ 330	$160	$100	$ 590
Direct labor	90	40	20	150
Factory overhead	108	48	24	180
Total cost of sales	$ 528	$248	$144	$ 920
Gross margin	$ 472	$152	$ 56	$ 680
Operating expenses				
Selling expenses				
Advertising	$ 50	$ 30	$ 20	$ 100
Commissions	50	40	20	110
Salaries and related benefits	30	20	10	60
Total selling expenses	$ 130	$ 90	$ 50	$ 270
General and administrative expenses				
Licenses	$ 50	$ 20	$ 15	$ 85
Salaries and related benefits	60	25	15	100
Total general and administrative expenses	$ 110	$ 45	$ 30	$ 185
Total operating expenses	$ 240	$135	$ 80	$ 455
Operating income before taxes	$ 232	$ 17	$(24)	$ 225

Other Data

1. *Cost of sales.* The company's inventories of raw materials and finished products do not vary significantly from year to year. The inventories at April 30, 19X8, were essentially identical to those at April 30, 19X7.

   Factory overhead was applied to products at 120 percent of direct-labor dollars. The factory overhead costs for the 19X7–X8 fiscal year were as follows:

Variable indirect labor and supplies	$ 15,000
Variable employee benefits on factory labor	30,000
Supervisory salaries and related benefits	35,000
Plant occupancy costs	100,000
	$180,000

   There was no overapplied or underapplied overhead at year-end.

2. *Advertising.* The company has been unable to determine any direct causal relationship between the level of sales volume and the level of advertising expenditures. However, because management believes ad-

vertising is necessary, an annual advertising program is implemented for each product line. Each product line is advertised independently of the others.

3. *Commissions.* Sales commissions are paid to the members of the sales force at the rates of 5 percent on the cereals and 10 percent on the breakfast bars and dog food.

4. *Licenses.* Various licenses are required for each product line. These are renewed annually for each product line.

5. *Salaries and related benefits.* Sales and general and administrative personnel devote time and effort to all product lines. Their salaries and wages are allocated on the basis of the management team's estimates of time spent on each product line.

Required □

1. The controller of Pralina Products Company has recommended that the company do a cost-volume-profit (C/V/P) analysis of its operations. As a first step, the controller has requested that you prepare a revised income statement for Pralina Products Company that employs a product-contribution margin format that will be useful in C/V/P analysis. The statement should show the profit contribution for each product line and the net income before taxes for the company as a whole.

2. What effect, if any, would there be on net income before taxes determined in requirement 1 if the inventories as of April 30, 19X8, had increased significantly over the inventory levels of April 30, 19X7? Explain your answer.

3. The controller of Pralina Products Company is going to prepare a report that he will present to the other members of top management explaining cost-volume-profit (C/V/P) analysis. Identify and explain the following points that the controller should include in the report.

a. The advantages that C/V/P analysis can provide to a company.
b. The difficulties Pralina Products Company could experience in the calculations involved in C/V/P analysis.
c. The dangers that Pralina Products Company should be aware of in using the information derived from the C/V/P analysis.

(CMA)

P11-19. The Columbus Hospital operates a general hospital but rents space and beds to separate entities for specialized areas such as pediatrics, maternity, and psychiatric. Columbus charges each separate entity for common services to its patients, such as meals and laundry, and for administrative services, such as billings and collections. All uncollectible accounts are charged directly to the entity. Space and bed rentals are fixed for the year.

C-V-P Analysis in the Health-Care Industry

For the entire year ended June 30, 19X3, the Pediatrics department at Columbus Hospital charged each patient an average of $65 per day, had a capacity of 60 beds, operated 24 hours per day for 365 days, and had revenue of $1,138,800.

Expenses charged by the hospital to the Pediatrics department for the year ended June 30, 19X3, were as follows:

| | Basis of allocation | |
	Patient-days	Bed capacity
Dietary	$ 42,952	
Janitorial		$ 12,800
Laundry	28,000	
Laboratory, other than direct charges to patients ...	47,800	
Pharmacy	33,800	
Repairs and maintenance	5,200	7,140
General administrative services		131,760
Rent		275,320
Billings and collections	40,000	
Bad-debt expense	47,000	
Other	18,048	25,980
	$262,800	$453,000

The only personnel directly employed by the Pediatrics department are supervising nurses, nurses, and aides. The hospital has minimum personnel requirements, based on total annual patient-days. Hospital requirements beginning at the minimum expected level of operation are as follows:

Annual patient-days	Aides	Nurses	Supervising nurses
10,000–14,000	21	11	4
14,000–17,000	22	12	4
17,000–23,725	22	13	4
23,726–25,550	25	14	5
25,551–27,375	26	14	5
27,376–29,200	29	16	6

The staffing levels given represent full-time equivalents, and it should be assumed that the Pediatrics department always employs only the minimum number of required full-time equivalent personnel.

Annual salaries for each class of employee are: supervising nurses, $18,000; nurses, $13,000; and aides, $5,000. Salary expense for the year ended June 30, 19X3, for supervising nurses, nurses, and aides was $72,000, $169,000, and $110,000, respectively.

The Pediatrics department operated at 100 percent capacity during 111 days for the past year. It is estimated that during 90 of these capacity days, the demand averaged 17 patients more than capacity and even went as high as 20 patients more on some days.

The hospital has an additional 20 beds available for rent for the year ending June 30, 19X4.

Required ☐

1. Calculate the minimum number of patient-days required for the Pediatrics department to break even for the year ending June 30, 19X4, if the additional 20 beds are not rented. Patient demand is unknown, but assume that revenue per patient-day, cost per patient-day, cost per bed, and employee salary rates will remain the same as for the year ended June 30, 19X3. Present calculations in good form.

2. Given that patient demand, revenue per patient-day, cost per patient-day, cost per bed, and employee salary rates for the year ending June 30, 19X4, remain the same as for the year ended June 30, 19X3, should the Pediatrics department rent the additional 20 beds? Show the annual gain or loss from the additional beds. Present calculations in good form.

(CPA)

P11-20. Hewtex Electronics manufactures two products—tape recorders and electronic calculators—and sells them nationally to wholesalers and retailers. The Hewtex management team is very pleased with the company's performance for the current fiscal year. Projected sales through December 31, 19X7, indicate that 70,000 tape recorders and 140,000 electronic calculators will be sold this year. The projected earnings statement, which appears below, shows that Hewtex will exceed its earnings goal of 9 percent on sales after taxes.

C-V-P Analysis with Changes in Sales Mix

The tape recorder business has been fairly stable the last few years, and the company does not intend to change the tape recorder price. However, the competition among manufacturers of electronic calculators has been increasing.

Hewtex's calculators have been very popular with consumers. In order to sustain this interest in the calculators and to meet the price reductions expected from competitors, management officials have decided to reduce the wholesale price of its calculator from $22.50 to $20.00 per unit effective January 1, 19X8. At the same time, the company plans to spend an additional $57,000 on advertising during fiscal year 19X8. As a consequence of these actions, management estimates that 80 percent of its total revenue will be derived from calculator sales as compared to 75 percent in 19X7. As in prior years, the sales mix is assumed to be the same at all volume levels.

The total fixed-overhead costs will not change in 19X8 nor will the variable-overhead cost rates (applied on a direct-labor hour base). However, the cost of materials and direct labor is expected to change. The cost of solid-state electronic components will be cheaper in 19X8. Hewtex estimates that material costs will drop 10 percent for the tape recorders and 20 percent for the calculators in 19X8. However, direct-labor costs for both products will increase 10 percent in the coming year.

HEWTEX ELECTRONICS
Projected Earnings Statement
For the Year Ended December 31, 19X7

	Tape recorders Total amount (in thousands)	Per unit	Electronic calculators Total amount (in thousands)	Per unit	Total (in thousands)
Sales	$1,050	$15.00	$3,150	$22.50	$4,200.0
Production costs					
Materials	$ 280	$ 4.00	$ 630	$ 4.50	$ 910.0
Direct labor	140	2.00	420	3.00	560.0
Variable overhead	140	2.00	280	2.00	420.0
Fixed overhead	70	1.00	210	1.50	280.0
Total production costs	$ 630	$ 9.00	$1,540	$11.00	$2,170.0

Gross margin	$ 420	$ 6.00	$1,610	$11.50	$2,030.0
Fixed selling and administrative					1,040.0
Net income before income taxes					$ 990.0
Income taxes (55%)					544.5
Net income					$ 445.5

Required □

1. How many tape recorder and electronic calculator units did Hewtex Electronics have to sell in 19X7 to break-even?

2. What volume of sales is required if Hewtex Electronics is to earn a profit in 19X8 equal to 9 percent on sales after taxes?

3. How many tape recorder and electronic calculator units will Hewtex have to sell in 19X8 to break-even?

(CMA)

CHAPTER OUTLINE

THE PRODUCT-MIX PROBLEM—A LINEAR-PROGRAMMING SOLUTION

CHAPTER 12

☐ **INTRODUCTION**

The single-product or constant sales-mix assumption restricts the use of cost-volume-profit analysis. Today, most firms produce more than a single product and can alter their sales mix by actions taken to influence behavior in the marketplace. For example, an automobile firm can advertise and influence people to purchase more expensive cars. If resources were un- limited, product-mix decisions would not present a managerial problem. However, since resources are limited, any shift in the output of a firm will change the demand for scarce resources. The impact of product-mix de- cisions on profit must also be considered by the management team. Each of these factors contribute to the complicated nature of product-mix de- cision making.

Linear programming is a powerful mathematical tool that permits the maximization or minimization of a linear-objective function subject to certain linear constraints. The oil refining, textile, chemical, and agricul- tural industries are some of the businesses in which linear programming is widely used. Though outputs from an oil refinery may vary, the objective is to maximize profits subject to market, inventory, and production con- straints. In agriculture, linear programming is used to determine the op- timal mix of feed grains for cattle and other livestock that will satisfy certain nutritional constraints and minimize cost. Other application areas of linear programming are scheduling production, formulating transpor- tation schedules, and assigning warehouse locations.

When linear programming is used to solve a product-mix problem, cost data are required because unit contribution margin is the criterion em- ployed in selecting the optimal output combination. Standard-resource inputs are also required to specify the resource constraints of the problem. A standard-cost system can often serve as the basis for constructing a linear-programming model since both have similar data requirements. Budgeted financial statements can be prepared based on a linear-pro- gramming solution.

When one employs linear programming, one assumes that all of the model coefficients are known with certainty. This assumption applies to the unit contribution margins, resource requirements per unit of output, and total available resources. However, from previous discussions concerning cost estimation and standard costing, you should recognize that these coefficients are not known with certainty and can change at different levels of production.

Thus, one performs sensitivity analysis on the linear-programming model to gain additional insight concerning the uncertainty of the coefficients and its impact on the optimal product mix. Since linear programming is an optimization technique that enables one to determine the optimal solution, one is also able to determine the opportunity costs associated with any resources that constrain the output of the system. This enables one to determine the contribution to profit per unit of resource input if the resource is used optimally.

In this chapter, the product-mix problem will be described by using an example. We will then discuss the graphic method of solving the problem. Although the graphic method has limited application to real-world problems, it does permit valuable insight into the problem.

The **simplex algorithm,** which is a general method for solving linear-programming problems, will also be employed in solving the problem. A major advantage of the simplex algorithm is that additional economic information about the problem can be obtained from the solution. We will explain how this economic information can be used in decision making and show how the solution can serve as the basis for preparing budgeted income statements.

□ THE PRODUCT-MIX PROBLEM AND SCARCE RESOURCES

Assume you are the manager of a two-product firm and you desire to determine the optimal production mix for the next month of operations. Let x_1 and x_2, respectively, represent the wooden benches and chairs produced by your firm. Two resources, wood and labor, are required to manufacture the benches and chairs. You estimate that you will have eighteen units of wood and ten units of labor available next month. From the standard-costing system, you determine that production of a bench (x_1) requires three units of wood and one unit of labor. A chair (x_2) requires two units of wood and two units of labor.

The output for the month of your two-product firm is constrained by the availability of the wood and labor. These resource **constraints** can be expressed as:[1]

$$3x_1 + 2x_2 \leq 18 \quad \text{(Wood constraint)}$$
$$x_1 + 2x_2 \leq 10 \quad \text{(Labor constraint)}$$

---

1. See the appendix of chapter 6 for a review of matrix algebra.

In matrix form, if we assume:

$$x = \begin{bmatrix} x_1 \\ x_2 \end{bmatrix}; \quad b = \begin{bmatrix} 18 \\ 10 \end{bmatrix}; \quad A = \begin{bmatrix} 3 & 2 \\ 1 & 2 \end{bmatrix}$$

Then, the resource constraints can be expressed as:

$$Ax \leq b \tag{12-1}$$

After substituting for A, x, and b, the constraints in matrix form can be expressed as:

$$\begin{bmatrix} 3 & 2 \\ 1 & 2 \end{bmatrix} \begin{bmatrix} x_1 \\ x_2 \end{bmatrix} \leq \begin{bmatrix} 18 \\ 10 \end{bmatrix}$$

The next step in formulating the problem involves determining the unit contribution margins of the benches and chairs. From the standard-costing system, you determine that the standard cost of a unit of wood is $8. The standard labor rate, including a charge for variable overhead, is $7 per unit. You could determine the variable unit costs of the benches and chairs with several simple manipulations. However, we will specify some matrix manipulations to make the calculations, since almost all cost systems are now computerized and since this is most likely how a computer will determine the variable unit costs and then the unit contribution margins.

Given that the row vector, p, contains the standard costs, then the unit variable cost vector, v, equals:

$$v = pA \tag{12-2}$$

In the example, equation (12-2) yields the variable unit costs of:

$$[\$31 \quad \$30] = [\$8 \quad \$7] \begin{bmatrix} 3 & 2 \\ 1 & 2 \end{bmatrix}$$

Assuming that the expected selling prices are $41 and $38 for x_1 and x_2, respectively, allows you to determine the unit contribution margins. Letting the row vector, s, contain the selling prices; then the c vector of unit contribution margins is:

$$c = s - v \tag{12-3}$$

In the problem, the unit contribution margins equal:

$$[\$10 \quad \$8] = [\$41 \quad \$38] - [\$31 \quad \$30]$$

In the **product-mix problem,** all possible production alternatives are considered. Unit contribution margins are used as the criterion elements for determining optimal product mix. The objective is to determine the specific combination of outputs that will maximize the total contribution margin.

Unit contribution margins rather than unit profits are employed as the criterion element because, over the relevant range, unit contribution margins are assumed to remain constant. One cannot employ unit profits because they change whenever the inclusion of fixed costs causes a shift in output. However, maximization of the total contribution margin is consistent with the profit-maximization criterion, since fixed costs are assumed to be constant over the relevant range and total contribution margin less fixed costs equals profit.

You should keep in mind the problems encountered in associating variable overhead with the output of the system. Any shift in the scheme of associating the variable overhead with the output could alter the unit contribution margins. Since unit contribution margins are used as the criterion for selecting the optimal product mix, any change in the unit contribution margins can alter the optimal mix.

Since negative production is not possible, it is necessary to introduce a set of nonnegativity constraints. These constraints eliminate negative production from the set of possible solutions to the problem. Now, the product-mix problem can be expressed as a linear-programming problem wherein the goal is to maximize total contribution margin (z). The problem is expressed as:

Maximize: $z = \$10x_1 + \$8x_2$ **(Objective function)**

Subject to: $3x_1 + 2x_2 \leq 18$ (Wood constraint)

$x_1 + 2x_2 \leq 10$ (Labor constraint)

$x_1, x_2 \geq 0$ (Nonnegativity constraints)

In matrix form, the general problem can be expressed as:

Maximize: $z = cx$

Subject to: $Ax \leq b$

$x \geq 0$

Now, we will consider the graphic method for solving the problem.

□ THE GRAPHIC SOLUTION

The first step in solving the problem by the graphic method involves plotting the constraints. Let x_1 (benches) be shown on the horizontal (X) axis and x_2 (chairs) be shown on the vertical (Y) axis. The inequality, $3x_1 + 2x_2 \leq 18$, can be located on a graph by determining the points where it intersects the horizontal and vertical axes. If one assumes that all the available wood is used to make benches, then six benches can be manufactured.

Thus, the point of intersection on the horizontal axis is (6,0), which is determined by manipulating the wood constraint as follows:

$$3x_1 + 2x_2 \leq 18$$

$$3x_1 + 2(0) \leq 18$$

$$x_1 \leq 6$$

If all the available wood is used to make chairs, then nine chairs can be made. The point of intersection on the vertical axis is (0,9), which is determined by manipulating the wood constraint as follows:

$$3x_1 + 2x_2 \leq 18$$

$$3(0) + 2x_2 \leq 18$$

$$x_2 \leq 9$$

Figure 12.1 shows the plot of the wood ($3x_1 + 2x_2 \leq 18$) and the two nonnegativity constraints. The nonnegativity constraints for x_1 and x_2 are the vertical and horizontal axes, respectively. Any combination of benches and chairs selected by the firm that lies in the region *ABC* does not exceed the constraint resulting from the limited supply of wood or the nonnegativity constraints.

The labor constraint ($x_1 + 2x_2 \leq 10$) intersects the horizontal and vertical axes at (10,0) and (0,5), respectively. Figure 12.2 shows the wood, labor, and nonnegativity constraints. Any combination of benches and chairs selected by the firm that lies in the region *ABEF* does not violate any of the four constraints. The region *ABEF* is called the **feasible region.**

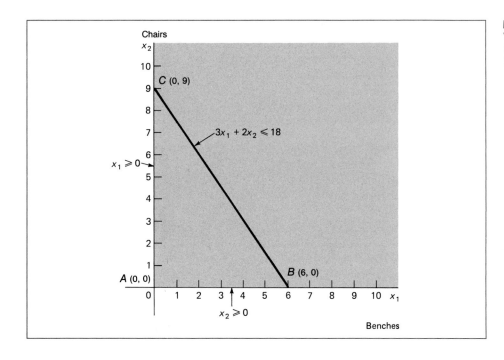

FIGURE 12.1
Wood and Nonnegativity Constraints

FIGURE 12.2
Wood, Labor, and
Nonnegativity
Constraints

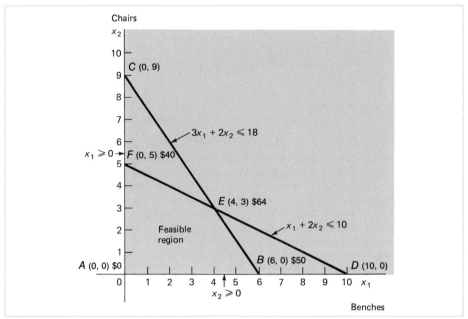

One of the basic theorems of linear programming is that the **optimal solution** occurs at a corner point of the feasible region. Therefore, one approach to solving a product-mix problem is to evaluate every corner point of the feasible region. When the corner points A, B, E, and F of the feasible region are evaluated with respect to the total contribution margin, one finds they equal $0, $60, $64, and $40, respectively. Based on this analysis, one would select point E as the optimal solution and produce four benches and three chairs, which would result in a total contribution margin of $64 $[(4 \times \$10) + (3 \times \$8) = \$64]$.

Another approach to graphically solving a linear-programming problem is shown in figure 12.3. This approach involves the use of iso-contribution margin lines. An iso-contribution margin line is a straight line such that for any product-mix combination on the line the total contribution margin is the same. An infinite number of iso-contribution margin lines are associated with any given objective function.

To draw accurate iso-contribution margin lines, their slopes must be known.[2] To determine the slope of the family of iso-contribution margin lines for any given linear-programming problem, the objective function is solved for the variable that is associated with the vertical axis. Thus, in the problem, one would solve for x_2 as follows:

$$z = \$10x_1 + \$8x_2 \qquad \text{(Objective function)}$$

$$\$8x_2 = z - \$10x_1$$

$$x_2 = z/\$8 - \$10/\$8x_1 \qquad \text{(Iso-contribution margin function)}$$

---

2. Since the total contribution margin, z, is not known, the x_2 intercept cannot be determined. Therefore, to draw the line, the slope must be known.

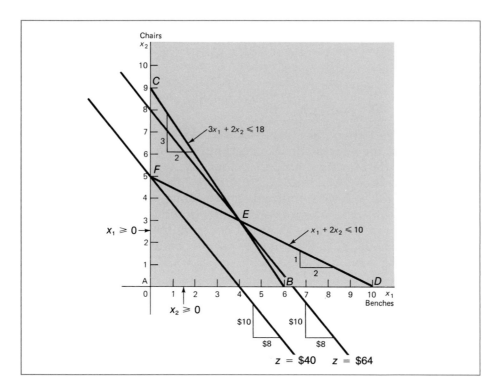

FIGURE 12.3
Iso-Contribution
Margin Lines

Examination of the iso-contribution margin function reveals that its slope is $-10/8$. After determining the slope, a series of iso-contribution margin lines are drawn on the graph as shown in figure 12.3. The iso-contribution margin line furthest from the origin and still in the feasible region determines the optimal solution. The $64 iso-contribution margin line specifies the optimal solution at the point where $x_1 = 4$ and $x_2 = 3$. Note that the $64 iso-contribution margin line crosses the x_1 axis at $x_1 = 6.4$ ($6.4 \times \$10 = \$64$) and the x_2 axis at $x_2 = 8$ ($8 \times \$8 = \$64$). However, both of these points are outside of the feasible region.

If the slope of the iso-contribution margin function is the same as the slope of one of the constraints, alternative optimal solutions will exist. Observe in figure 12.3 that if the contribution margin associated with x_1 is $12 rather than $10, then the iso-contribution margin lines will be parallel with the wood constraint. In this case, it would make no difference if the firm produced at B (6, 0, $72) or E (4, 3, $72) or anywhere along the line segment B–E. Thus, alternative optimal solutions exist. A similar condition is encountered if the contribution margin associated with x_1 is $4 rather than $10. In this case, the iso-contribution margin lines are parallel with the labor constraint and alternative optimal solutions exist along the line segment E–F.

Since drawing is possible in only three dimensions, graphic methods of solving linear-programming problems can only be used where there are no more than three variables in the objective function. We will now consider a mathematical algorithm for solving the product-mix problem. The advantage of the simplex algorithm is that it makes possible the solution of all linear-programming problems and provides additional insight into the economic relationship between the variables in the problem.

☐ THE SIMPLEX ALGORITHM

In 1947, George Dantzig and his associates developed the mathematical formulation of the general linear-programming problem along with the simplex algorithm for its solution. Technically, the general problem can be stated as follows: Maximize (or minimize) some dependent variable that is a function of several independent variables when the independent variables are subject to a set of constraints. In the product-mix problem, the dependent variable, z, is the total contribution margin, and the independent variable, x_j, is the possible output. Symbolically, the general problem can be expressed as:

$$\text{Maximize: } z = \sum_{j=1}^{n} c_j x_j \quad \text{(Objective function)}$$

$$\text{Subject to: } \sum_{i=1}^{m} \sum_{j=1}^{n} a_{ij} x_j \le b \text{ (Constraints)}$$

$$x_j \ge 0 \text{ (Nonnegativity constraints)}$$

$$i = 1, 2, \ldots m; \quad j = 1, 2, \ldots n$$

The dependent variable is z, x is an n-element vector of independent variables under the control of the decision maker, b is an m-element vector of constraints, c is an n-element vector of criterion elements, and A is an m-by-n matrix of structural coefficients.

The simplex algorithm is an iterative converging process for determining the optimal solution to a linear-programming problem. This process is characterized as *iterative* because it is repeated following the same routine until the optimal solution is determined. The routine involves exchanging variables in the solution so that the value of the objective function is increased with each iteration. The algorithm is converging in that each successive solution adds value to the objective function, thus moving closer to the optimal solution. Finally, the algorithm indicates when the optimal solution has been reached. Additional analysis of the tableaus employed in the simplex algorithm results in information that also has economic implications.

Setting Up the Initial Basic Solution

The first step in the simplex algorithm is to convert the constraints of the problem that are expressed as inequalities into equalities. We should recognize that all production combinations contained in the feasible region

ABEF (figure 12.2) do not require all of the wood and labor available. To account for the unused resources, or slack, a variable is added to each inequality. Such variables are called slack variables and make it possible to convert the inequalities to equalities. Let s_1 equal the unused wood available and s_2 equal the unused labor available. Our constraints can now be expressed as the following equalities:

$$3x_1 + 2x_2 + s_1 = 18$$
$$x_1 + 2x_2 + s_2 = 10$$

Perhaps further clarification of the slack-variable concept is needed. The slack variable s_1 is equal to the available wood less any wood used in production. Our first constraint can be expressed as:

$$s_1 = 18 - 3x_1 - 2x_2$$

At corner point A in figure 12.2, s_1 would assume a value of eighteen because both x_1 and x_2 equal zero. Since no production of chairs or benches is taking place at point A, eighteen units of wood are available. At point B, where six units of x_1 are produced, s_1 equals zero because all of the available wood is employed. The same situation exists at point E, where four units of x_1 and three units of x_2 are produced. At point F, where only five units of x_2 are produced, the slack variable s_1 assumes a value of eight. The eight represents the available wood not employed in producing the five units of x_2. Slack variable, s_2, can be evaluated in a similar manner.

In the simplex algorithm, any variable that appears in one equation must appear in all the other equations. Any variables that do not affect the equation assume zero coefficients. Our sample problem—including the slack variables—is now expressed as:

Maximize: $z = \$10x_1 + \$8x_2 + \$0s_1 + \$0s_2$

Subject to: $3x_1 + 2x_2 + s_1 + 0s_2 = 18$

$x_1 + 2x_2 + 0s_1 + s_2 = 10$

$x_1, x_2 \geqslant 0$

To simplify manipulation, the equations are placed in a tableau. The format we will use is shown in figure 12.4.

The initial tableau for our example is shown in tableau 12.1. In the initial simplex tableau, the solution is at corner point A (figure 12.2), and the variables s_1 and s_2 assume the values of eighteen and ten, respectively. Since x_1 and x_2 are not in the solution, they assume the value of zero. The value of the z_j row in the b column represents the total contribution margin from the solution. At this point, it is zero. This is determined by multiplying the units in the solution by the associated criterion element c_j, which in this problem is the unit contribution margin of the variable.

FIGURE 12.4
The Simplex
Tableau

c_j	Solution mix	b	c_1 x_1	c_2 x_2	c_3 s_1	c_4 s_2
	z_j					
	$c_j - z_j$					

TABLEAU 12.1 Initial Simplex Tableau

c_j	Solution mix	b	$10 x_1	$8 x_2	$0 s_1	$0 s_2
$0	s_1	18	3	2	1	0
$0	s_2	10	1	2	0	1
	z_j		$0	$0	$0	$0
	$c_j - z_j$		$10	$8	$0	$0

The symbols used in the tableau may be defined as follows:

c_j: The unit contribution margin of the jth variable. In the row, c_j represents the unit contribution margin of each variable in the objective function. In the column, c_j represents the unit contribution margin of the variables in the current solution.

Solution mix: The variables currently in the solution set, i.e., the variables that have nonzero values in the current solution.

b: In the initial tableau, these are the values of the constraints; as the simplex method converges toward a solution, these are the nonzero values assumed by the variables in the current solution.

Value of s_1 in solution		18
Associated-criterion element	×	$0
Subtotal		$0
Value of s_2 in solution	10	
Associated-criterion element	× $0	
Subtotal		$0
Total contribution margin z_j		$0

The values in the body of the tableau under a particular variable column (the structural coefficients) tell how much the variables in the present solution will be reduced if one unit of that particular variable is introduced into the solution. For example, if one unit of x_1 is introduced into the solution, s_1 will be reduced by three units.

The four values in the z_j row under the variable columns are the amounts the total contribution margin will be decreased if a unit of the variable is added to the solution. These z_j values are obtained by multiplying the values in the body of the tableau under the variable columns by the associated-criterion element, c_j. Since the criterion elements associated with s_1 and s_2 are zero, the contribution margin is not reduced by introducing a unit of x_1 into the solution.

Thus, in the example, elements in the z_j row under the variable columns are computed as follows:

$$z_j \text{ for column } x_1 = \$0(3) + \$0(1) = \$0$$
$$z_j \text{ for column } x_2 = \$0(2) + \$0(2) = \$0$$
$$z_j \text{ for column } s_1 = \$0(1) + \$0(0) = \$0$$
$$z_j \text{ for column } s_2 = \$0(0) + \$0(1) = \$0$$

In the problem, the criterion elements (c_j) have been defined as the unit contribution margins. Therefore, ($c_j - z_j$) is the **net** increase to the total contribution margin by introducing one unit of a variable into the solution. In the problem, if a unit of x_1 is introduced into the solution, the total contribution margin will be increased by \$10, since no loss is incurred (i.e., since the corresponding z_j element equals zero).

A positive element in the $c_j - z_j$ row indicates that the total contribution margin can be increased by adding a unit of the corresponding variable. The simplex algorithm involves substituting variables into the solution until all elements in the $c_j - z_j$ row are less than or equal to zero. When this situation is encountered, an optimal solution has been reached.

The Final Simplex Tableau

Manipulation of a simplex tableau is based on the same procedures employed to invert a matrix. A detailed description of these procedures is contained in the appendix to this chapter. Computer assistance is required in solving most complex linear-programming problems. However, some understanding of the simplex algorithm is necessary so that the initial tableau can be set up and the final results can be interpreted. The final tableau to the problem is contained in tableau 12.2. Here, once again, one finds the optimum mix to be four units of x_1 and three units of x_2 with a total contribution margin of \$64. It is now possible to consider constructing a budgeted income statement based on the final simplex tableau.

TABLEAU 12.2 Final Simplex Tableau

c_j			$10	$8	$0	$0
	Solution mix	b	x_1	x_2	s_1	s_2
$10	x_1	4	1	0	1/2	−1/2
$8	x_2	3	0	1	−1/4	3/4
	z_j	$64	$10	$8	$3	$1
	$c_j - z_j$		$0	$0	−$3	−$1

☐ BUDGETED INCOME STATEMENTS AND OPPORTUNITY COSTS

The input necessary to solve the product-mix problem plus the output from the final simplex tableau are sufficient to prepare a budgeted income statement. The selling prices, standard costs, standard-resource inputs, and the number of units to be produced have all been determined. Now, assuming that the B and C Company has monthly fixed costs of $40, we can prepare a budgeted income statement for the month of December, as shown in figure 12.5.

The income statement in figure 12.5 was prepared based on the assumption that eighteen units of wood and ten units of labor are available. For a moment, assume that nineteen units of wood and ten units of labor are available. The new optimal solution would be to produce 4.5 benches and 2.75 chairs.[3] This results in a total contribution margin of $67. A budgeted income statement for the solution is shown in figure 12.6.

Several things should be noted when comparing the two income statements. First of all, optimal linear-programming solutions are not always in integer units. If an integer solution is required, then integer programming should be employed. It is also important to note that the output of benches increased by one-half of a unit and the output of chairs decreased by one-fourth of a unit. Now, look at the elements in the s_1 column of the final simplex tableau in tableau 12.2. They are the same as the changes in the optimal output resulting from the availability of the additional unit of wood. That is, the x_1 element is one-half and the x_2 element is minus one-fourth.

These coefficients are called the substitution coefficients and specify the rate at which benches are substituted for chairs if additional wood is available.[4] (Since in the original problem the maximum number of benches that the firm could produce was constrained by the availability of wood, as additional wood becomes available, benches are substituted for chairs rather than vice-versa.) These coefficients are located in the s_1 column since s_1 is the slack variable associated with the wood. The coefficients in the s_2 column are the substitution coefficients for the labor.

Notice the differences between the total columns of the income statements. Optimal use of the additional unit of wood resulted in an increase in revenue of $11 ($289 vs. $278). The total variable costs increased $8 because it was assumed that the additional unit of wood had an $8 cost. Consequently, the total contribution increased $3, which is the same—except for the sign—as the amount in the $c_j - z_j$ row of the s_1 column in the final tableau. These $c_j - z_j$ elements under the slack columns are the opportunity costs, or shadow prices.

What do these **shadow prices** mean and how can they be used? In the case of the additional unit of wood, the shadow price indicates that if the firm purchases an additional unit of wood at the original cost and uses

3. Noninteger solutions are possible when linear programming is employed. If only integer solutions are acceptable, then integer programming is employed.

4. In the initial simplex tableau, the substitution coefficients are referred to as structural coefficients.

FIGURE 12.5
Budgeted Income
Statement

B and C COMPANY
Budgeted Income Statement
For Month Ending December 31, 19X0

	Benches $x_1 = 4$	Chairs $x_2 = 3$	Total
Sales	4 × $41 = $164	3 × $38 = $114	$278
Variable costs			
Materials	3 × 4 × $8 = $ 96	2 × 3 × $8 = $ 48	$144
Labor and overhead	1 × 4 × $7 = 28	2 × 3 × $7 = 42	70
Total variable costs	$124	$ 90	$214
Contribution margin	$ 40	$ 24	$ 64
Fixed costs			$ 40
Net income before taxes			$ 24

$$\text{Available resources } b = \begin{bmatrix} 18 \\ 10 \end{bmatrix}$$

FIGURE 12.6
Budgeted Income
Statement

B and C COMPANY
Budgeted Income Statement
For Month Ending December 31, 19X0

	Benches $x_1 = 4.5$	Chairs $x_2 = 2.75$	Total
Sales	4.5 × $41 = $184.50	2.75 × $38 = $104.50	$289
Variable costs			
Materials	3 × 4.5 × $8 = $108.00	2 × 2.75 × $8 = $ 44.00	$152
Labor and overhead	1 × 4.5 × $7 = $ 31.50	2 × 2.75 × $7 = 38.50	70
Total variable costs ...	$139.50	$ 82.50	$222
Contribution margins	45.00	22.00	$ 67
Fixed costs			40
Net income before taxes			$ 27

$$\text{Available resources } b = \begin{bmatrix} 19 \\ 10 \end{bmatrix}$$

the unit of wood optimally, then the total contribution margin will increase by $3. Another interpretation is that the firm is willing to pay up to a maximum of [$8 (unit costs) + $3 (opportunity costs)] for a marginal unit of wood if the wood can be used optimally.

Using the shadow prices, one can determine the opportunity cost of producing a bench or a chair by multiplying the units of wood and labor required to produce a bench or a chair by the respective opportunity costs. The opportunity cost of producing a bench or a chair is computed as follows:

	Units		Opportunity costs		Benches	Units		Opportunity costs		Chairs
Wood	3	×	$3	=	$ 9	2	×	$3	=	$6
Labor	1	×	$1	=	1	2	×	$1	=	2
Total opportunity cost per unit of output					$10					$8

Note that the opportunity cost of producing a bench or a chair if the resources are employed optimally equals the respective contribution margins of the output. If all eighteen units of wood and ten units of labor are employed optimally, then the total opportunity cost [(18 × $3) + (10 × $1) = $64] equals the total contribution margin.

A related question concerns the analysis if only seventeen units of wood are available. Figure 12.7 contains an income statement for the optimal output when this condition is encountered. From the original situation, in which eighteen units of wood were available, note that the revenue decreases by $11, the variable costs by $8, and the total contribution margin by $3. This is the opposite of what happened when the availability of wood increased. Note also that the output of benches decreased by one-half and the output of chairs increased by one-fourth. The substitution coefficients from the final tableau are still appropriate except that their sign must be changed.

In the next section, we will consider the limits of the analysis using the substitution coefficients. In addition, sensitivity analysis based on the simplex solution will be discussed.

☐ SENSITIVITY ANALYSIS

The next question one might ask concerns the range of the opportunity costs. How much additional wood can be made available and still increase the total contribution margin by $3 per unit? The analysis of parameter changes including the impact these changes have on a linear-programming solution is called **sensitivity analysis**. In this analysis, the assumption is made that only one parameter of the linear-programming problem changes, while the others remain constant.

Sensitivity analysis is helpful because the analyst generally does not know with certainty the parameters (c, b, A) of the linear-programming

FIGURE 12.7
Budgeted Income
Statement

B and C COMPANY
Budgeted Income Statement
For Month Ending December 31, 19X0

	Benches $x_1 = 3.5$	Chairs $x_2 = 3.25$	Total
Sales	3.5 × $41 = $143.50	3.25 × $38 = $123.50	$267
Variable costs			
Materials	3 × 3.5 × $8 = $ 84.00	2 × 3.25 × $8 = $ 52.00	$136
Labor and overhead	1 × 3.5 × $7 = 24.50	2 × 3.25 × $7 = 45.50	70
Total variable costs ...		$108.50	$ 97.50	$206
Contribution margin ...		$ 35.00	$ 26.00	$ 61
Fixed costs				40
Net income before taxes				$ 21

Available resources $b = \begin{bmatrix} 17 \\ 10 \end{bmatrix}$

problem. It is advantageous, therefore, to evaluate the effect of parameter changes on the optimal solution.

Recall the original linear-programming problem concerning the chairs and benches.

$$\text{Maximize:} \quad z = \$10x_1 + \$8x_2 \qquad \text{(Objective function)}$$

$$\text{Subject to:} \quad 3x_1 + 2x_2 \leqslant 18 \qquad \text{(Wood constraint)}$$

$$x_1 + 2x_2 \leqslant 10 \qquad \text{(Labor constraint)}$$

$$x_1, x_2 \geqslant 0 \qquad \text{(Nonnegativity constraints)}$$

The final simplex tableau is shown again in tableau 12.3.

If we increase one of the original b values ($b_1 = 18$, $b_2 = 10$) by an amount labeled Δ_1, we change the solution. Note in figure 12.8 how changing the available wood from eighteen to nineteen units moves the constraint and changes the optimal solution.

The next point of interest would be to develop a general approach for determining the new optimal solution when a b value is changed. It would also be desirable to specify the range over which this technique is appropriate. The new problem with the increased availability of wood can be expressed as:

$$\text{Maximize:} \quad z = \$10x_1 + \$8x_2$$

$$\text{Subject to:} \quad 3x_1 + 2x_2 \leqslant 18 + \Delta_1$$

$$x_1 + 2x_2 \leqslant 10 + 0$$

$$x_1, x_2 \geqslant 0 + 0$$

The final tableau for this problem is shown in tableau 12.4.

Since Δ_1 equals one, the tableau can be completed as shown in tableau 12.5. Note in the final simplex tableau that the optimal b values are a function of the s_1 values and that z_j has increased by $3, or the opportunity cost of the wood. These values could have been obtained by multiplying Δ_1 by the s_1 column values and adding them to the original optimal b values. The new z_j values can be obtained by multiplying the opportunity cost of wood by Δ_1. These manipulations are as follows:

$$x_1 = 4 + \tfrac{1}{2}(1) \quad = 4\tfrac{1}{2}$$

$$x_2 = 3 + (-\tfrac{1}{4})(1) = 2\tfrac{3}{4}$$

$$z_j = \$64 + \$3(1) = \$67$$

If three additional units of wood became available, then Δ_1 would equal three and the new optimal solution would be:

$$x_1 = 4 + \tfrac{1}{2}(3) \quad = 5\tfrac{1}{2}$$

$$x_2 = 3 - \tfrac{1}{4}(3) \quad = 2\tfrac{1}{4}$$

$$z_j = \$64 + \$3(3) = \$73$$

TABLEAU 12.3 Final Simplex Tableau

c_j				$10	$8	$0	$0
	Solution mix	b		x_1	x_2	s_1	s_2
$10	x_1	4		1	0	1/2	−1/2
$8	x_2	3		0	1	−1/4	3/4
	z_j	$64		$10	$8	$3	$1
	$c_j - z_j$			$0	$0	−$3	−$1

FIGURE 12.8
Wood, Labor, and
Nonnegativity
Constraints

$$b = \begin{bmatrix} 19 \\ 10 \end{bmatrix}$$

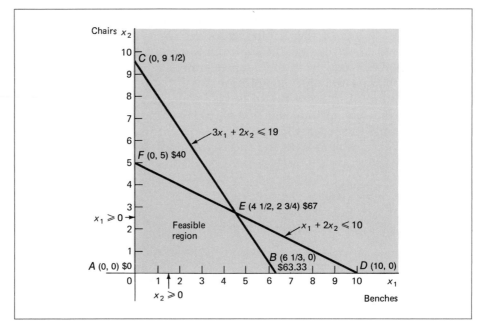

Now, assume that only eight units of labor were available. In this case, Δ_2 equals -2 and the coefficients from the s_2 column are employed. The new optimal solution is:

$$x_1 = 4 + (-\tfrac{1}{2})(-2) = 5$$
$$x_2 = 3 + (\tfrac{3}{4})(-2) \quad = 1\tfrac{1}{2}$$
$$z_j = \$64 + (\$1)(-2) = \$62$$

A logical question to be asked at this point is: how much can the availability of the wood or labor be adjusted without changing the analysis? Another way to express the question is to ask about the range of opportunity costs. In other words, what is the range of units of wood or labor that can be added or subtracted over which the respective opportunity costs will remain appropriate to the analysis?

From the earlier discussion of the simplex method, we know that it is necessary for a solution to remain positive in order to remain in the feasible

TABLEAU 12.4 Final Simplex Tableau before Substituting for s_1

c_j			$10	$8	$0	$0
	Solution mix	b	x_1	x_2	s_1	s_2
$10	x_1	$4 + 1/2 (\Delta_1)$	1	0	1/2	−1/2
$8	x_2	$3 − 1/4 (\Delta_1)$	0	1	−1/4	3/4
	z_j					
	$c_j − z_j$					

TABLEAU 12.5 Final Simplex Tableau

c_j			$10	$8	$0	$0
	Solution mix	b	x_1	x_2	s_1	s_2
$10	x_1	4 1/2	1	0	1/2	−1/2
$8	x_2	2 3/4	0	1	−1/4	3/4
	z_j	$67	$10	$8	$3	−$1
	$c_j − z_j$		$0	$0	−$3	−$1

region. Therefore, the range of wood (b_1) can be determined by solving the following inequalities:

$$x_1: \quad 4 + \tfrac{1}{2} \Delta_1 \geqslant 0$$
$$\tfrac{1}{2} \Delta_1 \geqslant -4$$
$$\Delta_1 \geqslant -8$$

$$x_2: \quad 3 - \tfrac{1}{4} \Delta_1 \geqslant 0$$
$$- \tfrac{1}{4} \Delta_1 \geqslant -3$$
$$\Delta_1 \geqslant 12$$

Since the original value of b_1 was 18, the range is:[5]

$$18 - 8 \leqslant b_1 \leqslant 18 + 12$$
$$10 \leqslant b_1 \leqslant 30$$

Figure 12.9 shows a graphic representation of the range of the wood constraint. Note that at the upper limit the feasible region is only constrained by the labor and nonnegativity constraints. At the lower limit, the feasible

5. If there are more than two constraints in the linear-programming problem, this manipulation, solving for the ranges of Δ, will provide more than one positive or negative number. In this case, the positive and negative numbers closest to zero are selected to determine the range.

FIGURE 12.9
Opportunity Cost
Range

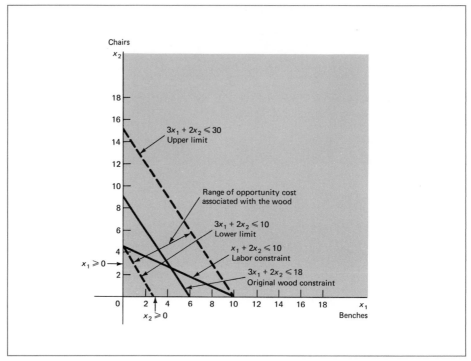

region is only constrained by the wood and nonnegativity constraints. These corner points are specified by the range of the wood constraint. The conclusion of the analysis is that the substitution coefficients and opportunity cost contained in the s_1 column of the final simplex tableau can be employed when the availability of the wood resources is in the range of $10 \leqslant b \leqslant 30$.

The range for the labor-substitution coefficients and opportunity costs is determined as follows:

$$x_1: \quad 4 - \tfrac{1}{2} \Delta_2 \geqslant \quad 0$$
$$- \tfrac{1}{2} \Delta_2 \geqslant -4$$
$$\Delta_2 \geqslant \quad 8$$

$$x_2: \quad 3 + \tfrac{3}{4} \Delta_2 \geqslant \quad 0$$
$$\tfrac{3}{4} \Delta_2 \geqslant -3$$
$$\Delta_2 \geqslant -4$$

$$10 - 4 \leqslant b_2 \leqslant 10 + 8$$
$$6 \leqslant b_2 \leqslant 18$$

Ranges for the unit contribution margins can also be determined from the final simplex tableau. Recall that for the solution to be optimal, all elements in the $c_i - z_i$ row of the tableau must be less than or equal to zero. From the final tableau in tableau 12.3, note that the z_j row associated with the slack variables is found to equal:

s_1: $\frac{1}{2}(\$10) + (-\frac{1}{4})(\$8) = \$3$

s_2: $(-\frac{1}{2})(\$10) + \frac{3}{4}(\$8) = \$1$

If the solution to either of these equations were less than zero, then the $c_j - z_j$ element would be positive and the optimal solution would not have been determined.

If it is desirable to find the range of the unit contribution margin associated with the benches (\$10), then one can set both equations equal to zero and solve for x.

$$\frac{1}{2}(x) + (-\frac{1}{4})(\$8) = 0$$

$$\frac{1}{2}x = \$2$$

$$x = \$4$$

$$-\frac{1}{2}(x) + \frac{3}{4}(\$8) = 0$$

$$-\frac{1}{2}x = -\$6$$

$$x = \$12$$

Therefore, the range of c_1 is:

$$\$4 \leq c_1 \leq \$12$$

and we know that the optimal solution will not change if the unit contribution remains in this range.

This range can be explained in the following way: Assume the unit contribution margin of x_2 remains \$8, but the unit contribution margin of x_1 is now \$12. In this case, the slope of the iso-contribution margin lines is $-\frac{3}{2}$ and this slope is the same as the slope of the wood constraint. Therefore, alternative optimal solutions exist. (That is, one is indifferent to the choice between producing four benches and three chairs ($z_j = \$72$) or producing six benches ($z_j = \$72$).) However, if the contribution margin of x_1 (benches) is any number greater than \$12, then the slope of the iso-contribution margin lines will be such that the line furthest from the origin and still in the feasible region will pass through point B (6,0) (figure 12.2). For example, if the contribution margin of x_1 is \$13, the iso-contribution margin lines will appear as in figure 12.10. Thus, the optimal solution has changed from point E (4,3) to point B (6,0).

Likewise, if the unit contribution margin of x_2 remains \$8 but the unit-contribution margin of x_1 is only \$4, then the slope of the iso-contribution margin lines is $\frac{1}{2}$, which is the same as the slope of the labor constraint. Thus, alternative optimal solutions will exist. (That is, one is indifferent to the choice of whether to produce four benches and three chairs ($z = \$40$) or to produce five chairs ($z = \$40$).) However, if the contribution

FIGURE 12.10
Iso-Contribution
Margin Lines
$(c_1 = \$13;$
$c_2 = \$8)$

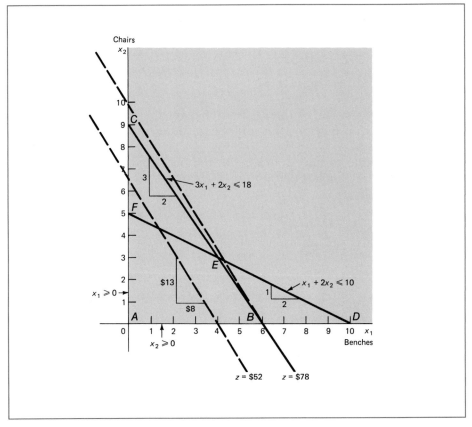

margin of x_1 (benches) is any number less than \$4, then the slope of the iso-contribution margin lines will be such that the line furthest from the origin and still in the feasible region will pass through point F (0,5). (See figure 12.2.) Thus, the optimal solution has changed from point E (4,3) to point F (0,5).

The above analysis allows one to determine how sensitive the optimal solution is to shifts in the unit contribution margins. In the example, one can see that if the contribution margin of x_2 remains constant, point E (4,3) will remain an optimal solution as long as the contribution margin of x_1 is not less than \$4 or not greater than \$12. If the contribution of x_1 drops below \$4, then an analysis indicates that, given the present resource constraints, one should no longer produce benches. In contrast, if the contribution margin of x_1 is greater than \$12, one should no longer produce chairs.

The range of the contribution margin for the chairs (x_2) is determined as follows:

$$\tfrac{1}{2}\,(\$10) + (-\tfrac{1}{4})x = \quad 0$$

$$-\tfrac{1}{4}x = -\$\ 5$$

$$x = \quad \$20$$

$$-\tfrac{1}{2}\ (\$10) + \tfrac{3}{4}(x) = \quad \$\ 0$$

$$\tfrac{3}{4}x = \quad \$\ 5$$

$$x = \quad \$\ 6.67$$

The range is $\$6.67 \leqslant c_2 \leqslant \$20$.

If there were more than two constraints, then there would be more than two equations to solve in determining the ranges of the contribution margins. Each equation yields a value, and the problem is then to determine the appropriate range for the unit contribution margins. In the case in which there are more than two constraints, the range is the smaller and larger values closest to the original c_j value.

Sensitivity analysis of the unit contribution margins is helpful when the impact of changes in selling prices is being evaluated in terms of shifting the optimal solution. In a similar vein, it can be used in analyzing the impact of shifts in resource costs on the optimal solution. However, a shift in a resource cost often affects the unit variable cost of more than one resource, and the analysis becomes rather complicated. The ranges of the contribution margins can be related to the allocation of variable overhead. If the unit contribution margin ranges are relatively small, it may be beneficial to review the basis upon which the variable overhead is associated with the output. A situation could exist whereby associating the overhead on some other basis (such as machine hours) might significantly alter the optimal mix.

☐ THE DUAL PROBLEM

If the objective function of a linear-programming problem is a maximization, then a corresponding problem in which the objective is a minimization also exists. The original formulation of a problem is referred to as the *primal* and the alternative formulation is called the *dual*. The primal could be a minimization problem; in that case, the corresponding dual problem would be a maximization problem.

The coefficients of the dual objective function are the primal constraints. Likewise, the coefficients of the primal objective function are the dual constraints. In the dual, the constraints are formulated by transposing the coefficients of the primal constraints. If the constraints are less or equal in the primal, then the dual constraints are greater or equal.

The primal and dual problems for the bench and chair firm are:

Primal	Dual
Maximize: $z = \$10x_1 + \$8x_2$	Minimize: $z = 18u_1 + 10u_2$
Subject to: $3x_1 + 2x_2 \leqslant 18$	Subject to: $3u_1 + u_2 \geqslant \$10$
$x_2 + 2x_2 \leqslant 10$	$2u_1 + 2u_2 \geqslant \$\ 8$
$x_1, x_2 \geqslant 0$	$u_1, u_2 \geqslant 0$

The objective function of the dual problem minimizes the total opportunity cost associated with employing the wood and labor in the manufacture of chairs and benches. The first constraint of the dual problem (which would be interpreted as the wood necessary to produce a bench, x_1, times the opportunity cost of wood, u_1, plus the labor to produce a bench, x_1, times the opportunity cost of labor, u_2) must be greater than or equal to the contribution margin of a bench ($10). A similar interpretation can be given to the second constraint concerning the chairs. The dual problem is solved in the appendix to this chapter.

From the final dual simplex tableau (tableau 12.6), one can see that the minimum opportunity cost associated with the wood (u_1) is $3 per unit, and the minimum opportunity cost associated with the labor (u_2) is $1 per unit. The minimum total opportunity cost is $64, which is the same as the maximum contribution margin found when the primal problem was solved. In the s_1 and s_2 columns of the $c_j - z_j$ row one has, respectively, the same quantities of chairs and benches to be produced as were found in solving the primal problem. Therefore, one can conclude the same results are achieved in solving a primal problem or the respective dual problem.

☐ SUMMARY

Linear programming is a powerful mathematical tool that has been widely employed in making decisions concerning the allocation of scarce resources. This chapter serves only as an introduction to an extensive body of knowledge that has evolved around the general linear-programming problem. Most linear-programming problems require data concerning resource inputs that are common to most standard-costing systems. Unit contribution margins are employed as the criterion for determining the optimal production mix when linear programming is employed.

A by-product of the solution to a linear-programming problem is the opportunity cost of the resources. These costs can be used to evaluate the contribution to profit of the various resource inputs that constrain the system. These opportunity costs also can be used in analyzing alternative solutions to the problem. The solution of a linear-programming problem can be used as the basis for constructing budgeted financial statements.

TABLEAU 12.6 Final Simplex Tableau

c_j			18	10	0	0	m	m
	Solution mix	b	u_1	u_2	s_1	s_2	a_1	a_2
18	u_1	$3	1	0	-1/2	1/4	1/2	-1/4
10	u_2	$1	0	1	1/2	-3/4	-1/2	3/4
	z_j	$64	18	10	-4	-3	4	3
	$c_j - z_j$		0	0	4	3	$m - 4$	$m - 3$

KEY TERMS

Constraints
Feasible region
Linear programming
Objective function
Optimal solution

Product-mix problem
Sensitivity analysis
Shadow prices
Simplex algorithm

REVIEW PROBLEM

Initial Simplex Tableau

c_j			$10	$8	$0	$0
	Mix	b	x_1	x_2	s_1	s_2
$0	s_1	80	2	4	1	0
$0	s_2	60	3	1	0	1
	z_j	$0	$0	$0	$0	$0
	$c_j - z_j$		$10	$8	$0	$0

Final Simplex Tableau

c_j			$10	$8	$0	$0
	Mix	b	x_1	x_2	s_1	s_2
$8	x_2	12	0	1	3/10	−1/5
$10	x_1	16	1	0	−1/10	2/5
	z_j	$256	$10	$8	$1.40	$2.40
	$c_j - z_j$		$0	$0	−$1.40	−$2.40

The units costs of the first and second resources are $7 and $3, respectively.

Required ☐

1. How many units of the first resource are required to make a unit of x_1?
2. How many units of the second resource are required to make a unit of x_1?
3. What is the selling price of output x_1?
4. How many units of x_2 should be produced and sold in the optimal solution?
5. What is the total contribution margin at the optimal solution?
6. How many units of the second resource are available?

7. What is the unit contribution margin of output x_2?

8. How many units of the first resource are available at the optimal solution?

9. How much would management personnel be willing to pay for an additional unit of the first resource?

10. If ten additional units of the first resource became available at a unit cost of $7, what is the new optimal solution and total contribution margin?

11. If five additional units of the second resource became available at a unit cost of $4, what is the new optimal solution and total contribution margin?

Solution ☐

1. 2 (From initial simplex tableau)

2. 3 (From initial simplex tableau)

3. Cost of first resource . . . . 2 × $7 = $14
Cost of second resource . . . . 3 × $3 =   9
Unit contribution margin   10
Unit selling price x_1 . . . . $33

4. 12 (From final simplex tableau)

5. $256 (From final simplex tableau)

6. 60 (From initial simplex tableau)

7. $8 (From initial simplex tableau)

8. $0 - s_1$ is not in the solution

9. $7.00 + $1.40 = $8.40

10. $x_2 = 12 + 10 \,(^3/_{10}) = 15$
$x_1 = 16 + 10 \,(-^1/_{10}) = 15$
$z_j = \$256 + 10 \,(\$8.40 - \$7.00) = \$270$

11. $x_2 = 12 + 5(-^1/_5) = 11$
$x_1 = 16 + 5(^2/_5) = 18$
$z_j = \$256 + 5 \,(\$5.40 - \$4.00) = \$263$

APPENDIX: Determining Improved Linear Programming Solutions Using the Simplex Algorithm

This appendix contains an example showing how the simplex algorithm is used in solving a linear-programming problem. The problem that is solved is the same problem that was described in the chapter. The initial simplex tableau is shown in appendix tableau 12.1.

There are three necessary steps in determining improved solutions when employing the simplex algorithm. The first step involves identifying the variable that will enter the solution. One *selects the variable with the largest positive* $c_j - z_j$ **value**. In the problem, x_1 enters the solution because $10 is the largest $c_j - z_j$ value.

The second step involves determining which variable will exit from the solution. This is accomplished by dividing the elements of the b-vector by the structural coefficients associated with the variable entering the solution. In the example, these ratios are:

APPENDIX TABLEAU 12.1 Initial Simplex Tableau

c_j			$10	$8	$0	$0
	Solution mix	b	x_1	x_2	s_1	s_2
$0	s_1	18	3	2	1	0
$0	s_2	10	1	2	0	1
	z_j	$0	$0	$0	$0	$0
	$c_j - z_j$		$10	$8	$0	$0

$$s_1 \text{ Row: } \frac{18 \text{ units of wood}}{3 \text{ units of wood/bench}} = 6 \text{ benches } (x_1)$$

$$s_2 \text{ Row: } \frac{10 \text{ units of labor}}{1 \text{ unit of labor/bench}} = 10 \text{ benches } (x_2)$$

The rule for determining which variable will exit the solution is to select the variable with the *minimum nonnegative ratio*. This results in the maximum number of units of the entering variable that can be introduced into the solution without violating any of the constraints. From figure 12.2, note that corner point D (10 benches) is out of the feasible region. Thus, one determines that the maximum number of benches that can be produced is six because at this point the wood supply is exhausted. It follows that since all of the available wood is being used to produce six benches, then the value of the slack variable associated with the wood (s_1) will be zero; and therefore, s_1 will exit from the solution.

The third step in the simplex algorithm involves manipulating the simplex tableau so that the constraints are expressed as a linear combination of the variables in the new solution (x_1 and s_2). To perform this manipulation, one must first identify the pivot element. The pivot element is the element in the tableau located at the intersection of the column of the entering variable and the row of the exiting variable. This is shown in appendix tableau 12.2.

The new x_1 row of the new simplex tableau is then determined by dividing each element in the old s_1 row by the pivot element:

$$^{18}/_3 = 6 \qquad ^3/_3 = 1 \qquad ^2/_3 = ^2/_3 \qquad ^1/_3 = ^1/_3 \qquad ^0/_3 = 0$$

APPENDIX TABLEAU 12.2 Determining the Pivot Element

Pivot element

c_j			$10	$8	$0	$0	
	Solution mix	b	x_1	x_2	s_1	s_2	
$0	s_1	18	③	2	1	0	← Exiting variable
$0	s_2	10	1	2	0	1	
	z_j	$0	$0	$0	$0	$0	
	$c_j - z_j$		$10	$8	$0	$0	

Entering variable

These elements are entered into the new simplex tableau as shown in appendix tableau 12.3. Note that x_1 now appears in the solution mix and its associated $10 criterion element appears in the c_j column.

The elements in the remaining rows of the new simplex tableau can be computed by the following formula:

$$\text{Element in old row} - \left[\begin{array}{c}\text{Element in entering variable} \\ \text{column}\end{array} \times \begin{array}{c}\text{Corresponding element in entering} \\ \text{variable row}\end{array}\right] = \begin{array}{c}\text{Element in new row}\end{array}$$

Employing the formula, computations for the new s_2 row are:

$$(10) - [(1) \times (6)] = 4$$
$$(1) - [(1) \times (1)] = 0$$
$$(2) - [(1) \times (\tfrac{2}{3})] = \tfrac{4}{3}$$
$$(0) - [(1) \times (\tfrac{1}{3})] = -\tfrac{1}{3}$$
$$(1) - [(1) \times (0)] = 1$$

Appendix tableau 12.4 contains the new s_2 row in the tableau. After computing the new z_j and $c_j - z_j$ rows, the completed tableau is shown in appendix tableau 12.5.

Since there is a positive value in the $c_j - z_j$ row ($413), one knows that the value of the objective function can be increased by entering x_2 into the solution. Appendix tableaus 12.6–12.9 show the development of the final tableau. We know that tableau 12.9 contains the optimum solution because all elements in the $c_j - z_j$ row are less than or equal to zero.

The final simplex tableau indicates that the optimum mix is four units of x_1 and three units of x_2, with a total contribution margin of $64. This is the same solution that was reached when the graphic method was employed. Complex problems do not lend themselves to manual solution of the simplex algorithm. Computers are used to solve such problems, but an understanding of the simplex algorithm is required so that the initial tableau can be set up and the results can be interpreted.

By introducing a break-even constraint into the product-mix problem, we can consider the notion of multiple break-even points and an additional refinement of linear programming. Since the simplex algorithm requires an initial feasible solution, the algorithm must be modified so that it can incorporate the break-even constraint. This will require the use of an artificial variable and the "Big M" method to introduce the initial basic solution.

APPENDIX TABLEAU 12.3 X_1 Enters Solution Mix

c_j			$10	$8	$0	$0
	Solution mix	b	x_1	x_2	s_1	s_2
$10	x_1	6	1	2/3	1/3	0
$ 0	s_2					
	z_j					
	$c_j - z_j$					

APPENDIX TABLEAU 12.4 New s_2 Row

c_j			$10	$8	$0	$0
	Solution mix	b	x_1	x_2	s_1	s_2
$10	x_1	6	1	2/3	1/3	0
$ 0	s_2	4	0	4/3	−1/3	1
	z_j					
	$c_j - z_j$					

APPENDIX TABLEAU 12.5 First Iteration Completed

c_j			$10	$8	$0	$0
	Solution mix	b	x_1	x_2	s_1	s_2
$10	x_1	6	1	2/3	1/3	0
$ 0	s_2	4	0	4/3	−1/3	1
	z_j	$60	$10	$20/3	$10/3	$0
	$c_j - z_j$		$0	$4/3	−$10/3	$0

APPENDIX TABLEAU 12.6 Identifying New Pivot Element

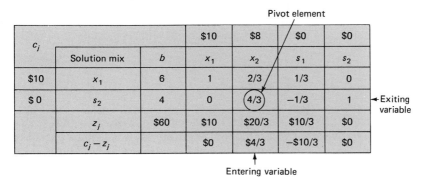

Pivot element

Entering variable

Exiting variable

c_j			$10	$8	$0	$0
	Solution mix	b	x_1	x_2	s_1	s_2
$10	x_1	6	1	2/3	1/3	0
$ 0	s_2	4	0	(4/3)	−1/3	1
	z_j	$60	$10	$20/3	$10/3	$0
	$c_j - z_j$		$0	$4/3	−$10/3	$0

APPENDIX TABLEAU 12.7 x_2 Enters Solution Mix

c_j			$10	$8	$0	$0
	Solution mix	b	x_1	x_2	s_1	s_2
$10	x_1					
$ 8	x_2	3	0	1	−1/4	3/4
	z_j					
	$c_j - z_j$					

APPENDIX TABLEAU 12.8 New x_1 Row

c_j			$10	$8	$0	$0
	Solution mix	b	x_1	x_2	s_1	s_2
$10	x_1	4	1	0	1/2	−1/2
$8	x_2	3	0	1	−1/4	3/4
	z_j					
	$c_j - z_j$					

APPENDIX TABLEAU 12.9 Final Simplex Tableau

c_j			$10	$8	$0	$0
	Solution mix	b	x_1	x_2	s_1	s_2
$10	x_1	4	1	0	1/2	−1/2
$8	x_2	3	0	1	−1/4	3/4
	z_j	$64	$10	$8	$3	$1
	$c_j - z_j$		$0	$0	−$3	−$1

Assume the chair and bench manufacturing firm has total fixed costs for one period of $40. The management team of the firm only wants to consider those production possibilities that will at least allow it to break-even. The break-even constraint can be expressed as:

$$\$10x_1 + \$8x_2 \geq \$40$$

Appendix figure 12.1 shows the new feasible region, GBEF, now that the break-even constraint has been incorporated into the problem. The firm can produce any combination of benches and chairs along the line segment FG and break-even. Therefore, the firm has multiple break-even points.

To express the break-even constraint as an equality, we will introduce an artificial and a slack variable and assign a very large negative criterion element $(-M)$ to the artificial variable. The artificial variable will appear in the initial solution because it represents how far one is from an initial feasible solution. The artificial variable will not appear in the final solution because of the large negative criterion element. If it did appear in the final solution, the z value would be negative. The break-even constraint expressed as an equality is:

$$\$10x_1 + \$8x_2 + a_1 - s_3 = \$40$$

where a_1 is the artificial variable and s_3 is a slack variable. The new objective function is:

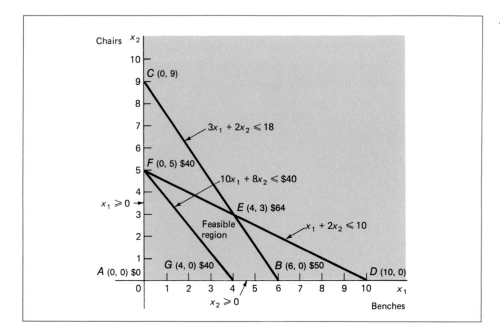

Maximize: $z = \$10x_1 + \$8x_2 + \$0s_1 + \$0s_2 - \$Ma_1 + \$0s_3$
(Objective function)

Subject to: $3x_1 + 2x_2 + s_1 + 0s_2 + 0a_1 + 0s_3 = 18$
(Wood constraint)

$x_1 + 2x_2 + 0s_1 + s_2 + 0a_1 + 0s_3 = 10$
(Labor constraint)

$\$10x_1 + \$8x_2 + 0s_1 + 0s_2 + a_1 - s_3 = \$40$
(Break-even constraint)

Appendix tableau 12.10 contains the initial simplex tableau. The tableaus developed in solving the problem are shown in appendix tableaus 12.11 and 12.12. In appendix tableau 12.13, which is the final tableau, note that s_3 is in the solution and equals \$24. If one substitutes in the break-even constraint expressed as an equality, one finds:

$$\$10x_1 + \$8x_2 + 1a_1 - s_3 = \$40$$
$$\$10(4) + \$8(3) + 1(0) - 24 = \$40$$
$$\$64 - \$24 = \$40$$

The \$24 in this case is the net income before taxes.

One should not assume that a break-even constraint is the only reason the origin would be eliminated from the solution. Consideration of production, marketing, labor, and resource factors could result in the same type of constraint. In these cases, the use of an artificial variable and the "Big M" method will make possible the solution of the problem.

APPENDIX TABLEAU 12.10 Initial Simplex Tableau

c_j			$10	$8	$0	$0	$-M$	$0	
	Solution mix	b	x_1	x_2	s_1	s_2	a_1	s_3	
$0	s_1	18	3	2	1	0	0	0	
$0	s_2	10	1	2	0	1	0	0	
$-M$	a_1	$40	⟨$10⟩	$8	0	0	1	-1	← Exiting variable
	z_j	$-40M$	$-10M$	$-8M$	$0	$0	$-M$	M	
	$c_j - z_j$		$10 + $10M	$8 + $8M	$0	$0	0	$-M$	

↑ Entering variable

APPENDIX TABLEAU 12.11 First Iteration

c_j			$10	$8	$0	$0	$-M$	$0	
	Solution mix	b	x_1	x_2	s_1	s_2	a_1	s_3	
$0	s_1	6	0	$-2/5$	1	0	$-3/10$	⟨3/10⟩	← Exiting variable
$0	s_2	6	0	6/5	0	1	$-1/10$	1/10	
$10	x_1	4	1	4/5	0	0	1/10	$-1/10$	
	z_j	$40	$10	$8	$0	$0	$1	$-$1	
	$c_j - z_j$		$0	$0	$0	$0	$-M-$1	$1	

↑ Entering variable

SOLUTION TO THE DUAL PROBLEM USING THE SIMPLEX METHOD

To solve the dual problem, we will introduce artificial variables and employ the "Big M" method to arrive at the solution. Introducing slack and artificial variables, the problem can be expressed as:

$$\text{Minimize: } z = 18u_1 + 10u_2 + 0s_1 + 0s_2 + Ma_1 + Ma_2$$

$$\text{Subject to: } 3u_1 + u_2 - s_1 - 0s_2 + a_1 + 0a_2 = \$10$$

$$2u_1 + 2u_2 - 0s_1 - s_2 + 0a_1 + a_2 = \$8$$

The initial simplex tableau is shown as appendix tableau 12.14. The criterion for determining the entering variable in a minimization problem is to select the most negative number in the $c_j - z_j$ row. The optimum solution has been reached when all elements in the $c_j - z_j$ row are greater than or equal to zero. In the minimization, the criterion for selecting the exiting variable is the same as that employed in the maximization problem.

APPENDIX TABLEAU 12.12 Second Iteration

c_j			$10	$8	$0	$0	−$M	$0	
	Solution mix	b	x_1	x_2	s_1	s_2	a_1	s_3	
$0	s_3	20	0	−4/3	10/3	0	−1	1	
$0	s_2	4	0	4/3	−1/3	1	0	0	← Exiting variable
$10	x_1	6	1	2/3	1/3	0	0	0	
	z_j	$60	$10	$6.66	$3.33	0	0	0	
	$c_j − z_j$		$0	$1.34	−$3.33	0	−M	$0	

Entering variable

APPENDIX TABLEAU 12.13 Final Simplex Tableau

c_j			$10	$8	$0	$0	−$M	$0
	Solution mix	b	x_1	x_2	s_1	s_2	a_1	s_3
$0	s_3	24	0	0	3	1	−1	1
$8	x_2	3	0	1	−1/4	3/4	0	0
$10	x_1	4	1	0	1/2	−1/2	0	0
	z_j	$64	$10	$8	$3	$1	0	0
	$c_j − z_j$		$0	$0	−$3	−$1	−$M	0

APPENDIX TABLEAU 12.14 Initial Simplex Tableau

c_j			18	10	0	0	M	M	
	Solution mix	b	u_2	u_2	s_1	s_2	a_1	a_2	
M	a_1	$10	③	1	−1	0	1	0	← Exiting variable
M	a_2	$8	2	2	0	−1	0	1	
	z_j	$18M	5M	3M	−M	−M	M	M	
	$c_j − z_j$		18 − 5M	10 − 3M	M	M	0	0	

Entering variable

APPENDIX TABLEAU 12.15 First Iteration

c_j			18	10	0	0	M	M	
	Solution mix	b	u_1	u_2	s_1	s_2	a_1	a_2	
18	u_1	$10/3	1	1/3	−1/3	0	1/3	0	
M	a_2	$4/3	0	④/3	2/3	−1	−2/3	1	← Exiting variable
	z_j	4/3M + 60	18	4/3M + 6	2/3M − 6	−M	6 − 2/3M	M	
	$c_j − z_j$		0	−4/3M + 4	−2/3M + 6	M	5/3M − 6	0	

Entering variable

APPENDIX TABLEAU 12.16 Final Simplex Tableau

c_j			18	10	0	0	M	M
	Solution mix	b	u_1	u_2	s_1	s_2	a_1	a_2
18	u_1	$3	1	0	−1/2	1/4	1/2	−1/4
10	u_2	$1	0	1	1/2	−3/4	−1/2	3/4
	z_j	$64	18	10	−4	−3	4	3
	$c_j - z_j$		0	0	4	3	M − 4	M − 3

QUESTIONS

Q12-1. Why does one employ unit contribution margin, rather than unit profit, as the criterion elements in a linear-programming problem?

Q12-2. In linear programming, every maximization problem has a corresponding minimization problem. In the maximization problems we have considered, we seek to maximize total contribution margin, which is consistent with profit maximization. In dual of these problems, what do we seek to minimize? Be specific in your answer.

Q12-3. Discuss how relevant-range assumptions could cause problems in determining unit contribution margins for use in a linear-programming problem.

Q12-4. Why are fixed costs not considered in determining the criterion elements in the objective function of a linear-programming problem?

For questions 5–18, which relate to applications of quantitative methods of accounting, select the best answer from the choices given. Choose only one answer for each item.

Q12-5. In a linear-programming maximization problem for business problem solving, the coefficients of the objective function usually are

 a. Marginal contributions per unit
 b. Variable costs
 c. Profit based upon allocations of overhead and all indirect costs
 d. Usage rates for scarce resources
 e. None of the above

Q12-6. The constraints in a linear-programming problem usually model

 a. Profits
 b. Restrictions
 c. Dependent variables
 d. Goals
 e. None of the above

Q12-7. If there are four activity variables and two constraints in a linear-programming problem, the most products that would be included in the optimal solution would be

a. 6
b. 4
c. 2
d. 0

Q12-8. Linear programming is used most commonly to determine

a. That mix of variables that will result in the largest quantity
b. The best use of scarce resources
c. The most advantageous prices
d. The fastest timing
e. None of the above

Q12-9. Assume the following data for the two products produced by Wagner Company:

	Product A	Product B
Raw material requirements (units)		
X	3	4
Y	7	2
Contribution margin per unit	$10	$4

If 300 units of raw material X and 400 units of raw material Y are available, the set of relationships appropriate for maximization of revenue using linear programming would be

a. $3A + 4B \geq 300$
$7A + 2B \geq 400$
$10A + 4B$ MAX
b. $3A + 7B \geq 300$
$4A + 2B \geq 400$
$10A + 4B$ MAX
c. $3A + 7B \leq 300$
$4A + 2B \leq 400$
$10A + 4B$ MAX
d. $3A + 4B \leq 300$
$7A + 2B \leq 400$
$10A + 4B$ MAX
e. None of the above

Q12-10. A final tableau for a linear-programming profit-maximization problem is:

	x_1	x_2	x_3	s_1	s_2	
x_1	1	0	4	3	−7	50
x_2	0	1	−2	−6	2	60
	0	0	5	1	9	1,200

If x_1, x_2, and x_3 represent products; s_1 refers to square feet (in thousands) of warehouse capacity; and s_2 refers to labor hours (in hundreds), then the number of x_1 that should be produced to maximize profit would be

a. 60
b. 50
c. 1
d. 0
e. None of the above

Q12-11. Assuming the same facts as in question 10, the contribution to profit of an additional 100 hours of labor would be

a. 9
b. 2
c. 1
d. -7
e. None of the above

Q12-12. Assuming the same facts as in question 10, an additional 1,000 square feet of warehouse space would

a. Increase x_1 by 3 units and decrease x_2 by 6 units
b. Decrease x_2 by 6 units and increase x_1 by 2 units
c. Decrease x_1 by 7 units and increase x_2 by 2 units
d. Increase x_1 by 3 units and decrease x_2 by 7 units
e. None of the above

Q12-13. The following is the final tableau of a linear-programming profit-maximization problem:

	x_1	x_2	s_1	s_2	
x_1	1	0	-5	3	125
x_2	0	1	1	-1	70
	0	0	5	7	500

The marginal contribution to profit of five for each added resource unit s_1 can be maintained if the added resource units do not exceed

a. 125
b. 100
c. 75
d. 25
e. None of the above

Q12-14. Assume the following per-unit raw material and labor requirements for the production of products A and B:

	Product A	Product B
Pounds of lead	5	7
Hours of labor	3	4

Assuming that 13,400 pounds of lead and 7,800 hours of labor are available, the production of products A and B required to use all of the available lead and labor hours is shown in the following final Gaussian Tableau:

1	0	-4	7	1,000
0	1	3	-5	1,200

If the available amounts were increased to 15,000 pounds of lead and 8,800 hours of labor, the matrix operation to perform to determine the production schedule that would fully utilize these resources is

a. $\begin{pmatrix} 5 & 7 \\ 3 & 4 \end{pmatrix} \begin{pmatrix} 15,000 \\ 8,800 \end{pmatrix}$

b. $\begin{pmatrix} 15,000 \\ 8,800 \end{pmatrix} \begin{pmatrix} -4 & 7 \\ 3 & -5 \end{pmatrix}$

c. $\begin{pmatrix} -4 & 7 \\ 3 & -5 \end{pmatrix} \begin{pmatrix} 1,000 \\ 1,200 \end{pmatrix}$

d. $\begin{pmatrix} -4 & 7 \\ 3 & -5 \end{pmatrix} \begin{pmatrix} 15,000 \\ 8,000 \end{pmatrix}$

e. None of the above

Q12-15. The following schedule provides data for product A, which is processed through processes 1 and 2, and product B, which is processed through process 1 only:

	Product A	Product B
Raw material cost per gallon	$ 4	$ 9
Process 1 (500 gallon input capacity per hour):		
Processing cost per hour	$60	$60
Loss in processing	30%	20%
Process 2 (300 gallon input capacity per hour):		
Processing cost per hour	$50	
Loss in processing	10%	
Selling price per gallon	$20	$40

If the objective is to maximize profit per eight-hour day, the objective function of a profit-maximizing linear-programming problem would be

a. $20A + 40B - 4A - 4B$

b. $20A + 40B - 4A - 4B - 60(A + B) - 50A$

c. $20(.63A) + 40(.80B) - 4(.63A) - 9(.8B)$

$$- 60\left(\frac{A + B}{500}\right) - 50\left(\frac{.7A}{300}\right)$$

d. $20(.63A) + 40(.80B) - 4A - 9B$

$$- 60\left(\frac{A}{500} + \frac{B}{500}\right) - 50\left(\frac{.7A}{300}\right)$$

e. None of the above

Q12-16. Assuming the same facts as in question 15, a constraint of the problem would be

a. $.63A \leqslant 2,400$

b. $.8A \leqslant 2,400$

c. $.7A + .8B \leqslant 4,000$

d. $.92 \leqslant 4,000$

Q12-17. Dancy, Inc., is going to begin producing a new chemical cleaner. The production process involves combining alcohol, peroxide, and an enzyme. Each quart of the new cleaner will require one-half quart of alcohol, one quart of peroxide, and one-third quart of enzyme. The costs per quart are 40¢ for alcohol, 60¢ for peroxide, and 20¢ for enzyme. The matrix operation to determine the cost of producing one quart of cleaner is

a. $(1/2, 1, 1/3) \begin{pmatrix} .40 \\ .60 \\ .20 \end{pmatrix}$

b. $\begin{pmatrix} 1/2 \\ 1 \\ 1/3 \end{pmatrix} \begin{pmatrix} .40 \\ .60 \\ .20 \end{pmatrix}$

c. $(1/2, 1, 1/3) \,(.40, .60, .20)$

d. $\begin{pmatrix} .40 \\ .60 \\ .20 \end{pmatrix} (1/2, 1, 1/3)$

e.   None of the above

Q12-18. A linear programming model is being used to determine for two products the quantities of each to produce to maximize profit over a one-year period. The two products have different profitabilities per unit. One component of cost is raw materials. If both products use the same amount of the same raw material,

a.   This cost may be ignored because it is the same for each product
b.   This cost must be ignored because it is the same for each product
c.   This cost must be included in the objective function since it varies with the independent variables in the model
d.   More information about the products and the other components of the objective function is needed to determine whether to include this cost
e.   None of the above

(Questions 12-5–12-18, CPA)

PROBLEMS

Initial and Final Simplex Tableau Analysis

P12-1. Based on the initial and final simplex tableaus that follow, answer the questions.

Initial Simplex Tableau

Final Simplex Tableau

Required ☐

1. From the initial tableau, the variable that would enter the solution is _____.

2. From the initial tableau, the variable that would exit the solution is _____.

Initial Simplex Tableau

c_j			5	4	0	0
	Mix	b	x_1	x_2	s_1	s_2
0	s_1	18	3	2	1	0
0	s_2	10	1	2	0	1
	z_j	0	0	0	0	0
	$c_j - z_j$		5	4	0	0

Final Simplex Tableau

c_j			5	4	0	0
	Mix	b	x_1	x_2	s_1	s_2
5	x_1	4	1	0	1/2	−1/2
4	x_2	3	0	1	−1/4	3/4
	z_j	32	5	4	3/2	1/2
	$c_j - z_j$		0	0	−3/2	−1/2

3. After the first iteration, what values would the following variables assume?

$x_1 =$ _____.

$x_2 =$ _____.

$s_1 =$ _____.

$s_2 =$ _____.

4. If one additional unit of the first resource became available, the new optimal solution and total contribution margin would be:

$x_1 =$ _____.

$x_2 =$ _____.

$s_1 =$ _____.

$s_2 =$ _____.

Total contribution margin = $ _____.

5. If ten additional units of the first resource became available, the new optimal solution and total contribution margin would be:

$x_1 =$ _____.

$x_2 =$ _____.

$s_1 =$ _____.

$s_2 =$ _____.

Total contribution margin = $ _____.

6. If two units of the first resource were not available, the new optimal solution and total contribution margin would be:

$x_1 =$ _____.

$x_2 =$ _____.

$s_1 =$ _____.

$s_2 =$ _____.

Total contribution margin = $ _____.

7. If six additional units of the second resource became available, the new optimal solution and total contribution margin would be:

$x_1 =$ _____ .
$x_2 =$ _____ .
$s_1 =$ _____ .
$s_2 =$ _____ .
Total contribution margin = $ _____ .

8. If four units of the second resource were not available, the new optimal solution and total contribution margin would be:

$x_1 =$ _____ .
$x_2 =$ _____ .
$s_1 =$ _____ .
$s_2 =$ _____ .
Total contribution margin = $ _____ .

9. Determine the ranges of the shadow prices.

LL	b_i	UL
_____	18	_____
_____	10	_____

10. Determine the ranges for the contribution margin.

LL	c_j	UL
_____	5	_____
_____	4	_____

11. If the unit cost of the resources are $4 and $5, respectively, determine the selling prices of x_1 and x_2.

$x_1 = $ _____ .
$x_2 = $ _____ .

12. If the unit cost of the resources are $5 and $4, respectively, determine the selling prices of x_1 and x_2.

$x_1 = $ _____ .
$x_2 = $ _____ .

13. If the unit cost of the first resource is $3 and six additional are available at a cost of $4 per unit:

   a. Would management consider the acquisition of the six units?
   b. If management acquired the six units, what is the optimal contribution margin?

14. If the unit cost of the second resource is $2.00 and six additional units are available at a cost of $2.75 per unit:

   a. Would management consider the acquisition of the six units?
   b. If management acquired the six units, what is the optimal contribution margin?

15. The opportunity costs are $1.50 and $.50, respectively:

   a. What is the opportunity cost of producing a unit of x_1? A unit of x_2?
   b. How are the opportunity costs of x_1 and x_2 related to their respective contribution margins?

16. The original problem can be expressed as:

Maximize: $5x_1 + 4x_2$
Subject to: $3x_1 + 2x_2 \leqslant 18$
$x_1 + 2x_2 \leqslant 10$
$x_1 \geqslant 0 \quad x_2 \geqslant 0$

Express the dual of the original problem.

P12-2. Based on the initial and final simplex tableaus that follow, answer the questions. *Initial and Final Simplex Tableau Analysis*

Initial Simplex Tableau

Final Simplex Tableau

Required ☐

1. Determine the ranges of the shadow prices.

LL	b_i	UL
———	———	———
———	———	———

2. Determine the ranges of the contribution margins.

LL	c_j	UL
———	———	———
———	———	———

Initial Simplex Tableau

c_j			$12	$16	$0	$0
	Mix	b	x_1	x_2	s_1	s_2
$0	s_1	80	4	8	1	0
$0	s_2	36	3	2	0	1
	z_j	$0	$0	$0	$0	$0
	$c_j \quad - \quad z_j$		$12	$16	$0	$0

Final Simplex Tableau

c_j			$12	$16	$0	$0
	Mix	b	x_1	x_2	s_1	s_2
$16	x_2	6	0	1	3/16	−1/4
$12	x_1	8	1	0	−1/8	1/2
	z_j	$192	$12	$16	$1.50	$2
	$c_j \quad - \quad z_j$		$0	$0	−$1.50	−$2

3. If the first resource cost is $3 a unit and the second is $4 a unit, determine the selling prices for x_1 and x_2.

x_1 = $ _____.
x_2 = $ _____.

4. If the first resource cost is $3 a unit, what is the *maximum* unit price management would be willing to pay for an additional unit of the first resource? Explain.

5. How many additional units would management consider buying at the price specified in your answer to question 4?

6. If the fixed costs for a firm are $96, express a break-even constraint for the linear-programming problem.

7. The original problem can be expressed as

Maximize: $Z = \$12x_1 + \$16x_2$
Subject to: $4x_1 + 8x_2 \leq 80$
$\qquad\qquad 3x_1 + 2x_2 \leq 36$
$\qquad\qquad x_1, x_2 \geq 0$

Identify what one seeks to maximize in the objective function. Explain why one seeks to maximize this rather than some other measure.

8. Express the dual of the original problem. Explain what one seeks to minimize and what each of the constraints means.

9. If the unit cost of the first resource were $3 and six additional units became available at a cost of $4 per unit:

   a. Would the management team consider the acquisition of the six units? Explain.
   b. If management personnel elected to acquire the six units, what is the new optimal contribution margin?

10. If the unit cost of the second resource is $4 and five additional units are available at a cost of $7 per unit:

    a. Would the management staff consider the acquisition of the five units? Explain.
    b. If management elected to acquire the five units, what is the new optimal contribution margin?

11. Based on the solution of the linear-programming problem, prepare a budgeted income statement. Assume the unit resource costs are $3 and $4, respectively, and the fixed costs are $96.

Initial and Final Simplex Tableau Analysis   **P12-3.**   Based on the initial and final simplex tableaus given, answer the following questions:

Required ☐

1. From the initial tableau, the variable that would enter the solution is _____.

2. From the initial tableau, the variable that would exit the solution is _____.

3. After the first iteration, what values would the following variables assume?

$x_1 = $ _____.

$x_2 = $ _____.

$s_1 = $ _____.

$s_2 = $ _____.

4. If one additional unit of the first resource became available, the new optimal solution and total contribution margin would be:

$x_1 = $ _____.

$x_2 = $ _____.

$s_1 = $ _____.

$s_2 = $ _____.

Total contribution margin = $_____.

5. If six additional units of the first resource became available, the new optimal solution and total contribution margin would be:

$x_1 = $ _____.

$x_2 = $ _____.

$s_1 = $ _____.

$s_2 = $ _____.

Total contribution margin = $_____.

6. If one unit of the first resource was not available, the new optimal solution and total contribution margin would be:

$x_1 = $ _____.

$x_2 = $ _____.

$s_1 = $ _____.

$s_2 = $ _____.

Total contribution margin = $_____.

Initial Simplex Tableau

c_j			8	6	0	0
	Mix	b	x_1	x_2	s_1	s_2
0	s_1	60	4	2	1	0
0	s_2	48	2	4	0	1
	z_j	0	0	0	0	0
	$c_j - z_j$		8	6	0	0

Final Simplex Tableau

c_j			8	6	0	0
	Mix	b	x_1	x_2	s_1	s_2
8	x_1	12	1	0	1/3	−1/6
6	x_2	6	0	1	−1/6	1/3
	z_j	132	8	6	5/3	2/3
	$c_j - z_j$		0	0	−5/3	−2/3

7. If six additional units of the second resource became available, the new optimal solution and total contribution margin would be:

$x_1 =$ _____.

$x_2 =$ _____.

$s_1 =$ _____.

$s_2 =$ _____.

Total contribution margin = $ _____.

8. If three units of the second resource were not available, the new optimal solution and total contribution margin would be:

$x_1 =$ _____.

$x_2 =$ _____.

$s_1 =$ _____.

$s_2 =$ _____.

Total contribution margin = $ _____.

9. Determine the ranges for the shadow prices.

LL	b_i	UL
_____	60	_____
_____	48	_____

10. Determine the ranges for the contribution margins.

LL	c_j	UL
_____	8	_____
_____	6	_____

11. If the unit cost of the resources are $2 and $3, respectively, determine the selling prices of x_1 and x_2.

$x_1 =$ _____.

$x_2 =$ _____.

12. If the unit cost of the resources are $3 and $2, respectively, determine the selling prices of x_1 and x_2.

$x_1 =$ _____.

$x_2 =$ _____.

13. If sixty additional units of the first resource became available, the new optimal solution and total contribution margin would be:

$x_1 =$ _____.

$x_2 =$ _____.

$s_1 =$ _____.

$s_2 =$ _____.

Total contribution margin = $ _____.

14. If the unit cost of the first resource is $2 and six additional units are available at a cost of $3.00 per unit:

   a. Would the management team consider the acquisition of the six units?

   b. If the management staff acquired the six units, what is the optimal contribution margin?

15. If the cost of the second resource is $3.00 and eight additional units are available at a cost of $3.75 per unit:

   a. Would the management personnel consider the acquisition of the eight units?

    b. If the management team acquired the eight units, what is the optimal contribution margin?

16. The original problem can be expressed as:

Maximize: $8x_1 + 6x_2$
Subject to: $4x_1 + 2x_2 \leq 60$
              $2x_1 + 4x_2 \leq 48$
              $x_1 \geq 0, x_2 \geq 0$

Express the dual of the original problem.

17. Explain why one seeks to maximize total contribution margin rather than profits.

P12-4. Based on the initial and final simplex tableaus given, answer the following questions:

Initial and Final Simplex Tableau Analysis

Required ☐

1. From the initial tableau, the variable that would enter the solution is _____.

2. From the initial tableau, the variable that would exit the solution is _____.

3. From the final tableau, the total contribution margin equals _____.

4. From the initial and final tableaus, the total profit equals _____.

Initial Simplex Tableau

c_j			$7	$6	$0	$0	$-M	$0
	Mix	b	x_1	x_2	s_1	s_2	a_1	s_3
0	s_1	36	2	4	1	0	0	0
0	s_2	24	3	1	0	1	0	0
$-M$	a_1	42	7	6	0	0	1	-1
	z_j	$-42M$	$-7M$	$-6M$	0	0	$-M$	M
	$c_j - z_j$		$7 + 7M$	$6 + 6M$	0	0	0	$-M$

Final Simplex Tableau

c_j			$7	$6	$0	$0	$-M	$0
	Mix	b	x_1	x_2	s_1	s_2	a_1	s_3
$6	x_2	6	0	1	3/10	-1/5	0	0
$0	s_3	36	0	0	11/10	8/5	-1	1
$7	x_1	6	1	0	-1/10	2/5	0	0
	z_j	$78	$7	$6	$1.10	$1.60	$0	$0
	$c_j - z_j$		$0	$0	-$1.10	-$1.60	$-M	$0

5. The total fixed costs of the firm are _____.

6. If the unit costs of the resources are $4 and $5, respectively, determine the selling prices of x_1 and x_2.
   $x_1 = \$$_____
   $x_2 = \$$_____

7. If the unit costs of the resources are $5 and $4, respectively, determine the selling prices of x_1 and x_2.

   $x_1 = \$$_____
   $x_2 = \$$_____

8. If one additional unit of the first resource became available, the new optimal solution would be:

   $x_1 =$ _____ $a_1 =$ _____
   $x_2 =$ _____ $z_j =$ _____
   $S_1 =$ _____
   $S_2 =$ _____
   $S_3 =$ _____

9. If two units of the first resource were found not to be available, the new optimal solution would be:

   $x_1 =$ _____ $S_3 =$ _____
   $x_2 =$ _____ $a_1 =$ _____
   $S_1 =$ _____ $z_j =$ _____
   $S_2 =$ _____

10. Determine the ranges of the shadow prices.

LL	b_i	UL
_____	36	_____
_____	24	_____

11. Determine the ranges for the contribution margins.

LL	c_j	UL
_____	$7	_____
_____	$6	_____

12. If the unit cost of the first resource is $3 and six additional units are available at a cost of $4 per unit:

    a. Would the management team consider the acquisition of the six units? Explain.
    b. If management acquired the additional six units, what is the optimum contribution?
    c. $z_j = \$$_____

13. If the unit cost of the second resource is $5.00 and six additional units are available at a cost of $6.75 per unit:

    a. Would the management staff consider the acquisition of the six additional units? Explain.
    b. If the management team acquired the additional six units, what is the optimum contribution margin?
    c. $z_j =$ _____

14. The opportunity costs are $1.10 and $1.60, respectively:

   a. What is the opportunity cost of producing a unit of x_1? A unit of x_2?

   $x_1 = \$$_____ $x_2 = \$$_____

   b. How are the opportunity costs of x_1 and x_2 related to their respective contribution margins?

15. If six additional units of the second resource became available, the new optimal solution and total contribution margin would be:

   $x_1 = $ _____ $s_3 = $ _____

   $x_2 = $ _____ $a_1 = $ _____

   $s_1 = $ _____ $z_j = $ _____

   $s_2 = $ _____

16. The original problem can be expressed as:

   Maximize: $7x_1 + 6x_2$

   Subject to: $2x_1 + 4x_2 \leq 36$

   $\qquad\qquad 3x_1 + x_2 \leq 24$

   $\qquad\qquad x_1 \geq 0; \qquad x_2 \geq 0$

   Express the dual of this original problem.

17. Why does one use contribution margin per unit instead of profit per unit in this objective function of a linear-programming problem?

P12-5. Solve graphically for the values of A and B that maximize the total contribution margin expressed as:

Graphic Solution of LP Problem

$Z = 3A + 4B$

Subject to:

$3A + 2B \leq 120$
$5A + 2B \leq 150$
$B \geq 20$
$A \geq 10$
$A \leq 25$

P12-6. Solve graphically for the values of A and B that maximize the total contribution margin expressed as:

Graphic Solution of LP Problem

$Z = .3A + .4B$

Subject to:

$A + B \leq 50$
$A \leq 40$
$B \leq 30$
$A \geq 0$
$B \geq 0$

P12-7. In the manufacture of product A, the TECH Company management team has determined that one hour of machine time and three units of raw materials are necessary. The production of product B requires two hours of machine time and two units of raw materials. Eight hours of machine time and twelve units of raw materials are available. The contribution margins are $2 and $3, respectively.

Graphic and Simplex Solution to LP Problem

Required ☐

1. Use the graphic method to solve this linear-programming problem.

2. Use the simplex algorithm to solve this linear-programming problem.

3. Determine the ranges of the opportunity costs and contribution margins.

4. Total fixed costs for the TECH Company are $6. Incorporate the break-even constraint into the problem, and solve using the simplex algorithm.

Graphic and Simplex Solution to LP Problem

P12-8. The L-K Corporation manufactures two products. Product x_1 requires one unit of materials and two units of labor. Product x_2 requires two units of materials and one unit of labor. The contribution margins are $3 and $2, respectively. Only six units of product x_1 can be sold. Sixteen units of material and fourteen units of labor are available.

Required ☐

1. Use the graphic method to solve this linear-programming problem.

2. Use the simplex algorithm to solve this linear-programming problem.

3. Determine the ranges of the opportunity costs and contribution margins.

4. Total fixed costs for the L-K Corporation are $12. Incorporate the break-even constraint into the problem, and solve using the simplex algorithm.

Simplex Solution to LP Problem

P12-9.

Maximize: $4A + 3B$
Subject to: $2A + B \leq 500$
$A + 3B \leq 1,000$

$A, B \geq 0$

Required ☐

1. Set up the initial simplex tableau for this problem.

2. Solve the problem.

3. Interpret each element in the final simplex tableau.

LP Problem Requiring Simplex Algorithm

P12-10. The LNK Corporation produces two products. Product x_1 requires three units of materials and one unit of labor. Product x_2 requires two units of materials and two units of labor. Sixty units of materials and forty units of labor are available. Material costs $3 a unit and labor, including variable overhead, is costed at $7 a unit. Selling prices for the products are estimated to equal $24 and $32, respectively. Total fixed costs for the firm are estimated to equal $96.

Required ☐

1. Determine the optimum production mix.

2. If six additional units of material were available at a cost of $4 a unit, should the firm acquire the material? Explain your answer.

P12-11. The DOT Corporation manufactures three products. Product x_1 requires four units of raw material one, five units of the second raw material, and twelve units of labor. Product x_2 requires six units of raw material one, eight units of the second raw material, and three units of labor. Product x_3 requires six units of the second raw material and ten units of labor. Forty units of the first raw material, sixty units of the second, and one hundred units of labor are available.

LP Problem Requiring Simplex Algorithm

The first material costs $3 a unit, the second $5 a unit, and labor, including variable overhead, is costed at $8 a unit. Selling prices are $200, $160, and $135, respectively.

Required ☐

1. Determine the optimum production mix.

2. Determine the ranges of the opportunity costs and the contribution margins.

P12-12. A refinery produces three grades of gasoline: premium, regular, and low-lead. Each grade of gasoline requires gasoline, octane, and additives. These inputs are available in the amount of 4 million, 3 million, and 1 million gallons per month, respectively. To produce a gallon of premium requires .6 gallon of gasoline, .3 gallon of octane, and .1 gallon of additives. A gallon of regular requires .7 gallon of gasoline, .2 gallon of octane, and .1 gallon of additives. The low-lead gasoline requires .6 gallon of gasoline, .1 gallon of octane, and .3 gallon of additives. The contribution margins for each grade of gasoline are .06, .03, and .04, respectively.

LP Problem Requiring Simplex Algorithm

Required ☐

1. How many gallons of each grade of gasoline should be produced each month to maximize profits?

2. The management team is considering investing in certain modifications to the refinery. The availability of which of the three inputs should they consider increasing by modifying the refinery? Comment on the cost of the modifications.

P12-13. The Williams Company produces two products, x_1 and x_2. These products require two resources of which there are fifty and forty units available, respectively. Product x_1 requires two units of the first resource and four units of the second. A unit of x_2 requires five units of the first resource and one unit of the second. The contribution margins are $6 and $4 for x_1 and x_2, respectively. Marketing considerations require that at least five units of product x_1 be sold.

LP Problem Requiring Simplex Algorithm

Required ☐

1. Determine the optimal mix of products x_1 and x_2 that the Williams Company should produce.

2. Determine the ranges of the opportunity costs and contribution margins.

LP Problem Requiring Simplex Algorithm

P12-14. The Parsons Chemical Company produces adhesive and wood glue in one of its plants. The adhesive requires four units of celluloid and one-half of a unit of cement. The glue requires two units of celluloid and one-fourth unit of cement. Seventy-six units of celluloid and twenty units of cement are available. Production restrictions require that at least six units of adhesive and twenty units of glue are produced. The contribution margins for the adhesive and glue are $3 and $2, respectively.

Required ☐

1. Determine the optimal mix of adhesive and glue that the Parsons Company should produce.

2. Determine the ranges of the opportunity costs and contribution margins.

LP Problem Requiring Simplex Algorithm

P12-15. The Levert Box Company manufactures wooden boxes and shipping crates. A box requires three units of wood and three units of labor, while a crate requires five units of wood and three units of labor. The standard cost of a unit of wood is $2, and labor, including the variable overhead, has a standard cost of $5 per unit. The boxes and crates sell for $25 and $30, respectively. Forty-five units of wood and thirty-six units of labor are available to the firm.

Required ☐

1. Determine the optimal mix of boxes and crates that the firm should produce.

2. Five additional units of wood are available at a cost of $3 per unit. Should the firm acquire the additional units? If the firm acquires the additional units, what is the optimal production mix, and what is the optimal contribution margin?

3. Additional labor can be purchased at 1.5 times the standard rate. If the labor rate is $3 per unit and the variable overhead is $2 per unit:

   a. Should the firm pay the overtime premium if both the labor and overhead are included in determining the overtime rate?
   b. Should the firm pay the overtime premium if only the labor cost of $3 is adjusted in determining the overtime rate?
   c. How many additional hours would the firm be willing to purchase and at what rate?

4. If the selling price of the crates increased to $37.50 and the selling price of the boxes remained at $25, how would this change your answer to requirement 1?

5. The management team has determined that they would not operate the plant unless at least twenty-four units of labor were employed. How would the constraint be incorporated into the original problem?

Review of LP Concepts

P12-16. The cost accountant of the Stangren Corporation, your client, wants your opinion of a technique suggested to him by a young accounting graduate he employed as a cost analyst. The following information was furnished to you for the corporation's two products, trinkets and gadgets:

1.

Exhibit 1
Daily Capacities in Units

	Cutting department	Finishing department	Sales price per unit	Variable cost per unit
Trinkets	400	240	$50	$30
Gadgets	200	320	$70	$40

2. The daily capacities of each department represent the maximum production for either trinkets or gadgets. However, any combination of trinkets and gadgets can be produced as long as the maximum capacity of the department is not exceeded. For example, two trinkets can be produced in the Cutting department for each gadget not produced and three trinkets can be produced in the Finishing department for every four gadgets not produced.

3. Material shortages prohibit the production of more than 180 gadgets per day.

4. Exhibit 2 is a graphic expression of simultaneous linear equations developed from the production information just cited.

Exhibit 2
Graph of Production Relationships

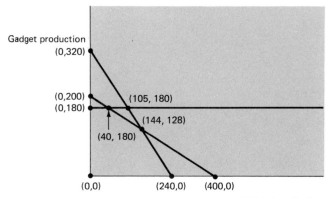

Required □

1. For what kinds of decisions are contribution-margin data (revenue in excess of variable cost) useful?

2. Comparing the information in Exhibit 1 with the graph in Exhibit 2, identify and list the graphic location (coordinates) of the

   a. Cutting department's capacity
   b. Production limitation for gadgets because of the materials shortage
   c. Area of feasible (possible) production combinations

3. *a.* Compute the contribution margin per unit for trinkets and gadgets.
   b. Compute the total contribution margin of each of the points of intersections of lines bounding the feasible (possible) production area.
   c. Identify the best production alternative.

(CPA)

Review of LP
Concepts

P12-17. Excelsion Corporation manufactures and sells two kinds of containers—paperboard and plastic. The company produced and sold 100,000 paperboard containers and 75,000 plastic containers during the month of April. Totals of 4,000 and 6,000 direct-labor hours were used in producing the paperboard and plastic containers, respectively.

The company has not been able to maintain an inventory of either product, owing to the high demand; this situation is expected to continue in the future. Workers can be shifted from the production of paperboard to plastic containers and vice versa, but additional labor is not available in the community. In addition, a shortage of plastic material used in the manufacture of the plastic container will occur in the coming months due to a labor strike at the facilities of a key supplier. The management team has estimated that only enough raw material to produce 60,000 plastic containers will be available during June.

The income statement for Excelsion Corporation for the month of April follows. The costs presented in the statement are representative of prior periods and are expected to continue at the same rates or levels in the future.

EXCELSION CORPORATION
Income Statement
For the month ended April 30, 19X8

	Paperboard containers	*Plastic containers*
Sales	$220,800	$222,900
Less: Returns and allowances	$ 6,360	$ 7,200
Discounts	2,440	3,450
	$ 8,800	$ 10,650
Net sales	$212,000	$212,250
Cost of sales		
Raw material cost	$123,000	$120,750
Direct labor	26,000	28,500
Indirect labor (variable with direct-labor hours)	4,000	4,500
Depreciation—machinery	14,000	12,250
Depreciation—building	10,000	10,000
Cost of sales	$177,000	$176,000
Gross profit	$ 35,000	$ 36,250
Selling and general expenses		
General expenses—variable	$ 8,000	$ 7,500
General expenses—fixed	1,000	1,000
Commissions	11,000	15,750
Total operating expenses	$ 20,000	$ 24,250
Income before tax	$ 15,000	$ 12,000
Income taxes (40 percent)	6,000	4,800
Net income	$ 9,000	$ 7,200

Required ☐

1. The management of Excelsion Corporation plans to use linear programming to determine the optimal mix of paperboard and plastic containers for the month of June to achieve maximum profits. Using data presented in the April income statement, formulate and label the

a. Objective function
b. Constraint functions

2. Identify the underlying assumptions of linear programming.

3. What contribution would the management accountant normally make to a team established to develop the linear-programming model and apply it to a decision problem?

(CMA)

P12-18. The Tripro Company produces and sells three products hereafter referred to as products A, B, and C. The company is currently changing its short-range planning approach in an attempt to incorporate some of the newer planning techniques. The controller and some of her staff have been conferring with a consultant on the feasibility of using a linear-programming model for determining the optimum product mix.

Formulation of LP Objective Function

Information for short-range planning has been developed in the same format as in prior years. This information includes expected sales prices and expected direct-labor and material costs for each product. In addition, variable- and fixed-overhead costs were assumed to be the same for each product because approximately equal quantities of the products were produced and sold.

Price and Cost Information (Per Unit)

	A	B	C
Selling price	$25.00	$30.00	$40.00
Direct labor	7.50	10.00	12.50
Direct materials	9.00	6.00	10.50
Variable overhead	6.00	6.00	6.00
Fixed overhead	6.00	6.00	6.00

All three products use the same type of direct material, which costs $1.50 per pound of material. Direct labor is paid at the rate of $5 per direct-labor hour. There are 2,000 direct-labor hours and 20,000 pounds of direct materials available in a month.

Required □

1. Formulate and label the linear-programming objective function and constraint functions necessary to maximize Tripro's contribution margin. Use Q_A, Q_B, and Q_C to represent units of the three products.

2. What underlying assumptions must be satisfied to justify the use of linear programming?

3. The consultant, upon reviewing the data presented and the linear-programming functions developed, performed further analysis of overhead costs. He used a multiple-linear-regression model to analyze the overhead cost behavior. The regression model incorporated observations from the past forty-eight months of total overhead costs and the

direct-labor hours for each product. The following equation was the result:

Where
$$Y = \$5,000 + 2X_A + 4X_B + 3X_C$$
Y = monthly total overhead in dollars
X_A = monthly direct-labor hours for product A
X_B = monthly direct-labor hours for product B
X_C = monthly direct-labor hours for product C

The total regression has been determined to be statistically significant as has each of the individual regression coefficients.

Reformulate the objective function for Tripro Company, using the results of this analysis.

(CMA)

Review of LP Concepts **P12-19.** The Frey Company manufactures and sells two products—a toddler bike and a toy high chair. Linear programming is employed to determine the best production and sales mix of bikes and chairs. This approach also allows Frey to speculate on economic changes. For example, the management team is often interested in knowing how variations in selling prices, resource costs, resource availabilities, and marketing strategies would affect company performance.

The demand for bikes and chairs is relatively constant throughout the year. The following economic data pertain to the two products:

	Bike (B)	Chair (C)
Selling price per unit	$12	$10
Variable cost per unit	8	7
Contribution margin per unit	$ 4	$ 3
Raw materials required		
Wood	1 board ft.	1 board ft.
Plastic	2 pounds	1 pound
Direct labor required	2 hours	2 hours

Estimates of the resource quantities available in a nonvacation month during the year are:

Wood	10,000 board feet
Plastic	10,000 pounds
Direct labor	12,000 hours

The graphic formulation of the constraints of the linear-programming model that the Frey Company has developed for nonvacation months is shown on the graph. The algebraic formulation of the model for the non-vacation months is as follows:

Objective function: Maximize: $Z = 4B + 3C$

Constraints
$$B + 2C \leq 10,000 \text{ board feet}$$
$$2B + C \leq 10,000 \text{ pounds}$$
$$2B + 2C \leq 12,000 \text{ direct-labor hours}$$
$$B, C \geq 0$$

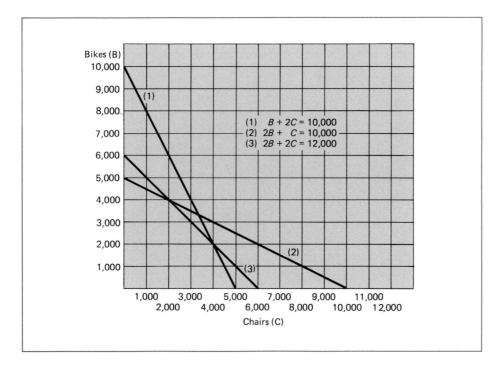

The results from the linear-programming model indicate that Frey Company can maximize its contribution margin (and thus profits) for a non-vacation month by producing and selling 4,000 toddler bikes and 2,000 toy high chairs. This sales mix will yield a total contribution margin of $22,000 in a month.

Required □

1. During the months of June, July, and August, the total direct-labor hours available are reduced from 12,000 to 10,000 hours per month due to vacations.

   a. What would be the best product mix and maximum total contribution margin when only 10,000 direct-labor hours are available during a month?

   b. The "shadow price" of a resource is defined as the marginal contribution of a resource or the rate at which profit would increase (decrease) if the amount of resource were increased (decreased). Based upon your solution for requirement 1a, what is the shadow price on direct-labor hours in the original model for a nonvacation month?

2. Competition in the toy market is very strong. Consequently, the prices of the two products tend to fluctuate. Can analysis of data from the linear-programming model provide information to management that will indicate when price changes made to meet market conditions will alter the optimum product mix? Explain your answer.

(CMA)

Review of LP
Concepts

P12-20. The Witchell Corporation manufactures and sells three grades, A, B, and C, of a single wood product. Each grade must be processed through three phases—cutting, fitting, and finishing—before it is sold.

The following unit information is provided:

	A	B	C
Selling price	$10.00	$15.00	$20.00
Direct labor	5.00	6.00	9.00
Direct materials	.70	.70	1.00
Variable overhead	1.00	1.20	1.80
Fixed overhead	.60	.72	1.08
Materials requirements in board feet	7	7	10
Labor requirements in hours			
Cutting	3/6	3/6	4/6
Fitting	1/6	1/6	2/6
Finishing	1/6	2/6	3/6

Only 5,000 board feet per week can be obtained. The cutting department has 180 hours of labor available each week. The Fitting and Finishing departments each have 120 hours of labor available each week. No overtime is allowed.

Contract commitments require the company to make 50 units of A per week. In addition, company policy is to produce at least 50 additional units of A and 50 units of both B and C each week to actively remain in each of the three markets. Because of competition, only 130 units of C can be sold each week.

Required □ Formulate and label the linear-objective function and the constraint functions necessary to maximize the contribution margin.

(CMA)

Review of LP
Concepts

P12-21. Girth, Inc., makes two kinds of men's suede leather belts. Belt A is a high-quality belt, while belt B is of somewhat lower quality. The company earns $7 for each unit of belt A that is sold and $2 for each unit of belt B sold. Each unit (belt) of type A requires twice as much manufacturing time as is required for a unit of type B. Further, if only type B is made, Girth has the capacity to manufacture 1,000 units per day.

Suede leather is purchased by Girth under a long-term contract that makes available to Girth enough leather to make 800 belts per day (A and B combined).

Belt A requires a fancy buckle, of which only 400 per day are available. Belt B requires a different (plain) buckle, of which 700 per day are available. The demand for the suede leather belts (A or B) is such that Girth can sell all that it produces.

The accompanying graph displays the constraint functions based upon the facts presented.

Required □

1. Using the graph, determine how many units of belt A and belt B should be produced to maximize daily profits.

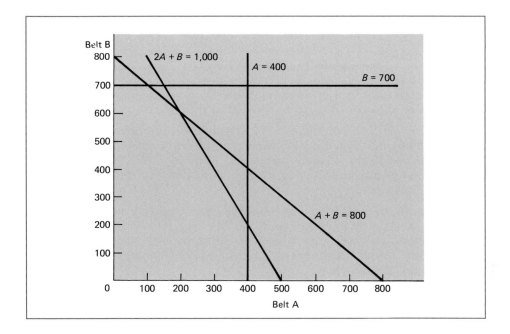

2. Assume the same facts above except that the sole supplier of buckles for belt A informs Girth, Inc., that it will be able to supply only 100 fancy buckles per day. How many units of each of the two belts should be produced each day to maximize profits?

3. Assume the same facts as in requirement 2 except that Texas Buckles, Inc., could supply Girth, Inc., with the additional fancy buckles it needs. The price would be $3.50 more than Girth, Inc., is paying for such buckles. How many, if any, fancy buckles should Girth, Inc., buy from Texas Buckles, Inc.? Explain how you determined your answer.

(CMA)

P12-22. Porta-Chick is an industrial caterer specializing in the sale of boxes of fried chicken to employees in various business organizations in the Atlanta area. The chicken is delivered daily, by truck, at various time intervals geared to meet demands for lunch and dinner hours at the various locations.

Comprehensive LP Problem

Demand for the product is of such a nature that Porta-Chick can sell all of the boxes produced per day. Production facilities at the plant, however, are limited so that only a maximum of 2,000 chickens can be prepared and fried daily. In addition, supply is restricted in that the wholesaler will sell chickens only in whole lots. Thus, the chickens must be cut up in usable pieces on the premises.

Based on the results of a number of investigations, studies, and market surveys, Ms. Stanley, proprietor of the concern, has established a number of guidelines in facilitating the production and sale of her product.

Surveys testing consumer preference have indicated that only eight pieces per chicken are desirable—two wings, two legs, two thighs, and two breast pieces. The remainder of the chicken (neck, etc.) possesses no market value and must be discarded or given away. In addition, Porta-Chick's facilities are inadequate for storing unused chicken overnight. Consequently, any leftover pieces must also be discarded in like manner (no tax concessions, etc., can be realized on this loss).

Customer-demand studies have also indicated an order of preference, from highest to lowest, for the various pieces of chicken: breast pieces, legs and thighs (of equal preference), and wings. All, however, are preferred by a large enough proportion of those surveyed to be included in the boxes sold.

Studies have also indicated that the most appealing size box contains eight pieces of chicken and that two different grades of boxes, predicated on the above preference studies, are demanded—economy and deluxe—containing different product mixes at a price level the public is willing to pay. For example:

A. Economy Box—not more than six wings per box at a price of $1.59
B. Deluxe Box—not more than two wings and not less than four breast pieces at a price of $1.99

Ms. Stanley has calculated the daily fixed and variable costs as follows:

Fixed
Labor (8 full-time employees @ $2 per hour) $128
Rent (including cooking, storing, and
  refrigeration equipment) 17
Overhead (utilities, etc.) 13
Miscellaneous (depreciation on truck, gasoline,
  various taxes, etc.) 15
                                                                  $173
Variables
Cost of frying batter and boxes
  (Available in unlimited supply and
  instantaneous delivery) .... $ .07 per box
Cost of chicken .... 1.08 each
  *Cost allocated according to what Ms. Stanley considers
  appropriate, predicated on customer preference for the
  various pieces of chicken:
Wings   = $.07 × 2 = $ .14
Leg/Thighs = $.13 × 4 = $ .52
Breasts   = $.21 × 2 = $ .42
                        $1.08

Required □ Ms. Stanley is interested in determining the best product mix (within the constraints outlined) for the two quality boxes that will result in production of the greatest number of boxes per day in order to maximize profits.

(This problem is an application of linear programming. It was prepared by Professor Dennis Grawoig and is taken from the Supplement to vol. XLVI of the 1971 *Accounting Review*, pp. 236–37. A computer is necessary to solve this problem.)

CHAPTER OUTLINE

THE USES OF COSTS IN MAKING NONROUTINE DECISIONS

CHAPTER **13**

☐ INTRODUCTION

In this chapter, a set of nonroutine decisions will be considered. Initially, we will introduce a general model for making decisions employing cost information. The key to the model is associating relevant revenues and costs with the alternative solutions to the problems. Whether to make or buy a part, whether to drop or add a product or department, and short-run pricing decisions are all considered in this chapter. Each problem is discussed by developing a comprehensive example. The problem is then evaluated by associating the relevant revenues and costs and evaluating the alternative solutions.

Once the quantitative evaluation is complete, qualitative factors related to the decision are discussed. These factors, although not quantifiable, are relevant to each problem and must be considered in making any decision.

☐ THE DECISION PROCESS

A general decision process can be developed for the nonroutine types of decisions considered in this chapter. A diagram of this process is shown in figure 13.1. Once the problem has been specified successfully, a set of **alternative solutions** must be identified. Most of the problems considered in this chapter have two alternative solutions: make or buy a part, add or drop a product, add or drop a department, and sell or not sell a special order.

After identifying the alternative solutions, the management accountant must consider **relevant revenue** and **cost** information associated with the alternatives. The revenues and costs that are relevant to an alternative are those revenues and costs that are different for each alternative. These relevant revenues and costs are also called differential revenues and costs. The adjective *differential* is used because the revenue or cost is different in amount for at least two of the alternatives under consideration. From another perspective, **differential-cost analysis** involves only current and future revenues and costs that are different in amount for at least two of the alternatives. Common revenues and costs that are the same amount

443

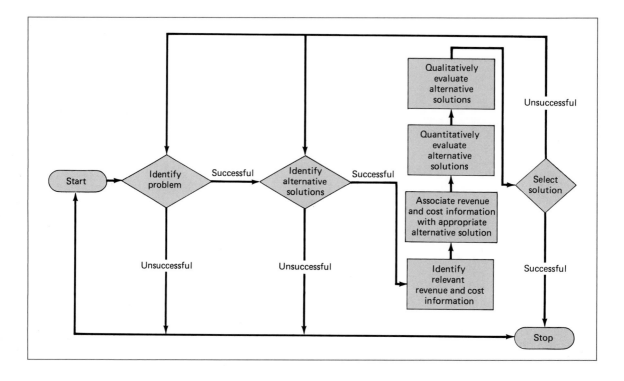

FIGURE 13.1
Diagram of
Decision Process

for all alternatives can be ignored in the decision analysis. Costs that were incurred in prior periods, namely sunk costs, are not relevant in analyzing the decision. The only exception to this statement is if the sunk cost may have some future value because of potential tax benefits derived from the disposal of an asset.

Once the relevant revenues and costs are associated with the alternative solutions, a solution is selected based on a maximum contribution to profit, or cost-minimization-decision criterion. Then, **qualitative factors** must be evaluated to determine their respective impact on the solution. For example, cost analysis might indicate that several workers should be laid off for a short time. The management team may reject this alternative because of potential morale problems with employees. In another case, revenue and cost data might indicate that the firm should eliminate a certain product. This alternative might be rejected because management personnel believe the sale of other products will be negatively affected by dropping the product.

After considering both the **quantitative** and qualitative factors, the management team selects a solution to the problem. While this is a relatively abstract description of the decision process, it does apply in a general way to all of the problems considered in this chapter.

☐ ADDING OR DROPPING A PRODUCT OR DEPARTMENT

Frequently, firms engage in an analysis to determine the contribution to profit of either a product or a department. The end result of such analysis is a decision—*add, drop,* or make no change concerning a *product* or a *department*. Assume the management team of Wades Grocery Company is analyzing the income statement shown in table 13.1. As a result of this analysis, company officials are considering eliminating the Dairy department because the department is losing $10,000 annually.

The problem with the income statement shown in table 13.1 is that the departmental operating profit is determined after allocating $125,000 of fixed costs among the departments. This results in evaluating the Dairy department on the basis of costs that are not relevant. The $25,000 in fixed costs allocated to the Dairy department will be incurred whether the Dairy department continues to operate or is eliminated. (Allocated costs are not relevant in most decision environments.) Because the $125,000 of allocated fixed costs are common to both alternatives, they are not relevant to the decision concerning operation of the Dairy department.

Table 13.2 contains a departmental income statement where no allocations have been made. Note that after subtracting all direct costs the Dairy department has a margin over direct costs of $15,000. Table 13.3 shows the departmental income statement after the Dairy department is dropped. Note that the operating profit is now $75,000 rather than the $90,000 shown when the Dairy department was assumed to be operating. The $15,000 difference in the operating profit is the margin over direct costs contributed by the Dairy department to the firm's net income. Therefore, based on a quantitative analysis, the Dairy department should not be eliminated.

Several qualitative factors should be considered in this problem. A very important assumption of the quantitative analysis is that the sales in the four departments are independent. This means that the sales in one department will in no way influence the sales in the other departments. If one assumes that Wades Grocery Company is a full-line grocery company, then an important question concerns potential customer reaction to eliminating the Dairy department. If indeed customers do change their shopping habits because Wades does not sell dairy products, then this factor must be considered in analyzing the problem.

Another qualitative factor is an evaluation to determine if all relevant revenues and costs have been considered in the analysis. For example,

TABLE 13.1 Departmental Income Statement

WADES GROCERY COMPANY
Departmental Income Statement
for Year Ended December 31, 19X3

Department	Groceries	Meats	Dairy	Drugs	Total
Sales	$680,000	$190,000	$150,000	$80,000	$1,100,000
Cost of goods sold	490,000	100,000	110,000	30,000	730,000
Gross margin	$190,000	$ 90,000	$ 40,000	$50,000	$ 370,000
Direct fixed and variable costs	$ 70,000	$ 50,000	$ 25,000	$10,000	$ 155,000
Allocated fixed costs	65,000	20,000	25,000	15,000	125,000
Total fixed costs	$135,000	$ 70,000	$ 50,000	$25,000	$ 280,000
Operating profit	$ 55,000	$ 20,000	$ (10,000)	$25,000	$ 90,000

TABLE 13.2 Departmental Income Statement—No Allocations

WADES GROCERY COMPANY
Departmental Income Statement
for Year Ended December 31, 19X3

Department	Groceries	Meats	Dairy	Drugs	Total
Sales	$680,000	$190,000	$150,000	$80,000	$1,100,000
Cost of goods sold	490,000	100,000	110,000	30,000	730,000
Gross margin	$190,000	$ 90,000	$ 40,000	$50,000	$ 370,000
Direct fixed and variable costs	70,000	50,000	25,000	10,000	155,000
Margin over direct costs	$120,000	$ 40,000	$ 15,000	$40,000	$ 215,000
Other fixed costs					125,000
Operating profit					$ 90,000

TABLE 13.3 Departmental Income Statement—Dairy Department Eliminated

WADES GROCERY COMPANY
Estimated Departmental Income Statement—Dairy Eliminated
for Year Ended December 31, 19X3

Department	Groceries	Meats	Drugs	Total
Sales	$680,000	$190,000	$80,000	$ 950,000
Cost of goods sold	490,000	100,000	30,000	620,000
Gross margin	$190,000	$ 90,000	$50,000	$ 330,000
Direct fixed and variable costs	70,000	50,000	10,000	130,000
Margin over direct costs	$120,000	$ 40,000	$40,000	$ 200,000
Other fixed costs				125,000
Operating profit				$ 75,000

other revenues and costs that might be relevant to the decision are (1) the potential revenues from items that could be sold in the space now occupied by the Dairy department, (2) the proceeds from disposal of refrigeration equipment in the dairy department, and (3) the impact on the cost of heating and air conditioning the store that results from the removal of dairy refrigeration units.

The independent sales assumption and questions concerning relevant revenues and costs are examples of qualitative factors that should be considered in this type of decision.

☐ MAKE-OR-BUY DECISION

Typical manufacturing firms produce products that consist of many components or parts. Just think of the number of different parts in a typewriter or an automobile. During the design phase of a product, a sourcing decision must be made for every part. Management must decide whether the firm should produce each part or purchase it from an outside supplier. Generally, a policy is developed based on marketing, capital budgeting, and production considerations for dealing with this long-run sourcing, or **make-or-buy decision**. Sourcing decisions have recently become an issue in union negotiations. In the U.S. automotive industry, unions are concerned when firms contract to have items produced by outside vendors (called out-sourcing) rather than produce the parts in the firm's own plants. The issue becomes especially acute from a union's point of view when the vendor employs nonunion labor. In this case, the unions contend that the vendor's lower costs are the result of employing labor at less than the union wage.

Even when a long-run sourcing policy has been developed, frequent decisions of this type must be made from a short-run perspective. A short-run decision will be considered in this section. Both full-cost and differential-cost analysis will be considered in evaluating the problem. When full-cost analysis is employed, the full costs of all alternatives are considered in the quantitative analysis of the problem. If differential-cost analysis is employed, then only incremental costs are considered when evaluating the alternative solutions.

Assume a firm requires 1,000 valves for a special nonrepetitive project. The estimated full cost to manufacture the valves is $57,000. An outside vendor has quoted a price of $50,000 for the valves. The full- and differential-cost analyses of the problem are shown in table 13.4. Additional explanation is necessary for the fixed overhead. It is assumed that $10,000 of the fixed overhead is allocated and will be incurred whether the valves are made or purchased. The other $5,000 of the fixed overhead is assumed to be direct and will be incurred only if the valves are manufactured. A savings of $3,000 ($60,000 − $57,000) is realized if the valves are manufactured rather than purchased.

The differential-cost analysis is also shown in table 13.4. As before, one determines that a savings of $3,000 ($50,000 − $47,000) is realized if the valves are manufactured rather than purchased. In the differential-cost analysis, only the $5,000 in direct fixed overhead is relevant for the manufacturing option. The $10,000 allocated fixed cost is not relevant because it is incurred in both the make and the buy options.

Note that the full- and differential-cost analyses both indicate that the manufacturing alternative is cheaper by $3,000. Both methods will always indicate the same preferred alternative, and the cost increment will be the same. In general, students initially find the full-cost approach easier to

TABLE 13.4 Analysis of Make-or-Buy Decision

	Full-cost analysis		Differential-cost analysis	
	Make	Buy	Make	Buy
Purchase cost		$50,000		$50,000
Direct material	$ 8,000		$ 8,000	
Direct labor	$24,000		$24,000	
Variable overhead	10,000		$10,000	
Fixed overhead*	$15,000	$10,000	$ 5,000	
Totals	$57,000	$60,000	$47,000	$50,000

*$10,000 allocated and $5,000 direct.

understand until they become familiar with determination of revenue and cost relevancy.

Other factors may complicate the make-or-buy problem. Assume that if the 1,000 valves were not manufactured, the capacity could be employed in manufacturing another product that would result in $5,000 of additional contribution margin. In other words, if the valves are manufactured, the $5,000 is foregone. The $5,000 is, therefore, an opportunity cost that will be incurred if the valves are manufactured.

Table 13.5 contains the full- and differential-cost analyses of the problem, incorporating the opportunity cost. In the full-cost analysis, the $5,000 opportunity cost is included with the make option. Under these conditions, it is $2,000 less expensive ($62,000 − $60,000) to purchase rather than manufacture the valves. Of course, this is based on the assumption that the manufacturing facilities are employed such that $5,000 in additional contribution margin is realized.

The same $2,000 difference ($52,000 − $50,000) is determined in the differential-cost analysis of the problem. Once again, the $5,000 opportunity cost is relevant in the make option, and the analysis indicates that the purchase option is the most profitable.

Some qualitative factors that would be considered in a make-or-buy decision are (1) the quality control of the vendor, (2) the ability of the vendor to meet the delivery date, (3) the customer reaction to purchasing a product containing outsourced components, (4) the labor and union reaction to the outsourcing decision, and (5) the impact on employee and management morale if the outsourcing option is selected. Potentially, each of the qualitative factors could cause management to select an option other than the one preferred based on the quantitative analysis.

☐ SHORT-RUN PRICING DECISION

Frequently, firms will have the opportunity to accept a special order for a product. This type of order typically requires the firm to quote a price or accept the order at a nonstandard price. In this section, several variations of a short-run pricing problem will be considered. An example will

TABLE 13.5 Analysis of Make-or-Buy Decision Including Opportunity Cost

| | Full-cost analysis | | Differential-cost analysis | |
	Make	Buy	Make	Buy
Purchase cost		$50,000		$50,000
Direct material	$ 8,000		$ 8,000	
Direct labor	$24,000		$24,000	
Variable overhead	$10,000		$10,000	
Fixed overhead*	$15,000	$10,000	$ 5,000	
Opportunity cost	$ 5,000		$ 5,000	
Totals	$62,000	$60,000	$52,000	$50,000

*$10,000 allocated and $5,000 direct.

be used to demonstrate the factors that should be considered in making this type of decision.

Assume the Ace Power Company manufactures a variable-speed gearbox that has a unit selling price of $500. The relevant cost information for the gearbox is shown in table 13.6. It takes six direct-labor hours to manufacture a gearbox, and Ace Power has the capacity to manufacture 100,000 gearboxes a year. Although the capacity is 600,000 direct-labor hours (100,000 gearboxes), Ace is presently operating at a production level of 450,000 hours (75,000 gearboxes).

A sales representative of Ace Power has found a customer that would be interested in purchasing 10,000 gearboxes during the next year. This customer, a small firm, produced its own gearboxes until a fire destroyed its factory. The factory is being rebuilt and will be back in production at the end of the year. The specifications of the Ace Power gearbox exceed the customer's specifications. The sales representative indicated that the 10,000 gearboxes will have to be sold at a unit price of $400 because of competition for the job.

The management team is faced with the problem of whether to accept this special order for the 10,000 gearboxes at the unit selling price of $400. Because of the short-run nature of this problem, the first step might be to reorder the cost information, as shown in table 13.7, to determine the unit contribution margin. From this analysis, one sees that any selling price over $360 will contribute to fixed costs or income. So, in the short run, this is the minimum selling price Ace Bearing would consider. In the long run, the selling price would have to exceed the full cost of a gearbox so that Ace could earn a profit.

The income statement in table 13.8 shows the impact of the special order on Ace's income for a year. If the special order were not accepted, and sales remained at 75,000 units, the operating profit would be $4.5 million (contribution margin of $10,500,000 minus fixed costs of $6,000,000). However, if the order for the 10,000 units is accepted, the total contribution margin and operating profit increases by $400,000 (10,000 × $40). Based on this quantitative analysis, one would conclude that Ace should accept the special order for the 10,000 gearboxes.

TABLE 13.6 Variable-Speed Gearbox Cost Information

Selling price		$500
Manufacturing costs		
Materials	$130	
Labor—six hours	120	
Variable overhead	80	
Fixed overhead	40	
Total	$370	
Selling and administrative		
Variable	$30	
Fixed	20	50
Total cost		420
Unit operating profit		$ 80

TABLE 13.7 Unit Contribution Margin of Variable-Speed Gearbox

Selling price		$500
Variable costs		
Materials	$130	
Labor—six hours	120	
Variable overhead	80	
Variable selling and administrative	30	360
Unit contribution margin		$140
Fixed overhead	$ 40	
Fixed selling and administrative	20	60
Unit operating profit		$ 80

TABLE 13.8 Income Statement

ACE POWER COMPANY
Income Statement
for Year Ending December 31, 19XX

	75,000 gearboxes at $500	10,000 gearboxes at $400	Total
Sales	$37,500,000	$4,000,000	$41,500,000
Variable costs			
Materials	$ 9,750,000	$1,300,000	$11,050,000
Labor	9,000,000	1,200,000	10,200,000
Variable overhead	6,000,000	800,000	6,800,000
Variable selling and administrative	2,250,000	300,000	2,550,000
Total variable costs	$27,000,000	$3,600,000	$30,600,000
Contribution margin	$10,500,000	$ 400,000	$10,900,000
Fixed costs			
Fixed overhead			4,000,000
Fixed selling and administrative			2,000,000
Total fixed costs			$ 6,000,000
Operating profit			$ 4,900,000

Assume Ace is operating at 75 percent capacity producing gearboxes. The 75,000 boxes require 450,000 direct-labor hours, leaving 150,000 hours available. These 150,000 hours are used to produce specialty gears that sell for $80 each. The variable costs associated with each specialty gear are

Selling price		$80
Variable costs:		
Materials	$30	
Labor—one hour	20	
Variable overhead	15	
Variable selling and administrative	5	70
Unit contribution margin		$10

Table 13.9 shows the yearly income for Ace when 75,000 gearboxes and 150,000 specialty gears are sold.

Now, assume again that the special order for the 10,000 gearboxes at a selling price of $400 is under consideration. In this case, if the order for the gearboxes is accepted, production will have to be curtailed on the specialty gears. One approach in analyzing this problem is to determine the contribution margin per direct-labor hour for each of the alternatives. The direct-labor hours are employed in this calculation because the capacity is expressed in terms of the direct-labor hours. The contribution margins per direct-labor hour are

Gearbox sold at $500 .... $\frac{\$140}{6}$ = $23.33 per direct-labor hour

Gearbox sold at $400 .... $\frac{\$40}{6}$ = $ 6.67 per direct-labor hour

Specialty gear sold at $80 .... $\frac{\$10}{1}$ = $10.00 per direct-labor hour

From this analysis, one would conclude that it is more profitable to manufacture the specialty gears rather than sell gearboxes at $400. Selling a gearbox at $400 results in a contribution margin of $40 and takes six direct-labor hours, whereas selling six specialty gears will also require six direct-labor hours but will result in a contribution margin of $60. If the special-order boxes could be sold for $420 (resulting in a unit contribution

TABLE 13.9 Income Statement

ACE POWER COMPANY
Income Statement
for Year Ending December 31, 19XX

	75,000 Gearboxes at $500	150,000 Specialty Gears at $80	Total
Sales	$37,500,000	$12,000,000	$49,500,000
Variable costs			
Materials	$ 9,750,000	$ 4,500,000	$14,250,000
Labor	9,000,000	3,000,000	12,000,000
Variable overhead	6,000,000	2,250,000	8,250,000
Variable selling and administrative	2,250,000	750,000	3,000,000
Total variable costs	$27,000,000	$10,500,000	$37,500,000
Contribution margin	$10,500,000	$ 1,500,000	$12,000,000
Fixed costs			
Fixed overhead			$ 4,000,000
Fixed selling and administrative			2,000,000
Total fixed costs			$ 6,000,000
Operating profit			$ 6,000,000

margin of $60), one would be indifferent as to whether Ace sold the specialty gears or the gearboxes.

In a case such as this where alternative uses exist for scarce resources, the minimum selling price for the special order is no longer the variable cost but the variable cost plus any opportunity cost incurred from employing the scarce resources. Therefore, the minimum acceptable selling price on the special-order gearboxes is the variable cost of $360 plus the opportunity cost for the six direct-labor hours of $60 (6 hours × $10 contribution margin per direct-labor hour of the specialty gears), or $420.

Now, assume that Ace is operating at capacity. The question now concerning the special order for the 10,000 gearboxes will result in a different conclusion. As shown in table 13.10, if the special order for the 10,000 gearboxes at a unit selling price of $400 is accepted, the operating profit for the firm will decrease by $1 million. This $1 million decrease in operating profit is caused by the $100 decrease in the selling price times the 10,000 special-order gearboxes. Therefore, when operating at capacity, based on the quantitative analysis, Ace Bearing would not be willing to accept the special order unless the order was at the existing market price of $500 per gearbox.

A major legal consideration that influences pricing decisions is the Robinson-Patman Act. This legislation forbids quoting different prices to competing customers unless the difference in price can be justified by differences in costs of manufacturing, sales, or delivery. Both the Federal Trade Commission and the courts have consistently interpreted cost to mean full cost rather than direct or differential cost. Therefore, in a case of competing customers for the same goods, prices cannot be defended solely on the basis that they cover incremental costs. It is important to note that the

TABLE 13.10 Income Statement—Operating at Capacity

	100,000 Gearboxes at $500	90,000 Gearboxes at $500 and 10,000 at $400	Difference
Sales	$50,000,000	$49,000,000	($1,000,000)
Variable costs			
Materials	13,000,000	$13,000,000	0
Labor	12,000,000	12,000,000	0
Variable overhead	8,000,000	8,000,000	0
Variable selling and administrative	3,000,000	3,000,000	0
Total variable costs	$36,000,000	$36,000,000	$0
Contribution margin	$14,000,000	$13,000,000	($1,000,000)
Fixed costs			
Fixed overhead	$ 4,000,000	$ 4,000,000	0
Fixed selling and administrative	2,000,000	2,000,000	0
Total fixed costs	$ 6,000,000	$ 6,000,000	0
Operating profit	$ 8,000,000	$ 7,000,000	($1,000,000)

Robinson-Patman Act relates to competing customers for the same goods. The act does not cover a competitive bidding situation, a situation in which idle capacity might be employed to produce output for a noncompeting market, or for the production of products that are not considered the normal output of the firm.

Several qualitative factors relate to short-run pricing decisions. The first concerns any possible reaction of regular customers if a special order is sold below the market price. Discounting, if excessive, can cause customer dissatisfaction and should be considered in short-run pricing decisions. Another consideration is that the customer may insist that future orders be sold at the discount price. If this situation develops, in the long run the firm will not be recovering its full cost on the sale of products.

When a firm consistently operates below its stated capacity, then this should be taken into consideration in determining the full cost of the output. When this situation is encountered, questions concerning the continued operation of the plant should be considered. However, the analysis presented in this chapter has a short-run perspective. If the problems begin to assume long-run characteristics, then the short-run analysis is no longer appropriate.

☐ SUMMARY

In this chapter, a set of nonroutine decisions was considered. Initially, a general model was described for making decisions. The key to the model was associating relevant revenue and cost data with the alternative solutions to permit the quantitative evaluation of each alternative. Another stage of the decision model is the consideration of qualitative factors before a final decision is made.

Throughout the chapter, the importance of segregating costs into their fixed and variable components was demonstrated. This generally was the initial step in solving all of the problems. Each problem has certain qualitative factors that should be considered by management personnel before making a decision. These factors, although not quantifiable, are important and must be considered in order to completely analyze the problem.

KEY TERMS

Alternative solutions   Quantitative factors
Differential-cost analysis   Relevant costs
Make-or-buy decision   Relevant revenue
Qualitative factors

REVIEW PROBLEM

Based on the departmental income statement prepared by the new accountant, the president of ABC Corporation is considering eliminating Department A.

Department	A	B	C	Total
Sales	$20,000	$40,000	$40,000	$100,000
Variable costs	$17,000	$23,000	$30,000	$ 70,000
Fixed costs*	4,000	8,000	8,000	20,000
Total costs	$21,000	$31,000	$38,000	$ 90,000
Operating profit (loss)	($ 1,000)	$ 9,000	$ 2,000	$ 10,000

*Allocation based on sales

Required ☐ Prepare a report for the president to assist her in making the decison concerning Department A.

Solution ☐

Departmental Contribution to Income
with Department A

Department	A	B	C	Total
Sales	$20,000	$40,000	$40,000	$100,000
Variable costs	17,000	23,000	30,000	70,000
Contribution to income	$ 3,000	$17,000	$10,000	$ 30,000
Less fixed costs				20,000
Operating profit				$ 10,000

Departmental Contribution to Income
without Department A

Department	B	C	Total
Sales	$40,000	$40,000	$ 80,000
Variable costs	23,000	30,000	53,000
Contribution to income	$17,000	$10,000	$ 27,000
Less fixed costs			20,000
Operating profit			$ 7,000

Conclusion ☐ Firm is better off by $3,000 by retaining Department A.

QUESTIONS

Q13-1. Identify some of the qualitative factors that are considered when deciding whether to add or drop a product.

Q13-2. Identify some of the qualitative factors that are considered when deciding whether to add or drop a department.

Q13-3. Identify some of the potential qualitative factors involved in a make-or-buy decision.

Q13-4. Why should the Robinson-Patman Act be considered when making a short-run pricing decision?

P13-1. The management of the Southwest Company is currently contemplating the elimination of one of its products, product D, because this product is now showing a loss. An annual income statement follows: *Dropping a Product*

SOUTHWEST COMPANY
Income Statement
for Year Ended August 1, 19XX
(in thousands)

Product	S	D	F	Total
Sales	$2,200	$1,400	$1,800	$5,400
Cost of sales	1,400	800	1,080	3,280
Gross margin	$ 800	$ 600	$ 720	$2,120
Direct fixed and variable costs	$ 630	$ 525	$ 520	$1,675
Allocated fixed costs	90	80	105	275
Total fixed costs	$ 720	$ 605	$ 625	$1,950
Operating profit	$ 80	$ (5)	$ 95	$ 170

Required □ Should the Southwest Company management team stop sales of product D? Support your answer with appropriate schedules. How would the net income of the company be affected by the decision?

P13-2. The Steele Corporation is now considering eliminating one of its existing products, product C, because decreased sales have resulted in a loss for product C. The following information is available for any typical operating year: *Dropping a Product*

	A	B	C
Units produced and sold	1,000	1,500	1,000
Sales price per unit	$2.00	$4.00	$2.10
Cost of goods sold:			
Material per unit	.80	2.00	1.05
Labor per unit	.30	.75	.80
Factory overhead per unit	.35	.45	.35
Selling and administrative expenses per unit	.15	.30	.20

The following information is also available:

1. If product C were eliminated, the sales of products A and B would remain the same.

2. Variable Factory Overhead is charged as follows: product A, $.25 per unit; product B, $.35 per unit; product C, $.20 per unit.

3. Variable Selling and Administrative Expenses are charged as follows: product A, $.10 per unit; product B, $.20 per unit; product C, $.15 per unit.

Required □ Prepare a schedule to help the Steele Corporation management staff decide on whether or not to eliminate product C. Give your choice and reasons for this choice.

Dropping a Product

P13-3.   Willie's Western Wear is considering dropping its line of boots because it is now showing a loss. Willie's last accountant raised the issue and submitted the following operating statement, which is typical for any year's operations:

	Shirts	Hats	Boots	Total
Revenue from sales	$110,000	$60,000	$35,000	$205,000
Cost of sales				
Raw material	$ 15,000	$22,000	$13,000	$ 50,000
Direct labor	27,000	10,000	10,000	47,000
Indirect overhead	13,000	8,500	7,000	28,500
	$ 55,000	$40,500	$30,000	$125,500
Gross margin on sales	$ 55,000	$19,500	$ 5,000	$ 79,500
Selling and administrative				
expenses	30,000	9,700	8,000	47,700
Operating profit (loss)	$ 25,000	$ 9,800	($ 3,000)	$ 31,800

Owing to unavoidable circumstances, the company's previous accountant is no longer employed by the firm. The management team would now like you to advise them on the issue brought to light. You examine the costs and conclude the following:

1. Variable costs include raw material, direct labor, variable overhead as follows: shirts, $6,000; hats, $4,250; boots, $3,500; and variable selling and administrative expenses as follows: shirts, $16,000; hats, $5,000; boots, $6,000.

2. Nonvariable costs include $14,750 overhead and $20,700 selling and administrative expenses. These costs have been allocated to the product lines.

Required □ Revise the operating statement so that it provides better information for the Willie management team to make a decision on the continuance or elimination of its line of western boots. Give your advice on the decision.

Dropping a Department

P13-4.   Active Sporting Goods Company is a large sporting goods manufacturer. Profitability has gone down in the past few years, and after a bitter internal struggle, Robert McIntyre has been appointed the new CEO. McIntyre's opinion is that profitability can be increased by discontinuing the Distribution department and hiring a trucking firm to transport the company's products to retail outlets. You have been given the task of determining if he is correct. The following information (given in thousands) is available for the preceding fiscal year:

	Manufacturing	Packaging	Distribution	Total
Salaries and wages	$4,000	$ 500	$1,950	$6,450
Material	2,000	750	—	2,750
Office supplies	500	350	350	1,200
Occupancy costs	420	300	300	1,020
General and administrative				
expense	650	310	450	1,410
Depreciation	200	75	90	365
Total	$7,770	$2,285	$3,140	$13,195

Additional information:

1. After a detailed review of the personnel, management decides to transfer the distribution supervisor at an annual cost of $35,000, an assistant distribution supervisor at an annual cost of $25,000, and six laborers at an average cost of $15,000 to the Packaging department to prepare goods for shipment.

2. Owing to more stringent requirements by trucking companies, an additional $100,000 will have to be expended for packaging materials.

3. The space for the Distribution department will be required by the Packaging department for storage of goods prior to shipment.

4. Office supplies for the Packaging department are expected to increase by $50,000.

5. Insurance costs included in General and Administrative Expenses are expected to decline by $50,000. Administrative costs are expected to increase, owing to the addition of three staff members in Accounts Payable at an annual rate of $12,000 per employee and two people in the Payroll department at annual salaries of $15,000 each. In addition, management will need to add four clerical positions at an annual rate of $10,000 each.

6. Equipment of the Distribution department, with an outstanding lien of $1,000,000 and a book value of 4,000,000, can be sold with no gain or loss. These funds in excess of termination pay will be invested in marketable securities at a yield of 10 percent.

7. A trucking company has offered to provide shipping for $2.5 million annually.

Required □ Prepare a statement setting forth in comparative form the costs of the Packaging department under the present arrangement and under the proposed change in operations. Determine the net savings or cost of accepting the proposal.

P13-5. The Stone Corporation requires 100 rock crushers to use in its gravel production. An outside vendor has offered a price of $4,000 per crusher. Costs to manufacture the crushers by Stone Corporation are shown. If the Stone Corporation does not manufacture the rock crushers, it can manufacture gravel grinders. The manufacture of gravel grinders would produce $6,000 of additional contribution margin.

Make-or-Buy Decision

Cost to Manufacture 100 Rock Crushers

Direct material	$130,000
Direct labor	150,000
Variable overhead	72,000
Fixed overhead*	120,000

*$70,000 allocated and $50,000 direct.

Required □ Would you advise the Stone Corporation to manufacture or to buy rock crushers?

Make-or-Buy **P13-6.** The Billings Company produces three products from three different ma-
Decision   terial inputs. A component on the production line is due for replacement.
                     The machine can be produced in-house or purchased from another firm
                     for $1,010,000. The following is the income statement for last year:

Sales	$6,210,000
Cost of goods sold	5,047,500
Selling and administrative expense	270,000
Operating profit	892,500

Additional information:

1. Plant capacity is 162,500 machine hours.

2. The material inputs (X, Y, and Z) for products A, B, and C are as follows:

Product	Input (in units)		
	X	Y	Z
A	7	2	5
B	4	6	3
C	5	3	2

3. Variable overhead is based on machine hours used at $12 per hour.
   Machine hours used for product A are 3.75 hours; for product B, 5
   hours; and for product C, 1.875 hours.

4. Costs for material inputs are as follows:

Input	Inventory cost	Replacement cost
X	5	6
Y	7	7
Z	3	5

5. Present material inventories are input X, 2,000 parts; input Y, 3,000
   parts; and input Z, 2,000 units.

6. Part Y is a high-technology part and has become obsolete for most
   uses. However, it is acceptable for the new machine. Beginning this
   year, part Y will be replaced by a new part that will cost $7 per unit.
   The only alternative use for part Y will be to sell it for scrap at $1
   per unit.

7. The requirements for the new machine in terms of materials are

Part X	2,000 units
Part Y	2,000 units
Part Z	1,000 units

   In addition, Billings Company will need to purchase materials totaling $150,000 to produce the machine.

8. Sales for last year were product A, 10,000 units; product B, 15,000
   units; and product C, 5,000 units.

9. Fixed production costs of $450,000 are allocated based on units pro-
   duced.

10. Direct-labor hours for product A are 3 hours; for product B, 4 hours; and for product C, 2.5 hours.

11. Selling and administrative expenses, fixed and variable, are allocated based on units sold. Fixed selling and administrative expenses are $150,000.

12. The selling price for product A is $186; for product B, $248; and for product C, $126.

13. If Billings builds the machine, it will use 30 percent of the machine-hours capacity. If building the machine and producing the three existing products exceeds total capacity, production of the product with the lowest contribution margin would be reduced.

14. Constructing the machine will require 10,000 direct-labor hours.

15. Billings expects unit sales and contribution margins to remain constant throughout the year.

Required □ Determine if Billings Company should purchase the new machine or produce it in-house.

P13-7. Rubert, Inc., is a manufacturer of generators. The company produces a light-weight, gasoline-driven generator with a selling price of $340 and a heavy-duty diesel model sold at $560. Unit sales for the current year are 15,000 units of the diesel model and 13,500 units of the gasoline model. The plant is currently operating at 90 percent of machine-hours capacity. The current income statement for the firm is given below.

Short-Run Pricing Decision

Sales		$12,990,000
Cost of goods sold		
Materials	$2,377,500	
Direct labor	4,215,000	
Overhead	4,747,500	11,340,000
Gross profit		$ 1,650,000
Selling and administrative expenses		313,500
Operating income		$ 1,336,500

Additional information:

1. Each diesel generator requires 15 machine hours, and each gasoline generator requires 10 machine hours. Variable overhead is assigned based on machine hours.

2. Twenty hours of direct labor are used to produce a diesel generator, and 9 hours are used in producing a gasoline generator. The firm's maximum direct-labor hours are 430,000 per year.

3. Managers of Rubert, Inc., think that they can obtain as much of the raw materials as needed. The diesel generator requires $100 per unit in material costs.

4. Total fixed costs are $570,000. Of this total, 25 percent is selling and administrative expense, and the remainder is manufacturing overhead.

Required □ (Solve each situation independently.)

1. Anders Company has offered to purchase 500 gasoline generators at a price of $280 each. Rubert would not incur any selling and administrative expenses for this purchase but would have to pay to ship the goods. The total cost of shipping would be $750. Should the company accept the offer from Anders?

2. Smith Company needs to purchase 1,000 diesel generators and will only purchase them from one source. Should Rubert, Inc., agree to provide the generators if the purchase price is $560 and they must either provide 1,000 or none?

Short-Run Pricing Decision

P13-8. You have been asked to advise Greengro Company on whether or not to accept a special order for Greengro's sole product, supersize planting containers. Greengro can produce enough containers to fill the special order without disrupting regular sales. The order is for 100 containers at $34 each. The buyer will pick up the containers at Greengro's plant.

Upon analyzing Greengro's production, you collect the following information about supersize planting containers:

1. It takes 4 pounds of material to produce each supersize planting container. The material costs $6 per pound.

2. Direct-labor costs for each container amount to $8.

3. Fixed indirect overhead costs are $3,000 at a normal volume of 1,000 units.

4. Variable indirect overhead costs total $.75 per unit.

5. Shipping expenses for each container are $1.30.

6. Greengro usually sells supersize planting containers for $37.75 each.

Required □ Should Greengro accept the special order? Support your answer.

Short-Run Pricing Decision

P13-9. The Scruffy Company manufactures heavy-duty razors at a unit selling price of $25. Each razor requires two hours of direct labor, and the company has the capacity to produce 100,000 razors. At present, production of razors is only 90 percent of capacity. The remaining capacity is used to produce hot-lather machines, which require five hours of direct labor. Hot-lather machines sell at a unit price of $40. Relevant costs for both razors and hot-lather machines are

	Razors	Lather machines
Selling price	$25	$40
Variable costs		
Materials	$ 9	$10
Labor	8	20
Variable overhead	2	4
Variable selling and administrative	1	2
Unit contribution margin	$ 5	$ 4

The fixed overhead is $70,000, and the fixed selling and administrative expense is $20,000.

The company has just received an offer for a special order of 10,000 razors at a price of $21.50 each.

Required ☐ Advise the Scruffy Company management team on whether or not to accept the order. Support your answer using unit contribution margins.

P13-10. The president of the Scott Company has called you in to help determine whether or not to suspend operations of the company. Due to a decrease in the demand for the company's product, it is now operating at a loss. Expectations are that sales will drop even more in the future. An operating statement for the present production level of 6,000 units per month is

Plant Shut-Down Decision

Revenue from sales—$4 per unit		$24,000
Less:		
Variable costs—$2.50 per unit	$15,000	
Nonvariable costs	10,000	25,000
Net loss		$(1,000)

The management team has also given you the following information about the nonvariable costs:

1. The plant manager will not be let go if the company shuts down. Her salary is $1,225 per month.

2. A security guard will also be retained with a salary of $825 per month.

3. Maintenance expense on the buildings and equipment comes to $450 per month.

4. Insurance premiums of $150 are due each month.

Required ☐ Would you advise Scott Company to shut down or continue operating under present conditions? Support your answer. If your answer is to advise Scott Company to continue operations, at what level of production should operations be suspended?

P13-11. The Anchor Company manufactures several different styles of jewelry cases. Management estimates that during the third quarter of 19X6 the company will be operating at 80 percent of normal capacity. Because the company desires a higher utilization of plant capacity, the company will consider a special order.

Short-Run Pricing Decision

Anchor has received special-order inquiries from two companies. The first order is from JCP, Inc., a company that would like to market jewelry cases similar to one of Anchor's cases. The JCP jewelry case would be marketed under JCP's own label. JCP, Inc., has offered Anchor $5.75 per jewelry case for 20,000 cases to be shipped by October 1, 19X6. The cost data for the Anchor jewelry case, which would be similar to the specifications of the JCP special order, are as follows:

Regular selling price per unit	$9.00
Costs per unit	
Raw materials	$2.50
Direct labor .5 hr @ $6	3.00
Overhead .25 machine hr @ $4	1.00
Total costs	$6.50

According to the specifications provided by JCP, Inc., the special-order case requires less expensive raw materials. Consequently, the raw materials will only cost $2.25 per case. The Management staff has estimated that the remaining costs, labor time, and machine time will be the same as those for the Anchor jewelry case.

The second special order was submitted by the Krage Co. for 7,500 jewelry cases at $7.50 per case. These jewelry cases, as with the JCP cases, would be marketed under the Krage label and would have to be shipped by October 1, 19X6. However, the Krage jewelry case is different from any jewelry case in the Anchor line. The estimated per-unit costs of this case are as follows:

Raw materials	$3.25
Direct labor .5 hr @ $6	3.00
Overhead .5 machine hr @ $4	2.00
Total costs	$8.25

In addition, Anchor will incur $1,500 in additional set-up costs and will have to purchase a $2,500 special device to manufacture these cases; this device will be discarded once the special order is completed.

The Anchor manufacturing capabilities are limited to the total machine hours available. The plant capacity under normal operations is 90,000 machine hours per year, or 7,500 machine hours per month. The budgeted fixed overhead for 19X6 amounts to $216,000. All manufacturing overhead costs are applied to production on the basis of machine hours at $4 per hour.

Anchor will have the entire third quarter to work on the special orders. The management team does not expect any repeat sales to be generated from either special order. Company practice precludes Anchor from subcontracting any portion of an order when special orders are not expected to generate repeat sales.

Required □ Should Anchor Company accept either special order? Justify your answer, and show your calculations.

(CMA)

Short-Run Pricing Decision **P13-12.** National Industries is a diversified corporation with separate and distinct operating divisions. Each division's performance is evaluated on the basis of total dollar profits and return on division investment.

The WindAir division manufactures and sells air conditioner units. The budgeted income statement for the coming year, which is based upon a sales volume of 15,000 units, is

WINDAIR DIVISION
Budgeted Income Statement
for the 19X9–X0 Fiscal Year

	Per unit	Total (in thousands)
Sales revenue	$400	$6,000
Manufacturing costs		
Compressor	$ 70	$1,050
Other raw materials	37	555
Direct labor	30	450

Variable overhead	45	675
Fixed overhead	32	480
Total manufacturing costs	$214	$3,210
Gross margin	$186	$2,790
Operating expenses		
Variable selling	$ 18	$ 270
Fixed selling	19	285
Fixed administrative	38	570
Total operating expenses	$ 75	$1,125
Net income before taxes	$111	$1,665

The WindAir divisional manager believes sales can be increased if the unit selling price of the air conditioners is reduced. A market research study conducted by an independent firm at the request of the manager indicates that a 5 percent reduction in the selling price ($20) would increase sales volume 16 percent, or 2,400 units. WindAir has sufficient production capacity to manage this increased volume with no increase in fixed costs.

At the present time, WindAir purchases its compressors from an outside supplier at a cost of $70 per compressor. The divisional manager of WindAir has approached the manager of the Compressor division regarding the sale of a compressor unit to WindAir. The Compressor division currently manufactures and sells a unit exclusively to outside firms. This unit is similar to the one used by WindAir. The specifications of the WindAir compressor are slightly different, and consequently the raw materials cost of the Compressor division would be reduced by $1.50 per unit. In addition, the Compressor division would not incur any variable selling costs in the units sold to WindAir. The manager of WindAir wants all of the compressors it uses to come from one supplier and has offered to pay $50 for each compressor unit.

The Compressor division has the capacity to produce 75,000 units. The Compressor division budgeted income statement for the coming year is shown below. It is based upon a sales volume of 64,000 units without considering WindAir's proposal.

COMPRESSOR DIVISION
Budgeted Income Statement
for the 19X9–X0 Fiscal Year

	Per unit	Total (in thousands)
Sales revenue	$100	$6,400
Manufacturing costs		
Raw materials	$ 12	$ 768
Direct labor	8	512
Variable overhead	10	640
Fixed overhead	11	704
Total manufacturing costs	$ 41	$2,624
Gross margin	$ 59	$3,776
Operating expenses		
Variable selling	$ 6	$ 384
Fixed selling	4	256
Fixed administrative	7	448
Total operating expenses	$ 17	$1,088
Net income before taxes	$ 42	$2,688

Required □

1. Should the WindAir division institute the 5 percent price reduction on its air conditioner units even if it cannot acquire the compressors internally for $50 each? Support your conclusion with appropriate calculations.

2. Without prejudice to your answer to requirement 1, assume WindAir needs 17,400 units. Should the Compressor division be willing to supply the compressor units for $50 each? Support your conclusions with appropriate calculations.

3. Without prejudice to your answer to requirement 1, assume WindAir needs 17,400 units. Would it be in the best interest of National Industries for the Compressor division to supply the compressor units at $50 each to the WindAir division? Support your conclusions with appropriate calculations.

(CMA)

*Short-Run
Pricing Decision* **P13-13.** Framar, Inc., manufactures automation machinery according to customer specifications. The company is relatively new and has grown each year. Framar, Inc., operated at about 75 percent of practical capacity during the 19X7–X8 fiscal year. The operating results for the most recent fiscal year are

FRAMAR, INC.
Income Statement
for the Year Ended September 30, 19X8
(in thousands)

Sales		$25,000
Less: sales commissions		2,500
Net sales		$22,500
Expenses		
Direct material		$ 6,000
Direct labor		7,500
Manufacturing overhead—variable		
Supplies	$ 625	
Indirect labor	1,500	
Power	125	2,250
Manufacturing overhead—fixed		
Supervision	$ 500	
Depreciation	1,000	1,500
Corporate administration		750
Total expenses		$18,000
Net income before taxes		$ 4,500
Income taxes (40 percent)		1,800
Net income		$ 2,700

Most of the management personnel had worked for firms in this type of business before joining Framar, Inc., but none of the top management had been responsible for overall corporate operations or for final decisions on prices. Nevertheless, the company has been successful.

The top-management staff of Framar, Inc., wants to have a more organized and formal pricing system to prepare quotes for potential customers. Therefore, it has developed the pricing formula presented. The formula is based upon the company's operating results achieved during the 19X7–X8 fiscal year. The relationships used in the formula are expected to continue during the 19X8–X9 year. The company expects to operate at 75 percent of practical capacity during the current 19X8–X9 fiscal year.

APA, Inc., has asked Framar, Inc., to submit a bid on some custom-designed machinery. Framar, Inc., used the new formula to develop a price and submitted a bid of $165,000 to APA, Inc. The calculations to arrive at the bid price are given next to the pricing formula.

Pricing Formula

Details of Formula		APA, Inc., Bid Calculations
Estimated direct-material cost	$XX	$ 29,200
Estimated direct-labor cost	XX	56,000
Estimated manufacturing overhead calculated at 50 percent of direct labor	XX	28,000
Estimated corporate overhead calculated at 10 percent of direct labor	XX	5,600
Estimated total costs excluding sales commissions	$XX	$118,800
Add 25 percent for profits and taxes	XX	29,700
Suggested price (with profits) before sales commissions	$XX	$148,500
Suggested total price equals suggested price divided by .9 to adjust for 10 percent sales commissions	$XX	$165,000

Required □

1. Calculate the impact the order from APA, Inc., would have on the net income after taxes of Framar, Inc., if its bid of $165,000 were accepted by APA, Inc.

2. Assume APA, Inc., has rejected the Framar, Inc., price but has stated it is willing to pay $127,000 for the machinery. Should Framar, Inc., manufacture the machinery for the counteroffer of $127,000? Explain your answer.

3. Calculate the lowest price Framar, Inc., can quote on this machinery without reducing its net income after taxes if it should manufacture the machinery.

4. Explain how the profit performance in 19X8–X9 would be affected if Framar, Inc., accepted all of its work at prices similar to the $127,000 counteroffer of APA, Inc., described in requirement 2?

(CMA)

P13-14. Stac Industries is a multi-product company with several manufacturing plants. The Clinton plant manufactures and distributes two household cleaning and polishing compounds—regular and heavy duty—under the

Short-Run Pricing Decision

Cleen-Brite label. The forecasted operating results for the first six months of 19X0—when 100,000 cases of each compound are expected to be manufactured and sold—are presented in the following statement:

CLEEN-BRITE COMPOUNDS—CLINTON PLANT
Forecasted Results of Operations
for the Six-Month Period Ending June 30, 19X0
(in thousands)

	Regular	Heavy duty	Total
Sales	$2,000	$3,000	$5,000
Cost of sales	1,600	1,900	3,500
Gross profit	400	1,100	1,500
Selling and administrative expenses			
Variable	$ 400	$ 700	$1,100
Fixed*	240	360	600
Total selling and administrative expenses	$ 640	$1,060	$1,700
Income (loss) before taxes	$ (240)	$ 40	$ (200)

*On the internal reports, the fixed selling and administrative expenses are allocated between the two products on the basis of dollar-sales volume.

The regular compound sold for $20 a case, and the heavy duty sold for $30 a case during the first six months of 19X0. The manufacturing costs by case of product are presented in the schedule below. Each product is manufactured on a separate production line. Annual normal manufacturing capacity is 200,000 cases of each product. However, the plant is capable of producing 250,000 cases of regular compound and 350,000 cases of heavy-duty compound annually.

	Cost per case	
	Regular	Heavy duty
Raw materials	$ 7	$ 8
Direct labor	4	4
Variable manufacturing overhead	1	2
Fixed manufacturing overhead	4	5
Total manufacturing overhead	$16	$19
Variable selling and administrative costs	$ 4	$ 7

*Depreciation charges are 50 percent of the fixed manufacturing overhead of each line.

The following schedule reflects the consensus of the top-management team regarding the price/volume alternatives for the Cleen-Brite products for the last six months of 19X0. These are essentially the same alternatives management had during the first six months of 19X0.

Regular compound		Heavy-duty compound	
Alternative prices (per case)	Sales volume (in cases)	Alternative prices (per case)	Sales volume (in cases)
$18	120,000	$25	175,000
20	100,000	27	140,000
21	90,000	30	100,000
22	80,000	32	55,000
23	50,000	35	35,000

Top-management personnel believe the loss for the first six months reflects a tight profit margin caused by intense competition. They also believe that many companies will be forced out of this market by next year and profits should improve.

Required ☐

1. What unit selling price should Stac Industries select for each of the Cleen-Brite compounds (regular and heavy duty) for the remaining six months of 19X0? Support your selection with appropriate calculations.

2. Without prejudice to your answer to requirement 1, assume the optimum price/volume alternatives for the last six months were a selling price of $23 and volume level of 50,000 cases for the regular compound and a selling price of $35 and volume of 35,000 cases for the heavy-duty compound.

    a. Should Stac Industries consider closing down its operations until 19X1 in order to minimize its losses? Support your answer with appropriate calculations.
    b. Identify and discuss the qualitative factors that should be considered in deciding whether the Clinton plant should be closed down during the last six months of 19X0.

(CMA)

P13-15. Helene's, a high-fashion women's dress manufacturer, is planning to market a new cocktail dress for the coming season. Helene's supplies retailers in the east and mid-Atlantic states. *Adding a Product*

Four yards of material are required to lay out the dress pattern. Some material remains after cutting. It can be sold as remnants.

The leftover material could also be used to manufacture a matching cape and handbag. However, if the leftover material is to be used for the cape and handbag, more care will be required in the cutting. This will increase the cutting costs.

The company expected to sell 1,250 dresses if no matching cape or handbag were available. Helene's market research reveals that dress sales will be 20 percent higher if a matching cape and handbag are available. The market research indicates that the cape and/or handbag will not be sold individually but only as accessories with the dress. The various combinations of dresses, capes, and handbags that are expected to be sold by retailers are

	Percent of total
Complete sets of dress, cape, and handbag	70%
Dress and cape	6
Dress and handbag	15
Dress only	9
Total	100%

The material used in the dress costs $12.50 a yard, or $50.00 for each dress. The cost of cutting the dress if the cape and handbag are not manufactured is estimated at $20.00 a dress, and the resulting remnants can be sold for $5.00 for each dress cut out. If the cape and handbag are to be manufactured, the cutting costs will be increased by $9.00 per dress.

There will be no saleable remnants if the capes and handbags are manufactured in the quantities estimated.

The selling prices and the costs to complete the three items once they are cut are

	Selling price per unit	Unit cost to complete (excludes cost of material and cutting operation)
Dress	$200.00	$80.00
Cape	27.50	19.50
Handbag	9.50	6.50

Required □

1. Calculate Helene's incremental profit or loss from manufacturing the capes and handbags in conjunction with the dresses.

2. Identify any nonquantitative factors that could influence the Helene's management team in its decision to manufacture the capes and handbags that match the dress.

(CMA)

Short-Run Pricing Decision **P13-16.** The Ashley Co. manufactures and sells a household product marketed through direct mail and advertisements in home improvement and gardening magazines. Although similar products are available in hardware and department stores, none is as effective as the Ashley model.

The company uses a standard-cost system in its manufacturing accounting. The standards have not undergone a thorough review in the past eighteen months. The general manager has seen no need for such a review because:

■ The material quality and unit costs were fixed by a three-year purchase commitment signed in July 19X9.

■ A three-year labor contract had been signed in July 19X9.

■ There have been no significant variations from standard costs for the past three quarters.

The standard cost for the product, as established in July 19X9, is presented below:

Material	.75 lb @ $1 per lb	$ .75
Direct labor	.3 hr @ $4 per hr	1.20
Overhead	.3 hr @ $7 per hr	2.10
Standard manufacturing cost per unit		$4.05

The standard for overhead costs was developed from the following budgeted costs, based upon an activity level of 1 million units (300,000 direct-labor hours).

Variable manufacturing overhead	$ 600,000
Fixed manufacturing overhead	1,500,000
Total manufacturing overhead	$2,100,000

The earnings statement and the factory costs for the first quarter are presented. The first quarter results indicate that Ashley probably will achieve its sales goal of 1.2 million units for the current year. A total of 320,000 units were manufactured during the first quarter in order to increase inventory levels needed to support the growing sales volume.

ASHLEY CO.
First Quarter Earnings
Period Ended March 31, 19X1

Sales (300,000 units)		$2,700,000
Cost of goods sold		
Standard cost of goods	$1,215,000	
Variation from standard costs	12,000	1,227,000
Gross profit		$1,473,000
Operating expenses		
Selling		
Advertising	$ 200,000	
Mailing list costs	175,000	
Postage	225,000	
Salaries	60,000	
Administrative		
Salaries	120,000	
Office rent	45,000	
Total operating expenses		$ 825,000
Income before taxes		$ 648,000
Income taxes (45 percent)		291,600
Net income		$ 356,400

ASHLEY CO.
Factory Costs
for the Quarter Ended March 31, 19X1

Materials	$ 266,000
Direct labor	452,000
Variable manufacturing overhead	211,000
Fixed manufacturing overhead	379,000
Total manufacturing costs	$1,308,000
Less: Standard cost of goods manufactured	1,296,000
Unfavorable variation from standard cost	$ 12,000

ACTION Hardware, a national chain, recently asked Ashley to manufacture and sell a slightly modified version of the product that ACTION would distribute through its stores.

ACTION has offered to buy a minimum quantity of 200,000 units each year over the next three years and has offered to pay $4.10 for each unit, f.o.b. shipping point.

The Ashley management team is interested in the proposal because it represents a new market. The company has adequate capacity to meet the production requirements. However, in addition to the possible financial results of taking the order, Ashley must consider carefully the other consequences of this departure from its normal practices. The president asked an assistant to the general manager to make an estimate of the financial aspects of the proposal for the first twelve months.

The assistant recommended that the order not be accepted and presented the following analysis to support the recommendation.

SALES PROPOSAL OF ACTION HARDWARE
First Twelve Months Results

Proposed sales	200,000 @ $4.10	$820,000
Estimated costs and expenses		
Manufacturing	200,000 @ $4.05	$810,000
Sales salaries		10,000
Administrative salaries		20,000
Total estimated costs		$840,000
Net loss		$ (20,000)

Note: None of the regular selling costs are included because this is a new market. However, a 16.6 percent increase in sales and administrative salaries has been incorporated because sales volume will increase by that amount.

Required □

1. Review the financial analysis of the ACTION Hardware proposal prepared by the general manager's assistant.

   a. Criticize the first-year financial analysis.
   b. Using only the data given, present a more suitable analysis for the first year of the order.

2. Identify the additional financial data that the Ashley Co. managers would need to prepare a more comprehensive financial analysis of the ACTION proposal for the three-year period.

3. Discuss the nonfinancial issues the Ashley management team should address in considering the ACTION proposal.

(CMA)

Dropping a Department **P13-17.** Ace Publishing Company is in the business of publishing and printing guide books and directories. The board of directors has engaged you to make a cost study to determine whether the company is economically justified in continuing to print, as well as publish, its books and directories. You obtain the following information from the company cost-accounting records for the preceding fiscal year:

	Departments			
	Publishing	Printing	Shipping	Total
Salaries and wages	$275,000	$150,000	$25,000	$ 450,000
Telephone and telegraph	12,000	3,700	300	16,000
Materials and supplies	50,000	250,000	10,000	310,000
Occupancy costs	75,000	80,000	10,000	165,000
General and administrative	40,000	30,000	4,000	74,000
Depreciation	5,000	40,000	5,000	50,000
	$457,000	$553,700	$54,300	$1,065,000

Additional data:

1. A review of personnel requirements indicates that, if printing is discontinued, the Publishing department will need one additional clerk

at $4,000 per year to handle correspondence with the printer. Two layout staff members and a proofreader will be required at an aggregate annual cost of $17,000; other personnel in the Printing department can be released. One mailing clerk, at $3,000, will be retained; others in the Shipping department can be released. Employees whose employment was being terminated would immediately receive, on the average, three months' termination pay. The termination pay would be amortized over a five-year period.

2. Long-distance telephone and telegraph charges are identified and distributed to the responsible department. The remainder of the telephone bill, representing basic service at a cost of $4,000, was allocated in the ratio of 10 to Publishing, 5 to Printing, and 1 to Shipping. The discontinuance of printing is not expected to have a material effect on the basic service cost.

3. Shipping supplies consist of cartons, envelopes, and stamps. It is estimated that the cost of envelopes and stamps for mailing material to an outside printer would be $5,000 per year.

4. If printing is discontinued, the company would retain its present building, but would sublet a portion of the space at an annual rental of $50,000. Taxes, insurance, heat, light, and other occupancy costs would not be significantly affected.

5. One cost clerk would not be required ($5,000 per year) if printing is discontinued. Other general and administrative personnel would be retained.

6. Included in administrative expenses is interest expense on a 5 percent mortgage loan of $500,000.

7. Printing and Shipping machinery and equipment having a net book value of $300,000 can be sold without gain or loss. These funds in excess of termination pay would be invested in marketable securities earning 5 percent.

8. The company has received a proposal for a five-year contract from an outside printer under which the volume of work done last year would be printed at a cost of $550,000 per year.

9. Assume continued volume and prices at last year's level.

Required □ Prepare a statement setting forth in comparative form the costs of operating of the Printing and Shipping departments under the present arrangement and under an arrangement in which inside printing is discontinued. Summarize the net savings or extra cost in case printing is discontinued.

(CPA)

P13-18. The Southwest Company, your audit client, requested your assistance in deciding whether the company should continue to manufacture or should purchase mansers, a component of its major product. The annual requirement for mansers is 10,000 units, and the part is available from an ouside supplier in any quantity at $5 per unit.

Make-or-Buy Decision

The following information is available:

1. The Machining department starts and substantially completes mansers, and minor finishing is completed by the use of direct labor in the Finishing department. The Assembly department places mansers in the finished product.

2. Machinery used to produce mansers could be sold for its book value of $15,000 and the proceeds invested at 6 percent per year if the mansers were purchased. Property taxes and insurance would decrease $300 per year if the machinery were sold. The machinery has a remaining life of ten years with no estimated salvage value.

3. The Machining department is about 25 percent devoted to the production of mansers, but labor and some other costs for mansers in this department could be reduced without affecting other operations. The costs of the Finishing department include direct labor totaling $800 devoted to mansers. If mansers were not manufactured, one-half of the resulting available direct labor would be used as indirect labor and the remaining one-half would result in paid idle time of employees.

4. In 19X7 when 10,000 mansers were produced, pertinent Machining department costs were

	Total costs	Costs allocated to mansers
Materials	$95,000	$24,200
Direct labor	39,400	12,200
Indirect labor	20,600	7,800
Heat and light	12,000	3,000
Depreciation	6,000	1,500
Property taxes and insurance	15,000	3,750
Production supplies	4,000	800

5. In addition, the Machining department total costs include $18,300 payroll taxes and other benefits.

6. Overhead allocated on the basis of 200 percent of direct-labor cost was $40,000 for the Finishing department and $20,000 for the Assembly department in 19X7. Overhead in these departments is 25 percent fixed and 75 percent variable.

7. If mansers are purchased, Southwest will incur added costs of $.45 per unit for freight and $3,000 per year for receiving, handling, and inspecting of the product.

Required ☐

1. Prepare a schedule comparing the total annual cost of mansers if the company manufactured them with the annual cost if purchased. (Ignore income taxes.)

2. Without regard to your solution to requirement 1, assume the total annual cost of mansers, if manufactured and if purchased is $60,000. Compute the annual net cash outflow. (Ignore income taxes.)

   a. If mansers are manufactured
   b. If mansers are purchased

3. Southwest's management staff must consider working-capital requirements in deciding whether to manufacture or to purchase mansers. Explain the working-capital requirements that should be considered.

(CPA)

P13-19. Your client, the Ocean Company, manufactures and sells three different products—Ex, Why, and Zee. Projected income statements by product line for the year ended December 31, 19X6, are presented.

Dropping a Product

	Ex	Why	Zee	Total
Unit sales	10,000	500,000	125,000	635,000
Revenues	$925,000	$1,000,000	$575,000	$2,500,000
Variable cost of units sold	285,000	350,000	150,000	785,000
Fixed cost of units sold	304,200	289,000	166,800	760,000
Gross margin	335,800	361,000	258,200	955,000
Variable general and administrative (G and A) expenses	270,000	200,000	80,000	550,000
Fixed G and A expenses	125,800	136,000	78,200	340,000
Income (loss) before tax	$ (60,000)	$ 25,000	$100,000	$ 65,000

Production costs are similar for all three products. The fixed G and A expenses are allocated to products in proportion to revenues. The fixed cost of units sold is allocated to products by various allocation bases, such as square feet for factory rent and machine hours for repairs, etc.

The Ocean management team is concerned about the loss for product Ex and is considering two alternative courses of corrective action.

Alternative A—Ocean would purchase some new machinery for the production of product Ex. This new machinery would involve an immediate cash outlay of $650,000. Management expects that the new machinery would reduce variable production costs so that total variable costs (cost of units sold and G and A expense) for product Ex would be 52 percent of product Ex revenues. The new machinery would increase total fixed costs allocated to product Ex to $480,000 per year. No additional fixed costs would be allocated to product Why or Zee.

Alternative B—Ocean would discontinue the manufacture of product Ex. Selling prices of products Why and Zee would remain constant. Management personnel expect that product Zee production and revenues would increase by 50 percent. Some of the present machinery devoted to product Ex could be sold at scrap value, which equals its removal costs. The removal of this machinery would reduce fixed costs allocated to product Ex by $30,000 per year. The remaining fixed costs allocated to product Ex include $155,000 of rent expense per year. The space previously used for product Ex could be rented to an outside organization for $157,500 per year.

Required ☐ Prepare a schedule analyzing the effect of alternative A and alternative B on projected total company income before tax.

(CPA)

Make-or-Buy
Decision

P13-20. When you had completed your audit of The Scoopa Company, the management staff asked for your assistance in arriving at a decision whether to continue manufacturing a part or to buy it from an outside supplier. The part, which is named Faktron, is a component used in some of the finished products of the company.

From your audit working papers and from further investigation, you develop the following data as being typical of the company operations:

1. The annual requirement for Faktrons is 5,000 units. The lowest quotation from a supplier was $8 per unit.

2. Faktrons have been manufactured in the Precision Machinery department. If Faktrons are purchased from an outside supplier, certain machinery will be sold and the company would realize its book value.

3. Following are the total costs of the Precision Machinery department during the year under audit when 5,000 Faktrons were made:

Materials	$67,500
Direct labor	50,000
Indirect labor	20,000
Light and heat	5,500
Power	3,000
Depreciation	10,000
Property taxes and insurance	8,000
Payroll taxes and other benefits	9,800
Other	5,000

4. The following Precision Machinery department costs apply to the manufacture of Faktrons: material, $17,500; direct labor, $28,000; indirect labor, $6,000; power, $300; other, $500. The sale of equipment used for Faktrons would reduce the following costs by the amounts indicated: depreciation, $2,000; property taxes and insurance, $1,000.

5. The following additional Precision Machinery department costs would be incurred if Faktrons were purchased from an outside supplier: freight, $.50 per unit; indirect labor for receiving, materials handling, inspection, etc., $5,000. The cost of the purchased Faktrons would be considered a Precision Machinery department cost.

Required □

1. Prepare a schedule showing a comparison of the total costs of the Precision Machinery department when

   a. Faktrons are made
   b. Faktrons are bought from an outside supplier

2. Discuss the considerations in addition to the cost factors that you would bring to the attention of the management team in assisting them to arrive at a decision whether to make or buy Faktrons. Include in your discussion the considerations that might be applied to the evaluation of the outside supplier.

(CPA)

P13-21. The Scio Division of Georgetown, Inc., manufactures and sells four related product lines. Each product is produced at one or more of the three manufacturing plants of the division. A product line profitability statement for the year ended December 31, 19X7, that shows a loss for the baseball equipment line is presented. A similar loss is projected for 19X8. *Dropping a Product*

The baseball equipment is manufactured at the Evanston plant. Some football equipment and all miscellaneous sports items also are processed through this plant. A few of the miscellaneous items are manufactured, and the remainder are purchased for resale. The items purchased for resale are recorded as materials in the records. A separate production line is used to produce the products of each product line.

A schedule presents the costs incurred at the Evanston plant in 19X7. Inventories at the end of the year were substantially identical to those at the beginning of the year.

The management of Georgetown, Inc., has requested a profitability study of the baseball equipment line to determine if the line should be discontinued. The Marketing department of the Scio Division and the Accounting department at the plant have developed the following additional data to be used in the study:

1. If the baseball equipment line is discontinued, the company will lose approximately 10 percent of its sales in each of the other lines.

2. The equipment now used in the manufacture of baseball equipment is quite specialized. It has a current salvage value of $105,000 and a remaining useful life of five years. This equipment cannot be used elsewhere in the company.

3. The plant space now occupied by the baseball equipment line could be closed off from the rest of the plant and rented out for $175,000 per year.

4. If the line is discontinued, the supervisor of the baseball equipment line will be released. In keeping with company policy, he would receive severance pay of $5,000.

5. The company has been able to invest excess funds at 10 percent per annum.

Required ☐

1. Should Georgetown, Inc., discontinue the baseball equipment line? Support your answer with appropriate calculations and qualitative arguments.

2. A member of the board of directors of Georgetown, Inc., has inquired whether the information regarding the discontinuance of product lines should be included in the financial statements on a regular monthly basis for all product lines. Draft a memorandum in response to the board member's inquiry. Your memorandum should

    a. State why or why not this information should be included in the regular monthly financial statements distributed to the board
    b. Detail the reasons for your response

Product Line Profitability—19X7
(in thousands)

	Football equipment	Baseball equipment	Hockey equipment	Miscellaneous sports items	Total
Sales	$2,200	$1,000	$1,500	$500	$5,200
Cost of goods sold					
Material	$ 400	$ 175	$ 300	$ 90	$ 965
Labor and variable overhead	800	400	600	60	1,860
Fixed overhead	350	275	100	50	775
Total	$1,550	$ 850	$1,000	$200	$3,600
Gross profit	$ 650	$ 150	$ 500	$300	$1,600
Selling expense					
Variable	$ 440	$ 200	$ 300	$100	$1,040
Fixed	100	50	100	50	300
Corporate administration expenses	48	24	36	12	120
Total	$ 588	$ 274	$ 436	$162	$1,460
Contribution to corporation	$ 62	$ (124)	$ 64	$138	$ 140

Evanston Plant Costs—19X7
(in thousands)

	Football equipment	Baseball equipment	Miscellaneous sports items	Total
Material	$100	$175	$ 90	$ 365
Labor	$100	$200	$ 30	$ 330
Variable overhead				
Supplies	$ 85	$ 60	$ 12	$ 157
Power	50	110	7	167
Other	15	30	11	56
Subtotal	$150	$200	$ 30	$ 380
Fixed overhead				
Supervision[1]	$ 25	$ 30	$ 21	$ 76
Depreciation[2]	40	115	14	169
Plant rentals[3]	35	105	10	150
Other[4]	20	25	5	50
Subtotal	$120	$275	$ 50	$ 445
Total costs	$470	$850	$200	$1,520

1. The supervision costs represent salary and benefit costs of the supervisors in charge of each product line.

2. Depreciation cost for machinery and equipment is charged to the product line on which the machinery is used.

3. The plant is leased. The lease rentals are charged to the product lines on the basis of square-feet occupied.

4. Other fixed overhead costs are the cost of plant administration and are allocated arbitrarily by management decision.

(CMA)

CHAPTER OUTLINE

CAPITAL BUDGETING AND CAPITAL-EXPENDITURE MANAGEMENT

CHAPTER **14**

☐ INTRODUCTION

In the capital-budgeting environment, management personnel are continually faced with a variety of investment decisions. Should we replace the packaging machine with a newer model? Our conveyor belt is down again and we need permission to buy a new one immediately. Can we afford to develop the new product? Should we invest in the new marketing territory? Management staff members face these kinds of decisions frequently, and they need relevant information for making the right investment decisions.

The purpose of this chapter is to acquaint you with capital budgeting and capital-expenditure management. While the emphasis will be on methods used to evaluate project proposals, you should also become familiar with the overall capital-expenditure management process. You will learn that the information needs in capital-expenditure management are somewhat different from those required in short-term planning decisions. The difference comes about because of the emphasis on specific projects rather than on normal responsibility centers, because of the emphasis on cash flows as opposed to revenues and expenses, and because of the emphasis on project life as opposed to accounting periods.

☐ THE MANAGEMENT FRAMEWORK

Although the capital-investment decision represents the most visible aspect of the capital-expenditure decision-making process, the total process is much more pervasive. It calls for comprehensive planning, proposal evaluation, control over selection and implementation of projects, and some type of project evaluation to see if implemented projects are performing as originally projected.

To begin, the meanings of capital budgeting and capital-expenditure management should be clarified. **Capital budgeting** can be defined as the process of determining how best to allocate a company's resources to long-term capital-facility proposals, new products, and various other project proposals. Capital-expenditure management involves the complete process—from the initial conception of investment possibilities to the performance evaluation of completed projects.

The process might be viewed as shown in figure 14.1. The schematic identifies four components in the capital-expenditure management system: (1) project origination, (2) project evaluation, (3) in-process control, and (4) post-audit. There are other ways to view the capital-expenditure management system, but the components identified in figure 14.1 reflect typical activities, though they may not be integrated as shown in the diagram.

Project Origination

The investment needs of a company should first be reflected in strategic planning or as part of the management-control process. If capital expen-

FIGURE 14.1
Model for Capital Expenditure Planning and Control

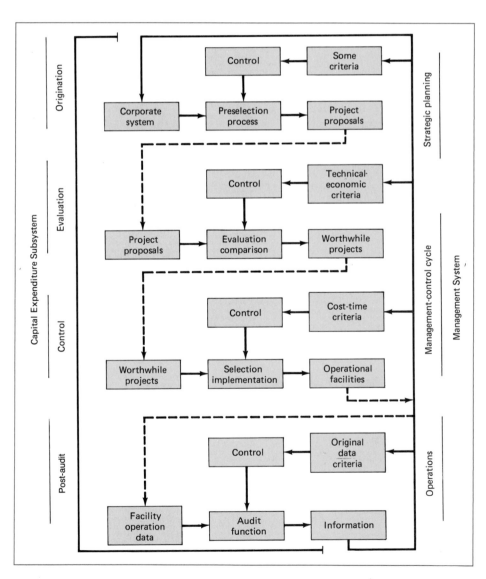

ditures are to be made, shouldn't funds be committed to the most attractive projects? But how does a company go about optimizing the project discovery phase? There is no easy answer to this question. Some companies are heavily involved in research and development for new products and projects. Others make sure that different management groups are kept abreast of emerging technologies and what their competitors are doing. Even employee incentive programs, whereby employees are encouraged to submit suggestions, have been successful in some companies as a means of identifying profitable projects.

Project Evaluation

After worthwhile projects have been discovered, they should be subjected to general and economic evaluation in order to decide which projects to undertake. The general evaluation should include consideration of company objectives along with legal and social concerns. Results of the economic evaluation should give management personnel some measure of the impact of a project on profitability of the company. This is a very important function in capital-expenditure management and will be discussed in detail later in the chapter.

In-Process Control

The determination of project acceptability should not be considered the final step in capital-expenditure management. After economic evaluation, some projects will be rejected for various reasons while others will be accepted and funds committed to make them operational. Once funds have been committed, management should establish control procedures to insure that cost and quality standards are met in acquiring the project and that the project is available within an acceptable time frame. Companies often find that actual costs far exceed original projections or that projects cannot be completed on a timely basis. An effective control system should act as an early warning system for cost and time overruns so that management pesonnel will have an opportunity to make appropriate modifications. For example, assume a project is expected to cost $200,000 with construction time projected to be eight months. Halfway through the project, the management team discovers that the project costs are in excess of $180,000 and that construction time has already exceeded five months. The management staff now needs information on expected costs to complete the project along with required time. With this information, another evaluation should be made to see if the project is to be continued or terminated.

Post-Audit

Post-audits should provide feedback to management on actual performance versus projected performance of projects. As in other aspects of management control, responsibility for estimates and actual performance should be fixed, and project sponsors and line managers should be informed that their ability to make valid projections is to be evaluated along with project performance.

☐ THE IMPORTANCE OF CASH FLOWS

Capital proposals should be evaluated on the basis of their expected total contribution. For this reason, neither accrual accounting nor accounting periods are relevant to the capital-budgeting decision. For example, if a decision is made to invest $100,000 in a capital project, management personnel should be concerned with the time required to recover the investment and the magnitude of expected benefits. While timing is important, the flows are not related to accounting periods. Cash flows rather than income are more important to the analysis.

Before a capital-budgeting decision can be made, information is needed on expected incremental cash flows on an after-tax basis. To illustrate, suppose a professional football team is planning to offer a contract to an outstanding college quarterback. The contract calls for a $500,000 bonus to be paid at the end of the first year with an annual salary of $200,000 per year for five years. In justifying the contract, the manager expects incremental revenues as follows:

Year 1	Year 2	Year 3	Year 4	Year 5
$100,000	$200,000	$400,000	$600,000	$1,000,000

If we can assume a simple tax structure (50 percent with no provision for loss carryovers), the expected net cash flows would be as follows:

	Year 1	Year 2	Year 3	Year 4	Year 5
Cash inflows	$ 100,000	$200,000	$400,000	$600,000	$1,000,000
Cash outflows	700,000	200,000	200,000	200,000	200,000
Before-tax cash flows	$(600,000)	$ 0	$200,000	$400,000	$ 800,000
After-tax cash flows	$(600,000)	0	$100,000	$200,000	$ 400,000

With this information, the management staff can begin to evaluate the attractiveness of the contract based on timing of the cash flows and overall benefit. Cash-flow projections are essential to the capital-budgeting decision. Once again it should be emphasized that cash flows need to be on an incremental and after-tax basis if the information is to be relevant.

Consider the following somewhat more complicated situation:

XYZ Company recently installed a piece of equipment that cost $40,000. Its present salvage value is $10,000 due to sudden and unexpected changes in technology. The equipment is to be depreciated on a straight-line basis with no salvage value at the end of five years. Incremental costs of operating the equipment are expected to be $30,000 a year for five years. Because of advances in technology, a replacement machine can now be purchased for $60,000, with related operating costs expected to be $10,000 a year for five years. Using straight-line depreciation, the replacement equipment is expected to have no salvage value at the end of five years. Assume a tax rate of 50 percent.

Working with incremental cash flows, the net cost of the new equipment would be $50,000 ($60,000 minus salvage value of existing equipment).

Savings in operating costs will be $20,000 ($30,000 − $10,000) before considering income taxes.

Depreciation must be considered in calculating cash flows, since it reduces the amount of taxes that would otherwise be paid. Consequently, to calculate the after-tax cash flows, the incremental depreciation must be determined and used in calculating the amount of taxes to be paid. Incremental depreciation is $4,000 per year [($60,000 ÷ 5) − ($40,000 ÷ 5)]. (The calculation for allowable depreciation has been simplified for purposes of this example. Current tax provisions will be discussed in the next chapter.) In addition, if the new asset is purchased, the firm can recognize a $30,000 tax loss ($40,000 cost − $10,000 salvage). The shielding effect of this loss would produce a $15,000 cash benefit (.50 × $30,000), which we assume would reduce net cash outflow in the first period from $50,000 to $35,000. After-tax cash flows can now be calculated as follows:

Expected cash savings	$20,000
Incremental depreciation	$ 4,000
Profit	$16,000
Tax liability (50% × $16,000)	$ 8,000
After-tax profit	$ 8,000
Add back the depreciation	$ 4,000
After-tax cash flows	$12,000

Consequently, the expected inflows and outflows are as follows:

	Year 1	Year 2	Year 3	Year 4	Year 5
Outflow for equipment	$(35,000)				
Inflow from savings	$ 12,000	$12,000	$12,000	$12,000	$12,000

Assuming the estimates are valid, the accountant's next step would be to develop a method for evaluating the equipment proposal.

☐ METHODS FOR EVALUATING PROPOSAL PROFITABILITY

After relevant cash flows have been developed for capital proposals, a method for evaluating proposal profitability should be developed. In the following sections, we will review four basic approaches to proposal evaluation—payback, accounting rate of return, internal rate of return, and the net present value method.

Payback

Payback provides a measure of the time required to recover the initial amount invested in a project. If the cash inflows occur at a uniform rate, it is the ratio of investment costs over expected annual cash inflows, or

$$\text{Payback} = \frac{\text{Investment costs}}{\text{Investment cash inflows}}$$

For sake of simplicity, when the payback method is employed, it is often assumed that the cash inflows occur at a uniform rate during the time period. For instance, in the earlier example on the replacement decision (p. 482), projected annual cash inflows were expected to be $12,000 a year for five years from an investment of $35,000. An assumption is made here that the investment was made at the beginning of the first year. Payback on this proposal is 2.92 years, which is calculated as follows:

$$\text{Payback} = \frac{\$35,000}{\$12,000} = 2.92$$

If annual cash inflows had not been equal, then the calculation would have been more difficult. Assume instead that the cash flows were $8,000 in the first year, $10,000 in the second year, $12,000 in the third year, $15,000 in the fourth year, and $15,000 in the fifth year. Given the initial cash investment of $35,000, the payback would be 3.33 years. In three years, all but $5,000 of the investment has been recovered. It takes one-third year ($5,000/$15,000) to recover the balance.

If the payback period is less than some acceptable time period set by management, then a proposal is considered acceptable. If it is greater than the acceptable time, it is rejected.

The major weakness of the payback method is its lack of emphasis on profitability. Simply because one proposal has a shorter payback period than another proposal does not justify its selection over the proposal with the longer payback. If two competing proposals, A and B, each require a $50,000 investment with cash inflows expected of $25,000 for each of the first two years, the two projects would be considered equally acceptable under the payback method. However, assume proposal B's cash inflows are expected to continue for an additional four years while proposal A's are not. The payback method ignores the greater profitability of project B's cash flows.

In spite of the limitations of payback, it continues to be widely used as a supplement to the other methods. It provides a rough measure of risk and liquidity, assuming that the shorter the recovery period the less risky the proposal. In summary, payback is often used (1) in preliminary screening of numerous proposals, (2) when profitability is not essential to the decision process, (3) when liquidity tends to be very important, and (4) when risk is significant.

Accounting Rate of Return

This method is also referred to as the average rate of return or accrual **accounting rate of return** method. The rate represents the ratio of average annual after-tax profits to the investment (or average investment) required in the proposal. The formula for calculating the accounting rate of return is:

$$\text{Accounting rate of return} = \frac{\text{Estimated increase in profits (average)}}{\text{Estimated increase in investment}}$$

As indicated, the denominator is sometimes expressed as an average increase in investment. Either method is considered acceptable as long as it is consistently applied. Referring back to our replacement example on page 482, the accounting rate of return is calculated as follows:

$$\text{Accounting rate of return} = \frac{\$8,000}{\$35,000} = 22.86 \text{ percent}$$

or

$$\text{Average accounting rate of return} = \frac{\$8,000}{\$35,000/2} = 45.71 \text{ percent}$$

The $8,000 represents the estimate of after-tax income calculated in the example. What if the equipment had a salvage value, or what if current assets also had to be committed for the duration of the project? If the accounting rate of return is to be calculated, salvage values and current asset investment need to be considered in the calculation approach. Consider the following example:

Singer Corporation is considering purchasing some new equipment that will cost $50,000 and is expected to be useful for four years with a salvage value of $10,000 at the end of the four years. After-tax income is expected to be $10,000 in the first year, $20,000 in the second year, $30,000 in the third year, and $40,000 in the fourth year. An investment in current assets, primarily of inventory, of $50,000 will also be required.

To calculate the accounting rate of return, it is necessary to calculate expected average income. This is done by adding the individual income figures and dividing by total years ($100,000/4 = $25,000). The total investment is $100,000 (new equipment cost + the additional inventory investment, or $50,000 + $50,000).

$$\text{Accounting rate of return} = \frac{\$25,000}{\$100,000} = 25 \text{ percent}$$

The calculation of the average accounting rate of return is more complicated. The average investment represented by the equipment is calculated as follows:

Year 0	$ 50,000
1	40,000
2	30,000
3	20,000
4	10,000
Total	$150,000/5 = $30,000 average investment

Where salvage values are involved, the average investment is usually defined as (Investment + Salvage value)/2. This results in the same answer (($50,000 + $10,000)/2 = $30,000). If it is assumed that the $50,000 invested in current assets will hold its value over the period of the investment, then the total average investment is $80,000 ($30,000 + $50,000).

$$\text{Average accounting rate of return} = \frac{\$25,000}{\$80,000} = 31.25 \text{ percent}$$

Although use of the accounting rate of return method has declined over the years, some managers still use it because they believe it to be acceptable and easily understood. Indeed, its primary advantages lie in its simplicity, its close ties to financial accounting, and its use of the return-on-investment ratio to evaluate segment performance (chapter 17). Once the rate has been calculated, it can be compared with the management team's required rate to see if the proposal is acceptable. Unlike the payback method, the accounting rate of return method does consider profitability. However, it gives no consideration to the timing of flows and uses income estimates rather than cash flows in the calculations.

☐ THE NEED FOR REQUIRED RATE OF RETURN

In the previous section, it was mentioned that the accounting rate of return is compared with the required rate to determine project profitability. Information on required rates becomes even more important as discounted cash flow methods are discussed. Investment decisions are linked to financing and risk decisions. Where are the funds coming from for upcoming capital projects? What kind of rate is needed to account for the risk involved? Whether the funds come from internal or external sources, there is some financing cost attached to their use.

The financing cost along with a risk rate results in a required rate for purposes of evaluating proposals under the accounting rate of return and discounted cash flow methods. This required rate is also often referred to as the minimum desired rate, hurdle rate, cost of capital rate, cutoff rate, and discount rate.

In this chapter, it is assumed that the rate has been calculated. Additional material relating to the required rate will be presented in the next chapter.

☐ DISCOUNTED CASH FLOW TECHNIQUES

Because of various limitations inherent in the payback and accounting rate of return models—both models ignore the time value of funds, and the payback method ignores profitability—**discounted cash flow methods** have been used increasingly to provide a more objective basis for evaluating proposals.

There are two discounted cash flow techniques used in capital budgeting, namely, the **internal rate of return** (IROR) and the **net present value** (NPV). Both recognize the time value of money. For sake of simplicity, it is assumed that expected cash flows take place at the end of the year in the examples in which discounted cash flow techniques are used.

A review of discounted cash flow methodology, along with the appropriate tables, is provided in an appendix to this chapter. If you are not familiar with the methodology, you should review the material before continuing.

The Internal Rate of Return

The internal rate of return is the discount rate that sets the present value of expected future cash flows equal to the initial investment. What is the internal rate of return for an investment of $3,388 with expected cash inflows of $4,000 at the end of the year? The answer can be calculated by using the following equation to determine the appropriate factor (and by referring to appendix 14.3):

$$\$3{,}388 = \$4{,}000 \, \frac{1}{(1+i)^1}$$

Substituting factor (F) for $\dfrac{1}{(1+i)^1}$

$$\$3{,}388 = \$4{,}000F$$
$$F = 3{,}388/4{,}000$$
$$F = .847$$

Referring to appendix table 14.3 for one year and reading across the row, one finds .847 around 18 percent. Thus, 18 percent is the internal rate of return, or the rate that will equate the inflow of $4,000 with the outflow of $3,388.

What is the internal rate of return in the earlier example (p. 482) in which there was a proposed investment of $35,000 that promised cash inflows of $12,000 a year for five years? Again, it is assumed that the $35,000 outflow was made at the beginning of the first year. The answer is calculated as follows:

$$\$35{,}000 = \$12{,}000 \, \frac{1 - \dfrac{1}{(1+i)^5}}{i}$$

Substituting F for $\dfrac{1 - \dfrac{1}{(1+i)^5}}{i}$

$$\$35{,}000 = \$12{,}000F$$
$$F = 35{,}000/12{,}000$$
$$F = 2.917$$

Referring to appendix table 14.4 for five periods and reading across the row, one finds the internal rate of return to be between 20 and 22 percent, or approximately 21.16 percent (Actual rate = 21.15) using interpolation.

The basic concept behind the internal rate of return model is presented in figure 14.2, using the cash outflow and inflows from the above example. As can be seen from figure 14.2, the internal rate of return method considers the amount of investment committed to the project from period to period. Having calculated the internal rate of return for a proposal, the management team would next compare it with the required rate of return. If the required rate is less than 21.16 percent, the project would be considered acceptable.

The internal rate of return method is easy to use as long as cash inflows are constant from period to period. Where the cash flows are irregular, the internal rate of return must be found by trial and error.

FIGURE 14.2
Basic Concept
behind Internal
Rate of Return

	Year				
	1	2	3	4	5
Unrecovered investment, begin	$35,000	$30,402	$24,832	$18,084	$ 9,909
Cash inflow	12,000	12,000	12,000	12,000	12,000
Interest @ 21.15%*	7,402	6,430	5,252	3,825	2,091†
Return of capital	4,598	5,570	6,748	8,175	9,907
Unrecovered investment, end	$30,402	$24,832	$18,084	$ 9,909	0

* Rate × unrecovered investment, beginning balance
† Adjusted for rounding differences

Assume that Armitage Corporation is considering an investment pro-posal that promises cash inflows of $40,000, $60,000, and $10,000 for each of the next three years for a given investment of $80,000. The management staff wants to know the internal rate of return expected from the invest-ment. The solution can be calculated only by a trial-and-error approach. The solution is found by selecting a rate and discounting the cash inflows. If the present value is greater than the initial investment, select a higher rate until one is found that equates the present value of the inflows with the initial investment. In this example, the internal rate is approximately 20 percent. Even this process has become easy in today's environment due to the sophistication of computers and calculators.

		Present values	
Inflows		20 percent	22 percent
$40,000		$33,320	$32,800
60,000		41,640	40,320
10,000		5,790	5,510
		$80,750	$78,630

One other problem exists with the use of the internal rate of return. In limited cases, where there are multiple reversals in the cash-flow streams, a person could have more than one internal rate of return for a given proposal.

The Net Present Value

Under the present value method, all cash flows are discounted to the pres-ent, using the required rate of return. A proposal is considered acceptable if the present value of cash inflows exceed the present value of the cash outflows. The major difference between the internal rate of return and the net present value method is that the internal rate of return compares a calculated rate with the required rate, whereas the net present value com-pares discounted cash inflows and outflows, using the required rate for discounting purposes.

Referring to the earlier example with a $35,000 required outlay and expected return of $12,000 per year for five years, what is the net present value? We have to know the required rate of return to make the calculation. Assume the management team has decided it needs a minimum return of

20 percent on the proposal. Using appendix table 14.4, the necessary calculations can quickly be made as shown.

Annual cash savings	12,000 × 2.991 = $35,892
Outlay required	35,000 × 1.000 = 35,000
Net present value	$ 892

What if the cash inflows had been irregular? Assume after-tax cash inflows are expected to be $20,000 at the end of the first year, $15,000 the second year, $10,000 the third year, $8,000 the fourth year, and $5,000 for the fifth year. Calculations would require reference to appendix table 14.3 and would be made as follows:

Year	Annual cash savings	Present value
1	$20,000 × .833 =	$16,660
2	15,000 × .694 =	10,410
3	10,000 × .579 =	5,790
4	8,000 × .482 =	3,856
5	5,000 × .402 =	2,010
Total present value from inflows		$38,726
Outlay required	$35,000 × 1.000 =	35,000
Net present value		$ 3,726

The logic of the net present value method is presented in figure 14.3, showing the amount left over after five years. The data from the preceding example, in which cash flows were constant, are used in the figure. The net present value method is quite easy to use and does not have the problems associated with the internal rate of return method.

☐ OTHER APPROACHES

In some cases, companies may not use any of the approaches just described. What happens when a major piece of equipment suddenly falls apart? Although, in well-managed companies, problems such as this tend to be minimized, they can happen. Typically, in such situations, the pressures of the situation lead management personnel to use the most expedient solution. Also, in some companies, capital-budgeting decisions are tied to a manager's ability to convince others of the merits of a particular in-

FIGURE 14.3
Basic Concept behind Present Value

	Year				
	1	2	3	4	5
Unrecovered investment, begin	$35,000	$30,000	$24,000	$16,800	$ 8,160
Cash inflow	12,000	12,000	12,000	12,000	12,000
Interest @ 20 percent	7,000	6,000	4,800	3,360	1,632
Return of capital	5,000	6,000	7,200	8,640	10,368
Unrecovered investment, end ...	$30,000	$24,000	$16,800	$ 8,160	$(2,208)*

*$2,208 × .402 = $888 present value, which approximates $892. Difference due to rounding.

vestment opportunity. In both of the above cases, economic considerations tend to become secondary, and decisions are likely to be made based on questionable information. For this reason, it is important that the management team provide for post-audits of capital-budgeting decisions and insist on objective evaluation of proposals.

☐ CONSOLIDATING EXAMPLE

The MRGK Company is considering the purchase of a computerized printing press for $150,000. The equipment must be depreciated over a five-year period on a straight-line basis with no consideration of salvage value. The current income tax rate is 40 percent.

A study made by the company indicates that, if the equipment is purchased, company officials should expect incremental cash savings of $80,000 for the first year, $60,000 for the second and third years, $40,000 for the fourth year, and $30,000 for the final year. The company's required rate of return is 16 percent.

Required ☐

The management team has asked you to calculate the payback, accounting rate of return, internal rate of return, and the net present value for the project proposal.

The first step in the solution process is to develop the relevant cash flows for the proposal. The only cash outflow is the $150,000 to be committed at the beginning of the first period. Calculation of after-tax cash flows is as follows:

	Year 1	Year 2	Year 3	Year 4	Year 5
Cash savings	$80,000	$60,000	$60,000	$40,000	$30,000
Depreciation	30,000	30,000	30,000	30,000	30,000
Profit	$50,000	$30,000	$30,000	$10,000	-0-
Tax liability	20,000	12,000	12,000	4,000	-0-
After-tax profit	30,000	18,000	18,000	6,000	-0-
Depreciation	30,000	30,000	30,000	30,000	30,000
After-tax cash flows	$60,000	$48,000	$48,000	$36,000	$30,000

After the relevant cash flows (incremental and after-tax) have been developed, the balance of the solution is one of the following procedures outlined in the chapter.

Payback. 2 42/48 years. After two years all but $42,000 has been recovered. So it should take 42,000/48,000 years to recover the balance.

Accounting rate of return. 9.60 percent. To calculate the accounting rate, it is necessary to first calculate the average income expected. This is done by adding the annual after-tax income projections and dividing by the number of years ($72,000 / 5 = $14,400). The total investment is limited to the initial outlay of $150,000.

$$\text{Accounting rate of return} = \frac{14,400}{150,000} = 9.60 \text{ percent}$$

Internal rate of return. 16.75 percent. The internal rate of return can be calculated through trial and error. To select a starting point in the trial-and-error process, 16 percent is used to see if the required rate of return provides a close approximation in this case. Using this as a starting point, the results are as follows:

| | Present values | |
Cash inflows	18 percent	16 percent
$60,000	$ 50,820	$ 51,720
48,000	34,464	35,664
48,000	29,232	30,768
36,000	18,576	19,872
30,000	13,110	14,280
Total	$146,202	$152,304

Using 18 percent, the discounted cash flows are less than $150,000. When 16 percent is used, the results are slightly higher. By using straight-line interpolation, the approximate internal rate of return of 16.75 percent is found.

Net present value. $2,978. The solution for the net present value method is rather straightforward since the required rate of return of 16 percent is used to discount the cash inflows. We also know that the net present value will be positive since the internal rate of return is greater than the required rate. Computations are as follows:

Year	Annual cash savings		Present value
1	$ 60,000 × .862	=	$ 51,720
2	48,000 × .743	=	35,664
3	48,000 × .641	=	30,768
4	36,000 × .552	=	19,872
5	30,000 × .476	=	14,280
Total present value from inflows			$152,304
Outlay required	150,000 × 1.0000	=	150,000
Net present value			$ 2,304

☐ SUMMARY

Capital budgeting is defined as a process of determining how best to allocate a company's resources to project proposals. Capital-expenditure management involves a complete process, from the initial conception of investment possibilities to the performance evaluation of completed projects.

Evaluation techniques typically used in capital budgeting are payback, accounting rate of return, internal rate of return, and the net present value method. The payback method continues to be used because it provides a rough measure of risk and liquidity. However, it does not consider profitability. The accounting rate of return method does consider profitability but only in terms of income flows. The accounting rate of return method also does not consider the timing of cash flows. To be valid, capital-budgeting analysis should consider incremental cash flows on a discounted basis.

Both the internal rate of return method and net present value method use incremental cash flows and consider the time value of money in the analysis. They tend to identify the same acceptable product proposals except in some cases with competing projects. The internal rate of return is compared with the required rate for decision-making purposes. The required rate is built into the net present value calculations.

All of the evaluation methods discussed continue to be used in practice. The two discounted cash flow methods appear to be conceptually superior and are increasingly being used in practice.

KEY TERMS

Accounting rate of return	**Internal rate of return**
Capital budgeting	**Net present value**
Discounted cash flow methods	**Payback**
	Post-audits

REVIEW PROBLEM

Select the best answer to the following multiple-choice items. Questions 1, 2, and 3 are based on the following information:

The George Company is planning to acquire a new machine at a total cost of $30,600. The estimated life of the machine is six years and estimated salvage value is $600. The George Company estimates annual cash savings from using this machine will be $8,000. Assume the company's cost of capital is 8 percent and its income tax rate is 40 percent. The present value of $1 at 8 percent for six years is .630. The present value of an annuity of $1 in arrears at 8 percent for six years is 4.623.

Required ☐

1. What are the annual after-tax net cash benefits of this investment?
a. $3,000
b. $4,800
c. $5,400
d. $6,800

2. If the annual after-tax net cash benefits of this investment were $5,000, what would the payback period be?
a. $30,600 ÷ $5,000
b. $30,000 ÷ $8,000
c. ($30,000 ÷ $5,000) × the appropriate present-value factor
d. ($30,000 ÷ $8,000) × the appropriate present-value factor

3. If the annual after-tax net cash benefits of this investment were $5,000, what would the net present value of this investment be?
a. $7,485 negative
b. $7,107 negative
c. $7,107 positive
d. $7,485 positive

Questions 4 and 5 are based on the following information:

The Apex Company is evaluating a capital-budgeting proposal for the current year. The relevant data follow:

Year	Present value of an annuity in arrears of $1 at 15%
1	$ .870
2	$1.626
3	2.284
4	2.856
5	3.353
6	3.785

The initial investment would be $30,000. It would be depreciated on a straight-line basis over six years with no salvage. The before-tax annual cash inflow due to this investment is $10,000, and the income tax rate is 40 percent paid the same year as incurred. The desired rate of return is 15 percent. All cash flows occur at year-end.

4. What is the after-tax accounting rate of return on the company's capital-budgeting proposal?
a. 10 percent
b. 16⅔ percent
c. 26⅔ percent
d. 33⅓ percent

5. What is the net present value of the company's capital-budgeting proposal?
a. $(7,290)
b. $280
c. $7,850
d. $11,760

Questions 6 and 7 are based on the following information:

The Gravina Company is planning to spend $6,000 for a machine that it will depreciate on a straight-line basis over a ten-year period. The machine will generate additional cash revenues of $1,200 a year. Gravina will incur no additional costs except for depreciation. The income tax rate is 50 percent.

6. What is the pay-back period?
a. 3.3 years
b. 4.0 years
c. 5.0 years
d. 6.7 years

7. What is the accounting (book-value) rate of return on the initial increase in required investment?
a. 5 percent
b. 10 percent
c. 15 percent
d. 20 percent

Questions 8 and 9 are based on the following information:

Heslin, Inc., invested in a machine with a useful life of five years and no salvage value. The machine was depreciated using the straight-line method. The annual cash inflow from operations, net of income taxes, was $1,000. The present value of an ordinary annuity of $1 in arrears for five periods at 12 percent is 3.605. The present value of $1 for five periods at 12 percent is 0.567.

8. Assuming that Heslin used a time-adjusted rate of return of 12 percent, what was the amount of the original investment?
a. $2,835
b. $3,605
c. $4,400
d. $5,670

9. Assuming that the minimum desired rate of return on this investment was 12 percent and the amount of the original investment was $3,500, what would be the net present value, rounded to the nearest dollar?
a. $0
b. $105
c. $198
d. $567

10. A planned factory expansion project has an estimated initial cost of $800,000. Using a discount rate of 20 percent, the present value of future cost savings from the expansion is $843,000. To yield exactly a 20 percent time-adjusted rate of return, the actual investment cost cannot exceed the $800,000 estimate by more than
a. $160,000
b. $ 20,000
c. $ 43,000
d. $ 1,075

Solution □

1. d
2. a
3. b
4. a
5. b
6. d
7. a
8. b
9. b
10. c

(CPA)

APPENDIX

DISCOUNTED CASH FLOW METHODOLOGY

Timing of cash flows is extremely important in the long-term investment decision. Whenever one is dealing with a long period of time, the cost of funds must be considered. Managers place a higher value on an investment promising returns over the next two years than one promising similar or maybe even slightly higher returns only in the third and fourth years. In other words, a dollar today is worth more than a dollar received a year from now—just how much is dependent on the relevant cost of funds.

COMPOUND INTEREST

In order to understand discounted cash flow methodology it is necessary to understand the basic notion of compound interest. Compound interest means that when interest is due, previously earned interest is added to the principal amount of the loan for purposes of calculating the interest due. Assume a person invests $1,000 at 10 percent compounded interest. After one year, the person would have $1,100 calculated as follows:

$$\text{Future value } (FV) = 1,000 + .10(1,000) = \$1,100$$

If the investment continued for a second year, the person would have $1,210, which is calculated as follows:

$$FV = 1,000 + .10(1,000) + .10[1,000 + .10(1,000)] = \$1,210$$

Simplifying, the last equation gives us

$$FV = 1,000 \, (1 + .10)^2$$

In general, we have the following equations for the compounded amount of $1:

$$FV = PV \, (1 + i)^n$$

where

$$
\begin{aligned}
FV &= \text{Future value} \\
PV &= \text{Present value} \\
i &= \text{Interest rate} \\
n &= \text{Time period}
\end{aligned}
$$

Appendix table 14.1 shows how much $1 invested now will accumulate in a given number of periods at various interest rates.

Now, assume that $1,000 is invested at the end of each year for two years at 10 percent compounded interest. After one year, the person would have $1,000 since the investment takes place at the end of the year. At the end of the second year, the investor would have $2,100, calculated as follows:

$$FV = \$1,000 \, (1 + .10)^1 + \$1,000 = \$2,100$$

If instead the individual invested $1,000 at end of each year for three years, the investment would be worth:

$$FV = \$1,000 \, (1 + .10)^2 + \$1,000 \, (1 + .10)^1 + \$1,000 = \$3,310$$

APPENDIX TABLE 14.1 Future Value of $1; $FV = PV(1 + i)^n$

N/R	2.0%	4.0%	6.0%	8.0%	10.0%	12.0%	14.0%	16.0%	18.0%	20.0%
1	1.0200	1.0400	1.0600	1.0800	1.1000	1.1200	1.1400	1.1600	1.1800	1.2000
2	1.0404	1.0816	1.1236	1.1664	1.2100	1.2544	1.2996	1.3456	1.3924	1.4400
3	1.0612	1.1249	1.1910	1.2597	1.3310	1.4049	1.4815	1.5609	1.6430	1.7280
4	1.0824	1.1699	1.2625	1.3605	1.4641	1.5735	1.6890	1.8106	1.9388	2.0736
5	1.1041	1.2167	1.3382	1.4693	1.6105	1.7623	1.9254	2.1003	2.2878	2.4883
6	1.1262	1.2653	1.4185	1.5869	1.7716	1.9738	2.1950	2.4364	2.6996	2.9860
7	1.1487	1.3159	1.5036	1.7138	1.9487	2.2107	2.5023	2.8262	3.1855	3.5832
8	1.1717	1.3686	1.5938	1.8509	2.1436	2.4760	2.8526	3.2784	3.7589	4.2998
9	1.1951	1.4233	1.6895	1.9990	2.3579	2.7731	3.2519	3.8030	4.4355	5.1598
10	1.2190	1.4802	1.7908	2.1589	2.5937	3.1058	3.7072	4.4114	5.2338	6.1917
11	1.2434	1.5395	1.8983	2.3316	2.8531	3.4785	4.2262	5.1173	6.1759	7.4301
12	1.2682	1.6010	2.0122	2.5182	3.1384	3.8960	4.8179	5.9360	7.2876	8.9161
13	1.2936	1.6651	2.1329	2.7196	3.4523	4.3635	5.4924	6.8858	8.5994	10.6993
14	1.3195	1.7317	2.2609	2.9372	3.7975	4.8871	6.2613	7.9875	10.1472	12.8392
15	1.3459	1.8009	2.3966	3.1722	4.1772	5.4736	7.1379	9.2655	11.9737	15.4070
16	1.3728	1.8730	2.5404	3.4259	4.5950	6.1304	8.1372	10.7480	14.1290	18.4884
17	1.4002	1.9479	2.6928	3.7000	5.0545	6.8660	9.2765	12.4677	16.6722	22.1861
18	1.4282	2.0258	2.8543	3.9960	5.5599	7.6900	10.5752	14.4625	19.6733	26.6233
19	1.4568	2.1068	3.0256	4.3157	6.1159	8.6128	12.0557	16.7765	23.2144	31.9480
20	1.4859	2.1911	3.2071	4.6610	6.7275	9.6463	13.7435	19.4608	27.3930	38.3376
21	1.5157	2.2788	3.3996	5.0338	7.4002	10.8038	15.6676	22.5745	32.3238	46.0051
22	1.5460	2.3699	3.6035	5.4365	8.1403	12.1003	17.8610	26.1864	38.1421	55.2061
23	1.5769	2.4647	3.8197	5.8715	8.9543	13.5523	20.3616	30.3762	45.0076	66.2474
24	1.6084	2.5633	4.0489	6.3412	9.8497	15.1786	23.2122	35.2364	53.1090	79.4968
25	1.6406	2.6658	4.2919	6.8485	10.8347	17.0001	26.4619	40.8742	62.6686	95.3962
26	1.6734	2.7725	4.5494	7.3964	11.9182	19.0401	30.1666	47.4141	73.9490	114.4755
27	1.7069	2.8834	4.8223	7.9881	13.1100	21.3249	34.3899	55.0004	87.2598	137.3706
28	1.7410	2.9987	5.1117	8.6271	14.4210	23.8839	39.2045	63.8004	102.9666	164.8447
29	1.7758	3.1187	5.4184	9.3173	15.8631	26.7499	44.6931	74.0085	121.5005	197.8136
30	1.8114	3.2434	5.7435	10.0627	17.4494	29.9599	50.9502	85.8499	143.3706	237.3763

This leads to the following equations for the compounded amount of $1 invested at the end of each period:

$$FV = (1+i)^n + (1+i)^{n-1}, \ldots, (1+i)^2 + (1+i)^1 + 1$$

or

$$FV = \frac{(1+i)^n - 1}{i}$$

Using the formula just given as the basis, appendix table 14.2 shows how much $1 invested at the end of each period will accumulate in a given number of periods at various interest rates.

PRESENT VALUES

In an earlier example in which a person invested $1,000 for a period of two years at 10 percent, the investment was worth $1,210 at the end of two years. By reversing the order, the present value of $1,210 to be received two years from now is $1,000,

APPENDIX TABLE 14.2 Future Value of Annuity; $FV = \dfrac{(1 + i)^n - 1}{i}$

N/R	2.00%	4.00%	6.00%	8.00%	10.00%	12.00%	14.00%	16.00%	18.00%	20.00%
1	1.0000	1.0000	1.0000	1.0000	1.0000	1.0000	1.0000	1.1000	1.0000	1.0000
2	2.0200	2.0400	2.0600	2.0800	2.1000	2.1200	2.1400	2.1600	2.1800	2.2000
3	3.0604	3.1216	3.1836	3.2464	3.3100	3.3744	3.4396	3.5056	3.5724	3.6400
4	4.1216	4.2465	4.3746	4.5061	4.6410	4.7793	4.9211	5.0665	5.2154	5.3680
5	5.2040	5.4163	5.6371	5.8666	6.1051	6.3528	6.6101	6.8771	7.1542	7.4416
6	6.3081	6.6330	6.9753	7.3359	7.7156	8.1152	8.5355	8.9775	9.4420	9.9299
7	7.4343	7.8983	8.3938	8.9228	9.4872	10.0890	10.7305	11.4139	12.1415	12.9159
8	8.5830	9.2142	9.8975	10.6366	11.4359	12.2997	13.2328	14.2401	15.3270	16.4991
9	9.7546	10.5828	11.4913	12.4876	13.5795	14.7757	16.0853	17.5185	19.0859	20.7989
10	10.9497	12.0061	13.1808	14.4866	15.9374	17.5487	19.3373	21.3215	23.5213	25.9587
11	12.1687	13.4864	14.9716	16.6455	18.5312	20.6546	23.0445	25.7329	28.7551	32.1504
12	13.4121	15.0258	16.8699	18.9771	21.3843	24.1331	27.2707	30.8502	34.9311	39.5805
13	14.6803	16.6268	18.8821	21.4953	24.5227	28.0291	32.0887	36.7862	42.2187	48.4966
14	15.9739	18.2919	21.0151	24.2149	27.9750	32.3926	37.5811	43.6720	50.8180	59.1959
15	17.2934	20.0236	23.2760	27.1521	31.7725	37.2797	43.8424	51.6595	60.9653	72.0351
16	18.6393	21.8245	25.6725	30.3243	35.9497	42.7533	50.9804	60.9250	72.9390	87.4421
17	20.0121	23.6975	28.2129	33.7502	40.5447	48.8837	59.1176	71.6730	87.0680	105.9306
18	21.4123	25.6454	30.9057	37.4502	45.5992	55.7497	68.3941	84.1407	103.7403	128.1167
19	22.8406	27.6712	33.7600	41.4463	51.1591	63.4397	78.9692	98.6032	123.4135	154.7400
20	24.2974	29.7781	36.7856	45.7620	57.2750	72.0524	91.0249	115.3797	146.6280	186.6880
21	25.7833	31.9692	39.9927	50.4229	64.0025	81.6987	104.7684	134.8405	174.0210	225.0256
22	27.2990	34.2480	43.3923	55.4568	71.4027	92.5026	120.4360	157.4150	206.3448	271.0307
23	28.8450	36.6179	46.9958	60.8933	79.5430	104.6029	138.2970	183.6014	244.4868	326.2369
24	30.4219	39.0826	50.8156	66.7648	88.4973	118.1552	158.6586	213.9776	289.4945	392.4842
25	32.0303	41.6459	54.8645	73.1059	98.3471	133.3339	181.8708	249.2140	342.6035	471.9811
26	33.6709	44.3117	59.1564	79.9544	109.1818	150.3339	208.3327	290.0883	405.2721	567.3773
27	35.3443	47.0842	63.7058	87.3508	121.0999	169.3740	238.4993	337.5024	479.2211	681.8528
28	37.0512	49.9676	68.5281	95.3388	134.2099	190.6989	272.8892	392.5028	566.4809	819.2233
29	38.7922	52.9663	73.6398	103.9659	148.6309	214.5828	312.0937	456.3032	669.4475	984.0680
30	40.5681	56.0849	79.0582	113.2832	164.4940	241.3327	356.7868	530.3117	790.9480	1181.8816

if discounted at 10 percent. Suppose you wanted to save for a vacation two years from now, and the vacation is expected to cost $1,210. How much would you have to put in some type of savings at 10 percent to have the $1,210 in two years? The answer is $1,000. The formula can be set up as follows:

$$\$1,210 = PV\,(1+.10)^2$$

or

$$PV = \frac{\$1,210}{(1 + .10)^2}$$

Consequently, the present value formula can be derived from the future value formula by solving for the present value instead of the future value.

$$FV = PV\,(1 + i)^n$$

$$PV = \frac{FV}{(1+i)^n}$$

APPENDIX TABLE 14.3 Present Value of $1; $PV = FV \dfrac{1}{(1+i)^n}$

n	2%	4%	6%	8%	10%	12%	14%	16%	18%	20%	22%	24%	26%	28%	30%	40%	50%
1	0.980	0.962	0.943	0.926	0.909	0.893	0.877	0.862	0.847	0.833	0.820	0.806	0.794	0.781	0.769	0.714	0.667
2	0.961	0.925	0.890	0.857	0.826	0.797	0.769	0.743	0.718	0.694	0.672	0.650	0.630	0.610	0.592	0.510	0.444
3	0.942	0.889	0.840	0.794	0.751	0.712	0.675	0.641	0.609	0.579	0.551	0.524	0.500	0.477	0.455	0.364	0.296
4	0.924	0.855	0.792	0.735	0.683	0.636	0.592	0.552	0.516	0.482	0.451	0.423	0.397	0.373	0.350	0.260	0.197
5	0.906	0.822	0.747	0.681	0.621	0.567	0.519	0.476	0.437	0.402	0.370	0.341	0.315	0.291	0.269	0.186	0.131
6	0.888	0.790	0.705	0.630	0.564	0.507	0.456	0.410	0.370	0.335	0.303	0.275	0.256	0.227	0.207	0.133	0.088
7	0.871	0.760	0.665	0.583	0.513	0.452	0.400	0.354	0.314	0.279	0.249	0.222	0.198	0.178	0.159	0.095	0.059
8	0.853	0.731	0.627	0.540	0.467	0.404	0.351	0.305	0.266	0.233	0.204	0.179	0.157	0.139	0.123	0.068	0.039
9	0.837	0.703	0.592	0.500	0.424	0.361	0.308	0.263	0.225	0.194	0.167	0.144	0.125	0.108	0.094	0.048	0.026
10	0.820	0.676	0.558	0.463	0.386	0.322	0.270	0.227	0.191	0.162	0.137	0.116	0.099	0.085	0.073	0.035	0.017
11	0.804	0.650	0.527	0.429	0.350	0.287	0.237	0.195	0.162	0.135	0.112	0.094	0.079	0.066	0.056	0.025	0.012
12	0.788	0.625	0.497	0.397	0.319	0.257	0.208	0.168	0.137	0.112	0.092	0.076	0.062	0.052	0.043	0.018	0.008
13	0.773	0.601	0.469	0.368	0.290	0.229	0.182	0.145	0.116	0.093	0.075	0.061	0.050	0.040	0.033	0.013	0.005
14	0.758	0.577	0.442	0.340	0.263	0.205	0.160	0.125	0.099	0.078	0.062	0.049	0.039	0.032	0.025	0.009	0.003
15	0.743	0.555	0.417	0.315	0.239	0.183	0.140	0.108	0.084	0.065	0.051	0.040	0.031	0.025	0.020	0.006	0.002
16	0.728	0.534	0.394	0.292	0.218	0.163	0.123	0.093	0.071	0.054	0.042	0.032	0.025	0.019	0.015	0.005	0.002
17	0.714	0.513	0.371	0.270	0.198	0.146	0.108	0.080	0.060	0.045	0.034	0.026	0.020	0.015	0.012	0.003	0.001
18	0.700	0.494	0.350	0.250	0.180	0.130	0.095	0.069	0.051	0.038	0.028	0.021	0.016	0.012	0.009	0.002	
19	0.686	0.475	0.331	0.232	0.164	0.116	0.083	0.060	0.043	0.031	0.023	0.017	0.012	0.009	0.007	0.002	
20	0.673	0.456	0.312	0.215	0.149	0.104	0.073	0.051	0.037	0.026	0.019	0.014	0.010	0.007	0.005	0.001	
21	0.660	0.439	0.294	0.199	0.135	0.093	0.054	0.044	0.031	0.022	0.015	0.011	0.008	0.006	0.004	0.001	
22	0.647	0.422	0.278	0.184	0.123	0.083	0.056	0.038	0.026	0.018	0.013	0.009	0.006	0.004	0.003		
23	0.634	0.406	0.262	0.170	0.112	0.074	0.049	0.033	0.022	0.015	0.010	0.007	0.005	0.003	0.002		
24	0.622	0.390	0.247	0.158	0.102	0.066	0.043	0.028	0.019	0.013	0.008	0.006	0.004	0.003	0.002		
25	0.610	0.375	0.233	0.146	0.092	0.059	0.038	0.024	0.016	0.010	0.007	0.005	0.003	0.002	0.001		
26	0.598	0.361	0.220	0.135	0.084	0.053	0.033	0.021	0.014	0.009	0.006	0.004	0.002	0.002	0.001		
27	0.586	0.347	0.207	0.125	0.076	0.047	0.029	0.018	0.011	0.007	0.005	0.003	0.002	0.001	0.001		
28	0.574	0.333	0.196	0.116	0.069	0.042	0.026	0.016	0.010	0.006	0.004	0.002	0.002	0.001	0.001		
29	0.563	0.321	0.185	0.107	0.063	0.037	0.022	0.014	0.008	0.005	0.003	0.002	0.001	0.001	0.001		
30	0.552	0.308	0.174	0.099	0.057	0.033	0.020	0.012	0.007	0.004	0.003						
40	0.453	0.208	0.097	0.046	0.022	0.011	0.005	0.003	0.001	0.001							

APPENDIX TABLE 14.4 Present Value of an Annuity of $1 in Arrears; $PV = \dfrac{1 - (1 + i)^{-n}}{i}$

n	2%	4%	6%	8%	10%	12%	14%	16%	18%	20%	22%	24%	25%	26%	28%	30%	40%	50%
1	0.980	0.962	0.943	0.926	0.909	0.893	0.877	0.862	0.847	0.833	0.820	0.806	0.800	0.794	0.781	0.769	0.714	0.667
2	1.942	1.886	1.833	1.783	1.736	1.690	1.647	1.605	1.566	1.528	1.492	1.457	1.440	1.424	1.392	1.361	1.224	1.111
3	2.884	2.775	2.673	2.577	2.487	2.402	2.322	2.246	2.174	2.106	2.042	1.981	1.952	1.923	1.868	1.816	1.589	1.407
4	3.308	3.630	3.465	3.312	3.170	3.037	2.914	2.798	2.690	2.589	2.494	2.404	2.362	2.320	2.241	2.166	1.848	1.605
5	4.713	4.452	4.212	3.993	3.791	3.605	3.433	3.274	3.127	2.991	2.864	2.745	2.689	2.635	2.532	2.436	2.035	1.737
6	5.601	5.242	4.917	4.623	4.355	4.111	3.889	3.685	3.498	3.326	3.167	3.020	2.951	2.885	2.759	2.643	2.168	1.824
7	6.472	6.002	5.582	5.206	4.868	4.564	4.288	4.039	3.812	3.605	3.416	3.242	3.161	3.083	2.937	2.802	2.263	1.883
8	7.325	6.733	6.210	5.747	5.335	4.968	4.639	4.344	4.078	3.837	3.619	3.421	3.329	3.241	3.076	2.925	2.331	1.922
9	8.162	7.435	6.802	6.247	5.759	5.328	4.946	4.607	4.303	4.031	3.786	3.566	3.463	3.366	3.184	3.019	2.379	1.948
10	8.983	8.111	7.360	6.710	6.145	5.650	5.216	4.833	4.494	4.192	3.923	3.682	3.571	3.465	3.269	3.082	2.414	1.965
11	9.787	8.760	7.887	7.139	6.495	5.988	5.453	5.029	4.656	4.327	4.035	3.776	3.656	3.544	3.335	3.147	2.438	1.977
12	10.575	9.385	8.384	7.536	6.814	6.194	5.660	5.197	4.793	4.439	4.127	3.851	3.725	3.606	3.387	3.190	2.456	1.985
13	11.343	9.986	8.853	7.904	7.103	6.424	5.842	5.342	4.910	4.533	4.203	3.912	3.780	3.656	3.427	3.223	2.458	1.990
14	12.106	10.563	9.295	8.244	7.367	6.628	6.002	5.468	5.008	4.611	4.265	3.962	3.824	3.695	3.459	3.249	2.477	1.993
15	12.849	11.118	9.712	8.559	7.606	6.811	6.142	5.575	5.092	4.675	4.315	4.001	3.859	3.726	3.483	3.268	2.484	1.995
16	13.578	11.652	10.106	8.851	7.824	6.974	6.205	5.669	5.162	4.730	4.357	4.033	3.887	3.751	3.503	3.283	2.489	1.997
17	14.292	12.166	10.477	9.122	8.022	7.120	6.373	5.749	5.222	4.775	4.391	4.069	3.910	3.771	3.518	3.295	2.492	1.998
18	14.992	12.659	10.828	9.372	8.201	7.250	6.467	5.818	5.273	4.812	4.419	4.080	3.928	3.786	3.529	3.304	2.494	1.999
19	15.678	13.134	11.158	9.604	8.365	7.366	6.550	5.877	5.316	4.844	4.442	4.097	3.942	3.799	3.539	3.311	2.496	1.999
20	16.351	13.590	11.470	9.818	8.514	7.469	6.623	5.929	5.353	4.870	4.460	4.110	3.954	3.808	3.546	3.316	2.497	1.999
21	17.011	14.029	11.764	10.017	8.649	7.562	6.687	5.973	5.384	4.891	4.476	4.121	3.963	3.816	3.551	3.320	2.498	2.000
22	17.658	14.451	12.042	10.201	8.772	7.645	6.743	6.011	5.410	4.909	4.488	4.130	3.970	3.822	3.556	3.323	2.498	2.000
23	18.292	14.857	12.303	10.371	8.883	7.718	6.792	6.044	5.432	4.925	4.499	4.137	3.976	3.827	3.559	3.325	2.499	2.000
24	18.914	15.247	12.550	10.529	8.985	7.784	6.835	6.073	5.451	4.937	4.507	4.143	3.981	3.831	3.562	3.327	2.499	2.000
25	19.523	15.622	12.783	10.675	9.077	7.843	6.873	6.097	5.467	4.948	4.514	4.147	3.986	3.834	3.564	3.329	2.499	2.000
26	20.121	15.983	13.003	10.810	9.161	7.896	6.906	6.119	5.480	4.956	4.520	4.151	3.988	3.837	3.566	3.330	2.500	2.000
27	20.707	16.330	13.211	10.935	9.237	7.943	6.935	6.136	5.402	4.964	4.524	4.154	3.989	3.839	3.567	3.331	2.500	2.000
28	21.281	16.663	13.466	11.051	9.307	7.984	6.961	6.152	5.502	4.970	4.528	4.157	3.992	3.840	3.568	3.331	2.500	2.000
29	21.844	16.984	13.591	11.158	9.370	8.022	6.983	6.166	5.510	4.975	4.531	4.159	3.994	3.841	3.569	3.332	2.500	2.000
30	22.396	17.292	13.765	11.258	9.427	8.055	7.003	6.177	5.517	4.979	4.534	4.160	3.995	3.842	3.569	3.332	2.500	2.000
40	27.355	19.793	15.106	11.925	9.779	8.244	7.105	6.234	5.543	4.997	4.544	4.166	3.999	3.846	3.571	3.333	2.500	2.000

In present value calculations, the interest rate is frequently referred to as the discount rate. Appendix table 14.3 gives us the proper discount factors at various rates.

What is the present value, using a discount rate of 10 percent, of $1,000 to be received at the end of each year for two years? Using appendix table 14.3, one can calculate the answer by taking the present value of $1,000 for one year and the present value of $1,000 for two years and totaling the results as indicated by the following:

$$PV = \frac{1,000}{(1+.10)^1} + \frac{1,000}{(1+.10)^2} = \$1,735$$

In general, the present value of an ordinary annuity of $1 in arrears can be expressed as

$$PV = \frac{1}{(1+i)^1} + \frac{1}{(1+i)^2} +, \ldots, + \frac{1}{(1+i)^{n-1}} + \frac{1}{(1+i)^n}$$

or

$$PV = \frac{1 - \dfrac{1}{(1+i)^n}}{i}$$

Using this formula as the basis, appendix table 14.4 gives the proper factors for discounting a series of constant cash flows at various discount rates. By comparing appendix table 14.4 with appendix table 14.3, you can see that the latter is nothing more than an aggregation of factors from appendix table 14.3. For instance, the factor 3.274, taken from appendix table 14.4, fifth period at 16 percent can be duplicated in appendix table 14.3 by summing the factors under 16 percent for the first five periods.

QUESTIONS

Q14-1. What is capital budgeting?

Q14-2. Describe the components of an effective capital-expenditure management system.

Q14-3. Why are cash flows more important than income flows in capital budgeting?

Q14-4. Discuss the significance of depreciation in capital budgeting.

Q14-5. Discuss payback along with its strengths and weaknesses.

Q14-6. What is meant by discounted cash flow techniques?

Q14-7. Discuss the limitations of the accounting rate of return method.

Q14-8. What is meant by the required rate of return?

Q14-9. Discuss the impact of emergency replacement situations on use of evaluation techniques.

Q14-10. Discuss some of the practical problems associated with capital budgeting.

Q14-11. The president of XYZ Company approved a capital-investment proposal calling for the construction of a new warehouse. The warehouse was to cost $100,000 and was expected to be completed in six months. You are in the process of reviewing the status of the project and find that $80,000 has been expended and five months have elapsed since the start of construction. Identify the items you will want to review in your analysis.

Q14-12. A company is considering two proposals. Proposal A and B are competing for funds and require a $100,000 outlay each. Project A promises a return of $40,000 a year for five years. Project B promises a return of $60,000 per year for two years. Utilizing the payback method, which project would be accepted? What is wrong with this approach?

PROBLEMS

P14-1. XYZ Company is considering a project proposal that requires an outlay of $180,000. A return of $40,000 a year is expected for five years. At the end of the first year, the salvage value of the project is expected to be $100,000. It decreases by $10,000 each year after the first year.   *Payback*

Required ☐

1. Calculate the payback period.

2. Discuss the significance of the residual values.

P14-2. Homebuilder's management team is considering the purchase of some building equipment costing $100,000. The equipment is expected to have a life of five years with no salvage value at the end of five years. Returns for the first two years are expected to be $60,000 each year, and they will be $20,000 a year for the next three years.   *Accounting Rate of Return*

Required ☐ Calculate the accounting rate of return and discuss its advantages and disadvantages as they relate to this problem situation.

P14-3. Willburger, Inc., is planning to purchase some new equipment that promises to improve productivity. The equipment will cost $40,000 with an expected useful life of eight years and no salvage value. After-tax cash savings are expected as follows: *Payback*

Year	After-tax cash flows
1	$15,000
2	10,000
3	10,000
4	8,000
5	8,000
6	6,000
7	6,000
8	2,000

Required ☐ Calculate the payback period, and discuss the significance as it relates to this problem.

Payback and Accounting Rate of Return   **P14-4.**   The town manager of Blacksburg is considering two mutually exclusive investment proposals for the town's water utility. Both proposals, A and B, promise cash inflows of $40,000 per year based on an investment of $120,000. Expected useful lives are as follows:

Proposal	Life
A	4
B	5

Required ☐

1. Using the payback method, evaluate the two projects.

2. Using the accounting rate of return method, evaluate the two projects.

3. Comment on the results.

Payback and Accounting Rate of Return   **P14-5.**   The manager of Bindiya Company is considering two mutually exclusive investment proposals for the company's manufacturing operations. The two proposals, X and Y, promise the following cash inflows:

Year	X	Y
1	$20,000	$60,000
2	40,000	40,000
3	60,000	20,000
4	20,000	40,000
5	60,000	

An initial investment of $120,000 is required in each case.

Required ☐

1. Using the payback method, evaluate the two projects.

2. Using the accounting rate-of-return method, evaluate the two projects.

3. Comment on the results.

Incremental Costs and Cash Flows   **P14-6.**   The Amex Company is considering the introduction of a new product that will be manufactured in an existing plant; however, new equipment costing $150,000 with a useful life of five years (no salvage value) will be necessary. The space in the existing plant to be used for the new product is currently used for warehousing. When the new product takes over the warehouse space, on which the actual depreciation is $20,000, Amex Company will rent warehouse space at an annual cost of $25,000. An accounting study produces the following estimates of incremental revenue and expense on an average annual basis:

Sales	$500,000
Cost of merchandise sold (excluding depreciation)	385,000
Depreciation of equipment (straight-line)	30,000
Marketing expense	10,000

The company requires an accounting rate of return of 11 percent (after income taxes) on average investment proposals. The effective income tax rate is 46 percent. Ignore the time value of money.

Required ☐

1. Compute the average annual incremental costs for the first five years (including income taxes) that must be considered in evaluating this decision.

2. Calculate the minimum annual net income needed to meet the company's requirement for this investment.

3. Determine the estimated incremental cash flow during the third year.

(CPA)

P14-7. The Laura Bernstein Company installed equipment costing $50,000 on January 1, 19X1. Due to sudden advances in technology, the equipment's value was reduced to $12,000 by January 5, 19X1. The equipment is to be depreciated on a straight-line basis with no salvage value planned at the end of four years. Incremental costs of operating the equipment are projected to be about $40,000 a year for four years. Due to the technological advances, a replacement machine can now be acquired for $60,000 with related operating costs expected to be $15,000 a year for four years. The replacement equipment is not expected to have a salvage value at the end of four years, and straight-line depreciation is to be used. Assume a tax rate of 40 percent.

Accounting Rate of Return

Required ☐

1. Calculate the relevant cash flows.

2. Calculate the accounting rate of return.

3. Calculate the average accounting rate of return.

P14-8. Globe, Inc., invested in a machine with a useful life of five years and no salvage value. The machine was depreciated using the straight-line method. The annual cash inflow from operations, net of income taxes, was $2,500.

Internal Rate of Return

Required ☐ Assuming that Globe used the internal rate of return method and the rate of return was 14 percent, what was the amount of the original investment? Assuming that the minimum desired rate of return on this investment was 14 percent and the amount of the original investment was $6,500, what would be the net present value, rounded to the nearest dollar?

(CPA)

P14-9. 1. What is the internal rate of return for a project costing $60,000 with returns of $20,000 per year for four years?

Internal Rate of Return

2. What would the rate be if the return were $30,000 a year for the first two years and $10,000 a year for the next two years? Ignore taxes.

General Capital Budgeting Techniques

P14-10. The Irene Co. plans to buy a vending machine costing $50,000. For tax purposes, the machine will be depreciated over a five-year period using the straight-line method and no salvage value. Assume that the investment tax credit or other tax incentives are not applicable to the purchase. Company managers estimate that this machine will yield an annual after-tax cash inflow of $15,000. The desired rate of return on the Irene Co. investments is 12 percent.

Required □

1. Calculare the Irene Co.'s accounting rate of return on its initial investment in the machine.

2. Calculate the expected payback period for the investment.

3. Calculate the internal rate of return.

4. Calculate the net present value.

Internal Rate of Return

P14-11. The management staff of Town Company has decided not to accept a project unless they can get at least a 20 percent return. Project A will cost $140,000 with an expected return of $60,000 a year for four years. The equipment will have a salvage value of $20,000 at the end of four years.

Required □ Calculate the expected internal rate of return for project A. Ignore taxes.

Accounting Rate of Return and Net Present Value

P14-12. The Apex Company is evaluating a capital-budgeting proposal for the current year. The initial investment would be $30,000. It would be depreciated on a straight-line basis over six years with no salvage. The before-tax annual cash inflow due this investment is $10,000, and the income tax rate is 40 percent paid the same year incurred. The desired rate of return is 16 percent. All cash flows occur at year-end.

Required □

1. What is the after-tax accounting rate of return on the company's capital-budgeting proposal?

2. What is the net present value of the company's capital-budgeting proposal?

3. How much would Apex have had to invest five years ago at 16 percent compounded annually to have $30,000 now?

(CPA)

General Capital-Budgeting Techniques

P14-13. The George Company is planning to acquire a new machine at a total cost of $30,600. The estimated life of the machine is six years, and estimated salvage value is $600. George Company officials estimate that annual cash savings from using this machine will be $8,000. Assume the company's cost of capital is 8 percent, and its income tax rate is 40 percent.

Required □

1. Calculate the annual after-tax net cash benefits of this investment proposal. (Use straight-line depreciation.)

2. Calculate the payback period.

3. Calculate the net present value.

4. Calculate the accounting rate of return.

(CPA)

P14-14. Jack, Henry, and Smith, three franchised home appliance dealers, have requested short-term financing for their company. The dealers have agreed to repay the loans within three years and to pay Benjamin Industries 6 percent of net income for the three-year period for the use of the funds. The following table summarizes by dealer the financing requested and the total remittance (principal plus 6 percent of net income) expected at the end of each year: *Net Present Value Calculations*

	Jack	Henry	Smith
Financing requested	$ 80,000	$40,000	$30,000
Remittances expected			
Year 1	$ 10,000	$25,000	$10,000
Year 2	40,000	30,000	15,000
Year 3	70,000	5,000	15,000
	$120,000	$60,000	$40,000

Management officials believe these financing requests should be granted only if the annual pre-tax return to the company exceeds the target internal rate of 22 percent on investment.

Required ☐ Prepare a schedule to compute the net present value of the investment opportunities of financing Jack, Henry, and Smith. The schedule should determine if the discounted cash flows expected from (1) Jack, (2) Henry, and (3) Smith would be more or less than the amount of Benjamin Industries investments in loans to each of the three dealers.

(CPA)

P14-15. An individual is faced with two different investment alternatives. In one case, she can invest $100,000 with an expected growth in that investment of 12 percent per year for the next six years. Alternatively, she can purchase some equipment for $100,000 that will provide her with revenues of $30,000 a year for four years and $10,000 a year for the last two years. *Capital Budgeting, Comparison of Alternatives*

Required ☐ Using discounted cash flow methods, prepare an analysis of the alternatives for the individual's use. Ignore taxes in this problem. Assume the equipment will have no salvage value.

P14-16. The Beta Corporation manufactures office equipment and distributes its products through wholesale distributors. *Comprehensive Capital-Budgeting Problem*

Beta Corporation recently learned of a patent on the production of a semiautomatic paper collator that can be obtained at a cost of $60,000 cash. The semiautomatic model is vastly superior to the manual model that the corporation now produces. At a cost of $40,000, present equipment could be modified to accommodate the production of the new semiautomatic model. Such modifications would not affect the remaining useful life of four years or the salvage value of $10,000 that the equipment now has. Variable costs, however, would increase by $1 per unit. Fixed costs, other than relevant amortization charges, would not be affected. If the equipment is modified, the manual model cannot be produced.

The current income statement relative to the manual collator appears as follows:

Sales (100,000 units @ $4)		$400,000
Variable costs	$180,000	
Fixed costs*	120,000	
Total costs		$300,000
Net income before income taxes		$100,000
Income taxes (40%)		40,000
Net income after income taxes		$ 60,000

*All fixed costs are directly allocable to the production of the manual collator and include depreciation on equipment $20,000, calculated on the straight-line basis with a useful life of ten years.

Market research has disclosed three important findings relative to the new semiautomatic model. First, a particular competitor will certainly purchase the patent if Beta Corporation does not. If this were to happen, Beta Corporation sales of the manual collator would fall to 70,000 units per year. Second, if no increase in the selling price is made, Beta Corporation could sell approximately 190,000 units per year of the semiautomatic model. Third, because of the advances being made in this area, the patent will be completely worthless at the end of four years.

Because of the uncertainty of the current situation, the raw materials inventory has been almost completely exhausted. Regardless of the decision reached, substantial and immediate inventory replenishment will be required. The Engineering department estimates that if the new model is to be produced, the average monthly raw materials inventory will be $20,000. If the old model is continued, the inventory balance will average $12,000 per month.

Required ☐

1. Prepare a schedule that shows the incremental after-tax cash flows for the comparison of the two alternatives. Assume that the corporation will use the sum-of-the-years'-digits method for depreciating the costs of modifying the equipment.

2. Assuming that the incremental after-tax cash flows calculated in requirement 1 and the annual incomes for the two alternatives are as given in the following schedule, will Beta Corporation, if it has a cost of capital of 18 percent, decide to manufacture the semiautomatic collator? Use the net present value decision rule and assume all operating revenues and expenses occur at the end of the year.

Year	Incremental cash flow (in thousands)	Annual income (in thousands) Manual	Annual income (in thousands) Semiautomatic
1 Beginning	− $110	—	—
1 End	+ 40	$24	$39
2 End	+ 40	24	39
3 End	+ 40	24	39
4 End	+ 50	24	39

3. Calculate the accounting rate of return for each project. Using this method, would you recommend Beta manufacture the semiautomatic collator? Explain.

4. What concerns would you have about using the information, as given in the problem, to reach a decision in this case?

(CMA)

P14-17. The Baxter Company manufactures toys and other short-lived, fad-type items.

Comprehensive Capital- Budgeting Problem

The Research and Development department came up with an item that would make a good promotional gift for office equipment dealers. Aggressive and effective effort by the Baxter sales personnel has resulted in almost firm commitments for this product for the next three years. It is expected that the product's value will be exhausted by that time.

In order to produce the quantity demanded, Baxter will need to buy additional machinery and rent some additional space. About 25,000 square feet will be needed; 12,500 square feet of currently unused, but leased, space is available now. (Baxter's present lease, with ten years to run, costs $3.00 per foot.) Another 12,500 square feet adjoin the Baxter facility which Baxter will rent for three years at $4.00 per square foot per year if it decides to manufacture this product.

The equipment will be purchased for about $900,000. It will require $30,000 in modifications, $60,000 for installation, and $90,000 for testing; all of these activities will be done by a firm of engineers hired by Baxter. All of the expenditures will be paid for on January 1, 19X3.

The equipment should have a salvage value of about $180,000 at the end of the third year. No additional general overhead costs are expected to be incurred.

The following estimates of revenues and expenses for this product for the three years have been developed:

	19X3	19X4	19X5
Sales	$1,000,000	$1,600,000	$800,000
Material, labor, and incurred overhead	400,000	750,000	350,000
Assigned general overhead	40,000	75,000	35,000
Rent	87,500	87,500	87,500
Depreciation	450,000	300,000	150,000
	$ 977,500	$1,212,500	$622,500
Income before tax	$ 22,500	$ 387,500	$177,500
Income tax (40 percent)	9,000	155,000	71,000
	$ 13,500	$ 232,500	$106,500

Required ☐

1. Prepare a schedule that shows the incremental, after-tax cash flows for this project.

2. If the company requires a two-year payback period for its investment, would it undertake this project? Show your supporting calculations clearly.

3. Calculate the after-tax accounting rate of return for the project.

4. A newly hired business school graduate recommends that the company consider the use of the net present value analysis to study this project. If the company sets a required rate of return of 20 percent after taxes, will this project be accepted? Show your supporting calculations clearly. (Assume all operating revenues and expenses occur at the end of the year.)

(CMA)

Comprehensive Capital-Budgeting Problem

P14-18. The owner of XYZ Store operates a Service department for his customers. Cost of operating the Service department is expected to be about $40,000 per year, and it is expected to be required for another six years based on present market conditions.

A representative of a service company has approached the owner about assuming the service responsibilities for him. If the owner disposed of the Service department, he could sell equipment at an estimated price of $36,000. The representative indicated that the service company would charge the XYZ Store $6 per customer for providing the outside service.

About 8,000 customers use the service, although the owner would expect to lose about 2,000 customers immediately if the owner-operated service were discontinued. This amounts to about $4 profit per customer. Growth in customers is expected to be about 10 percent per year under either alternative.

Required □ Determine the best alternative for the owner of XYZ Store, using the net present value method and a 12 percent discount rate. Ignore taxes.

Comprehensive Capital-Budgeting Problem

P14-19. The Wyle Co. is considering a proposal to acquire new manufacturing equipment. The new equipment has the same capacity as the current equipment, but will provide operating efficiencies in direct and indirect labor, direct-material usage, indirect supplies, and power. Consequently, the savings in operating costs are estimated at $150,000 annually.

The new equipment will cost $300,000 and will be purchased at the beginning of the year when the project is started. The equipment dealer is certain that the equipment will be operational during the second quarter of the year it is installed. Therefore, 60 percent of the estimated annual savings can be obtained in the first year. Wyle will incur a one-time expense of $30,000 to transfer the production activities from the old equipment to the new equipment. No loss of sales will occur, however, because the plant is large enough to install the new equipment without interfering with the operations of the current equipment. The equipment dealer states that most companies use a five-year life when depreciating this equipment.

The current equipment has been fully depreciated and is carried in the accounts at zero book value. The management team has reviewed the condition of the current equipment and has concluded that it can be used an additional five years. Wyle Co. would receive $5,000 net of removal costs if it elected to buy the new equipment and dispose of its current equipment at this time.

Wyle currently leases its manufacturing plant. The annual lease payments are $60,000. The lease, which will have five years remaining when the equipment installation would begin, is not renewable. Wyle Co. would be required to remove any equipment in the plant at the end of the lease. The cost of equipment removal is expected to equal the salvage value of either the old or new equipment at the time of removal.

The company uses the sum-of-the-years'-digits depreciation method for tax purposes. A full year's depreciation is taken in the first year the asset is put into use.

The company is subject to a 40 percent income tax rate and requires an after-tax return of at least 12 percent on any investment.

Required ☐

1. Calculate the annual incremental after-tax cash flows for the Wyle Co. proposal to acquire the new manufacturing equipment.

2. Calculate the net present value of the Wyle Co. proposal to acquire the new manufacturing equipment using the cash flows calculated in requirement 1, and indicate what action Wyle Co. management should take. For ease in calculation, assume all recurring cash flows take place at the end of the year.

(CMA)

P14-20. Hazman Company plans to replace an old piece of equipment that is obsolete and is expected to be unreliable under the stress of daily operations. The equipment is fully depreciated, and no salvage value can be realized upon its disposal.

Comprehensive Capital-Budgeting Problem

One piece of replacement equipment being considered would provide annual cash savings of $7,000 before income taxes. The equipment would cost $18,000 and have an estimated useful life of five years. No salvage value would be used for depreciation purposes because the equipment is expected to have no value at the end of five years.

Hazman uses the straight-line depreciation method on all equipment for both book and tax purposes. The company is subject to a 40 percent tax rate. Hazman has an after-tax cost of capital of 14 percent.

Required ☐

1. Calculate for the Hazman Company's proposed investment in new equipment the after-tax

   a. Payback period
   b. Accounting rate of return
   c. Net present value
   d. Internal rate of return

   Assume all operating revenues and expenses occur at the end of the year.

2. Identify and discuss the issues Hazman Company should consider when deciding which of the four decision models identified in requirement 1 it should employ to compare and evaluate alternative capital investment projects.

(CMA)

CHAPTER OUTLINE

ADDITIONAL CAPITAL BUDGETING TOPICS

CHAPTER **15**

☐ INTRODUCTION

Chapter 14 provided a basic introduction to capital budgeting and capital-expenditure management. In this chapter, a number of additional topics are introduced. These topics either represent additional tools for analysis or touch upon substantial problems faced by the capital-budgeting analyst. We will review the reasons for a conflict in rankings between the internal rate of return and net present value methods; capital rationing; sensitivity and risk analysis; required rate of return considerations; and the role of taxes in analysis.

☐ NET PRESENT VALUE vs.
INTERNAL RATE OF RETURN

Where mutually exclusive projects are being evaluated, use of both the net present value and internal rate of return may provide conflicting acceptance decisions. The basic problem stems from different assumptions made concerning the reinvestment of intermediate cash flows. The internal rate of return method assumes that these funds are reinvested at the internal rate of return throughout the life of the investment. The net present value method assumes that intermediate funds are reinvested at the required rate of return set by the management team.

While differences in the reinvestment assumption alone are not sufficient to cause a difference in rankings, they can cause a ranking difference when competing projects with different outlay requirements (size differences), differences in timing of expected cash flows (timing differences), or different expected lives (useful life differences) are being evaluated.

Size Differences

Consider the following example in which a difference in the initial investment required between mutually exclusive projects exists. For purposes of the example, a required rate of 12 percent is assumed.

	Project X	Project Y
Initial investment	250,000	50,000
Cash inflows	75,000	20,000
Expected life (no salvage)	10 years	10 years

Net present value
  Project X $75,000 (5.650) = $423,750 − $250,000 = $173,750
  Project Y $20,000 (5.650) = $113,000 − $ 50,000 = $ 63,000

Internal rate of return
  Project X 250,000 ÷ 75,000 = 3.33, IROR = 28 percent
  Project Y   50,000 ÷ 20,000 = 2.50, IROR = 40 percent

Acceptance criterion

	X	Y
Net present value	$173,750	$63,000
Internal rate of return	28%	40%

This conflict can be viewed graphically as shown in figure 15.1.

The point of intersection for the two curves can be found by solving for the incremental internal rate of return as follows:

Incremental investment	$200,000
Incremental inflows	55,000

IROR = 200,000/55,000 = 3.64 ≈ 24 percent

The graph points out that to the left of the point of intersection there is a conflict in rankings between the net present value method and the internal rate of return method. By using a discount rate of 24 percent (point of intersection) or higher, both methods will rank project Y as the more desirable project.

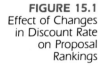

FIGURE 15.1
Effect of Changes in Discount Rate on Proposal Rankings

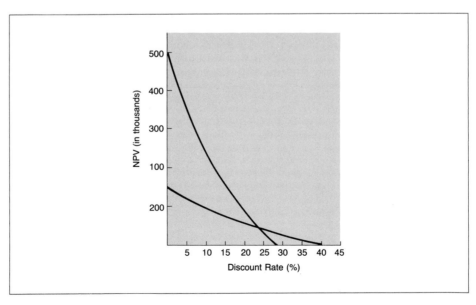

In conflicts of this type, the key to a successful solution is found by focusing attention on the incremental cash outlay required, $200,000 for project X in this specific case. Are there other alternatives totaling $200,000 that promise a higher return (net present value or internal rate of return) than the $55,000 ($75,000 from X minus $20,000 from Y) incremental inflows expected from project X? If not, project X should be considered the more desirable project.

Timing Differences

A conflict similar to the one just discussed can occur when timing of cash inflows varies between competing projects. For example, assume that a decision must be made between the following two mutually exclusive proposals, using a required rate of 10 percent:

Year	Project X	Project Y
0	$(20,000)	$(20,000)
1	5,000	17,000
2	9,000	5,000
3	16,000	5,000

Net present value and internal rate of return for the two projects are:

	X	Y
Net present value	$3,995	$3,338
Internal rate of return	18%	22%

The conflict can again be viewed graphically as shown in figure 15.2. As before, a conflict exists at any discount rate to the left of the point of intersection, 14 percent. The full impact of the differences in the reinvestment assumption can be seen in this example. The only way to resolve the conflict is first to find a common rate that reflects a realistic reinvestment rate and then to incorporate that rate in both proposals. For instance, if one believed that funds could be realistically reinvested at 14 percent, this rate could be incorporated in the alternative by using the factors for

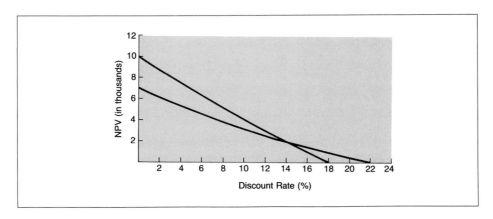

FIGURE 15.2
Effect of Changes in Discount Rate on Proposal Ranking

the future value of an annuity (appendix table 14.1) at 14 percent so as to determine the total value of the inflows from each project at the end of three years. This is shown in the following:

	Project X			Project Y		
Year	Cash flows	Appendix table 14.1 factor	Amount	Cash flows	Appendix table 14.1 factor	Amount
1	5,000 ×	1.30	= $ 6,500	17,000 ×	1.30	= $22,100
2	9,000 ×	1.14	= 10,260	5,000 ×	1.14	= 5,700
3	16,000 ×	1.00	= 16,000	5,000 ×	1.00	= 5,000
	Total		$32,760	Total		$32,800

These total values would then be used to calculate net present value and internal rate of return.

NPV	Future value	Appendix table 14.3 factor	Present value	Initial investment	Net present value
X	$32,760 ×	.675	= $22,113 −	$20,000	= $2,113
Y	32,800 ×	.675	= $22,140 −	$20,000	= $2,140

IROR	IROR factor		From appendix table 14.3
X	20,000 ÷ 32,760	= .61	≈ 18%
Y	20,000 ÷ 32,800	= .61	≈ 18%

As indicated, by using the same reinvestment rate one obtains consistent rankings when comparing the net present value and internal rate of return methods.

Useful Life Differences

In evaluating mutually exclusive projects, competing proposals often do not have a common termination point. One suggested way of handling this problem is to assume reinvestment in one or both proposals until a common terminal point can be found. For instance, consider the following example, assuming a 10 percent discount rate:

Year	Project X	Project Y
0	$(100,000)	$(100,000)
1	120,000	
2		
3		
4		175,000

Ignoring the differences in useful lives, the following results are obtained under the net present value and internal rate of return methods:

	X	Y
Net present value	$9,080	$19,527
Internal rate of return	20%	15%

Looking at the competing proposals, you can see that the analysis is deficient since it gives no consideration to investment possibilities of cash inflows from project X. If you assume a common terminal point of four years and reinvestment in project X, then the analysis yields the following results:

Year	Project X*	Project Y
0	$(100,000)	$(100,000)
1	20,000	
2	20,000	
3	20,000	
4	120,000	175,000

*Assuming reinvestment every year would result in net cash inflows of $20,000 ($100,000 − $120,000) for years 1 through 3.

Net present value and internal rate of return would then provide the following results:

	X	Y
Net present value	$31,698	$19,527
Internal rate of return	20%	15%

Using the indicated reinvestment assumption shifts the net present value preference from proposal Y to X, making it consistent with the IROR preference. But what about those situations when it becomes difficult to find a realistic common terminal point? Similar results can be developed by calculating an **equivalent annual charge**. The equivalent annual charge is derived by dividing the net present value for each alternative by the applicable factor from the present value of $1 received per year table. For proposal X, the applicable factor, namely, .909, is determined by using 10 percent and one year. For proposal Y, the proper factor would be 3.107, using 10 percent and four years. Results are as follows:

Equivalent annual charge for X = $ 9,080 ÷ .909 = $10,000

Equivalent annual charge for Y = 19,527 ÷ 3.170 = $ 6,160

Again, proposal X is preferred over proposal Y.

One other potential problem should be recognized when considering net present value versus internal rate of return. Certain cash flow patterns, where a proposal has one or more negative cash flows subsequent to the initial outlay, can result in multiple internal rates of return for the proposal. Under such conditions, there is no valid internal rate of return. For instance, assume the following pattern of cash flows:

Time period	Cash flows
0	− 72,727
1	170,909
2	− 100,000

The internal rate of return for this example is 10 percent and 26 percent.

At 10 percent: −72,727 + (.909)170,909 − (.826)100,000 ≈ 0

At 26 percent: −72,727 + (.794)170,909 − (.630)100,000 ≈ 0

Which Method Should Be Used?

The use of net present value assumes that intermediate cash flows generated by the investment are reinvested at the required rate of return. Use of the internal rate of return assumes, unrealistically, reinvestment at the internal rate. Also, due to the multiple internal rate of return problem mentioned earlier, it is possible that a valid internal rate of return would not exist in some situations. For these reasons the net present value method is considered theoretically superior to the internal rate of return method.

In spite of the theoretical preference for net present value, managers in many large corporations tend to prefer the internal rate of return method. This apparent contradiction is due to the fact that managers often use various rates of return rather than financial returns. Segment performance is often evaluated in terms of rates of return on investment (chapter 17). Managers are comfortable talking about various profitability rates, interest rates, and various benefits relative to amounts invested.

☐ CAPITAL RATIONING

Companies often find that there are more acceptable projects than they have the money to undertake because of limits placed on the amount of funds to be committed to capital investments in a given period. Under such operating conditions, managers must attempt to select that continuation of acceptable proposals that will maximize the overall return to the company.

Why wouldn't the management team commit funds to all project proposals that promise to enhance long-term profitability of the company? Realistically, managers are often under pressure to improve short-term profits and sometimes consciously make selections based on maximizing short-term profits. Uncertainty causes managers to avoid some commitments. As a result, funds are simply not available for all promising proposals.

Assume a company expects to have $1 million for investment purposes, and the following proposals are available with indicated returns based on the net present value and internal rate of return methods:

Project	Cash outlay required	Net present value @ 12%	Internal rate of return %
A	$ 500,000	$100,000	20
B	400,000	60,000	18
C	600,000	80,000	16
D	200,000	50,000	15
E	100,000	10,000	14
F	200,000	40,000	14
Total	$2,000,000		

As indicated by the schedule, all projects promise a positive net present value and an internal rate greater than the required rate. Rankings under the net present value method and internal rate of return methods would be

	Net present value			Internal rate of return	
Project	Outlay	NPV	Project	Outlay	NPV
A	$ 500,000	$100,000	A	$ 500,000	$100,000
D	200,000	50,000	B	400,000	60,000
E	100,000	10,000	E	100,000	10,000
F	200,000	40,000			
Total	$1,000,000	$200,000		$1,000,000	$170,000

The net present value is highest when projects A, D, E, and F are selected. This is the same as maximizing net present value because the rationed budget is viewed as the initial investment for which maximum present value of benefits must be obtained. When the number of alternatives and fund availability become more complex, it is extremely difficult to arrive at the best combination by a single visual ranking. In such cases, it is usually best to resort to analytical methods such as integer programming for an optimal allocation of resources.

☐ REQUIRED RATE OF RETURN

Throughout the material on capital budgeting, a certain **required rate of return** has been assumed for purposes of working through examples using the net present value or internal rate of return methods. It was noted that companies use different terms to refer to this rate, which expresses their minimum return expectations regarding a particular proposal. Although finance theorists have been dealing with the topic for many years, management accountants have not developed adequate methods for advising members of management on how to arrive at a meaningful rate for analysis purposes. Conceptually, one knows the required rate combines a risk-free rate (frequently associated with the interest rate for government securities) with a risk premium reflecting investors' perceptions of the risk related to the company. At present, the premium is identifiable for individual projects only by highly subjective means.[1]

Until financial theory provides the business community with an acceptable means for calculating the risk premium—through risk analysis, application of the capital asset pricing model, or other comparable techniques—managers will continue to develop highly subjective rates for their use.[2] For instance, some managers are assigning what they consider to be meaningful target rates based on expectations for individual divisions or programs in a company. Other managers are attempting to find listed companies with risk exposures comparable to their individual divisions so that the identified company's historical return might be used as a basis for developing the division's required return.

1. An introduction to this topic is provided in a subsequent section of this chapter.

2. See chapters 6 and 7 in James C. Van Horne, *Financial Management and Policy*, 5th ed. (Prentice-Hall: New York, 1980).

Still other managers continue to use a single rate for all projects of the company. The single rate (weighted-average method) may be appropriate if the following criteria are met:

1. A market for the company's securities is well established.

2. The relative portion of the components in the company's capital structure is constant.

3. Commitment to various capital projects does not alter the investing public's perception of the company's risk.

The weighted-average approach looks on cost of capital as an average cost of the various means of financing, both externally and internally generated. Consider the following example:

Capital structure
Market value of bonds .... $10,000(1/3)
Market value of stock .... 20,000(2/3)
   Total $30,000

Projected income data
Expected operating profit .... $ 2,000
Interest expense 400
Net profit .... $ 1,600

Debt costs = 400/10,000 = .04
Internal costs = 1,600/20,000 = .08
Weighted-average costs = .066 [1/3(.04) + 2/3(.08)]

In many cases, this basic approach is expanded. Debt cost might refer to interest on new debt financing. Internal financing costs through retained earnings are represented by dividing earnings per share anticipated by market value of the stock, while common stock financing costs might be developed by dividing earnings anticipated by net proceeds of common stock issuance. In this case, the cost of equity capital refers to a rate of return that stockholders might require before they will invest their funds. Calculations might be made as follows:

XYZ COMPANY
Capital Structure

Long-term debt (5 percent) .... $ 50,000   .20
Equity 200,000   .80
  Invested capital $250,000   1.00

Expected earnings per share .... $ 2
Market value of stock $20

Debt cost (given above) 5%
Equity cost (2 ÷ 20) 10%

Weighted-average cost of capital
  5% × 20% = ... 1%
  10% × 80% = ... 8%
   Cost of capital 9%

Consider the following example:[3]

Calculate the average cost of capital with the following information given:

The capital structure of Niebuhr Corporation follows:

	Amount	Percent
Short-term notes at 5 percent interest	$ 3,500,000	10%
4 percent cumulative preferred stock, $100 par	1,750,000	5
Common stock	12,250,000	35
Retained earnings	17,500,000	50
Total	$35,000,000	100%

Additional data available is:

	Current market price	Expected EPS	Expected dividend per share
Preferred stock, noncallable	$120	—	$4.00
Common stock	50	$3.20	1.60

The average marginal income tax rate for Niebuhr stockholders is estimated to be 25 percent. Assume that the corporate income tax rate is 50 percent.

Required ☐

The budget committee has asked you to check the reasonableness of the cutoff rate. You realize that one of the factors to be considered is an estimate of the average cost of capital to this firm. Prepare a schedule, supported by computations in good form, to compute the average cost of capital weighted by the percentage of the capital structure that each element represents.

This particular problem is closely related to the previous discussion on cost of capital and in addition considers (1) short-term notes, (2) preferred stock financing, and (3) after-tax costs. Short-term notes are handled in the same manner as long-term debt. Preferred stock financing is similar to long-term debt in determining an interest factor but is less desirable because its cost is not reduced by taxes. Taxes in the problem serve to reduce cost of debt and retained-earnings financing. The solution is given as follows:

Computation of average cost of capital

Capital structure	%		Cost		Average cost
Notes	10%	×	2.50%	(1)	.25%
Preferred stock	5	×	3.33	(2)	.17
Common stock	35	×	6.40	(3)	2.24
Retained earnings	50	×	4.80	(4)	2.40
Average cost of capital					5.06%

(1) 5% interest rate ≈ (5% × (1 − 50% tax rate)) = 2.50% cost
(2) $4 dividend ÷ $120 market price = 3.33% cost
(3) $3.20 EPS ÷ $50.00 market price = 6.40% cost
(4) $3.20 (1 − .25 marginal tax rate)/$50.00 market price = 4.80% cost

Cost of capital theory remains an unsettled issue. Nevertheless, it is an essential part of capital-expenditure analysis, and accountants should be

3. Adapted from problem appearing on the May 1967 CPA examination.

familiar with different approaches to determination of the required rate. Additional exposure to risk analysis will be given in a subsequent section.

At this point, you should at least be aware that required rates are a function of a risk-free rate, risk premium, and sometimes an inflation premium. When applicable, attempts should be made to make use of probabilities through risk analysis in evaluating proposals. In most instances, however, managers will have to rely on their judgment with respect to proposal requirements.

☐ SENSITIVITY ANALYSIS

The capital-budgeting problem exists because accountants must estimate future cash flows. Even the discount rates used with the net present value method are nothing more than estimates of a company's required return from projects. Indeed, in an actual situation, practically all data used are estimates and thus subject to error. What happens when an estimated value included in the analysis is incorrect? Through the use of **sensitivity analysis,** additional information relating to problems can be provided. By means of this type of analysis, upper and lower limits—which should be of some value to the decision maker—can be placed on the various values. In order to provide an orientation to sensitivity analysis, sample cash flow values and the required rate will be ranged.

Ranging Cash Flow Values

Using the **net present value** method to evaluate a proposal, the decision rule can usually be stated in the following manner:

If estimated cash inflows are greater than cash outflows, both multiplied by appropriate factors, accept the proposed project.

For example, using the following format as a basis, assume that a proposal estimated to cost $10,000 is expected to provide a return of $4,000 a year for four years. Company management requires a return of 14 percent. Since the $4,000 cash inflows are nothing more than an estimate, the management staff wants to know the lower limit of this estimate that will still provide a favorable result. The answer is developed as follows:

$X(2.914) = \$10,000$, (where X equals the cash inflow) is the minimum acceptance point. Solving for X:

$X(2.914) = \$10,000$
$X = \$10,000 \div 2.914$
$X = \$3,432$

This analysis indicates that the company management officials could expect favorable results from the project even if cash inflows were as small as $3,432. By means of ranging, management personnel have been given additional information regarding the proposal.

Ranging Required Rates

There is always a possibility that the management team's estimate of the required return may be of some concern. Through an analysis similar to the one just cited, an upper limit for the required rate can also be determined. Assume from the preceding problem that the management personnel desire to know the highest discount rate that will yield a favorable decision on the proposed projects. The solution is as follows:

$4,000($Y$) = $10,000, (where Y equals the discount factor) is the minimum acceptance point

Solving for Y:
$4,000 ($Y$) = $10,000
$Y = 2.5$

From appendix table 14.4, the 2.5 value for Y yields a discount rate of about 22 percent. The management team again is provided with additional insight into the problem situation by means of sensitivity analysis.

Other Considerations

Although it may be possible to increase the management officials' awareness by means of sensitivity analysis, uncertainty cannot be eliminated. Since all data relating to the problem are estimates, any one or more data elements are subject to change, thereby creating potentially much more complicated problems for analysis. In many cases, cash flows involved cannot be expected to be consistent from year to year. In such cases, sensitivity analysis as outlined cannot be depended on as a useful tool. Nevertheless, the technique suggests that it is desirable to range all significant estimates involved in capital-expenditure analysis.

☐ RISK ANALYSIS

Cash flows in capital-budgeting proposals reflect single-point estimates. Consequently, the projected cash flows for any future year may be represented by a range of values. Typically, there are varying expectations regarding the individual values within a range. If these expectations can be converted to probabilities, they can be used to develop expected values of the net present value and a standard deviation for the project. The standard deviation then provides a measure of the amount of *risk* (or uncertainty) surrounding a project proposal. Use of statistical analysis also simplifies some of the complexities in deriving a required rate since risk is a major factor in determining the rate. For instance, if cash flows could be adjusted for risk, then the adjusted cash flows could be discounted at the risk-free rate.

Suppose you were considering mutually exclusive proposals **X** and **Y** with the expected cash flows for four years shown as follows:

Competing Proposals*

	X (in thousands)			Y (in thousands)	
Probability	Cash flows	Weighted value	Probability	Cash flows	Weighted value
.10	$2.0	$ .20	.10	$2.0	$ .20
.30	4.0	1.20	.25	3.0	.75
.40	4.5	1.80	.30	4.0	1.20
.10	5.0	.50	.25	5.0	1.25
.10	3.0	.30	.10	6.0	.60
Expected cash flows (E.V.)		$4.00	Expected cash flows (E.V.)		$4.00

*Adapted from James C. Van Horne, *Financial Management and Policy*, 5th ed. (Prentice-Hall: New York, 1980), p. 149.

Both proposals have the same expected values. In order to assess the relative riskiness of the two projects, one needs to calculate the standard deviation for each proposal. Using the formula,

$$S.\,D. = \left[\sum_{x=1}^{n} (CF_x - EV)^2 P_x \right]^{1/2} \text{ where}$$

$S.\,D.$ = Standard Deviation
CF = Cash flow
EV = Mean of expected values
P = Probability attached to cash flow

One can calculate the standard deviation for projects X and Y as follows:

Project X
$(\$2 - \$4)^2 \times .10 = \$ .40$
$(\$4 - \$4)^2 \times .30 = —$
$(\$4.5 - \$4)^2 \times .40 = .10$
$(\$5 - \$4)^2 \times .10 = .10$
$(\$3 - \$4)^2 \times .10 = \underline{.10}$
$\$ .70$ $S.D. = \sqrt{.70} = \$.84$

Project Y
$(\$2 - \$4)^2 \times .10 = \$ .40$
$(\$3 - \$4)^2 \times .25 = .25$
$(\$4 - \$4)^2 \times .30 = —$
$(\$5 - \$4)^2 \times .25 = .25$
$(\$6 - \$4)^2 \times .10 = \underline{.40}$
$\$1.30$ $S.D. = \sqrt{1.30} = \$1.14$

The standard deviation for **Y** is larger, indicating a greater degree of risk for **Y** even though both proposals had the same expected value. If the proposals had different expected values, a coefficient of variation (standard deviation divided by expected value) could be used to provide a relative measure of the risk.

Continuing with the previous example, assume it was necessary to calculate the net present value for the two projects, X and Y. The company's required rate, using risk analysis, is currently 12 percent. Both projects require an initial investment of $8,000.

Net present value (in thousands)
Project X
$\quad$ NPV $= \$4(3.037) - \$8$
$\quad$ NPV $= \$4.15$
Project Y
$\quad$ NPV $= \$4(3.037) - \$8$
$\quad$ NPV $= \$4.15$

Since the net present value of the expected values is the same for both projects, management personnel should review the standard deviations, or coefficients of variation if applicable, before choosing between the projects. Assuming the cash flows are perfectly correlated, the standard deviations would be calculated as follows:

Project X

$$\text{S.D.} = \frac{.84}{(1.12)} + \frac{.84}{(1.12)^2} + \frac{.84}{(1.12)^3} + \frac{.84}{(1.12)^4} = 2.5515$$

Project Y

$$\text{S.D.} = \frac{1.14}{(1.12)} + \frac{1.14}{(1.12)^2} + \frac{1.14}{(1.12)^3} + \frac{1.14}{(1.12)^4} = 3.4626$$

If there is serial independence with respect to the cash flows, the standard deviations would then be calculated:

Project X

$$\text{S.D.} = \left[\frac{(.84)^2}{(1.12)^2} + \frac{(.84)^2}{(1.12)^4} + \frac{(.84)^2}{(1.12)^6} + \frac{(.84)^2}{(1.12)^8} \right]^{1/2} = 1.2858$$

Project Y

$$\text{S.D.} = \left[\frac{(1.14)^2}{(1.12)^2} + \frac{(1.14)^2}{(1.12)^4} + \frac{(1.14)^2}{(1.12)^6} + \frac{(1.14)^2}{(1.12)^8} \right]^{1/2} = 1.7450$$

While the foregoing example introduces the notion of risk analysis, it is obviously an oversimplification of the problem for several reasons. Each year's cash flow projections cannot be expected to have the same risk. Indeed, greater uncertainty would be expected for each succeeding year in the future. Moreover, correlation of cash flows over time would have to be considered and the specific model to be used determined only after considering the degree of correlation.

Use of **risk analysis** requires a great deal of sophistication on the part of the management team and the accountant. This brief material only suggests possibilities. Substantial material exists for those who want to consider the subject in more detail.[4]

4. See for instance, David B. Hertz, "Risk Analysis in Capital Investment," *Harvard Business Review*, January-February 1964, pp. 95–06, and James Van Horne, *Financial Management and Policy*, pp. 147–80.

☐ CAPITAL BUDGETING AND INFLATION

The general decline in the purchasing power of the monetary unit has become a way of life in most of the world. In the 1970s, substantial inflation was present in a number of different economies, and it is possible that continued difficulties will be experienced over the balance of the 1980s as accountants provide and analyze information for management planning and control. Therefore, capital-budgeting models should be appropriately adjusted to give recognition to inflationary effects.

Sometimes, management officials adjust the required rate for investments by an inflation factor so that the required rate consists of:

Required rate = [(Risk-free rate + Business-risk rate) × (Expected inflation rate)]^n

n = Time period

If this is done, then the cash flows should also be adjusted to reflect the expected effects of inflation. In making these adjustments, one must remember that the tax effects of depreciation are based on the unadjusted (historical) cost of the fixed asset. Consider the following example:

The president of Lan Corporation is considering the purchase of certain equipment that promises to provide cost reductions of about $200,000 per year to the already profitable operations of the plant. The equipment will cost $500,000 installed and is expected to last for five years. Straight-line depreciation is to be used and no residual value is anticipated. The existing required rate for equipment of this type is 15 percent, but the company's economist has forecast a 10 percent rate of inflation for the next five to eight years. The approximate tax rate for Lan Corporation is 40 percent.

After-tax Cash Flow Calculation

	Year 0	Year 1	Year 2	Year 3	Year 4	Year 5
Cash flows	$(600,000)	$200,000	$200,000	$200,000	$200,000	$200,000
Inflation factor	(1.00)	(1.10)	$(1.10)^2$	$(1.10)^3$	$(1.10)^4$	$(1.10)^5$
Inflation adjusted cash flows	(600,000)	220,000	242,000	266,200	292,820	322,102
Depreciation		120,000	120,000	120,000	120,000	120,000
Before-tax income		100,000	122,000	146,200	172,820	202,102
After-tax income		60,000	73,200	87,720	103,692	121,261
Depreciation		120,000	120,000	120,000	120,000	120,000
After-tax cash flow		$180,000	$193,200	$207,720	$223,692	$241,261

Net Present Value Calculation

$$PV = \frac{\$180,000}{[(1.15)(1.10)]} + \frac{\$193,200}{[(1.15)(1.10)]^2} + \frac{\$207,720}{[(1.15)(1.10)]^3} + \frac{\$223,692}{[(1.15)(1.10)]^4} + \frac{\$241,261}{[(1.15)(1.10)]^5}$$

PV = $527,475

NPV = $527,475–$500,000

NPV = $27,475

The overall impact of inflation is to add more uncertainty to the capital-budgeting decision. When inflation becomes a significant factor, decision makers appear to have a tendency to rely more heavily on evaluation methods that favor the short term—such as payback or even the internal rate of return method—which would tend to favor proposals with shorter lives.

☐ CURRENT TAX IMPLICATIONS

If capital-budgeting analysis is to be properly performed, it must be done with a sound understanding of the tax implications of each proposal being considered. Tax laws vary widely from country to country, and they change rather frequently in individual countries.

The Economic Recovery Tax Act of 1981 was designed in large part to increase savings and spur investment. Significant changes were made with respect to depreciation for tangible assets placed in service after 1980. Under the 1982 act, the **Accelerated Cost Recovery System** (ACRS) is to be used for most tangible depreciable property placed in service after 1980. Under this method, the cost of eligible assets is recovered over a three-year, five-year, ten-year, or fifteen-year period on an accelerated basis (straight-line optional) established by the system.

While the examples in the preceding material give recognition to the tax implications of depreciation, they do not attempt to reflect specific provisions of the ACRS.

Unless specific provisions are revised, ACRS does away with other accelerated methods of depreciation and residual values on new capital asset acquisitions for tax purposes, but retains certain features of the straight-line method, which might be elected by taxpayers.

Since tax provisions change frequently, there is no particular advantage to providing examples on specific areas of the current law. This section is included only to highlight the importance of tax provisions to capital-budgeting analysis and to indicate that the management accountant must be aware of current tax provisions before attempting to evaluate investment proposals.

☐ SUMMARY

The primary goal of capital-expenditure analysis is to provide management personnel with relevant information for decision-making purposes. Basic tools used to develop this information were discussed in chapter 14. This chapter builds on this basic knowledge by discussing certain complicating factors and by introducing additional tools for analysis.

The reasons for the conflict between net present value and internal rate of return with respect to mutually exclusive projects was explained. The problem exists because of differences in the reinvestment assumption and timing, size, and asset-life differences. Capital rationing and inflation were introduced as "facts of life" in today's environment. Given the fact that the manangement team is going to limit the amount of capital investment, ways must be developed to optimize the rationing process. Inflation introduces additional uncertainty into the evaluation process and makes projections even more difficult. Nevertheless, analysis is not complete without a proper consideration of the impact of inflation.

With respect to capital budgeting, sensitivity analysis and risk analysis can improve information provided to the management team. Sensitivity analysis requires that ranges be developed by varying critical variables in the analysis. Its main value lies in the fact that managers are provided with a better understanding of the effect of changes in the value used in the projections. Risk analysis, as its name implies, is an attempt to quantify and measure the risk inherent in different proposals by using probabilities and calculating the standard deviation about expected values. When used, it reduces the problems associated with determining the proper required rate for a particular proposal.

Finally, the importance of a good working knowledge of taxes and their effect on the analysis of capital proposals was emphasized. Tax laws are constantly changing. These changes are frequently directly applicable, in large part, to capital investments.

KEY TERMS

Accelerated Cost Recovery System (ACRS)
Capital rationing
Equivalent annual charge

Net present value
Required rate of return
Risk analysis
Sensitivity analysis

REVIEW PROBLEM

The owner of the Atlas Company is planning to purchase new equipment that promises to provide cost reductions of $50,000 per year to the profitable operations of the company. The equipment is expected to cost $90,000 and should last for three years. Cost recovery (depreciation) will be spread evenly over the three years. The required rate of return for equipment of this type is 12 percent. The tax rate for Atlas Company is 50 percent. A rate of inflation of 4 percent per year has been projected for the next four years.

Required □ Calculate the net present value of the planned purchase, giving appropriate consideration to inflation.

Solution □ After-tax cash flow calculation:

Cost savings per year	$50,000
Cost recovery	30,000

Profit before taxes	$20,000
Taxes	10,000
Net profit	$10,000
Add-back cost recovery	30,000
Cash flow	$40,000*

*Cash flows of $25,000 plus $15,000 due to tax effect of cost recovery.

$PV =$

$$\frac{(25,000)(1.04) + 15,000}{[(1.12)(1.04)]} + \frac{(25,000)(1.04)^2 + 15,000}{[(1.12)(1.04)]^2} + \frac{(25,000)(1.04)^3 + 15,000}{[(1.12)(1.04)]^3} = \$93,469$$

$NPV = \$93,469 - \$90,000$

$NPV = \$3,469$

QUESTIONS

Q15-1. In evaluating mutually exclusive proposals, describe the conditions under which you might have a conflict between the net present value and internal rate of return methods.

Q15-2. In evaluating competing proposals with useful life differences, how would you attempt to eliminate the problem of unequal lives?

Q15-3. What conditions would cause a project proposal to have multiple internal rates of return?

Q15-4. Discuss the significance of the difference in reinvestment assumptions between the net present value and internal rate of return methods.

Q15-5. What is meant by capital rationing?

Q15-6. What procedures are followed for ranking investment proposals under the net present value method?

Q15-7. What is meant by the required rate of return?

Q15-8. Discuss how the required rate of return might be derived.

Q15-9. What is the purpose of sensitivity analysis as used in the capital-budgeting decision?

Q15-10. What is your assessment of the value of sensitivity analysis?

Q15-11. What is the purpose of risk analysis as used in capital budgeting?

Q15-12. What changes are brought about in the required rate of return when using risk analysis?

Q15-13. What is the function of the standard deviation in risk analysis?

Q15-14. Describe the problems found by the accountant in using risk analysis.

Q15-15. Describe the impact of inflation on the capital-budgeting decision.

Q15-16. Why should the capital-budgeting analyst be knowledgeable about current tax provisions?

PROBLEMS

Comparison of Net Present Value and Internal Rate of Return

P15-1. Project proposal A requires an outlay initially of $4,000 with expected returns of $2,700 a year for two years. Proposal B, a competing project, requires an outlay of $10,000 with expected returns of $6,600 a year for two years. The company uses a 10 percent required rate of return.

Required ☐ Calculate the net present value and internal rate of return for each project. Which project should be chosen? Justify your answer to the extent possible.

Comparison of Net Present Value and Internal Rate of Return

P15-2. Margaret Meyer, controller of Ocean Engineering Corporation, has asked you to evaluate two mutually exclusive proposals, Compression (C) and Decompression (D). C requires an initial outlay of $200,000 with a promised return of $240,000 at the end of the year. D requires an initial investment of $200,000 with a single return of $350,000 at the end of the fourth year. The company's required rate of return is 10 percent.

Required ☐

1. Calculate the net present value for each project.

2. Calculate the internal rate of return for each project.

3. Evaluate the overall results.

Comparison of Net Present Value and Internal Rate of Return

P15-3. The controller of the Easy Corporation has asked you to evaluate two mutually exclusive projects, A and B. A requires an initial outlay of $5,000 with promised return of $2,000 per year for five years. B requires a $5,000 outlay but returns are expected to be about $1,500 per year for eight years. The company's cost of capital rate is 10 percent.

Required ☐

1. Calculate the net present value for the projects.

2. Calculate the internal rate of return for the projects.

3. Evaluate the projects, using the equivalent annual charge.

Comparison of Net Present Value and Internal Rate of Return

P15-4. Two mutually exclusive projects are being considered by the management team of Standard Company. Proposal 1 will cost $5,000 and will provide a return of $2,000 per year for five years. Proposal 2 will also cost $5,000, but returns are expected to be about $3,500 per year for two years. Neither proposal is expected to have a salvage value at the end of its estimated useful life. The declining value for each proposal can be approximated by straight-line depreciation. The required return is 16 percent.

Required ☐

1. Calculate the net present value for each project.

2. Calculate the internal rate of return for each project.

3. Evaluate the projects using a common terminal point.

P15-5. XYZ Company is considering the following mutually exclusive investment proposals. Proposal A is expected to cost $20,000 with promised returns of $15,500 each year for two years. Proposal B is expected to cost $20,000 also; however, it offers a single return of $33,900 expected at the end of the second year. The required rate of return is set at 12 percent. *Comparison of Net Present Value and Internal Rate of Return*

Required ☐

1. Calculate the net present value for each project.

2. Calculate the internal rate of return for each project.

3. Indicate which proposal should be selected.

P15-6. The production manager of LISA Company finds that a decision must be made between two competing proposals—project X and project Y. The following cash flows have been projected for the two projects: *Comparison of Net Presdent Value and Internal Rate of Return*

Year	Project X	Project Y
0	$(10,000)	$(10,000)
1	2,500	8,500
2	4,500	2,500
3	8,000	2,500

The required rate of return is 10 percent.

Required ☐

1. Calculate the net present value for each proposal.

2. Calculate the internal rate of return for each proposal.

3. Select the best proposal.

P15-7. PAUL, Inc., has $200,000 available for commitment to capital expenditures in the next fiscal period. By means of capital-budgeting techniques, all available proposals have been screened and the following proposals offer an opportunity to increase the company's profits: *Capital Rationing*

Proposal	Required investment	Net present value
N	$ 55,000	$ 6,000
O	25,000	12,000
P	110,000	60,000
Q	100,000	56,000
R	10,000	5,000
S	40,000	8,000
T	15,000	4,000
U	50,000	14,000
V	200,000	85,000

Required ☐ Which proposals should be accepted? Why?

P15-8. The capital budgeting director of the Dot Company has been asked to identify the best group of projects from those in the following schedule. She has been given a limit on total expenditures of $1 million. *Capital Rationing*

Proposal	Required investment	Net present value
I	$800,000	$160,000
II	500,000	70,000
III	100,000	25,000
IV	300,000	84,000
V	200,000	10,000
VI	900,000	90,000
VII	100,000	50,000
VIII	250,000	10,000

Required ☐ Which proposals should be accepted?

Capital Rationing **P15-9.** Assume the same facts given in 15-8 except that we now know that expected useful life of each proposal is four years except for proposal IV. Proposal IV's estimated life is one year.

Required ☐ Which proposals should be accepted? Why?

Sensitivity Analysis **P15-10.** The manager of Shaindasani International, Inc., is considering a project proposal expected to cost $100,000. Cash inflows are expected to average about $20,000 a year for ten years. The company requires a return of 14 percent for projects of this type.

Required ☐

1. Calculate the lower limit for estimated inflows.

2. Calculate the upper limit for the required rate.

Sensitivity Analysis **P15-11.** The XYZ Company is considering a project proposal expected to cost $25,000. Returns are expected to average about $8,000 per year for the next five years. Company management officials have set a required return of 12 percent for all projects.

Required ☐ Range all relevant estimates and write an explanation of their meaning.

Sensitivity Analysis **P15-12.** The management team of the Town Company has decided not to accept a project unless they can get at least a 20 percent return. Project A will cost $140,000 with an expected return of $60,000 a year for four years.

Required ☐ Range all relevant estimates and explain.

Risk Analysis **P15-13.** The investment manager of the XYZ Company is considering a capital expenditure proposal that will require a cash outlay of $50,000, with constant cash savings promised for each of the next four years. Probabilities associated with the cash savings are shown as follows:

Annual savings	Probability
$ 5,000	20%
15,000	20%
30,000	50%
40,000	10%

Required ☐ Calculate the expected value and standard deviation for the proposal.

P15-14. The accountant at the Singapore Shipping Company is attempting to *Risk Analysis*
evaluate two mutually exclusive proposals, A and B. Both require an
initial investment of $10,000. The company's required rate of return is 10
percent. Cash inflows are expected for ten years on each project. Assume
each year's cash flows are perfectly correlated. A schedule of expected
cash flows follows:

Project	Probability	Cash inflows per year
A	.25	$1,500
	.50	3,000
	.25	2,500
B	.25	$2,000
	.50	2,500
	.25	4,000

Required ☐

1. Calculate the expected net present value for each project.

2. Calculate the standard deviation for each of the projects. Which project
should be accepted? Why?

P15-15. The capital budgeting manager of Hawa Construction Company is in the *Risk Analysis*
process of evaluating two investment proposals, X and Y. Either will
require a $20,000 investment. Cash flows are expected for five years and
are perfectly correlated. The company's required rate, when using risk
analysis, is 12 percent. A schedule of estimated cash flows is as follows:

Proposal	Probability	Cash inflows per year
X	.20	$ 3,000
	.20	4,000
	.40	6,000
	.20	8.000
Y	.10	$10,000
	.30	4,000
	.40	5,000
	.20	8,000

Required ☐

1. Calculate the expected net present value for each project.

2. Develop an analysis of each of the projects, showing which should be
accepted based on standard deviation calculations.

P15-16. The city council of York, Pennsylvania, has decided to purchase a mini- *Capital*
computer for $9,000. The equipment is expected to have a five-year life *Budgeting and*
with no residual value at the end of five years. Cash savings in data *Inflation*
processing costs are expected to be $2,800 per year. The required rate for
projects of this type is 8 percent. The town manager has projected an
inflation rate of 6 percent per year for the next six years.

Required ☐ Calculate the net present value, giving proper consideration
to the impact of inflation.

Capital Budgeting and Inflation

P15-17. The PANDAN Company is planning to acquire a new machine at a total cost of $30,600. The estimated life of the machine is six years and estimated salvage value is $600. PANDAN Company officials estimate annual cash savings from using this machine will be $8,000. Assume the company's cost of capital is 8 percent and its income tax rate is 40 percent. An inflation rate of 4 percent per year is expected for the next six years.

Required ☐

1. Calculate the annual after-tax net cash benefits of this investment proposal. (Use straight-line depreciation.)

2. Calculate the net present value.

Comprehensive Capital Budgeting Problem

P15-18. Carol Corporation is beginning its first capital budgeting program and has retained you to assist the budget committee in the evaluation of a project to expand operations designated as Proposed Expansion Project #12 (PEP #12).

    a. The following capital expenditures are under consideration:

$ 300,000	Fire sprinkler system
100,000	Landscaping
600,000	Replacement of old machines
800,000	Projects to expand operations (including PEP #12)
$1,800,000	Total

    b. The corporation requires no minimum return on the sprinkler system or the landscaping. However, it expects a minimum return of 6 percent on all investments to replace old machinery. It also expects investments in expansion projects to yield a return that will exceed the average cost of the capital required to finance the sprinkler system and the landscaping, in addition to the expansion projects.

    c. Under Proposed Expansion Project #12 a cash investment of $75,000 will be made one year before operations begin. The investment will be depreciated by the sum-of-the-years'-digits method over a three-year period and is expected to have a salvage value of $15,000. Additional financial data for PEP #12 follow:

Time period	Revenue	Variable costs	Maintenance, property taxes, and insurance
0–1	$80,000	$35,000	$ 8,000
1–2	95,000	41,000	11,000
2–3	60,000	25,000	12,000

The amount of the investment recovered during each of the three years can be reinvested immediately at a rate of return approximating 15 percent. Each year's recovery of investment, then, will have been reinvested at 15 percent for an average of six months at the end of the year.

    d. The capital structure of Carol Corporation follows:

	Amount	Percentage
Short-term notes at 5 percent interest	$ 3,500,000	15%
4 percent cumulative preferred stock, $100 par . .	1,750,000	10
Common stock	12,250,000	35
Retained earnings	17,500,000	40
Total	$35,000,000	100%

e. Additional data available to you are summarized below:

	Current market price	Expected earnings per share	Expected dividends per share
Preferred stock, noncallable	$120	—	$4.00
Common stock	50	$4.20	1.60

The average marginal tax rate for Carol stockholders is estimated to be 25 percent.

f. Assume that the corporate income tax rate is 50 percent.

g. The present value of $1.00 due at the end of each year and discounted at 15 percent is:

End of year	Present value
2 years before 0	$1.32
1 year before 0	1.15
0	1.00
1 year after 0	.87
2 years after 0	.76
3 years after 0	.66

h. The present values of $1.00 earned uniformly throughout the year and discounted at 15 percent follow:

Year	Present value
0–1	$.93
1–2	.80
2–3	.69

Required □

1. Assume that the cutoff rate for considering expansion projects is 15 percent. Prepare a schedule calculating the:

   a. Annual cash flows from operations for PEP #12
   b. Present value of the net cash flows for PEP #12

2. The budget committee has asked you to check the reasonableness of an estimate of the average cost of capital to this firm. Prepare a schedule, supported by computations in good form, to compute the average cost of capital weighted by the percentage of the capital structure that each element represents.

3. a. Assume that the average cost of capital computed in part 2 is 9 percent. Prepare a schedule to compute the minimum return (in

dollars) required on expansion projects to cover the average cost of capital for financing the sprinkler system and the landscaping, in addition to expansion projects. Assume that it is necessary to replace the old machines.

   b.   Assume that the minimum return computed in part 3a is $150,000. Calculate the cutoff rate on expansion projects.

(CPA)

PART OUTLINE

PART IV

MANAGEMENT-CONTROL

CHAPTER OUTLINE

MANAGEMENT INFORMATION SYSTEMS

CHAPTER 16

☐ INTRODUCTION

A management information system (MIS) is a formalized, computer-based system that is able to integrate data from various sources to provide information necessary for management decision making.[1] The data processing system supports the management information system. Much of the information that the MIS uses is initially captured and stored in the data processing system. To contrast the two, data processing is oriented toward the capture, processing, and storage of data, whereas MIS is oriented toward using that data to produce management information. The data processing system performs transaction processing; in other words, it processes such data as orders, sales, and payments on account. In the course of processing these transactions, the data processing system collects and stores a large amount of detailed information. This information provides the data base for the management information system.

In this chapter, we will examine the relationship of the management information system to management accounting activities within an organization. The informational needs of management personnel will be described in the context of several information-system environments. Consideration will be given to techniques available to tailor data to meet these informational requirements. The concept of a responsibility-accounting system will then be developed. Concluding sections of the chapter contain an overview of basic data storage, processing modes, and information processing applications.

☐ MANAGEMENT INFORMATION SYSTEMS

Considering the design properties of information systems along a continuum, the two extremes are a hierarchical and an integrated information

---

1. Much of this chapter is adapted from James O. Hicks, Jr., and Wayne E. Leininger, *Accounting Information Systems*, 2d ed. (St. Paul, Minn.: West Publishing Company, 1986).

system.[2] Although no information system can be classified as strictly hierarchical or integrated, description of the extremes highlights the structural characteristics that are necessary to understand how an information system operates. The location of the data base or bases within the organization is the major factor that differentiates the systems.

A **data base** is the collection of data upon which the information system depends to produce information. Literally, the data base contains the raw material necessary to operate the information system. Data is stored in computer- or noncomputer-accessible media. Magnetic tape, disk packs, and machine-readable paper media are examples of computer-accessible storage. Filing cabinets, ledgers, and tub files are examples of noncomputer-accessible storage.

In an information system based on hiererachical design principles, segregated data bases are divided among functional, departmental, or divisional lines. An example of information flow in an information system characterized as hierarchical is shown in figure 16.1. The data bases and management functions are segregated along functional lines.[3] They just as easily could have been segregated along departmental or divisional lines. In addition to the segregated data bases, a hierarchical system features subordinate-superior relationships in the processing of data and the flow of information. Queries by superiors to subordinates in a functional area trigger data processing activities to provide information.

Data processing activities may be centralized or decentralized in a **hierarchical information system.** When the data processing activities are centralized, the majority of the data processing is performed by a separate organizational unit. In this situation, one might initially conclude that the information system is integrated. However, if separate data bases are maintained and controlled by each functional area, division, or department, then the information is hierarchical. Control in this context usually means that the department controls access to the data base. If someone from another department desires to access that data base, permission must be obtained from the department head who has control over the data base. When the data processing activities are decentralized, each functional area, division, or department still possesses the facilities to satisfy its own data processing needs.

An **integrated information system** is characterized by a common data base and a separation of the data processing activities from the functional areas of the business. The management functions are separate from the data processing activities. The flow of information in an integrated information system is shown in figure 16.2. An integrated information system can respond quickly to queries via remote terminals and, therefore, contains significant amounts of online storage. This online storage, usually a disk, is necessary so that the data base can be accessed on demand.

The common data base consists of a number of files stored on a media so that the output can be provided on a timely basis. A representative list

2. This material is based on John G. Burch and Felix R. Strater, Jr., *Information Systems: Theory and Practice* (Santa Barbara, Calif.: Hamilton Publishing Company, 1974).

3. Refer to chapter 1 for a discussion of strategic planning, management control, and operating control. Figure 1.1 diagrams the relationship between the management system and the management information system.

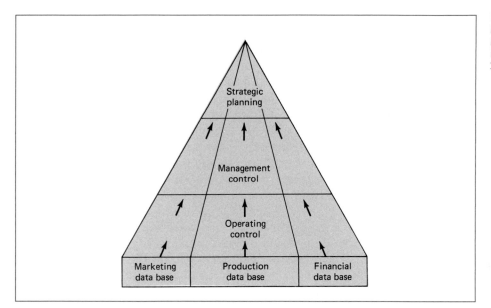

FIGURE 16.1
Data Flow in a
Hierarchical
Information
System

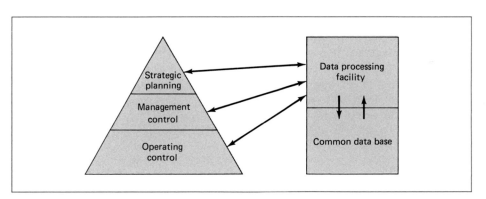

FIGURE 16.2
Data Flow in an
Integrated
Information
System

of these files would include inventory, production, accounting, receivables, customers, and sales. These files are constructed in such a fashion as to reduce redundancy. Redundancy is reduced, for example, when one file contains all the relevant customer information and can be accessed by all appropriate users. In a hierarchical system, customer information must be maintained by each functional area in a separate data base.

Advances in data processing technology in both the hardware and software fields have made it possible for firms to move along the continuum from hierarchical information systems toward more integrated information systems. Although this trend will continue into the foreseeable future, most information systems will be hybrids, containing certain characteristics of both the integrated and hierarchical systems. An understanding of these characteristics and their implications is beneficial to the cost accountant.

For example, the preparation of a comprehensive budget would require the accumulation of considerable amounts of data. If the information system is hierarchical, the accountant may have to gain access to several data bases controlled by functional area managers. In some cases, he or she may have to request the data from the area manager. Consequently, the accountant will receive a response that has been reviewed by the functional area manager. This may result in some bias being introduced because of the political environment that exists within the organization and the desire of the manager of a functional area to control the content of information leaving the department.

After gathering the data from the several data bases in a hierarchical system, the accountant may find that, because of the structure and format of the files in the different data bases, the data is not compatible. This may prove to be a handicap if a computer is to be employed in analyzing the data.

In an integrated system, these problems would not be encountered because the common data base would insure compatibility of the data. Access to the common data base would be the only administrative clearance necessary. This would considerably reduce the communication necessary to gather the data. However, the generalized aspects of the integrated system limit its capability to prepare reports tailored to meet the specific needs of a user. Therefore, a user may not be able to obtain a report to his or her exact specifications because of technical or cost constraints.

When a high degree of integration exists in the information system, the manager of the information system holds a very influential position within the organization. Rather than having to deal with several different managers to obtain data, the accountant in this situation may find that he or she has to deal with one very influential manager. Indeed, in a highly integrated management information system, there may not be a need for a separate accounting department. It would be the function of the information system to perform all the traditional accounting functions.

☐ SATISFYING THE INFORMATIONAL NEEDS OF MANAGEMENT

To this point, it should be evident that information requirements vary depending on the activities of management. At the operational control level, required information is generally very detailed and comes from internal sources. However, at the strategic planning level, there is a great deal of aggregation, and the information often comes from sources external to the organization. For example, at the operating control level, there may be a request for the line item budgeted amounts for a particular department. The budget information requested at the management control level may be the total operating budget for a particular department.

One technique available for satisfying the information requirements of management personnel is to build **filters** into the system that aggregate information and as a result reduce detail. This results in a significant reduction in voluminous listings when every detail is included in a report or budget.

Such filters in a university information system may operate as follows: Instructors of specific courses receive a listing of all students registered in that course. At the departmental level, the information would include only the total number of students in each section of each of the courses offered during the semester. At the college level, the dean would require a report on the total number of students and the number of sections of courses offered at the freshman, sophomore, junior, senior, and graduate level in each department. The dean also might require information concerning the average class size. At the university level, the information required may be in the form of total student contact hours classified by department, college, and course level. At each level within the university organization, a filter is introduced to aggregate data in order to better meet the informational requirements of management personnel. In a hierarchical system, the filters are under the control of the managers at the various levels within the organization. Queries in an integrated system would specify the degree of filtering desired.

A second technique available to satisfy the informational requirements of management personnel is to make use of *exception reporting*. A standard-cost system is a classic example of this technique. Recall that in a standard-cost system the variances result from deviations from a standard. These variances show up as entries in the accounting system and are highlighted to managers. As long as the system operates according to standard, no variances are reported to management personnel. Only the significant exceptions from standard are reported.

The two techniques for satisfying the informational needs of management team members are not totally unrelated, since filtering also takes place in exception reporting. For example, in a job-order cost system, labor rate and efficiency variances are reported for each project at the operating control level. At the management control level, the labor rate variance would be reported as a total to make possible an evaluation of scheduling and overall labor efficiency.

A third means of satisfying the information requirements of management personnel is dependent upon the computer hardware configuration in the information system. In an integrated information system, where aspects of the common data base are stored online, managers can interrogate the data base if the proper supporting software is available. Managers then have the capability to specify the level of detail required. For example, managers may query the system concerning the dollar value of the raw-material inventory. If this did not prove to be satisfactory, they would query the system concerning the inventory level of classes or specific items in the inventory. Similar interrogation of this type is possible concerning accounts receivable, accounts payable, work-in-process, and other files stored online.

☐ TYPES OF REPORTS

We have discussed management decision making and the need for information to support these decisions. But in what form is this information produced? There are four types of computer reports: (1) scheduled reports, (2) demand reports, (3) exception reports, and (4) predictive reports.

Although they are called reports, which implies a hard-copy printout on a printer, they could just as easily be displayed on a CRT screen. In fact, as the use of CRTs becomes more widespread, many of these reports are being displayed on CRTs. The user thus interacts directly with the computer to obtain information.

Scheduled Reports

Scheduled reports are produced on a regularly scheduled basis, such as daily, weekly, or monthly. These reports are widely distributed to users and often contain information that is not used regularly. As the use of CRTs becomes more widespread, scheduled reports will diminish in importance. A manager will not feel compelled to ask for information on a scheduled report just in case he or she may need it in the future. With a CRT, the information can be retrieved on demand.

Demand Reports

A **demand report** is generated upon request. These reports fill irregular needs for information. In the earlier days of computing, the contents of a demand report had to be previously anticipated because the user often experienced a delay of weeks or months before receiving the data. It simply took time to modify programs to produce information that filled unanticipated demands. Today, largely through the query languages of data base management systems, we can fulfill unanticipated demands for information very quickly, often within minutes. This is possible because users and managers themselves can use the query languages to produce reports. Of course, if the data required to produce the information is not in the data base, then even query languages will not solve the problem of unanticipated demands for information.

Exception Reports

One of the most efficient approaches to management is the management by exception approach. Management by exception means that the manager spends his or her time dealing with exceptions, or those situations that are out of control. Activities proceeding according to plan are in control and therefore do not need the manager's attention. *Exception reports* notify management when an activity or system is out of control so that corrective action can be taken. An example of an exception report is a listing that identifies all customers having overdue account balances. Another type of exception report is an error listing, which identifies input or processing errors that have occurred during the computer's execution of a particular application.

Predictive Reports

Predictive reports are useful in planning decisions. They make use of statistical and modeling techniques such as regression, time series analysis, and simulation. These reports assist management in answering "what if" questions. For example: What if sales increased by 10 percent? What impact would the increase have on net profit? The statistical and modeling techniques that produce predictive reports depend largely on historical data. Such data must be readily accessible by the MIS in a form that can be used by the models; otherwise, these models will be of little use to management.

☐ PREPARATION OF RESPONSIBILITY-ACCOUNTING REPORTS

A management information system will output product costs for inventory valuation and profit determination. Responsibility accounting is a design feature that should be incorporated into all management information systems. An organization is viewed as consisting of a group of responsibility centers, and the MIS is designed so that revenues, costs, assets, and liabilities, when appropriate, can be traced to a responsibility center. The principle employed in tracing revenues, costs, assets, or liabilities to a responsibility center is controllability. Controllable revenues, costs, assets, or liabilities are traced to that center where decisions are made concerning the item in question. Therefore, only those financial items under the control of the managers at the responsibility center are incorporated into the performance reports for a responsibility center.

The performance report for a responsibility center should contain both budgeted and actual financial information for the period. Flexible budgets and standard costs serve as the basis for the budgeted information contained in the performance report. Only those costs and revenues under the control of the managers of the responsibility center are incorporated into the performance reports. No allocated costs are included in such reports because they are not controllable by the managers of the center. Process and job-order cost systems include allocated costs from service departments; a process-cost system, in which costs are assigned to departments and then averaged over the output, includes costs from prior departments. Neither allocated service department costs nor prior department costs are included on a performance report for a responsibility center.

Hierarchies of responsibility centers develop in most organizations. For example, a Machining department can be a responsibility center within a factory. Other responsibility centers within the factory could be the Foundry, Finishing, and Shipping departments, and a warehouse. All of these responsibility centers then could be under the control of the factory manager. The factory manager might report to a divisional vice-president. The divisional vice-president would report to the corporate president.

Performance measurement in these responsibility or decision centers is based on some definition of controllable profit, return on investment, or cost. Ideally, all revenues and costs can be directly associated with a manager who made the appropriate decision. Although the identification may at times be clouded, the principle of associating revenues and costs with responsibility centers must be employed to satisfy the informational requirements of management personnel for performance measurement. In the next chapter, various performance measures for responsibility centers will be considered.

The following are some characteristics that typify responsibility-accounting reports. These characteristics should be considered when preparing or analyzing the reports.

1. Responsibility-accounting reports should primarily address short-run performance.

2. Responsibility reports should only contain controllable revenue, costs, and assets.

3. Responsibility-accounting reports should be issued on a prompt and regular basis.

4. Responsibility-accounting reports should contain sufficient but not excessive detail. Care must be exercised so that the appropriate level of aggregation is achieved on each report.

5. Responsibility-accounting reports should contain comparative figures. Actual results should be compared with budgeted amounts.

6. Responsibility-accounting reports may appropriately include physical units in some situations, rather than convert everything into dollars.

☐ MIS AND DATA BASE MANAGEMENT SYSTEMS

Data is the central resource of an MIS. The management of this resource is crucial. A **data base management system** (DBMS) is a program that serves as an interface between applications programs and a set of coordinated and integrated files called a data base. Prior to the use of DBMS, little, if any, data were shared or integrated among the functional information systems. However, there are now many opportunities for these systems to share the same data. For example, the payroll application within the accounting information system could share data with the personnel information system. Examples of data that might be shared are employee names, addresses, and pay rates.

Figure 16.3 illustrates the statement above that data base management systems are an interface between the functional applications and the data base. The DBMS allows the various functional systems to access the same data, and can pool together related data from different files as in the case of a personnel file and a payroll file. The DBMS is perhaps the most important tool in making an MIS possible.

☐ MIS AND DECISION-SUPPORT SYSTEMS

Management information systems in the past have been most successful in providing information for routine, structured, and anticipated types of decisions. In addition, they have been successful in acquiring and in storing large quantities of detailed data concerning transaction processing. They have been less successful in providing information for semistructured or unstructured decisions, particularly unanticipated ones. A **decision-sup-**

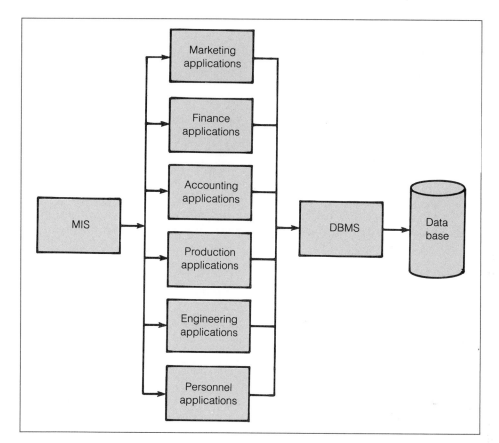

FIGURE 16.3
Relationship between a DBMS and an MIS

port system provides a set of integrated computer tools that allows a decision maker to interact directly with computers to retrieve information useful in making semistructured and unstructured decisions. Examples of these decisions include such things as plant expansion, merger and acquisition, and new product decisions.

A decision-support system is an extension of an MIS. It provides user-friendly languages, data retrieval, data processing, and modeling capabilities for the decision maker's direct use.

☐ BASIC DATA STORAGE

The Data Hierarchy

Listed below in ascending order of complexity are the components of the information system data hierarchy.

1. Bit

2. Byte

3. Field or item

4. Record

5. File or data set

6. Data base

Bit The term **bit** is short for binary digit. It can assume either of two possible states and therefore can be represented by either a 1 or 0. Typically, a bit represents data through the positive or negative polarity of an electrical charge on a magnetic recording medium such as a tape or disk. In the case of semiconductor storage, a bit is represented by an electrical circuit that is either conducting or not conducting electricity.

Byte The ability to represent only binary information in a computer system is not sufficient for business information processing. Numeric, alpha-

TABLE 16.1 EBCDIC Coding Scheme

Character	EBCDIC Binary
A	1100 0001
B	1100 0010
C	1100 0011
D	1100 0100
E	1100 0101
F	1100 0110
G	1100 0111
H	1100 1000
I	1100 1001
J	1101 0001
K	1101 0010
L	1101 0011
M	1101 0100
N	1101 0101
O	1101 0110
P	1101 0111
Q	1101 1000
R	1101 1001
S	1110 0010
T	1110 0011
U	1110 0100
V	1110 0101
W	1110 0110
X	1110 0111
Y	1110 1000
Z	1110 1001
0	1111 0000
1	1111 0001
2	1111 0010
3	1111 0011
4	1111 0100
5	1111 0101
6	1111 0110
7	1111 0111
8	1111 1000
9	1111 1001

betic, and a wide variety of special characters such as dollar signs, question marks, and quotation marks must be stored. In a computer system, a character of information is called a **byte.** A byte of information is stored by using several bits in specified combinations. One widely used coding scheme is IBM's Extended Binary Coded Decimal Interchange Code (EBCDIC), an eight-bit code illustrated in table 16.1. Each 1 or 0 in the table corresponds to a single bit. The first four bits, called zone bits, are used in combination with the last four bits, called digit bits, for coding alphabetic and other special characters.

Field or Item The next level in the data hierarchy is a field or item of data. A **field** of data is one or more bytes that contain data about an attribute of an entity in the information system. For example, an entity in a payroll system is an individual employee. Attributes are the employee's name, hourly rate, and so on. The hourly rate is a field or item of data. Figure 16.4 shows a payroll record with typical fields of data.

Record A **record** is a collection of fields relating to a specific entity. For example, the payroll record shown in figure 16.4 contains fields of data relating to a specific employee. An analogy can be made between a computer-based record and the concept of an individual folder in a manual file. A folder in a manual employee file may contain much the same information as a record in a computer-based payroll file. The field that uniquely identifies a record from all other records in a file is the *record key.* For example, the record key in a payroll is normally the employee's social security number.

Payroll Master File Record
First name, middle initial
Last name
Street address
City, state
Zip code
Social security number
Sick leave eligibility date
Effective date of salary increase
Date of birth
Department number
Hourly rate
Sick hours
Overtime earnings
Regular earnings
Federal tax year-to-date
Marital status
Number of dependents
Total voluntary deductions year-to-date
FICA year-to-date
State tax year-to-date
City tax year-to-date
Net earnings year-to-date

FIGURE 16.4
Example of Data Fields
in a Payroll Master File Record

File or Data Set A **file** consists of a collection of related records. For example, all the payroll records for all of a company's employees are a payroll master file. The seven basic types of files are (1) master files, (2) transaction files, (3) table files, (4) index files, (5) summary files, (6) program libraries, and (7) backup files.

Master files contain relatively permanent data. Examples include payroll, material inventory, furnished goods, work-in-process, accounts receivable, and accounts payable. A typical payroll master file record might contain an employee's name, address, job description, pay rate, number of exemptions, and year-to-date totals of wages, FICA, and income tax withheld, as shown in figure 16.4. A registrar's file containing student information such as name, address, courses taken, and grades is another example of a master file record. Business data processing revolves around master files, which are an organization's central files. They contain the information necessary for the organization to operate. All other types of files are auxiliary to and support the maintenance of master files or facilitate the retrieval and reporting of information from them.

Transaction files contain records used to change (update) master files. Any change to a master file is termed a transaction even though it may not be a transaction under the traditional accounting definition—that is, an exchange by the company with an outside party. For example, the change in an employee's address is a transaction to the payroll master file. Most transactions occur between the organization and external parties—for example, orders and payments on account. The data for these transaction records are taken from invoices, receiving reports, employee hiring and termination records, and the like.

Table files contain relatively permanent information that is used to facilitate processing. An example is the freight rate table used to assign freight charges to customer invoices.

Index files are used to indicate the physical address of records stored on secondary storage devices. They are analogous to a card catalog in a library, allowing computer systems to locate individual records without having to search the entire file.

Summary files contain data extracted and summarized from other files. Examples include temporary work files used by the computer in processing and report files that contain the necessary information for specific management reports.

Program libraries are files containing the production copy of programs. These are the programs that are used in the day-to-day execution of data processing jobs. Program files contain both source and object copies of production programs. This is because it is wasteful to recompile a frequently executed program each time the program is run. Therefore, production program libraries actually used in the execution of jobs are kept in object form. When a production program is changed, the source copy of the program is changed, tested, and recompiled. The compilation produces an object module, which is then stored in the production program library.

Backup files are either copies of current files or the only copy of noncurrent files used to reconstruct current files in case they are partially or totally destroyed. Backup files should be kept for all the different types of files. In addition, they are sometimes kept for long periods of time to serve as archival files. Archival files contain information that is not on current files but that may be useful in the future for long-term studies or for support documentation, as in the case of income tax returns.

Data Base A *data base* consists of all the files of an organization that are structured and integrated to facilitate information retrieval and update. Technically, a data base consists of the files that are part of a data-base management system. However, the term data base also designates all the files of an organization.

File Organization

Basically, the two types of file organization are those that allow sequential access to the data and those that allow direct access. Under **sequential file organization,** the computer typically begins searching for a record by examining the first record in the file and then examining the rest in sequence until the required record is located. Certain storage media (i.e., magnetic tape) will allow only sequential file organization. To locate a record on a reel of magnetic tape, the tape must be read sequentially beginning with the first record.

On the other hand, **direct file organization** allows immediate, direct access to individual records in the file. Several techniques are used to accomplish direct file organization. Magnetic disks are by far the most widely used device for storage of direct-access files. Direct-access file organization must be used whenever the application requires immediate access to individual records. It is widely used today whenever the computer configuration includes CRT (cathode ray tube) terminals, which will display management information upon demand.

□ PROCESSING MODES

In the preceding section we discussed two basic types of file organization—sequential and direct. These can be combined with two information processing modes—batch and immediate—to form three information processing approaches: (1) **batch sequential,** (2) **batch direct,** and (3) **immediate direct.**

Batch Processing

With **batch processing,** changes and queries to a file are stored for a period of time. Then a processing run is made periodically to update the file and to produce responses to queries. The batch runs can be made on a scheduled basis, such as daily, weekly, or monthly, or they can be made as needed. Figure 16.5 illustrates batch sequential processing with a file stored on magnetic tape. Batch processing can also be performed with direct or-

FIGURE 16.5
Overview of
Batch Sequential
Processing Using
Tape Files

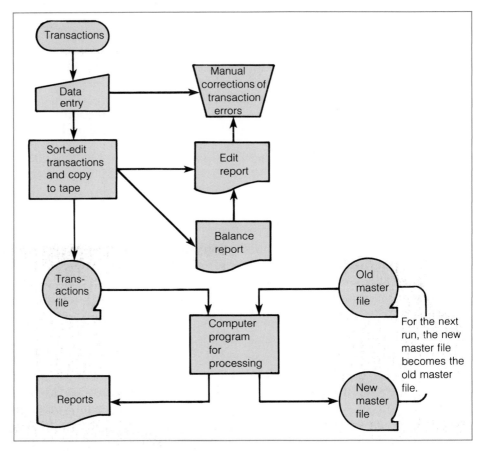

ganized files. Figure 16.6 illustrates batch direct processing with a file stored on disk.

Immediate Processing

With **immediate processing,** transactions are processed to update the file immediately or shortly after a real-world event occurs. Immediate processing is illustrated in figure 16.7. Quite often information processing applications using the immediate mode are real-time applications. A real-time application can immediately capture data about ongoing events or processes and provide the information necessary to manage them. Examples of real-time systems are process-control and airline-reservation systems.

An essential component of a real-time system is updating of master files immediately after an event occurs. Consequently, at any point in time, the data in real-time master files should accurately reflect the status of the real-world variables that they represent. For example, when a customer reserves a seat on an airline flight, the reservations agent keys in that fact, and the inventory of nonreserved seats on the flight is immediately updated

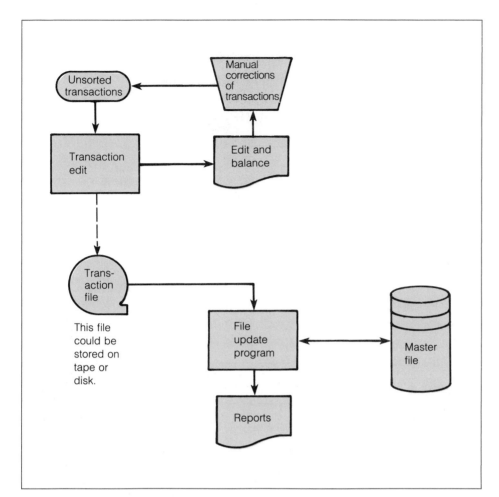

FIGURE 16.6
Batch Direct
Processing

to reflect one less available seat. Immediate processing requires direct-access files—using sequential files would be impractical because of the time required to search for individual records. However, batch processing can occur either with sequential or direct files.

□ OVERVIEW OF INFORMATION PROCESSING APPLICATIONS

Figure 16.8 provides an overview of typical information processing applications in a business environment. The flow lines between the various applications in the figure illustrate the flow of data between applications. Arrows on the flow lines indicate direction of the data flow from one application to another.

Data needed for multiple applications should be shared between relevant applications in machine-readable form. This obviously eliminates much manual processing and recapture of data. In the remainder of this chapter we will discuss each of the applications illustrated in Figure 16.8.

FIGURE 16.7
Immediate
Processing

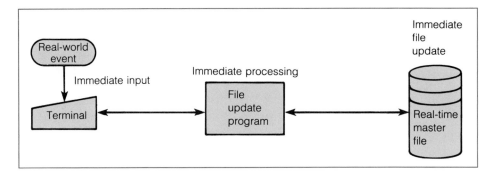

FIGURE 16.8
Overview of
Typical Business
Data Processing
Applications

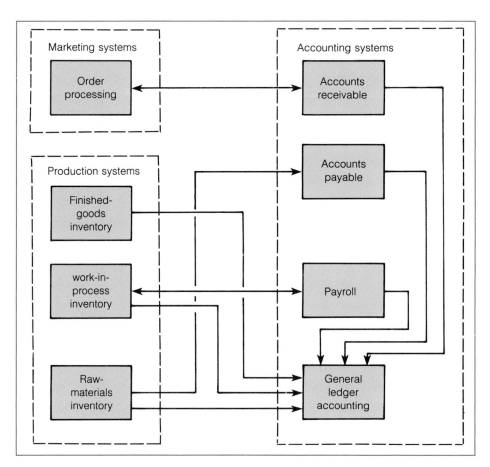

Inventory

In a manufacturing firm, there are three types of inventory systems: (1) *raw materials*, (2) *work-in-process*, and (3) *finished goods*. Of course, a merchandising firm has only one type of inventory: finished goods or *merchandise inventory*. However, regardless of the type of inventory, an inventory system has two primary objectives: (1) minimize costs due to out-of-stock situations and (2) minimize the inventory carrying costs.

At the finished goods level, out-of-stock situations can result in loss of sales; at the raw materials level, out-of-stock conditions may result in the unnecessary idling of production employees and facilities. However, a company cannot simply keep large quantities of inventory on hand to avoid out-of-stock situations. Such an approach would certainly increase inventory carrying costs beyond acceptable levels. Inventory carrying costs include such things as the interest that could be made on funds invested in inventory, insurance costs, and warehousing costs. Obviously, as the amount of inventory carried increases, carrying costs also increase. As you can see, these two objectives conflict. We could certainly minimize inventory carrying costs by not carrying any inventory. However, out-of-stock costs might then be unacceptable. Furthermore, we could avoid out-of-stock situations by carrying large amounts of inventory, but this would increase inventory carrying costs. Inventory must be closely monitored to minimize both costs. Computer-based inventory systems have been very useful in providing this close monitor. In fact, computers can be programmed to automatically make inventory reorder decisions that minimize these two costs. Such systems are based on mathematical economic-order quantity (EOQ) formulas.

The work-in-process inventory system monitors goods while they are being produced. It has two important objectives in addition to the two discussed above: (1) to provide scheduling control over individual production jobs so that an accurate prediction of their completion date can be made and (2) to accumulate the unit costs of individual products. In large companies these two objectives are often met by two separate applications that support the work-in-process system. These applications are a scheduling system and a cost-accounting system.

Since the three types of inventory systems are similar in many respects, we will simplify our presentation of them in this chapter by using the example of a merchandising firm. Understanding how a merchandise inventory system operates will give you a good idea of how all three systems are run. Figure 16.9 provides an overview of a merchandise inventory system that maintains a merchandise inventory master file. Some of the data fields that could be contained in each record in this file are listed in figure 16.10. At any point in time, the master file should accurately reflect the quantities indicated in figure 16.10.

The two primary inputs that update the merchandise inventory master file are quantities of goods shipped (input by the order processing system) and quantities of goods received (input by the receiving department).

The merchandise inventory system produces outputs updating the general ledger system in the areas of current inventory on hand and the cost of goods sold. The system also provides the purchasing department with a purchase order notice. This notice identifies the items whose quantities are at or below the reorder level. Quite often the merchandise inventory system will produce a purchase order instead of a purchase order notice. This purchase order is sent to the purchasing department for approval prior to sending it to a vendor. Figure 16.11 illustrates three typical kinds of inventory management reports. These reports may be printed on paper or displayed on a CRT screen.

FIGURE 16.9
Overview of the
Merchandise
Inventory System

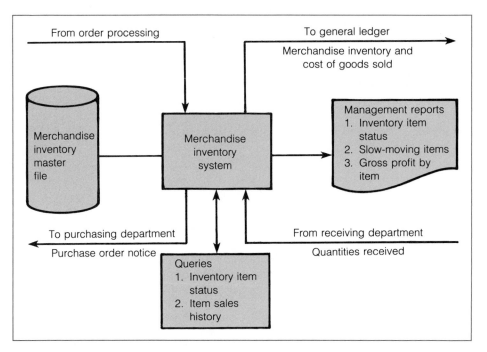

FIGURE 16.10
Typical Fields in a
Merchandise
Inventory Master
File Record

Inventory item number
Item description
Location in warehouse
Current quantity on hand
Current quantity on order
Quantity sold—Year-to-date
Quantity backordered
Standard cost

Order Processing

Figure 16.12 provides an overview of the order processing system. The **order processing** system is the place of entry for customer orders, and it initiates the shipping of orders. The system is also often called an order entry system. The primary objectives of an order processing system are (1) to initiate shipping orders, (2) to maintain a record of backordered items (a **backorder** occurs when an item is out of stock and will be shipped later), and (3) to produce various sales analysis reports.

A shipping order is illustrated in figure 16.13. The shipping order is issued in triplicate—a picking copy sent to the warehouse to tell the warehouse employees which goods are to be shipped, a packing copy put inside the box when the goods are shipped, and a copy to be kept on hand for record purposes. Some companies will also produce a fourth copy, which serves as a customer acknowledgment and is sent to the customer as soon as the shipping order is produced.

```
                                                                         PAGE 1
                                                              RUN DATE 11—5—8X
                              GROSS PROFIT BY ITEM
                                    REPORT
                            MONTH ENDING 10—31—8X

                                                       QTY
ITEM   ITEM                       QTY      GROSS      SOLD
NO     DESCRIPTION       SALES    SOLD     PROFIT     YTD
```

ITEM NO	ITEM DESCRIPTION	SALES	QTY SOLD	GROSS PROFIT	QTY SOLD YTD
1003	PAPER,3H,LOOSE LEAF	187.50	250	40.00	3520
1004	PAPER,TYPING,BOND	7187.50	1250	1000.00	7500
1005	PAPER,MIMEO,8.5X11	2835.00	750	885.00	6000
7085	PEN,BALLPOINT	3185.00	3500	385.00	24500
4106	PENCIL,DRAWING 3H	1425.00	475	209.00	1900
8165	STAPLER REMOVER	675.00	1500	90.00	16500

```
                                                                         PAGE 1
                                                              RUN DATE 11—5—8x
                              SLOW MOVING ITEMS
                                    REPORT
                              AS OF 10—31—8X
```

ITEM NO	ITEM DESCRIPTION	STD UNIT COST	DAY OF LAST SALES	QTY ON HAND	QTY SOLD YTD
6405	BOOKCASE,37.5X55X5	133.03	041583	1000	250
6408	CHAIR,SWIVEL,ARMS	138.29	061083	75	20
8082	CUSHION,15X16	5.74	082383	60	15
3015	FAN,WINDOW	38.28	053083	25	10
6440	TABLE,MULTI-PURPOSE	121.68	072583	30	7
6017	TRANSPARENCY,8.5X11	20.93	072383	550	325

```
                                                                         PAGE 1
                                                              RUN DATE 11—5—8X
                              INVENTORY ITEM
                              STATUS REPORT
                              AS OF 10—31—8X
```

ITEM NO	ITEM DESCRIPTION	WAREHOUSE LOCATION	QTY ON HAND	QTY ON ORDER	QTY BACK ORDER	QTY SOLD YTD	UNIT	STD UNIT COST
6045	BOOKCASE,37.5X55X5	7340	1000	500	0	350	EA	133.03
3403	CABINET FILE,8"	7340	400	0	0	150	EA	162.15
8002	CALENDAR,PAD,#SD 170	7428	75	60	0	25	EA	.98
3403	CLOCK,WALL,8",ELECT	7428	20	50	30	35	EA	27.88
9005	FOLDER,MANILA,LETTER	7419	50	750	250	950	BOX	3.78

Most order processing systems access the merchandise inventory file to determine if particular goods are on hand prior to producing a shipping order. If given items are not on hand, they are placed on backorder. The inventory master file is updated to reflect quantities of goods that are actually shipped. Backorder quantities must be maintained on the current

FIGURE 16.11
Typical Inventory
Management
Reports

FIGURE 16.12
Overview of the
Order Processing
System

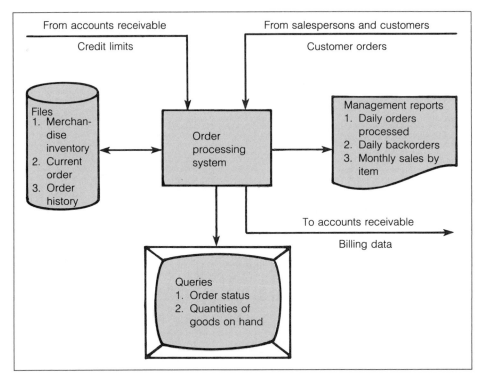

order file so that when the goods are available the order processing system can initiate a shipping order.

In addition to the inventory file, the order processing file maintains a current order file and an order history file. The order history file is identical in format to the current order file. The typical fields within a record of these two files contain the same information that is displayed on the shipping order in figure 16.13.

After a short period of time (for example, 3 months), records are deleted from the current order file and placed in the order history file. This procedure prevents the current order file from growing too large. Normally, the records in the order history file are maintained for at least a year to support various sales analysis reports that the system can produce.

Figure 16.14 illustrates representative order processing reports. The daily-orders-processed report is primarily a control report providing daily information concerning orders processed. Management can also use the totals on this report to monitor trends and the amount of orders processed. The daily backorder report is also a control report, enabling management to monitor the level of backorders. If the quantity of backorders becomes excessive, relations with customers may be damaged. The monthly sales-by-item report is just one example of the many different types of sales analysis reports that can be produced. This particular report enables management to monitor sales trends by following the numbers of individual items sold.

```
                                                                        PAGE  1
                                                             RUN  DATE  11—5—8X
                                        SHIPPING  ORDER
                                      ORDER  DATE  10—31—8X
     SHIP  TO:

       NAME:    PERDUE  PROCESSORS
     ADDRESS:    104  LANDSDOWNE  LANE
                 BLACKSBURG,  VA        24060

      PACKAGE  NO:    764290
     SHIPMENT  NO:      1721

     ITEM     ITEM                      QTY             QTY                      UNIT
     NO       DESCRIPTION               ORDERED         SHIPPED       UNIT       PRICE

     1003     PAPER,3H,LOOSE  LEAF        100             100         PKG          .75
     1004     PAPER,TYPING,BOND           500             500         PKG        5.75
     1005     PAPER,MIMEO,8.5X11           30              30         RM         3.65
     9090     PAD,SCRATCH,4X6              12              12         DOZ        1.69
     8039     RUBBER  BANDS,1/8X3          10              10         BOX         .79
     1035     STENCIL,8.5X14              12              12         DOZ        3.10
```

Accounts Receivable

The objectives of the *accounts receivable* system are threefold: (1) to bill customers for orders shipped, (2) to maintain account records of the amounts that customers owe and records of payments on these accounts, and (3) to provide the information necessary to assist in the collection of past-due accounts. We are assuming here that the billing function is performed by the accounts receivable system. The billing function is the sending of the initial invoice to the customer. Actually, this function can be performed either by the order processing system, a separate billing system, or by the accounts receivable system.

Figure 16.15 provides an overview of the accounts receivable system. The accounts receivable system maintains one file—the accounts receivable master file. Typical fields contained within a record in this file are illustrated in figure 16.16. This file is updated with billing data from order processing. All the other data in the file is input from the accounts receivable department.

Queries to the accounts receivable system display information such as account status and payment history. The account status screen displays unpaid purchases and recent payments, while the payment history screen provides detailed information about the payment habits of a particular customer.

Figure 16.17 displays three typical kinds of management reports from the accounts receivable system. The *aged trial balance* is a very important and valuable report for collection purposes since it indicates the accounts that are past due and how far they are past due, either 30–60 days, 60–90 days, or over 90 days. The *customer status* report provides detailed information concerning a specific customer. This information can be very valuable to the salesperson assigned to a given customer.

FIGURE 16.13
Shipping Order

DAILY ORDERS PROCESSED
REPORT
FOR 10-31-8X

ORDER NO	CUSTOMER NO	CUSTOMER NAME	ITEM NO	SHIPMENT NO	SHIPPING DATE
764290	25190	PERDUE PROCESSORS	1004	1721	12-31-83
764290	25190	PERDUE PROCESSORS	1005	1721	12-31-83
764290	25190	PERDUE PROCESSORS	9090	1721	12-31-83
889233	27300	KINKO'S	1005	2930	12-31-83
889233	27300	KINKO'S	1750	2930	12-31-83
931240	31790	POLYSCIENTIFIC	9005	3501	12-31-83

PAGE 1
RUN DATE 11-5-8X

SALES-BY-ITEM
REPORT
MONTH ENDING 10-31-8X

ITEM NO	ITEM DESCRIPTION	QUANTITY	CURRENT MONTHLY SALES	SALES YTD
1003	PAPER,3H,LOOSE LEAF	250	187.50	2640.00
1004	PAPER,TYPING,BOND	1250	7187.50	43125.00
1005	PAPER,MIMEO,8.5X11	750	2835.00	22680.00
7085	PEN,BALLPOINT	3500	3185.00	22295.00
4106	PENCIL,DRAWING 3H	475	1425.00	4864.00
8165	STAPLER REMOVER	1500	675.00	6435.00

PAGE 1
RUN DATE 11-5-8X

DAILY BACKORDER REPORT
FOR 10-31-8X

ITEM NO	ITEM DESCRIPTION	QTY ORDERED	QTY BACK ORDERED	UNIT	UNIT PRICE
3403	CLOCK,WALL,8",ELECT	50	30	EA	27.88
9005	FOLDER,MANILA,LETTER	750	250	BOX	3.78
6412	LETTER TRAY,LEGAL	50	20	EA	6.88
9090	PAD,SCRATCH,4X6	625	300	DOZ	1.04
4106	PENCIL,DRAWING 3H	200	150	DOZ	2.56

FIGURE 16.14
Typical Order
Processing Reports

Since the accounts receivable system is the primary cash receipt system, it can provide very useful cash forecasts. This information is normally based on statistics maintained concerning customer payment habits, such as the average number of days the customer is late in making payments.

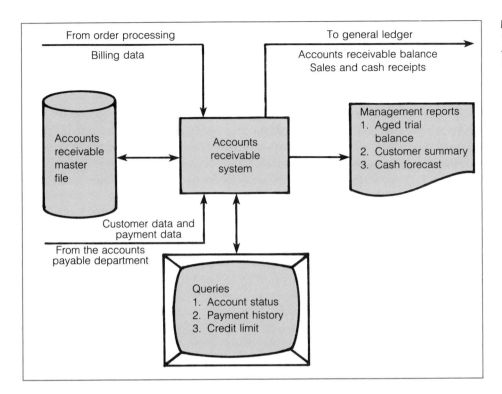

FIGURE 16.15
Overview of the Accounts Receivable System

Customer number
Customer name
Customer address
Credit rating
Average days late
Credit limit
Purchase date
Purchase reference
Purchase amounts
Payment date
Payment reference
Payment amounts
Current balance

FIGURE 16.16
Typical Fields in an Accounts Receivable Master File Record

Accounts Payable

The accounts payable system tends to be a mirror image of the accounts receivable system. The accounts receivable keeps records of the amounts owed to the firm, whereas the *accounts payable* system keeps records of amounts owed to suppliers of the firm. The objectives of the accounts payable system are (1) to provide control over payments to vendors of goods and suppliers of services, (2) to issue checks to these vendors and suppliers, and (3) to provide information for effective cash management.

```
                                                                              PAGE 1
                                                                  RUN DATE 11-5-8X
                                      CASH FORECAST
                                          REPORT
                                      AS OF 10-31-8X

PROBABLE
PYMT          DUE        INVOICE    CUSTOMER          PYMT          DISC      AMOUNT
DATE          DATE       NO         NAME              TERMS         AMT       DUE          PYMT

010184        011584     23910      PERDUE PROCESSORS  2/10,N/30     10.00     490.00       490.00
011584        013184     24920      PERDUE PROCESSORS  2/10,N/30      9.00     441.00       441.00
013184        020584     39011      KINKO'S            3/10,N/30      7.50     242.50       242.50
013184        020584     39015      KINKO'S            3/10,N/30      2.25      47.75        47.75
013184        021584     39120      KINKO'S            3/10,N/30      1.50      38.50        38.50
020584        021584     45270      DORN,HC            *****          .00     125.00        75.00

                                                             TOTAL CASH FORECASTED $ 1334.75
```

```
                                                                              PAGE 1
                                                                  RUN DATE 11-5-8X
                                  ACCOUNTS RECEIVABLE
                                   CUSTOMER STATUS
                                        REPORT
                                    AS OF 10-31-8X

CUST      CUST                    CREDIT      CREDIT      AMNT        AMNT
NO        NAME                    RATING      LIMIT       DUE         REC'D       BALANCE

25190     PERDUE PROCESSORS        9         5000.00     2695.50      1500.00     1195.50
27300     KINKO'S                  7         3500.00     1325.00       750.00      575.00
31790     POLYSCIENTIFIC          10         7500.00     5290.00      3900.00     1790.00
51230     BANDY,MW               * 0             .00      750.00          .00      750.00
61359     DORN,HD                  6         1000.00      625.00       375.00      250.00
73401     JONES,LT               * 0             .00      100.00          .00      100.00
```

```
                                                                              PAGE 1
                                                                  RUN DATE 11-5-8X
                                  AGED TRIAL BALANCE
                                        REPORT
                                    AS OF 10-31-8X

                       AMOUNT      AMOUNT       AMOUNT      AMOUNT       TOTAL
CUSTOMER   CUSTOMER    NOT         1-30 DAYS    31-60       >60 DAYS     BALANCE
NO         NAME        DUE         OVERDUE      OVERDUE     OVERDUE      DUE

25190      PERDUE PROCESSORS  1000.00    195.00       .00         .00      1195.00
27300      KINKO'S             550.00     25.00       .00         .00       575.00
31790      POLYSCIENTIFIC     1500.00    200.00     90.00         .00      1790.00
51230      BANDY,MW               .00    350.00    400.00         .00       750.00
61359      DORN,HD             195.00     55.00       .00         .00       250.00
73401      JONES,LT               .00     25.00     75.00                   100.00
```

FIGURE 16.17
Typical Accounts
Receivable
Management
Reports

Figure 16.18 provides an overview of the accounts payable system. The accounts payable system maintains an accounts payable master file. Typical fields contained in an accounts payable master file record are illustrated in figure 16.19. The accounts payable department provides the input

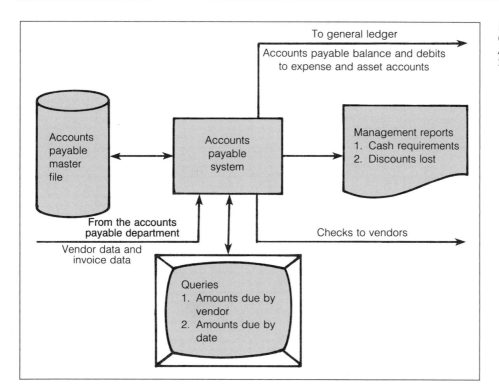

FIGURE 16.18
Overview of the
Accounts Payable
System

to the accounts payable system. The primary types of input are data concerning vendors, such as vendor name, address, etc., and data from new invoices received from vendors and suppliers.

Representative accounts payable management reports are illustrated in figure 16.20. They include a *cash requirements* report, which is based on amounts owed and dates when these amounts are due. The *discounts lost* report is an important type of cash management report. Many vendors allow customers to take a discount on payments, say 2 percent off the invoice, if payments are made within 10 days. If enough cash is available, or can be borrowed, discounts generally should be taken. The discounts lost report identifies payables where the discounts were not taken. These situations are usually derivations from management policy and therefore require investigation.

The accounts payable system also produces checks that are sent to vendors after review by the accounts payable department. Queries to the system normally are related to amounts due to be paid. Management may need to know the amount due a particular vendor or the amount due by a certain date.

Payroll

Payroll is often the first system that a company converts to computer processing because it is a relatively simple operation that does not interface with many other application systems. The primary objectives of the

FIGURE 16.19
Typical Fields in
an Accounts
Payable Master
File

Vendor number
Vendor name
Vendor address
Payment terms
Amounts owed by invoice
Payments—Year-to-date
Discounts taken—Year-to-date
Discounts lost—Year-to-date

payroll system are (1) to pay both hourly and salaried employees on a timely basis, (2) to maintain records of payments to employees and the taxes withheld from employee payments, and (3) to provide management with the reports necessary to manage the payroll function. Figure 16.21 provides an overview of a payroll system. This system maintains a payroll master file. Typical contents of a record within the payroll master file are illustrated in figure 16.22. The payroll department provides most of the payroll system input in the form of personal employee data, such as name, address, pay rate, and hours worked during a pay period. The sales department, in some cases, provides sales commission data for commission payments to

FIGURE 16.20
Typical Accounts
Payable
Management
Reports

PAGE 1
RUN DATE 11-5-8X

DISCOUNTS LOST
REPORT
AS OF 10-31-8X

VOUCHER NO	VENDOR NO	VENDOR NAME	INVOICE AMOUNT	AMOUNT LOST	EFF APR	DAYS LATE
15270	25190	INTERNATIONAL PAPER	7500.00	150.00	24%	10
29563	31723	LLOYD'S MANUFACTURIN	1350.00	13.50	13%	5
14021	45310	ABDICK	1080.00	21.60	13%	4
83910	51377	IBM	2532.00	75.96	25%	9
85674	63784	PENTEL	950.00	9.50	15%	4
93201	72111	XEROX	1500.00	30.00	22%	6

PAGE 1
RUN DATE 11-5-8X

CASH REQUIREMENT
REPORT
AS OF 10-31-8X

DUE DATE	VENDOR NO	VENDOR NAME	PYMT TERMS	INVOICE NO	AMOUNT DUE	DISC AMOUNT	BALANCE DUE	PYMT
013184	25190	INTERNATIONAL PAPER	2/10,N/30	07519	450.00	9.00	441.00	441.00
021084	31723	LLOYD'S MANUFACTURIN	*****	21340	652.00	.00	652.00	200.00
021584	45310	ABDICK	2/10,N/30	17001	107.50	2.15	105.40	105.40
021584	61377	IBM	3/10,N/30	00910	963.00	28.89	934.11	934.11
022884	63784	PENTEL	*****	50003	93.00	.00	93.00	50.00
030184	72111	XEROX	1/10,N/30	43000	70.00	7.00	63.00	63.00

TOTAL CASH REQUIREMENTS 10—31—8X $ 1793.51

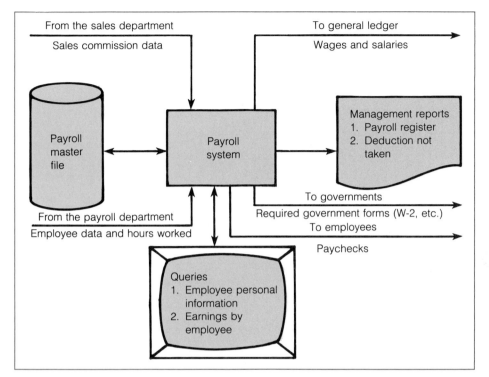

FIGURE 16.21
Overview of the
Payroll System

Employee number
Employee name
Employee address
Department
Occupation
Pay rate
Vacation time
Sick leave time
Gross pay year-to-date
Federal income tax withheld
State income tax withheld
FICA tax withheld
Health insurance withheld
Credit union savings withheld
Bank code

FIGURE 16.22
Typical Contents
of a Payroll Master
File Record

sales representatives. The output from the payroll system includes required government forms such as the W-2 form. This form is produced annually to report wages that have been earned for the year as well as other income tax information. The system also produces paychecks for employees. Management reports (illustrated in figure 16.23) include the *deductions-not-taken* report and the *payroll register,* which is a record of wages paid and withholding amounts for each employee. The deductions-not-taken report shows payroll deductions not taken on schedule due to an employee's insufficient pay. Queries to the payroll system generally are

```
                                                                        PAGE 1
                                                                RUN DATE 11-5-8X
                                  PAYROLL REGISTER
                                      REPORT
                                   AS OF 10-31-8X

  EMP     EMP                  REG     OT     TOTAL      FEDERAL   FICA    STATE    EARNINGS
  NO      NAME         RATE    HOURS   HOURS  EARNINGS   TAX       TAX     TAX      YTD

  00001   TURNBALL,JW   4.51   40      10     248.05     32.20    25.41   13.04    7840.21
  00002   CLARK,TC      5.37   40       0     214.80     16.81    12.10    6.75    8250.00
  00003   JONES,FL      3.35   21       0      70.35      6.91     4.21    2.10    2615.00
  00004   SMITH,AJ      3.35   30       0     100.50      9.22     6.90    4.12    3700.12
  00005   JAMES,CL      5.37   40       5     255.08     41.90    31.76   15.02    9215.91
  00006   FREDERICKSON,JR 4.51 40       0     180.40     12.13    10.91    5.33    7651.00
```

```
                                                                        PAGE 1
                                                                RUN DATE 11-5-8X
                                DEDUCTIONS NOT TAKEN
                                      REPORT
                                   AS OF 10-31-8X

  EMP     EMP                 DEDUCTION        AMOUNT        AMOUNT        NOT TAKEN
  NO      NAME                DESC             TAKEN         NOT TAKEN     BALANCE

  00001   TURNBALL,JW         UNITED FUND        .00         25.00         25.00
  00001   TURNBALL,JW         CREDIT UNION     40.00           .00         57.00
  00002   CLARK,TC            HOSPITALIZATION  26.00           .00          5.00
  00003   JONES,FL            PENSION          45.00           .00         40.00
  00003   JONES,FL            BONDS              .00         65.00         70.00
  00005   JAMES,CL            CREDIT UNION     40.00           .00         40.00
```

FIGURE 16.23
Typical Payroll
Management
Reports

for information concerning individual employees, such as personal information or earnings by the employee.

Other Applications

The general ledger is becoming a very common computer application. The *general ledger system* maintains the financial accounts of the business. It is responsible for producing such financial statements as the *income statement,* the *statement of financial position,* and the *statement of changes in financial position.* This application maintains a record of all assets, liabilities, owner's equities, revenues, and expenses of the firm.

Sometimes the general ledger system will also have the capability of maintaining a budget, especially for revenues and expenses. Reports can be prepared comparing actual revenues and expenses to budgeted amounts. Such reports are very valuable in maintaining control of a business organization.

Another application is the **manufacturing resource planning (MRP) system.** This system is closely related to our earlier discussion concerning inventory systems. However, an MRP system is a much more sophisticated approach to the materials inventory area than a simple inventory system.

Based on production schedules and material requirements for individual products, the MRP system can efficiently order materials so that they will be on hand when required in production. Along with the MRP system, many manufacturing firms maintain a **production scheduling system.** This system helps control the flow of materials and production jobs through the factory.

Under order processing, we previously discussed the possibility of producing a few sales analysis reports from the order processing system. A separate **marketing analysis system** can go far beyond the scope of these few reports. In addition to providing information about past sales, the system can assist in estimating future sales and even help in optimizing the marketing strategy for certain products through a market research approach.

Several other types of systems are used by specialized industries. Examples of such systems are the reservation systems used by motels and airlines.

□ SUMMARY

In this chapter, the linkage between decision making by managers and a management-information system was specified. A data base contains the raw material used to produce the information output from the information system. Hierarchical and integrated designs of information systems were described. In a hierarchical system, the data bases are segregated along functional lines, whereas an integrated system is characterized by a common data base. The demands of management personnel for information depend on the type of decision being made. A management information system should be capable of providing information tailored to the information requirements of all managers.

A management information system should incorporate the design features of a responsibility-accounting system. This feature views an organization as a group of responsibility centers. Therefore, revenues, costs, assets, and liabilities—when appropriate—should be traced to a responsibility center within the organization. The principle employed in tracing revenues, costs, assets or liabilities is controllability. These items are traced to that center in which decisions are made. Then, these controllable financial items are used in preparing performance reports. These reports serve as a basis for evaluating the performance of the managers of the responsibility center. (The next chapter contains a rather detailed description of accounting-based performance measures.)

The remainder of the detailed material contained in the chapter can be summarized as follows:

■ The management information system is a formalized computer-based system able to integrate data from various sources to provide the information necessary for management decision making. Scheduled reports are produced on a regularly scheduled basis, such as daily, weekly, or monthly. A demand report is generated upon request. Exception reports notify management when an activity or system is out of control. Predictive reports assist management in answering "what if" questions.

■ A data base management system is a program that serves as an interface between application programs and a set of coordinated and integrated files called a data base. The components of the information system data hierarchy, in ascending order of complexity, are (1) bit, (2) byte, (3) field or item, (4) record, (5) file or data set, and (6) data base.

■ The two basic types of file organization, sequential and direct, are combined with two data process modes, batch and immediate, to form three data processing strategies: batch sequential, batch direct, and immediate direct. Under the batch mode, changes and queries to a file are stored for a period of time and then a processing run is made periodically to update the master file, produce scheduled reports, and produce responses to queries. Under the immediate mode, transactions are processed to update the master file immediately or shortly after a real-world event occurs. One type of application using immediate processing is a real-time system. A real-time application can immediately capture data about ongoing events or can process and provide the information necessary to manage them. There are two primary objectives of an inventory system: (1) minimize costs due to out-of-stock situations and (2) minimize the inventory carrying costs. These two objectives are in conflict with one another.

■ The primary objectives of an order processing system are (1) to initiate shipping orders, (2) to maintain a record of backordered items, and (3) to update various sales analysis reports. Objectives of the accounts receivable system are threefold: (1) to bill customers for orders shipped, (2) to maintain records of the amounts that customers owe and to maintain a record of payments on account, and (3) to provide the information necessary to assist in collection of past-due accounts. The objectives of the accounts payable system are (1) to provide control over payments to vendors of goods and suppliers of services, (2) to issue checks to vendors and suppliers, and (3) to provide information for effective cash management. The objectives of the payroll system are to (1) pay both hourly and salaried employees on a timely basis, (2) maintain records of payments to employees and the taxes withheld from employee payments, (3) provide management with the reports necessary to manage the personnel function. The general ledger maintains the financial accounts of the business and produces financial statements. Other typical applications include material requirements planning, production scheduling, and marketing analysis.

KEY TERMS

Backorder	Data base
Batch direct	Data base management system
Batch processing	Decision-support system
Batch sequential	Demand reports
Bit	Direct file organization
Byte	Field or item

File
Filters
Hierarchical information system
Immediate direct
Immediate processing
Manufacturing resource planning
(MRP) system

Marketing analysis system
Order processing
Predictive reports
Production scheduling system
Record
Sequential file organization

QUESTIONS

Q16-1. How does exception reporting reduce the volume and size of reports?

Q16-2. How is information filtered?

Q16-3. What are some of the advantages of a hierarchical information system?

Q16-4. What are some of the disadvantages of a hierarchical information system?

Q16-5. What are some of the advantages of an integrated information system?

Q16-6. What are some of the disadvantages of an integrated information system?

Q16-7. Discuss some of the problems that would be encountered in preparing cost estimates if a firm had a hierarchical information system.

Q16-8. Discuss some of the problems that would be encountered in preparing a comprehensive budget if a firm had a hierarchical information system.

Q16-9. How does the capability to interrogate a data base allow the management staff to specify the threshold of detail required?

Q16-10. What is a controllable cost? Does the concept of controllability vary with the level of the organization? How?

Q16-11. What are the components of the information systems date hierarcy?

Q16-12. Define and explain each of the components in the information systems data hierarchy.

Q16-13. Identify the two basic types of file organization.

Q16-14. Outline the difference between batch and immediate data processing modes.

Q16-15. What are the similarities and differences among batch sequential, batch direct, and immediate direct processing approaches?

Q16-16. What is a real-time system?

Q16-17. What are the primary objectives of an inventory system?

Q16-18. For the merchandise inventory system, identify the following: primary inputs, typical data maintained on the master file, and some examples of output.

Q16-19. What are the primary objectives of the order processing system?

Q16-20. For the order processing system, identify the following: primary inputs, typical data maintained on the master file, and some examples of output.

Q16-21. What are the primary objectives of the accounts receivable system?

Q16-22. For the accounts receivable system, identify the following: primary inputs, typical data maintained on the master file, and some examples of output.

Q16-23. What are the primary objectives of the accounts payable system?

Q16-24. For the accounts payable system, identify the following: primary inputs, typical data maintained on the master file, and some examples of output.

Q16-25. What are the primary objectives of the payroll system?

Q16-26. For the payroll system, identify the following: primary inputs, typical data maintained on the master file, and some examples of output.

Q16-27. What is a general ledger system?

Q16-28. What is a manufacturing resources planning system?

PROBLEMS

Preparation of a Production Report

P16-1. The Accounting department prepares monthly production reports for each department of the Potter Manufacturing Company. A report for department S for the month of September 19X6 is given along with some production statistics. Cost allocations are made on the following basis:

a. Materials handling—number of requisitions
b. Warehouse cost—cost of materials requisitioned
c. Holding cost—cost of materials requisitioned
d. Ordering cost—number of requisitions
e. Supervision—number of employees
f. Taxes—cost of machinery
g. Insurance—cost of machinery
h. Inspection—units produced
i. Heat—floor space
j. Building occupancy

POTTER MANUFACTURING COMPANY
Production Report
Department S
Month of September 19X6

Direct materials cost		
Cost of materials requisitioned		$15,000
Materials handling cost		750
Warehouse costs		500
Inventory holding costs		150
Ordering costs		100
Total direct-material cost		$16,500
Direct-labor cost		32,000
Factory overhead cost		
Supervision	$2,000	
Depreciation	3,000	
Taxes on machinery	200	
Insurance	150	
Inspection	750	
Supplies and tools	800	
Heat	1,600	
Light and power	500	
Building occupancy	1,000	
Total factory overhead		10,000
Total manufacturing costs		$58,500

Production Statistics

	Department	Percent of factory
Number of units produced	5,000	
Number of employees in department	25	5%
Number of direct-labor hours worked	4,000	6%
Number of material requisitions made	600	40%
Floor space occupied—sq ft	3,000	10%

Required ☐ Prepare a production report for department S for the month of September 19X6, where the costs incurred in the department and the costs allocated to the department are segregated.

P16-2. The Promotion department of the Doxolby Co. is responsible for the design and development of all promotional campaigns and related literature, pamphlets, and brochures. Top-management personnel are reviewing the effectiveness of the Promotion department to determine if the department's activities could be managed better and more economically by an outside promotion agency. As a part of this review, the top-management staff has asked for a summary of the Promotion department's costs for the most recent year. The following cost summary was supplied:

Responsibility- Accounting Reports

Promotion Department
Costs for the Year Ended November 30, 19X8

Direct department costs	$257,500
Charges from other departments	44,700
Allocated share of general	
administrative overhead	22,250
Total costs	$324,450

The direct department costs consist of those costs that can be traced directly to the activities of the Promotion department, such as staff and clerical salaries (including related employee benefits, supplies, etc.). The charges from other departments represent the costs of services that are provided by other departments of Doxolby at the request of the Promotion department.

The company has developed a charging system for such interdepartmental uses of services. For instance, the in-house Printing department charges the Promotion department for the promotional literature printed. All such services provided to the Promotion department by other departments of Doxolby are included in the "Charges from other departments."

General administrative overhead is comprised of such costs as top-management personnel salaries and benefits, depreciation, heat, insurance, property taxes, etc. These costs are allocated to all departments in proportion to the number of employees in each department.

Required ☐ Discuss the usefulness of the cost figures as presented for the Promotion department of Doxolby, Inc., as a basis for a comparison with a bid from an outside agency to provide the same type of activities as Doxolby's own Promotion department.

(CMA)

P16-3. George Johnson was hired on July 1, 19X9, as assistant general manager of the Botel Division of Staple, Inc. It was understood that he would be elevated to general manager of the division on January 1, 19X1, when the then current general manager retired. This was done. In addition to becoming acquainted with the division and the general manager's duties, Johnson was specifically charged with the responsibility for development of the 19X0 and 19X1 budgets. As general manager in 19X1, he was, obviously, responsible for the 19X2 budget.

The Staple Company is a multiproduct company that is highly decentralized. Each division is quite autonomous. The corporation staff approves division-prepared operating budgets, but seldom makes major changes in them. The corporate staff actively participates in decisions requiring capital investment (for expansion or replacement) and makes the final decisions. The divisional management team is reponsible for implementing the capital program.

The major method used by the Staple Corporation to measure division performance is contribution return on division net investment.

The budgets presented were approved by the corporation. Revision of the 19X2 budget is not considered necessary even though 19X1 actually departed from the approved 19X1 budget.

Botel Division (in thousands)

	Actual			Budget	
Accounts	*19X9*	*19X0*	*19X1*	*19X1*	*19X2*
Sales	1,000	1,500	1,800	2,000	2,400
Less division variable costs					
Material and labor	250	375	450	500	600
Repairs	50	75	50	100	120
Supplies	20	30	36	40	48
Less division managed costs					
Employee training	30	35	25	40	45
Maintenance	50	55	40	60	70
Less division committed costs					
Depreciation	120	160	160	200	200
Rent	80	100	110	140	140
Total	600	830	871	1,080	1,223
Division net contribution	400	670	929	920	1,177
Division investment					
Accounts receivable	100	150	180	200	240
Inventory	200	300	270	400	480
Fixed assets	1,590	2,565	2,800	3,380	4,000
Less: Accounts and wages payable	(150)	(225)	(350)	(300)	(360)
Net investment	1,740	2,790	2,900	3,680	4,360
Contribution return on net investment	23%	24%	32%	25%	27%

Required □

1. Identify Mr. Johnson's responsibilities under the management and measurement program described.

2. Appraise the performance of Mr. Johnson in 19X1.

3. Recommend to the president any changes in the responsibilities assigned to managers or in the measurement methods used to evaluate divisional management staff members based upon your analysis.

(CMA)

P16-4. The Arment Co. has sales in the range of $25 to $30 million, has one manufacturing plant, employs 700 people, including fifteen national account salespeople and eighty traveling sales representatives. The home office and plant is in Philadelphia, and the product is distributed east of the Mississippi River. The product is a line of pumps and related fittings used at construction sites, in homes, and in processing plants.

Development of Profit Plans

The company has total assets equal to 80 percent of sales. Its capitalization is: accruals and current liabilities, 30 percent; long-term debt, 15 percent; and shareholders' equity, 55 percent. In the last two years, sales have increased 7 percent each year, and income after-tax has amounted to 5 percent of sales.

Required □

1. Strategic decisions by top management personnel on a number of important topics serve as a basis for the annual profit plan. What are these topics? Why are they important?

2. What specific procedures will be followed each year in developing the annual profit plan?

(CMA)

P16-5. The Parsons Co. compensates its field sales force on a commission and year-end bonus basis. The commission is 20 percent of standard gross margin (planned selling price less standard cost of goods sold on a full absorption basis), contingent upon collection of the account. Customer's credit is approved by the company's Credit department. Price concessions are granted on occasion by the top sales management staff, but sales commissions are not reduced by the discount.

Evaluation of an Employee Compensation Plan

A year-end bonus of 15 percent of commissions earned is paid to salespeople who equal or exceed their annual sales target. The annual sales target is usually established by applying approximately a 5 percent increase to the prior year's sales.

Required □

1. What features of this compensation plan would seem to be effective in motivating the sales force to accomplish company goals of higher profits and return on investment? Explain why.

2. What features of this compensation plan would seem to be counter-effective in motivating the salespeople to accomplish the company goals of higher profits and return on investment? Explain why.

(CMA)

Responsibility-
Accounting
Reports

P16-6.   The board of trustees of the First Baptist Church is meeting to prepare a budget for the next year. The treasurer of the church has given each member of the board the following statement:

FIRST BAPTIST CHURCH
Statement of Cash Receipts and Disbursements
For Year Ended December 31, 19XX

Cash receipts		$127,987.50
Cash disbursements		
Wages and salaries	$29,850.00	
Mortgage	25,000.00	
Operating expenses	14,378.15	
Transportation	5,800.00	
Missions	35,000.00	
Miscellaneous	2,517.29	
Total disbursements		122,545.44
Excess of receipts over disbursements		$ 5,442.06

One of the members of the board states that this statement is not adequate for the board to use in preparing the budget. The treasurer states that this is the report that has always been presented to the members of the church, and he believes that it is adequate for the purposes of preparing a budget. The board member states that they are responsible for the financial management of the church. He states that management needs additional information than that which is provided to the congregation.

Required □

1. Do you agree with the board member or the treasurer? Explain your answer.

2. What additional information would the board of trustees require concerning the cash receipts of the church?

3. What additional information would the board of trustees require concerning the cash disbursements of the church?

CHAPTER OUTLINE

PERFORMANCE MEASUREMENT AND EVALUATION IN DIVISIONALIZED ORGANIZATIONS

CHAPTER **17**

☐ INTRODUCTION

Many varied patterns of business structure have emerged at the corporate level during the last several decades. Perhaps the most pronounced of these trends is the increased size and complexity of the modern corporation. As a result of the increased size of corporations, a trend in the areas of decision making and control is also observable.

Decentralization is the term that best describes this second trend.[1] Decentralization does not refer to geographic dispersion of units within an organization; rather it is a management philosophy that involves the delegation of decision-making prerogatives within the organization. The goal of decentralization is to delegate decision-making authority to the lowest possible level within the organizational hierarchy so that the majority of the decision making is done by those knowledgeable individuals who are directly affected by the decision.

Although the concept of decentralization can be introduced into an organization without structural changes, generally the organizational structure is arranged around a set of responsibility centers. The structural counterpart of decentralization is called **divisionalization**. When the corporation is divisionalized, each division is regarded as a separate entity for purposes of performance evaluation.

The task of evaluating divisional performance would be considerably less complicated if there were no transactions between divisions of the same corporation. Unfortunately, this is seldom the case, and rather involved relationships among divisions are often encountered. Whenever a service or product is transferred from one division to another, a value must be attached to make accounting-based **performance measurement** possible. (The problems relating to the attached value or transfer price will be considered in the next chapter.)

---

1. For an extended discussion on decentralization, see James L. Gibson, John M. Ivancevich, James H. Donnelly, Jr., *Organizations: Structure, Processes, Behavior* (Dallas: Business Publications, Inc., 1973).

577

The focus in this chapter will be directed toward gaining an understanding of the criteria that are employed in evaluating performance. Particular attention will be given to the accounting problems encountered when cost, profit, or investment criteria may elicit different behavioral patterns from divisional managers. Our discussion of accounting-based performance-measurement criteria will identify the functional and dysfunctional behavior patterns that may result.

□ THE OBJECTIVES OF THE MEASUREMENT SYSTEM

Any benefits that may accrue to an organization because of its divisionalized structure can be lost if there is no clear statement of the objectives of the measurement system. A comprehensive list of objectives is perhaps not possible to identify, but most objectives can be classified into one of the three following categories:

1. Measures designed to determine the contribution that the division makes to the performance of the total organization.

2. Measures designed to permit comparative and qualitative evaluations of the performance of the divisional managers.

3. Measures designed to influence the divisional managers to operate the division within the confines of corporate policies and to achieve the goals established by the corporate management team.

Since corporate performance is gauged in terms of profits, a frequent objective of measurement systems will be to determine the direct or indirect contribution of each division to overall corporate profits. The measures will be employed in making comparative evaluations among divisions of the firm. At the same time, evaluations will be made concerning the profitability of a division as compared with industry averages.

One aim of a performance-measurement system should be to provide input into the performance-evaluation process in an objective manner. However, **performance evaluation** is the function of management personnel and involves a considerable degree of subjective judgment. Users of any performance-measurement system should realize that corporate managers—and not the measurement system—are charged with making the performance evaluations and any related decisions. Therefore, in the design of any measurement system, careful consideration must be given to how the system will influence the behavior of the divisional managers. In many respects, the measurement system specifies the "rules of the game" as far as divisional managers are concerned. Any influence the systems will have on the behavior of divisional managers must be considered in terms of the overall goals of the corporation.

Perhaps an example will help clarify some of the concepts presented here. Assume your task is to identify the number-one accounting student graduating from your university this year. Assuming a four-point scale, you identify two students who have overall grade-point averages of 3.94

and 3.87, respectively. The grade-point averages are the performance measures that are the result of a technical process involving calculating quality points and determining the grade-point average.

Now, suppose you are given some additional information about the two students. You learn that the first student only took the required accounting courses and all of the student's electives were identified as easy grades by other students. In addition, you learn that this student is either in class, studying, eating, or sleeping. This student is not involved in any outside activities. You determine that the second student took elective courses in accounting, computer science, and economics. The second student also participates in a varsity sport, works part-time in the library, and is president of a student organization. At this point, you might conclude that the objective of the first student is to maximize the grade-point average while the second student is concerned with obtaining an education and developing as an individual.

If only one performance measure (grade-point average) is used, the first student described would be the number-one accounting student in the senior class. In this case, the performance measure dictates the decision. However, if you take into account the additional information concerning the two students, you then engage in performance evaluation. You used the performance measure plus the environmental information and engaged in the social/human judgment process in making the selection. This example should help clarify the difference between performance measurement and performance evaluation. Some insight also should have been gained as to how the performance-measurement system can influence behavior.

☐ ORGANIZATIONAL STRUCTURE

When divisionalization underlies decentralization, each division is regarded as a separate economic unit worthy of independent evaluation. If decentralization is to be successful, certain ground rules must be established. Perhaps the most prominent ground rule is that authority must be commensurate with responsibility.[2] The divisional manager should only be held responsible for that over which he or she has control. This is necessary so that the advantages associated with decision making and control in the smaller firm can be realized. For example, divisional managers would be held responsible for television advertising expense only if the decision to run the advertising was made at the divisional level of the corporation.

A rigid interpretation of the authority and responsibility proposition leads to some very interesting conclusions. Carried to the extreme, a divisional manager would have control over the sources of supply of raw materials, the acquisition of plant and equipment, maintenance policies,

---

2. For an extended discussion on organization of a performance-measurement system, see David Solomons, *Divisional Performance: Measurement and Control* (New York: Financial Executives Research Foundation, 1965).

product pricing, advertising, research and development activities, and any other factors that would influence revenues or expenses. A situation in which a divisional manager would have this degree of control over all aspects of a division would be difficult to imagine and could present problems. If every divisional manager exercised this degree of control over his or her division, suboptimization certainly would be likely. This occurs when divisions seeking to maximize profits for themselves as separate entities prevent the corporation from optimizing its profits as a whole.

Assume a divisionalized firm in which one division manufactures refrigerators and a sister division manufactures electric motors. Each refrigerator requires a motor and all intradivisional transfers are made at market price. Assume the Refrigerator division has just received a rush order for 100 units at a premium price. In turn, the Refrigerator division places a rush order for the required 100 motors. Managers of the Motor division refuse the rush order because it will require working a significant amount of overtime to meet the delivery date. The overtime premium will reduce divisional profits. This decision may be optimal as far as the Motor division is concerned. However, if the premium on the purchase price of the refrigerators exceeds the overtime cost, it would be optimal from the firm's point of view to accept the order for the refrigerators.

To avoid suboptimization and to insure that the best interests of the company are served, certain policies are established and administered at the corporate level to coordinate divisional operations. Of course, such policies are in conflict with the proposition concerning divisional control over all aspects of the divisional operation. Therefore, some balance must be achieved between the delegation of authority to the divisional managers and the establishment of policies to avoid corporate suboptimization.

From the discussion to this point, one might conclude that all performance measures are based on some definition of profit. However, most organizations have some divisions that do not lend themselves to evaluation based on a measure of profit contribution. For example, data processing, research, or administrative centers often do not permit profit determination because of the difficulty associated with expressing the output of these centers in financial terms.

First, let us consider performance measures in cost centers employing either standard costs or a budgetary system. Then, we will review several definitions of net income that can be employed in measuring performance in a profit center. In conclusion, investment centers and the capital-investment-based-valuation possibilities will be considered. In each case, we will look at some of the behavioral implications of each of the accounting-based performance measures.

☐ COST CENTERS

A **cost center** is an entity within a firm or divison in which performance is measured by comparing actual costs with budgeted costs for a specified period of time. This type of performance-measurement system is only concerned with financial inputs. In most cases, cost centers are employed when difficulties are encountered in measuring output in financial terms. Activities often associated with cost centers are accounting, corporate planning, data processing, legal services, marketing, personnel administration, plant engineering, and public relations. Such activities are required for a firm to function effectively and each has, to some degree, an identifiable output. However, it is difficult to express in financial terms outputs such as employee morale, legal advice, or good public relations.

Nonprofit and governmental units are often evaluated as cost centers. Appropriations are made to centers based on budget requests. Performance measures relate expenditures to line-item budget amounts and evaluations are generally based on the ability of the management team to achieve levels of output within the constraints of the budget.

For purposes of measuring the performance of cost center managers, only those costs that are controllable by the center's managers are considered. Controllable costs are those costs that are incurred as a result of decisions made by the managers of the cost center. Therefore, any allocations resulting from costs common to two or more divisions would not be included in the performance report. If such allocated costs are included in the report, they should be segregated and clearly labeled. A sample cost-center performance report is shown in table 17.1.

One problem concerning performance evaluation that should be recognized is that the performance of a Legal Services department cannot be evaluated simply in terms of costs. This report serves as a device for measuring the spending in the Legal Services department. Many other factors would have to be considered in evaluating departmental performance. For example, the number of legal opinions, contracts written, or contracts reviewed might give some indication as to the level of activity in the Legal Services department. The firm's ability to avoid litigation and successful settlement of legal claims are two other possible indications of successful operations in the department.

Expenditures in cost centers are frequently authorized by being included in the budget. A problem encountered with cost centers revolves around this authorization function of a budget. Often, a budget is based

TABLE 17.1 Cost-Center Performance Report

GENERAL TECH CORPORATION
Legal Services Department
19X4 Expense Report

	Actual cost	Budgeted cost	Spending variance
Professional staff salaries	$194,750	$200,000	$ 5,250
Secretarial staff	53,000	50,000	(3,000)
Librarian	15,000	15,000	0
Library supplies	25,000	30,000	5,000
Office supplies	27,275	25,000	(2,275)
Travel	14,650	15,000	350
Professional development	21,730	25,000	3,270
Consulting fees	29,000	40,000	11,000
Total	$380,405	$400,000	$19,595

on past performance, and managers have learned certain lessons from playing the "budgeting game." For example, if an amount that has been authorized is not spent, the budget for the next period may be reduced to reflect this. As a result, managers often adopt the attitude that if a budgeted amount is not spent, they will lose it. Many people have received new office furniture, typewriters, and calculators near the end of a budget period simply because "money was left in the budget."

Another behavioral pattern attributable to budgeting in cost centers that may result in dysfunctional activity relates to managers' freedom concerning the line items in the budget. For example, assume that the office supplies line item in the budget has been exhausted in the first ten months of a calendar year. In addition, assume that the line item relating to travel has a more than ample balance for the remaining two months. Cost-center managers might react in several ways depending on corporate operating procedures. If the cost-center manager can transfer budgeted amounts between accounts without much difficulty, then the manager in the situation just mentioned would probably make a transfer from travel to office supplies. If, however, corporate procedures did not allow such a transfer, employees would find themselves without the necessary office supplies until the next budget period, or the manager may resort to some "creative accounting procedure" so that additional office supplies would be purchased and charged to the travel account. Finally, the manager may elect to overspend for office supplies and to accept any possible negative sanctions.

Such actions do not improve cost-center performance and instead cause the entire budgeting, performance measurement, and evaluation process to assume many of the attributes of a game. The activities of managers are directed more toward playing the game according to the rules than obtaining improved performance from the cost center. This is not necessarily bad if the rules of the game are such that the players' actions are directed towards improved performance. Frequently, however, the rules are such that the resulting behavior can be dysfunctional when evaluated in terms of the organizational goals.

The designer of a performance-measurement system must anticipate possible dysfunctional behavior that may result from the policies and procedures underlying the system. A periodic evaluation of the system is advisable to assess the behavioral patterns that are attributed to the system. If dysfunctional behavior is observed, then system modifications may be appropriate. An adequately designed and administered performance-measurement system provides the management team with a means for controlling costs and the basis for evaluating performance.

☐ PROFIT CENTERS

A **profit center** is a division of a firm in which performance measurement is based on controllable revenues and expenses that are matched to determine the division's income. It is a more sophisticated performance-measurement system than a cost center because both inputs and outputs are measured in financial terms. In addition to the matching problems encountered in determining income, cost-allocation problems among profit centers may frequently complicate performance measurement in a profit center. Therefore, different definitions of income may be employed in performance-measurement systems.

When net income is employed in determining divisional performance, the income of a division includes both direct and allocated revenues and expenses. Therefore, the sum of the revenues, expenses, and net incomes reported for the various divisions of a firm will equal the total revenues, expenses, and net income of the entire firm.

Generally, a divisional income statement is prepared so that the direct and allocated items are segregated. This is illustrated in table 17.2. The danger of such a statement, especially in the short run, is that the divisional operating income before-tax figure will be used as a basis for performance evaluation or decision making. Such actions fail to recognize the implications of the arbitrary cost allocation employed in determining the divisional operating income before taxes.

Perhaps the most relevant question concerns the appropriateness of income as a measure of short-run performance. Even when income is measured according to generally accepted accounting principles, many problems in the areas of performance evaluation must be considered.

For example, maintenance and repairs can be deferred, resulting in a short-run increase in income. Advertising or research and development expenditures may be reduced to favorably influence income in the short run. If standard-costing variances are closed to cost of goods sold, income in the short-run can be increased by increasing production. This will decrease an unfavorable capacity variance and result in a decrease in cost of goods sold.

Some of the shortcomings of reporting divisional income are overcome when controllable divisional income is employed. Under this method, a division's revenues include only revenues generated by the division. Ex-

TABLE 17.2 Divisional Income Statement (Net-Income Basis)

K & L DIVISION
Divisional Income Statement
for Year Ended December 31, 19X1

Sales		$1,500,000
Less		
Standard cost of sales	$750,000	
Factory cost variances (net)	25,000	775,000
		$ 725,000
Less		
Direct divisional selling and administrative expenses	$225,000	
Allocated selling and administrative expenses	85,000	310,000
Divisional operating income		$ 415,000
Less—Allocated financial charges		95,000
Divisional operating income before taxes		$ 320,000

TABLE 17.3 Division Income Statement (Controllable-Income Basis)

K & L DIVISION
Divisional Income Statement
for Year Ended December 31, 19X1

Sales		$1,500,000
Less		
Standard cost of sales	$750,000	
Factory cost variances (net)	25,000	775,000
Divisional gross profit		$ 725,000
Less		
Controllable divisional selling and		
administrative expenses		225,000
Controllable divisional income		$ 500,000

penses include only those directly attributable to the division. A sample divisional income statement is shown in table 17.3.

Any selling and administrative expenses incurred at the corporate level specifically for and at the request of the divisional managers are charged to the division. Manufacturing, selling, and administrative fixed costs, which are to a large degree controlled by the divisional managers, are employed in this income calculation. However, no allocated costs are used in determining controllable divisional income.

The advantage of this method is that the controllable income results from revenue and expenses controllable at the divisional level. This certainly comes closer to the objective of controllability initially established for a performance-measurement system. However, there are several weaknesses encountered when this technique is employed. Variable and fixed costs are not segregated in the statement shown in table 17.3. This can be remedied by modifying the statement, as shown in table 17.4.

A second weakness in income-based performance-measurement systems results from various methods employed in asset valuation. When LIFO is employed during a period of rising price levels, net income can increase

TABLE 17.4 Divisional Income Statement (Direct-Income Basis with Variable and Fixed Costs Segregated)

K & L DIVISION
Divisional Income Statement
for Year Ended December 31, 19X1

Sales		$1,500,000
Less		
Variable standard cost of sales	$600,000	
Factory cost variances (net)	10,000	
Variable selling and administrative		
expenses	150,000	760,000
Divisional contribution margin		$ 740,000
Less		
Controllable fixed costs		240,000
Controllable divisonal income		$ 500,000

significantly if base stocks from inventory are sold. The different methods of computing depreciation expense directly affect net income and make direct comparisons hazardous.

There is a human tendency to rank items when numbers are associated with them. This seems to lend a degree of objectivity to what is most likely a subjective evaluation. Consequently, there is a tendency to employ net-income figures to rank divisions based on the reported net incomes. Sole reliance on profitability with no consideration given to the investment employed results in measurements of dubious value for making comparisons. This can be overcome by employing return-on-investment measurements of performance, which are discussed in the next section.

☐ INVESTMENT CENTERS

An **investment center** is a division of a firm in which performance is measured by relating the net income to the capital investment employed in the division. One method of measuring performance in an investment center is **return on investment (ROI)**, where:

$$\text{ROI} = \frac{\text{Income}}{\text{Capital investment}}$$

The equation is often expanded to include two intermediate calculations. The first intermediate calculation shows the percentage of income on sales.

$$\text{Percentage of income on sales} = \frac{\text{Income}}{\text{Sales}}$$

Relating sales to capital investment results in the capital turnover.

$$\text{Capital turnover} = \frac{\text{Sales}}{\text{Capital investment}}$$

ROI can be expressed as

$$\text{ROI} = \frac{\text{Income}}{\text{Sales}} \times \frac{\text{Sales}}{\text{Capital investment}}$$

The relationship expressed with the two intermediate calculations emphasizes the three factors that cause changes in the ROI. They are

1. Increases or decreases in sales

2. Increases or decreases in costs

3. Increases or decreases in capital investment

The first two factors cause changes in the income and the third factor takes into account changes in the capital investment. Table 17.5 shows how a

TABLE 17.5 Divisional Return-on-Investment

	Period 1	*Period 2*	*Period 3*
Changes in Sales			
Sales	$1,000,000	$1,200,000	$750,000
Variable costs	$ 500,000	$ 600,000	$375,000
Fixed costs	250,000	250,000	250,000
Operating income	$ 250,000	$ 350,000	$125,000
Capital investment	$2,000,000	$2,000,000	$2,000,000
Return on sales	25 %	29.17%	16.67 %
Capital turnover	.5	.6	.375
Return on investment	12.5 %	17.5 %	6.25 %
Changes in Costs			
Sales	$1,000,000	$1,000,000	$1,000,000
Variable costs	$ 500,000	$ 600,000	$ 400,000
Fixed costs	250,000	300,000	250,000
Operating income	$ 250,000	$ 100,000	$ 350,000
Capital investment	$2,000,000	$2,000,000	$2,000,000
Return on sales	25 %	10%	35 %
Capital turnover	.5	.5	.5
Return on investment	12.5%	5%	17.5%
Changes in Capital Investment			
Sales	$1,000,000	$1,000,000	$1,000,000
Variable costs	$ 500,000	$ 500,000	$ 500,000
Fixed costs	250,000	250,000	250,000
Operating income	$ 250,000	$ 250,000	$ 250,000
Capital investment	$2,000,000	$1,750,000	$2,500,000
Return on sales	25 %	25 %	25 %
Capital turnover	.5	.57	.4
Return on investment	12.5%	14.25%	10 %

division's ROI is influenced by changes in these factors over three different periods.

In determining ROI, income before taxes is used because divisional managers do not have control over income-tax expense. Generally, all tax decisions are made at the corporate level. Frequently, accounting methods employed for tax purposes are not consistent with the methods employed for performance measurement.

Along with the various definitions of income possible in determining divisional ROI, several alternatives exist for determining the capital investment. Initially, problems are encountered in determining assets that should be included in the divisional capital investment. Once a determination has been made as to which assets are to be included in the divisional investment, then an investment-based valuation procedure must be selected. We will consider the asset-inclusion problem initially and then direct attention to the valuation problem.

As a general rule, the capital-investment base used in an ROI computation should include assets directly employed in generating the income. Both the assets and the income should be under the control of the divisional manager. In most cases, all of the assets of a corporation will not be directly traceable to the divisions. Problems are encountered with assets that are employed in servicing the divisions but are under the control of corporate managers. For example, a division may make use of corporate assets in the areas of marketing, data processing, research, and personnel. Generally, such assets are not allocated for purposes of determining divisional ROI. Facilities under construction also can be a problem, but generally they are included only if the divison has committed the funds for the new asset.

When considering asset valuation, a timing question exists concerning whether the opening, average, or closing amount of the capital investment should be employed. If the ROI is determined for periods of time over which no significant change in the asset base has taken place, then it is not necessary to employ an average investment. Generally, for periods in excess of a quarter, the average between the opening and closing amount of investment capital is employed.

In the area of asset valuation, perhaps the problem most frequently encountered concerns inventories. Since inventories often account for 50 percent or more of divisional capital investment, any LIFO-based inventory should be adjusted to a FIFO or replacement-value basis of valuation. This is consistent with the adjustment suggested for inventory valuation when income is being determined for internal-reporting purposes.

Several alternatives for valuing the investment base employ historical cost concepts. The assets included in the capital-investment base may be valued at (1) historical cost, (2) book value, or (3) book value less total liabilities. When historical cost is employed for valuing the capital investment, accummulated depreciation is not recognized in computing the ROI. If price levels and productivity of the asset base remained constant, this procedure would tend to produce a diminishing ROI because of increased maintenance costs. It is also unlikely that the productivity of any asset will remain constant, hence a diminishing ROI (assuming stable price levels) is inevitable.

Any tendency toward a diminishing ROI could be overcome by employing book values (cost less accumulated depreciation) in asset valuation. The limitation resulting from employing book values is that depreciation is an arbitrary allocation scheme, and the book value rarely approximates asset replacement cost. Therefore, the economic significance of an ROI employing book value is generally meaningless.

Assume an asset costs $16,852 and has an estimated useful life of three years with a zero salvage value. Yearly operating cash flows are estimated to equal $8,000. Table 17.6 shows the yearly ROI calculations for three different methods of determining the depreciation expense. Assets are valued at the book value at the beginning of the year in calculating the ROI. Note that when straight-line and sum-of-the-years'-digits depreciation are used, the ROI increases dramatically in later years. Compound-interest depreciation is a possible solution to this problem. When the actual results correspond with expectations, this method results in a constant ROI over the life of the asset. This ROI is equal to the internal rate of return on the project.

TABLE 17.6 Impact of Depreciation on ROI

Straight-line depreciation	Year 1	Year 2	Year 3
Operating cash flow	$ 8,000	$ 8,000	$ 8,000
Depreciation	5,617	5,617	5,618
Operating income	$ 2,383	$ 2,383	$ 2,382
Book value—start of year	$16,852	$11,235	$ 5,618
Return on investment	14%	21.2%	42.4%
Sum-of-the-years'-digits depreciation			
Operating cash flow	$ 8,000	$ 8,000	$ 8,000
Depreciation	8,426	5,617	2,809
Operating income	($ 426)	$ 2,383	$ 5,191
Book value—start of year	$16,852	$ 8,426	$ 2,809
Return on investment	(2.5%)	28.3%	184.8%
Compound-interest depreciation			
Operating cash flow	$ 8,000	$ 8,000	$ 8,000
Depreciation	4,629.60	5,555.52	6,666.62
Operating income	$ 3,370.40	$ 2,444.48	$ 1,333.38
Book value—start of year	$16,852	$12,222.40	$ 6,666.88
Return on investment	20%	20%	20%
Cash flow	$ 8,000	$ 8,000	$ 8,000
Less: interest at 20% on unrecovered investment (book value) at beginning of year	3,370.40 *	2,444.48	1,333.38
Depreciation	$ 4,629.60	$ 5,555.52	$ 6,666.62[†]
Book value—start of year	$16,852	$12,222.40	$ 6,666.88[†]

$$\frac{\$16,852}{\$8,000} = 2.1065$$

* Book value—start of year	$16,852.00
Interest rate	.20
Interest	$ 3,370.40

From Appendix Table 14.4, for *n* = 3, *i* = 20%   [†]Rounding error

Book value of the assets less the total liabilities of the division is equal to the divisional net assets. An ROI based on book value less total liabilities represents the return on the corporate investment in the division. Although an ROI based on net assets is frequently employed in external evaluation, it is not frequently used for internal evaluations because it does not include all revenue-producing assets. Studies indicate that most firms employing ROI in performance measurement employ total assets available in the investment base, and about two-thirds of these firms deduct accumulated depreciation.[3]

Since the plant and equipment of any division remains relatively unchanged for substantial periods of time, it is difficult to justify that in the short run they are controlled by the divisional managers. In most divisionalized firms, decisions concerning major capital expenditures are made

3. See National Association of Accountants, Research Report 35, "Return on Capital as a Guide to Managerial Decisions" (New York: 1959); and Solomons, *Divisional Performance: Measurement and Control.*

at the corporate and not the divisional level. Therefore, divisional managers have limited control over their divisional capital investment. Their major efforts are directed toward achieving sales increases and cost reductions.

An ROI Example

The income statement in table 17.7 shows the results of operations for the K & L Division for the year ended December 31, 19X1. Assume operating results are the same for 19X2 and 19X3. Table 17.8 shows the balance sheets at the end of each year. K & L Division pays no dividends, uses straight-line depreciation, and all assets have a three-year useful life. Cost of goods sold and selling and administrative expenses contain $150 and $50 in depreciation expense, respectively. Therefore, the total divisional yearly depreciation expense is $200.

Table 17.9 contains the rates of return for each year, calculated using the three methods suggested for valuing assets. In the first set of calculations, the end-of-year asset balances are used to determine the returns on investment. The second set of calculations employs the average yearly balances in determining the returns on investment. Recall that in this

TABLE 17.7 Divisional Income Statement

K & L DIVISION
Divisional Income Statement
for Year Ended December 31, 19X1

Sales	$500
Cost of goods sold	300*
Gross margin	$200
Selling and administrative expense	100†
Divisional operating income	$100

*Includes $150 depreciation expense.
†Includes $50 depreciation expense.

TABLE 17.8 Divisional Balance Sheets

K & L DIVISION
Divisional Balance Sheets

	December 31, 19X0		December 31, 19X1		December 31, 19X2		December 31, 19X3	
Current Assets		$200		$500		$ 800		$1,100
Fixed Assets	$600		$600		$600		$600	
Accumulated depreciation	0	600	200	400	400	200	600	0
Total assets		$800		$900		$1,000		$1,100
Current liabilities		$200		$200		$ 200		$ 200
Long-term liabilities		400		400		400		400
Owners' equity		200		300		400		500
Total liabilities and equity		$800		$900		$1,000		$1,100

TABLE 17.9 Divisional ROI Calculations

Investment bases	Year 1	Year 2	Year 3
	End-of-Year Balances Used to Determine ROI		
Historical cost	$\dfrac{\$100}{\$1,100} = 9.1\%$	$\dfrac{\$100}{\$1,400} = 7.1\%$	$\dfrac{\$100}{\$1,700} = 5.9\%$
Book value	$\dfrac{\$100}{\$900} = 11.1\%$	$\dfrac{\$100}{\$1,000} = 10\%$	$\dfrac{\$100}{\$1,100} = 9.1\%$
Book value less total liabilities	$\dfrac{\$100}{\$300} = 33.3\%$	$\dfrac{\$100}{\$400} = 25\%$	$\dfrac{\$100}{\$500} = 20\%$
	Average Yearly Balances Used to Determine ROI		
Historical cost	$\dfrac{\$100}{\left(\dfrac{\$800 + \$1,100}{2}\right)} = 10.5\%$	$\dfrac{\$100}{\left(\dfrac{\$1,100 + \$1,400}{2}\right)} = 8\%$	$\dfrac{\$100}{\left(\dfrac{\$1,400 + \$1,700}{2}\right)} = 6.5\%$
Book value	$\dfrac{\$100}{\left(\dfrac{\$800 + \$900}{2}\right)} = 11.8\%$	$\dfrac{\$100}{\left(\dfrac{\$900 + \$1,000}{2}\right)} = 10.5\%$	$\dfrac{\$100}{\left(\dfrac{\$1,000 + \$1,100}{2}\right)} = 9.5\%$
Book value less total liabilities	$\dfrac{\$100}{\left(\dfrac{\$200 + \$300}{2}\right)} = 40\%$	$\dfrac{\$100}{\left(\dfrac{\$300 + \$400}{2}\right)} = 28.6\%$	$\dfrac{\$100}{\left(\dfrac{\$400 + \$500}{2}\right)} = 22.2\%$

example the divisional operating income is assumed to be the same for each year. Notice that in the example the rates of return are larger when the average yearly balances are employed rather than the end-of-year balances. This is because the division is accumulating assets as a result of yearly operations. Therefore, the average-assets base is smaller than the end-of-year balances, which result in higher rates of return. Also note that the smallest rates of return are obtained when cost is used in valuing assets. When book value is employed, a higher rate of return results. Finally, the highest rate of return results when book value less total liabilities is employed in valuing the assets.

It is of interest to note from table 17.8 that after the third year of operation the division's current assets have increased by $900. The source of the $900 is $300 of divisional operating income plus the $600 depreciation expense that is added back because depreciation expense does not result in an outflow of working capital. To this point, no changes in the value of the dollar have been considered in the example.

Now, to make the situation more complex, assume that the overall price level increases 10 percent each year during years two and three. Therefore, assume the operating costs and replacement cost of the fixed assets will increase by 10 percent each year during years two and three. Table 17.10 contains yearly divisional income statements for three different sets of assumptions. The following discussion will highlight some of the problems encountered in performance measurement when there are changes in the price level.

In the first set of income statements, selling prices have been adjusted upward to reflect the 10 percent increase in the operating costs during years two and three. The constant profit of $100 has been maintained. As

TABLE 17.10 Yearly Divisional Income Statements with Various Assumptions

	Year 1	Year 2	Year 3
Yearly income statements—10% increase in costs—Pricing to maintain constant profits			
Sales	$500	$520	$542
Cost of goods sold	$150 + $150 = 300	$165 + $150 = 315	$181.50 + $150 = 331.50
Gross margin	$200	$205	$210.50
Selling and administrative expense	$ 50 + $ 50 = 100	$ 55 + $ 50 = 105	$ 60.50 + $ 50 = 110.50
Divisional operating income	$100	$100	$100.00
Yearly income statements—10% increase in costs—Depreciation to recover increased cost of assets—Pricing to maintain constant profit			
Sales	$500	$560	$628
Cost of goods sold	$150 + $150 = 300	$165 + $180 = 345	$181.50 + $214.50 = 396
Gross margin	$200	$215	$232
Selling and administrative expense	$ 50 + $ 50 = 100	$ 55 + $ 60 = 115	$ 60.50 + $ 71.50 = 132
Divisional operating income	$100	$100	$100
Yearly income statements—10% increase in costs—Depreciation to recover increased cost of assets—Pricing to maintain 10% increase in profits			
Sales	$500	$570	$649
Cost of goods sold	$150 + $150 = 300	$165 + $180 = 345	$181.50 + $214.50 = 396
Gross margin	$200	$225	$253
Selling and administrative expense	$ 50 + $ 50 = 100	$ 55 + $ 60 = 115	$ 60.50 + $ 71.50 = 132
Divisional operating income	$100	$110	$121

TABLE 17.11 Depreciation Calculations

End of year	Replacement cost	Depreciation percentage	Accumulated depreciation	Yearly depreciation expense	Cost of goods sold	Selling and administrative
1	$600	1/3	$200	$200	$150.00	$50.00
2	$660	2/3	$440	$240	$180.00	$60.00
3	$726	1	$726	$286	$214.50	$71.50

a result of employing this strategy, after the third year the division's current assets will have increased by $900. This is the same result as was achieved in the original example when constant dollars were assumed. The only difference is that now the cost to replace the fixed assets at the end of year three is $726 (refer to table 17.11 for calculations) rather than $600 when constant dollars were assumed. This will require additional financing of $126 from internal or external sources to replace the assets. Divisional rates of return for the three years will remain the same as those in the constant-dollars example. Profit as a percentage of sales will decrease in this situation.

In the second set of income statements in table 17.10, the yearly depreciation expense is adjusted to reflect the increased replacement cost of the assets. The depreciation calculations to determine the catch-up depreciation expense are shown in table 17.11. Pricing policies have been adjusted to maintain the yearly operating income of $100. As a result of employing this strategy, after the third year of operations, divisional current assets have increased by $1,026. The sources of the $1,026 increase are the $300 in divisional operating income and $726 recovered from depreciation. Therefore, the additional financing required to replace the assets has been internally generated by the increased sales revenue. Now, consider the rates of return. If the asset base is valued using historical cost, the rates of return will be the same as in the constant-dollar assumption. However, if replacement cost is used in valuing the assets, the rates of return in all cases will decrease because of the increase in the asset base and the constant-income assumption.

Finally, the third set of income statements in table 17.10 was prepared under the circumstances in which selling prices were adjusted upward to reflect the increase in operating and depreciation expenses and a 10 percent increase in divisional net income. This strategy results in divisional current assets increasing by $1,057 after the third year. Sources of the $1,057 increase are the $331 in divisional operating income and $726 recovered from depreciation. Table 17.12 shows the rates of return for the three years under the three different sets of assumptions.

It is difficult to generalize concerning the impact of inflation on rate-of-return calculations. However, the following general observations can be made. If historical cost is employed to value divisional assets and to determine divisional depreciation expense, resources will not be internally generated to replace retired assets. Also, when historical cost is used to value assets and income is increasing because of the impact of inflation, rates of return may be increasing while at the same time the entity may experience difficulty in financing the replacement assets. In general, one can conclude that when inflation rates are significant, inflation must be considered in some manner in accounting-based performance measures.

Residual Income

Another investment-based method that has gained some degree of popularity in performance measurement is **residual income.** This measurement

TABLE 17.12 Rates of Return

	Year 1	Year 2	Year 3
Constant profit Recover historical cost Gross assets at historical cost	$\dfrac{\$100}{\$1,100} = 9.1\%$	$\dfrac{\$100}{\$1,400} = 7.1\%$	$\dfrac{\$100}{\$1,700} = 5.9\%$
Constant profit Recover replacement cost Gross assets at replacement cost	$\dfrac{\$100}{\$1,100} = 9.1\%$	$\dfrac{\$100}{\$1,500^*} = 6.7\%$	$\dfrac{\$100}{\$1,952} = 5.1\%$
Increase in profit Recover replacement cost Gross assets at replacement cost	$\dfrac{\$100}{\$1,100} = 9.1\%$	$\dfrac{\$110}{\$1,510} = 7.3\%$	$\dfrac{\$121}{\$1,983} = 6.1\%$

*Calculation of asset base—Gross assets at replacement cost

Beginning balance		Net income		Depreciation expense		Increase in asset value		Assets base— end of year
$1,100	+	$100	+	$240	+	($660 − $600)	=	$1,500

TABLE 17.13 Divisional Income Statement (Residual Income)

K & L DIVISION
Divisional Income Statement
for Year Ended December 31, 19X1

Sales		$1,500,000
Less		
Variable standard cost of sales	$600,000	
Factory standard cost variances (net)	10,000	
Variable selling and administrative expenses	150,000	760,000
Divisional contribution margin		$ 740,000
Less		
Direct fixed costs		240,000
Direct divisional income		$ 500,000
Less		
Investment charge*		300,000
Residual income		$ 200,000

*Controllable investment, $3,000,000, and rate of investment charge, 10%.

system takes into account that divisional managers focus on operating problems and allows for normal return on divisional controllable investment. This is accomplished by charging each divison for controllable investments. The profit-contribution figure that remains is referred to as the residual income. Table 17.13 contains a performance-measurement report based on residual income. Residual income is the excess of net earnings after the cost of capital has been considered.

The theoretical justification for employing residual income can be explained by evaluating figure 17.1. The investment charge is represented by the straight line coming out of the origin, and the slope of the line represents the percentage of the charge against the investment. As the amount of divisional investment increases, the investment charge in-

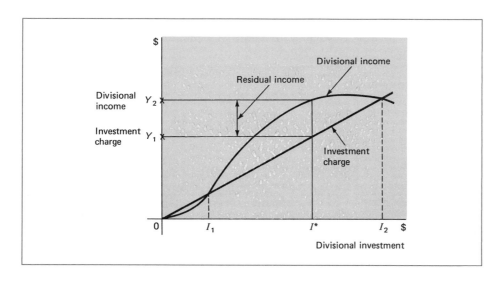

FIGURE 17.1
Residual Income
and Divisional
Investment

creases proportionately. On the other hand, divisional income, represented by the curve coming out of the origin, does not change in direct proportion to increases in divisional investment. Divisional income is influenced by increasing and decreasing returns to scale as the divisional-investment level is increased.

Therefore at investment points I_1 and I_2, residual income for the divison equals zero. Theoretically, there exists an optimal investment level, represented by I^*, where the residual income is a maximum. The objective is to have each division operate at this optimal investment level, at which residual income is maximized.

The advantage of residual income over return on investment is that a manager will seek to expand investment as long as the return exceeds the rate of the investment charges. In contrast, when return on investment is employed, a manager would be unwilling to make additional investments if it lowered the divisional rate of return, even though the investment opportunity has a return that exceeds the cost of capital.

Performance measurement based on residual income overcomes this problem because the divisonal manager seeks to maximize residual income. The manager will, therefore, consider all investment opportunities where the return exceeds the cost of capital of the firm. Residual income, like ROI, is subject to problems encountered in measuring divisional profit and identifying controllable assets to determine the investment base. It does offer the advantage of encouraging divisional managers to consider all investment opportunities that will aid the firm.

No accounting-based performance-measurement system is appropriate for all situations. Careful judgment must be exercised in selecting any performance-measurement system because it will have a significant influence on the behavior of all members of the organization.

These systems have been successfully used in industry as an integral part of the management-control system. They are a major component in the successful management of a divisionalized corporation. Fortunately, management has the freedom to select the system that has the most favorable impact on performance. For example, one is not limited to employing only historical costs in the preparation of internal reports. Price-level adjustment and replacement costs are just two examples of other asset-valuation systems that can be employed. Also, modifications to generally accepted accounting principles can be made in determining divisional net income.

☐ SYSTEM ASSUMPTIONS

Underlying any accounting-based measurement system are certain assumptions relating to the capabilities of the system and human behavior. To some degree, each of the assumptions presented in this section has been alluded to in the previous discussion. Explicit identification of the assumptions should afford additional insight into some of the problems encountered with divisionalized performance-measurement systems.

The following assumptions have been found to be implicit in all accounting-based performance-measurement systems in a divisionalized corporation:[4]

1. The management-accounting system makes possible goal allocation that enables managers to select operational objectives and allocate them among the divisions of the corporation.

2. The management-accounting system allows for an accurate comparison between responsibility and performance that makes neutral performance measurement possible.

3. Lower levels of a corporate organization are accountable to the upper levels of management.

4. Corporate personnel strive to attain the operational objectives as determined by the management team.

The first two assumptions relate to the accounting system. After considering some of the problems in determining divisional profit on investment, one might question the appropriateness of these assumptions. Experience shows that corporate managers often act as if there were no problems concerning the selection of operational objectives or in achieving a neutral evaluation.

The authors of this text have had contact with several divisionalized conglomerates that maintain large scoreboards in the parent corporation boardroom. Divisions are ranked according to their profit contribution or return on investment. No consideration is given to the fact that the divisions operate in different industries facing different market conditions. The asset requirements vary in different industries, and this makes comparisons among divisions questionable. Because of the cost allocations and transfer-pricing policies (which will be discussed in the next chapter) that greatly influence the performance measures of the divisions, the neutrality of any performance measure must be considered.

The third and fourth assumptions relate to how individuals within the organization are influenced by the performance-evaluation system. These assumptions can be inferred from the performance measures generally employed in management accounting. There is no consideration given to the possibility that individuals or groups within the organization might not accept the objectives as specified by members in the organization to which they are supposedly accountable. There are no controls in most performance-measurement systems to determine if divisional managers are attempting to realize their own personal objectives at the expense of overall corporate performance. In our presentation of the various performance-measurement systems, we have attempted to indicate how situa-

4. Similar lists can be found in Edwin H. Caplan, "Behavioral Assumption of Management Accounting," *The Accounting Review* 41, no. 3 (July 1966): 496–509; and G. H. Hofstede, *The Game of Budget Control* (Assen, The Netherlands: Koninklijke Van Garcum & Comp., N.V., 1967).

tions can develop in which individual goals are not consistent with divisional or corporate goals.

In 1952, Chris Argyris undertook a study to determine the sociopsychological implications of budgeting.[5] His research involved using open-ended interviews of line and staff supervisors in four medium-sized manufacturing organizations. His findings can be summarized as follows:

1. Budget pressure tends to unite employees against management personnel and tends to place factory supervisors under tension.

2. Finance staff can obtain feelings of success only by finding fault with factory employees.

3. The use of budgets as "needlers" by top-management personnel tends to make the factory supervisors see only the problems of their own department.

4. Supervisors use budgets as a way of expressing their own patterns of leadership.

This study was revolutionary because it identified some unintended effects of basing performance measurement on budgets and emphasized some of the behavioral problems related to the budgeting process. Of course, a budgetary system is only one type of performance-measurement system. One does not have to gain much experience in the business world before realizing that Argyris's results can be generalized to apply to most performance-measurement systems.

Any attempt to influence performance by managers at any level is going to create tension. Employees will attempt to reduce this tension. One way they do this is to engage in some unified activity against managers. This is the case when dealing with crew supervisors or divisional managers. At the divisional level, the division managers will unite in their efforts to reduce tension they perceive emanating from corporate management employees.

Management accountants must recognize that in any reporting system it appears to others that they justify their existence by identifying and following up deviations. This is especially the case if the evaluation of negative variances is emphasized. Overemphasis on divisional performance measurement will cause divisional managers to turn inward in problem situations. That is, consideration of what is best for the corporation as a whole will become secondary to consideration of what is most beneficial to the division. Cooperation among divisions in this situation will be reduced because of the environment created by the actions of management personnel. For example, a divisional manager may refuse a rush order for a component required by a sister division because the required overtime will reduce divisional income. The external sales by the sister division may be profitable from the corporate standpoint.

---

5. See Chris Argyris, "The Impact of Budgets on People" (Ithaca, N.Y.: The Controllership Foundation, 1952); and Chris Argyris, "Human Problems with Budgets," *Harvard Business Review* 31, no. 1 (January-February 1953):97–110.

Performance measures and evaluation are a means of expressing managerial leadership styles. For example, managers who overemphasize detail may not consider some of the relevant subjective factors in performance evaluation. Other managers may continually change and revise the performance-measurement system. There are other managers who would not consider a change in the performance-measurement system even when one was clearly necessary.

In summary, it is necessary to understand of how others in an organization perceive the functions and activities of the accounting staff. The four assumptions concerning a performance-measurement system may have no validity as far as the accounting staff is concerned. However, many managerial accountants behave as if these assumptions were true, which in turn influences the perceptions of other members of the management team.

The same holds true concerning the findings in Argyris's study. Performance-measurement systems based on budgets can be employed by management personnel in various ways. Argyris points out some of the possible reactions by those whose behavior managers are attempting to influence. Although these reactions can only be identified in general terms, the important thing to keep in mind is that a reaction of some kind will occur as the result of performance evaluation.

□ SUMMARY

Throughout this chapter, the emphasis has been upon performance evaluation in divisionalized organizations. We considered cost, profit, and investment-based performance measures that may be employed in evaluation. One should keep in mind that variations of these systems can be employed in measuring individual and departmental performance.

The chapter concluded by discussing some of the implicit assumptions that underlie performance-measurement systems. It is important to remember that the performance-measurement system and the behavior of the management accountant influences the behavior of the individual or group whose performance is being measured. This influence can be functional or dysfunctional in terms of the benefits realized by the total organization.

KEY TERMS

Cost center
Decentralization
Divisionalization
Investment center
Performance evaluation

Performance measurement
Profit center
Residual income
Return on investment (ROI)

REVIEW PROBLEM

The P division of Seago Company reported the following income for the most recent year of operation.

P DIVISION OF SEAGO COMPANY
Income Statement
for the Year Ended December 31, 19X4

Sales	$500,000
Variable costs	250,000
Contribution margin	$250,000
Divisional fixed costs	125,000
Divisional interest expense	25,000
Controllable income	$100,000
Capital investment	$500,000
Rate of return	20%

Rate of return for the company as a whole is 15 percent.

Assume the following investment opportunity for P division:

Expected annual sales	$100,000
Expected annual variable costs	50%
Expected annual fixed costs	$ 23,000
Expected outlay	$150,000

Required □

1. As the manager of P division, would you accept or reject the investment opportunity? Why?

2. As the head of Seago Company, would you accept or reject the investment opportunity? Why?

3. How can Seago Company avoid this type of problem in the future?

Solution □

1. Sales	$100,000
Variable costs	50,000
Contribution margin	50,000
Fixed costs	23,000
Controllable income	$ 27,000

$$ROI = \frac{\$27,000}{\$150,000} = 18\%$$

No, divisional ROI is 20 percent, and project ROI is only 18 percent. If project is accepted, divisional ROI will be lowered.

2. Yes, ROI for the firm is 15 percent; therefore, if project is accepted with an ROI of 18 percent, the ROI for the firm will increase.

3. Yes, residual income as a performance measure. If capital charge is 15 percent, P division would accept project because of the positive residual income.

Sales	$100,000
Variable costs	50,000
Contribution margin	$ 50,000
Fixed cost	23,000
Controllable income	$ 27,000
Capital charge 15% × 150,000	= 22,500
Residual income	$ 4,500

QUESTIONS

Q17-1. Is an organization that is decentralized necessarily divisionalized?

Q17-2. What is the difference between decentralization and divisionalization?

Q17-3. Why is corporate performance gauged in terms of profits?

Q17-4. Discuss several problems that are frequently encountered in attempting to measure divisional profit.

Q17-5. Discuss several reasons why a divisional manager would not have complete control over a division. What are some of the implications in performance evaluation when the divisional manager has less than complete control?

Q17-6. What is a cost center? What is a profit center? What is an investment center? What type of performance measures are used in these organizational units?

Q17-7. Why do problems develop about the authorization function of a budget?

Q17-8. What type of dysfunctional activity on the part of management personnel can be associated with budgets?

Q17-9. What are some of the definitions of net income that are employed in performance-measurement systems? Evaluate the relative merits of each definition in relation to performance measurement.

Q17-10. What are some of the problems encountered in determining return on investment? Why are the intermediate calculations often shown when determining the return on investment?

Q17-11. Besides cost, what are some alternative bases of asset valuation that can be employed?

Q17-12. Define residual income. Evaluate residual income as a measure of performance.

PROBLEMS

P17-1. Golf course maintenance at the Feasterville Country Club is managed by the greenskeeper and treated as a cost center. Performance measurement is based on comparing the budgeted amounts with the actual expenses

Cost-Center Performance Evaluation

for the year. The following statement was prepared by the bookkeeper of the club.

FEASTERVILLE COUNTRY CLUB
Golf Course Expenses
for the Year Ended December 31, 19X3

Line item	Budgeted amount	Expense incurred	Difference
Payroll and payroll taxes	$54,000	$54,500	$ (500)
Sand and gravel	300	500	(200)
Topsoil	1,000	800	200
Fertilizer	5,000	8,500	(3,500)
Fungicide	1,000	1,400	(400)
Grass seed	800	300	500
Parts	2,500	1,800	700
Petroleum products	1,800	3,100	(1,300)
Golf equipment	500	100	400
Uniforms	300	—	300
Training	300	—	300
Equipment rental	2,500	250	2,250
Utilities	3,000	5,100	(2,100)
Depreciation	5,000	5,000	—
Total	$78,000	$81,350	$(3,350)

The budget for the golf course is prepared by the greens committee and Mr. Paul Walls, the greenskeeper. The budget is approved by the board of directors of the club and is used in evaluating the performance of Mr. Walls at the end of the year. As a part of this evaluation, the following conversation takes place between Mr. Beard, the president of the club, and Mr. Walls:

MR. BEARD: Paul, you should realize that the golf course budget represents the best judgment of the greens committee and the board of directors as to how resources should be used on the golf course. It is my opinion that differences between each budgeted amount and the expense incurred should be minor if you operate the course as directed by the committee with the approval of the board. The only items on this report where I view the differences as insignificant are payroll and depreciation. In many areas, such as fertilizer, petroleum products, and utilities, you significantly exceeded the budgeted amounts. To cover up these excesses, you failed to carry out our wishes concerning golf equipment, uniforms, and I can't explain the problem with equipment rental. I have received several complaints from our members about the condition of our markers, ball-washers, and the appearance of the help on the course. I now see how this is reflected in this report. Besides that, we have had many complaints as to the condition of the course.

MR. WALLS: My understanding has been that I am to run the golf course and try to remain within the total budget. I can explain all of the differences that show up on this report. The cost of fertilizer, fungicide, petroleum products, and utilities went up significantly this year. Because of this, we only put out a minimum of fertilizer. It was either this or incur a significant budget overrun. The late summer was very dry, which required excessive pumping and this added to the increased utility cost.

MR. BEARD: Paul, you are telling me that the budget did not allow for any price increases, but I know this is not the case.

MR. WALLS: I know price increases were built into the budget, but they in no way covered the actual increases for the year. No one could anticipate the short supply of fertilizer and fungicide that existed this year.

MR. BEARD: You should have limited your expenditures for these items to the amount in the budget and bought the new uniforms, golf equipment, and started some of the reseeding that was included in your budget.

MR. WALLS: In my opinion, I did the best job possible to maintain the course, given the economic and weather conditions during the year. These things cannot be anticipated in preparing a budget. I must use my professional judgment in some of these matters. In addition, concerning the depreciation, I have nothing to do with it! It just shows up at the end of each year.

MR. BEARD: I am not sure that helps the situation.

Required ☐

1. Explain the difference between Mr. Beard and Mr. Walls in the way that they interpret the budget and in the way they believe Mr. Walls' performance is to be evaluated.

2. Suggest how some of the differences in requirement 1 can be reconciled.

3. Do you see any problem with how the depreciation is handled on the golf course budget?

4. Should Mr. Walls' performance be evaluated by the greens committee or the board of directors? Explain.

P17-2. The town of Old Salem, Virginia, is governed by a town council. Day-to-day operations of the town are under the control of the town manager, who serves at the pleasure of the town council. Each year the town manager prepares a line-item budget that is revised and then approved by the town council.

Responsibility Accounting Problems

Recently, a member of the town council became quite upset when she learned that the town manager was shifting amounts among line items in the budget. For example, he might increase the budget of the Fire Department and decrease the budget of the Recreation Department. The town manager argued that such shifts were insignificant in amount and were necessary so that he could effectively manage the operations of the town. It was his opinion that his performance evaluation was based upon his ability to operate the town government for the total amount in the annual town budget. He believes he must possess the authority to make these line-item shifts to insure some flexibility in managing the town.

The member of the town council who raised the question has a different opinion concerning the budget shifts. She believes that the performance of the elected members of the council is evaluated by the electorate every two years. In her opinion, the budget reflects the consensus of the council as to how resources should be allocated in operating the town. She believes that the town manager is exceeding his authority in making any budgetary shifts. In her opinion, all such shifts should be approved by the council.

In the opinion of the town manager, such shifts, although they are frequent, are insignificant in amount. He believes it would involve a great deal of time for the council to approve all shifts, and there are times when he cannot wait for the monthly council meetings. He points out that the last shift he made in the Police Department budget involved shifting funds from the training to the petroleum products line item. He pointed out that such a shift was necessary to keep the police cars on patrol during the last two weeks of the year.

Required ☐

1. Evaluate the position of the town manager concerning making line-item shifts in the budget.

2. Evaluate the position taken by the member of the town council concerning the line-item shifts in the budget.

3. Recommend several possible solutions to the problem.

Divisional Performance Measurement

P17-3. Division A, B, and C of Robin Industries report the following income and investment:

Division	A	B	C
Operating income	$ 25,000	$ 150,000	$ 200,000
Asset investment	$100,000	$1,000,000	$2,000,000
Rate of return	25%	15%	10%

Required ☐

1. Assuming the company charges each division 10 percent for the capital employed, determine the residual income for each division.

2. Based on the above information, which division is most efficient? Why?

3. Discuss some of the problems encountered using rate of return and residual income in performance measurement.

4. What is the difference between performance measurement and performance evaluation?

Divisional Performance Measurement

P17-4. Divisions of A and B of the Terry Corporation report the following income and investments:

Division	A	B
Operating income	$10,000	$ 17,000
Asset investment	50,000	100,000
Rate of return	20%	17%

Required ☐

1. Assuming the company charges each division 10 percent for the capital employed, determine the residual income for each division.

2. Based on the above information, which division is most efficient? Why?

3. Relate the controversy between rate of return and residual income to the controversy in capital budgeting between internal rate of return and excess present value.

P17-5. The Lansing Corporation has recently shifted to the LIFO method of valuing inventory for tax and external-reporting purposes. Lansing is divisionalized and employs ROI as a performance measure. The president of Lansing is undecided as to whether inventories valued using LIFO should be used in computing divisional ROI. On the average, inventories make up 50 percent of a division's asset base.

Inventory Valuation and ROI

Required □

1. Prepare a memo for the president of Lansing discussing the inventory-valuation problem and make a specific recommendation.

2. Would your recommendation in requirement 1 change if inventories on the average were only 5 percent of a division's asset base? Explain.

P17-6. The Givens Company is a divisionalized multinational firm that uses ROI in measuring divisional performance. Annual ROI calculations for each division have traditionally employed the closing amount of the divisional invested capital. The ROI calculations for the Homet Divisions of Givens Company are:

ROI Evaluation

$$19X4 \quad \frac{\$1,000,000}{\$10,000,000} \times \frac{\$10,000,000}{\$5,000,000} = 20\%$$

$$19X5 \quad \frac{\$1,200,000}{12,500,000} \times \frac{\$12,500,000}{\$7,500,000} = 16\%$$

Management personnel are disappointed in the performance of Homet for 19X5, since the additional investment had a budgeted ROI of 23 percent.

Required □

1. Discuss some factors that may have contributed to the decreased ROI for Homet in 19X5.

2. Compare the ROI for Homet in 19X5, using the average divisional invested capital. Explain how this might be a better basis for performance measurement.

P17-7. Divisional income statements and balance sheets for the Eastview Company for the current year are:

ROI Calculations with Different Assumptions

EASTVIEW COMPANY
Divisional Income Statements
for Year Ended December 31, 19X3

	Division A	Division B
Sales	$500,000	$730,000
Variable costs	270,000	420,000
Contribution margin	$230,000	$310,000
Divisional interest expense	17,000	43,000
Divisional fixed expenses (depreciation)	30,000	49,000

Controllable income	$183,000	$218,000
Allocated costs	78,000	93,000
Divisional income	$105,000	$125,000

EASTVIEW COMPANY
Divisional Balance Sheets
December 31, 19X3

	Division A	Division B
Current assets	$127,000	$ 185,000
Fixed assets cost	940,000	1,680,000
Accumulated depreciation	(220,000)	(330,000)
Total assets	$847,000	$1,535,000
Current liabilities	$ 98,000	$ 134,000
Long-term debt—6 percent annual interest	240,000	570,000
Owners' equity	509,000	831,000
Total liabilities and owners' equity	$847,000	$1,535,000

Required ☐

1. Determine the rate of return for each division of Eastview Company using:

   a. Assets valued at cost and controllable income
   b. Assets valued at book value and controllable income
   c. Assets valued at book value less total liabilities and controllable income

2. If maintenance costs, price levels, and productivity of the asset base remain constant and assets are valued at book value, what would happen to the ROI through time? Explain.

3. If price levels generally remain constant, what would happen to the ROI through time if assets are valued at cost? Explain. What would happen if the assets were valued at book value? Explain.

Cost-Center Performance Evaluation

P17-8. The Advertising department of Sporting Goods, Inc., is evaluated as a cost center. The fiscal year for the company ended on July 30, and divisional managers are evaluated on their ability to "live" within their budgets. For the last several years, the Advertising department, has run out of office supplies in June, and the advertising manager makes a vigorous attempt to control the volume of mail leaving the department.

During the period, office equipment is not repaired, photo supplies run short, the signing of advertising and printing contracts is deferred, and all travel is eliminated. Because of these shortages, there are frequent complaints from sales personnel and manufacturer's representatives because they do not receive adequate service during this period of time. Several employees in the Advertising department have observed that this condition is being encountered earlier each year. Some employees have been known to stockpile office supplies during the year so that they can function at the year's end.

Required ☐

1. Comment on the probable causes of the problems in the Advertising department.

2. Suggest several means by which some of these problems can be corrected.

P17-9. The Fillep Co. operates a standard-cost system. The variances for each department are calculated and reported to the department manager. It is expected that the manager will use the information to improve operations and that the manager will recognize that it is used by superiors when they are evaluating his or her performance. *Standard Costs and Performance Measurement*

John Swanson was recently appointed manager of the Assembly department of the company. He has complained that the system as designed is disadvantageous to his department. Included among the variances charged to the departments is one for rejected units. The inspection occurs at the end of the Assembly department. The inspectors attempt to identify the cause of the rejection so that the department where the error occurred can be charged with it. Not all errors can be easily identified with a department. These are totaled and apportioned to the departments according to the number of identified errors. The variance for rejected units in each department is a combination of the errors caused by the department plus a portion of the unidentified causes of rejects.

Required □

1. Is John Swanson's claim valid? Explain the reason(s) for your answer.

2. What would you recommend the company do to solve its problem with John Swanson and his complaint?

(CMA)

P17-10. Divisional income statements and balance sheets for the Ajax Company for the current year are *ROI Calculations with Different Assumptions*

AJAX COMPANY
Divisional Income Statements
for Year Ended December 31, 19X4

	Division A	Division B
Sales	$200,000	$300,000
Variable costs	90,000	185,000
Contribution margin	$110,000	$115,000
Divisional fixed costs	65,000	50,000
Controllable income	$ 45,000	$ 65,000
Allocated costs	25,000	33,000
Divisional income	$ 20,000	$ 32,000

AJAX COMPANY
Divisional Balance Sheets
December 31, 19X4

	Division A	Division B
Current assets	$ 60,000	$ 95,000
Fixed assets—cost	150,000	260,000
Accumulated depreciation	(30,000)	(65,000)
Total assets	$180,000	$290,000
Current liabilities	$ 40,000	$ 55,000
Long-term debt—8% annual interest	75,000	105,000
Owners' equity	65,000	130,000
Total liabilities and owners' equity	$180,000	$290,000

Required □

1. Determine the rate of return for each division of Ajax Company using

   a. Gross assets and controllable income
   b. Gross assets and net income
   c. Book value and controllable income
   d. Book value and net income
   e. Owners' equity and controllable income
   f. Owners' equity and net income

2. Discuss the advantages and disadvantages of each of the above measures of performance.

Performance Measurement and Transfer Pricing

P17-11. Conveyor Systems is a firm made up of three divisions that are evaluated as profit centers. The two Systems divisions are located in Philadelphia and Los Angeles. They engineer and manufacture all types of materials handling and transportation systems. The Steel Fabricating division is located in Chicago and does all the steel fabricating and erection for the Systems divisions. About 40 percent of the work of the Fabricating division is for its sister divisions, with the remaining work performed for outside contractors.

When one of the Systems divisions bids on a job, the Fabricating division estimates the cost of the steel fabrication and erection required on the job. The Systems divisions submit the final bid on such jobs, and they adjust the bid to reflect the competitive situation and the company's desire to obtain the work.

All transfers are made from the Fabricating division to the Systems division at full-absorption cost. Since adjustments are made to the total price bid on the job, the transfer prices in no way reflect the bid submitted by the fabricator. The Systems divisions complain that the Fabricating division "pads" the costs on all jobs transferred. The internal auditors have detected evidence that such a practice does exist.

The manager of the Fabricating division believes that he should be able to transfer on a cost-plus basis since his division is treated as a profit center. Both managers of the Systems divisions are opposed to this recommendation and suggest that the transfer price should in some way be tied to the original fabrication and erection estimated cost.

Required □

1. Explain why the Systems division managers are against transfers at cost plus.

2. Suggest a modification for the performance evaluation and transfer-pricing policies.

ROI Calculations

P17-12. Rumsey Company uses ROI as a measure of divisional performance. Controllable income and net assets are employed to determine the ROI. The manager of division B claims that this is not a useful means of measuring performance when comparisons are made between divisions. He indicates that the price level has increased 15 percent between the time divisions A and B were constructed. The manager of division A counters his argument by stating that division B is a new plant and incorporates many technological improvements. He states that ROI is a good measure of performance.

RUMSEY COMPANY
Divisional Income Statements
for Year Ended December 31, 19X4

	Division A	Division B
Sales	$300,000	$200,000
Variable costs	210,000	48,000
Contribution margin	$ 90,000	$152,000
Division interest expense	11,000	23,000
Division fixed expense (depreciation)	20,000	35,000
Controllable income	$ 59,000	$ 94,000
Allocated costs	25,000	37,000
Divisional income	$ 34,000	$ 57,000

RUMSEY COMPANY
Divisional Balance Sheets
December 31, 19X4

	Division A	Division B
Current assets	$ 75,000	$120,000
Fixed assets cost	250,000	370,000
Accumulated depreciation	(90,000)	(45,000)
Total assets	$235,000	$445,000
Current liabilities	$ 40,000	$ 75,000
Long-term debt—10% annual interest	100,000	200,000
Owners' equity	95,000	170,000
Total liabilities and owners' equity	$235,000	$445,000

Required □

1. From the statement just given, determine the ROI for each division, using controllable income and assets at book value.

2. Determine the ROI by adjusting for price levels and then by using the controllable income and net assets.

3. Comment on the arguments presented by the divisional managers.

P17-13. Assume the JF Division was established to manufacture a product with an expected life of three years. All assets of the division are to be depreciated over three years using straight-line depreciation. Assume any divisional profits are retained by the division. Below are the budgeted income statements for each of the three years of operation for the division. The balance sheet was prepared at the start of the first year of operation. *Impact of Inflation on Depreciation*

JF DIVISION
Budgeted Income Statement
for Years Ending December 31, 19X1, 19X2, and 19X3

Sales	$1,000	
Cost of goods sold	500	(a)
Gross margin	$ 500	
Selling and administrative expense	200	(b)
Divisional operating income	$ 300	

(a) Includes $200 depreciation expense
(b) Includes $50 depreciation expense

JF DIVISION
Balance Sheet
January 1, 19X1

Current assets		$ 250	Current liabilities		$ 200
Fixed assets	$750		Long-term liabilities		400
Accumulated depreciation	0	750	Owners' equity		400
Total assets		$1,000	Total Liabilities and equity		$1,000

Required □

1. If the Division operates for three years according to the budget, what will the balance of the current assets be at the end of the third year? Identify the source of the funds in the current asset account.

2. Prepare a depreciation schedule for the fixed assets of the division, assuming that costs are increasing at a yearly rate of ten percent.

3. Determine the additional yearly cost that must be recovered each year if the replacement cost of the asset is to be recovered through depreciation.

Divisional Income Measurement

P17-14. The Walcott Division is one of several divisions of DMP Industries. The divisional manager has a high degree of autonomy in operating the division. Walcott's management staff consists of a division controller, division sales manager, and division production manager, all reporting to the division manager. The division manager reports to the executive vice-president at corporate headquarters, while the division controller has a functional reporting relationship to the corporate controller.

The members of the management staff of the Walcott Division have developed good working relationships with each other over the past several years. Regularly scheduled staff meetings are held, and most of the management process is carried out by the daily contact among the members of the staff.

An important staff meeting is held each September for making decisions required to finalize the annual budget to be submitted to corporate headquarters for the coming calendar year. The fourth quarter plans are finalized and the current year's forecasted results are reviewed at this meeting prior to completing the budget for the coming year.

For the first time in recent years, the budgeted amounts of the Walcott Division for the coming year show no growth and lower profits than the forecast for the current year. A review of the coming year's plans did not uncover any alternatives that could improve the sales and profits. This unusual situation was of concern to the divison manager because he has developed the reputation for producing growing profits. In addition, growth and profits affect the division manager's performance evaluation and annual bonus. During the meeting in September 19X9, he stated that he would like to see some of the profits shifted from 19X9 to 19X0.

The division manager heard that another company had shifted profits. He believes the following actions were used to accomplish this objective:

1. Shipments made to customers in the last two weeks of December were not billed until January.

2. The sales force was instructed to encourage customers to specify January delivery rather than December wherever possible.

3. Abnormally generous amounts were used when establishing accruals for:

   a. Warranties
   b. Bad debts
   c. Other expenses

4. Purchased raw materials for which title had passed and that were in-transit at the end of December were recorded as purchased in December; however, the raw materials were not included in the year-end inventory.

5. Sales on account for the last day of December were not recorded until the first business day in January.

6. The cleaning and painting of the exterior of the plant was rescheduled to be completed in the current year rather than in the coming year as planned.

The dollar amounts involved in these actions were material and would be material for Walcott Division if similar actions were taken. The division manager asked the division controller if profits would be shifted from the 19X9 to 19X0 if actions similar to these were carried out at Walcott Division.

Required □

1. For each of the six items enumerated in the text, indicate whether there would be a shift in Walcott Division's profit from 19X9 to 19X0 if similar actions were implemented by the division.

2. Assume you are the controller of the Walcott Division. Are the suggestions presented by the division manager proper actions for a division to take, given its profit record? Explain your answer.

3. Without prejudice to your answer to requirement 2, assume that at least one of the actions presented would be inappropriate if implemented. If you were the division controller, what step(s) is (are) available for you to report the inappropriate action and which one(s) would you take? Explain your answer.

(CMA)

P17-15. The Darmen Corporation is one of the major producers of prefabricated houses in the home-building industry. The corporation consists of two divisions: (1) Bell Division, which acquires the raw materials to manufacture the basic house components and assembles them into kits, and (2) the Cornish Division, which takes the kits and constructs the homes for final home buyers. The corporation is decentralized, and the management of each division is measured by its income and return on investment.

Management Performance Evaluation

Bell Division assembles seven separate house kits using raw materials purchased at the prevailing market prices. The seven kits are sold to

Cornish for prices ranging from $45,000 to $98,000. The prices are set by corporate management of Darmen, using prices paid by Cornish when it buys comparable units from outside sources. The smaller kits with the lower prices have become a larger portion of the units sold because the final house buyer is faced with prices that are increasing more rapidly than personal income. The kits are manufactured and assembled in a new plant just purchased by Bell this year. The division had been located in a leased plant for the past four years.

All kits are assembled upon receipt of an order from the Cornish Division. When the kit is completely assembled, it is loaded immediately on a Cornish truck. Thus, Bell Division has no finished-goods inventory.

The accounts and reports of Bell Division are prepared on an actual-cost basis. There is no budget, and standards have not been developed for any product. A factory-overhead rate is calculated at the beginning of each year. The rate is designed to charge all overhead to the product each year. Any over- or underapplied overhead is allocated to the cost-of-goods-sold account and work-in-process inventories.

Bell Division's annual report follows. This report forms the basis of the evaluation of the division and its management by the corporation management team.

Additional information regarding corporate and division practices is as follows:

1. The corporation office does all the personnel and accounting work for each division.

2. The corporate personnel costs are allocated on the basis of number of employees in the division.

3. The accounting costs are allocated to the division on the basis of total costs excluding corporate charges.

4. The division administration costs are included in factory overhead.

5. The financing charges include a corporate-imputed interest charge on division assets and any divisional lease payments.

6. The division investment for the return-on-investment calculation includes division inventory and plant and equipment at gross book value.

Required □

1. Using the information in the problem to illustrate your discussion, discuss the value of the Bell Division annual report in evaluating the division and its management in terms of:

   a. The accounting techniques employed in the measurement of division activities
   b. The manner of presentation
   c. The effectiveness with which it discloses differences and similarities between years

2. Present specific recommendations you would make to the management of Darmen Corporation that would improve its accounting and financial-reporting system.

BELL DIVISION
Performance Report
for the Year Ended December 31, 19X0

	19X0	19X9	Increase or (decrease) from 19X9	
			Amount	Percent change
Summary data				
Divisional income (in thousands)	$ 34,222	$ 31,573	$ 2,649	8.4
Return on investment	37%	43%	(6)%	(14.0)
Kits shipped (units)	2,000	2,100	(100)	(4.8)
Production data (in units)				
Kits started	2,400	1,600	800	50.0
Kits shipped	2,000	2,100	(100)	(4.8)
Kits in-process at year-end	700	300	400	133.3
Increase (decrease) in kits in-process at year-end	400	(500)	—	—
Financial data (in thousands)				
Sales	$138,000	$162,800	$(24,800)	(15.2)
Production costs of units sold				
Raw material	$ 32,000	$ 40,000	$ (8,000)	(20.0)
Labor	41,700	53,000	(11,300)	(21.3)
Factory overhead	29,000	37,000	(8,000)	(21.6)
Cost of units sold	$102,700	$130,000	$(27,300)	(21.0)
Other costs				
Corporate charge for				
Personnel services	$ 228	$ 210	$ 18	8.6
Accounting services	425	440	(15)	(3.4)
Financing costs	300	525	(225)	(42.9)
Total other costs	$ 953	$ 1,175	$ (222)	(18.9)
Adjustments to income				
Unreimbursed fire loss	—	$ 52	$ (52)	(100.0)
Raw material losses due to improper storage	$ 125	$ —	$ 125	—
Total adjustments	$ 125	$ 52	$ 73	(140.4)
Total deductions	$103,778	$131,227	$(27,449)	(20.9)
Division income	$ 34,222	$ 31,573	$ 2,649	8.4
Division investment	$ 92,000	$ 73,000	$ 19,000	26.0
Return on investment	37%	43%	(6)%	(14.0)

(CMA)

P17-16. An important managerial function is coordination. Coordination is the organizational integration of tasks and activities. In general, effective coordination can be attained by the proper assignment of responsibility and delegation of authority within the context of the formal organiza-   *Responsibility-Accounting Concepts*

Required ☐

1. Define the concepts of responsibility and authority.

2. Explain what basic principles of management should be observed if delegation of authority is to be effective.

3. Identify actions of superiors that frequently undermine the effectiveness of the delegation of authority.

4. Identify actions of subordinates that frequently undermine the effectiveness of the delegation of authority.

(CMA)

Responsibility-Accounting Concepts

P17-17. RV Industries manufactures and sells recreation vehicles. The company has eight divisions strategically located to be near major markets. Each division has a sales force and two to four manufacturing plants. These divisions operate as autonomous profit centers responsible for purchasing, operations, and sales.

John Collins, the corporate controller, described the divisional performance-measurement system as follows:

We allow the divisions to control the entire operation from the purchase of raw materials to the sale of the product. We, at corporate headquarters, only get involved in strategic decisions, such as developing new product lines. Each division is responsible for meeting its market needs by providing the right products at a low cost on a timely basis. Frankly, the divisions need to focus on cost control, delivery, and services to customers in order to become more profitable.

While we give the divisions considerable autonomy, we watch their monthly income statements very closely. Each month's actual performance is compared with the budget in considerable detail. If the actual sales or contribution margin is more than 4 or 5 percent below the budget, we jump on the division people immediately. I might add that we don't have much trouble getting their attention. All of the management people at the plant and division level can add appreciably to their annual salaries with bonuses if actual net income is considerably greater than budget.

The budgeting process begins in August when division sales managers, after consulting with their sales personnel, estimate sales for the next calendar year. These estimates are sent to plant managers who use the sales forecasts to prepare production estimates. At the plants, production statistics, including raw material quantities, labor hours, production schedules and output quantities, are developed by operating personnel. Using the statistics prepared by the operating personnel, the plant accounting staff determines costs and prepares the plant's budgeted variable cost of goods sold and other plant expenses for each month of the coming calendar year.

In October, each division's accounting staff combines plant budgets with sales estimates and adds additional division expenses. After the divisional management is satisfied with the budget, I visit each division to go over their budget and make sure it is in line with corporate strategy and projections. I really emphasize the sales forecasts because of the volatility in the demand for our product. For many years, we lost sales to our competitors because we didn't project high enough production and sales, and we couldn't meet the market demand. More recently, we were caught with large excess inventory when the bottom dropped out of the market for recreational vehicles.

I generally visit all eight divisions during the first two weeks in November. After that the division budgets are combined and reconciled by my staff, and they are ready for approval by the board of directors in early December. The board seldom questions the budget.

One complaint we've had from plant and division management employees is that they are penalized for circumstances beyond their control. For example, they failed to predict the recent sales decline. As a result, they didn't make their budget and, of course, they received no bonuses. However, I point out that they are well rewarded when they exceed their budget. Furthermore, they provide most of the information for the budget, so it's their own fault if the budget is too optimistic.

Required ☐

1. Identify and explain the biases the corporate management team of RV Industries should expect in the communication of budget estimates by its division and plant personnel.

2. What sources of information can the top-management personnel of RV Industries use to monitor the budget estimates prepared by its divisions and plants?

3. What services could top-management of employees of RV Industries offer the divisions to help them in their budget development without appearing to interfere with the division budget decisions?

4. The top-management staff of RV Industries is attempting to decide whether it should get more involved in the budget process. Identify and explain the variables the staff needs to consider in reaching its decision.

P17-18. Rouge Corporation is a medium-sized company in the steel fabrication industry. There are six divisions located in different geographical sectors of the United States. Considerable autonomy in operational management is permitted in the divisions due in part to the distance between corporate headquarters in St. Louis and five of the six divisions. Corporate management employees establish divisional budgets using prior year data adjusted for industry and economic changes expected for the coming year. Budgets are prepared by year and by quarter, with the top-management team attempting to recognize problems unique to each division in the divisional budget-setting process. Once the year's divisional budgets are set by the corporate managers, they cannot be modified by the division managers.

Responsibility-Accounting Concepts

The budget for calendar year 19X0 projects total corporate net income before taxes of $3,750,000 for the year, including $937,500 for the first quarter. Results of first-quarter operations presented to corporate managers in early April showed corporate net income of $865,000, which was $72,500 below the projected net income for the quarter. The St. Louis Division operated at 4.5 percent above its projected divisional net income, while the other five divisions showed net incomes with variances ranging from 1.5 to 22 percent below budgeted net income.

Corporate managers are concerned with the first-quarter results because they believe strongly that differences between divisions had been recognized. An entire day in late November of last year had been spent presenting and explaining the corporate and divisional budgets to the division managers and their division controllers. A mid-April meeting of the corporate and division management teams has generated unusual candor. All five out-of-state division managers cited reasons why first quarter results in their respective divisions represented effective management and was the best that could be expected. Corporate management staff members have remained unconvinced and have informed divisional managers that "results will be brought into line with the budget by the end of the second quarter."

Required □

1. Identify and explain the major disadvantages in the procedures employed by Rouge Corporation's corporate management team in preparing and implementing the divisional budgets.

2. Discuss the behavioral problems that may arise by requiring the Rouge Corporation division managers to meet the quarterly budgeted net income figures as well as the annual budgeted net income.

(CMA)

Performance Evaluation **P17-19.** The ATCO Co. purchased the Dexter Co. three years ago. Prior to the acquisition, Dexter manufactured and sold plastic products to a wide variety of customers. Dexter has since become a division of ATCO and now only manufactures plastic components for products made by ATCO's Macon Division. Macon sells its products to hardware wholesalers.

ATCO's corporate management team gives the Dexter Division managers considerable authority in running the division's operations. However, corporate management staff members retain authority for decisions regarding capital investments, price setting of all products, and the quantity of each product to be produced by the Dexter Division.

ATCO has a formal performance-evaluation program for the management employees of all of its divisions. The performance-evaluation program relies heavily on each division's return on investment. The Income Statement of the Dexter Division provides the basis for the evaluation of Dexter's divisional management employees.

The financial statements for the divisions are prepared by the corporate accounting staff. The corporate general services costs are allocated on the basis of sales dollars, and the Computer department's actual costs are apportioned among the divisions on the basis of use. The net division investment includes division fixed assets at net book value (cost less depreciation), division inventory, and corporate working capital apportioned to the divisions on the basis of sales dollars.

DEXTER DIVISION OF ATCO CO.
Income Statement
for the Year Ended October 31, 19X0
(in thousands)

Sales	$4,000
Costs and expenses	
Product costs	
Direct materials	$ 500
Direct labor	1,100

Factory overhead	1,300	
Total	$2,900	
Less: Increase in inventory	350	$2,550
Engineering and research		120
Shipping and receiving		240
Division administration		
Manager's office	$ 210	
Cost accounting	40	
Personnel	82	332
Corporate costs		
Computer	$ 48	
General services	230	$ 278
Total costs and expenses		$3,520
Divisional operating income		$ 480
Net plant investment		$1,600
Return on investment		30%

Required □

1. Discuss the financial reporting and performance evaluation program of ATCO Co. as it relates to the responsibilities of the Dexter Division.

2. Based on your response to requirement 1, recommend appropriate revisions of the financial information and reports used to evaluate the performance of Dexter's divisional managers. If revisions are not necessary, explain why revisions are not needed.

(CMA)

P17-20. Bio-grade Products is a multiproduct company manufacturing animal feeds and feed supplements. The need for a widely based manufacturing and distribution system has led to a highly decentralized management structure. Each divisional manager is responsible for production and distribution of corporate products in one of eight geographical areas of the country.

Performance Evaluation

Residual income is used to evaluate divisional managers. The residual income for each division equals each division's contribution to corporate profits before taxes less a 20 percent investment charge on a division's investment base. The investment base for each division is the sum of its year-end balances of accounts receivable, inventories, and net plant fixed assets (cost less accumulated depreciation). Corporate policies dictate that divisions minimize their investments in receivables and inventories. Investments in plant fixed assets are a joint division/corporate decision based on proposals made by divisional plant managers, available corporate funds, and general corporate policy.

Alex Williams, divisional manager for the southeastern sector, prepared the 19X9 and preliminary 19X0 budgets in late 19X8 for her division. Final approval of the 19X0 budget took place in late 19X9 after adjustments for trends and other information developed during 19X9. Preliminary work on the 19X1 budget also took place at that time. In early October of 19X0, Williams asked the divisional controller to prepare a report that presents performance for the first nine months of 19X0. The report is presented.

Required □

1. Evaluate the performance of Alex Williams for the nine months ending September 19X0. Support your evaluation with pertinent facts from the problem.

2. Identify the features of Bio-grade Products divisional performance-measurement reporting and evaluating system that need to be revised if it is to reflect effectively the responsibilities of the divisional managers.

(CMA)

BIO-GRADE PRODUCTS—SOUTHEASTERN SECTOR
(in thousands)

	Annual budget	19X0 Nine-month budget[1]	Nine-month actual	19X9 Annual budget	Actual results
Sales	$2,800	$2,100	$2,200	$2,500	$2,430
Divisional costs and expenses					
Direct materials and labor	$1,064	$ 798	$ 995	$ 900	$ 890
Supplies	44	33	35	35	43
Maintenance and repairs	200	150	60	175	160
Plant depreciation	120	90	90	110	110
Administration	120	90	90	90	100
Total divisional costs and expenses	$1,548	$1,161	$1,270	$1,310	$1,303
Divisional margin	$1,252	$ 939	$ 930	$1,190	$1,127
Allocated corporate fixed costs	360	270	240	340	320
Divisional contribution to corporate profits	$ 892	$ 669	$ 690	$ 850	$ 807
Imputed interest on divisional investment (20%)	420	321[2]	300[2]	370	365
Divisional residual income	$ 472	$ 348	$ 390	$ 480	$ 442

	Budgeted balance 12/31/X0	Budgeted balance 9/30/X0	Actual balance 9/30/X0	Budgeted balance 12/31/X9	Actual balance 12/31/X9
Division investment					
Accounts receivable	$ 280	$ 290	$ 250	$ 250	$ 250
Inventories	500	500	650	450	475
Plant fixed assets (net)	1,320	1,350	1,100	1,150	1,100
Total	$2,100	$2,140	$2,000	$1,850	$1,825
Imputed interest (20%)	$ 420	$ 321[2]	$ 300[2]	$ 370	$ 365

1. Bio-grade's sales occur uniformly throughout the year.
2. Imputed interest is calculated at only 15 percent to reflect that only nine months or three-fourths of the fiscal year has passed.

Performance Evaluation   **P17-21.** The Notewon Corporation is a highly diversified company that grants its divisional executives a significant amount of authority in operating the divisions. Each division is responsible for its own sales, pricing, production, costs of operations, and the management of accounts receivable, inventories, accounts payable, and use of existing facilities. Cash is managed by corporate headquarters; all cash in excess of normal operating needs of the divisions is transferred periodically to corporate headquarters for redistribution or investment.

The divisional executives are responsible for presenting requests to corporate managers for investment projects. The proposals are analyzed and documented at corporate headquarters. The final decision to commit funds to acquire equipment, to expand existing facilities, or for other investment purposes rests with the corporate managers. This procedure for investment projects is necessitated by Notewon's capital-allocation policy.

The corporation evaluates the performance of division executives by the return-on-investment (ROI) measure. The asset base is composed of fixed assets employed plus working capital, exclusive of cash.

The ROI performance of a divisional executive is the most important appraisal factor for salary changes. In addition, the annual performance bonus is based on the ROI results, with increases in ROI having a significant impact on the amount of the bonus.

The Notewon Corporation adopted the ROI performance measure and related compensation procedures about ten years ago. The corporation did so to increase the awareness of divisional managers of the importance of the profit/asset relationship and to provide additional incentive to the divisional executives to seek investment opportunities.

The corporation seems to have benefited from the program. The ROI for the corporation as a whole increased during the first years of the program. Although the ROI has continued to grow in each division, the corporate ROI has declined in recent years. The corporation has accumulated a sizeable amount of cash and short-term marketable securities in the past three years.

The corporation management team is concerned about the increase in the short-term marketable securities. A recent article in a financial publication suggested that the use of ROI was overemphasized by some companies with results similar to those experienced by Notewon.

Required ☐

1. Describe the specific actions that division managers might have taken to cause the ROI to grow in each division but decline for the corporation. Illustrate your explanation with appropriate examples.

2. Explain, using the concepts of goal congruence and motivation of divisional executives, how Notewon Corporation's overemphasis on the use of the ROI measure might result in the recent decline in the corporation's return on investment and the increase in cash and short-term marketable securities.

3. What changes could be made in Notewon Corporation's compensation policy to avoid this problem? Explain your answer.

(CMA)

P17-22. During your examination of the financial statements of Benjamin Industries, the president requested your assistance in the evaluation of several *ROI Concepts* financial management problems in the Home Appliances division, which he summarized for you as follows:

1. Management wants to determine the best sales price for a new appliance that has a variable cost of $4 per unit. The sales manager has estimated probabilities of achieving annual sales levels for various selling prices as shown in the following chart:

Sales level (units)	$4	$5	$6	$7
20,000	—	—	20%	80%
30,000	—	10%	40%	20%
40,000	50%	50%	20%	—
50,000	50%	40%	20%	—

Selling price

2. The division's current profit rate is 5 percent on annual sales of $1.2 million; an investment of $400,000 is needed to finance these sales. The company's basis for measuring divisional success is return on investment.

3. Management is also considering the following two alternative plans submitted by employees for improving operations in the Home Appliances division:

> David Green believes that sales volume can be doubled by greater promotional effort, but his method would lower the profit rate to 4 percent of sales and require an additional investment of $100,000. Mary Gold favors eliminating some unprofitable appliances and improving efficiency by adding $200,000 in capital equipment. Her methods would decrease sales volume by 10 percent, but improve the profit rate to 7 percent.

4. Black, White, and Gray, three franchised home appliance dealers, have requested short-term financing from the company. The dealers have agreed to repay the loans within three years and to pay Benjamin Industries 5 percent of net income for the three-year period for the use of the funds. The following table summarizes by dealer the financing requested and the total remittances (principal plus 5 percent of net income) expected at the end of each year.

Financing requested	$ 80,000	$40,000	$30,000
Remittances expected at end of:			
Year 1	$ 10,000	$25,000	$10,000
Year 2	40,000	30,000	15,000
Year 3	70,000	5,000	15,000
	$120,000	$60,000	$40,000

Management personnel believe these financing requests should be granted only if the annual pre-tax return to the company exceeds the target internal rate of 20 percent on investment. Discount factors (rounded) that would provide this 20 percent rate of return are:

Year 1	.8
Year 2	.7
Year 3	.6

Required □

1. Prepare a schedule computing the expected incremental income for each of the sales prices proposed for the new product. The schedule should include the expected sales levels in units (weighted according to the sales manager's estimated probabilities), the expected total monetary sales, expected variable costs, and the expected incremental income.

2. Prepare schedules computing:

   a. The company's current rate of return on investment in the Home Appliances division
   b. The anticipated rates of return under the alternative suggestions made by David Green and Mary Gold

3. Prepare a schedule to compute the net present value of the investment opportunities of financing Black, White, and Gray. The schedule should determine if the discounted cash flows expected from (a) Black, (b) White, and (c) Gray would be more or less than the amounts of Benjamin Industries' investment in loans to each of the three dealers.

(CPA)

CHAPTER OUTLINE

TRANSFER PRICING IN DIVISIONALIZED ORGANIZATIONS

CHAPTER 18

□ INTRODUCTION

Electro Corporation is a multinational, divisionalized electronics firm that operates plants in the Far East and the United States. Each division of the firm manufactures electronic subassemblies that are sold to computer, calculator, and television manufacturers. There are no sales transactions between divisions, and for purposes of performance measurement, each division is considered an investment center. Divisional managers receive a bonus based on their ability to exceed a budgeted rate of return on investment.

The president of Electro is convinced that the firm can assemble and market color televisions in the United States at a considerable profit. She wants to establish an assembly division in California that will use components from the tube division in Taiwan and the circuit division in the Philippine Islands. After reviewing cost data provided by the component divisions, the president concludes that Electro cannot assemble televisions any cheaper than the existing competition in the United States. The reason for this, she believes, is that the supplying divisions have quoted the same prices as are used in sales to outside firms.

She believes that with this cost data she cannot determine the cost to Electro of assembling a color television in the United States. Therefore, she requests that the supplying division's managers indicate the cost for the tubes and circuits required for the televisions. During a meeting in Hawaii with the divisional managers, she meets considerable resistance concerning the request. This resistance centers around two points.

The divisional managers believe that the Television Assembly division is becoming a favored project of the president and that she desires that the intracompany transfers be made to the detriment of the supplying divisions. Since the divisional managers' performance evaluations—and to some degree their compensation—is based on their return on investment, they view such a transfer policy as working to their disadvantage. The president indicates that all she wants is information so that a decision can be made in the best interest of Electro Corporation. The divisional managers also point out that neither host government will permit transfers to be made at cost because of corporate tax regulations.

The president is now faced with a complex problem. She would like to establish **transfer-pricing** policies that will to some degree be appropriate for decision making, performance measurement, and tax purposes.

The preceding example highlights some of the problems that occur when goods or services are transferred among divisions within a corporation. These and other considerations will be the focus of this chapter.

When considering the problem of divisional-performance evaluation, it would be ideal if there were no transactions between divisions of a corporation. This would eliminate the accounting problems resulting from such transactions and the related complicating factors in appraising divisional performance. This ideal situation is seldom encountered since the nature of most corporate structures results in rather involved relationships among the divisions. A value must be associated with any products or services involved in transactions between divisions.

Determination of this attached value or transfer price is of equal importance to both the selling and purchasing divisions. The sales revenue of a selling division is determined in part or entirely by the transfer price. In a purchasing division, the cost of goods sold is influenced by the transfer price. As a result, the profits of both the selling and purchasing divisions are affected by the transfer price employed. When transfer prices are used in divisions located in different states or countries, tax regulations must be considered in establishing the transfer price. As a result, a transfer-pricing policy will influence decision making at both the selling and purchasing divisions.

Another dimension of the transfer-pricing problem can be viewed at extreme points along a continuum. At one end of the continuum is the situation in which divisional managers have the freedom to choose whether or not they wish to trade with other divisions within the firm. At the other extreme is the case in which corporate policy requires that divisions trade appropriate services and products with each other.

In the first situation, divisional performance measures are not contaminated by artificial market conditions created by corporate policy. However, when divisions are required to trade, potential problems are present in information created for performance evaluation and decision making at the divisional levels. If a division operates as a profit center and is required to purchase components from a sister division at a transfer price above the market price, then the divisional profits for both the selling and purchasing divisions do not reflect the operating efficiencies.

We will now consider several of the transfer-pricing policies that are employed by divisionalized firms. After an initial description, the relative merits of the policies as they relate to inventory valuation, decision making, and performance evaluation will be discussed.

☐ MARKET-BASED TRANSFER PRICING

If divisions of a firm were separate business entities, any transaction between them would be recorded at the market price. In the U.S. economy, independent business entities are evaluated on their ability to profitably buy and sell in the marketplace. This same rationale is the basis for employing **market-based transfer prices** in exchanges between divisions of a firm.

If the division cannot show a profit while paying market prices for its purchases, then it should not be sheltered by permitting internal transfers at other than market price. The logic of the argument can be extended to include the selling division. If a division can sell externally at the market price, it should not be penalized by having to sell internally for less than the market price. The elimination of any external competitive pressure that results from a market-based transfer price is considered undesirable. Transfer prices should have some relationship with the economic reality of the situation, and only a market-based transfer price meets the criterion. The logical conclusion of this argument is that if transfer prices are not market based, they should not be employed in the determination of divisional profit.

The preceding discussion summarized the arguments in favor of a market-based transfer price. However, we should recognize that there are several significant problems that are often encountered when trying to implement a market-based transfer-pricing system.

Often, transactions between divisions involve intermediate products for which it is difficult to determine a market price. The intermediate goods may not be traded frequently or in sufficient quantities to determine the market price. A special quote might be requested from an outside vendor to ascertain the market price. However, price quotes by a prospective supplier might reflect more than the current market price. On the other hand, the price might reflect the desire to obtain an initial order or ignorance concerning job requirements and resulting costs. These and other factors can make a quoted price unreliable. Furthermore, the continued practice of seeking quotes with no intention of buying is unethical. After a time, this practice may result in unreliable quotes because a vendor will not continue to develop adequate cost estimates if there is no opportunity to receive any work.

Another factor that may make it difficult to specify a market price is that items may not be frequently traded on the open market. Electronic equipment, machinery, and other specialty items are generally built to specification, and market prices are difficult to determine. In this respect, one must recognize that small variations in size, weight, quality, grade, performance specifications, and appearance may distort any true sense of equality.

In performance evaluation, if a market-based transfer price is employed, advantages will generally accrue to the selling division. One reason for this is that marketing costs are minimized when sales are made to a sister divison. This is especially true if corporate policy requires internal transfers where possible. Also, credit costs are eliminated when dealing with a sister division. Finally, if demand from a consuming division is known, then certain economies would be expected to be realized in purchasing, production, warehousing, and shipping activities. For these reasons, transfers are often made at an adjusted market price. Market prices are marked down to reflect some of the advantages that accrue to the selling division.

The objective is to adjust the external price so that it reflects more accurately the existing conditions in the internal market. Such an adjusted market-based transfer price might be computed as follows:

Adjusted Market-Based Transfer Price

	Percent
Market price	100
Less	
Selling costs	15
Credit costs	3
Production costs	2
Warehousing and shipping costs	5
Total deductions	25
Transfer price as a percentage	
of market price	75

If market prices are used to record transfers, then interdivisional profit must be eliminated from inventories for financial-reporting purposes. For decision-making purposes, there is one major problem that must be considered when a market-based transfer price is used. Fixed costs of the selling division are regarded as variable costs in the buying division. Market-based transfer prices are nearly useless in the analysis of make-or-buy or elimination-of-product-line decisions at the corporate level. In making these decisions, incremental costs and revenues are relevant.

□ NEGOTIATED TRANSFER PRICES

Under a **negotiated transfer-pricing system,** divisional managers are free to negotiate with each other to determine a mutually acceptable transfer price. Generally, for this type of system to function effectively, a market for the intermediate product must exist. The existence of an outside market will tend to narrow any bargaining range in determining the transfer price. Also, the presence of an outside market assures both divisions an alternative of either purchasing or selling the intermediate product. Any negotiated price would reflect the availability of this option.

If negotiation is unsuccessful and no outside option is available, then the prospective purchasing division can only manufacture the intermediate product or stop selling the final product. The selling division can either manufacture the final product or cease manufacturing the intermediate product.

One problem area that can develop in a negotiated transfer-pricing system is the amount of time spent in negotiation. Such exchanges can involve different levels of divisional management personnel and can significantly contribute to overhead costs. As a practical matter, this time consideration rules out negotiation where a large number of individual products are involved.

In cases where divisional management employees cannot agree on a transfer price, a member of the corporate management team will enter the dispute as an umpire. Based on the information available, the umpire will determine the transfer price to be employed. When disputes are carried this far, it is questionable how useful the transfer price will be for purposes of performance evaluation. Also, circumstances and personalities of the divisional managers must be considered when the information is used for performance evaluation. It is quite possible that a divisional manager could dominate a negotiating relationship and exploit another division. Certainly, the factors contributing to such a situation should be considered in performance evaluation.

If negotiated transfer prices are employed, interdivisional profits must be eliminated from inventories for financial-reporting purposes. Fixed costs of the selling division being considered as variable costs by the buying division would limit the value of the transfer price for short-run decision making. This is the same situation that exists when a market-based system of transfer pricing is employed.

☐ TRANSFER PRICING AT COST

Perhaps the most straightforward method of transfer pricing employs some measure of cost. However, one should recognize that there are numerous concepts of cost and each will have a different impact on inventory valuation, decision making, and performance evaluation. Transfer prices based on absorption, standard costs, and variable costs will be discussed in this section.

Absorption or full-manufacturing cost, by definition, includes direct material, direct labor, and both variable and fixed overhead. This information is routinely generated by the cost-accounting system for financial-reporting purposes. No additional expense would be incurred in determining transfer prices based on absorption cost. Since this method is in agreement with generally accepted accounting principles concerning inventory valuation, financial statements can be prepared directly from the accounts with no adjustments for intercompany profit.

The major problem encountered when transfer prices are based on cost is that, from the firm's point of view, suboptimal short-run decisions may be made by the divisions due to the fact that the fixed costs of the selling division will be treated as variable costs by the purchasing division. This problem is compounded if transfers are made between several divisions before a product is sold externally.

To illustrate, assume four divisions of a firm transfer products at full cost. From the following assumed costs, one can demonstrate how a less-than-optimal decision from the point of view of the firm might result.

Division	A	B	C	D
Direct materials	$2	$ 3	$ 3	$ 2
Direct labor	2	3	3	2
Variable overhead	1	2	4	6
Fixed overhead*	3	2	4	5
Total cost	$8	$10	$14	$15

*Based on normal production.

Now, if division B requires a unit of output from division A, and division C likewise from B, and D likewise from C before the product is sold externally, the following costs are appropriate for each division:

Division	A	B	C	D
Transferred cost	$0	$ 8	$18	$32
Direct materials	2	3	3	2
Direct labor	2	3	3	2
Variable overhead	1	2	4	6
Fixed overhead*	3	2	4	5
Total cost	$8	$18	$32	$47

*Based on normal production.

Assume the management of division D is faced with a short-run decision in which the variable costs are relevant. Question: what are the variable costs? From the perspective of division D managers, the unit variable cost is $42 ($32 + $2 + $2 + $6). However, from the firm's point of view, the unit variable cost is $33 (A($5) + B($8) + C($10) + D($10)). Using the unit variable cost figure of $42, the management of division D could make a decision that is optimal from the point of view of the division but not from the point of view of the firm. For example, assume division D is faced with a short-run make-or-buy decision and is quoted a unit price of $37 from a vendor. If the managers compare the $37 with the $42, then the proper decision is to buy. However, if the $37 is compared with the $33, then the proper decision is to make the item. Thus, in this case, the decision that seems proper from the division's viewpoint is not the decision that benefits the firm as a whole. This is just one of a series of examples of how a full-absorption transfer-pricing policy might result in suboptimal short-run decision making at the divisional level.

In the area of performance evaluation, when transfers are made at cost, regardless of the definition of cost being employed, the selling division's income is understated because there is no profit margin on the goods transferred. Income is overstated for the purchasing division since the transfers are made at an artificially low price. Thus, cost is an inappropriate transfer price for the purpose of profit or investment-center evaluation unless total transfers are insignificant. However, when divisions are evaluated as expense centers, cost is an appropriate transfer price.

Standard costs can be used as a transfer price. The previous discussion concerning absorption costs also applies when transfers are made at standard cost. In addition, however, the disposition of variances must be weighed when standard costs are employed as a transfer price. Minor efficiencies and inefficiencies reflected in materials and labor variances are generally charged to the selling division. It should be recognized that substantial shifts in volume can negatively influence both materials and labor variances. To satisfy a rush order, a division may be forced to place rush orders for materials or hire additional production workers. These actions will most likely unfavorably influence the materials price and usage and the labor rate and efficiency variances. If the majority of the output of a division is transferred to sister divisions within the firm, then it is questionable whether it is appropriate to hold the division responsible for the variances.

This is especially true in the case of an unfavorable volume variance. When a division manufactures an intermediate product and has little responsibility in the area of marketing, this must be considered in performance evaluation. To evaluate such a division based on an unfavorable volume variance is inconsistent with the philosophy of responsibility accounting, since this would result in divisional management personnel being evaluated on the basis of factors over which they have no control.

When internal transfers are required by corporate management policy and the principal objective is to provide management personnel with useful information for making short-run decisions, then transfer prices set at the variable costs are appropriate. However, transfer prices based on variable costs are not useful in making long-run decisions, since full cost information is then relevant. Potential problems exist in the area of pricing when transfers are made at variable cost.

To value inventory for financial-reporting purposes, items transferred at variable cost must be adjusted to reflect their full-absorption cost. Transfer pricing at variable cost is not compatible with the purpose of treating divisions as either investment or profit centers. As discussed previously, such policies result in an excessive advantage to purchasing divisions.

☐ TRANSFER PRICING AT COST PLUS A MARKUP

A direct means of transforming a **cost-based transfer price** to one that included a profit margin is to employ cost-plus transfer prices. This results in a predetermined profit margin being added to interdivisional transactions, causing the selling division to realize a profit. In valuing inventories for financial-reporting purposes, any interdivisional profit must be eliminated.

What constitutes an appropriate markup is the initial problem confronted when establishing a cost-plus system. If the markup is established so that both selling and purchasing divisions will share relatively equally in the profit realized from the external sale, then divisional profit is questionable as far as performance evaluation is concerned. If the cost-plus transfer price approaches the market price, then some useful information concerning performance evaluation can be obtained.

In addition to the problems just discussed, a potentially unfavorable situation is created in the selling divisions where any cost or cost-plus transfer pricing system is employed. One does not have to delve deeply into cost accounting before realizing that the discipline is replete with allocation problems. There is a subjective element involved in the solution of any cost-allocation problem. Keeping this in mind, we will now consider how the management team of a selling division might act in making an allocation decision about when any cost-based transfer price is employed.

A simplified example will aid in illustrating the point. Assume a division has two jobs with the following direct costs:

Job	A10	X14
Direct materials	$100	$100
Direct labor	200	400
Total direct costs	$300	$500

Assume Job A10 has a fixed price of $700, whereas Job X14 is to be transferred to another division at cost plus 10 percent. Also assume there are $300 in overhead costs to be allocated between the two jobs. When the allocation is made in proportion to the value of the direct materials used, the results for the division are:

Job	A10	X14	Total
Selling price	$700	$715	$1,415
Direct material	$100	$100	$ 200
Direct labor	200	400	600
Overhead	150	150	300
Total cost	$450	$650	$1,100
Operating profit	$250	$ 65	$ 315

In contrast, if the allocation is based on the direct labor, the results are as follows:

Job	A10	X14	Total
Selling price	$700	$770	$1,470
Direct material	$100	$100	$ 200
Direct labor	200	400	600
Overhead	100	200	300
Total cost	$400	$700	$1,100
Operating profit	$300	$ 70	$ 370

By employing another cost-allocation scheme, the cost accountant has increased the division's operating profit by $55 or 17½ percent. The point to be made from the example is that whenever transfers are based on cost, a situation exists in which there is the temptation to overallocate costs to items that will be transferred. This condition is compounded when cost-plus transfer prices are used.

Another problem frequently encountered in a divisionalized enterprise concerns the preparation of contract bids. One division bidding on an outside job may require certain components that are manufactured by a sister division. The sister division, in preparing cost estimates, must make several decisions. The estimated costs are influenced by how desirable the division views the potential job. In addition, if corporate policy dictates that the transfer must be made at the lesser of the actual or estimated cost, the estimated cost would probably be related to the division's need for work. Such practices can jeopardize the chances of the corporation receiving an order and greatly distort the value of cost estimates.

If corporate policy directs that transfers are made at actual cost or cost plus, then a different pattern of behavior may result. If the supplying division needs work, managers probably will submit a low estimated cost. If the contract is received, the supplying division knows it will not be penalized because it can transfer at actual cost or actual cost plus a markup. When such conditions are encountered, one must be careful if any profit-based performance-evaluation procedure is employed.

A COMPREHENSIVE TRANSFER-PRICING PROBLEM

To this point in this chapter, much of the discussion concerning transfer pricing has been at the policy level. In this section, a transfer-pricing situation will be described. Then, by changing several assumptions, a series of problems will be analyzed. Most of these problems can be analyzed from three different points of view. From the firm's point of view, the transfer-pricing policy should result in decisions at the divisional level that are optimal from the firm's point of view. The other points of view to be considered in a transfer-pricing problem regard the purchasing and the selling divisions. At the divisional level, the performance-measurement system is the primary determinant of management's behavior.

The Setting

K & L Corporation is a conglomerate consisting of many divisions operating in many different industries. All divisions within the K & L Corporation are evaluated as profit centers. All transfers between divisions of the K & L Corporation are made at market price. If no market price exists for an intermediate product, the transfer is made at the full-absorption standard cost.

The Spinfree division of K & L Corporation manufactures a washing machine for household use. All of the washing machines are sold to appliance distributors at an average unit selling price of $400. Spinfree manufactures every component for the washing machine except for a one-horsepower watertight electric motor. These motors are purchased by Spinfree from the Electric Power division of K & L Corporation. Currently, Spinfree is operating at 80 percent of capacity, resulting in an annual production of 40,000 washers.

The Electric Power division of K & L Corporation produces many types of small-horsepower electric motors. Spinfree is the only division of the K & L Corporation that purchases motors from Electric Power. Each motor produced by Electric Power requires a control unit. Electric Power purchases all of the required control units from the Controls division of the K & L Corporation. The relationships among the divisions are shown in figure 18.1.

Standard-cost data for each division are shown in table 18.1. In most decision-making situations at the corporate level, it will be necessary to know the variable cost to the firm of producing a washing machine. The variable costs to the Spinfree division include the $100 cost of the motor. This cost includes profit and variable and fixed costs from the Electric

FIGURE 18.1
Relationships
among Divisions

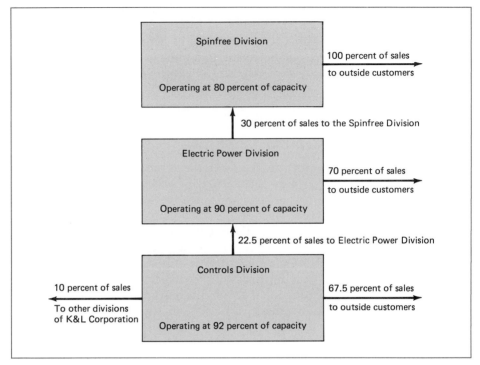

Power and Controls divisions. Therefore, it is necessary to calculate the unit variable cost and contribution margin as shown in table 18.2. The $301 and $99 are the unit variable cost and contribution margin, respectively, to the firm for a washing machine.

A Purchase-Quantity Problem

Assume S-H Corporation is building 5,000 apartments and wishes to purchase a washing machine for each apartment. A competitor of Spinfree has agreed to supply S-H Corporation the 5,000 washing machines at $320 each. Management of S-H Corporation has indicated that it will purchase the 5,000 washing machines from the Spinfree division at the $320 unit cost. Quantity sales of washing machines of this magnitude are extremely rare.

This problem can be evaluated from two points of view. From the point of view of the management team of the Spinfree division, which is evaluated as a profit center, the problem would be analyzed as follows. From table 18.1, one sees that the unit variable cost is the $325 at the divisional level. Therefore, the division would lose $5 a unit ($320 − $325) for each machine sold to S-H Corporation. Since Spinfree is evaluated as a profit center, the divisional managers would not be interested in accepting the order for the 5,000 machines at a unit selling price of $320 because the division will lose $25,000 ($5 × 5,000).

TABLE 18.1 Divisional Cost Data

Spinfree Division—
Washing Machine

Selling price			$400
Material		$ 75	
Labor	10 hours × $10 =	100	
Variable overhead	10 hours × $ 5 =	50	
Purchased component—motor		100	325
Unit contribution margin			$ 75
Fixed overhead—10 hours × $2.50			25
Unit gross profit			$ 50

Annual capacity	500,000 hours	
Current operating level	400,000 hours	

Electric Power Division—
One-Horsepower Electric Motor

Selling price			$100
Material		$ 20	
Labor	2 hours × $10 =	20	
Variable overhead	2 hours × $10 =	20	
Purchased component—control		20	80
Unit contribution margin			$ 20
Fixed overhead	2 hours × $ 5		10
Unit gross profit			$ 10

Annual capacity	300,000 hours	
Current operating level	270,000 hours	

Controls Division—
Control for One-Horsepower Electric Motor

Selling price			$ 20
Materials		$ 6	
Labor	1 hour × $8 =	8	
Variable overhead	1 hour × $2 =	2	16
Unit contribution margin			$ 4
Fixed overhead	1 hour × $1		1
Unit gross profit			$ 3

Annual capacity	650,000 hours	
Current operating level	600,000 hours	

However, from the point of view of the corporate management team, the analysis will lead to a different conclusion. As shown in table 18.2, the firm's unit variable cost for a washing machine is $301. Therefore, since sufficient excess capacity exists in all three divisions concerned with the manufacture of washing machines, the firm will profit from supplying the machines. The unit contribution margin from the firm's point of view is $19 ($320 − $301) and the firm will profit by $95,000 ($19 × 5,000). This is an example of how a performance-measurement system in conjunction with the transfer pricing may result in suboptimal decisions when decisions are made at the divisional level.

To solve this problem, corporate management personnel must get the divisional managers to agree on how the unit contribution margin of $19 is to be allocated among the three divisions. The current situation leaves

TABLE 18.2 Washing Machine Cost Data—Corporate Level

K & L Corporation
Cost of washing machine produced by Spinfree Division with
components produced by Electric Power and Controls Divisions

Selling price			$400
Variable costs			
Spinfree Division			
Material	$ 75		
Labor	100		
Variable overhead	50	$225	
Electric Power Division			
Materials	$ 20		
Labor	20		
Variable overhead	20	60	
Controls Division			
Materials	$ 6		
Labor	8		
Variable overhead	2	16	
Total variable costs			301
Unit contribution margin			$ 99
Fixed costs			
Spinfree Division		$ 25	
Electric Power Division		10	
Controls Division		1	
Total fixed costs			36
Unit gross profit			$ 63

the Controls division with a unit contribution margin of $4 and the Electric Power division with a unit contribution margin of $20. However, the Spinfree division has a negative unit contribution margin of $5 that makes the contract appear unattractive. Since it is desirable for the divisions to operate autonomously, the corporate management team does not want to impose an allocation on the divisional managers. This behavioral dimension makes this type of problem difficult to solve from the corporate point of view.

A Sourcing Problem

Assume another independent situation develops with the divisions of K & L Corporation. An outside supplier offers to sell 40,000 electric motors annually to the Spinfree division at $90 each. These motors meet the specifications for the washing machines produced by Spinfree. Assume that if the Electric Power division did not sell the 40,000 motors to Spinfree that they could not sell the motors on the open market.

Managers of the Spinfree division will be in favor of accepting the $90 offer. At the divisional level, the unit contribution margin will be increased by $10 because the cost of a motor is decreased from $100 to $90. Therefore, divisional profitability will increase by $400,000 ($10 × 40,000) annually if the motors are purchased externally.

From the K & L management team's perspective, the motors should be manufactured by the Electric Power division rather than be purchased from the outside vendor. The variable cost of a motor is $90 if purchased externally and $76 ($16 for the control and $60 for the motor) if it is manufactured by the Electric Power division. Therefore, if the motors are purchased by Spinfree from the vendor, K & L will realize a $560,000 ([$90 − $76] × 40,000) decrease in income. From the corporate point of view, the motors should be manufactured by the Electric Power Division unless they can be purchased for less than $76.

If the Spinfree division purchases the motor from the outside vendor, the Electric Power division will see its annual profits reduced $800,000 (($100 − $80) × 40,000). The $90 selling price only covers the full cost of the Electric Power division and, therefore, they will be unwilling to make a long-run commitment to supply motors at $90. Profits of the Control division will be reduced by $160,000 ($4 × 40,000) annually if the motors are purchased externally.

Now, let us slightly change the facts concerning this situation. Assume that the outside supplier will sell the 40,000 motors annually at $90 each and that the Electric Power division is operating at capacity and can sell all the motors it produces (including the 40,000 now transferred to Spinfree) on the open market for an average unit selling price of $100. This situation need only be evaluated from the K & L Corporate perspective. Electric Power will prefer to sell the motor for $100 rather than transfer to Spinfree at $90 and Spinfree will prefer purchasing the motors at $90 rather than from Electric Power for $100.

From the point of view of the firm, the variable cost of a motor is $76 ($16 for the control and $60 for the motor). Therefore, the unit contribution margin resulting from the sale of a motor is $24 ($100 − $76). Now, to purchase the motor is more expensive by $14 a unit ($90 − $76) than to have them manufactured by Electric Power. Therefore, the firm is better off by $400,000 (40,000 × [$24 − $14]) by having Spinfree purchase the motors from the outside supplier and having Electric Power sell the motors externally.

☐ TRANSFER PRICING AND DECISION MAKING

Transfer prices are used in performance measurement and can result in suboptimal decisions at the divisional level. Students frequently become confused when dealing with transfer prices because there is no algorithm that can be employed to determine the "correct" transfer price. Frequently, the appropriate transfer price for use in performance measurement is inappropriate for decision making.

A theoretically correct transfer price for decision-making purposes can be specified. However, this transfer price involves opportunity-cost concepts, and, therefore, in many cases measurement problems are encountered. This transfer price equals:

1. The incremental costs (in most cases these can be approximated by the variable costs) plus

2. Opportunity costs to the firm

This transfer can be demonstrated from the K & L Corporation example. In the initial problem in which excess capacity existed in all three divisions, the theoretically correct transfer price for a motor is the variable costs in the Control division of $16 plus the variable costs in the Electric Power division of $60. There are no opportunity costs, since the divisions have no alternative uses for their facilities. In this situation, the $76 is the correct transfer price for decision-making purposes.

Now, if we alter the facts concerning the K & L Corporation, a different transfer price for decision making can be determined. Assume that the Controls division is operating at capacity. If an additional control is supplied to the Electric Motor division, then an outside sale is lost. The theoretically correct transfer price for decision making in this case is the $16 variable cost in the Controls division plus the $60 variable cost in the Power division. In addition, an opportunity cost of $4 must be included in the transfer price. This is the profit foregone, since the outside sale of a control unit is lost if the internal transfer is made. In this situation, the correct transfer price for decision-making purposes is $80.

☐ THE ECONOMICS OF TRANSFER PRICING

The market environment of the intermediate and final products must be considered in any economic analysis of transfer prices.[1] Assume the markets for both the intermediate and final products are perfectly competitive. A selling division in a competitive market will maximize its profit by equating its marginal revenue (*MR*), which is equal to price under the assumption of perfect competition, to its marginal cost (*MC*). The price of the intermediate good plus any additional costs incurred before the final sale is the marginal cost of the purchasing division. The demand curve for the purchasing division is equal to a net marginal-revenue curve ($Pp - MCp$) where Pp is the market price of the final product and MCp is the marginal-processing cost.

Given this situation, the purchasing division will only acquire units of the intermediate product as long as its incremental revenue ($Pp - MCp$) is greater than the price of the intermediate good. If the purchasing division's equilibrium quantity demanded is greater than the selling division's equilibrium supply, the purchasing division can, of course, satisfy the additional demand through purchases on the outside market. In a like manner, if the selling division has an excess supply, it can sell it on the outside market. Under these conditions, the analysis indicates that the market price is the appropriate transfer price.

In addition to assumptions concerning the market environment, the foregoing analysis requires that several other conditions exist. From an accounting point of view, perhaps the most significant condition is that one must be able to determine the marginal costs for both products. Other requirements of this analysis are that (1) each division produces only one

1. See Jack Hirshleifer, "On the Economics of Transfer Pricing," *Journal of Business* 29, no. 7 (July 1956):172–84.

product, (2) the products have external markets, (3) the demands for each division's product are independent, and (4) the cost functions of each division are independent of each other.

Let's extend the discussion by assuming imperfect markets for the intermediate and final products. The selling division now faces a downward sloping demand curve. Similarly, the purchasing division's demand curve slopes downward. The optimal solution is to equate the joint marginal cost of production with the net marginal revenue in each market. The purchasing division will set its quantity demanded at a level at which the transfer price is equal to its net marginal revenue $(MRp - MCp)$. Similarly, the producing division will set the transfer price against its marginal cost of manufacturing and produce that quantity. The result of this analysis is that the transfer price of the intermediate good equals the marginal cost of production.

If the producing divisions did transfer at their marginal costs, then only the division producing the end-product would report profit from goods involved in internal transfers. One then encounters the same problems as when transfers are made at cost. All that has been accomplished is that the definition of cost has been changed.

The economic approach to the transfer-pricing problem breaks down when one is confronted with multidivisions making multiproducts. The two-dimensional price-theory graphs on which the economic analysis is based cannot be employed to cover multiconditions. Thus, linear programming has been suggested as a means of determining an optimal approach.

☐ PROGRAMMED TRANSFER PRICES

The general linear-programming problem (refer to chapter 12 for a detailed discussion of linear programming) is expressed as

$$\text{Max } Z = cx \text{ subject to } Ax \leqslant b \text{ for all } x \geqslant 0$$

This model has been suggested as a means for determining the optimal outputs for a divisionalized firm.[2] For a multinational firm, it has been demonstrated how this model could incorporate tax and foreign exchange rates in determining the optimal output.[3] From chapter 12, you know that one of the outputs from a linear-programming model is the opportunity cost associated with each resource constraining the system. These opportunity costs could be employed as transfer prices within the divisionalized firm.

However, problems might result in determining transfer prices for resources that do not constrain the system. The opportunity cost associated

2. See Nicholas Dopuch and David F. Drake, "Accounting Implications of a Mathematical Programming Approach to the Transfer Pricing Problem," *Journal of Accounting Research* 2 (Spring 1964):10–24.

3. See John William Petty, II, *An Optimal Transfer Pricing System for the Multinational Firm: A Linear Programming Approach* (Austin, Texas: The University of Texas at Austin, 1971).

with these resources is equal to zero. If unconstrained resources are transferred at a zero price, the producing division cannot recoup its variable costs. This problem can be overcome if the variable costs are added to the opportunity costs in determining the transfer price.

The major problem encountered in employing either the economic or the programming approach to determine transfer prices can best be expressed as a paradox. If all of the information required by either approach were available, then the management personnel is equipped to engage in centralized planning activities. When an optimization model of the firm can be constructed, then why would management adopt a divisionalized organization structure? Attempts to model a firm strongly suggest a movement away from decentralization and divisionalization toward more centralization.

□ TAX CONSIDERATIONS

The technical aspects of the tax considerations in transfer pricing are beyond the scope of this text. However, you should be aware of potential tax-related transfer-pricing problems that can develop in a divisionalized enterprise.

Assume transfer prices are used as the bases for tax computations by divisions located in different states or countries. A multinational divisionalized firm must deal with the U.S. Treasury Department and taxing authorities of any host countries in which it operates.

Prior to 1962, a U.S.-based firm realized a substantial tax advantage by showing profit in a country with a comparatively low tax rate. This was accomplished by transferring at less than the market price from a division located in the United States to a division located in a country with a corporate tax rate less than that of the United States. The division located in the United States would realize minimum profit (hence, minimum tax), and the foreign division would realize a profit after the final sale. Taxes paid to the foreign government by the foreign division would be less than the taxes that would have been paid to the U.S. government. Amendments to the Internal Revenue Code that took effect at the end of 1962 ruled out practically all tax benefits from such practices.

Section 482 of the Internal Revenue Code permits the I.R.S. to distribute, apportion, or allocate gross income, deductions, or credits between two or more organizations, trades, or businesses that are controlled by the same interests if the I.R.S. determines that such allocation is necessary to prevent tax evasion or to clearly reflect the income of the entities involved. If divisions of a firm do not file a consolidated tax return and there are transfers between the divisions or if it suspects tax evasion, then the I.R.S. can allocate divisional income to clearly reflect income.

If the I.R.S. took such action, the firm would have to justify any internal transactions questioned. The I.R.S. applies two tests in evaluating internal transactions. The first is the arm's-length test of a transfer price. This test employs three standards specified by U.S. Treasury Department regulations.[4]

4. Internal Revenue Code Regulation 1.482-2(e)(1).

1. Comparable uncontrolled price method. Is the transfer price substantially the same price at which uncontrolled parties sell?

2. Resale price method. When a firm markets through a subsidiary, the transfer price should be comparable to the resale price, since little value is added by the division that acts as a distributor. Under this test, it is assumed that no value is added by the division to which goods have been transferred.

3. Cost-plus method. If the first two tests are not appropriate, then the cost-plus test is employed. Under this test, the transfer price should be equivalent to cost plus a profit margin as determined by comparable uncontrolled sales.

The second test employed in evaluating internal transactions is referred to as the business-purpose test. Each transaction must have a business as contrasted with a tax purpose. That is, if the only purpose of the transaction is to avoid taxes, then the I.R.S. most likely will allocate income between the questioned divisions.

Of course, any allocation of income must also be acceptable to any foreign country involved. When entering a foreign country, firms have found it necessary to enter into negotiations with authorities representing both the host country and the United States to determine acceptable transfer prices. The position of most taxing authorities in opposing the exportation of profits has both corporate and national implications. If corporate policy permits a foreign division to purchase inside or outside of the corporate structure, transfer prices imposed by taxing authorities could be at a level that would make it advantageous for the division to purchase from outside sources. From the firm's point of view, such action might be less than optimal. It also could limit the export markets of a country if the transfer prices are not competitive in world markets.

Market or adjusted market-based transfer prices generally prove to be most acceptable to the tax authorities. Of course, the host country of a selling division would prefer the market price. Authorities in the country of the purchasing division prefer an adjusted market-based transfer price. However, oftentimes a market price cannot be established. Rather than resorting to a negotiated transfer-pricing system, most firms employ a cost-plus formula for pricing. This method permits them to demonstrate a consistent method of establishing the transfer price. The method also is acceptable as far as it relates to the I.R.S. third test for an arm's-length price. Foreign custom and tariff laws generally require that the fair market value be employed. These taxing authorities generally reserve the right to determine the fairness of the prices.

Similar tax situations can also be encountered when a firm operates in different states where corporate incomes are taxed. Several states have fair-trade-practice laws that make illegal the sale of goods at less than full cost. A transfer price set at less than full cost, therefore, may be in violation of state law.

The SEC requires that firms report profits by line of business in registration statements and annual 10-K reports. FASB Statement no. 14, which was issued in 1976, requires that firms that issue a complete set of financial statements disclose as a part of those statements information relating to the firm's operations in different industries, its foreign operations, its export sales, and its major customers.[5] When this is done, transfer prices are the basis for internal and external performance evaluation. Certainly, cost and perhaps cost-plus transfer-pricing systems could lead to financial reports that might be misleading to investors.

☐ SUMMARY

In this chapter, we have surveyed the transfer-pricing problem that is encountered by the management team of a divisionalized enterprise. We considered the advantages and disadvantages associated with several market and cost-based transfer-pricing systems. From the discussion, one can conclude that transfer prices are a multidimensional problem that include motivational, organizational, tax, and legal aspects. Overemphasis or neglect of any of these aspects of the transfer-pricing problem can have far-reaching impacts on both divisional and corporate performance.

Decision making in a transfer-pricing environment has several dimensions. Generally, a problem can be evaluated from the corporate and divisional points of view. Management personnel at these levels may not reach the same conclusion because of the performance-measurement system. The decision as to whether an item should be purchased from a sister division or an external supplier is an example of a problem where the transfer-pricing policy will influence behavior at the divisional level. Corporate management personnel will compare the market prices from the outside supplier with the unit variable cost of its manufacturing division. The Purchasing division, if evaluated as a profit or investment center, will compare the market price with the transfer price in making the sourcing decision.

Finally, it was concluded that the optimal transfer price for decision making was the unit variable cost plus any opportunity cost. However, it was recognized that in many situations it is not possible to measure the opportunity-cost component of the transfer price.

KEY TERMS

Cost-based transfer prices	**Negotiated transfer pricing system**
Market-based transfer prices	**Transfer pricing**

REVIEW PROBLEM

The Miller Corporation has twenty operating divisions that are evaluated as profit centers. All internal transfers in the Miller Corporation are made at market price. If no market price is available, the divisional managers negotiate a transfer price.

---

5. "Financial Reporting for Segments of a Business Enterprise," *Statement of Financial Accounting Standards* no. 14 (Stamford, Conn.: FASB, 1976). A number of pronouncements have been issued since 1976 that modify certain disclosure requirements.

The Petty division of Miller Corporation manufactures precision roller chains that have many uses. All the products of the Petty division are sold externally to many customers; therefore, a market price has been established.

The Power division of Miller Corporation requires several thousand links of PRC-80 roller chains. Power proposes to pay $.95 a link for the chain because it will be used on a special order that will be sold in an extremely cost-competitive market. The market price for the PRC-80 chains is $1 a link and Petty managers have determined that its variable cost per link is $.75. Both the Petty and Power divisions have the capacity to produce the chain and the new product. The special order will be filled in three months, and it is unlikely there will be any repeat orders.

Required ☐

1. From the point of view of the Power division, what is the variable cost of the PRC-80 chain?

2. From the point of view of the Petty division, what is the variable cost of the PRC-80 chain?

3. From the point of view of the Miller Corporation, what is the variable cost of the PRC-80 chain?

4. Should the Petty division supply the PRC-80 chain to the Power division at $.95 a link?

5. From the point of view of the Miller Corporation management team, should the Petty division supply the PRC-80 chain to the Power division?

Solution ☐

1. $.95 a link (the proposed transfer price)

2. $.75 a link

3. $.75 a link (the variable cost of the Petty division)

4. This is a short-run decision, since it is unlikely there will be any additional orders. Another factor is that the Petty division is not at present operating at full capacity. If the chain is transferred at $.95 a link, Petty division will realize a contribution to profit of $.20 ($.95 − $.75) a link.

5. Assuming the Power division will sell the special order for an amount greater than its variable cost, the Miller Corporation will benefit from the transfer of the chain and the external sale of the Power division because both divisions are not at present operating at capacity.

QUESTIONS

Q18-1. What is a transfer price? Is a transfer price the same as the market price of goods exchanged between firms in a normal market exchange?

Q18-2. Explain why the problems of performance evaluation and transfer pricing are closely related.

Q18-3. Under what circumstances might standard cost be an acceptable transfer price?

Q18-4. Under what circumstances might variable cost be an acceptable transfer price?

Q18-5. Under what circumstances might market price be an acceptable transfer price?

Q18-6. Under what circumstances might adjusted market price be an acceptable transfer price?

Q18-7. Under what circumstances might a negotiated transfer price be acceptable?

Q18-8. What are some of the tax implications that must be considered in establishing a transfer-pricing policy?

Q18-9. What are some of the problems encountered when the economic approach to the transfer-pricing problem is employed?

Q18-10. Linear programming has been suggested as a means of establishing transfer prices. What is the major conceptual problem relating to the application of linear programming to the transfer-pricing problem?

Q18-11. Is a competitive market necessary to maintain divisionalized profit responsibility?

Q18-12. Identify examples of transfer prices encountered on a university campus.

Q18-13. Discuss the following statement: "The complexity of the transfer-pricing problem is a function of the size and growth rate of a company."

Q18-14. Discuss the following statement: "If no market price exists upon which to base a transfer price, then the division should not be evaluated as a profit center."

Q18-15. Discuss the following statement: "For a division to be evaluated as a profit center, divisional managers must have the freedom to decide whether purchases are made within the firm or on the open market."

Q18-16. Discuss the following statement: "We evaluate the performance of our divisions only on the results of outside sales. All internal transfers are made at standard cost. This policy eliminates any transfer-pricing problem."

PROBLEMS

General Transfer-Pricing Policy Considerations

P18-1. The Virginia Instruments Company is considering establishing a division in Scotland to manufacture integrated circuits. Some of the circuits will be shipped to the United States and incorporated into VIC's line of electronic calculators. The remaining output from the Scotland division will be sold on the world market. VIC plans to operate the Scotland division as a profit center.

Required □ Discuss some of the problems related to transfer pricing that VIC must consider in establishing the Scotland division.

Transfer-Pricing Tax Considerations

P18-2. The A.G.S. Corporation manufactures baseballs in Taiwan, which are then transferred to a United States Marketing division for distribution. Corporate policy at A.G.S. directs that all transfers are made at cost. Tax authorities in Taiwan have questioned the A.G.S. transfers at cost. Tax accountants for A.G.S. have suggested that the I.R.S. should be consulted before an agreement is reached with the Taiwan authorities.

Required □

1. Why would the Taiwan tax authorities question the A.G.S. transfer-pricing policy?

2. Why do the tax accountants want to consult with the I.R.S.?

P18-3.   The General Sound Corporation assembles car radios in Salem, Virginia, for sale nationwide in large discount stores. The speakers are made in Quesenberry, Alabama, and the tuners are made in Amherst, Massachusetts, by divisions of General Sound. All other parts of the radios are manufactured in Salem.   *Transfer-Pricing Tax Considerations*

General Sound operates a Marketing division that is located in New York City. All transfers within General Sound Corporation are made at market prices. All divisions are evaluated as profit centers except the Marketing division, which is evaluated as a revenue center. The Marketing division operates at a loss since it transfers the radios in at the market price for which they are sold to the discount stores.

The highest corporate tax rates are in the states of New York and Massachusetts. Lower corporate tax rates are found in Virginia and Alabama.

Required □ Identify questions that state corporate tax authorities might raise concerning the organization of General Sound Corporation.

P18-4.   All transfers in the Ten Company are made at cost plus 10 percent. The Atlantic Boat Division of the Ten Company has a contract to construct a research submarine for the U.S. Navy. Terms of the contract for the submarine are cost plus 10 percent. The Steel Casting Division of Ten Company casts the propeller and several pipe fittings for the submarine. They were transferred to the Atlantic Boat Division at cost plus 10 percent.   *Transfer Pricing and Auditing*

Representatives from the Naval Audit Service are coming to audit the books of the Steel Casting Division. The divisional manager is concerned and cannot understand why he is being subjected to their harassment.

Required □ Prepare a memo addressed to the divisional manager explaining why the Naval Audit Service wants to review Steel Castings' accounting records with regard to the submarine contract. Include in your memo some specific items that the Naval Audit Service will want to review.

P18-5.   Clark Industries consists of eight divisions that are evaluated as profit centers. All transfers between divisions are made at market price. Ace Bearing is a division of Clark that sells approximately 20 percent of its output externally. The remaining 80 percent of the output from the Bearing division is transferred to other divisions within Clark. No other division of Clark Industries transfers internally more than 10 percent of its output.   *Transfer Pricing and Performance Measurement*

Based on any profit-based measure of performance, Ace Bearing is the leading division within Clark Industries. Other divisional managers within

Clark always find that their performance is compared to that of the Bearing division. These managers argue that the transfer-pricing situation gives Ace a competitive advantage.

Required □

1. What factors may contribute to any advantage that the Ace Bearing division might have over the other divisions?

2. What alternative transfer price or performance measure might be more appropriate in this situation?

Transfer Pricing and Management Behavior

P18-6. Bell Grocery Company operates ten large supermarkets on Cape Cod in Massachusetts. Each store is evaluated as a profit center, and store managers have complete control over purchases and their inventory policy. The policy is that if a store runs short of an item and a sister store has a sufficient supply, a transfer will be made between stores. Company policy requires that all such transfers be made at cost.

During a recent period of rapid increases in food prices, company management officials have noted that transfers between stores have decreased sharply. Store managers have indicated that if they ran short of a particular item, they could not locate a sister store with sufficient inventory to make a transfer.

Company management officials have observed several recent cases in which a store manager inquired about the availability of a particular item and was told that the sister store did not have sufficient inventory to make a transfer. Further checking indicated that the sister store had more than sufficient inventory to make the transfer.

Required □

1. Why were the store managers reluctant to make transfers?

2. How could the transfer-pricing policy be changed to avoid this situation?

Transfer Pricing and Decision Making

P18-7. The Clutch division of Bergstrum Industries manufactures a variable-speed clutch that it sells commercially at $500 per unit. Standard unit costs for the variable-speed clutch are:

Direct materials	$ 75
Direct labor	150
Overhead	150
Total unit cost	$375

The standard direct-labor rate is $10 per hour, and overhead is assigned at 100 percent of the direct-labor rate. Normal direct-labor hours are 75,000, and the overhead rate is $4 variable and $6 fixed. The Clutch division is operating at 80 percent of capacity.

A coal-handling system is being rebuilt by the Materials Handling division of Bergstrum Industries. This job requires fifty variable-speed clutches. A clutch that meets the job specifications can be purchased for $450 a unit from an outside supplier. The clutch manufactured by the Clutch division exceeds the specifications for the coal-handling system job. Interdivisional transfers in Bergstrum Industries are made at market price when available, and all divisions are evaluated as profit centers.

Required ☐

1. From the point of view of corporate management officials, is Bergstrum Industries better off if the Materials Handling division purchases the clutches from the outside supplier at $450 a unit or from the Clutch division at $500 a unit? Would your answer change if the Clutch division agreed to transfer the clutches at $450 a unit? Explain.

2. From the point of view of the Materials Handling divisional manager, should the division purchase the clutches externally at $450 a unit or internally at $500 a unit? Would your answer change if the Clutch division agreed to transfer the clutches at $450 a unit? Explain.

3. If the Clutch division is operating at 80 percent of normal capacity, what is the lowest price at which they would consider transferring the clutches to the Materials Handling division? Would your answer change if the Clutch division was operating at 100 percent of capacity? Explain.

4. Since both divisions are evaluated as profit centers, what is the most useful transfer price if the Clutch division is operating at 80 percent of capacity? Explain. Would your answer change if the Clutch division were operating at 100 percent of capacity? Explain.

P18-8. The Controls division of Electric Motors Corporation manufactures a starter with the following standard costs: *Transfer Pricing and Decision Making*

Direct materials	$ 5
Direct labor	30
Overhead	15
Total unit cost	$50

The standard direct-labor rate is $15 per hour, and overhead is assigned at 50 percent of the direct-labor rate. Normal direct-labor hours are 20,000, and the overhead rate is $2.50 variable and $5.00 fixed per direct-labor hour.

The starters sell for $75 and the Controls division is currently operating at a level of about 16,000 direct-labor hours for the year. All transfers in Electric Motor Corporation are made at market price. If mutually agreed upon, the divisional managers are permitted to negotiate a transfer price.

The Motor division currently purchases 2,000 starters annually from the Controls division at the market price. The divisional manager of the Motor division indicates he can purchase the starters from a foreign supplier for $65. Since he is free to select a supplier, he has indicated that he would like to negotiate a new transfer price with the Controls division. The managers of the Controls division indicate that they believe that the foreign supplier is attempting to "buy in" by selling the starters at what they consider an excessively low price.

Required ☐

1. From the point of view of the firm, should the Motor division purchase the starters internally or externally? How much will the firm's net income change if the starters are purchased from the foreign supplier?

2. From the point of view of the Motor division, should the starters be purchased from the Controls division or the foreign supplier? How much will the net income of the division change if the starters are purchased from the foreign supplier?

3. From the point of view of the Controls division, how much will its net income change if the starters are purchased from the foreign supplier? What is the minimum price at which the Controls division would transfer the starters? What is the change in the net income of the Controls division if the transfers are made at $65 a unit?

4. If the Controls division were operating at 100 percent of capacity and the Motor division wanted to purchase the starters externally, from the point of view of the firm, the Motor division, and the Controls division, what should be done if:

   a. The Controls division could not sell the additional starters externally to continue operating at full capacity?
   b. The Controls division could sell the additional starters externally to continue operating at full capacity?

Transfer Pricing and ROI

P18-9. Kenley Corporation uses ROI for divisional performance measurement. The manager of the Claude division proposed purchasing 1,000 units monthly of a component from the Sarah division at $75 each. The controller of the Sarah division has determined that the variable unit cost of the component is $70 and that no additional fixed costs will be incurred if the component is supplied to Claude.

The controller of the Sarah division has determined that the raw materials of the component cost $30 a unit and that a two-month supply will have to be maintained in inventory. In addition, a two-month supply of the finished component will be required in the finished-goods inventory. Variable cost is used in valuing divisional inventories.

Corporate policy of Kenley provides for a one-month credit on intracompany transfers. Therefore, Sarah division will have a receivable and Claude division a payable for one month's sales. Gross assets are used in determining divisional ROI. Today, Sarah division has an ROI of 25 percent, and the ROI for the corporation is 20 percent.

Required ☐

1. Determine if the Sarah division would be interested in selling the components to the Claude division. Explain your answer.

2. From the point of view of the Kenley Corporation, is the firm better off if the transfer is made internally or if the Claude division purchases the component from an external supplier for $75 each.

3. Evaluate the firm's policy of recognizing intracompany receivables and payables in determining the divisional investment basis.

Transfer Pricing and ROI

P18-10. Neece Corporation uses ROI for divisional performance measurement. The manager of the Digger division proposed an annual purchase of 6,000 units of a part at $200 each from the Clark division of Neece Corporation. The controller of the Clark division estimates the variable unit cost of the part to be $125, and additional fixed costs of $300,000 will be incurred if the 6,000 parts are supplied to Digger.

The controller of the Clark division has determined that the raw materials of the part cost $35 a unit and a two-month supply will have to be maintained in inventory. In addition, a two-month supply of the finished part will be required in the finished-goods inventory. Manufacture of the parts will require additional capital investment of $640,000 by the Clark division. Gross assets are used in determining divisional ROI. Currently, Clark division has an ROI of 25 percent and the average ROI for Neece Corporation is 15 percent.

Required ☐

1. Determine if the Clark division would be interested in transferring the parts at $200 each to the Digger division. Support your answer.

2. Determine the minimum transfer price the Clark division would accept for the parts from the Digger division.

3. If Clark division will not supply the parts to the Digger division at $200 each, Digger managers intend to purchase the parts from an outside vendor for $210 each. If the Digger managers purchase the parts from the outside vendor, what is the additional annual cost to the Neece Corporation?

P18-11. Anderson Corporation is divisionalized and uses ROI as a means of evaluating divisional performance. The firm has an average cost of capital of 10 percent and a corporate ROI of 13 percent.

Transfer Pricing and Residual Income

Patsy division of Anderson Corporation manufactures high-speed printers for computers. The managers of the Patsy division have requested that the Sally division supply it with eighty motors annually for its new high-speed page printer. Managers in the Patsy division have identified an outside vendor who will supply the motors at $500 each.

Sally division of Anderson Corporation manufactures precision miniature electric motors and has a divisional ROI of 18 percent. The division is not operating at capacity and has determined that manufacturing the motors for the page printer will require an additional investment of $100,000. The estimated variable cost for the motors is $300 each. After evaluating the proposal from Patsy division for the motors, Sally division managers declined the order unless the Patsy division was willing to pay $525 each for the motors. The management staff of the Patsy division has indicated that it intends to purchase the motors at $500 each from the outside vendor.

Required ☐

1. Explain why the Sally division required a transfer price of $525 for the motors.

2. From the point of view of Anderson Corporation, should the motors be purchased from the vendor or manufactured by the Sally division?

3. Would the Sally division managers consider supplying the motors at $500 if residual income was used to measure divisional performance?

P18-12. Assume the same facts given in problem 18-11 except that Sally division is operating at capacity and that outside sales will be lost if the motors are supplied to Patsy for the page printer. As a result of operating at capacity, Sally division has an ROI of 18 percent.

Transfer Pricing and Opportunity Costs

Required □

1. From the point of view of Anderson Corporation, should the motors for the page printer be purchased from the vendor or manufactured by the Sally division?

2. Would Sally division managers consider supplying the motors at $500 if residual income were used to measure divisional performance?

Transfer Pricing and Opportunity Costs

P18-13. The Electric Power division of General Power Corporation produces two types of five-horsepower electric motors. The basic motor has been in production for almost twenty years and has been subject to minor modifications. It is an extremely reliable piece of equipment, and Electric Power can sell all of these motors that it produces. Recently, a Super-Efficient motor was developed; the division has only two customers at this time. These customers purchase 5,000 of the Super-Efficient motors annually. If the Super-Efficient motor is not available, the customers will accept the basic motor.

The following information relates to the two motors:

	Basic motor	Super-efficient motor
Selling price	$105	$300
Materials and parts	$ 45	$ 75
Labor 3 hours @ $15 =	45	
10 hours @ $15 =		150
Total variable cost	$ 90	$225
Unit contribution margin	$ 15	$ 75

Capacity at the Electric Power division is 150,000 hours, and annual overhead is $500,000, all fixed.

The Air Compressor division of General Power produces precision electric air compressors. These compressors use a special explosion-proof motor that is purchased from an outside vendor. Costs for the air compressor are

Materials—Motor	$285
Other	25
Labor 5 hours @ $15	75
Total variable cost	$385

Annual overhead costs at the Air Compressor division are $300,000, all fixed. The market price for the air compressor is $500. Annual sales of the air compressor have averaged 4,000 units. Engineers at the Air Compressor division have just determined that the Super-Efficient motor meets the specifications for the Air Compressor. Managers of the Air Compressor division have asked managers of the Electric Power division to declare a transfer price for 4,000 of the Super-Efficient motors. Both of the divisions are evaluated as investment centers.

Required □

1. From the corporate point of view at General Power, should the 4,000 Super-Efficient motors be transferred to replace the explosion-proof motors? Support your answer.

2. Specify a transfer price that will ensure proper decisions from the corporate point of view. Support your answer.

3. If demand for the air compressor increases to 6,000 units annually, and Electric Power can produce only 10,000 Super-Efficient motors, from the corporate point of view, how many air compressors should be built using the Super-Efficient motor?

P18-14. The Ketz Corporation has several operating divisions that are evaluated as profit centers. Ace Paint division manufactures specialty paints for industrial use. In the past, 99 percent of the output from Ace was sold to outside customers. Any paint sold to sister divisions was transferred at the standard variable cost.

Transfer Pricing at Variable Cost

Recently, the Office Furniture division has started to purchase significant quantities of paint from the Ace division. The manager of Ace Paint has determined that now 5 percent of the output is transferred to other divisions within Ketz Corporation. Initially, when Ace was not operating at capacity, the additional internal transfers did not affect divisional profitability. Recently, however, Ace has been operating at capacity and divisional profitability has declined because corporate policy requires that internal transfers take priority over external sales.

Required ☐

1. Comment on the standard-variable-cost-transfer-pricing policy when Ace was transferring internally 1 percent of its output and not operating at capacity.

2. Comment on the standard-variable-cost-transfer-pricing policy when Ace was transferring internally 5 percent of its output but not operating at capacity.

3. Comment on the standard-variable-cost-transfer-pricing policy when Ace was transferring internally 5 percent of its output and operating at capacity.

4. Comment on the corporate policy of giving priority to internal transfers and evaluating the divisions as profit centers.

P18-15. The Hicks Corporation is a large manufacturing firm with a centralized data processing facility. Most data processing costs are fixed, and each department that uses the facility is charged based on its actual use for the period. Costs for the data processing facility are itemized for the following categories: (1) lines printed, (2) printer setups, (3) CPU time (seconds), (4) memory (kilobyte–minutes), (5) time-sharing (CPU–seconds), (6) tape setups, and (7) other.

Data Processing and Transfer Pricing

Managers of the new departments are held responsible for data processing costs. The Billing department has received the following charges for computer use for the last two months:

	Month 1		Month 2	
	Number	*Charge*	*Number*	*Charge*
Lines printed	654,883	$ 622.08	515,803	$ 490.02
Printer setups	16	56.00	22	77.00
CPU time	23,938	29.37	25,917	33.14

Memory	346,950	328.93	235,293	211.87
Time-sharing	221,719	89.47	365,252	130.75
Tape setups	34	23.80	130	91.00
Other	—	29.75	—	34.87
Total		$1,179.40		$1,068.65

The manager of the Billing department is concerned because she is consistantly over her $900 monthly budget for data processing.

Required ☐

1. Comment on the system the firm uses for establishing data processing transfer prices. Would you recommend any changes?

2. Comment on the policy of holding the departmental managers responsible for data processing costs. Would you recommend any changes?

Cost Structure and Break-Even

P18-16. The Dempsey Corporation has several operating divisions. The Steve division manufactures circulating fans for ceilings. Although these fans have different designs, their costs are the same because the only difference is in the outside casings. The Steve division sells 90 percent of its output externally and transfers 10 percent of its output to a sister division that manufactures mobile and modular homes. The Dempsey Corporation uses market prices for all internal transfers. Selling and cost information relating to the fans follows:

Selling price	$139
Variable manufacturing costs	57
Fixed manufacturing costs*	10
Variable selling and administrative expenses	15
Fixed selling and administrative expenses*	5

*Based on normal production and sales of 100,000 units.

Required ☐

1. What is the variable cost of a fan from the Dempsey Corporation's point of view?

2. What is the variable cost of a fan from the Mobile and Modular Home division's point of view?

3. What is the variable cost of a fan from the Steve division's point of view?

4. If the Steve division has fixed costs of $1.5 million, how many fans must the division sell to break-even?

5. Would the break-even volume of the Steve division change if it sold more than 10 percent of its output to the Mobile and Modular Home division?

Transfer Pricing and Decision Making

P18-17. The Ajax division of the Cunnco Corp., which is operating at capacity, has been asked by the Defco division of Cunnco Corp. to supply it with electrical fitting number 1726. Ajax sells this part to its regular customers for $7.50 each. Defco, which is operating at 50 percent capacity, is willing to pay $5.00 for the fitting. Defco will put the fitting into a brake unit that it is manufacturing on essentially a cost-plus basis for a commercial airplane manufacturer.

Ajax has a variable cost of producing fitting number 1726 of $4.25. The cost of the break unit as being built by Defco is as follows:

Purchased parts—outside vendors	$22.50
Ajax fitting—1726	5.00
Other variable costs	14.00
Fixed overhead and administration	8.00
	$49.50

Defco believes the price concession is necessary to get the job.

The company uses return on investment and dollar profits in the measurement of division and divisional manager performance.

Required □

1. Assume that you are the division controller of Ajax. Would you recommend that Ajax supply fitting 1726 to Defco? (Ignore any income tax issues.) Why or why not?

2. Would it be to the short-run economic advantage of the Cunnco Corp. for the Ajax division to supply Defco division with fitting 1726 at $5 each? (Ignore any income tax issues.) Explain your answer.

3. Discuss the organizational and manager behavior difficulties, if any, inherent in this situation. As the Cunnco controller, what would you advise the Cunnco Corp. president to do in this situation?

(CMA)

P18-18. A. R. Oma, Inc., manufactures a line of men's perfumes and after-shave lotions. The manufacturing process is basically a series of mixing operations with the addition of certain aromatic and coloring ingredients; the finished product is packaged in a company-produced glass bottle and packed in cases containing six bottles.

Transfer Pricing and Income Measurement

A. R. Oma management officials feel that the sale of the product is heavily influenced by the appearance and appeal of the bottle and has, therefore, devoted considerable managerial effort to the bottle-production process. This has resulted in the development of certain unique bottle-production processes in which the management team takes considerable pride.

The two areas (i.e., perfume production and bottle manufacture) have evolved over the years in an almost independent manner; in fact, a rivalry has developed between management personnel as to "which division is the more important" to A. R. Oma. This attitude is probably intensified because the bottle manufacturing plant was purchased intact ten years ago and no real interchange of management personnel or ideas (except at the top corporate level) has taken place.

Since the acquisition, all bottle production has been absorbed by the perfume manufacturing plant. Each area is considered a separate profit center and evaluated as such. As the new corporate controller, you are responsible for the definition of a proper transfer value to use in crediting the bottle-production profit center and in debiting the packaging profit center.

At your request, the Bottle division general manager has asked certain other bottle manufacturers to quote a price for the quantity and sizes demanded by the Perfume division. These competitive prices are

Volume (millions)	Total price (millions)	Price per case
2 equivalent cases*	$ 4	$2.00
4	7	1.75
6	10	1.67

*An *equivalent case* represents six bottles each.

A cost analysis of the internal bottle plant indicates that they can produce bottles at these costs:

Volume (millions)	Total price (millions)	Price per case
2 equivalent cases	$3.2	$1.60
4	5.2	1.30
6	7.2	1.20

(Your cost analysts point out that these costs represent fixed costs of $1.2 million and variable costs of $1 per equivalent case.)

These figures have given rise to considerable corporate discussion as to the proper value to use in the transfer of bottles to the Perfume division. This interest is heightened because a significant portion of a division manager's income is an incentive bonus based on profit-center results.

Volume (millions)	Total price (millions)	Cost per case
2 cases	$16.4	$8.20
4	32.4	8.10
6	48.4	8.07

After considerable analysis, the Marketing Research department has furnished you with the following price-demand relationship for the finished product:

Sales volume (millions)	Total sales revenue (millions)	Sales price per case
2 cases	$25.0	$12.50
4	45.6	11.40
6	63.9	10.65

Required □

1. A. R. Oma, Inc., has used market-price transfer prices in the past. Using the current market prices and costs and assuming a volume of 6 million cases, calculate the income for

 a. The Bottle division
 b. The Perfume division
 c. The corporation

2. Is this production and sales level the most profitable volume for

 a. The Bottle division
 b. The Perfume division
 c. The corporation

3. A. R. Oma uses the profit-center concept for divisional operation.

  a. Define a profit center.

  b. What conditions should exist for a profit center to be established?

  c. Should the two divisions of A. R. Oma be organized as profit centers?

(CMA)

P18-19. MBR, Inc., consists of three divisions that were formerly three independent manufacturing companies. Bader Corporation and Roach Company merged in 1975, and the merged corporation acquired Mitchell Co. in 1976. The name of the corporation was subsequently changed to MBR, Inc., and each company became a separate division retaining the name of its former company.

Transfer Pricing and Management Behavior

The three divisions have operated as if they were still independent companies. Each division has its own sales force and production facilities. Each division management team is responsible for sales, cost of operations, acquisition and financing of divisional assets, and working-capital management. The corporate management team of MBR evaluates the performance of the divisions and division managements on the basis of return on investment.

The Mitchell division has just been awarded a contract for a product that uses a component that is manufactured by the Roach division as well as by outside suppliers. Mitchell used a cost figure of $3.80 for the component manufactured by Roach in preparing its bid for the new product. This cost figure was supplied by Roach in response to Mitchell's request for the average variable cost of the component and represents the standard variable manufacturing cost and variable selling and distribution expense.

Roach has an active sales force that is continually soliciting new prospects. Roach's regular selling price for the component Mitchell needs for the new product is $6.50. Sales of this component are expected to increase. However, the Roach management team has indicated that it could supply Mitchell with the required quantities of the component at the regular selling price less variable selling and distribution expenses. Mitchell's managers have responded by offering to pay standard variable manufacturing cost plus 20 percent.

The two divisions have been unable to agree on a transfer price. Corporate management personnel have never established a transfer-price policy because interdivisional transactions have never occurred. As a compromise, the corporate vice-president of finance has suggested a price equal to the standard full manufacturing cost (i.e., no selling and distribution expenses) plus a 15 percent markup. This price has also been rejected by the two divisional managers because each considered it grossly unfair.

The unit cost structure for the Roach component and the three suggested prices are

Regular selling price	$6.50
Standard variable manufacturing cost	$3.20
Standard fixed manufacturing cost	1.20
Variable selling and distribution expenses	.60
	$5.00

Regular selling price less variable selling and distribution expenses ($6.50 − .60)	$5.90
Variable manufacturing plus 20% ($3.20 × 1.20)	$3.84
Standard full manufacturing cost plus 15% ($4.40 × 1.15)	$5.06

Required ☐

1. Discuss the effect each of the three proposed prices might have on the Roach division manager's attitude toward intracompany business.

2. Is the negotiation of a price between the Mitchell and Roach divisions a satisfactory method of solving the transfer-price problem? Explain your answer.

3. Should the corporate management of MBR, Inc., become involved in this transfer-price controversy? Explain your answer.

(CMA)

Transfer Pricing and Decision Making

P18-20. The Lorax Electric Company manufactures a large variety of systems and individual components for the electronics industry. The firm is organized into several divisions with divisional managers given the authority to make virtually all operating decisions. Management control over divisional operations is maintained by a system of divisional profit and return on investment measures, which are reviewed regularly by top-management personnel. The top-management staff of Lorax has been quite pleased with the effectiveness of the system they have been using and believe that it is responsible for the company's improved profitability over the last few years.

The Devices division manufactures solid-state devices and is operating at capacity. The Systems division has asked the Devices division to supply a large quantity of integrated circuit IC378. The Devices division currently is selling this component to its regular customers at $40 per hundred.

The Systems division, which is operating at about 60 percent capacity, wants this particular component for a digital clock system. It has an opportunity to supply large quantities of these digital clock systems to Centonic Electric, a major producer of clock radios and other popular electronic home-entertainment equipment. This is the first opportunity any of the Lorax divisions have had to do business with Centonic Electric. Centonic Electric has offered to pay $7.50 per clock system.

The Systems division managers prepared an analysis of the probable costs to produce the clock systems. The amount that could be paid to the Devices division for the integrated circuits was determined by working backward from the selling price. The cost estimates employed by the division reflected the highest per unit cost the Systems division could incur for each cost component and still leave a sufficient margin so that the division's income statement could show reasonable improvement. The cost estimates are summarized as follows:

Proposed selling price		$7.50
Costs excluding required integrated circuits (IC378)		
Components purchased from outside suppliers	$2.75	
Circuit board etching—labor and variable overhead	.40	

Assembly, testing, packaging—labor and variable overhead	1.35	
Fixed overhead allocations	1.50	
Profit margin	.50	6.50
Amount that can be paid for integrated circuits IC378 (5 @ $20 per hundred)		$1.00

As a result of this analysis, the Systems division offered the Devices division a price of $20 per hundred for the integrated circuit. This bid was refused by the manager of the Devices division because he felt the Systems division should at least meet the price of $40 per hundred that regular customers pay. When the Systems division found that it could not obtain a comparable integrated circuit from outside vendors, the situation was brought to an arbitration committee, which had been set up to review such problems.

The arbitration committee prepared an analysis that showed that $.15 would cover variable costs of producing the integrated circuit, $.28 would cover the full cost including fixed overhead, and $.35 would provide a gross margin equal to the average gross margin on all of the products sold by the Devices division. The manager of the Systems division reacted by stating, "They could sell us that integrated circuit for $.20 and still earn a positive contribution toward profit. In fact, they should be required to sell at their variable cost and not be allowed to take advantage of us."

Lou Belcher, manager of Devices, countered by arguing, "It doesn't make sense to sell to the Systems division at $20 per hundred when we can get $40 per hundred outside on all we can produce. In fact, Systems could pay us up to almost $60 per hundred and they would still have a positive contribution to profit."

The recommendation of the committee—to set the price at $.35 per unit ($35 per hundred), so that Devices could earn a "fair" gross margin—was rejected by both divisional managers. Consequently, the problem was brought to the attention of the vice-president of operations and her staff.

Required □

1. What is the immediate economic effect on the Lorax Company as a whole if the Devices division were required to supply IC378 to the Systems division at $.35 per unit, which is the price recommended by the arbitration committee? Explain your answer.

2. Discuss the advisability of intervention by top-management personnel as a solution to transfer-pricing disputes between divisional managers.

3. Suppose that Lorax adopted a policy of requiring that the price to be paid in all internal transfers by the buying division would be equal to the variable costs per unit of the selling division for that product and that the supplying division would be required to sell if the buying division decided to buy the item. Discuss the consequences of adopting such a policy as a way of avoiding the need for the arbitration committee or for intervention by the vice-president.

(CMA)

CHAPTER OUTLINE

INTRODUCTION

THE PRODUCTIVITY PROBLEM

HOW PRODUCTIVITY IS MEASURED

PARTIAL PRODUCTIVITY MEASURES
USING ACTUAL- AND STANDARD-
LABOR HOURS

HOW MANAGEMENT PERSONNEL
USE PRODUCTIVITY INFORMATION

SUMMARY

KEY TERMS

QUESTIONS

PROBLEMS

PRODUCTIVITY MEASUREMENT AND COST ACCOUNTING

CHAPTER 19

☐ **INTRODUCTION**

The typical cost-accounting text does not include material on productivity or productivity measurement. Of course, the logical next question is, "Why include this chapter in this text?" You will recall that some of the objectives of the cost-managerial system are to provide management with information for decision making and performance measurement. The vast majority of this information is in terms of dollars and involves attaching costs to inputs and outputs.

One cannot read a current business periodical without encountering an article dealing with productivity. Concern is frequently expressed about productivity problems at the national level. Other literature concerns productivity at the industry, corporate, divisional, departmental, and on down to the individual-worker levels. Much research is currently being undertaken both in the public and private sectors to develop effective productivity measures at all levels within the economy. Many firms have or are in the process of introducing productivity-measurement systems and are incorporating these measures into their performance-measurement systems.

It certainly is not possible for any student to become an expert in productivity measurement after reading only one chapter of a text. However, it is possible to gain some insight into the **productivity problem** and to understand some of the basic concepts involved in measuring productivity. As the major provider of information to management, management accountants should be familiar with some basic concepts concerning productivity. That is the purpose of this chapter. In addition, the relationship between a productivity measurement and a standard-cost system will be demonstrated.

The opening section of this chapter contains a description of the productivity problem on a national level in the United States. Potential problems and possible implications from decreased productivity are also discussed. The concluding sections of the chapter contain a discussion and evaluation of various productivity measures and how management can use productivity information in decision making.

□ THE PRODUCTIVITY PROBLEM

Problems in the United States concerning productivity have become more evident in recent years. The data contained in table 19.1 reveals a trend in productivity at the national level that has been a source of concern for leaders in both business and government. The noticeable decline in annual productivity gains at the national level during the 1970s culminated with an absolute decline during 1980.

What are some of the general factors that contributed to this decline in productivity? One major factor is the growth of employment relative to growth of plant and equipment or capital. Table 19.2 contains the average annual growth rates in employment and capital. Note that since 1973 there has been a significant decrease in the average annual growth rate in capital while the growth rate in labor has remained relatively constant. Another way to view this situation is to consider the growth rate of the ratio of capital to labor. Table 19.3 contains the average annual growth rates of the **capital/labor ratio.** Once again a decline is observed. What this means is that business is increasingly substituting labor for capital. The decline in the capital/labor ratio has accompanied the decline in productivity.

Other factors also contribute to the decline in the growth rate of productivity. The tendency in the United States has been to consume rather than save. The percentage of disposable income that is saved in the United States is less than the rate in any other major industrial country. This

TABLE 19.1 National Manufacturing Productivity Gains

Time period	Average annual manufacturing productivity gains (%)
1947–1966	3.2
1959–1969	2.8
1969–1973	2.5
1973–1978	1.7
1979	1.0
1980	(0.5)
1981	1.9
1982	.2
1983	2.8

Source: U.S. Bureau of Labor Statistics

TABLE 19.2 Growth Rate in Employment and Capital

Time period	Average annual growth rate in employment (%)	Average annual growth rate in capital
1948–1965	1.2	2.3
1965–1973	2.2	3.0
1973–1979	2.3	1.3
1980	.6	1.0
1981	.8	1.0
1982	(1.7)	1.4
1983	.6	3.3

Source: U.S. Bureau of Labor Statistics

decline in the rate of savings results in higher interest rates, which discourages investment and contributes to the substitution of labor for capital. Inflation certainly contributes to decreased rates of savings and increases in consumption. Other factors that have contributed to decreased growth in productivity are decreased research and development expenditures and increases in government regulation.

What do these decreases in the rate of growth in productivity mean to individual citizens? Real per capita income is one measure of the standard of living within an economy. During the decade of the seventies, per capita income in real terms in the United States grew at an annual rate of 2.4 percent. If the trends in productivity during the later years of the 1970s continue, the United States Bureau of Labor Statistics estimates that the growth rate in real per capita income for the eighties will be 1.2 percent. They estimate the real per capita income will only increase from $6,476 in 1979 to $7,410 in 1990 if there isn't an increase in the rate of productivity growth.

At the corporate level, a relationship between productivity and income exists. Firms that do not remain competitive in the area of productivity will suffer from increased price competition and, as a result, decreased profits. At the national level, the United States will become less competitive in international markets if productivity growth does not remain competitive with the rate of growth of foreign competition.

☐ HOW PRODUCTIVITY IS MEASURED

Productivity is generally defined as the ratio of some measure of output to some measure of input over various time periods. The most common potential productivity measure used is *output per labor hour*. The primary use of a productivity measure is to monitor changes in the ratio over two or more time periods. The objective is to determine whether increasing or decreasing amounts of output are being realized for each unit of input consumed. This time dimension requires that the units employed in one period to calculate a productivity ratio be comparable to the units used in the calculations for prior periods.

TABLE 19.3 Growth Rates in Capital/Labor Ratios

Time period	Average annual growth rate capital / labor ratio (%)
1948–1965	1.9
1965–1973	1.4
1973–1978	(0.6)
1978–1979	(1.5)
1979–1980	1.0
1980–1981	1.0
1981–1982	1.1
1982–1983	1.0

Source: U.S. Bureau of Labor Statistics

The two distinct types of productivity ratios can be expressed as follows:

$$\text{Total productivity} = \frac{\text{Total output}}{\text{Total input}}$$

$$\text{Partial productivity} = \frac{\text{Total output}}{\text{Partial input}}$$

These ratios can employ dollar units or physical units. Generally, dollar units are employed in calculating a total productivity ratio, and physical units are employed in calculating a partial productivity ratio. Performance measures such as tons of coal mined per labor hour or bushels of corn produced per labor year are examples of how many people conceive of productivity.

A **total productivity ratio**[1] of a firm for time period T can be expressed as

$$P = \frac{O}{M + L + C + H} \times 100$$

where

P = Productivity ratio for period T

O = Output for period T

M = Raw material and purchased parts input for period T

L = Labor input for period T

C = Capital input for period T

H = Overhead input for period T

Outputs and inputs must be stated in a common unit, generally constant dollars. To make the productivity ratios comparable from period to period, all dollar values must be adjusted to a base-period value. Typically, the dollar figures are deflated to comparable values for the first year the ratio is produced. It is important that the base year be one that is representative in terms of activity and overall conditions. A year during a major recession or an oil embargo would not be satisfactory.

In measuring total productivity, output is the sum of the units produced multiplied by their respective selling prices. Units produced rather than units sold is used because productivity is a ratio of ability to convert inputs into outputs. To determine outputs in base-year dollars, base-year selling prices can be employed.

New products and quality changes can present difficulties. If a product line changes significantly, it might be appropriate to establish a new base year. Additionally, an index may need to be developed to account for quality changes.

---

1. The total productivity model was developed by Charley E. Craig and R. Clark Harris and was published in the *Sloan Management Review* (Spring 1973):13–29.

Dividends received on capital stock owned and interest income should be included in the output for the period. Both labor and capital inputs are used to produce outputs such as dividends and interest. Extraordinary gains and losses should not be included in the output unless some input was consumed in producing them.

Raw-materials and purchased-parts inputs for period T are determined by multiplying the quantities consumed in the production process by the base-year prices. The labor input for period T is determined by multiplying the labor hours worked by the wage rates in the base period. Overhead input includes the costs of all resources employed except materials, labor, and capital.

The measurement of capital inputs presents the most difficult measurement problem. A simplified approach is to use depreciation expense as a measure of the capital input. Another approach is to use the weighted-average cost of capital and determine the sum of the annuity values for each asset using the base-year cost and an estimate of the productive life. These measurement problems, especially for the inputs, limit the use of total-productivity measures.

The **partial productivity ratio** is defined as the ratio of some measure of output to some partial measure of input. Output per labor hour is an example of a partial productivity measure because direct-labor hours are the only input considered. The major advantage of using partial-productivity measures is that measurement problems with the capital and overhead inputs are avoided.

However, problems can develop when partial productivity measures are used and one input is substituted for another. For example, an electric utility might use kilowatt hours of electricity generated per ton of coal consumed as a partial productivity measure. Kilowatt hours generated might increase because a higher quality of coal is purchased (more BTUs per ton). Therefore, the productivity index would indicate an increase when, in fact, the increased output might be more than offset by the increased cost of the coal. Although the partial productivity index has increased, the use of the higher-grade coal cannot economically be justified.

A similar situation could develop if the partial input is labor hours. A higher-quality raw material might result in a reduction of the hours required to produce the output. In this case, if a partial productivity measure is used, management might believe that productivity has increased when, in fact, the increased output is more than offset by the increased cost of the raw materials. These limitations must be considered whenever a partial productivity index is employed.

Now we will develop an extended example using actual- and standard-labor hours as the input for a partial productivity index.

□ PARTIAL PRODUCTIVITY MEASURES USING ACTUAL- AND STANDARD-LABOR HOURS

In this section, we will demonstrate methods for calculating productivity changes that use both actual direct-labor hours and standard hours to

TABLE 19.4 Simple Example

	Base period			Period T		
Product	Labor hours per unit	Units made	Total hours	Units made	Actual hours	Current units times base-period hours
A	5	4	20	8		5 × 8 = 40
B	10	2	20	3		10 × 3 = 30
C	4	5	20	2		4 × 2 = 8
Total			60		70	78

Index of output = (78 ÷ 60) × 100 = 130%
Index of labor hours = (70 ÷ 60) × 100 = 116.67%
Index of output per labor hour = (130% ÷ 116.67%) × 100 = 111.42%
Productivity gain = (111.42% − 100%) = 11.42%

estimate a measure of output.[2] The illustrations used will progress from the fairly simple to those that are somewhat more realistic and complex. Throughout these illustrations, the key objective is to devise a measure of productivity that links several time periods in terms of a common or base unit of measure. You should keep in mind that the methods demonstrated in this chapter are not the only methods for measuring productivity using standard costs. For example, material inputs could be used in developing a partial productivity index.

Table 19.4 contains an illustration showing how output is measured for two periods using a common, or base, unit of measure. Output is expressed here in terms of the total labor hours required to produce the actual output. Thus, in the base period, "output" is 60 hours (i.e., $(5 \times 4) + (10 \times 2) + (4 \times 5) = 60$). To maintain a common unit of measure over both periods, output in period T is calculated by using the hours that would have been required to produce the output in the base period. Thus, period T output is 78 hours (i.e., $(5 \times 8) + (10 \times 3) + (4 \times 2) = 78$). In standard-cost terminology, the per-unit labor hours in the base period are the standard hours. The 78 hours in period T represent the total standard hours for the actual output in time period T.

To determine any increase or decrease in productivity, several manipulations are required. Initially, an index of output is determined by dividing the total standard hours for time period T by the total standard hours for the base period and multiplying by one hundred. In one example, the index of output equals

$$\frac{78}{60} \times 100 = 130 \text{ percent}$$

An index of labor hours is determined by dividing the actual hours in time period T by the total standard hours for the base period and multiplying by one hundred. In our example, the index of labor hours equals

2. This section is based on a paper by Robert M. Brown and Kent F. Murrmann entitled "Productivity Management in Manufacturing Firms," published in *Cost and Management* (January–February 1984):25–29.

$$\frac{70}{60} \times 100 = 116.67 \text{ percent}$$

Now, an index of output per labor hour is determined by dividing the index of output by the index of hours and multiplying by one hundred. In this example, the index of output per labor hour equals

$$\frac{130 \text{ percent}}{116.67 \text{ percent}} \times 100 = 111.42 \text{ percent}$$

Since the productivity index in the base period is one hundred in the example, an 11.42 percent gain in productivity has been realized. This is determined by subtracting the index of output per labor hour from the base period index. In our example, the increase in productivity is calculated as follows

$$111.42 \text{ percent} - 100 \text{ percent} = 11.42 \text{ percent}$$

The basic procedure for calculating changes in productivity will be employed in the examples in the remainder of the chapter. The base period labor standard will be used as the basis for measuring productivity changes in future periods.

Few, if any, firms have a product line that is perfectly stable. Table 19.5 contains an example of a company that adds a new product to its line. Here one would use the same procedure, expressing output in terms of base-period hours, to maintain a common unit of measure. In addition, since product D was not produced in the base period, one would extrapolate back to estimate the hours it would have taken had product D been produced in the base period. This procedure assumes that if product D had been produced in the base period, then the average ratio of produc-

TABLE 19.5 Simple Example—New Product

Product	Base period			Period T		
	Labor hours per unit	Units made	Total hours	Units made	Actual hours	Current units times base-period hours
A	5	4	20	2	9	5 × 2 = 10
B	10	2	20	4	30	10 × 4 = 40
C	4	5	20	5	11	4 × 5 = 20
D	5.6*	0	__	10	40	5.6 × 10 = 56
Total			60		90	126

*Estimated by $(70 \div 50) \times 4 = 5.6$.

Index of outputs = $(126 \div 60) \times 100 = 210\%$
Index of labor hours = $(90 \div 60) \times 100 = 150\%$
Index of output per labor hour = $(210\% \div 150\%) \times 100 = 140\%$
Productivity gain = $(140\% - 100\%) = 40\%$

Note: 50 = Actual hours to produce A, B, and C in period T (i.e., 9 + 30 + 11);
     70 = Period T output of A, B, and C in base-period hours
        (i.e., 10 + 40 + 20);
     4 = 40 hours ÷ 10 units of D in period T.

TABLE 19.6 Linking Procedure

Period 1

Product	Labor hours per unit	Units made	Total hours	Total* hours based on period 2
A	4.0	30	120	105
B	3.0	40	120	120
Total			240	225

Period 2

Product	Labor hours per unit	Units made	Total hours	Total* hours based on period 3
A	3.5	20	70	64
B	3.0	20	60	60
C	4.5	20	90	72
Total			220	196

Period 3

Product	Labor hours per unit	Units made	Total hours
A	3.2	20	64
B	3.0	0	—
C	3.6	40	144
D	5.0	10	50
			258

Productivity from

Period 1
  to
    Period 2

Output—$(220 \div 225) \times 100 = 97.78\%$
Labor hours—$(220 \div 240) \times 100 = 91.67\%$
Output per labor hour—$(97.78\% \div 91.67\%) \times 100 = 106.67\%$
Productivity gain $= (106.67\% - 100\%) = 6.67\%$

Period 1
  to
    Period 3

Output—$(97.78\% \times 131.63\%) \div 100 = 128.71\%$
Labor hours—$(91.67\% \times 117.27\%) \div 100 = 107.50\%$
Output per labor hour—$(106.67\% \times 112.25\%) \div 100 = 119.74\%$
Productivity gain $= (119.74\% - 100\%) = 19.74\%$

Period 2
  to
    Period 3

Output—$(258 \div 196) \times 100 = 131.63\%$
Labor hours—$(258 \div 220) \times 100 = 117.27\%$
Output per labor hour—$(131.63\% \div 117.27\%) \times 100 = 112.25\%$
Productivity gain $= (112.25\% - 100\%) = 12.25\%$

*Calculated by multiplying the number of units made in period i by the hours required to make those products in period i + 1.

tivity growth would have been realized on the product between the base period and period T. This procedure is outlined at the bottom of table 19.5.

The procedures demonstrated in tables 19.4 and 19.5 would work only in relatively simple situations. In manufacturing concerns with changing product lines, more complex and realistic procedures must be used. For instance, if products change but retain substantial common elements, the measurement system could be set up to retain the major common elements from one period to the next and treat the "embellishments" as new products. However, a better approach uses linkage to compare products and trace productivity from one period to the next. This technique is illustrated in table 19.6.

Table 19.6 depicts a situation in which products are added and deleted from time period to time period. The basic premise is that product changes do not occur with great frequency between adjacent time periods. For example, from time period 1 (the base period) to time period 2, only one product is changed; from time period 2 to time period 3, two product changes occur. However, if the period 1 to period 3 time frame is examined, then only one product is in common. Therefore, to determine productivity changes over this period, the indices of adjacent time periods should be used. The indices for output, labor hours of input, and productivity are calculated at the bottom of table 19.6.

In this illustration, the base hours used for calculating output are those established in the current year rather than the prior year, which was the case in tables 19.4 and 19.5. Either approach may be used as long as it is applied consistently.

Let us incorporate some features of a standard-cost system into the partial productivity measure. In table 19.7, one product with an initial standard time of one hour is manufactured. If the efficiency ratio is the only index monitored, then it would appear that the decision to purchase the new machine in time period 4 was a bad decision as the efficiency rate (col. 6) went from 111 down to 90. Only by looking at the productivity index of 114 is the decision placed in proper perspective. Ths index (col. 9) tells us that from period 1 to period 4 a productivity gain of 14 percent was achieved. Furthermore, a productivity gain of 8.44 percent was experienced from period 3, a very efficient period, to period 4, which was

TABLE 19.7 Efficiency Ratio versus the Productivity Index

(1)	(2)	(3)	(4) (2) × (3) Standard hours allowed	(5)	(6) Efficiency ratio (4 ÷ 5)*100	(7) Output base-period units	(8) Productivity ratio (7 ÷ 5)*100	(9) Productivity index (8) ÷ 105.26 (Base period)
Time period	Standard time unit	Units made		Actual hours				
1	1 hr	200	200	190	105	200	105.26	100
2	1 hr	210	210	205	102	210	102.44	97.32
3	1 hr	250	250	225	111	250	111.11	105.56
4*	.75 hr	300	225	250	90	300	120.00	114.00
5	.75 hr	300	225	225	100	300	133.33	126.67

*Purchased a new machine

an inefficient period. Without productivity measures, these subtleties could very easily be overlooked.

The example in table 19.7 deals with only one product, and as previously stated, is not realistic. The example in table 19.6 shows how to calculate productivity changes in the more likely situation in which multiple products are produced and products are added and deleted from the product line. However, this example is also somewhat limited. For instance, in the situation in which none of the goods produced in period $T+1$ were produced in period T, productivity calculations depend on the use of engineered labor standards to provide a common unit of measure from period to period. This is illustrated in tables 19.8, 19.9, and 19.10, which combine the features of a standard-cost system introduced in table 19.7, with the more complex manufacturing environment demonstrated in table 19.6, which showed production figures for four time periods. Table 19.9 shows how to calculate productivity changes between adjacent time periods based on the data in table 19.8. Table 19.10 contains an illustration of how to calculate productivity changes over the several time periods that previously were calculated in table 19.9.

With respect to table 19.8, note in particular that product D is produced only in periods 2 and 4. Also, observe that the standard hours required to make product D decrease from period 2 to period 4. Under these circumstances, the method for calculating productivity demonstrated in table 19.6 must be changed. In table 19.6, actual production times in period $T+1$ are used to determine output in period T. In table 19.9, the standard hours used in period T are used to calculate the output in period $T+1$. If a product manufactured in period $T+1$ was not manufactured in period

TABLE 19.8 Production Report

Period	Product	Current standard hours	Previous standard hours	Units made	Allowed hours— current standards	Allowed hours— previous standards	Actual hours
1	A	4.0	4.0	30	120	120	125
(Base period)	B	3.0	3.0	40	120	120	119
	Total for period			70	240	240	244
2	A	3.5	4.0	20	70	80	65
	B	3.0	3.0	20	60	60	60
	C	4.0	4.0	10	40	40	42
	D	5.0	5.0	4	20	20	18
	Total for period			54	190	200	185
3	A	3.5	3.5	30	105	105	100
	B	3.0	3.0	30	90	90	85
	C	4.0	4.0	20	80	80	82
	Total for period			80	275	275	267
4	A	3.5	3.5	30	105	105	105
	C	4.0	4.0	25	100	100	85
	D	4.0	5.0	10	40	50	42
	Total for period			65	245	255	232

TABLE 19.9 Productivity—Adjacent Periods

	Output* of current period		Output Index Output of previous period				Index of output (%)
1 to 2	(200	÷	240)	×	100	=	83.33
2 to 3	(275	÷	190)	×	100	=	144.74
3 to 4	(255	÷	275)	×	100	=	92.73

	Input of current period		Input Index Input of previous period				Index of input (%)
1 to 2	(185	÷	244)	×	100	=	75.82
2 to 3	(267	÷	185)	×	100	=	144.32
3 to 4	(232	÷	267)	×	100	=	86.89

Productivity Index

	Output index		Input index		Index of output per input unit (%)	Productivity gain (%) (Loss)
1 to 2	(83.33%	÷	75.82%)		109.91	9.91
2 to 3	(144.74%	÷	144.32%)	× 100 =	100.29	0.29
3 to 4	(92.73%	÷	86.89%)	× 100 =	106.72	6.72

*Current output is determined by using the most recent past time standard. If a product is a new product, the current period's standard is used.

TABLE 19.10 Productivity Change Over Several Time Periods Illustrated

	Change from period 1 to period 3 Index 1 to 2		Index 2 to 3				
Output	(83.33%	×	144.74%)	÷	100	=	120.61%
Input	(75.82%	×	144.32%)	÷	100	=	109.42%
Productivity	(109.91%	×	100.29%)	÷	100	=	110.23%

	Change from period 1 to period 4 Index 1 to 3		Index 3 to 4				
Output	(120.61%	×	92.73%)	÷	100	=	111.84%
Input	(109.42%	×	86.89%)	÷	100	=	95.08%
Productivity	(110.23%	×	106.72%)	÷	100	=	117.64%

T, but was manufactured in some previous period, then the standard used in that previous period is used to determine output in period $T+1$. Without this modification, the manufacturing change that allowed the standard time for making a unit of D to change from five to four hours would not be reflected in the productivity indices when a productivity gain obviously took place.

In this section, a method for incorporating productivity measurement into a standard-cost system has been presented. Individual circumstances may dictate that alternate methods be developed. However, the fact that there is increasing competition and emphasis upon productivity would seem to indicate that productivity measures derived from a standard-cost system will become more widely used.

☐ HOW MANAGEMENT PERSONNEL USE PRODUCTIVITY INFORMATION

The major advantage of productivity data is that it is based on constant units. Therefore, the impact of inflation, changing costs, and changing selling prices has been eliminated from the productivity ratio since every unit is expressed in terms of the base period. Hence, management officials can evaluate any trends in the productivity ratios over time. In addition, comparisons can be made between operating units of the same firm. When this is attempted, and a partial productivity ratio has been employed, the relative quality of the inputs must be considered.

Comparisons between firm and industry productivity measures can also be used in evaluating performance. Trade organizations and government agencies publish industry productivity ratios. Care must be taken to assure that the industry and firm ratios have been calculated on the same basis before detailed comparisons are made.

Because productivity ratios are frequently expressed in terms of trend lines, computer graphics are often employed in presenting productivity information to management personnel. Then, not only do key decision makers have the raw data available for analysis, but they also can observe the trends in any partial productivity ratios. Modern computer graphics systems in color make effective presentations of productivity trends possible.

☐ SUMMARY

Productivity is a ratio of some measure of output to some measure of input. Total productivity is the ratio of total output to total input. When measuring total productivity, dollar units are employed. The inputs consist of materials, labor, capital, and overhead.

Partial productivity is the ratio of total output to some partial measure of input. Generally, physical units are employed in determining a partial productivity measure. Labor hours are the most commonly used partial-input measure. In this chapter, several examples were developed using actual- and standard-labor hours to determine a partial productivity measure.

Productivity on a national level in the United States has been decreasing. Several reasons are given for the decline of productivity. Among these factors is the increased use of labor instead of capital. The tendency in the United States to consume rather than save contributes to the decrease in capital investment. Growth in real per capita income is highly correlated with increases in productivity rates. As the rate of growth in productivity growth has decreased, so has the rate of growth in per capita income. This productivity problem has received attention at both the national and corporate levels.

Management personnel are becoming more involved in developing productivity indices at various levels within a firm. Management accountants are becoming involved in productivity measurement, and the purpose of this chapter was to introduce the topic.

We demonstrated a partial productivity measurement system based on standard-labor hours. Similar systems could be developed using standard raw-material input measures. Much of the data required to develop productivity measures exists in a standard-costing system. Where both systems exist, linkages between the data bases will result in decreased costs for data processing.

KEY TERMS

Capital/labor ratio   **Productivity problem**
Partial productivity ratio   **Total productivity ratio**
Productivity

QUESTIONS

Q19-1. In general terms, what is the "productivity problem"? What are some factors that contribute to the problem?

Q19-2. Why would a management accountant be concerned with the measurement of productivity?

Q19-3. How is the growth rate of capital related to productivity?

Q19-4. How is the growth rate of the capital/labor ratio related to productivity?

Q19-5. In general terms, how is productivity measured? What are the differences between total and partial productivity measures? What are the advantages and disadvantages of total and partial productivity measures?

Q19-6. What problems are encountered in measuring capital inputs when measuring productivity?

Q19-7. Why are units produced rather than units sold used when measuring outputs?

Q19-8. What problems are encountered when measuring outputs?

Q19-9. Describe how the data base from a standard-costing system can be used in measuring productivity.

Q19-10. What are some procedures that can be used in measuring outputs when a firm has changes in its product lines?

Q19-11. In productivity measurement, explain why the concept of a base period is important.

Q19-12. If an economy is shifting from manufacturing to service, in general what can be expected to happen to productivity at the national level?

Q19-13. How is the rate of saving related to productivity growth in a country?

Q19-14. How is real per capita income related to productivity growth in a country?

Q19-15. How is profitability of a company related to its productivity rate?

PROBLEMS

Basic   **P19-1.**
Productivity
Calculations

	Base period			Period T		
Product	Labor hours per unit	Units made	Total hours	Units made	Actual hours	Current units times base-period hours
S	8	10	80	10		80
D	1	10	10	20		20
F	60	6	360	4		240
			450		395	340

Required ☐ Compute the index of output, the index of labor hours, the index of output per labor hour, and the productivity gain or loss. Show your computations.

Calculating   **P19-2.** The LNK Corporation added a new product in period *T* and the following
Productivity with   data relate to both period *T* and the base period.
New Product

	Base period			Period T		
Product	Labor- hours per unit	Units made	Total hours	Units made	Actual hours	Current units times base-period hours
X	6	5	30	6	34	36
Y	14	2	28	3	32	42
Z	3	10	30	15	31	45
Q	A	0	—	4	44	B
			88		141	C

Required ☐ Fill in the letters in the above chart, and compute the index of outputs, the index of labor hours, the index of output per labor hour, and the productivity gain or loss. Support your answers.

Calculating   **P19-3.** The following data are for three production periods at the K & L Corpo-
Productivity over   ration:
Three Periods

Period 1

Product	Labor hours per unit	Units made	Total hours	Total hours based on period 2 times
M	5	15	75	75
I	3	10	30	20
			105	95

Period 2

Product	Labor hours per unit	Units made	Total hours	Total hours based on period 3 times
M	5	15	75	75
I	2	7	14	21
K	6	12	72	72
			161	168

		Period 3	
Product	Labor hours per unit	Units made	Total hours
M	5	—	—
I	3	12	36
K	6	10	60
E	10	10	100
			196

Required ☐ Use the linking procedure to compute the output, labor hours, output per labor hour, and productivity gain or loss for periods 1 to 3. Show all supporting computations.

P19-4. The following data are from four production periods for the K & L Corporation.

Calculating Productivity over Four Periods

Production Report

Period	Product	Current standard hours	Previous standard hours	Units made	Allowed hours—current standards	Allowed hours—previous standards	Actual hours
1	L	5	5	20	100	100	105
	C	3	3	10	30	30	29
	D	4	4	5	20	20	24
				35	150	150	158
2	L	4	5	20	80	100	75
	D	4	4	15	60	60	60
	M	6	6	12	72	72	76
	F	3	3	10	30	30	24
				57	242	262	235
3	C	3	3	30	90	90	87
	D	4	4	14	56	56	56
	M	5	6	20	100	120	140
	F	4	3	8	32	24	26
				72	278	290	309
4	C	5	3	23	115	69	100
	D	4	4	20	80	80	80
	M	6	5	15	90	75	110
	F	4	4	10	40	40	36
				68	325	264	326

Required ☐ Using the above information, compute the output, input, and productivity indices for periods 1 to 2, 2 to 3, and 3 to 4. Then, use that information to compute the same indexes for periods 1 to 3 and 1 to 4. Show *all* computations.

P19-5. The following data are for four production periods at the D&G Corporation:

Calculating Productivity over Four Periods and Use of Computer Graphics

Period	Product	Current standard hours per unit	Units made	Actual hours used
1	A	5.00	200	1,050
	C	3.00	60	200
	M	4.00	75	250

2	A	5.50	210	1,000
	M	4.50	85	400
	N	6.00	100	500
	P	8.00	50	300
3	C	3.00	180	600
	M	4.00	120	400
	P	8.50	88	700
	R	7.00	40	300
4	A	6.00	190	1,050
	M	5.00	150	700
	P	9.00	70	700
	R	7.00	20	180
	S	4.00	35	160

Required ☐

1. Using the above information,

    a. Compute the output, input, and productivity indices for the four periods.
    b. Graph the results to show the trend in productivity.

2. Briefly identify and discuss the limitations of your productivity measurements.

3. What alternative productivity-measurement approach would you recommend for D&G?

Calculating Productivity over Four Periods and Use of Computer Graphics

P19-6. The following data are from the production records of M&C, Inc.:

Period 1

Products	Labor hours per unit	Units made	Total hours
A	8.50	15	128
B	10.00	25	250
C	12.50	50	625
			1,003

Period 2

Products		Units made	Total hours
A		17	125
B		24	228
C		54	620
			973

Period 3

Products		Units made	Total hours
A		20	140
B		30	290
C		560	660
			1,090

Period 4

Products		Units made	Total hours
A		10	130
B		45	465
C		75	915
			1,510

M&C, Inc., is a small corporation that produces three products at a labor-intensive plant. According to the production manager, period 1 has been the only "normal" production period the plant has had over the past four periods. Toward the end of period 3, a major accident occurred in the area where product A is assembled. As a result, the company decided to increase production of product B and C. The plant manager now needs to investigate the impact of the recent problems on labor productivity.

Required □ Using graphs and appropriate tables, briefly discuss the trend in productivity over the past four periods.

P19-7. At State University, faculty teaching productivity is evaluated by determining departmental average-weighted student credit hours per faculty member. All courses are three hours, and the weights assigned for lower-division undergraduate (freshman and sophomore), upper-division undergraduate (junior and senior), and graduate courses are 1.0, 1.2, and 1.5, respectively. For example, if 30 students were in a junior-level course, the weighted student credit hours for the course are $30 \times 3 \times 1.2 = 108$. The average-weighted student credit hours per faculty member for a department are determined by dividing the total weighted student credit hours for the department by the number of faculty members.

Productivity-Measurement Concepts

Required □

1. What type of productivity measure is average-weighted student credit hours per faculty member?

2. What are some factors that might explain some significant differences among the average-weighted student credit hours per faculty member for various departments at a university?

3. How could this productivity measure be manipulated by department administrators?

P19-8. The presidents of two large department store chains were discussing the methods they employ for evaluating the performance of individual stores. Mr. Jones indicated that his firm uses sales-per-square-foot as the basis for evaluating the performance of each store. He believes that this simple ratio between sales in a store and the square footage of the store is understandable, and a major advantage is that no allocations are involved. Jones believes that this is a good measure of the productivity of management personnel and his firm's investment in the store.

Productivity-Measurement Problems

Ms. Smith states that her firm uses return-on-investment as a basis for measuring performance. This is the ratio between the net income generated by the store over the total assets employed by the store. She believes that this method is superior because it considers profits and that is the basis upon which the firm is evaluated.

Required □

1. What type of productivity measure is Mr. Jones describing?

2. What potential problems exist with the productivity measure used by Mr. Jones?

3. Can return-on-investment be considered a productivity measure? Explain.

4. What, if any, measurement problems will be encountered if return-on-investment is used as a productivity measure over an extended number of periods?

Productivity- **P19-9.** A productivity measure that is used in banks is assets-per-employee. The
Measurement   ratio is determined by dividing the total assets of the bank by the number
Concepts   of employees. Assume two banks: the first has $20 billion in assets and
7,000 employees, and the second has $5 billion in assets and 12,000 employees.

Required □

1. What type of productivity measure is assets-per-employee?

2. Compute the assets-per-employee for each of the banks. What factors might contribute to the significant difference in the ratios of the two banks?

3. Discuss how the productivity measure assets-per-employee might be used through time by each bank to evaluate its productivity. Also, discuss problems that may be encountered in using this productivity measure in comparing the banks.

Productivity **P19-10.** Miller Products Company is a medium-sized manufacturer of durable goods.
Concepts   Nearly half of the company's costs are associated with the wages and
employee benefits of its labor force. Miller Products is one of fifteen firms
in its industry, all with similar labor-intensive production methods.

Industry wages and benefits are set in industry-wide bargaining with a
labor union. The settlements have led to rapidly escalating labor costs for
several years. The current contract continues the 10 percent increase for
wages and benefits for each of the next two years. Because of the industry-
wide bargaining, all competitors face similar labor-cost problems.

However, labor-productivity advances have varied within the industry. The
productivity increase at the Miller Products Company, which has averaged
1 percent per year over the past five years, is much lower than the average
3 percent advance in the industry. The company's management team is
distressed about the increased labor cost and lower relative increase in
productivity and is attempting to evaluate the effect on company costs,
profitability, and position within the industry.

Required □

1. Discuss the interrelationships among labor costs, productivity, and cost
of production. Specifically, define the marginal productivity of labor
and marginal cost of production as a part of your discussion.

2. Explain the impact the lower relative increase in productivity is likely
to have on Miller Products'

   a. Costs
   b. Profitability
   c. Position within the industry

Use economic arguments to support your conclusions.

3. Identify alternative actions the management team of Miller Products Company could undertake to correct its dilemma of increased labor costs and lower relative increase in productivity. Explain how the actions you identify would affect the results of company operations.

(CMA)

PART OUTLINE

PART V

QUANTITATIVE MODELS FOR COST AND PROJECT ANALYSIS

CHAPTER OUTLINE

THE USE OF COSTS IN INVENTORY DECISIONS

CHAPTER **20**

☐ INTRODUCTION

Because the alternative is more costly, a business should hold inventory. Factors that contribute to making it a necessity to hold inventory can be related to the reasons individuals and firms maintain cash balances.[1] The expected demand for a product most likely requires a minimum inventory level (the transaction motive). Any uncertainty associated with the expected demand would influence the amount of inventory held (the precautionary motive). Finally, in times of accelerated price changes, a business may elect to speculate by accumulating inventories (the speculative motive).

In 1915, F. W. Harris developed the economic-order-quantity (EOQ) model.[2] The objective of the equation was to minimize the total of the carrying and ordering costs in situations where the demand was known and constant.[3] By incorporating factors such as probabilistic demand, lead time, and stockouts, inventory models have undergone extensive development since World War II.

The objective of this chapter is to introduce two groups of inventory models. In the first group, the demand is assumed to be known and constant. In the second group, it is assumed that only one order can be placed and that the probability distribution of the demand is known. Emphasis will be placed upon identifying the necessary properties of an inventory system so that an analytic-decision model can be formulated. Solutions to the models will be derived so that cost-accounting problems resulting from employing formal inventory models can be considered.

---

1. First suggested by K. Arrow in K. Arrow, S. Karlin, and H. Scarf, *Studies in Mathematical Theory of Inventory and Production* (Stanford, Cal.: Stanford University Press, 1959), chapters 2 and 3.

2. F. W. Harris, *Operations and Cost,* Factory Management Series (Chicago: A. W. Shaw Co., 1915).

3. For example, refer to: R. H. Wilson and W. A. Mueller, *Harvard Business Review* 5, no. 2 (1926–27):197–205; R. H. Wilson, *Harvard Business Review* 13, no. 1 (1929):116–28.

The relationships between cost assumptions and the resulting inventory policies will be demonstrated. This will aid in understanding how decisions that minimize the total cost of an inventory system might be altered if the cost assumptions were modified. Keep in mind that the decision to acquire and hold inventory is not independent of investment considerations such as other investment alternatives and the cash position of the firm. However, these factors are not considered in this chapter.

The following notation will be adopted:

q = Order quantity

q^* = Optimal order quantity

T_c = Total system cost per period[4]

D = Demand rate in units per period

N = Number of orders per period

t = Time between orders

R = Replenishment rate in units per period

$\bar{I}$ = Average inventory during a period

T = Lead time expressed as a fractional part of a period

L = Procurement level

m = Maximum inventory

C_o = Cost of ordering per order

C_c = Carrying cost per unit per period

C_s = Stockout cost per unit per period

C_p = Item purchase cost per unit

☐ THE ABC METHOD

The material presented in this chapter describes some rather sophisticated techniques employed in making inventory-related decisions. Complex manufacturing and retailing firms maintain inventories of hundreds or even thousands of items. Thus, it is unrealistic to assume that the same techniques are applied in making decisions relating to all the items held in inventory. In practice, many companies divide the items held in inventory into subclassifications for control purposes. These classifications may be based on the cost or profitability of items held in inventory.

The classifications are often referred to as A, B, and C. The greatest degree of control would be exercised over those items in the A classification either because they represent the greatest percentage of the total cost or because they are the most profitable items held in the inventory. A per-

4. In the examples developed in this chapter, a period will be considered as a calendar year. It should be kept in mind that any length of time could be employed.

petual-inventory record system is probably appropriate for items in the A classification, and the techniques suggested in this chapter would most likely be employed for determining order or procurement levels and safety stocks. When the order level is reached, a purchase order is placed to replenish the inventory. Safety stock is inventory that is carried for the purpose of avoiding a stockout between the time a purchase order is placed and the time the inventory is received.

Items in the C classification that represent less costly or less profitable items might be controlled by a two-bin system. In this case, two storage bins are kept; and after the first bin is emptied, a withdrawal from the second bin triggers a purchase order. Another example of this type of system involves painting a line in the storage bin at the procurement level. When the level of the stock falls below the line, a purchase order is placed. Placing some stock in a plastic bag and then placing the purchase order when the bag is opened is another system sometimes employed. Generally, high-safety stocks are maintained for class C items since they do not represent a large investment.

Items falling into the B classification are subjected to some combination of the techniques described for those items in the A and C classifications.

The ABC method is demonstrated in the following example. For the sake of simplicity, assume a firm carries ten items in inventory. The estimated yearly demand and unit costs are shown in table 20.1, which has the units arranged according to their respective unit costs. The highest cost items are listed first and the lowest unit cost items last. Percentages of the total for the units and costs are determined as shown in table 20.1. Then, these percentages are graphed as shown in figure 20.1.

Investment in inventory is the criterion employed to direct the attention of management personnel to important items in the inventory. The arbitrary classification scheme developed in this example is

■ 16.67 percent of items contain 78.56 percent of cost class A items.

■ 60.00 percent of items contain 19.79 percent of cost class B items.

■ 23.33 percent of items contain 1.65 percent of cost class C items.

TABLE 20.1 ABC Classification Scheme

	Item	Number of units required for year	Percent of total		Unit cost	Total cost	Percent of total	
A	1	12,000	4	16.67	$30	$360,000	37.21	78.56
	2	8,000	2.67		20	160,000	16.54	
	3	30,000	10		8	240,000	24.81	
B	4	15,000	5	60	1.60	24,000	2.48	19.79
	5	25,000	8.33		1.50	37,500	3.88	
	6	100,000	33.34		1.00	100,000	10.33	
	7	40,000	13.33		.75	30,000	3.10	
C	8	6,000	2	23.33	.50	3,000	.31	1.65
	9	4,000	1.33		.25	1,000	.10	
	10	60,000	20		.20	12,000	1.24	
Totals		300,000	100.00			$967,500	100.00	

FIGURE 20.1
Inventory Usage
and Total Cost
(Cumulative
Percentages)

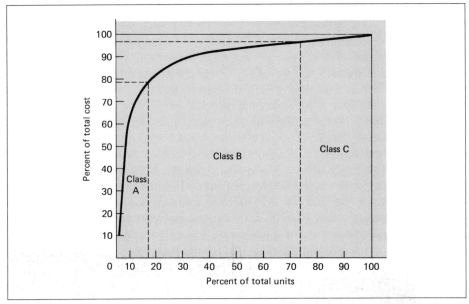

In the example, 16.67 percent of the items contain 78.56 percent of the total inventory cost. The greatest control effort will be directed toward these items. Economic-order-quantity models, which will be subject to frequent review, will be employed for these items. Generally, it will be expected that these items will have high turnover rates and low safety-stock levels. Additionally, one expects that frequent orders will be placed. Inventory records relating to the class A items will be very complete.

At the other extreme, the low-value (class C) items will not require complete inventory records, and inventory turnover will be low. The amount of safety stock will be high, and few orders will be placed each year. Economic-order-quantity models may be used, but most likely a two-bin system will be employed. Also, the inventory system will not be subjected to frequent review. Inventory procedures associated with the class B items will be a combination of those procedures for the class A and C categories.

There are no decision rules that are used to classify the items. The analyst merely looks for break points in the percentage of total cost that in some way correspond with the percentage of the total units. In our example, it might be considered desirable to classify item six in the A category because of its relatively high (10.33%) percentage of the total cost. Such decisions are made based on the particular characteristics of the inventory system.

☐ INVENTORY COSTS

When referring to inventory models, we will use the term cost in a broader sense than it is normally used throughout this book. Cost is the common measure of performance used in evaluating inventory systems. The cost of ordering, the cost of carrying inventory, and the cost of stockout are the significant inventory costs. An inventory decision model is employed for the purpose of minimizing at least two, or if possible all three, of these costs. Such costs are not found directly in a chart of accounts. For example, a stockout cost may include a penalty that results from losing a customer. In this section, those factors that would be considered in determining costs for an inventory system will be described.

Ordering Costs

Ordering costs are those associated with placing an order with a vendor. The costs of maintaining an ordering system (staff, supplies, order-processing equipment) are one aspect of ordering costs. Additional ordering costs would be incurred when inventory is received and inspected. The payment for purchases would complete the order cycle and any costs associated with this activity would also be included in the ordering costs. In a production system, ordering costs are referred to as setup costs and include machine setup and other production line start-up costs.

Carrying Costs

Carrying costs of inventory can be classified into two categories: (1) any costs associated with the physical presence of the goods and (2) the cost of capital invested in the inventory. Costs associated with the physical presence of goods would include such items as warehousing, insurance, taxes, breakage, obsolescence, and handling. It should be noted that some of these costs include both fixed and variable components. The cost of the money tied up in the inventory would include financing costs. Opportunity costs may be considered if an investment opportunity exists that is better than the investment in the inventory. In practice, carrying costs are often estimated as a percentage of the purchase price.

Stockout Costs

Stockout costs are incurred when the demand for an item exceeds the supply. Factors considered when determining stockout costs are loss of a sale, loss of goodwill, and the additional administrative effort required to process a back order. Direct measures of stockout costs are difficult to estimate. In practice, a stockout cost is often implied and related to a given service level. Management would then select a particular service level at which they would prefer to operate.

☐ THE EOQ MODEL

Perhaps the most common inventory problem encountered in business is that of deciding order quantities for staple items. Such items are considered staple in the sense that they are carried for a significant period of time and their demand rate tends to be constant. Under these circumstances, management wishes to adopt an inventory policy that seeks to minimize the total of the inventory ordering and carrying costs. The **economic-order-quantity (EOQ)** model determines the order size that minimizes the total annual cost of ordering and carrying inventory.

Concepts of Average Inventory and Number of Orders

Consider a case in which the demand rate for a product is uniform and totals 12,000 units for the year. Let D equal the total demand for the year, and also assume the order quantity, q, is 12,000 units. Therefore, only one order would be placed during the year. As illustrated in figure 20.2, the maximum inventory level is q, and it diminishes at a uniform rate until it reaches zero. The average inventory carried during the year is 6,000 units, or $q/2$.

The same system is depicted in figure 20.3, but now the order quantity, q, has been changed to 4,000 units. Three orders are necessary during the year, and the average inventory during the year is 2,000 units or $q/2$. From these two examples, we shall generalize to express the average inventory, $\bar{I}$, and number of orders, N, as

$$\bar{I} = \frac{q}{2} \tag{20-1}$$

$$N = \frac{D}{q} \tag{20-2}$$

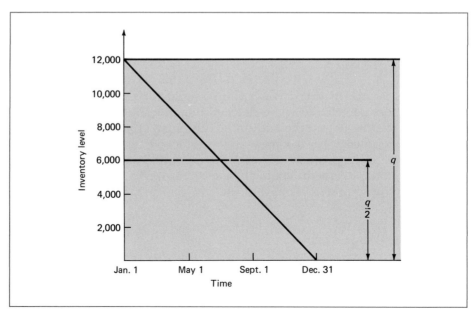

FIGURE 20.2
Average Inventory
for One Order

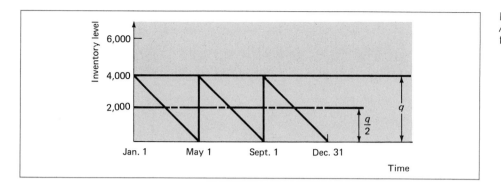

FIGURE 20.3
Average Inventory
for Three Orders

Tabular Solution for the EOQ

Building upon the original example, assume the cost accountants have determined the cost of ordering, C_o, is $500 per order and the cost of carrying, C_c, is $3 per unit for a year. Constructing a table, such as table 20.2, is one possible approach to finding the EOQ. From the table, note that the company should place six orders of 2,000 units on the average in order to minimize total ordering and carrying costs for the year. Figure 20.4 graphically indicates the same EOQ as determined in the table. One can mathematically derive a formula that will prove to be more efficient for determining the EOQ.

Mathematical Solution for the EOQ with Stockout Costs

To mathematically determine the EOQ, one must formulate the equation of the total cost line in figure 20.4. From the equation, one can determine the q that will result in the minimum cost. The equations for the ordering and carrying cost lines are, respectively:

$$\text{Total ordering cost} = NC_o = \frac{D}{q} C_o \qquad\qquad \textbf{(20-3)}$$

TABLE 20.2 Determining the EOQ

Number of orders	Order quantity	Order cost	Carrying cost	Total cost
N	$q = \dfrac{D}{N}$	$N \times C_o$	$\dfrac{q}{2} \times C_c$	
1	12,000	$ 500	$18,000	$18,500
2	6,000	1,000	9,000	10,000
3	4,000	1,500	6,000	7,500
4	3,000	2,000	4,500	6,500
5	2,400	2,500	3,600	6,100
6	2,000	3,000	3,000	6,000*
7	1,714	3,500	2,571	6,071
8	1,500	4,000	2,250	6,250

*Optimal number of orders and order quantity.

FIGURE 20.4
EOQ Cost Curves

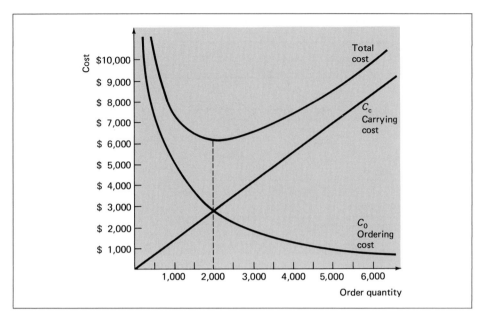

Total carrying cost $= \dfrac{q}{2}\, C_c$ **(20-4)**

Adding equations (20-3) and (20-4) results in the total cost (T_c) equation:

$$T_c = \dfrac{D}{q}\, C_o + \dfrac{q}{2}\, C_c \qquad\qquad\qquad\text{(20-5)}$$

To find the optimal EOQ, q^*, we differentiate T_c with respect to q, set the result equal to zero, and solve for q^* as follows:[5]

$$\dfrac{d\,T_c}{d\,q} = \dfrac{-C_o D}{q^2} + \dfrac{C_c}{2}$$

$$0 = \dfrac{-C_o D}{q^2} + \dfrac{C_c}{2} \qquad\qquad\qquad\text{(20-6)}$$

$$q^* = \sqrt{\dfrac{2C_o D}{C_c}}$$

Given q^*, the optimal EOQ, from (20-6) we can determine the optimal number of orders:

$$N^* = \dfrac{D}{q^*} = \dfrac{D}{\sqrt{2C_0 D/C_c}} = \sqrt{\dfrac{DC_c}{2C_0}} \qquad\qquad\text{(20-7)}$$

5. In equation (20-6) there are actually two values of Q because a square root is involved. We will not consider the negative value since negative purchases are not possible.

Assume an interval of time elapses between the time an order is placed and the time it is received. This interval is referred to as **lead time.** It is, therefore, necessary to take into account the lead time when determining the procurement level (the level of inventory at which the next order should be placed). The procurement level would be

$$L = DT \qquad \qquad \text{(20-8)}$$

where L is the procurement level and T is the lead time.

Since the time period in our problem is a year, assume a lead time of thirty days of the period or 1/12 (30/360) of a year. Employing formulas (20-6), (20-7), (20-8), and (20-5), respectively, we find that in our example:

$$q^* = \sqrt{\frac{(2)(\$500)(12,000)}{\$3.00}} = \sqrt{4,000,000} = 2,000 \text{ units}$$

$$N^* = \sqrt{\frac{(12,000)(\$3)}{(2)(\$500)}} = \sqrt{36} = 6 \text{ orders/year}$$

$$L = 12,000(1/12) = 1,000 \text{ units}$$

$$T_c = \frac{12,000}{2,000}(\$500) + \frac{2,000}{2}(\$3) = \$3,000 + \$3,000 = \$6,000/\text{year}$$

From the information just cited, note that every time the inventory level reaches 1,000 units, an order for 2,000 units should be placed. The average number of orders to be placed each year equals six, and the total cost of the system is $6,000.

A technical problem concerning the procurement level can be encountered if the length of the cycle time is less than the lead time. For example, assume the same problem as above except the lead time now equals 90 days. The procurement level now equals

$$L = 12,000 \left(\frac{90}{360} \right) = 3,000 \text{ units}$$

Since the maximum inventory is 2,000 units, the procurement level will never be reached. However, when the physical inventory reaches 1,000 units (a 30-day supply), another order for 2,000 units must have been placed 60 days earlier. Therefore, by including the outstanding order of 2,000 units and the physical inventory of 1,000 units, the procurement level of 3,000 units has been reached, and another order for 2,000 units should be placed.

☐ ASSUMPTIONS OF THE EOQ MODEL

A model is an abstraction and, as such, does not incorporate every aspect of the real-world system. It is, therefore, necessary to understand what assumptions have been made concerning the real-world system in constructing the model. The objective here is to review and explain the assumptions underlying the EOQ model. Since we will elaborate on the EOQ model by relaxing some of these assumptions, this will serve as a basis for the rest of the chapter.

1. *Demand Rate.* It is assumed that the demand rate is deterministic at a constant rate of D units per unit of time. In most of the cases we will consider, the demand will be stated in terms of a year. It should be recognized that the demand could be stated in terms of any unit of time.

2. *Replenishment Time.* It is assumed that replenishments are made whenever the inventory level reaches zero so that no stockouts can occur.

3. *Replenishment Quantity.* The replenishment quantity is assumed to be a constant lot size of q.

4. *Replenishment Rate.* It is assumed that the replenishment rate (R) is infinite. Therefore, it takes no time to replenish the system with a lot size q.

5. *Lead Time.* It is assumed that the lead time (T) is known and constant. Orders are placed when the inventory reaches the procurement level (L) so that no stockouts occur.

6. *Order Cost.* The unit-order cost (C_o) is assumed to be constant and measured in terms of dollars.

7. *Carrying Cost.* The unit carrying cost (C_c) is assumed to be constant over the same time period as that of the demand and is measured in terms of dollars.

8. *Stockout Cost.* Since no stockouts are permitted, the stockout cost (C_s) is assumed to be infinite.

9. *Unit Purchase Cost.* The unit purchase cost (C_p) is assumed to be constant and does not vary as the order quantity changes.

☐ ALLOWING FOR STOCKOUTS

Since costs of stockouts are assumed to be infinite in the EOQ model (assumption 8), no stockouts are permitted. We will now relax that assumption and assume that the stockout costs are finite. It is also assumed that if the merchandise is not on hand, the customer will place a back order that will be filled as soon as the merchandise becomes available. Such an inventory system is represented in figure 20.5, where m represents the maximum inventory level when the order has been received and after back orders have been filled.

During time segment t_1, the company is holding inventory at the average level of $m/2$. In time segment t_2, the company is accumulating back orders and the average level of back orders is $(q - m)/2$. Therefore, the company will be holding inventory m/q percent of the time. The same line of reasoning would result in the conclusion that the firm was short $(q - m)/q$ percent of the time. We are now ready to develop the total cost equation

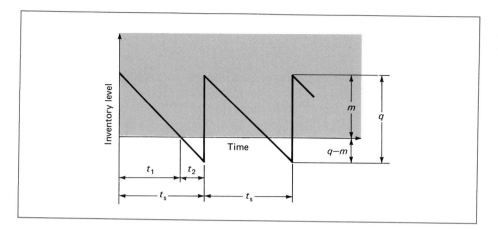

FIGURE 20.5
Allowing for
Stockouts

for this system in which purchase, carrying, and stockout costs will be considered.

The Total Cost Equation

The equations for the ordering, carrying, and stockout costs are, respectively:

$$\text{Ordering cost} = NC_o = \frac{D}{q}\,C_o \tag{20-9}$$

$$\text{Carrying cost} = \frac{m}{2}\cdot\frac{m}{q}\,C_c = \frac{m^2}{2q}\,C_c \tag{20-10}$$

$$\text{Stockout cost} = \frac{q-m}{2}\cdot\frac{q-m}{q}\,C_s = \frac{(q-m)^2}{2q}\,C_s \tag{20-11}$$

Adding equations (20-9), (20-10), and (20-11) results in the total cost equation:

$$T_c = \frac{D}{q}\,C_o + \frac{m^2}{2q}\,C_c + \frac{(q-m)^2}{2q}\,C_s \tag{20-12}$$

Mathematical Solution for the EOQ with Stockout Costs

To determine an optimal q^{**} and m^{**} when stockouts are permitted, one must differentiate (20-12) with respect to m and q, set the result equal to zero, and solve. This results in the following:[6]

$$q^{**} = \sqrt{\frac{2C_oD}{C_c}}\cdot\sqrt{\frac{C_c + C_s}{C_s}} \tag{20-13}$$

6. Refer to Appendix A on page 000 for the derivation of q^{**} and m^{**}.

$$m^{**} = \sqrt{\frac{2C_oD}{C_c}} \cdot \sqrt{\frac{C_s}{C_c + C_s}} \tag{20-14}$$

It is of interest to note that as C_s approaches infinity, the second expression in both (20-13) and (20-14) approaches the value of one and the result is the original EOQ formula. Therefore, the EOQ formula is a special case of (20-13), where the stockout costs are infinite. The procurement level when stockouts are permitted equals

$$L = DT - (q-m) \tag{20-15}$$

$$L = DT - \sqrt{\frac{2C_oD}{C_s(1 + (C_s/C_c))}} \tag{20-16}$$

Assuming a stockout cost of $1 per unit per year, one can now extend the original example to include stockout costs. From (20-13), (20-14), (20-12), and (20-16), one finds that

$$q^{**} = \sqrt{\frac{(2)(\$500)(12,000)}{\$3}} \cdot \sqrt{\frac{\$1 + \$3}{\$1}}$$

$$= 2,000 \cdot 2 = 4,000 \text{ units}$$

$$m^{**} = \sqrt{\frac{(2)(\$500)(12,000)}{\$3}} \cdot \sqrt{\frac{\$1}{\$1 + \$3}}$$

$$= 2,000 \cdot 1/2 = 1,000 \text{ units}$$

$$T_c = \frac{12,000}{4,000}(\$500) + \frac{(1,000)^2}{2(4,000)}(\$3) + \frac{(4,000 - 1,000)^2}{2(4,000)}(\$1)$$

$$= \$1,500 + \$375 + \$1,125 = \$3,000$$

$$L = (12,000 \cdot 1/12) - 3,000 = -2,000 \text{ units}$$

It should be noted that by assuming a finite stockout cost of $1, as opposed to the infinite stockout cost assumed with the EOQ model, the total inventory cost of the system was reduced by $3,000 ($6,000 − $3,000). Also, the model balances the ordering cost ($1,500) with the carrying plus the stockout costs ($375 + $1,125 = $1,500). Maximum holding and stockout inventory levels are balanced in the same ratio as the respective costs are to the sum of the carrying and holding costs. An order for 4,000 units should be placed when the inventory level equals −2,000 units (i.e., back orders have reached 2,000 units). When the order of 4,000 units is received, back orders will equal 3,000 units. At this time, the back orders will be filled and the remaining 1,000 units placed in inventory.

An additional example will aid in understanding how the model balances the three inventory costs. Let us now assume a stockout cost of $3 per unit per year. Solving the appropriate equations,

$$q^{**} = \sqrt{\frac{(2)(\$500)(12,000)}{\$3}} \cdot \sqrt{\frac{\$3 + \$3}{\$3}}$$

$$= 2,000 \cdot 1.414214 = 2,828.43 \text{ units}$$

$$m^{**} = \sqrt{\frac{(2)(\$500)(12,000)}{\$3}} \cdot \sqrt{\frac{\$3}{\$3 + \$3}}$$

$$= 2,000 \cdot .707 = 1,414.21 \text{ units}$$

$$T_c = \$2,121.32 + \$1,060.66 + \$1,060.66 = \$4,242.64$$

$$L = (12,000 \cdot 1/12) - 1,414 = -414 \text{ units}$$

Observe now that the total carrying and ordering costs are equal because $C_c = C_s$. Note that the maximum holding and stockout inventory levels are equal.

The service level of the model is defined as

$$\text{Service level} = \frac{m}{q} = \frac{C_s}{C_c + C_s} \qquad \textbf{(20-17)}$$

In the example just given, the service level equals

$$\text{Service level} = \frac{1,414}{2,828} = \frac{\$3}{\$3 + \$3} = .50$$

It is often the case that the stockout cost is not known and is imputed by specifying a **service level**. Employing the previous example and assuming a service level of 90 percent, the imputed stockout is

$$\frac{C_s}{C_c + C_s} = .9$$

$$\frac{C_s}{\$3 + C_s} = .9$$

$$C_s = \$27$$

Now, q^{**} equals 2,108 using (20-13) and m^{**} is 1,897 using (20-14) with a service level of

$$\text{Service level} = \frac{1,897}{2,108} = .9$$

Because of the inherent difficulties in measuring stockout costs, it is often imputed in this manner by allowing management to specify a service level.

☐ UNIFORM REPLENISHMENT RATE

In the preceding models, we assumed that stock was replenished instantaneously. This assumption may be unrealistic in cases where a vendor delivers orders in partial shipments over a period of time. In other cases, it may be that production of batches takes time to complete, and inventory replenishment is being accomplished while demand is being met. Therefore, we are no longer assuming that inventory rises to its maximum level instantaneously.

A uniform replenishment system is illustrated in figure 20.6. It should be noted that inventory is being used while new inventory is being received and that the inventory does not build up immediately to its maximum level. Let R equal the inventory replenishment rate. The maximum inventory is $(R - D)t_1$, and the average inventory equals:

$$\bar{I} = \frac{(R - D)t_1}{2} \tag{20-18}$$

Since $q = Rt_1$, substituting in (20-18) for t_1 where $t_1 = q/R$ and simplifying we get

$$\bar{I} = \frac{(1 - D/R)q}{2} \tag{20-19}$$

The carrying cost for this system is

$$\text{Carrying cost} = \frac{(1 - D/R)qC_c}{2} \tag{20-20}$$

and the total cost of the system using (20-4) for the ordering cost is

$$T_c = \frac{D}{q}C_o + \frac{(1 - D/R)qC_c}{2} \tag{20-21}$$

FIGURE 20.6
Uniform
Replenishment
Rate

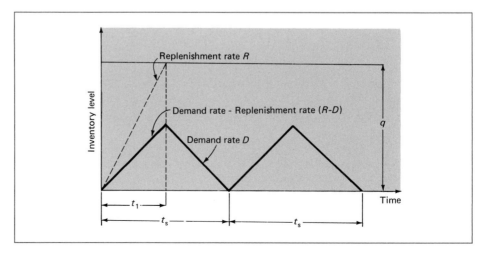

Once again, to determine the optimal EOQ, one differentiates T_c with respect to q, sets the result equal to zero, and solves for q^* as follows:

$$\frac{dT_c}{dq} = \frac{-C_oD}{q^2} + \frac{(1 - D/R)C_c}{2} \qquad\qquad \textbf{(20-22)}$$

$$0 = \frac{-C_oD}{q^2} + \frac{(1 - D/R)C_c}{2}$$

$$q^* = \sqrt{\frac{2C_oD}{C_c}} \cdot \sqrt{\frac{R}{R - D}}$$

From the original example, assume that R is 24,000 units a year, employ formulas (20-22) and (20-21), and find

$$q^* = \sqrt{\frac{(2)(\$500)(12,000)}{\$3}} \cdot \sqrt{\frac{24,000}{24,000 - 12,000}}$$

$$= 2,000 \cdot 1.414214 = 2,828.43 \text{ units}$$

$$L = 12,000 \cdot 1/12 = 1,000 \text{ units}$$

$$T_c = \frac{12,000}{2,828.43} (\$500) + \frac{(1 - 12,000/24,000)(2,828.43)(\$3.00)}{2}$$

$$= \$2,121.32 + \$2,121.32 = \$4,242.64$$

Note that this model also balances the ordering and carrying costs, and that the total cost is less than those determined when one assumed an infinite replenishment rate.

☐ PRICE BREAKS

To this point we have assumed that inventory policies are not affected by purchase prices. This assumption is valid if prices do not vary with volume. However, in this country it is traditional to quote reduced prices as the quantity purchased increases. In this case, it is necessary to consider the purchase price when determining economic-order quantities.

From the previous example where we assumed the demand D to equal 12,000 units a year, ordering costs C_o to equal \$500, and carrying costs C_c to equal \$3 per unit per year, let us also assume a vendor quoted the following prices:

Unit price	Units
\$1.05	0–1,999
1.00	2,000–2,999
.95	3,000–3,999
.90	4,000–5,999
.80	6,000– ∞

FIGURE 20.7
Cost Curve with
Price Breaks

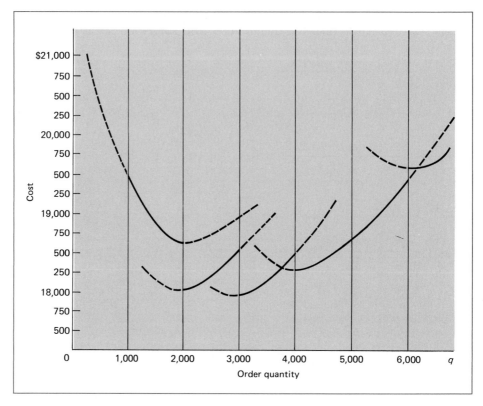

Now, the total cost equation for the EOQ model can be modified to include the purchase price.

$$T_c = \frac{D}{q} C_o + \frac{q}{2} C_c + C_p D \qquad \qquad \text{(20-23)}$$

If one solved the equation for the EOQ, one would get the same results obtained in (20-6), since the purchase price is not expressed as a function of q. Plotting the total cost curve for the problem as shown in figure 20.7, we find the curve is discontinuous at each **price break**. The reason for the breaks in the total cost curve is that the purchase price is a step function. Each of the curves can be continued (as shown with the dotted lines in figure 20.7), which results in each curve assuming the general shape of the total cost curve of the EOQ model.

With the price breaks at 2,000 units, 3,000 units, 4,000 units, and 6,000 units, the problem involves determining whether the price breaks offset any additional inventory related costs that would be incurred from ordering other than the optimal quantity. For example, if the firm ordered in lots of 1,999 units, the total cost by (20-23) is approximately $18,600. However, if the firm ordered in lots of 2,000 units, the total cost is $18,000. The savings of $600 results from taking advantage of the price break ($1.05

versus $1.00) at 2,000 units. Since the EOQ in this problem is 2,000 units, one might conclude that this order level will minimize total costs. It is true that ordering lots of 2,000 units will result in minimizing inventory cost (ordering and carrying costs), but one cannot be sure that total costs are at a minimum when price breaks are considered.

If the next price break at 3,000 units ($1.00 versus $.95) is evaluated, the total cost of 2,999 units is approximately $19,000. If lots of 3,000 units are ordered, the total cost is $17,900, which is lower than the $18,000 incurred when 2,000 units are ordered each time. When lots of 3,000 units are ordered, the inventory costs total $6,500 as opposed to inventory costs of $6,000 with an order quantity of 2,000 units. This $500 increase in inventory cost is offset by the $600 savings (.05 × 12,000) realized from decreased purchase prices. Checking the price breaks at 4,000 and 6,000 units, respectively, total costs are found to be $18,300 and $19,600. Therefore, in this problem the EOQ, taking into account the price breaks, is 3,000 units.

The reason for checking at the price break rather than some intermediate point is that any point farther away from the EOQ has increased inventory costs (refer to figure 20.7). Also, at the price break, one realizes the maximum savings resulting from reduced purchase prices.

A general approach for solving problems with price breaks is to solve for the EOQ and then determine the total costs at the price breaks. If the EOQ falls within the range of the lowest price, then further testing is not necessary. When the EOQ does not fall in the range of the lowest price, it is then necessary to check at the price breaks to determine the minimum cost order quantity.

☐ LEAD TIME AND SAFETY STOCK

Safety stock is extra inventory retained as a hedge against the possibility of a stockout. When a safety stock is carried, it will increase carrying cost and reduce the costs of stockouts. The optimum level of safety stock to carry is determined by minimizing the carrying costs and the expected stockout costs.

In our approach to this problem we will assume a constant lead time. Under this assumption, a stockout can only occur because of increased demand during the lead time. If demand increased before the procurement level was reached, a purchase order would be placed as soon as the inventory level reached the procurement level. Figure 20.8 illustrates the situation. To determine the optimal level of safety stock, we will assume known probabilistic demand during lead time and then evaluate the problem.

Assume a company has determined the EOQ to equal 2,000 units with an average time of 60 working days between orders. Lead time is 15 days with an expected demand of 500 units, and 4 orders are placed each year. Further analysis of the demand during lead time reveals that the following probabilities can be assigned to various levels of demand:

Demand during lead time	Demand probability
650	.05
600	.07
550	.12
500	.55
450	.10
400	.08
350	.03
	1.00

If the firm places a purchase order when the procurement level reaches 500 units, the company will have adequate stock on hand 76 percent of the time (.03 + .08 + .10 + .55) and will incur stockouts 24 percent of the time (.12 + .07 + .05).

To reduce or eliminate the possibility of stockouts, the firm could elect to carry safety stock. Since the demand distribution is discrete, we will evaluate safety-stock policies of 50, 100, and 150 units and select the one that results in the lowest expected total stockout and carrying cost.

If we assume carrying costs of $5 per unit and stockout costs of $20 per unit, we then can determine the expected total costs. The computation of the expected stockout costs is shown in table 20.3. The carrying costs and the total expected costs are computed in table 20.4.

For this case, the minimum expected costs occur when a safety stock of 100 units is held. The carrying cost of $500 results from carrying the safety stock of 100 units for the entire year. In practice, it is not uncommon

FIGURE 20.8
Increased Demand before Procurement Level Is Reached

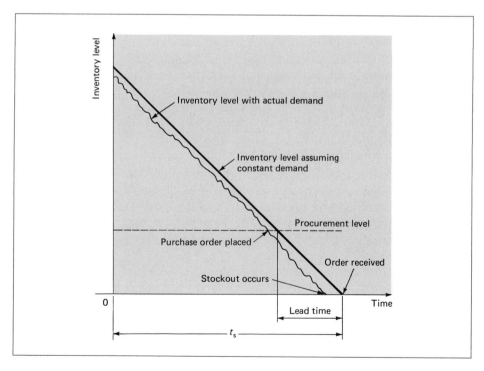

TABLE 20.3 Expected Stockout Costs

Safety stock	Number short	Probability of stockout	Number of orders × number short × probability of being short × cost of being short	Total expected stockout costs
0	50	.12	4 × 50 × .12 × $20 = $480	
	100	.07	4 × 100 × .07 × $20 = 560	
	150	.05	4 × 150 × .05 × $20 = 600	$1,640
50	50	.07	4 × 50 × .07 × $20 = $280	
	100	.05	4 × 100 × .05 × $20 = 400	680
100	50	.05	4 × 50 × .05 × $20 = $200	200
150	0	0		0

TABLE 20.4 Carrying and Total Expected Costs

Safety stock	Annual carrying costs	Total expected stockout costs	Total expected costs
0	0 × $5 = 0	$1,640	$1,640
50	50 × $5 = $250	680	930
100	100 × $5 = $500	200	700*
150	150 × $5 = $750	0	750

*Optimal safety stock.

for a firm to adopt a service-level policy because of difficulties encountered in measuring stockout costs. For example, the firm might adopt a service level of 88 percent. This means that the firm wants to be able to supply items 88 percent of the time. To achieve an 88 percent service level, the firm would maintain a safety stock of 50 units. Therefore, stockouts would be expected to occur only 12 percent of the time the system was in operation.

☐ STATIC-INVENTORY PROBLEMS UNDER RISK

The static-inventory problem is distinguished from the dynamic-inventory problems we have dealt with in the previous sections in that only one order is possible. At first, this might appear to be a very unrealistic situation; however, this type of problem is often encountered in business. When a retailer is selling a seasonal item, there might not be an opportunity to place a second order. Christmas trees, Valentine candy, Easter eggs, Halloween costumes, high-fashion apparel, and newspapers are just some examples of seasonal items that can be treated as a static-inventory problem.

Static problems in which the demand is known with certainty do not present an analytical problem. Since the quantities of the item required are known, and only one order is possible, the profitability of the item determines whether or not the order should be placed. We are going to consider a series of static-inventory problems in which the probability distribution of the demand is assumed to be known.[7]

Determining the probability distribution of the demand is a forecasting problem that will not be considered in this text. This topic is generally covered in business statistics or sales forecasting textbooks. The static-inventory problem under risk will provide a vehicle by which we will consider profit maximization and opportunity costs as criteria for decision making.

Profit Maximization

Assume a flower shop in Philadelphia is considering how many corsages to order for the Army-Navy football game. Corsages sell for $5 and cost $2. Our florist estimates the demand for corsages before the game to equal

Demand	Probability
4	.1
5	.25
6	.4
7	.15
8	.1
Total	1.00

The probabilities are to be interpreted as follows: the probability is .25 that the demand will equal five corsages.

If we assume that the florist will always order at least four corsages, since she is certain of selling that number, our florist has five strategies available. This assumes that the profit from selling four corsages exceeds the purchasing cost. Generally, purchasing costs are not considered in this model since they are fixed for all alternatives except not placing an order. Of course, the number of strategies available to the florist is also fixed since we will assume that she will never order more than eight corsages because it is not possible for her to sell any more than this number. Therefore, the strategies available to the florist are to order between four and eight corsages.

Since there are five possible strategies and five possible levels of demand, we can then conclude that there are a total of $5 \times 5 = 25$ possible combinations of one strategy and one level of demand. We will now construct a profit matrix in which the ordering strategies are on the rows and the possible demand on the columns.[8] The profit matrix for the florist is shown in table 20.5.

If the florist orders five corsages and the demand is for eight, profit will be $15, which is determined by subtracting costs of $10 [(5)($2)] from sales of $25 [(5)($5)]. (Remember the florist can only sell the number she orders.) This is the element in the second row and fifth column of the profit matrix.

---

7. In the literature, this is often referred to as the "newsboy problem."

8. In this case, since we have not considered fixed costs, profit is used in place of contribution margin.

TABLE 20.5 Profit Matrix

Order \ Demand	4	5	6	7	8
4	$12	$12	$12	$12	$12
5	10	15	15	15	15
6	8	13	18	18	18
7	6	11	16	21	21
8	4	9	14	19	24

On the other hand, if the florist ordered eight corsages and the demand is only for five, the sales will equal $25 [(5)($5)] and the costs will be $16 [(8)($2)]; thus, a profit of only $9 will result. This is the element in the fifth row and second column of the profit matrix. You would benefit from verifying additional elements in the matrix.

Since we do not know what level of demand will occur, we will determine the expected profit for each strategy. To accomplish this, we will weight each event with the probability of the event occurring to arrive at the expected profit for each strategy. For the first strategy of ordering four corsages, the expected profit equals

$$.1(\$12) + .25(\$12) + .4(\$12) + .15(\$12) + .1(\$12) = \$12$$

For the fourth strategy of ordering seven corsages, the expected profit equals

$$.1(\$6) + .25(\$11) + .4(\$16) + .15(\$21) + .1(\$21) = \$15$$

Employing the same procedure, we find the expected profit for each of the five strategies to equal

Order	Expected profit
4	$12.00
5	14.50
6	15.75*
7	15.00
8	13.50

*Maximum

Thus, we would recommend that the florist order six corsages to maximize profit.

Although the optimal strategy is to order six corsages with an expected profit of $15.75, we observe from the profit matrix that when the florist orders six corsages the profit never equals $15.75. If six corsages are ordered, the profit is either $8, $13, or $18. An expected profit of $15.75 means that if the florist orders six corsages for many Army-Navy games and the demand, costs, and selling prices remain stable, the average profit will be $15.75.

Constructing a profit matrix and then determining the expected profit is one means of specifying the optimal strategy of a static-inventory problem under risk. Now let us formulate the problem so that we can determine a general solution. There are two conditions encountered in this problem that initially will be considered separately. The first is where the demand is less than or equal to the supply (supply being the number ordered). In this case, the florist would be holding corsages after the football game. In the other condition, the demand would exceed the supply and the florist would be short corsages.

If we let p equal the selling price and c equal the cost, then when holding corsages ($D \leq S$) the profit equals

$$\text{Profit} = Dp - Sc \quad \text{(holding)} \tag{20-24}$$

In this case, the revenue equals the demand times the selling price, while the cost equals the supply times the unit cost. When the florist is short ($S < D$), the profit equals

$$\text{Profit} = Sp - Sc = S(p - c) \quad \text{(short)} \tag{20-25}$$

In this case, the revenue equals the supply times the selling price, while the cost equals the supply times the unit cost. Combining (20-24) and (20-25) and incorporating the demand probabilities $P(D)$, we now can express the expected profit where

$$E(\text{profit}) = \sum_{D=4}^{S} (Dp - Sc)\, P(D) + \sum_{D=S+1}^{8} S(p - c)\, P(D) \tag{20-26}$$

Note that the first summation in equation (20-26) is from the lower limit of the demand up to the supply S. This encompasses all cases in which the florist would be left holding excess corsages. The second summation in (20-26) is from the supply plus one to the upper limit of the demand. This encompasses all cases where the florist would be short corsages.

If we differentiate (20-26) with respect to S, set the expression equal to zero, and solve (refer to Appendix B on page 000), we find:

$$\sum_{D=4}^{S} P(D) = \frac{p - c}{p} \tag{20-27}$$

This expression can be interpreted as follows: The maximum expected profit is found where the sum of the probabilities from the lower limit of the demand up to the supply equals the price minus the cost (the contribution margin) over the price. In the example, using (20-27) we find

$$\sum_{D=4}^{S} P(D) = \frac{\$5 - \$2}{\$5} = \frac{\$3}{\$5} = .6$$

Therefore, the florist should order six corsages because as we sum the probabilities (.1 + .25 + .4), .5 is included in demand of six corsages.

Expression (20-27) is a general solution to this type of problem and will always indicate the optimal strategy. Therefore, it is not necessary to construct a profit matrix to solve the static-inventory problem under risk.

Opportunity Costs—Profit Situation

We will now consider the static-inventory problem under risk, employing opportunity costs as the criterion for decision making. In this situation, we will consider the profit that could have been made if the right decision had been made and the profit earned as a result of the decision that was made. The difference between these two profit figures is the opportunity cost associated with a particular stragegy and demand occurrence. The opportunity-cost matrix in table 20.6 is based on the flower shop example described in the previous sections.

Assume the florist ordered four corsages and the demand was for six. If the right decision (ordering six corsages) had been made, profit would equal $18 [(6)($3)]. However, the profit earned equals only $12 [(4)($3)] and results in an opportunity cost of $6 ($18 − $12). This is the element in the first row and the third column of the opportunity-cost matrix. Now, assume seven corsages were ordered and the demand was for five. If the right decision has been made, profit would equal $15 [(5)($3)]. However, the profit earned equals $11 (refer to the profit matrix) and results in an opportunity cost of $4 ($15 − $11). This is the element in the fourth row and the second column of the opportunity-cost matrix.

We will now determine the expected cost for each strategy by the same means as the expected profit was determined. For the second strategy of ordering five corsages, the expected cost equals

$$.1(\$2) + .25(0) + .4(\$3) + .15(\$6) + .1(\$9) = \$3.20$$

For the fifth strategy of ordering eight corsages, the expected cost equals

$$.1(\$8) + .25(\$6) + .4(\$4) + .15(\$2) + .1(0) = \$4.20$$

TABLE 20.6 Opportunity Cost Matrix—Profit Situation

Order \ Demand	4	5	6	7	8
4	$0	$3	$6	$9	$12
5	2	0	3	6	9
6	4	2	0	3	6
7	6	4	2	0	3
8	8	6	4	2	0

Employing the same procedure, we find the expected cost for each of the five strategies to equal

Order	Expected cost
4	$5.70
5	3.20
6	1.95*
7	2.70
8	4.20

*Minimum

Thus, the florist should order six corsages to minimize the opportunity cost. As expected, this is the same strategy as was adopted when the maximization of profits was sought. If the opportunity-cost problem was formulated to determine the general solution, a similar result as that found in (20-27) is obtained.

Cost Minimization

Another set of static-inventory problems is often encountered when cost minimization is the criterion employed in decision making. For example, assume the florist from the previous section is going to purchase a new heating system for her greenhouses. Her problem this time is that she is not sure how many sets of spare parts to acquire with the new heater. Any spare parts acquired would become part of the inventory held by the Maintenance department. Sets of spare parts for the heating system cost $200 each. If the heating system should break down and spare parts were not immediately available, the florist estimates the cost to equal $1,500.

The heating system has an estimated life of ten years and the probability distribution of the number of failures during the life of the system is:

Failure	Probability
0	.15
1	.4
2	.2
3	.15
4	.1
Total	1.00

The total-cost matrix for the example is shown in table 20.7. If the florist ordered two sets of spare parts and the system broke down three times, the total cost is $1,900 [(2 × $200) + $1,500)]. This is the element in the third row and fourth column of the total-cost matrix. The expected cost for the second strategy of ordering one set of spare parts equals:

$$.15(\$200) + .4(\$200) + .2(\$1,700) + .15(\$3,200) + .1(\$4,700) = \$1,400$$

Employing this procedure, we find the expected cost for each of the five strategies is:

TABLE 20.7 Total Cost Matrix

Order \ Failure	0	1	2	3	4
0	$ 0	$1,500	$3,000	$4,500	$6,000
1	200	200	1,700	3,200	4,700
2	400	400	400	1,900	3,400
3	600	600	600	600	2,100
4	800	800	800	800	800

Order	Expected cost
0	$2,475
1	1,400
2	925
3	750*
4	800

*Minimum

Placing an order for three sets of spare parts minimizes the expected cost; thus, this is the strategy that should be adopted by the florist.

As might be expected, this problem can be formulated so that we can determine a general solution. Let b equal the penalty cost if spare parts are short and c equals the cost of a set of spare parts. If we are holding spare parts ($D \leq S$), the cost equals

$$\text{Cost} = cS \quad \text{(holding)} \tag{20-28}$$

If we are caught short of spare parts ($D > S$), the cost equals

$$\text{Cost} = cS + b(D - S) \quad \text{(short)} \tag{20-29}$$

Combining (20-28) and (20-29) and incorporating the demand probabilities $P(D)$, we can express the expected cost as

$$E(\text{cost}) = \sum_{D=0}^{S} (cS)\, P(D) + \sum_{D=S+1}^{4} [cS + b(D - S)\, P(D)] \tag{20-30}$$

If (20-30) is differentiated with respect to S and solved (refer to Appendix B on page 706), we find

$$\sum_{D=0}^{S} P(D) = \frac{b - c}{b} \tag{20-31}$$

The minimum cost is found when the sum of the probabilities, from the lower limit of the demand for spare parts to the supply, equals the penalty cost minus the normal cost divided by the penalty cost. In the example, using (20-31) we find

$$\sum_{D=0}^{S} P(D) = \frac{\$1,500 - \$200}{\$1,500} = \frac{\$1,300}{\$1,500} = .87$$

In the case, this means that the florist should order three sets of spare parts because as we sum the probabilities (.15 + .4 + .2 + .15), .87 is included in the demand for three sets. Expression (20-31) is a general solution for this type of problem.

Opportunity Costs—Cost Situation

Our last static-inventory problem involves minimizing opportunity costs in the cost-minimization problem. In this case, the opportunity cost equals the total cost minus the cost if the right decision had been made. Considering the florist and her spare parts problem, the opportunity-cost matrix is shown in table 20.8. If the florist ordered one set of spare parts and the system broke down three times, the total cost is $3,200 [$200 + (2 × 1,500)] and the cost if the right decision had been made is $600 (3 × $200). The opportunity cost is $2,600; this is the demand in the second row and fourth column of the opportunity-cost matrix. If three sets of spare parts were ordered and the system did not break down, the total cost is $600 (3 × $200) and the cost would have been zero if the right decision had been made. The opportunity cost of $600 appears in the fourth row and first column of the opportunity-cost matrix.

The expected opportunity cost for the fifth strategy of ordering four sets of spare parts is

$$.15(\$800) + .4(\$600) + .2(\$400) + .15(\$200) + .1(0) = \$470$$

We find the expected opportunity cost for each of the five strategies to equal

Order	Expected opportunity cost
0	$2,145
1	1,070
2	595
3	420*
4	470

*Minimum

TABLE 20.8 Opportunity Cost Matrix—Cost Situation

Order \ Failure	0	1	2	3	4
0	$ 0	$1,300	$2,600	$3,900	$5,200
1	200	0	1,300	2,600	3,900
2	400	200	0	1,300	2,600
3	600	400	200	0	1,300
4	800	600	400	200	0

By ordering three sets of spare parts, the florist minimizes the expected opportunity cost. This problem can also be formulated so that a general solution can be determined. The result would be the same as (20-31) for the cost-minimization problem.

☐ JUST-IN-TIME INVENTORIES

Recently, inventory control methods employed by American businesses have been challenged by Japanese innovations. The dramatic differences between Japanese and American inventory-control procedures are the result of two critical problems encountered in the Japanese production environment. Space is a great problem in Japan, and therefore plant sites must be designed with considerable attention directed toward the efficient use of space. In addition, Japanese products often travel great distances before they reach their ultimate consumer. Therefore, space and distance have made inventory and quality control critical factors for Japanese management.

The inventory control systems used in Japan and the United States can generally be described respectively as **just-in-time** (JIT) and just-in-case (JIC). The Japanese employ what can be described as a "pull" system in which the final assembly line pulls only what is needed from the various work centers to produce a specific output. The goal of this system is to produce and deliver goods just in time to be sold, to produce subassemblies just in time to be assembled into finished goods, and to manufacture fabricated parts just in time to be assembled into subassemblies. The United States counterpart, Just-in-Case, is a "push" system. Here, mass-produced items are pushed into inventory to offset lead time and to meet economic-order-quantity (EOQ) requirements. This inventory philosophy holds that a certain level (safety stock) of inventory is necessary to act as a buffer against stockouts, machine breakdowns, and defective parts. It is estimated that as much as 40 percent of all American industry assets are invested in inventory. Inventory can be viewed as a means of hiding a firm's production inefficiencies and accumulating mistakes. Of course, just-in-time will expose these types of problems.

Under the just-in-time product system, all manufacturing facilities are viewed as a single conduit or trunk, and all movement between facilities is viewed as a uniform flow of materials, parts, and subassemblies. Advocates of the JIT system claim it results in (1) reduced space needs, (2) reductions in raw material, work-in-process, and finished-goods inventories, (3) increases in employee productivity, (4) increased equipment utilization, and (5) improved quality of output.

The JIT process is facilitated by a device called **Kanban.** In the Japanese language, the meaning of a word rests heavily on the sense in which the word is used. The connotation of Kanban in manufacturing means a marker to control the sequencing of job activities through sequential processes. In reference to just-in-time, Kanban refers to the tickets employed to control work flow. A Kanban consists physically of a plate about four by eight inches in dimension, made of plastic, cardboard, or sometimes metal. It displays information about production of a specific product at a specific point. Kanbans are strategically placed in factories so that all of the employees can read them and take instructions from them.

Many American corporations such as IBM, Hewlett-packard, Xerox, and General Motors have begun to implement JIT concepts. These and other firms claim to have benefited significantly from the system. A detailed description of the JIT system is beyond the scope of this text. It is not a complicated statistical tool but simply a reorganization of the production flow process.

Certain aspects of JIT, such as a limited number of suppliers, may not be appropriate for the American economy. For the JIT system to operate efficiently, a company must commit to use only a few suppliers. Also, a very open relationship is necessary between suppliers and manufacturer. In Japan, large manufacturers merely tell vendors if they require a change in a product line and then work with the vendor to bring it about. This is possible in Japan because large manufacturing companies own or have financial control over their suppliers. In addition, many suppliers only sell to one large company. Therefore, if a manufacturer wants a change, there is little argument.

In a world economy, we should recognize that there may be management philosophies that operate better than those employed in this country. JIT is a proven technique, and change may be necessary in the American economy to take advantage of the economies that can be realized from this system.

☐ SUMMARY

This chapter began with a brief discussion of why it is necessary for a business to hold inventory. How the ABC method is used for identifying those items in inventory that require the greatest degree of control was demonstrated. Next, three costs (ordering, carrying, and stockout) that are incurred in maintaining inventory were discussed. Ordering and carrying costs were then considered, and the elementary EOQ model was developed. By relaxing assumptions concerning stockouts and replenishment rates, we were able to develop two additional models. These models still require us to make simplifying assumptions about real-world inventory systems, but they have been extensively used in applying scientific principles to inventory management.[9]

The study of these models gives some understanding of how the costs resulting from maintaining inventories influence optimal-ordering policies. We have demonstrated how modification of assumptions concerning stockout costs, replenishment rates, and demand influence order quantities in attempting to minimize inventory costs.

In the final sections of the chapter, the static-inventory problem under risk was developed. Insight was gained concerning the interaction of costs and profits and an optimal inventory policy. Opportunity cost concepts were also integrated into the discussion of these models.

---

9. For example, refer to: J. Buchan and E. Koenigsbert, *Scientific Inventory Management* (Englewood Cliffs, N.J.: Prentice-Hall, 1963).

The concluding section of the chapter contained a description of the Japanese just-in-time inventory- and production-control system. This system views production as a flow process. It can be described as a "pull" system in that final assembly line pulls only what is needed from the other work centers to produce a specified output. American industry is attempting to incorporate some features of the just-in-time system into its inventory- and production-control systems.

KEY TERMS

Carrying cost	Ordering cost
Economic-Order Quantity (EOQ)	Price break
Just-in-time (JIT)	Safety stock
Kanban	Service level
Lead time	Stockout cost

REVIEW PROBLEM

Demand for a special electrical switch is 2,500 units per year. The switches cost $10 each, and the annual carrying costs are $2 per switch per year. Incremental ordering costs equal $25.

The firm has determined that existing equipment can be used to produce the switches. The equipment can produce 30,000 switches per year, and the estimated setup cost is $50. The estimated variable manufacturing costs are $9.75 for each switch.

Required ☐

1. Determine the unit cost if the firm purchases the switches.
2. Determine the unit cost if the firm manufactures the switches.

Solution ☐

1. $q^* = \sqrt{\dfrac{2 \times \$25 \times 2,500}{\$2}} = 250$ units $\qquad\qquad$ **(20-6)**

$T_c = \dfrac{2,500}{250}\,(\$25) + \dfrac{250}{2}\,(\$2) + 2,500\ (\$10)$ $\qquad\qquad$ **(20-5)**

$T_c = \$25,500$

Unit cost $= \dfrac{\$25,500}{2,500} = \$10.20$/unit

2. $q^* = \sqrt{\dfrac{2 \times \$50 \times 2,500}{\$2}}\sqrt{\dfrac{30,000}{30,000 - 2,500}} = 369$ units $\qquad$ **(20-22)**

$T_c = \dfrac{2,500}{369}\,(\$50) + \dfrac{(1 - 2,500/30,000)\ 369\ (\$2)}{2} + 2,500\ (\$9.75)$ $\qquad$ **(20-21)**

$T_c = \$25,052$

Unit cost $= \dfrac{\$25,052}{2,500} = \$10.02$/unit

APPENDIX A: Derivation of the Inventory Model with Stockouts Permitted

$$TC = \frac{D}{q} C_0 + \frac{m^2}{2q} C_c + \frac{(q-m)^2\, C_s}{2q} \qquad \textbf{(20 A-1)}$$

$$\frac{dTC}{dm} = \frac{mC_c}{q} + \frac{mC_s}{q} - C_s$$

$$0 = \frac{mC_c}{q} \cdot \frac{mC_s}{q} - C_s$$

$$\frac{dTC}{dq} = \frac{-DC_0}{q^2} + \frac{-m^2 C_c}{2q^2} + \frac{C_s}{2} + \frac{-m^2 C_s}{2q^2} \qquad \textbf{(20 A-2)}$$

$$0 = \frac{-DC_0}{q^2} + \frac{-m^2 C_c}{2q^2} + \frac{C_s}{2} + \frac{-m^2 C_s}{2q^2}$$

$$q^2 = \frac{2DC_0 + m^2 C_c + m^2 C_s}{C_s}$$

Substitute (20 A-2) for m, and solve for q.

$$q = \sqrt{\frac{2C_0 D}{C_c}} \sqrt{\frac{C_c + C_s}{C_s}} \qquad \textbf{(20 A-3)}$$

Substitute (20 A-3) for q in (20 A-2), and solve for m.

$$m = \sqrt{\frac{2C_0 D}{C_c}} \sqrt{\frac{C_s}{C_c + C_s}}$$

APPENDIX B

Using finite calculus, we determine (20-27) as follows:

$$E(\text{Profit}) = \sum_{D=4}^{S} (Dp - S^1 c)\, P(D) + \sum_{D=S+1}^{8} S^1(p-c)\, P(D)$$

$$\frac{d\, E(\text{Profit})}{dS} = \sum_{D=4}^{S} -c\, P(D) + \sum_{D=S+1}^{8} (p-c)\, P(D)$$

$$0 = -c \sum_{D=4}^{S} P(D) + (p-c) \sum_{D=S+1}^{8} P(D)$$

$$0 = -c \sum_{D=4}^{S} P(D) + (p-c) \sum_{D=S+1}^{8} P(D) + (p-c) \sum_{D=4}^{S} P(D) - (p-c) \sum_{D=4}^{S} P(D)$$

$$0 = (-c-p+c) \sum_{D=4}^{S} P(D) + p - c$$

$$p \sum_{D=4}^{S} P(D) = p - c$$

$$\sum_{D=4}^{S} P(D) = \frac{p-c}{p}$$

In the opportunity-cost (profit situation) problem, let $g = p - c$, and (20-27) is determined as follows:

$$E(\text{opportunity cost}) = \sum_{D=4}^{S} c(S-D)\, P(D) + \sum_{D=S+1}^{8} g(D-S)\, P(D)$$

$$\frac{dE(\text{opportunity cost})}{dS} = c \sum_{D=4}^{S} P(D) - g \sum_{D=S+1}^{8} P(D)$$

$$0 = c \sum_{D=4}^{S} P(D) - g \sum_{D=S+1}^{8} P(D)$$

$$0 = c \sum_{D=4}^{S} P(D) - g \sum_{D=S+1}^{8} P(D) + g \sum_{D=4}^{S} P(D) - g \sum_{D=4}^{S} P(D)$$

$$0 = c + g \sum_{D=4}^{S} P(D) - g$$

$$\sum_{D=4}^{S} P(D) = \frac{g}{c+g} = \frac{p-c}{c+p-c}$$

$$\sum_{D=4}^{S} P(D) = \frac{p-c}{p}$$

We solve the cost minimization (20-31) as follows:

$$E(\text{Cost}) = \sum_{D=0}^{S} (cS)\, P(D) + \sum_{D=S+1}^{4} (cS + b(D-S))\, P(D)$$

$$\frac{d\,E\,(\text{Cost})}{dS} = c \sum_{D=0}^{S} P(D) + (c-b) \sum_{D=S+1}^{4} P(D)$$

$$0 = c \sum_{D=0}^{S} P(D) + (c-b) \sum_{D=S+1}^{4} P(D)$$

$$0 = c \sum_{D=0}^{S} P(D) + (c-b) \sum_{D=S+1}^{4} P(D) + (c-b) \sum_{D=0}^{S} P(D) - (c-b) \sum_{D=0}^{S} P(D)$$

$$0 = b \sum_{D=0}^{S} P(D) + (c-b)$$

$$\sum_{D=0}^{S} P(D) = \frac{b-c}{b}$$

The opportunity cost (cost situation) is solved as follows:

$$E(\text{opportunity cost}) = \sum_{D=0}^{S} c(S-D)\,P(D) + \sum_{D=S+1}^{4} (b-c)(D-S)\,P(D)$$

$$\frac{d\,E(\text{opportunity cost})}{ds} = c\sum_{D=0}^{S} P(D) - (b-c)\sum_{D=S+1}^{4} P(D)$$

$$0 = c\sum_{D=0}^{S} P(D) - (b-c)\sum_{D=S+1}^{4} P(D)$$

$$0 = c\sum_{D=0}^{S} P(D) - (b-c)\sum_{D=S+1}^{4} P(D) + (b-c)\sum_{D=0}^{S} P(D) - (b-c)\sum_{D=0}^{S} P(D)$$

$$0 = b\sum_{D=0}^{S} P(D) - (b-c)$$

$$\sum_{D=0}^{S} P(D) = \frac{b-c}{b}$$

QUESTIONS

Q20-1. In this chapter, we considered three inventory models. The following questions refer to the models as depicted in the following figure:

D = Demand rate in units per period
R = Replenishment rate in units per period
q = Order quantity
q^* = Optimal order quantity
N = Number of orders per period
C_o = Cost of ordering
C_c = Carrying cost per unit per period
C_s = Shortage cost per unit per period
C_p = Item purchase cost per unit

a. In model B, during time t_1, inventory is accumulating at a rate equal to:

1. D
2. R
3. $D - R$
4. Infinite
5. None of the above

b. In model C, during time t_1:

1. Demand and back orders are being filled at a rate D
2. Demand and back orders are being filled at a rate $D - R$
3. Inventory is being depleted at a rate D

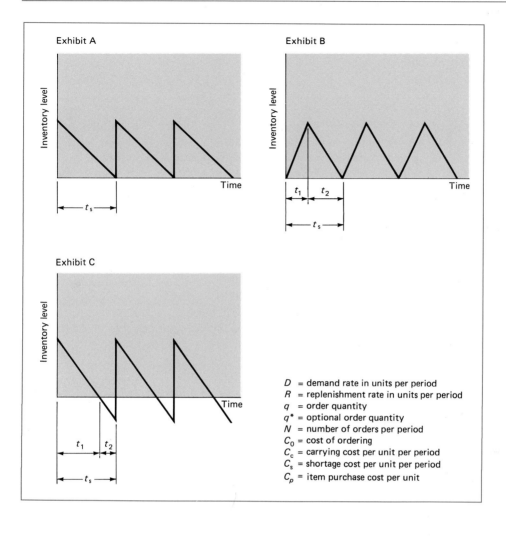

Exhibit A

Exhibit B

Exhibit C

D = demand rate in units per period
R = replenishment rate in units per period
q = order quantity
q^* = optional order quantity
N = number of orders per period
C_0 = cost of ordering
C_c = carrying cost per unit per period
C_s = shortage cost per unit per period
C_p = item purchase cost per unit

   4. Inventory is being depleted at a rate $D - R$
   5. None of the above

c. The number of orders N equals $\dfrac{D}{q}$ for model(s):

   1. A
   2. A and B
   3. A, B, and C
   4. B and C
   5. None of the above

d. The average inventory equals $\dfrac{q}{2}$ for model(s):

   1. A
   2. A and B
   3. A, B, and C
   4. B and C
   5. None of the above

e. In model B during time t_2, inventory is depleted at a rate equal to:

   1. R
   2. $D - q$
   3. $D - q^*$
   4. $D - R$
   5. None of the above

f. In model C, during time t_2:

   1. Inventory is depleted at a rate D
   2. Back orders are accumulating at a rate $D - R$
   3. Inventory is depleted at a rate $D - R$
   4. Back orders are accumulated at a rate D
   5. None of the above

g. In model A, during time t_s:

   1. Inventory is depleted at a rate $D - \dfrac{N}{q}$

   2. Inventory is depleted at a rate R
   3. Inventory is depleted at a rate $D - q$
   4. Inventory is depleted at a rate D
   5. None of the above

h. In which model(s) is it assumed the $C_s = \infty$?

   1. A and C
   2. B
   3. B and C
   4. A and B
   5. None of the above

i. For which model(s) is it assumed that $R > D$?

   1. B
   2. A and C
   3. A, B, and C
   4. C
   5. None of the above

j. If $C_c = \infty$, in model A:

   1. $N = \infty$
   2. $N = D$
   3. $N = O$
   4. $C_o = \infty$
   5. None of the above

k. For which models is it assumed that $R = \infty$?

   1. A and B
   2. B
   3. C
   4. A, B, and C
   5. None of the above

Q20-2. In this chapter, we considered three inventory models as depicted in problem 1. The following questions refer to either none, one, two, or three of the models.

a. Which of the models assumes a constant demand rate?
b. Which of the models assumes a finite replenishment rate?
c. Which of the models assumes a finite stockout cost?

    d. Which of the models assumes an infinite replenishment rate?

    e. Which of the models assumes back ordering during stockout?

    f. Which of the models assumes the replenishment rate exceeds the demand rate?

    g. Which of the models assumes a probabilistic replenishment rate?

    h. Which of the models assumes both a finite replenishment rate and an infinite stockout cost?

    i. Which of the models assumes both a finite replenishment rate and a finite stockout cost?

    j. Which of the models assumes an infinite stockout cost?

    k. Which of the models assumes both an infinite replenishment rate and an infinite stockout cost?

    l. Which of the models assumes the demand rate exceeds the replenishment rate?

    m. Which of the models assumes an infinite demand rate?

    n. Which of the models assumes probabilistic demand during lead time?

    o. Which of the models assumes a finite purchase cost?

Q20-3. What are the philosophical differences between the just-in-time and the typical American inventory system?

PROBLEMS

P20-1.   **1.** Assuming that problems with stockouts can be ignored, the problem of optimal order quantities can be related to a set of opposing cost curves. Indicate the nature of these curves in graphical form, and *identify all significant elements* relating to the graph.   *Basic EOQ Model*

  2. Express total costs in equation form, and derive the model for determining the economic-order quantity from the equation. (Identify all variables.)

  3. State the assumptions of the economic-order-quantity model.

P20-2. Carrying costs are often expressed as a percentage of the unit purchase cost, C_p. Assume a carrying cost of i percent of the purchase cost, and derive expressions for the total cost and the optimal order quantity for such a system.   *Developing EOQ Model*

P20-3. Each of the following questions requires some manipulation of an inventory model.   *Basic EOQ Model and EOQ Model with Stockouts*

  Required ☐

  1. The economic-order-quantity model assumes the cost of stockouts is infinite. Express the total cost equation for the EOQ model, and derive the optimal q^*. Identify the independent and dependent variables and the parameters of the model.

  2. When stockouts with back orders are assumed, the economic-order quantity changes. Diagram and label the system. Develop the total cost equation and identify each term in the equation.

3. In the original economic-order-quantity model, instead of setting up and solving for the optimal q, set up and solve for the optimal N (number of orders).

Basic EOQ Calculations   **P20-4.**   Assume the following:

D = 500 units per year
C_o = \$20 per order
C_c = \$2 per unit per year

Required □

1. Prepare a table similar to table 20.2 to determine the EOQ.

2. Determine the EOQ by formula (20-6) and the total cost by formula (20-5).

EOQ Model with Price Break   **P20-5.**   The demand for a product is 40,000 units a year. The carrying cost is estimated to equal \$2 per unit per year, and ordering cost is \$100. The firm purchases in lots of 2,000 units at a cost of \$3.00 a unit. If the firm purchased in lots of 4,000 units, the vendor would be willing to lower the unit price to \$2.98.

Required □

1. How much of a savings or loss would the firm realize if it purchased in lots of 4,000 units?

2. At what unit price should the firm consider purchasing in lots of 4,000 units?

EOQ Model with Price Break   **P20-6.**   Demand for a product is 20,000 units a year. Annual carrying cost is estimated to equal 20 percent of the purchase price. Incremental ordering costs are estimated to equal \$75. The estimated unit cost is \$75.

Required □

1. Determine the economic-order quantity and minimum inventory cost for the firm.

2. The vendor is willing to lower the price to \$74 if the firm will purchase in lots of 5,000. Should the firm accept the offer? Show calculations.

EOQ Model with Price Break   **P20-7.**   Demand for a product is estimated to be 40,000 units a year. Ordering costs are \$50, and carrying costs per unit per year are estimated to equal \$4.00. In lots of 1,000 or less units, the vendor quoted a unit price of \$3.00. In lots of 4,000 units, the vendor quoted a unit price of \$2.85, and the firm has been placing orders at this price for several years.

Required □

1. How much has the firm saved annually by ordering in lots of 4,000 rather than 1,000 units?

2. If the vendor quoted a unit price of \$2.75 for lots of 8,000 units, should the firm revise its order policy?

P20-8. Assume the following:

EOQ Model with Sensitivity Analysis

D = 5,000 units per year
C_o = \$100 per order
C_c = \$4 per unit per year
C_p = \$25 per unit

Required ☐

1. Calculate q^* and the total cost of the inventory system.

2. Using the data, calculate the effect on q^* and TC of a possible error of +20 percent in C_o, C_c.

P20-9. A manufacturing plant requires 10,000 castings a year for use in assembling lawn and garden tractors. The foundry can produce 30,000 castings a year. The cost associated with setting up the production line is \$25, and the holding cost is \$2 per unit per year. The lead time is sixty days.

Production-Lot Model

Required ☐

1. Find the production quantity that minimizes cost.

2. Calculate the total cost of the system for a year.

3. Determine the procurement level.

P20-10. The setup cost on a production line averages \$25 for the CP Corporation. The carrying costs are \$5 a unit per year, and the annual demand is 10,000 units. Production capacity is 30,000 units per year and stockouts are not permitted in the system.

Production-Lot Model

Required ☐

1. Determine the number of setups that result in the minimum cost.

2. What are the minimum setup and carrying costs?

3. Assuming that the variable unit cost of production is \$5, what is the maximum purchase price C_p would be willing to pay from an outside vendor? Assume the cost of ordering is \$15.

P20-11. A contractor has a requirement for cement that amounts to 80,000 bags per year. No shortages are allowed. Cement costs \$4 a bag, holding cost is \$6 per unit per year, and it costs \$24 to process a purchase order. The lead time is thirty days.

EOQ Model with Shortage Cost

Required ☐

1. Find the purchase quantity that minimizes cost.

2. Calculate the total cost of the system for a year. (Include purchase cost.)

3. Determine the procurement level.

4. What additional cost is incurred if the firm orders in lots of 4,000 bags?

In addition to the information just given, assume the cost of shortage is $2 per bag per year.

5. Find the purchase quantity that minimizes cost.

6. Find the maximum inventory level.

7. Determine the new procurement level.

8. Explain any difference between your answer for requirement 2 and the total cost of the system when shortage cost is considered.

EOQ and Production-Lot Models   **P20-12.** A manufacturing plant requires 10,000 slip rings a year for use in assembly operations. The machine shop can produce 18,000 units per year. The cost associated with initiating manufacturing action (setup cost) is $18, and the holding cost is $1 per unit per year. Manufacturing cost is $10 per unit. No stockouts are permitted. The lead time is sixty days.

Required □

1. Find the manufacturing quantity that minimizes cost.

2. Calculate the total cost of the system per year.

3. Determine the procurement level.

A subcontractor has been found that can supply slip rings to the manufacturer. Procurement cost is estimated at $18 per purchase order, and storage cost remains at $1 per unit per year. No shortages are to be allowed. Purchase price is $9.97 per slip ring. The lead time is thirty days.

Required □

4. Find the purchase quantity that minimizes cost.

5. Find the total inventory cost of the system.

6. Determine the new procurement level.

7. Considering only the inventory and production or purchasing costs, should the firm manufacture or purchase the slip rings?

8. The cost accountant calls an error he has made to your attention. He says the setup cost is correct at $18, but that the cost per purchase order is $32 rather than the original $18 used in the previous situation. Based on this, would your answer to requirements 4 and 7 change? Show computations and explain.

Developing an Inventory Model   **P20-13.** The Beams Corporation has a completely computerized accounting-information system. The firm must process a yearly average of 10,000 checks for payment of accounts payable. The average amount of each check is $100. Interest is charged at an average annual rate of 18 percent for late payment on these accounts. Assume the payables are due upon receipt. The Beams computer system is so efficient that it can process any quantity of checks in a matter of seconds. However, preparing the system to process the checks costs $100 each time the accounts-payable program is run.

Required □

1. Specify the equation for the total annual cost of the accounts-payable system.

2. Determine from requirement 1 the optimal number of accounts payable that should be processed each time the accounts payable program is run. This should be the general solution of your model.

3. Draw and label a diagram of the accounts-payable system. (The diagram should not be of the cost curves.)

4. Determine the minimum total cost and optimal number of accounts payable to be processed for Beams Corporation.

P20-14. The Accounting Society at Virginia Tech has daily cash needs of $30, or $10,800 a year. The only source of cash for the Accounting Society is running a car wash at a local shopping center. For each day the car wash is run, the net cash receipts average $200. If the Accounting Society ran the car wash all year, their total cash receipts would be $72,000. Every time the car wash is started, a fee of $100 must be paid to the shopping center.   *Developing an Inventory Model*

Because the Accounting Society is a student organization, all funds must be deposited with the university's central accounting office. To cover the expense of operating this office, the university charges each organization 5 percent annually of their average cash balance. Since the Accounting Society cannot borrow, it can never have a negative balance in its account with the university.

Required □

1. On the average, how many car washes should the Accounting Society run each year to minimize its costs?

2. How many days on the average should the car wash last?

3. What is the minimum total average cost the accounting society can incur in managing its cash?

P20-15. A criterion employed to evaluate the efficiency of a firm's inventory policies is the inventory-turnover ratio: *EOQ Model and Inventory Turnover*

$$\frac{\text{Cost of goods sold}}{\text{Average inventory on hand}}$$

The following relates to the inventory system of two firms:

Firm A		*Firm B*	
D	= 12,000	D	= 24,000
C_o	= $200 per order	C_o	= $200 per order
C_c	= $3 per unit per year	C_c	= $3 per unit per year
C_p	= $30	C_p	= $30

Required ☐

1. Determine the optimal order quantity for each of the firms.

2. Determine the inventory-turnover ratio for the two firms.

3. If Firm A determines $C_s = \$15$ per unit per year, what is the new inventory-turnover ratio for Firm A?

4. Discuss the use of this ratio in light of your answers.

EOQ Model and Inventory Turnover
P20-16. A criterion employed to evaluate the efficiency of a firm's inventory policies is the inventory-turnover ratio:

$$\frac{\text{Cost of goods sold}}{\text{Average inventory on hand}}$$

The following relates to the inventory systems of two firms:

Firm A	Firm B
D = 9,000 units per year	D = 36,000 units per year
C_o = \$100 per order	C_o = \$100 per order
C_c = \$5 per unit per year	C_c = \$5 per unit per year
C_p = \$50 per unit	C_p = \$50 per unit.

Required ☐

1. Determine the optimal order quantity for each of the firms.

2. Determine the inventory-turnover ratio for the two firms.

3. Discuss the use of this ratio in light of your first answer.

Estimating Shortage Costs
P20-17. A sporting goods dealer estimates his annual demand for blank golf balls to equal 80,000. When a customer purchases these golf balls, the shop will print up to fifteen letters on each ball. The cost of placing an order is \$5, and the carrying cost is \$.10.

The owner of the store indicates that he would like to be able to service 60 percent of his customers on demand. Assume that the other 40 percent of the customers would place back orders.

Required ☐ What shortage cost can be inferred from the owner's service-level policy?

Estimating Shortage Costs
P20-18. A record shop owner estimates the shop's annual demand for blank tape cartridges to equal 10,000 units. The cost of placing an order is \$50, and the carrying cost is estimated to be \$1. The manager is unable to determine shortage costs but would like to maintain a service level of 90 percent (i.e., 90 percent of the customers receive their tapes on demand, and 10 percent are forced to place back orders).

Required ☐ Determine the shortage cost that can be inferred from the company's service-level policy.

P20-19. Assume that a firm can purchase units at five different prices at the number of units indicated.

Price Breaks and EOQ Model

Units	Price
0– 99	$1.00
100–199	.95
200–299	.90
300–399	.85
400–∞	.80

Required ☐ If the ordering cost is $5 and the demand is 3,000 units annually, determine the economic-order quantity when the carrying cost is estimated to equal 20 percent of the purchase price.

P20-20. Assume that a firm can purchase units at four different prices at the number of units indicated.

Price Breaks and EOQ Model

Units	Price
0– 999	$1.10
1,000–1,999	1.00
2,000–2,999	.90
3,000–∞	.80

Required ☐ If the ordering cost is $50, carrying cost is $3, and the demand is 120,000 units annually, find the economic-order quantity, considering the price breaks.

P20-21. Assume a firm has an EOQ of 300 for an item and six orders are placed each year. The procurement level is 100 units and demand during lead time is assigned the following probabilities:

Determining Safety Stock

Demand during lead time	Probability of demand
120	.10
110	.20
100	.35
90	.25
80	.10

Required ☐ Assume the annual carrying costs of $5 per unit per year and shortage costs of $10 per unit. Determine the minimum cost-safety stock.

P20-22. Lead time for the Paul Wayne Company is 20 days, and the optimum number of orders per year is five. Shortage costs are estimated to be $10 per unit and carrying costs are $3 per unit per year. Estimated demand during lead time is 300 units.

Determining Safety Stock

Demand during lead time	Demand probability
150	.05
200	.06
250	.14
300	.5
350	.12
400	.08
450	.05

Required □

1. What level of safety stock should be carried to minimize costs?

2. What level of safety stock should be carried if Paul Wayne wants to maintain a 100 percent service level during lead time? What additional cost is incurred by maintaining the 100 percent service level during lead time?

Static Inventory under Risk   **P20-23.** A florist is trying to decide how many mums to order for the homecoming football game. The selling price is $5 and the cost is $3 each. According to past experience, the florist estimates the demand and its associated probabilities to be:

Demand	1	2	3	4	5	6
Probability	.06	.15	.25	.30	.20	.04

Required □

1. Prepare a profit matrix, and determine the expected profit for each strategy available to the florist.

2. Prepare an opportunity-cost matrix, and determine the expected opportunity cost for each strategy available to the florist.

3. Review your answer to requirement 1 by using the appropriate formula to determine the optimum strategy.

Static Inventory under Risk   **P20-24.** Paul's Bait Shop is preparing for a three-day July 4th holiday by buying minnows for resale. Tanked minnows only survive approximately four days, so it is imperative that Paul buy enough minnows to last him only through the holiday. Demand is based solely on weather conditions. The Farmer's Almanac, local television reports, and Paul's rheumatism indicate the following:

Weather	Probability	Demand for minnows in pounds
Showers	.1	0
Fair but overcast	.3	100
Partly sunny	.4	200
Sunny and mild	.2	300

Minnows sell at $2.00 a pound and cost $1.50 a pound, including delivery.

Required □

1. Prepare a profit matrix, and determine the expected profit for each strategy available to Paul.

2. Prepare an opportunity-cost matrix, and determine the expected opportunity cost for each strategy available to Paul.

3. Review your answer to requirement 1 by using the appropriate formula to determine the optimum strategy.

P20-25. In the construction business, government regulations require that everyone on a job site wear a hard hat. A spare hat costs $50. If no spare is on hand, the cost associated with replacing the hat is $150 (special ordering costs, lost time, etc.). The probabilities associated with damaging a hat during a three-year period are:

Static Inventory under Risk

Number of damaged hats	Probability
0	.2
1	.2
2	.4
3	.2

If, after three years, a hat is still in usable condition, it must be replaced.

Required □

1. Prepare a cost matrix, and determine the expected cost for each strategy available to the contractor.

2. Prepare an opportunity-cost matrix, and determine the expected opportunity cost of each strategy available to the contractor.

3. Review your answer to requirement 2 by using the appropriate formula to determine the optimum strategy.

P20-26. In purchasing a new dishwasher, the buyer has the opportunity to purchase a service contract that will cover all repairs for one year. The service contract costs $25, and a breakdown, based on previous experience, will cost $35. From past maintenance records, the probabilities of the dishwasher breaking down during the year are:

Static Inventory under Risk

Number of breakdowns	Probability
0	.2
1	.4
2	.4

Required □

1. Prepare a cost matrix, and determine the expected cost of each strategy available to the buyer.

2. Prepare an opportunity cost matrix, and determine the expected opportunity cost of each strategy available to the buyer.

P20-27. A firm has the option of self insuring, purchasing insurance that will cover 50 percent of the loss due to fire, or buying insurance that will cover 100 percent of the loss due to fire. The average expected loss caused by a fire is $1,000.

Static Inventory under Risk

	0%	50%	100%
Purchase insurance			
Cost	0	$150	$280

Number of fires	Probability
0	.6
1	.3
2	.1

Required ☐

1. Prepare a cost matrix, and determine the expected cost of each strategy available to the firm.

2. Prepare an opportunity-cost matrix, and determine the expected opportunity cost of each strategy available to the firm.

Static Inventory under Risk and Cost of Perfect Information

P20-28. Fast Food purchases sandwiches from a vendor that delivers every Monday. Demand per week for cases of sandwiches is shown. A case of sandwiches costs $75 and is sold for $150. Any cases of sandwiches over a week old are sold to a pig farm for $10 a case. Management desires the vendor to leave the same number of cases each week.

Demand per week in cases	Probability of demand
1	.2
2	.5
3	.3

Required ☐

1. Prepare a profit matrix, and determine the maximum expected profit.

2. Prepare an opportunity-cost matrix, and determine the minimum expected opportunity cost.

3. Determine how much the firm would be willing to pay for perfect information.

4. Formulate a general expression for the expected profit for Fast Food.

Static Inventory under Risk and Cost of Perfect Information

P20-29. A grocery store buys bread from a truck that delivers every Monday. Demand per week for cases of 144 loaves of bread is shown. A case of bread costs $40 and is sold for $60.

Demand per week in cases	Probability of demand
1	.10
2	.50
3	.40

We want the delivery truck to leave the same amount of bread each Monday. Once the new delivery arrives, the old bread must be thrown away.

Required ☐

1. Prepare a profit matrix, and determine the supply of bread that will maximize the expected profit.

2. Prepare an opportunity-cost matrix, and determine the supply of bread that will minimize the expected opportunity cost.

3. How much would the firm be willing to pay for perfect information?

EOQ-Model Manipulations

P20-30. The Robney Company is a restaurant supplier that sells a number of products to various restaurants in the area. One of the products is a special meat cutter with a disposable blade.

The blades are sold in packages of twelve blades for $20 per package. After a number of years, it has been determined that the demand for the replacement blades has a constant rate of 2,000 packages per month. The packages cost the Robney Company $10 each from the manufacturer and require a three-day lead time from date of order to date of delivery. The ordering cost is $1.20 per order, and the carrying cost is 10 percent per annum.

Robney is going to use the economic-order-quantity formula:

$$EOQ = \sqrt{\frac{2 \text{ (annual requirements) (cost per order)}}{\text{(price per unit) (carrying cost)}}}$$

Required □

1. Calculate:

   a. The economic-order quantity
   b. The number of orders needed per year
   c. The total cost of buying and carrying blades for the year

2. Assuming there is no reserve (e.g., safety stock) and that the present inventory level is 200 packages, when should the next order be placed? (Use 360 days equals one year.)

3. Discuss the problems that most firms would have in attempting to apply this formula to their inventory problems.

(CMA)

P20-31. Breakon, Inc., manufactures and distributes machine tools. The tools are assembled from approximately 2,000 components manufactured by the company. For several years, the production schedule called for one production run of each component each month. This schedule has resulted in a high inventory-turnover rate of four times but requires twelve setups for each component every year. In a normal year, $3,500 of cost is incurred for each component to produce the number of units sold. The company has been successful in not letting the year-end inventory drop below $100 for each component. *Production Scheduling*

The production manager recommends that the company gradually switch to a schedule of producing the annual needs of each component in one yearly production run. He believes this would reduce costs, because only one setup cost would be incurred each year for every component rather than twelve. At the present time, the costs for each setup are $36. Estimated annual costs associated with carrying inventory, per $1 of inventory value, are: property, 4 percent; insurance, 2 percent; and storage cost, 20 percent. The firm estimates its cost of capital to be 10 percent after taxes and pays income taxes at 40 percent of taxable income.

Required □

1. If Breakon converts to the once-a-year production schedule for its components, calculate the total investment released or additional investment required once the changeover is completed.

2. If Breakon converts to the once-a-year production schedule, calculate the after-tax savings or added expenses once the changeover is completed.

3. What factors other than those referred to in requirements 1 and 2 should be considered in reaching a decision to change the production policy?

3. Do your calculations support a change to the proposed policy? Explain your answer.

(CMA)

Identifying Inventory Costs

P20-32. You have been engaged to install an accounting system for the Kaufman Corporation. Among the inventory-control features the Kaufman management personnel desire as a part of the system are indicators of how much and when to order. The following information is furnished for one item, called a komtronic, which is carried in inventory:

1. Komtronics are sold by the gross (twelve dozen) and have a list price of $800 per gross F.O.B. shipper. Kaufman receives a 40 percent trade discount off list price on purchases in gross lots.

2. Freight cost is $20 per gross from the shipping point to Kaufman's plant.

3. Kaufman uses about 5,000 komtronics during a 259-day production year and must purchase a total of thirty-six gross per year to allow for normal breakage.

4. Normal delivery time to receive an order is twenty working days from the date a purchase request is initiated. A rush order in full gross lots can be received by air freight in five working days at an extra cost of $52 per gross. A stockout (complete exhaustion of the inventory) of komtronics would stop production, and Kaufman would purchase komtronics locally at list price rather than shut down.

5. The cost of placing an order is $10; the cost of receiving an order is $20.

6. Space storage cost is $12 per year per gross stored.

7. Insurance and taxes are approximately 12 percent of the net delivered cost of average inventory, and Kaufman expects a return of at least 8 percent on its average investment (ignore return on order and carrying cost for simplicity).

Required ☐

1. Prepare a schedule computing the total annual cost of komtronics based on uniform order lot sizes of one, two, three, four, five, and six gross of komtronics. (The schedule should show the total annual cost according to each lot size.) Indicate the economic-order quantity (economic lot size to order).

2. Prepare a schedule computing the minimum stock-reorder point for komtronics. The komtronics inventory should not fall below this point without reordering so as to guard against a stockout. Factors to be

considered include average lead-period usage and safety-stock requirements.

3. Prepare a schedule computing the cost of a stockout of komtronics. Factors to be considered include the excess costs for local purchases and for rush orders.

(CPA)

P20-33. The Hermit Company manufactures a line of walnut office products. Hermit executives estimate the demand for the double walnut letter tray, one of the company's products, at 6,000 units. The letter tray sells for $80 per unit. The costs relating to the letter tray are estimated to be as follows for 19X7:

Determining Inventory-cost Savings

1. Standard manufacturing cost per letter tray unit—$50

2. Costs to initiate a production run—$300

3. Annual cost of carrying the letter tray in inventory—20 percent of standard manufacturing cost

In prior years, the company has scheduled the production for the letter tray in two equal production runs. The company is aware that the economic-order-quantity (EOQ) model can be employed to determine optimum size for production runs. The EOQ formula as it applies to inventories for determining the optimum order quantity is shown below.

$$\text{EOQ} = \sqrt{\frac{2 \text{ (annual demand)(cost per order)}}{\text{(cost per unit)(carrying cost)}}}$$

Required □ Calculate the expected annual cost savings Hermit Company could experience if it employed the economic-order-quantity model to determine the number of production runs that should be initiated during the year for the manufacture of the double walnut letter trays.

(CMA)

P20-34. ROAT Company is a regional manufacturing company that operates with a typical manufacturing plant utilizing a raw material, work-in-process, and finished-goods inventory system. Raw materials are purchased and stored until their introduction into the manufacturing process. Upon completion, the finished product is stored in the company's warehouse until final sale.

Inventory-Cost Issues

The company controller recently read an article that stated that the annual cost of carrying inventory from the raw-material phase through the finished-goods phase can cost between 15 and 30 percent of the average value of the total inventory. As a consequence of the article, the controller asked the company's Cost Accounting department to prepare an analysis and estimate of the company's inventory carrying cost. The analysis indicated that carrying costs were greater than 25 percent of the average inventory value. The study confirmed the controller's belief that inventory carrying costs might be an excellent area in which to implement cost reductions.

At a management meeting, the production manager suggested that the inventory carrying costs be shifted to suppliers and customers. This could be accomplished by not requesting raw materials from suppliers until needed in the manufacturing process and by transferring the finished goods to customers immediately following completion.

Required □

1. Identify three types of inventory carrying costs, and give specific examples of each type of cost.

2. The production manager of ROAT Company has suggested that inventory carrying costs be shifted to suppliers and customers. Identify and discuss the circumstances that would have to exist to make such a proposal feasible with respect to:

   a. Raw-materials inventories
   b. Finished-goods inventories

3. Suppose ROAT Company is successful in shifting a portion or all of its inventory carrying costs to suppliers and customers.

   a. Identify the inventory carrying costs ROAT might be able to reduce by shifting the inventory burden.
   b. Identify possible areas of increased costs that could offset, in whole or part, the reduction of inventory carrying costs.

(CMA)

Determining **P20-35.** Evans, Inc., is a large wholesale distributor that deals exclusively in baby
Inventory Costs   shoes. Due to the substantial costs related to ordering and storing the shoes, the company has decided to employ the economic-order-quantity method (EOQ) to help determine the optimum quantities of shoes to order from the different manufacturers. The EOQ formula is

$$EOQ = \sqrt{\frac{2C_oD}{PC_s}}$$

where

EOQ = Optimum number of units per purchase order
D = Annual demand
P = Purchase price per unit
C_o = Cost of placing an order
C_s = The annual cost of storage per dollar of investment in inventory

Before Evans, Inc., can employ the EOQ model, they need to develop values for two of the cost parameters—ordering costs (C_o) and storage costs (C_s). As a starting point, the management staff has decided to develop the values for the two cost parameters by using cost data from the most recent fiscal year, 19X5.

The company placed 4,000 purchase orders during 19X5. The largest number of orders placed during any one month was 400 orders in June, and the smallest number of orders placed was 250 in December. Select cost data for these two months and the year for the purchasing, accounts payable, and warehousing operations are:

	Costs for high-activity month (June, 400 orders)	Costs for low-activity month (December, 250 orders)	Annual costs
Purchasing Department			
Purchasing manager ..	$ 1,750	$ 1,750	$ 21,000
Buyers	2,500	1,900	28,500
Clerks	2,000	1,100	20,600
Supplies	275	150	2,500
Accounts-Payable Department			
Clerks	2,000	1,500	21,500
Supplies	125	75	1,100
Data processing	2,600	2,300	30,000
Warehouse			
Crew supervisor	1,250	1,250	15,000
Receiving clerks	2,300	1,800	23,300
Receiving supplies	50	25	500
Shipping clerks	3,800	3,500	44,000
Shipping supplies	1,350	1,200	15,200
Freight out	1,600	1,300	16,800
	$21,600	$17,850	$240,000

The Purchasing department is responsible for placing all orders. The costs listed for the Accounts-Payable department relate only to the processing of purchase orders for payment. The warehouse costs reflect two operations—receiving and shipping. The receiving clerks inspect all incoming shipments and place the orders in storage. The shipping clerks are responsible for processing all sales orders to retailers.

The company leases space in a public warehouse. The rental fee is priced according to the square feet occupied during a month. The annual charges during 19X5 totaled $34,500. Annual insurance and property taxes on the shoes stored in the warehouse amounted to $5,700 and $7,300, respectively. The company pays 8 percent a year for a small amount of short-term, seasonal bank debt. Long-term capital investments are expected to produce a rate of return of 12 percent after taxes. The effective tax rate is 40 percent.

The inventory balances tend to fluctuate during the year depending upon the demand for baby shoes. Selected data on inventory balances is:

Inventory, January 1, 19X5 .... $160,000
Inventory, December 31, 19X5 120,000
Highest inventory balance (June) 220,000
Lowest inventory balance (December) 120,000
Average monthly inventory 190,000

The boxes in which the shoes are stored are all approximately the same size. Consequently, the shoes all occupy about the same amount of storage space in the warehouse.

Required □

1. Using the 19X5 data, determine estimated values appropriate for

    a. C_o—cost of placing an order
    b. C_s—the annual cost of storage per dollar of investment in inventory

2. Should Evans, Inc., use the cost parameters developed solely from the historical data in the employment of the EOQ model? Explain your answer.

(CMA)

Determining
Inventory Costs

P20-36. The Pointer Furniture Company manufactures and sells office furniture. In order to compete effectively in different quality and price markets, it produces several brands of office furniture. The manufacturing operation is organized by the item produced rather than by the furniture line. Thus, the desks for all brands are manufactured on the same production line. For efficiency and quality-control reasons, the desks are manufactured in batches. For example, ten high-quality desks might be manufactured during the first two weeks in October and fifty units of a lower-quality desk during the last two weeks. Because each model has its own unique manufacturing requirement, the change from one model to another requires the factory's equipment to be adjusted.

The Pointer management team wants to determine the most economical production run for each of the items in its product lines. The manager of the Cost Accounting department is going to adapt the economic-order-quantity (EOQ) inventory model for this analysis.

One of the cost parameters that must be determined before the model can be employed is the setup cost incurred when there is a change to a different furniture model. The Cost Accounting department has been asked to determine the setup cost for the desk (Model JE 40) in its junior-executive line as an example.

The Equipment Maintenance department is responsible for all of the changeover adjustments on production lines in addition to the preventive and regular maintenance of all the Production equipment. The equipment maintenance staff has a forty-hour work week; the size of the staff is changed only if there is a change in the workload that is expected to persist for an extended period of time.

The Equipment Maintenance department had ten employees last year, and they each averaged 2,000 hours for the year. They are paid $9 an hour, and employee benefits average 20 percent of wage costs. The other departmental costs, which include such items as supervision, depreciation, insurance, etc., total $50,000 per year.

Two men from the Equipment Maintenance department are required to make the change on the desk line for Model JE 40. They spend an estimated five hours in setting up the equipment as follows:

Machinery changes	3 hours
Testing	1 hour
Machinery readjustments	<u>1 hour</u>
Total	<u>5 hours</u>

The desk-production line on which Model JE 40 is manufactured is operated by five workers. During the changeover, these workers assist the maintenance workers when needed and operate the line during the test run. However, they are idle for approximately 40 percent of the time required for the changeover.

The production workers are paid a basic wage rate of $7.50 an hour. Two overhead bases are used to apply the indirect costs of this production line because some of the costs vary in proportion to direct-labor hours while others vary with machine hours. The overhead rates applicable for the current year are as follows:

	Based on direct-labor hours	Based on machine hours
Variable	$2.75	$ 5.00
Fixed	2.25	15.00
	$5.00	$20.00

These department overhead rates are based upon an expected activity of 10,000 direct-labor hours and 1,500 machine hours for the current year. This department is not scheduled to operate at full capacity because production capability currently exceeds sales potential at this time.

The estimated cost of the direct materials used in the test run totals $200. Salvage material from the test run should total $50.

Required ☐

1. Prepare an estimate of the Pointer Furniture Company setup cost for desk Model JE 40 for use in the economic production run model. For each cost item identified in the problem, justify the amount and the reason for including the cost item in your estimate. Explain the reason for excluding any cost item from your estimate.

2. Identify the cost items that would be included in an estimate of the Pointer Furniture Company cost of carrying the desks in inventory.

(CMA)

CHAPTER OUTLINE

COST ESTIMATION USING LINEAR REGRESSION

CHAPTER **21**

☐ INTRODUCTION

We have previously described how the high-low technique and flexible budgets can be employed in associating costs with some measure of input or output. Linear regression is a statistical technique for specifying a relationship between variables. The major advantage of regression over the high-low technique is that all of the data rather than just the high and low points are employed in specifying the relationship. This chapter contains a description of several linear-regression techniques that can be employed to specify a mathematical function to estimate costs.

In mathematics, the concept of the function plays an important role. For example, consider the following function:

$$y = 5 + 3x$$

Points are found to satisfy the equation by assigning a value to x and then computing the corresponding value of y. Free choice is exercised in selecting a value of x; it is called the independent variable. The expression $5 + 3x$ is a rule that specifies how to compute a value for y given the value for x. This rule is called the function of x, and the outcome is the value assigned to the dependent variable y.

In cost estimation, one seeks to identify some independent variable and the functional relationship that will permit computation of the corresponding value of the dependent variable. The dependent variable will then be some measure of cost. For example, assume the independent variable, x, is units of output, and the dependent variable, y, is total cost. If the function of x is $5 + 3x$ and we seek to estimate total cost for producing seven units, the value of the dependent variable y is

$$y = 5 + 3(7)$$
$$y = 26$$

We will consider several regression techniques for estimating the functional relationship between an independent variable and the dependent variable, cost. Over a relevant range, discussed in chapter 2, costs can be classified as either variable, fixed, semivariable, or semifixed. If we ignore the discontinuity of the step function for semifixed costs and treat the cost as either variable or semivariable, we then can assume linear-cost functions. Such a linear-cost function can be expressed as

$$y = A + Bx$$

where

y = Total cost (dependent variable)
A = Intercept
B = Variable cost
x = Measure of activity (independent variable)

In this linear cost function, x is the independent variable, and y is the dependent variable. If the cost were variable, A would equal zero in the cost function. On the other hand, if the cost were fixed, then B would equal zero. For semivariable costs, both A and B would have positive values.

We assume a linear relationship between x and y for cost estimation. The problem is that we do not know the values of A and B that specify this relationship. Regression analysis is a set of methods for estimating the relationship between a dependent variable and one or more independent variables. When the relationship between a dependent variable and one independent variable is studied, the analysis is called **simple regression.** If more than one independent variable is considered, the analysis is called **multiple regression.**

Regression analysis involves manipulating sample data to derive an equation that specifies a relationship between an independent and dependent variable. This linear regression equation is expressed as

$$\hat{y} = a + bx$$

Here $\hat{y}$ (y hat) indicates that the value of the dependent variable has been estimated given some sample value of the independent variable, x. In the regression equation, a and b are estimates of the true population values A and B that are inferred when we assumed a linear relationship.

☐ CHARACTERISTICS OF A LINEAR-REGRESSION LINE

Assume we are given the linear-regression equation $\hat{y} = 10 + 5x$ as shown in figure 21.1. A regression equation is formulated by observing the value assumed by the dependent variable (y) at given levels of the independent variable (x), and then, using criteria that will be discussed later, selecting the equation that best describes the observed relationship between the two variables. Notice that when the value of x is observed to be 10, the corresponding observed value of the dependent variable (y) is 65. When the value 10 is substituted for x into the regression equation, the estimated value of the dependent variable, $\hat{y}$, is

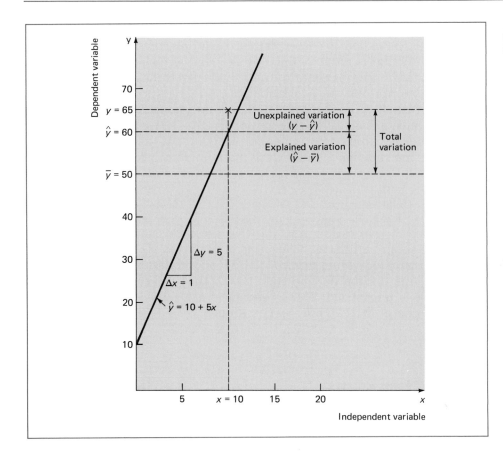

FIGURE 21.1
Characteristics of a
Regression Line

$$\hat{y} = 10 + 5(10)$$
$$\hat{y} = 60$$

Also, assume that the mean, or average, of all of the y values, $\bar{y}$ (y bar), is 50.

Therefore, as shown in figure 21.1, we have three values of the dependent variable. The first, y equals 65, is the observed value when x equals 10. This data point, along with many others, was used in determining the regression equation. The second value, $\hat{y}$ equals 60, was obtained using the regression equation. The third value, $\bar{y}$ equals 50, is the mean of all observed values of the dependent variable.

Characteristics of a linear-regression line are expressed in terms of the differences among these three values of the dependent variable. The difference between $\hat{y}$ (the estimated value) and $\bar{y}$ (the mean) equals ten and is called the **explained variation.** It is explained in the sense that if we knew nothing about the relationship between x and y and were told that x equaled 10 and were asked to estimate a value for y, a rational person would estimate $\hat{y}$ to equal the mean, or 50. Since the regression line explains something about this relationship, we estimate the $\hat{y}$ value to equal 60. Therefore, the difference of 10 is the variation in y that is explained by variation of x.

The difference between y (the observed value) and $\hat{y}$ (the estimated value) equals 5 and is called the **unexplained variation,** or the error. It is the variation in y that is not explained by the regression equation. Later, we will discuss assumptions about the distribution of these error terms. Based on these assumptions, we can make probabilistic statements about our regression results. Keep in mind that we are only considering one observed value of x and the corresponding value for y. As shown in figure 21.1, the same difference can be determined for all points in the original data.

A regression line has the following mathematical properties:

$$\Sigma(y - \hat{y}) = 0$$
$$\Sigma(y - \hat{y})^2 = \text{minimum}$$

That is, the first expression indicates that the regression line fits the data so that the sum of all the error terms (the deviation of the observed value from the estimated value) is zero. The second equation tells us that the regression line fits the data in such a way that the sum of the squared error terms is minimized. These conditions are satisfied by the simultaneous solution of the two normal equations:[1]

$$\Sigma y = na + b\Sigma x$$
$$\Sigma xy = a\Sigma x + b \Sigma x^2$$

where n is the number of observations in the sample. Solving the normal equations, the value of a and b are

$$b = \frac{\Sigma(x - \bar{x})(y - \bar{y})}{\Sigma (x - \bar{x})^2}$$

$$a = \bar{y} - b\bar{x}$$

where $\bar{x}$ and $\bar{y}$ are respectively the means of x and y.

---

1. The two normal equations are obtained by taking the partial derivatives of the sum-of-the-squared-error terms equation as follows:

$$s = \Sigma (y - \hat{y})^2$$
$$= \Sigma (y - a - bx)^2$$
$$\frac{ds}{da} = -2\Sigma(y - a - bx)$$
$$\frac{ds}{db} = -2\Sigma x(y - a - bx)$$

Then, the partial derivatives are set equal to zero:

$$-2\Sigma (y - a - bx) = 0$$
$$\Sigma y - na - b\Sigma x = 0$$
$$\Sigma y = na + b\Sigma x$$
$$-2\Sigma x(y - a - bx) = 0$$
$$\Sigma xy - a\Sigma x - b\Sigma x^2 = 0$$
$$\Sigma xy = a\Sigma x - b\Sigma x^2$$

Thus, this procedure assumes that the values of a and b obtained by solving the normal equations minimize the sum-of-the-squared-error terms.

To aid in computation, these equations can be modified as follows:

$$b = \frac{n(\Sigma xy) - (\Sigma x)(\Sigma y)}{n(\Sigma x^2) - (\Sigma x)^2} \tag{21-1}$$

$$a = \frac{(\Sigma y)(\Sigma x^2) - (\Sigma x)(\Sigma xy)}{n(\Sigma x^2) - (\Sigma x)^2} = \frac{\Sigma y}{n} - b\frac{\Sigma x}{n} \tag{21-2}$$

The sum of squared deviations of the observed dependent variable (y) from the mean of the dependent variable ($\bar{y}$) can be decomposed into the sum of squares regression (or the explained sum of squares and the sum of squares error).

Total sum of squares	=	Sum of squares regression	+	Sum of squares error
$(y - \bar{y})^2$	=	$(\hat{y} - \bar{y})^2$	+	$(y - \hat{y})^2$

For a given total sum of squares, minimizing[2] the sum of squares error $(y - \hat{y})^2$ results in a maximum sum of squares regression $(\hat{y} - \bar{y})^2$. Therefore, the regression line explains the average maximum variation in y through variation in x.

The coefficient of determination, R^2, is defined as

$$R^2 = \frac{\text{Sum of squares regression}}{\text{Total sum of squares}} = \frac{\Sigma(\hat{y} - \bar{y})^2}{\Sigma(y - \bar{y})^2} \tag{21-3}$$

or

$$= 1 - \frac{\text{Sum of squares error}}{\text{Total sum of squares}} = 1 - \frac{\Sigma(y - \hat{y})^2}{\Sigma(y - \bar{y})^2}$$

The **coefficient of determination** ranges in value from zero to one. It measures the percentage of variation in y that is explained by changes in x. In the case of a perfect fit, the regression line will pass through every observed value of y. In such a case, the sum of the squared error terms will be zero and R^2 will equal one. At the other extreme, if b equals zero, then a will equal y, every error term will equal $(y - \bar{y})$, and R^2 will equal zero.

☐ DESCRIPTIVE LINEAR REGRESSION—AN EXAMPLE

Table 21.1, which contains the data to be used in this example, gives the overhead cost and direct-labor hours for twenty-four periods. The objective is to determine a linear-regression equation so that it is possible to estimate overhead cost, given some level of direct-labor hours. The first step is to plot the data and then evaluate the relationship between the two variables. As shown in figure 21.2, there appears to be a linear relationship between the variables, although the relationship certainly is not perfect.

---

2. This is the second mathematical property of a regression line.

TABLE 21.1 Simple Regression Data

Observation number	Overhead cost y	Direct-labor hours x
1	$55,000	5,010
2	57,200	5,100
3	56,800	5,350
4	57,900	5,200
5	58,400	5,100
6	54,700	5,300
7	54,100	4,100
8	53,900	4,100
9	54,200	5,700
10	56,900	5,800
11	62,100	6,300
12	62,700	6,250
13	61,900	6,300
14	63,400	6,800
15	64,100	6,900
16	64,500	7,100
17	62,200	6,850
18	61,100	7,050
19	60,800	6,650
20	59,700	6,400
21	58,400	6,050
22	59,400	5,900
23	60,900	5,950
24	65,100	6,150

Manipulating the data from table 21.1 and substituting in equations (21-1) and (21-2), the regression coefficients are found to equal:[3]

$$b = \frac{24(8,455,900,000) - (141,410)(1,425,400)}{24(849,770,100) - (19,996,788,100)}$$

$$b = \$3.4594$$

$$a = \frac{(1,425,400)(849,770,100) - (141,410)(8,455,900,000)}{24(849,770,100) - 19,996,788,100}$$

$$a = \$39,008.56$$

Substituting the values for a and b in the regression equation, we have

$$\hat{y} = \$39,008.56 + \$3.4594x$$

where $\hat{y}$ is the estimated overhead cost and x is the direct-labor hours. The resulting linear-regression line is shown in figure 21.3. For example, if we

3. Generally, a computer program is employed to determine regression coefficients.

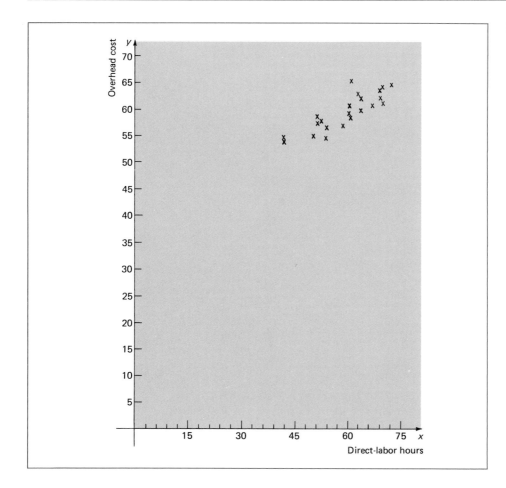

FIGURE 21.2
Plot of Simple
Regression Data

planned to work 5,900 hours during the next period, then the estimated overhead cost based on the regression equation is

$\hat{y} = \$39,008.56 + \$3.4594(5,900)$
$\hat{y} = \$59,419$

The coefficient of determination (R^2) by formula (21-3) equals

$$R^2 = \frac{198,308,424}{284,978,333} = .6959$$

This means that on the average 69.59 percent of the variation in the overhead cost is explained by variation in the direct-labor hours.

Now we can evaluate some of the mathematical properties of the regression equation. The explained and unexplained variation for the first observation ($x = 5,010$ DLH) can be determined as follows:

$\hat{y} = \$39,008.56 + \$3.4594(5,010) = \$56,340$

FIGURE 21.3
Regression Line
and Plotted
Observations

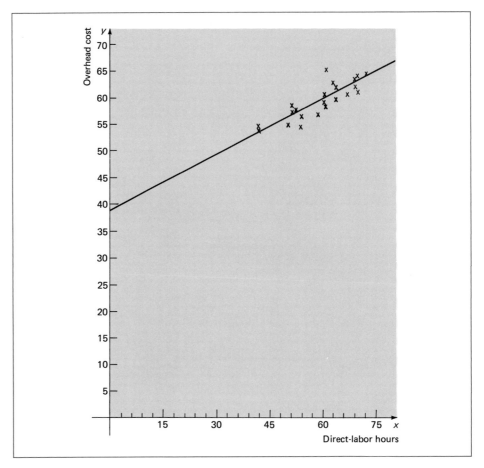

Explained variation $= (\hat{y} - \bar{y}) = \$56,340 - \$59,392 = (\$3,052)$

Unexplained variation $= (y - \hat{y}) = \$55,000 - \$56,340 = (\$1,340)$

Table 21.2 contains the error terms for each of the observations. Note that the sum of the error terms as expected equals zero.
The sum of squares for this example is:

$$\begin{array}{ccc}
\text{Total sum of} & = & \text{Sum-of-squares} & + & \text{Sum-of-squares} \\
\text{squares} & & \text{regression} & & \text{error}
\end{array}$$

$$284,978,333 = 198,308,424 + 86,669,909$$

The sum-of-squares error is minimized and, therefore, there exists no line that would result in a lower sum-of-squares error.

The example to this point has been based on the assumption that a linear relationship exists between the direct-labor hours and the overhead cost. This approach is called descriptive regression. By making additional assumptions about the error terms, additional statistical inferences can be drawn from the regression results. When these assumptions are made,

TABLE 21.2 Simple Regression Cost Estimates—Direct-Labor Hours Independent Variable

Observation number	Overhead cost y	Estimated overhead cost ŷ	Error terms (y − ŷ)
1	$55,000	$56,340	$(1,340)
2	57,200	56,662	548
3	56,800	57,516	(716)
4	57,900	56,997	903
5	58,400	56,652	1,748
6	54,700	57,343	(2,643)
7	54,100	53,192	908
8	53,900	53,192	708
9	54,200	58,727	(4,527)
10	56,900	59,073	(2,173)
11	62,100	60,803	1,297
12	62,700	60,630	2,070
13	61,900	60,803	1,097
14	63,400	62,533	867
15	64,100	62,878	1,222
16	64,500	63,570	930
17	62,200	62,704	(506)
18	61,100	63,397	(2,297)
19	60,800	62,014	(1,214)
20	59,700	61,149	(1,449)
21	58,400	59,938	(1,538)
22	59,400	59,419	(19)
23	60,900	59,592	1,308
24	65,100	60,284	4,816
		Total	0

the analysis is called classical regression. In the next section, we will discuss the assumptions that underlie classical-regression analysis.

☐ CLASSICAL REGRESSION ANALYSIS—THE ASSUMPTIONS

Regression analysis, like all modeling techniques, requires the user to make certain assumptions about the real world.[4] The availability of canned computer programs has resulted in regression analysis being employed where some, if not all, of the regression assumptions are violated. The material in this chapter should be viewed as an introduction to an extremely complex statistical tool. The assumptions described in this section must be considered carefully if the various statistical tests are to be employed to test the fit of the regression line and to make probabilistic statements about the regression results. If, however, the assumptions are not tenable, regression analysis can only be employed, as previously described, to spec-

4. For an extended discussion of the regression analysis assumptions, see George Benston, "Multiple Regression Analysis of Cost Behavior," *The Accounting Review* XLI (October 1966): 657–72; and Robert Jensen, "Multiple Regression Models for Cost Control—Assumptions and Limitations," *The Accounting Review* XLII (April 1967): 265–72.

ify the structural relationship between the independent and dependent variables.

The basic assumption underlying linear regression is that a linear relationship exists between the independent and dependent variables. It is necessary to plot the data to justify this assumption. Many computer-regression programs have a plot routine that is very helpful in determining whether the linearity assumption is reasonable.

Any deviation between the observed value, y, and the estimated value, $\hat{y}$, is called the error term, u. The error terms are defined as $y - \hat{y}$, and the average or expected value of all the error terms is zero. In addition, in classical regression it is assumed that the variance, and, therefore, the standard deviation, of the error terms is constant. Technically, this constant variance assumption is referred to as homoscedasticity.

For constant variance to exist, the observed points should be uniformly distributed around the regression line. After examining figures 21.4 and 21.5, it is apparent that the constant variance assumption is not appropriate in figure 21.5. If the constant variance assumption is not satisfied, heteroscedasticity exists and the tests of statistical significance regarding the regression coefficients are not appropriate because the variances of the regression parameters are overestimated. A practical test for heteroscedasticity is to plot the distribution of the squared-error terms to determine if there is a significant difference over the range of observations.

In classical regression it is also assumed that the error terms $(y - \hat{y})$ are independent. This means that the error included in one observation is independent of the errors in all the other observations. This assumption often presents problems when analyzing costs because much of the data are time series. Unfortunately, conditions in one time period often influence conditions in the next time period, such that the error terms cannot be assumed to be independent. This condition is called autocorrelation

FIGURE 21.4
Observations when Error Terms Have a Constant Variance

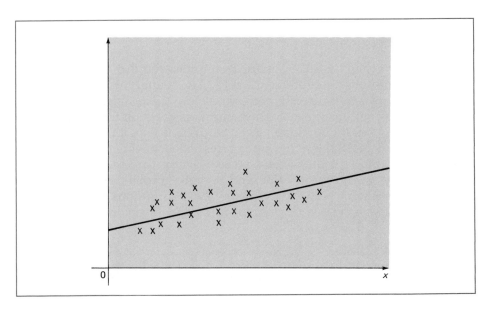

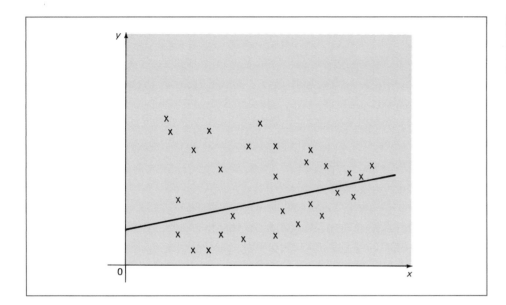

FIGURE 21.5
Observations when Error Terms Do Not Have a Constant Variance

and refers to the lack of serial independence in the error terms. The Durbin-Watson test may be used to determine if significant autocorrelation exists. If the autocorrelation is significant, the estimates of the b values are unbiased, but the variances of the regression coefficients are over or under-estimated. This, in turn, renders the statistical tests inappropriate. At times, the autocorrelation problem can be overcome by introducing additional independent variables, transforming the data, or regressing cost changes against changes in output.

☐ CLASSICAL LINEAR REGRESSION—AN EXAMPLE

When the classical-regression model is used, the regression line is the same as the line determined when using the descriptive-regression model. Therefore, we will use the same data in this section that was employed in the descriptive-regression example. When applying classical-linear regression, we assume the relationship between x and y is linear. In addition, we assume that the error terms are independent, are normally distributed, and have a constant variance.

If the classical assumptions are met, the standard error of the estimate can be used to estimate the variation between estimates of y based on the regression equation and the true value of y. The standard error of the estimate measures the dispersion of the observed values around the regression line. The **standard error of the estimate** for a population is estimated from a sample as follows:

$$s_e = \sqrt{\frac{\Sigma(y - \hat{y})^2}{n - k - 1}}$$

(21-4)

where n is the sample size and k is the number of slopes. The numerator is the sum of squares error, and the denominator, $n-k-1$, is called the degrees of freedom. We lose one degree of freedom for each value that has been estimated. In the example, we estimated the intercept and one slope to determine the regression line; therefore, two degrees of freedom are lost. The number of slopes, k, will be greater than one when multiple regression is employed. A computational form for finding the standard error of the estimate is

$$s_e = \sqrt{\frac{\Sigma y^2 - a\Sigma y - b\Sigma xy}{n - k - 1}} \qquad \textbf{(21-5)}$$

From the previous example with twenty-four observations, the standard error of the estimate using equation (21-4) equals

$$s_e = \sqrt{\frac{86,669,909}{24 - 1 - 1}} = \$1,985$$

If the classical-regression assumptions are reasonably satisfied, then the standard error of the estimate can be used in evaluating the fit of a regression line. It is a measure of the average amount the y values (overhead costs) vary around the regression line. The smaller the standard error of the estimate, the better the regression line fits the data. Refer to figure 21.6 to see how the standard error of the estimate is related to the regression line.

Suppose, however, that it is of interest to predict and make inferences concerning the value of y for some given value of the independent variable (x). In addition to the variance associated with the dispersion of the observed values around the regression line, the formula for computing the estimated standard error of the prediction must take into account another source of variation. This variance component arises due to the fact that with repeated sampling the expected value of y will vary. Recall that the expected value of y for any given x value is $\hat{y}$, the point on the regression line corresponding to that particular x value. With each new sample the estimates of the intercept and slope coefficients will vary somewhat. Therefore, each sample will yield a slightly different regression line and, thus, a different $\hat{y}$ value for any given value of x.

It can be shown that the following equation yields the estimated standard error of the predicted value of y given some value of x:

$$s_p(\hat{y}_j|x_j) = s_e \sqrt{1 + \frac{1}{n} + \frac{(x_j - \bar{x})^2}{\Sigma x_i^2 - \frac{(\Sigma x_i)^2}{n}}} \qquad \textbf{(21-6)}$$

This conditional standard error of the prediction can be used in making probabilistic statements and constructing a prediction interval about the predicted value of y. The prediction interval equals

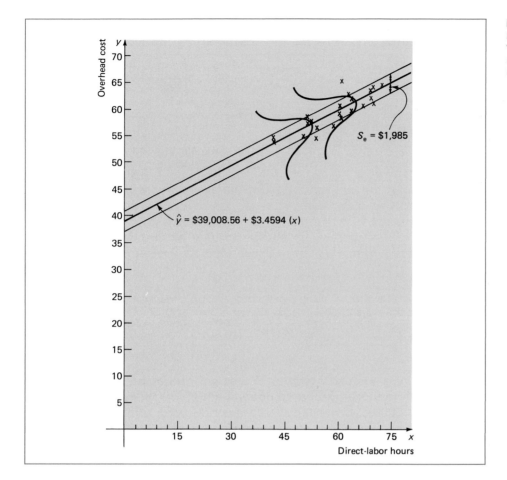

FIGURE 21.6
Regression Line
with Standard
Error of the
Estimate

$S_e = \$1,985$

$\hat{y} = \$39,008.56 + \$3.4594\,(x)$

Overhead cost

Direct-labor hours

$$\hat{y} \pm t_{\alpha/2}\, s_p(\hat{y}_j|x_j) \qquad \qquad \textbf{(21-7)}$$

We have already determined that if 5,900 direct-labor hours are worked, the estimated overhead cost is $59,419. Based on the assumptions of the classical-regression model, if 5,900 hours are worked, we are 50 percent certain that the actual overhead cost will be less than or equal to $59,419. We are also 50 percent certain that the actual overhead cost will be greater than or equal to $59,419.

A 99 percent **confidence interval** can be constructed around the estimate of $59,419 by using formulas (21-6) and (21-7) and using a t-value obtained from table 21.3. Since table 21.3 contains the area of the curve outside the interval for one tail, to construct a $1 - \alpha$ (99 percent) prediction interval, the t-value is selected from the $t_{\alpha/2}$ ($t_{.01/2} = t_{.005}$) column of the table with $n - k - 1$ ($24 - 1 - 1 = 22$) degrees of freedom. For the 99-percent prediction interval, from the $t_{.005}$ column with twenty-two degrees of freedom, a t-value of 2.819 is selected.

Then, using formulas (21-6) and (21-7), the prediction interval is

TABLE 21.3 Values of t

d.f.	$t_{.100}$	$t_{.050}$	$t_{.025}$	$t_{.010}$	$t_{.005}$
1	3.078	6.314	12.706	31.821	63.657
2	1.886	2.920	4.303	6.965	9.925
3	1.638	2.353	3.182	4.541	5.841
4	1.533	2.132	2.776	3.747	4.604
5	1.476	2.015	2.571	3.365	4.032
6	1.440	1.943	2.447	3.143	3.707
7	1.415	1.895	2.365	2.998	3.499
8	1.397	1.860	2.306	2.896	3.355
9	1.383	1.833	2.262	2.821	3.250
10	1.372	1.812	2.228	2.764	3.169
11	1.363	1.796	2.201	2.718	3.106
12	1.356	1.782	2.179	2.681	3.055
13	1.350	1.771	2.160	2.650	3.012
14	1.345	1.761	2.145	2.624	2.977
15	1.341	1.753	2.131	2.602	2.947
16	1.337	1.746	2.120	2.583	2.921
17	1.333	1.740	2.110	2.567	2.898
18	1.330	1.734	2.101	2.552	2.878
19	1.328	1.729	2.093	2.539	2.861
20	1.325	1.725	2.086	2.528	2.845
21	1.323	1.721	2.080	2.518	2.831
22	1.321	1.717	2.074	2.508	2.819
23	1.319	1.714	2.069	2.500	2.807
24	1.318	1.711	2.064	2.492	2.797
25	1.316	1.708	2.060	2.485	2.787
26	1.315	1.706	2.056	2.479	2.779
27	1.314	1.703	2.052	2.473	2.771
28	1.313	1.701	2.048	2.467	2.763
29	1.311	1.699	2.045	2.462	2.756
inf.	1.282	1.645	1.960	2.326	2.576

The t-value describes the sampling distribution of a deviation from a population value divided by the standard error. Probabilities indicated in the subordinate of t in the heading refer to the sum of the two-tailed areas under the curve that lie outside the points $\pm t$. Degrees of freedom are listed in the first column.

For example, in the distribution of the means of sample size $n = 12$, $df = n - 2 = 12 - 2$; then .05 of the area under the curve falls in the two tails of the curve outside the interval $t \pm 2.228$, which is taken from the $t_{.025}$ column of the table.

$$s_p(\$59,419|5,900) = \$1,985 \quad 1 + \frac{1}{24} + \frac{(5,900 - 5,892.08)^2}{849,770,100 - \frac{(141,410)^2}{24}}$$

$$s_p(\$59,419|5,900) = \$1,985 \sqrt{1.041670452}$$

$$s_p(\$59,419|5,900) = \$2,026$$

$$\hat{y} = \$59,419 \pm 2.819(\$2,026)$$

$$\hat{y} = \$59,419 \pm \$5,711$$

We are 99 percent certain that if 5,900 hours are worked, the actual overhead cost will be between \$53,708 and \$65,130. Frequently in cost estimation, we are only interested in the larger estimate. We can say that

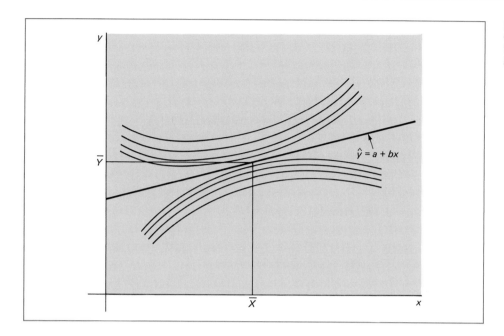

FIGURE 21.7
Confidence
Interval around a
Regression Line

we are 99½ percent certain that the actual overhead cost will not exceed $65,130.

From formula (21-6) we observe the further the value of the independent variable (5,900) is from the mean of the observed values of the independent variable, the larger $s_p(\hat{y}_i|x_i)$ will be. Therefore, the further we move from the mean of the direct-labor hours, the wider will be the prediction interval. This relationship is shown in figure 21.7.

The b coefficient of the regression equation is of primary interest in cost estimation. If there is no relationship between the independent and dependent variables, the slope of the true regression line will be zero. From this we can infer that x and y are independent of each other and no variation in y will be explained by variation in x. We can test to determine if our sample value b is significantly different from zero. If it is significantly different, then we infer that there is a relationship between the independent and dependent variables.[5]

The *null hypothesis* H_0 is that $B=0$ and the alternative hypothesis H_1 is $B \neq 0$. These hypotheses may be expressed as

$H_0: B = 0$
$H_1: B \neq 0$

To test the hypotheses, we calculate how many standard errors b is away from B, and compare this observed *t-value* with Student's t distribution:

$$t_{obs} = \frac{b - B}{S_b} \sim t_{(\alpha/2,\ n-2)}$$

5. This technique is appropriately used only with simple linear regression.

Under the null hypothesis, H_0, then,

$$t = \frac{b - 0}{s_b}$$

We must, therefore, determine the *standard error* of the *b regression coefficient*. This standard error may be expressed as

$$s_b = \frac{s_e}{\sqrt{\Sigma x^2 - \bar{x}\Sigma x}} \tag{21-8}$$

In the example, the standard error of b is

$$s_b = \frac{1{,}985}{\sqrt{849{,}770{,}100 - 5{,}892.08(141{,}410)}} = .4876$$

We can employ the s_b to compute the number of standard errors the sample value b (3.4594) is from zero. In the example, the number of standard errors b is from zero is

$$\frac{b}{s_b} = \frac{3.4594}{.4876} = 7.09 = \text{observed } t\text{-value}$$

Therefore, b is 7.09 standard errors from zero, and we conclude that it is extremely unlikely that a deviation of 7.09 standard errors could occur by chance. The number of standard errors is sometimes referred to as the *t*-value of the regression coefficient. A high *t*-value is an indication that the coefficient is a good estimate of the population parameter. Such a high *t*-value would result in more confidence in the estimated cost. Generally, *t*-values of greater than two are desired.

Using the standard error of the regression coefficient and the *t*-value, we can construct confidence intervals. A 95-percent confidence interval can be computed with the appropriate *t*-value from table 21.3. Since table 21.3 gives the area of the curve outside the interval for one tail, then for a 95-percent confidence interval we select a *t*-value in the $t_{.025}$ column of the table. This gives the interval under 95 percent of the curve. The degrees of freedom are *n-k*-1. For the example with 24-1-1 = 22 degrees of freedom, the 95-percent confidence interval equals

$b \pm t_{.025}\, s_b$

$3.4594 \pm 2.074(.4876)$

3.4594 ± 1.0113

Therefore, if all the relevant classical-regression assumptions hold, a 95-percent confidence interval for the true population parameter B is \$2.4481 $\leq B \leq$ \$4.4707. Another way of expressing the relationship is to say that if many independent samples are taken with the same levels of x (the direct-labor hours) being observed in these other samples as were observed in the original sample, and if a 95-percent confidence interval is constructed for each sample, then 95-percent of the intervals will contain the true value of B. In the same manner, we can construct a 99-percent confidence interval using $t_{.005}$. This confidence interval equals \$3.4594 ± \$1.3745.

The standard error and confidence intervals can also be constructed for the intercept (a) of the regression line. However, this is rarely done in cost estimation since the origin is out of the relevant range. In addition, we are more concerned with the marginal cost estimate (b) than with estimating the fixed cost.

☐ SUMMARY

In this chapter, the characteristics of the least-squares linear-regression model were described. This model fits a line to sample data so that the error terms sum to zero and the sum of the squares of the error terms is minimized. The descriptive-linear-regression model only assumes a linear relationship between the independent and dependent variables. This assumption can be evaluated by plotting the data and evaluating the coefficient of determination, R^2.

The classical-linear-regression model was also presented. The only difference between the descriptive and classical models is the assumptions. In addition to linearity, the classical model assumes that the error terms are normally distributed with a mean of zero and a constant variance.

When the classical assumptions are met, it is possible to make probabilistic statements about the cost estimates and regression coefficients. The analysis also provides information (i.e., t-values, standard error of regression coefficients, and standard error of the estimate) that can be used in selecting the independent variable employed in cost estimation.

KEY TERMS

Classical-linear regression
Coefficient of determination
Confidence interval
Descriptive-linear regression
Explained variation

Multiple regression
Simple regression
Standard error of estimate
Unexplained variation

REVIEW PROBLEM

Using direct-labor hours as the independent variable and overhead cost as the dependent variable, twenty-four months of data were employed to obtain the following regression results:

Variable	Coefficient	Standard error	t-value
Intercept	39,008.56		
(B)	3.4594	.4876	7.09

$R^2 = .6959$

Standard error of the estimate	1,985
Sum-of-squares regression	198,308,424
Sum-of-squares error	86,669,909
Total sum of squares	284,978,333

Required ☐

1. What is the slope of the regression line?
2. Show how the *t*-value was determined.
3. Show how R^2 was determined.
4. Show how the standard error of the estimate was determined.
5. If the firm planned to work 5,000 direct-labor hours, determine the estimated overhead cost.

Solution ☐

1. 3.4594

2. $t = \dfrac{b}{s_b} = \dfrac{3.4594}{.4876} = 7.09$

3. $\dfrac{SSR}{TSS} = \dfrac{198,308,424}{284,978,333} = .6959$

4. $s_e = \sqrt{\dfrac{SSE}{n-k-1}} = \sqrt{\dfrac{86,669,909}{24-1-1}} = 1,985$

5. $\hat{y} = \$39,008.56 + 5,000\,(\$3.4594)$
   $\hat{y} = \$56,305.56$

APPENDIX: Multiple Regression

Multiple regression involves using more than one independent variable to estimate the dependent variable. The general equation of the linear-multiple-regression model is

$$y = a + b_1x_1 + b_2x_2 + b_3x_3 + \ldots + b_nx_n + u$$

Once again y is the estimated value of the dependent variable; $x_1, x_2, x_3, \ldots x_n$ are the independent variables; $a, b_1, b_2, b_3, \ldots b_n$ are the regression coefficients; and u is the error term. There are cases where using two or more independent variables may improve the ability to predict costs. Consider the data in appendix table 1 where the overhead cost can be estimated using direct-labor hours and machine hours as independent variables. Now we can determine three regression equations. The results obtained from a computer program for the three regressions are shown in appendix table 2.

APPENDIX TABLE 1 Multiple-Regression Data

Observation number		Overhead cost (cost)	Direct-labor hours (A)	Machine hours (B)
1	....	$55,000	5,010	10,400
2	....	57,200	5,100	10,700
3	....	56,800	5,350	10,800
4	....	57,900	5,200	9,800
5	....	58,400	5,100	10,500
6	....	54,700	5,300	9,600
7	....	54,100	4,100	9,100
8	....	53,900	4,100	8,700
9	....	54,200	5,700	9,400
10	....	56,900	5,800	10,100
11	....	62,100	6,300	10,500
12	....	62,700	6,250	10,600
13	....	61,900	6,300	10,400
14	....	63,400	6,800	11,000
15	....	64,100	6,900	11,200
16	....	64,500	7,100	11,300
17	....	62,200	6,850	10,800
18	....	61,100	7,050	11,100
19	....	60,800	6,650	10,900
20	....	59,700	6,400	11,000
21	....	58,400	6,050	10,800
22	....	59,400	5,900	10,400
23	....	60,900	5,950	11,000
24	....	65,100	6,150	11,200

Note that multiple-linear regression results in a higher coefficient of determination (R^2) and a smaller standard error of the estimate than the cases where only one independent variable is used. Also note that both t-values are greater than two. The equation for estimating overhead costs using multiple regression is

$$\hat{y} = \$26,248.25 + \$2.2264x_1 + \$1.9125x_2$$

If in the next period we planned to work 6,000 direct-labor hours and use 11,000 machine hours, the estimated overhead cost is

$$\hat{y} = \$26,248.25 + \$2.2264(6,000) + \$1.9125(11,000)$$

$$\hat{y} = \$26,248.25 + \$13,358.40 + \$21,037.50$$

$$\hat{y} = \$60,644.15$$

The statistical significance of a multiple-regression equation is evaluated by employing the F statistic where

$$F = \frac{\Sigma(\hat{y} - \bar{y})^2}{k} \div \frac{\Sigma(y - \hat{y})^2}{n - k - 1} \qquad \textbf{(21A-1)}$$

APPENDIX TABLE 2 Results from Solving Regression Problems with a Computer

(1)   *Independent variable—Direct-labor hours*

Variable	Coefficient	Standard error	t-value
Intercept	39,008.56		
(A)	3.4594	.4876	7.09

$R^2 = .6959$
Standard error of the estimate = 1,985

Sum-of-squares regression	198,308,424
Sum-of-squares error	86,669,909
Total sum-of-squares	284,978,333

(2)   *Independent variable—Machine hours*

Variable	Coefficient	Standard error	t-value
Intercept	16,907.98		
(B)	4.0573	.6479	6.26

$R^2 = .6406$
Standard error of the estimate 2,158

Sum-of-squares regression	182,556,456
Sum-of-squares error	102,421,877
Total sum-of-squares	284,978,333

(3)   *Independent variable—Direct-labor hours and machine hours*

Variable	Coefficient	Standard error	t-value
Intercept	26.248.25		
(A)	2.2264	.7354	3.03
(B)	1.9125	.8989	2.13

$R^2 = .7498$
Standard error of the estimate = 1,843

Sum-of-squares regression	213,676,775
Sum-of-squares error	71,301,558
Total sum-of-squares	284,978,333

The *F* statistic is the ratio between two mean squares where

$$\text{Mean square regression} = \frac{\Sigma(\hat{y} - \bar{y})^2}{k}$$

$$\text{Mean square error} = \frac{\Sigma(y - \hat{y})^2}{n - k - 1}$$

What we are testing here is the null hypothesis that $x_1, x_2, x_3, \ldots x_k$ contribute no information in predicting y. This is the equivalent of hypothesizing that the true value of the regression coefficients equals zero. This can be expressed as

$$B_1 = B_2 = B_3 = \ldots B_k = 0$$

where the *B*s are the actual values and the *b*s are the estimated values of the coefficients used in the regression equation.

In the multiple-regression example, the F statistic is:

$$F = \frac{213,676,775}{2} \div \frac{71,301,558}{21} = 31.47$$

From appendix table 3 using 2 (k) and 21 ($n-k-1$) degrees of freedom, we determine the critical value to be 3.47. Since the F statistic of 31.47 is greater than 3.47, we conclude that the multiple-regression equation is significant at the .05 level. This means that there is only one chance in twenty that the regression results we obtained resulted from a chance relationship among the variables. As will be discussed in the next section, the F test is frequently used in selecting the appropriate independent variable or variables to be used in the regression equation.

☐ POSSIBLE REGRESSIONS

The previous classical-regression example was solved using the two independent variables. However, two other regression equations can be determined from the data base. These equations would have the direct-labor hours and machine hours, respectively, as the independent variable. The problem, then, is to determine which regression model is "best" and should be employed according to a set of criteria. In this section, several criteria will be discussed for evaluating a set of regression equations.

When faced with the problem of selecting a regression equation, there is almost always a multiple-regression equation available for consideration. In this situation, it is desirable that the number of observations substantially exceed the number of regression coefficients. A commonly used rule is that the number of observations should be five times greater than the number of independent variables. For example, if there were five independent variables and only ten observations, the multiple regression results are very suspect. This rule would require twenty-five observations if five independent variables were employed.

The coefficient of determination (R^2) is used as a criterion for selecting a regression equation. Selection is based on the fact that the equation with the highest R^2 on average explains most of the variation in the dependent variable. However, this criterion must be interpreted differently when multiple regression is involved. Recall that the denominator employed in determining R^2 is the total sum of squares. This denominator is constant over all possible regressions for a given data set since the total sum of squares is independent of any regression equation. It can be shown that the sum-of-squares error can never increase as additional independent variables are added to the regression equation. Consequently, the coefficient of determination will be at a maximum when all possible independent variables are included in the regression model.

When multiple-regression equations are being evaluated, the criterion cannot be to maximize the value of R^2. Instead, we seek to determine at what point adding another independent variable does not significantly increase the value of R^2. Frequently, the inclusion of only one or two independent variables results in a satisfactory value of R^2. The addition of more independent variables will increase the value of R^2, but not by a significant amount.

The standard error of the estimate is another criterion that has been suggested for evaluating possible regression equations. In calculating the standard error of the estimate, the number of coefficients is considered in the determination of the degrees of freedom. The standard error of the estimate can increase as a result of introducing another independent variable if the reduction of the sum-of-squares error is not sufficient to offset the loss of the additional degree of freedom [refer to equation (21-4)].

When employing this criterion, the objective is to find the set of independent variables that minimizes the standard error of the estimate or is so close to the minimum that adding additional independent variables will not significantly re-

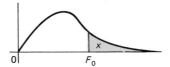

APPENDIX TABLE 3 Percentage Points of the *F* Distribution

Degrees of freedom   *(y = .05)*

v_2 \ v_1	1	2	3	4	5	6	7	8	9
1	161.4	199.5	215.7	224.6	230.2	234.0	236.8	238.9	240.5
2	18.51	19.00	19.16	19.25	19.30	19.33	19.35	19.37	19.38
3	10.13	9.55	9.28	9.12	9.01	8.94	8.89	8.85	8.81
4	7.71	6.94	6.59	6.39	6.26	6.16	6.09	6.04	6.00
5	6.61	5.79	5.41	5.19	5.05	4.95	4.88	4.82	4.77
6	5.99	5.14	4.76	4.53	4.39	4.28	4.21	4.15	4.10
7	5.59	4.74	4.35	4.12	3.97	3.87	3.79	3.73	3.68
8	5.32	4.46	4.07	3.84	3.69	3.58	3.50	3.44	3.39
9	5.12	4.26	3.86	3.63	3.48	3.37	3.29	3.23	3.18
10	4.96	4.10	3.71	3.48	3.33	3.22	3.14	3.07	3.02
11	4.84	3.98	3.59	3.36	3.20	3.09	3.01	2.95	2.90
12	4.75	3.89	3.49	3.26	3.11	3.00	2.91	2.85	2.80
13	4.67	3.81	3.41	3.18	3.03	2.92	2.83	2.77	2.71
14	4.60	3.74	3.34	3.11	2.96	2.85	2.76	2.70	2.65
15	4.54	3.68	3.29	3.06	2.90	2.79	2.71	2.64	2.59
16	4.49	3.63	3.24	3.01	2.85	2.74	2.66	2.59	2.54
17	4.45	3.59	3.20	2.96	2.81	2.70	2.61	2.55	2.49
18	4.41	3.55	3.16	2.93	2.77	2.66	2.58	2.51	2.46
19	4.38	3.52	3.13	2.90	2.74	2.63	2.54	2.48	2.42
20	4.35	3.49	3.10	2.87	2.71	2.60	2.51	2.45	2.39
21	4.32	3.47	3.07	2.84	2.68	2.57	2.49	2.42	2.37
22	4.30	3.44	3.05	2.82	2.66	2.55	2.46	2.40	2.34
23	4.28	3.42	3.03	2.80	2.64	2.53	2.44	2.37	2.32
24	4.26	3.40	3.01	2.78	2.62	2.51	2.42	2.36	2.30
25	4.24	3.39	2.99	2.76	2.60	2.49	2.40	2.34	2.28
26	4.23	3.37	2.98	2.74	2.59	2.47	2.39	2.32	2.27
27	4.21	3.35	2.96	2.73	2.57	2.46	2.37	2.31	2.25
28	4.20	3.34	2.95	2.71	2.56	2.45	2.36	2.29	2.24
29	4.18	3.33	2.93	2.70	2.55	2.43	2.35	2.28	2.22
30	4.17	3.32	2.92	2.69	2.53	2.42	2.33	2.27	2.21
40	4.08	3.23	2.84	2.61	2.45	2.34	2.25	2.18	2.12
60	4.00	3.15	2.76	2.53	2.37	2.25	2.17	2.10	2.04
120	3.92	3.07	2.68	2.45	2.29	2.17	2.09	2.02	1.96
∞	3.84	3.00	2.60	2.37	2.21	2.10	2.01	1.94	1.88

duce the standard error of the estimate. A means of employing both the coefficient of determination (R^2) and the standard error of the estimate (S_e) as criteria for selecting a regression equation is to plot both as shown in appendix figure 1.

The basis for the selection of a regression equation is, then, to arbitrarily determine from the graph where R^2 does not increase and S_e does not decrease significantly by the addition of another variable. Other criteria have been suggested, but they are beyond the scope of this text. The interested student can find additional material on this subject in the list of references at the end of the chapter.

In many cases, it is not possible to determine the regression equation for all possible combinations of the independent variables. Therefore, a search procedure is necessary to find the equation that "best" fits the data. Variable-selection techniques are available with most computer statistical-analysis packages. All variable-selection techniques are based on the extra sum of squares principle. The incre-

10	12	15	20	24	30	40	60	120	∞	
241.9	243.9	245.9	248.0	249.1	250.1	251.1	252.2	253.3	254.3	1
19.40	19.41	19.43	19.45	19.45	19.46	19.47	19.48	19.49	19.50	2
8.79	8.74	8.70	8.66	8.64	8.62	8.59	8.57	8.55	8.53	3
5.96	5.91	5.86	5.80	5.77	5.75	5.72	5.69	5.66	5.63	4
4.74	4.68	4.62	4.56	4.53	4.50	4.46	4.43	4.40	4.36	5
4.06	4.00	3.94	3.87	3.84	3.81	3.77	3.74	3.70	3.67	6
3.64	3.57	3.51	3.44	3.41	3.38	3.34	3.30	3.27	3.23	7
3.35	3.28	3.22	3.15	3.12	3.08	3.04	3.01	2.97	2.93	8
3.14	3.07	3.01	2.94	2.90	2.86	2.83	2.79	2.75	2.71	9
2.98	2.91	2.85	2.77	2.74	2.70	2.66	2.62	2.58	2.54	10
2.85	2.79	2.72	2.65	2.61	2.57	2.53	2.49	2.45	2.40	11
2.75	2.69	2.62	2.54	2.51	2.47	2.43	2.38	2.34	2.30	12
2.67	2.60	2.53	2.46	2.42	2.38	2.34	2.30	2.25	2.21	13
2.60	2.53	2.46	2.39	2.35	2.31	2.27	2.22	2.18	2.13	14
2.54	2.48	2.40	2.33	2.29	2.25	2.20	2.16	2.11	2.07	15
2.49	2.42	2.35	2.28	2.24	2.19	2.15	2.11	2.06	2.01	16
2.45	2.38	2.31	2.23	2.19	2.15	2.10	2.06	2.01	1.96	17
2.41	2.34	2.27	2.19	2.15	2.11	2.06	2.02	1.97	1.92	18
2.30	2.31	2.23	2.16	2.11	2.07	2.03	1.98	1.93	1.88	19
2.35	2.28	2.20	2.12	2.08	2.04	1.99	1.95	1.90	1.84	20
2.32	2.25	2.18	2.10	2.05	2.01	1.96	1.92	1.87	1.81	21
2.30	2.23	2.15	2.07	2.03	1.98	1.94	1.89	1.84	1.78	22
2.27	2.20	2.13	2.05	2.01	1.96	1.91	1.86	1.81	1.76	23
2.25	2.18	2.11	2.03	1.98	1.94	1.89	1.84	1.79	1.73	24
2.24	2.16	2.09	2.01	1.96	1.92	1.87	1.82	1.77	1.71	25
2.22	2.15	2.07	1.99	1.95	1.90	1.85	1.80	1.75	1.69	26
2.20	2.13	2.06	1.97	1.93	1.88	1.84	1.79	1.73	1.67	27
2.19	2.12	2.04	1.96	1.91	1.87	1.82	1.77	1.71	1.65	28
2.18	2.10	2.03	1.94	1.90	1.85	1.81	1.75	1.70	1.64	29
2.16	2.09	2.01	1.93	1.89	1.84	1.79	1.74	1.68	1.62	30
2.08	2.00	1.92	1.84	1.79	1.74	1.69	1.64	1.58	1.51	40
1.99	1.92	1.84	1.75	1.70	1.65	1.59	1.53	1.47	1.39	60
1.91	1.83	1.75	1.66	1.61	1.55	1.50	1.43	1.35	1.25	120
1.83	1.75	1.67	1.57	1.52	1.46	1.39	1.32	1.22	1.00	∞

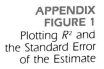

**APPENDIX
FIGURE 1**
Plotting R^2 and
the Standard Error
of the Estimate

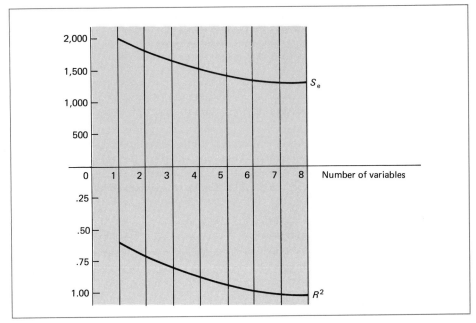

mental change in the regression sum of squares is calculated and the F test (discussed previously) is employed to determine whether or not the change is significant.

In the forward-selection technique, a variable is added only if it results in a significant increase in the regression sum of squares. The backward-elimination technique starts with the full model. It discards a variable if its elimination does not result in a significant decrease in the regression sum of squares. Stepwise regression is a compromise between forward selection and backward elimination. It starts as forward selection does, but after the addition of each variable, backward elimination is used to ascertain whether any variable can be discarded. Backward elimination has the advantage that if a good subset of variables exists, it will be detected by the backward-elimination technique.

Employing the backward-elimination technique on the data set, the results indicate that both independent variables (direct-labor hours and machine hours) are significant at the 10-percent level.

QUESTIONS

Q21-1. The high-low technique only takes into account partial information, while the least-squares technique takes into account all of the information available in determining a cost-estimation equation. Explain.

Q21-2. Why is it suggested that before using regression analysis the data should be plotted?

Q21-3. What are the differences between the structural and classical regression models?

Q21-4. Employing the least-squares technique, you find the following regression equation for estimating overhead cost.

$$\hat{y} = -\$2,550 + \$2.75x$$

Interpret each of the regression coefficients. Are they reasonable?

Q21-5. Employing the least-squares technique where direct-labor hours are the independent variable and overhead cost is the dependent variable, you find the following regression equation:

$$\hat{y} = \$5,758 - \$3.57x$$

Interpret each of the regression coefficients. Are they reasonable?

Q21-6. Identify each of the following terms or expressions as they relate to regression.

a. y d. $\Sigma(y - \bar{y})^2$
b. $\bar{y}$ e. $\Sigma(\hat{y} - \bar{y})^2$
c. $\hat{y}$ f. $\Sigma(y - \hat{y})^2$

Q21-7. Identify the assumptions concerning the error terms or residuals when the classical-regression model is employed.

Q21-8. Is the relevant-range assumption important when regression analysis is employed in cost estimation? Explain.

Q21-9. Explain the meaning of R squared, the coefficient of determination.

Q21-10. Explain the meaning of S_e, the standard error of the estimate. How can S_e be used in cost estimation?

Q21-11. Explain the meaning of S_b, the standard error of the regression coefficient. How can S_b be used in cost estimation?

Q21-12. Explain the meaning of the t-value. How can the t-value be used in cost estimation?

PROBLEMS

P21-1. Armer Company is accumulating data to be used in preparing its annual profit plan for the coming year. The cost-behavior pattern of the maintenance costs must be determined. The accounting staff has suggested that linear regression be employed to derive an equation in the form of $y = a + bx$ for maintenance costs. Data regarding the maintenance hours and costs for last year and the results of the regression analysis are as follows:

Multiple Choice

	Hours of activity	Maintenance costs
January	480	$ 4,200
February	320	3,000
March	400	3,600
April	300	2,820
May	500	4,350
June	310	2,960
July	320	3,030
August	520	4,470
September	490	4,260
October	470	4,050
November	350	3,300
December	340	3,160
Sum	4,800	43,200
Average	400	3,600

Average cost per hour (43,200 ÷ 4,800) = $9

a coefficient	684.65
b coefficient	7.2884
Standard error of the a coefficient	49.515
Standard error of the b coefficient	.12126
Standard error of the estimate	34.469
r^2	.99724
t-value a	13.827
t-value b	60.105

Single-tailed values of t

Degrees of freedom	$t_{.100}$	$t_{.05}$	$t_{.025}$	$t_{.01}$
8	1.40	1.86	2.31	2.90
9	1.38	1.83	2.26	2.82
10	1.37	1.81	2.23	2.76
11	1.36	1.80	2.20	2.72
12	1.36	1.78	2.18	2.68
13	1.35	1.77	2.16	2.65
14	1.35	1.76	2.15	2.62

Required ☐

1. In the standard regression equation of $y = a + bx$, the letter b is best described as the

  a. Independent variable
  b. Dependent variable
  c. Constant coefficient
  d. Variable coefficient
  e. Coefficient of determination

2. The letter y in the standard regression equation is best described as the

  a. Independent variable
  b. Dependent variable
  c. Constant coefficient
  d. Variable coefficient
  e. Coefficient of determination

3. The letter x in the standard regression equation is best described as the

    a. Independent variable
    b. Dependent variable
    c. Constant coefficient
    d. Variable coefficient
    e. Coefficient of determination

4. If the Armer Company uses the high-low method of analysis, the equation for the relationship between hours of activity and maintenance cost would be

    a. $y = 400 + 9.0x$
    b. $y = 570 + 7.5x$
    c. $y = 3{,}600 + 400x$
    d. $y = 570 + 9.0x$
    e. Some equation other than those given

5. Based on the data derived from the regression analysis, 420 maintenance hours in a month would mean the maintenance costs would be budgeted at

    a. $3,780
    b. $3,461
    c. $3,797
    d. $3,746
    e. Some amount other than those given

6. The coefficient of correlation for the regression equation for the maintenance activities is

    a. $34.469 \div 49.515$
    b. .99724
    c. $\sqrt{.99724}$
    d. $(.99724)^2$
    e. Some amount other than those given

7. The percent of the total variance that can be explained by the regression equation is

    a. 99.724
    b. 69.613
    c. 80.982
    d. 99.962
    e. Some amount other than those given

8. What is the range of values for the marginal maintenance cost such that Armer can be 95 percent confident that the true value of the marginal maintenance cost will be within this range?

    a. $7.02 − 7.56
    b. $7.17 − 7.41
    c. $7.07 − 7.51
    d. $6.29 − 8.29
    e. Some range other than those given

9. At 400 hours of activity, Armer management officials can be approximately two-thirds confident that the maintenance costs will be in the range of

  a. $3,550.50 − 3,649.53
  b. $3,551.37 − 3,648.51
  c. $3,586.18 − 3,613.93
  d. $3,565.54 − 3,634.48
  e. Some range other than those given

(CMA)

Analyzing Regression Results for Cost Estimation

P21-2. This data base and the regression results should be used to answer the following questions:

Period	Y Period overhead cost	X Direct-labor hours
1	$78,200	5,300
2	81,500	5,430
3	94,800	6,020
4	92,000	5,590
5	84,600	5,480
6	89,700	5,510
7	73,300	5,050
8	90,000	5,570
9	77,400	5,210
10	88,100	5,520

Regression results
$\hat{y} = -52,807 + 25.2X$
$S_b = 3.84$ *t*-value   6.56
$S_e = 2,988$ $R^2 = .843$

Sum-of-squares regression	384,548,096
Sum-of-squares error	71,451,392

Required □

1. If the firm planned to work 6,000 hours in the next period, determine the estimated overhead cost.

2. If the firm planned to work 8,000 hours in the next period, determine the estimated overhead cost. Would you have any reservations concerning this estimate? Explain.

3. If $\bar{y} = \$84,960$, for the first period, compute $\hat{y}$ and then find the explained and the unexplained variation or error term for this observation.

4. From the regression equation, explain the constants −52,807 and 25.2.

5. Show how the R^2 (coefficient of determination) of .843 was determined. What does R^2 mean?

6. Show how the S_e (standard error of the estimate) was determined. What does S_e measure?

7. What is the relationship between S_b and the t-value? What does each measure?

8. What are the assumptions made when the classical-regression model is used?

9. Compute a 95-percent confidence interval for the slope of the regression line. Explain what the confidence interval means.

10. Determine the total sum of squares. Explain the relationships among the total sum of squares, the sum of squares regression, and the sum-of-squares error.

P21-3. As a cost analyst for Kida, Inc., you have recorded the feet of twine used in manufacturing volleyballs and the overhead cost for the last twenty-four months.

Analyzing Regression Results for Cost Estimation

Month	Overhead cost	Feet of twine
1	1,500	23,500
2	1,700	28,000
3	1,700	20,000
4	1,800	24,000
5	1,900	35,000
6	1,900	30,000
7	1,925	24,000
8	2,100	28,000
9	2,150	34,500
10	2,200	26,000
11	2,225	40,000
12	2,300	31,000
13	2,400	44,000
14	2,425	29,000
15	2,475	39,500
16	2,575	43,000
17	2,650	38,000
18	2,700	33,500
19	2,850	39,000
20	2,900	45,000
21	2,950	49,000
22	3,050	43,000
23	3,100	48,000
24	3,200	45,000

The data was run on a computer using a standard-regression program and the following results were obtained:

	DF	Sum of squares
Regression	1	3,980,815.3092
Error	22	1,589,158.6491
Total		5,569,973.9583

	Coefficient	Standard error	t-value
Intercept	668.78060		
B	0.04836	0.0065	7.4236

R squared $= 0.7147$ $S_e = 268.7647$

Observation	Observed value	Predicted value	Residual
1	1,500.	1,805.2927	−305.2927
2	1,700.	2,022.9227	−322.9227
3	1,700.	1,636.0250	63.9749
4	1,800.	1,829.4739	−29.4739
5	1,900.	2,361.4583	−461.4583
6	1,900.	2,119.6472	−219.6472
7	1,925.	1,829.4739	95.5260
8	2,100.	2,022.9227	77.0772
9	2,150.	2,337.2772	−187.2772
10	2,200.	1,926.1983	273.8016
11	2,225.	2,603.2694	−378.2694
12	2,300.	2,168.0094	131.9905
13	2,400.	2,796.7183	−396.7183
14	2,425.	2,071.2850	353.7149
15	2,475.	2,579.0883	−104.0883
16	2,575.	2,748.3561	−173.3561
17	2,650.	2,506.5449	143.4550
18	2,700.	2,288.9150	411.0849
19	2,850.	2,554.9072	295.0927
20	2,900.	2,845.0805	54.9194
21	2,950.	3,038.5294	−88.5294
22	3,050.	2,748.3561	301.6438
23	3,100.	2,990.1672	109.8327
24	3,200.	2,845.0805	354.9194

Required □

1. If the firm planned to use 41,000 feet of twine in the next period, determine the estimated overhead cost.

2. Show how the R^2 (coefficient of determination) of .7147 was determined.

3. Show how the S_e (standard error of the estimate) was determined. What does S_e measure?

4. What does the S_b of 0.0065 measure? How is it used?

5. Show how the t-value of 7.4236 was determined. What does it mean?

6. What are the relationships among the three sums of squares? What are the unique characteristics of the sum-of-squares regression and the sum-of-squares error?

7. What is the difference between descriptive regression and classical regression?

8. Plot the residual (error terms) with time (observation) on the x axis and the residuals on the x axis. From your graph, evaluate whether the assumptions of the classical-regression model are satisfied.

Analyzing Regression Results for Cost Estimation

P21-4. You have gathered the following information concerning overhead costs for the Sego Corporation.

Month	Overhead cost	Direct-labor hours	Weight of output
1	35,500	18,600	77,000
2	42,000	19,100	81,500

3	24,000	15,200	65,000
4	28,000	16,200	69,500
5	43,000	20,600	84,000
6	38,000	19,000	80,500
7	39,000	19,300	82,500
8	43,000	20,200	79,000
9	48,000	24,000	86,000
10	45,000	20,750	84,500
11	36,750	18,600	77,200
12	33,000	17,800	76,500
13	40,000	19,700	83,000
14	31,250	16,900	71,000
15	22,500	16,200	72,500
16	30,500	15,000	77,000
17	37,500	15,500	74,000
18	39,000	16,900	75,500
19	31,250	18,000	68,000
20	30,000	18,700	80,000
21	37,250	20,100	85,000
22	47,500	18,900	81,000
23	42,500	21,200	86,000
24	48,500	20,800	84,000

The data was run on a computer using a standard-regression program and the following results were obtained:

Independent variable: Direct-labor hours

	DF	Sum of squares
Regression	1	738,818,696
Error	22	469,139,637
Total		1,207,958,333

	Coefficient	Standard error	t-value
Intercept	− 11,352.8		
B	2.61	.4427	5.8861

R squared $= .6116$ $S_e = 4,617.85$

Independent variable: Weight of output

	DF	Sum of squares
Regression	1	760,547,180
Error	22	447,411,152
Total		1,207,958,333

	Coefficient	Standard error	t-value
Intercept	− 38,524.96		
B	.9667	.1581	6.1145

R squared $= .6296$ $S_e = 4,509.64$

Required ☐ Which model (if any) would you employ to estimate overhead costs? Justify your answer.

P21-5. The following data was used to generate the following regression results: *Analyzing Regression Results for Cost Estimation*

Month	Overhead cost	Direct-labor hours	Machine hours
1	29,000	17,250	2,925
2	26,000	17,500	2,575

3	28,000	19,500	2,500
4	24,000	19,000	2,800
5	24,000	19,750	3,000
6	20,000	20,250	3,750
7	28,000	20,250	3,450
8	23,500	22,000	3,400
9	39,000	22,000	4,875
10	33,500	20,500	4,325
11	39,000	21,800	4,075
12	39,500	21,000	4,575
13	31,000	22,000	4,250
14	34,500	24,250	4,800
15	30,000	23,800	5,350
16	35,000	23,600	5,900
17	45,000	27,000	5,450
18	48,000	28,000	5,000
19	43,000	27,250	5,500
20	49,000	26,000	5,200
21	45,000	25,500	6,200
22	43,000	25,500	6,400
23	44,000	24,250	6,100
24	40,000	27,800	6,000

Variable	B value	Standard error	t-value
Intercept	−13,399.42		
Direct-labor hours	2.13	.345	6.16

	DF	Sum of squares
Regression	1	1,080,220,687
Error	22	628,737,646
Total	23	1,708,958,333

R squared $= .632$ $S_e = 5,345.93$

Variable	V-value	Standard error	t-value
Intercept	10,488.77		
Machine hours	5.44	.925	?

	DF	Sum of squares
Regression	1	?
Error	22	664,644,613
Total	23	?

R squared $= ?$ $S_e = ?$

Required ☐

1. Explain the meaning of the following expressions:

   a. $\Sigma (\hat{Y} - \bar{Y})^2$
   b. $\Sigma (Y - \bar{Y})^2$
   c. $\Sigma (Y - \hat{Y})^2$

2. Using the results where direct-labor hours was the independent variable, show how the R^2 of .632 was determined. Explain what R^2 means.

3. Using the results where direct-labor hours was the independent variable, show how the t-value of 6.16 was determined. Explain what the t-value means.

4. Using the results where the direct-labor hours was the independent variable, show how the standard error of the estimate of 5,345.93 was determined. Explain what the standard error of the estimate measures.

5. Using the results where the direct-labor hours was the independent variable, determine the estimated overhead cost if 5,000 direct-labor hours were worked. Explain your answer.

6. Using the results where the direct-labor hours was the independent variable, if $\overline{Y}$ = $35,042, for the first month compute Y and then determine the explained, unexplained, and total variation for this observation.

7. Determine the sum-of-squares regression for the second case where machine hours was the independent variable.

8. Determine the standard error of the estimate for the second case where machine hours was the independent variable.

9. Determine the t-value for the second case where machine hours was the independent variable.

10. Determine R^2 for the second case where machine hours was the independent variable.

P21-6. Based on the data and regression results contained in problem 21-5, answer the following questions:

Classical Regression and Cost Estimation

Required ☐

1. Using the results where direct-labor hours was the independent variable, explain the negative intercept of $-13,399.42$.

2. Using the results where direct-labor hours was the independent variable, explain the relationship between the standard error of the regression coefficient, .346, and the t-value of 6.16. What does the standard error of the regression coefficient measure? What does the t-value measure?

3. Construct a 99-percent confidence interval around the slope of the regression line when direct-labor hours is the independent variable. Explain the meaning of the confidence interval. Why it is important in cost estimation?

4. If the firm plans to work 23,000 direct-labor hours next month, determine the estimated overhead cost and construct a 99-percent confidence interval for the estimate. Explain the meaning of the confidence interval. Why it is important in cost estimation?

5. Find the total sum of squares for the regression results where machine hours was the independent variable. Explain the relationship between the sum of squares for the two regression equations.

6. Explain the difference between structural regression and classical regression.

7. Identify the assumptions of classical regression, and state how they are evaluated.

8. Define the following terms:

    a. Explained variation
    b. Unexplained variation
    c. Homoscedasticity
    d. Heteroscedasticity
    e. Error term

Classical Regression and Cost Estimation

P21-7. The Timmons Co. management team wants to develop a method of forecasting overhead cost. The company's new cost accountant volunteered to come up with a method for forecasting overhead cost.

The cost accountant examined accounting and production records for the past twenty-four months. During the course of her investigation, she found that monthly overhead cost ranged from $53,900 to $65,100, direct-labor hours ranged from 4,100 to 7,100, and machine hours ranged from 8,700 to 11,300.

She obtained the following results from Timmons' SAS software package:

Independent variable—Direct-labor hours

Variable	Coefficient	Standard error	t-value
Intercept	39,008.52		
(B)	3.4594	.4876	7.09

R^2 = ?
Standard error of estimation = 1,985

Sum-of-squares regression	198,308,424
Sum-of-squares error	86,669,909
Total sum of squares	284,978,333

Independent variable—Machine hours

Variable	Coefficient	Standard error	t-value
Intercept	16,907.98		
(B)	4.0573	.6479	6.26

R^2 = .6406
Standard error of estimation = ?

Sum-of-squares regression	182,556,456
Sum-of-squares error	?
Total sum of squares	284,978,333

Independent variable—Direct-labor hours and machine hours

Variable	Coefficient	Standard error	t-value
Intercept	26,248.25		
(B₁)	2.2264	.7354	3.03
(B₂)	1.9125	.8989	2.13

R^2 = ?
Standard error of estimation = ?

Sum-of-squares regression	?
Sum-of-squares error	71,301,558
Total sum of squares	284,978,333

Required ☐

1. For the model using direct-labor hours as the independent variable, determine the coefficient of determination.

2. For the model using machine hours as the independent variable, determine the standard error of the estimate.

3. For the model using direct-labor hours and machine hours as the independent variables, determine the coefficient of determination and standard error of the estimate.

4. Identify the best model for forecasting overhead cost. Why did you select this model?

5. Upon reflection, the accountant concluded that there is an unacceptably high level of multicollinearity between direct-labor hours and machine hours. Now identify the best regression model for forecasting overhead cost. Why did you select this model?

6. The controller has asked for an estimate of next month's overhead cost. Manufacturing engineering estimates that 4,000 direct-labor hours and 9,000 machine hours will be used next month. Based on your model in requirement 5, estimate next month's overhead cost.

7. The chief cost accountant is concerned about the accuracy of the forecasting models. To provide some insight, calculate a 95-percent confidence interval for the slope of the regression line that uses direct-labor hours as the independent variable.

8. Based on your answer to requirement 7, calculate the range (high and low values) of estimated overhead at 4,000 direct-labor hours.

9. Using a forecasting model based on 5,000 direct-labor hours, the controller wanted to know the probability of actual overhead being greater than $60,400.

10. The cost accountant is preparing a quotation for a contract that will require 10,000 machine hours. She is very concerned about the possibility that actual cost could exceed her quotation. What overhead cost estimate should she use so that she will be 99 percent certain that actual overhead will not exceed the quoted cost?

P21-8. The weekly direct-labor hours and the overhead costs for the Taffy Co. are presented.

Estimating and Calculating Regression Coefficients

OBS	Cost	Direct-labor hours
1	$12,000	4,100
2	12,750	4,300
3	13,250	4,500
4	12,750	4,875
5	13,125	5,600
6	13,750	6,325
7	13,500	6,550
8	14,000	6,750
9	14,000	7,100
10	13,125	4,700
11	12,500	5,050
12	12,300	5,275
13	12,800	5,400
14	13,750	5,650
15	14,125	5,800
16	14,250	6,000
17	14,300	6,850
18	14,200	7,050

Required ☐

1. Plot the data, and visually fit a linear cost function.

2. Compute the cost function using the high-low method.

3. Compute the cost function using the least-squares technique.

4. How much of the variance in overhead is explained by the quantity of production?

5. Is there a significant relationship between the quantity of production and overhead cost?

6. Compare the three methods.

Calculating Regression Coefficients **P21-9.** From the following data, identify the simple regression equation that will best estimate overhead costs. Justify your answer.

Month	Overhead cost	Direct-labor hours	Machine hours
1	$11,250	1,500	3,050
2	12,250	1,700	3,900
3	12,750	1,700	3,755
4	12,000	1,925	3,575
5	13,500	2,100	3,500
6	13,125	2,200	4,625
7	13,250	2,300	4,500
8	14,500	2,425	5,250
9	14,500	2,575	5,300
10	14,125	2,650	5,325
11	15,900	2,850	5,250
12	15,000	2,950	5,025
13	16,750	3,050	5,000
14	16,000	3,100	5,275
15	12,750	1,300	4,375
16	11,500	1,300	3,950
17	11,375	2,050	4,750
18	12,500	2,325	4,900
19	13,250	2,700	3,900
20	14,250	2,925	4,400
21	13,750	1,775	4,700
22	15,500	2,550	4,600
23	16,500	2,700	4,500

Regression and Break-Even Analysis **P21-10.** The W & L Company is a simple-product firm. The output from the firm sells at $10 a unit. The firm used regression analysis to determine the total cost function of

$$\hat{Y} = \$500 + \$5X$$

where X is units of output and twenty-four observations were used in estimating the cost function. The firm sells its output as fast as it can manufacture it; therefore, there is no finished-goods inventory. This information was obtained from the computer in determining the regression equation:

$$R^2 = .92 \qquad S_b = \$.50$$
$$S_e = \$75$$

Required ☐

1. What is the break-even volume for the firm?

2. At what price should the firm sell its product if it wants to be 50 percent certain of at least breaking-even at a volume of 200 units?

3. At what price should the firm sell its product if it wants to be 97½ percent certain that it will at least break-even at a volume of 200 units?

4. If the firm sells 200 units at a price of $10, what is the probability of the firm making a profit of $500 or more? What is the probability of the firm making a profit of $425 or more?

P21-11. The K & L Company is a single-product firm. Output from the firm sells at $5 a unit. Regression analysis was used to determine the total cost function of

$$\hat{Y} = \$250 + \$3X$$

where X is units of output and twenty-four observations were used in estimating the cost function. The firm sells its output as fast as it can manufacture it; therefore, there is no finished-goods inventory. This information was obtained from the computer in determining the regression equation:

$R^2 = .87 \qquad S_b = \$.25$

$S_e = \$50$

Regression and Break-Even Analysis

Required ☐

1. If the firm sells 250 units at a price of $5, what is the probability of the firm making a profit of $300 or more?

2. If the firm sells 250 units at a price of $5, what is the probability of the firm making a profit of more than $100?

3. At what price would the firm have to sell 200 units to be 97½ percent certain of earning a profit of at least $400?

4. At what price would the firm have to sell 150 units to be 50 percent certain of earning a profit of at least $50?

P21-12. The JFG Company is a single-product firm that over the last ten periods has produced the following units with the related costs:

Simple Regression Calculations and Break-Even Analysis

Period	Units produced	Costs
1	845	$4,075
2	815	4,010
3	870	4,240
4	775	3,850
5	950	4,620
6	825	3,980
7	1,080	4,990
8	1,020	4,880
9	985	4,525
10	905	4,790

Required ☐

1. What price should JFG set for its product if it wishes to break-even at a volume of 750 units?

2. What is the expected profit if 1,000 units are sold and the price is established so that the firm will break-even at a volume of 750 units?

3. If the price is set so that JFG will break-even at a volume of 600 units, what is the expected profit if 1,000 units are sold?

4. At what price should the product be sold if JFG wants to be 97½ percent certain of breaking-even at a volume of 750 units? What assumptions are necessary to analyze the problem in this manner?

Simple **P21-13.** The PWL Company is a single-product firm that over the last ten periods
Regression has produced the following units with the related costs:
Calculations and
Break-Even
Analysis

Period	Units produced	Costs
1	1,780	$40,200
2	1,650	38,100
3	1,860	43,300
4	1,750	43,100
5	1,930	43,900
6	1,690	38,800
7	1,980	44,700
8	1,500	37,650
9	1,810	42,400
10	1,720	39,200

Required ☐

1. What price should PWL set for its product if it expects to break-even at a volume of 1,400 units?

2. What is the expected profit if 1,800 units are sold and the price was set so that the firm could expect to break-even at 1,400 units?

3. What is the range that contains 99 percent of the expected profits the firm can expect to earn if 1,800 units are sold and the price was set so that the firm can expect to break-even at a volume of 1,200 units? What assumptions are made if the problem is analyzed in this manner?

4. At what price should the product be sold if PWL wants to be 99½ percent certain of break-even at volume of 1,400 units?

Analyzing **P21-14.** The Johnstar Co. makes a very expensive chemical product. The costs
Regression average about $1,000 per pound, and the material sells for $2,500 per
Results pound. The material is very dangerous; therefore, it is made each day to fill the customer orders for the day. Failure to deliver the quantity required results in a shutdown for the customers and high cost penalty for Johnstar (plus customer ill will).

Predicting the final weight of a batch of the chemical being processed has been a serious problem. This is critical because of the serious cost of failure to meet customer needs.

A consultant recommended that the batches be weighed halfway through the six-hour processing period. He proposed that linear regression be used to predict the final weight from the midpoint weight. If the prediction indicated that too little of the chemical would be available, then a new batch could be started and still delivered in time to satisfy customers' needs for the day.

Included in the consultant's report of a study made during a one-week period were the following items:

Observation number	Weight at three hours	Final weight	Observation number	Weight at three hours	Final weight
1	55	90	11	60	80
2	45	75	12	35	60
3	40	80	13	35	80
4	60	80	14	55	60
5	40	45	15	35	75
6	60	80	16	50	90
7	50	80	17	30	60
8	55	95	18	60	105
9	50	100	19	50	60
10	35	75	20	20	30

Data from the regression analysis:

Coefficient of determination	0.4126
Coefficient of correlation	0.6423
Coefficients of the regression equation	
Constant	+28.6
Independent variable	+1.008
Standard error of the estimate	14.2
Standard error of the regression coefficient for the	
independent variable	0.2796
The t-statistic for a 95 percent confidence	
Interval (18 degrees of freedom)	2.101

Required ☐

1. Using the results of the regression analysis by the consultant, calculate the estimate of today's first batch, which weighs forty-two pounds at the end of three hours processing time.

2. Customer orders for today total sixty-eight pounds. The nature of the process is such that the smallest batch that can be started will weigh at least twenty pounds at the end of six hours. Using only the data from the regression analysis, would you start another batch? (Remember that today's first batch weighed forty-two pounds at the end of three hours.)

3. Is the relationship between the variables such that this regression analysis provides an adequate prediction model for the Johnstar Co.? Explain your answer.

(CMA)

P21-15. The Alma Plant manufactures the industrial product line of CJS Industries. Plant management officials want to be able to get a good, yet quick, estimate of the manufacturing overhead costs that can be expected to be incurred each month. The easiest and simplest method to accomplish this task appears to be to develop a flexible-budget formula for the manufacturing overhead costs.

Analyzing Regression Results

The plant accounting staff suggested that simple linear regression be used to determine the cost-behavior pattern of the overhead costs. The regression data can provide the basis for the flexible-budget formula. Sufficient evidence is available to conclude that manufacturing overhead costs vary with direct-labor hours. The actual direct-labor hours and the corresponding manufacturing overhead costs for each month of the last three years were used in the linear-regression analysis.

The three-year period contained various occurrences not uncommon to many businesses. During the first year, production was severely curtailed during two months due to wildcat strikes. In the second year, production was reduced in one month because of material shortages and materially increased (overtime scheduled) during two months to meet the units required for a one-time sales order. At the end of the second year, employee benefits were raised significantly as the result of a labor agreement. Production during the third year was not affected by any special circumstance.

Various members of the accounting staff raised some issues regarding the historical data collected for the regression analysis. These issues were as follows:

1. Some members of the accounting staff believed that the use of data from all thirty-six months would provide a more accurate portrayal of the cost behavior. While they recognized that any of the monthly data could include efficiencies and inefficiencies, they believed these efficiencies/inefficiencies would tend to balance out over a longer period of time.

2. Other members of the accounting staff suggested that only those months that were considered normal should be used so that the regression would not be distorted.

3. Still other members felt that only the most recent twelve months should be used because they were the most current.

4. Some members questioned whether historical data should be used at all to form the basis for a flexible-budget formula.

The Accounting department staff ran two regression analyses of the data—one using the data from all thirty-six months and the other using only the data from the last twelve months. The information derived from the two linear regressions is shown.

Least-squares Regression Analyses

	Data from all thirty-six months	Data from most recent twelve months
Coefficients of the regression equation:		
Constant	$123,810	$109,020
Independent variable (DLH)	$1.6003	$4.1977
Coefficient of correlation	.4710	.6891
Standard error of the estimate	13,003	7.473
Standard error of the regression coefficient for the independent variable	.9744	1.3959
Calculated *t*-statistic for the regression coefficient	1.6423	3.0072

t-statistic required for a 95-percent
  confidence interval
    34 degrees of freedom (36 – 2) 1.960
    10 degrees of freedom (12 – 2) 2.228

Required □

1. From the results of Alma Plant's regression analysis that used the data from all thirty-six months:

   a. Formulate the flexible-budget equation that can be employed to estimate monthly manufacturing overhead costs
   b. Calculate the estimate of overhead costs for a month when 25,000 direct-labor hours are worked

2. Using only the results of the two regression analyses, explain which of the two results (twelve-months versus thirty-six-months) you would use as a basis for the flexible-budget formula.

3. How would the four specific issues raised by the members of Alma's accounting staff influence your willingness to use the results of the statistical analyses as the basis for the flexible-budget formula? Explain your answer.

(CMA)

P21-16. The controller of the Connecticut Electronics Company believes that the identification of the variable and fixed components of the firm's costs will enable the firm to make better planning and control decisions. Among the costs the controller is concerned about is the behavior of indirect supplies expense. He believes there is some correlation between the machine hours worked and the amount of indirect supplies used.   *Review of Regression Concepts*

A member of the controller's staff has suggested that a simple linear-regression model be used to determine the cost behavior of the indirect supplies. The regression equation shown was developed from forty pairs of observations using the least-squares method of regression. The regression equation and related measures are as follows:

$$S = \$200 + \$4H$$

where

   S = Total monthly costs of indirect supplies
   H = Machine hours per month

Standard error of estimate: $S_e = 100$

Coefficient of correlation: $r = .87$

Required □

1. When a simple linear-regression model is used to make inferences about a population relationship from sample data, what assumptions must be made before the inferences can be accepted as valid?

2. Assume the assumptions identified in requirement 1 are satisfied for the indirect supplies expense of Connecticut Electronics Company, then:

   a. Explain the meaning of "200" and "4" in the regression equation $S = \$200 + \$4H$.

   b. Calculate the estimated cost of indirect supplies if 900 machine hours are to be used during a month.

   c. In addition to the estimate for the cost of indirect supplies, the controller would like the range of values for the estimate if a 95-percent confidence interval is specified. He would use this range to judge whether the estimated costs indicated by the regression analysis was good enough for planning purposes. Calculate, for 900 machine hours, the range of the estimate for the cost of indirect supplies with a 95-percent confidence interval.

3. Explain briefly what the

   a. Coefficient of correlation measures

   b. Value of the coefficient of correlation ($r = .87$) indicates in this case if Connecticut Electronics Company wishes to predict the total cost of indirect supplies on the basis of estimated machine hours

Comprehensive Regression and Linear-Programming Problem

P21-17. In November 19X0, the Bayview Manufacturing Company was in the process of preparing its budget for 19X1. As the first step, it prepared a pro forma income statement for 19X0 based on the first ten months' operations and revised plans for the last two months. This income statement, in condensed form, was as follows:

Sales		$3,000,000
Materials	$1,182,000	
Labor	310,000	
Factory overhead	775,000	
Selling and administrative expense	450,000	2,717,000
Net income before taxes		$ 283,000

These results were better than were expected, and operations were close to capacity, but Bayview's management team was not convinced that demand would remain at present levels and hence had not planned any increase in plant capacity. Its equipment was specialized and made to its order; over a year's lead time was necessary on all plant additions.

Bayview produces three products; sales have been broken down by product, as follows:

100,000 of Product A @ $20.00	$2,000,000
40,000 of Product B @ 10.00	400,000
20,000 of Product C @ 30.00	600,000
	$3,000,000

The managers have ordered a profit analysis for each product and have available the following information:

	A	B	C
Material	$ 7.00	$ 3.75	$16.60
Labor	2.00	1.00	3.50
Factory overhead	5.00	2.50	8.75

Selling and administrative expense	3.00	1.50	4.50
Total costs	$17.00	$ 8.75	$33.35
Selling price	20.00	10.00	30.00
Profit	$ 3.00	$ 1.25	($ – 3.35)

Factory overhead has been applied on the basis of direct-labor costs at a rate of 250 percent; management officials assert that approximately 20 percent of the overhead is variable and does vary with labor costs. Selling and administrative costs have been allocated on the basis of sales at the rate of 15 percent; approximately one-half of this is variable and does vary with sales in dollars. All of the labor expense is considered to be variable.

As the first step in the planning process, the Sales department has been asked to make estimates of what it could sell; these estimates have been reviewed by the firm's consulting economist and by top management. They are as follows:

A	130,000 units
B	50,000 units
C	50,000 units

Production of these quantities was immediately recognized as being impossible. Estimated cost data for the three products, each of which requires activity of both departments, were based on the following production rates:

	Product		
	A	B	C
Department 1	2 per hour	4 per hour	3 per hour
Department 2	4 per hour	8 per hour	4/3 per hour

Practical capacity in department 1 is 67,000 hours and in department 2, 63,000 hours, and the Industrial Engineering department has concluded that this cannot be increased without the purchase of additional equipment. Thus, while last year department 1 operated at 99 percent of its capacity and department 2 at 71 percent of its capacity, anticipated sales would require operating both departments 1 and 2 at more than 100 percent capacity.

These solutions to the limited-production problem have been rejected: (1) subcontracting the production out to other firms is considered to be unprofitable because of problems of maintaining quality; (2) operating a second shift is impossible because of shortage of labor; (3) operating overtime would create problems because a large number of employees are "moonlighting" and would therefore refuse to work more than the normal forty-hour week. Price increases have been rejected; although they would result in higher profits this year, the long-run competitive position of the firm would be weakened, resulting in lower profits in the future.

The treasurer then suggested that the product C has been carried at a loss too long and that now was the time to eliminate it from the product line. If all facilities are used to produce A and B, profits would be increased.

The sales manager objects to this solution because of the need to carry a full line. In addition, she maintains that there is a group of customers who have provided and will continue to provide a solid base for the firm's activities, and these customers' needs must be met. She provided a list of these customers and their estimated purchases (in units), which total as follows:

A	80,000
B	32,000
C	12,000

It was impossible to verify these contentions, but they appeared to be reasonable and they served to narrow the bounds of the problem so that the president concurred.

The treasurer reluctantly acquiesced but maintained that the remaining capacity should be used to produce A and B. Because A produced 2.4 times as much profit as B, he suggested that the production of A (in excess of the 80,000 minimum set by the sales manager) be 2.4 times that of B (in excess of the 32,000 minimum set by the sales manager).

The production manager made some quick calculations and said that this would result in budgeted production and sales of:

A	104,828
B	42,344
C	12,000

The treasurer then made the following calculations of what profits would be:

A	104,828 @ $3.00	$314,484
B	42,344 @ $1.25	52,930
C	12,000 @ ($ − 3.35)	(− 40,200)
		$327,214

As this would represent an increase of almost 15 percent over the current year, there was a general feeling of self-satisfaction. Before final approval was given, however, the president said that he would like to have his new assistant check over the figures. Somewhat piqued, the treasurer agreed and at that point the group adjourned.

The next day the above information was submitted to you as your first assignment on your new job as the president's assistant. Prepare an analysis showing the president what he should do.

Exhibits A and B contain information that you are able to obtain from the accounting system.

Exhibit A

	Direct-labor expense (in thousands)			Overhead expense (in thousands)		
Department	1	2	Total	1	2	Total
Year						
19X0	$140	$170	$310	$341	$434	$775
19W9	135	150	285	340	421	762*
19W8	140	160	300	342	428	770
19W7	130	150	280	339	422	761

19W6	130	155	285	338	425	763
19W5	125	140	265	337	414	751
19W4	120	150	270	335	420	755
19W3	115	140	255	334	413	747
19W2	120	140	260	336	414	750
19W1	115	135	250	335	410	745

*Rounding error

Exhibit B

Sales (in thousands)

Year	Product A	Product B	Product C	Total	Selling and administrative expense (000)
19X0	$2,000	$400	$600	$3,000	450
19W9	1,940	430	610	2,980	445
19W8	1,950	380	630	2,960	445
19W7	1,860	460	630	2,950	438
19W6	1,820	390	640	2,850	433
19W5	1,860	440	580	2,880	437
19W4	1,880	420	570	2,870	438
19W3	1,850	380	580	2,810	434
19W2	1,810	390	580	2,780	430
19W1	1,770	290	610	2,670	425

This problem is taken from the Supplement to vol. XLVI of the 1971 *Accounting Review*, pp. 229–31. A computer is necessary to solve this problem.

CHAPTER OUTLINE

LEARNING CURVES AND COST ANALYSIS

CHAPTER **22**

☐ INTRODUCTION

The discussion in previous chapters was limited to the consideration of linear variable costs. In this chapter, the behavioral phenomenon called learning and the resulting nonlinear cost functions will be considered. As a person performs any activity repeatedly, learning occurs. Consequently, less time is required for each repetition. Such decreases in time can be attributed to physical conditioning of the body to the required motions and to learning that occurs because of human intelligence. Consideration of this phenomenon has important cost-behavior implications for an organization.

Several learning models will be considered in this chapter. Methods for estimating the learning rate and other model parameters will be discussed. The assumptions and limitations of the models will also be presented. In the concluding sections of the chapter, the relationships among learning, standard costs, and net income will be considered.

☐ AVERAGE-TIME MODEL

In the airframe industry during World War II, the rate of progress, or **learning,** was found to be approximately 80 percent for a doubling of unit output.[1] This mathematical relationship can be expressed as

$$y = ax^b \tag{22-1}$$

where

y = Average time per unit
a = Time required for the first unit

1. Frank J. Andress, "The Learning Curve as a Production Tool," *Harvard Business Review* (January-February 1954): 88.

x = Cumulative number of units produced
b = A measure of learning (learning index)[2]

The log transformation of this function is linear and is expressed as

$$\log y = \log a + b \log x \tag{22-2}$$

The value of b is determined by

$$b = \frac{\log (\% \text{ of learning})}{\log (\% \text{ of output increase})} \tag{22-3}$$

By convention, the doubling points are considered the percentage of output increase, so equation (22-3) can be expressed as

$$b = \frac{\log (\% \text{ of learning})}{\log 2} \tag{22-4}$$

For example, assume it takes 100 hours to assemble the first hydraulic lift and it has been determined that an 80 percent **learning curve** is appropriate for estimating assembly time. The hourly labor cost is $10. Table 22.1 contains estimates of the hours and labor costs at the points where output is doubled. Note that the average times at the doubling points of output are determined by multiplying the learning rate by the average time at the previous doubling point. The total time is determined by multiplying the average time by the units of output.

The marginal time and cost estimates are the respective differences between the estimates at the current and previous doubling points. This procedure can be used for estimating times and costs at all doubling points if the time to produce the first unit and the estimated rate of learning are known.

Often it is necessary to estimate average times and costs at points other than where the output doubles. When this is the case, the procedure becomes more complicated. For example, to determine the average time to produce three units, it is necessary to determine b by using equation (22-4) and to find the average time by using equation (22-2).

$$b = \frac{\log .80}{\log 2.0}$$

$$b = \frac{9.903090 - 10}{0.3010300} = \frac{-0.09691}{0.301030} = -.3219$$

$$y = 100(3)^{-.3219}$$

---

2. The solution of exponential functions such as (22-1) with electronic calculators eliminates the necessity of employing logs. However, understanding how the learning function can be transformed using logs aids in understanding the learning phenomenon. The appendix to this chapter contains a brief review of logs and a table of common logarithms.

TABLE 22.1 Times and Costs at Doubling Points—80 Percent Average-Time Learning Curve

Additional output	Cumulative units	Average time	Total time	Total cost	Marginal units	Marginal time	Marginal cost
1	1	100	1 × 100 = 100	$1,000.00	1	100	$1,000.00
1	2	.8 × 100 = 80	2 × 80 = 160	$1,600.00	1	60	$ 600.00
2	4	.8 × 80 = 64	4 × 64 = 256	$2,560.00	2	96	$ 960.00
4	8	.8 × 64 = 51.2	8 × 51.2 = 409.6	$4,096.00	4	153.6	$1,536.00
8	16	.8 × 51.2 = 40.96	16 × 40.96 = 655.36	$6,553.60	8	245.76	$2,457.60

$$\log y = \log 100 + (-.3219) \log 3$$

$$\log y = 2.000000 + (-.3219).477121$$

$$\log y = 1.846415$$

$$y = 70.21 \text{ hours}$$

The same procedure was used to determine the other average times in table 22.2. In figure 22.1, the outputs (x) and average times (y) from table 22.2 are graphed. As the value of x increases, the value of y decreases and the relationship is described by an exponentially decreasing function.

In table 22.3, the logs of the outputs and average times are given. Now perhaps a better understanding of b (the **learning index**) can be obtained by using regression analysis. If the logs of the outputs are the independent variable and the logs of the average times are the dependent variable, solving for the regression coefficients we find

$$\log y = 2.000000 - .3219 \log x$$

Plotting $\log y$ against $\log x$ as shown in figure 22.2, we have the linear function found using regression. This function has an intercept of 2.000000

TABLE 22.2 Times and Costs—80 Percent Average-Time Learning Curve

Additional output	Cumulative units	Average time	Total time	Total cost	Marginal units	Marginal time	Marginal cost
1	1	100.00	100.00	$1,000.00	1	100.00	$1,000.00
1	2	80.00	160.00	$1,600.00	1	60.00	$ 600.00
1	3	70.21	210.63	$2,106.30	1	50.63	$ 506.30
1	4	64.00	256.00	$2,560.00	1	45.37	$ 453.70
1	5	59.56	297.80	$2,978.00	1	41.80	$ 418.00
1	6	56.17	337.02	$3,370.20	1	39.22	$ 392.20
1	7	53.45	374.15	$3,741.50	1	37.13	$ 371.30
1	8	51.20	409.60	$4,096.00	1	35.45	$ 354.50
1	9	49.30	443.70	$4,437.00	1	34.10	$ 341.00
1	10	47.66	476.60	$4,766.00	1	32.90	$ 329.00
1	11	46.21	508.31	$5,083.10	1	31.71	$ 317.10
1	12	44.93	539.16	$5,391.60	1	30.85	$ 308.50
1	13	43.80	569.40	$5,694.00	1	30.24	$ 302.40
1	14	42.76	598.64	$5,986.40	1	29.24	$ 292.40
1	15	41.83	627.45	$6,274.50	1	28.81	$ 288.10
1	16	40.96	655.36	$6,553.60	1	27.91	$ 279.10

FIGURE 22.1
Cumulative
Average Labor
Hours

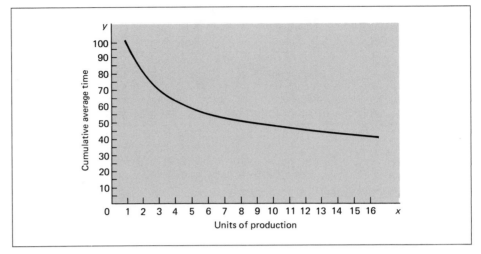

and a slope of − .3219. The antilog of 2.000000 is the time to produce the first unit (100 hours). The slope of − .3219 is the learning index for an 80 percent learning curve. Frequently used learning indexes are contained in table 22.4.

In all of the examples to this point, the learning rate has been given. Frequently, the learning rate is not known and it is necessary to estimate the rate from observed times. Consider the outputs and times in table 22.5. Taking the logs of the outputs and average times, the following regression equation is found.

$$\log y = 2.009926 - .169801 \log x$$

From table 22.4 or using formula (22-4), an 89 percent learning rate is found. Note that the log of the intercept in the regression equation is

TABLE 22.3 Logs of Outputs and Average Times

Output	Log of outputs	Average times	Log of average times
1	0.000000	100.00	2.000000
2	0.301030	80.00	1.903090
3	0.477121	70.21	1.846399
4	0.602060	64.00	1.806180
5	0.698970	59.56	1.774955
6	0.778151	56.16	1.749427
7	0.845098	53.45	1.727948
8	0.903090	51.20	1.709270
9	0.954243	49.30	1.692847
10	1.000000	47.66	1.678154
11	1.041393	46.21	1.664736
12	1.079181	44.93	1.652536
13	1.113943	43.80	1.641474
14	1.146128	42.76	1.631038
15	1.176091	41.83	1.621488
16	1.204120	40.96	1.612360

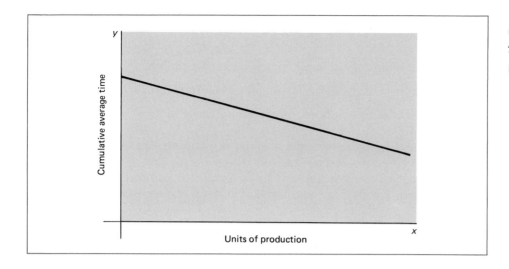

FIGURE 22.2
Cumulative
Average Labor
Time Plotted on a
Log-Log Scale

TABLE 22.4 Learning Indexes—Average-Time Learning Curves

Learning rate	b	Learning rate	b	Learning rate	b
95%	−.0740	88%	−.1844	81%	−.3040
94%	−.0893	87%	−.2009	80%	−.3219
93%	−.1047	86%	−.2176	79%	−.3401
92%	−.1203	85%	−.2345	78%	−.3585
91%	−.1361	84%	−.2515	77%	−.3771
90%	−.1520	83%	−.2688	76%	−.3959
89%	−.1681	82%	−.2863	75%	−.4150

TABLE 22.5 Observed Data

Output	Log of output	Total time	Average time	Log of average times
1	0.000000	103	103.00	2.012837
2	0.301030	178	89.00	1.949390
3	0.477121	263	87.67	1.942851
4	0.602060	316	79.00	1.897627
5	0.698970	390	78.00	1.892095
6	0.778151	454	75.67	1.878924
7	0.845098	511	73.00	1.863323
8	0.903090	580	72.50	1.860338

2.009926, whereas the log from the observed data is 2.012837. This discrepancy is caused by the fact that the regression equation is the best fit of a line for all eight observed points. In this case, the coefficient of determination (R^2) is .9783, which indicates that the regression line is an exceptionally good fit for the observed data.

It has been found that the rate of learning depends largely on the proportion of people-paced to machine-paced operations. When data are not available to estimate the learning rate, the following percentages are often employed as general guidelines:[3]

75 percent assembly labor, 25 percent machine labor = 80 percent curve

50 percent assembly labor, 50 percent machine labor = 85 percent curve

25 percent assembly labor, 75 percent machine labor = 90 percent curve

Observe that the higher the percentage of people-paced labor (assembly labor), the higher the learning rate.[4]

There are occasions when it is appropriate to compute the total time directly when learning is considered. The total time equals

$$t = ax^{b+1} \qquad\qquad\qquad \textbf{(22-5)}$$

The log transformation of this function is

$$\log t = \log a + (b+1) \log x \qquad\qquad\qquad \textbf{(22-6)}$$

Continuing with the original example from table 22.2, the total time to produce eight units using formula (22-6) is

$$\log t = \log 100 + (-.3219 + 1)\log 8$$

$$\log t = 2.000000 + (.6781)(.903090)$$

$$\log t = 2.612385$$

$$t = 409.6 \text{ hours}$$

In table 22.2, marginal times are determined by subtracting the total time of the previous output from the total time to produce the units under consideration. For example, the marginal time of the second unit (60 hours) is determined by subtracting 100 hours (the time to produce the first unit) from 160 hours (the total time to produce the first two units). This is the discrete approach to determining the marginal time. When determining marginal times for the first several hundred units, the discrete approach is most appropriate.

However, the learning curve is a continuous function, and the marginal time (n) can be found by taking the first derivative of the total time function with respect to the output.

$$n = \frac{dt}{dx} = ax^{(b+1)}$$

$$n = a(b+1)x^{b} \qquad\qquad\qquad \textbf{(22-7)}$$

3. Thomas G. Vayda, "How to Use the Learning Curve for Planning and Control," *Cost and Management* (July-August 1972): 28.

4. The lower limit for the learning rate is 100 percent. At this rate, no reduction of time is realized in producing the next unit. The upper limit for the learning rate is 50 percent. At this rate of learning, it would take zero time to produce additional output.

$$\log n = \log a + \log (b+1) + b \log x \qquad \text{(22-8)}$$

Using the original example from table 22.2 and employing equation (22-8), the marginal time for the second unit is

$$\log n = \log 100 + \log(-.3219 + 1) + (-.3219)\log 2$$

$$\log n = 2.000000 + (9.831294 - 10) + (-.3219)(.301030)$$

$$\log n = 1.734392$$

$$n = 54.24 \text{ hours}$$

This estimate of the marginal time (54.24) does not compare favorably with the 60 hours obtained using the discrete method. However, using the discrete approach, the marginal time for unit number 500 is 9.175 hours. Using the continuous approach, the marginal time for unit number 500 is 9.173 hours. Generally, over 200 units, the answers obtained using the two approaches are essentially equivalent. The continuous approach does reduce some of the required calculations.

☐ MARGINAL-TIME MODEL

Another learning-curve model that recently has been used for some labor operations is based on the observation that the marginal time decreases by a constant percent when the cumulative production doubles. This mathematical relationship can be expressed as

$$m = ax^b \qquad \text{(22-9)}$$

where

m = Marginal time
a = Time required for the first unit
x = Cumulative number of units produced
b = A measure of learning (learning index)

TABLE 22.6 Times and Cost—80 Percent Marginal-Time Learning Curve Model

Additional output	Cumulative units	Average time	Total time	Total cost	Marginal units	Marginal time	Marginal cost
1	1	100.000	100.00	$1,000.00	1	100.00	$1,000.00
1	2	90.000	180.00	$1,800.00	1	80.00	$ 800.00
1	3	83.400	250.21	$2,502.10	1	70.21	$ 702.10
1	4	78.550	314.21	$3,142.10	1	64.00	$ 640.00
1	5	74.756	373.78	$3,737.80	1	59.57	$ 595.70
1	6	71.660	429.95	$4,299.50	1	56.17	$ 561.70
1	7	69.060	483.40	$4,834.00	1	53.45	$ 534.50
1	8	66.825	534.60	$5,346.00	1	51.20	$ 512.00

The log transformation of this function is linear and is expressed as

$$\log m = \log a + b \log x \qquad\qquad \textbf{(22-10)}$$

The value of b is the same value used in the average-time model and is determined by formula (22-4).

Employing the example with the hydraulic lift that took 100 hours to assemble, table 22.6 contains the marginal and total times, assuming an 80 percent learning curve marginal-time model.[5] The marginal time for the second unit is $.8 \times 100 = 80$ hours. The total time for the second unit is $100 + 80 = 180$ hours. For the fourth unit, the marginal time is $.8 \times 80 = 64$ hours, and the total time is $100 + 80 + 70.21 + 64 = 314.21$ hours. The algorithm at the doubling points is similar to that used in the average-time model except that the marginal time is computed.

The marginal time for the third unit is determined using formula (22-10) as follows:

$$\log m = \log(100) + (-.3219)\log(3)$$

$$\log m = 2.000000 + (-.3219)\,.477121$$

$$\log m = 1.846415$$

$$m = 70.21 \text{ hours}$$

Total time using the marginal-time model is

$$T = \frac{a}{b+1} x^{b+1} \qquad\qquad \textbf{(22-11)}$$

This formula is obtained by integrating the marginal-time expression (22-9) over the range of x. When a small number of units are involved, the total time determined by adding the marginal times will be different from the total time obtained using formula (22-11). This discrepancy between the total time occurs because using formula (22-9) is the discrete approach, whereas formula (22-11) is the continuous approach to computing the total times. When the number of units exceeds 100, the discrepancy between the total time obtained using the discrete approach and the total time obtained using the continuous approach is immaterial.

Except for the initial doubling of production, the average-time and marginal-time learning models have the same slope when plotted on a log-log scale. Figure 22.3 shows the average-time and marginal-time 80 percent learning curves plotted on a log-log scale. Since the two lines are parallel, it is possible to convert from the average-time model to the marginal-time model by employing a constant. Table 22.7 contains some of the constants for converting from the average-time model to the marginal-time model.

For example, assume that it takes 100 hours to complete the first unit and that an 80 percent learning curve is appropriate. Assuming the mar-

5. Although the same example is used for both learning-curve models, it should be noted that in any given situation where learning is present either the average-time or the marginal-time model will be appropriate, but not both.

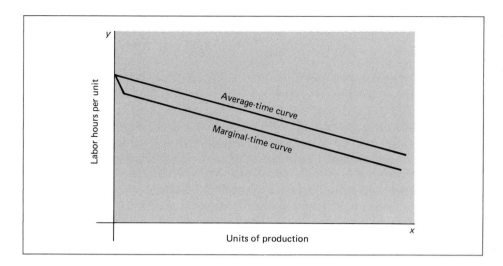

FIGURE 22.3
Average-Time and
Marginal-Time
Curves Plotted on
a Log-Log Scale

TABLE 22.7 Conversion Factors

Learning rate	Conversion factor	Learning rate	Conversion factor	Learning rate	Conversion factor
95%	.9260	88%	.8156	81%	.6960
94%	.9107	87%	.7991	80%	.6781
93%	.8953	86%	.7824	79%	.6599
92%	.8797	85%	.7655	78%	.6415
91%	.8639	84%	.7485	77%	.6229
90%	.8480	83%	.7312	76%	.6041
89%	.8319	82%	.7137	75%	.5850

ginal-time model, using formula (22-9), the marginal time for unit number 120 is

$$m = ax^b$$

$$m = 100(120)^{-.3219}$$

$$m = 21.41$$

Now, assuming the average-time model, the marginal time for unit number 120 can be found using formula (22-7).

$$n = a(b+1)x^b$$

$$n = 100(-.3219 + 1)120^{-.3219}$$

$$n = 14.52$$

From table 22.7, the relationship between the two models can be shown by using the conversion factor for an 80 percent learning curve.

$$n = cm \qquad \textbf{(22-12)}$$

$$14.52 = .6781(21.41)$$

☐ MODEL ASSUMPTIONS

The basic assumption underlying any learning-curve model is that the rate of learning is sufficiently regular to be predictable, and that learning will exist no matter how long the production cycle. The following examples are often cited as evidence to support this assumption. From 1909—when the first Model T Ford was produced—until 1926—when the production cycle was terminated—the improvement in productivity followed an 86 percent learning curve.[6] Results from a longitudinal study in the aircraft industry covering fourteen years showed that productivity followed an 80 percent learning curve.[7]

In a people-paced operation involving the assembly of candy boxes, learning was found to exist over many years involving millions of boxes. Assembly by one person over a period of sixteen years involving 16 million boxes of candy was found to follow a learning curve.[8] In machine-paced operations, learning has been found to exist during the production of tens of millions of units.[9]

In the majority of cases cited in the literature, the application of learning curves is made to a work group. This is usually the case when attempting to estimate costs. Learning curves have been found to be applicable in the petroleum refining and the basic chemical industries.[10] In fact, it has been found that learning curves are applicable to most industries.

Besides the learning index, *b*, the other parameter of a learning model is the time to produce the initial unit or production lot. It is assumed that this initial time is known and that the rate of learning can be measured from this first unit. When the model is employed, problems have been encountered in determining this initial time estimate. If a single employee is used in an assembly operation, the skill level of the employee will influence the time required to assemble the initial unit. Therefore, it is common practice to have several people perform the task and use the average time to estimate the model parameter. Of course, the assembly of an airplane or ship does not permit using an average to estimate the initial time.

☐ LEARNING AND STANDARD COSTS

A standard cost has been defined as reflecting reasonable approximations of actual costs with reasonably competent management. It furnishes a medium by which the effectiveness of current results can be measured and the responsibility for deviations can be placed. A standard-cost system

6. Winifred B. Huschmann, "Profit from The Learning Curve," *Harvard Business Review* (January 1964): 138.

7. Frank J. Andress, "The Learning Curve as a Production Tool," *Harvard Business Review* (January-February 1954): 88.

8. Huschmann, "Profit from The Learning Curve," p. 136.

9. Ibid., p. 136.

10. Ibid., p. 128.

TABLE 22.8 Actual and Standard Hours

Unit	Total actual hours	Total standard hours (55-hour standard)	Total standard hours (80 percent learning curve)
1	100	55	100.0
2	165	110	160.0
3	217	165	210.6
4	264	220	256.0
5	302	275	297.8
6	342	330	337.0
7	379	385	374.2
8	412	440	409.6

allows measurement of inefficiencies. Most explanations of direct-labor standards suggest that a constant of direct labor is required per unit. For example, after a job is set up, if the direct-labor standard is 50 hours, then a standard of 50 hours is associated with each unit of output. If one unit is produced, the standard direct-labor input is 50 hours, the standard for 25 units is 1,250 hours (50 × 25), and the standard for N units is $50N$.

Now, consider the impact of learning on the labor-efficiency variance. Assume the actual hours for the production of eight units as shown in the left column of table 22.8. If a standard of fifty-five hours per unit is assumed with a standard hourly rate of $10, the labor-rate and labor-efficiency variances are calculated as follows, assuming an actual labor rate of $10.25.

Labor-rate variance = ($10.25 − $10.00) × 412 hours
                    = $103.00 unfavorable

Labor-efficiency variance = (412 hours − 440 hours) × $10.00
                          = $280.00 favorable

In terms of hours, we see in table 22.9 what happens to the labor-efficiency variance when a constant standard of fifty-five hours is employed. The total labor-efficiency variance originally is unfavorable; however, as production increases the variance gradually becomes favorable. The marginal or unit variance as shown in table 22.9 also is unfavorable originally, but it rapidly becomes favorable as production increases.

TABLE 22.9 Labor-Efficiency Variances (Hours)

Unit	Hour standard — Total efficiency variance (hours)	Hour standard — Marginal unit efficiency variance (hours)	80% Average-time learning curve standard — Total efficiency variance (hours)	80% Average-time learning curve standard — Marginal unit efficiency variance (hours)
1	(55 − 100) = 45 U	(55 − 100) = 45 U	(100 − 100) = 0	(100 − 100) = 0
2	(110 − 165) = 55 U	(55 − 65) = 10 U	(160 − 165) = 5.0 U	(60 − 65) = 5.0 U
3	(165 − 217) = 52 U	(55 − 52) = 3 F	(210.6 − 217) = 6.4 U	(50.6 − 52) = 1.4 U
4	(220 − 264) = 44 U	(55 − 47) = 8 F	(256 − 264) = 8.0 U	(45.4 − 47) = 1.6 U
5	(275 − 302) = 27 U	(55 − 38) = 17 F	(297.8 − 302) = 4.2 U	(41.8 − 38) = 3.8 F
6	(330 − 342) = 12 U	(55 − 40) = 15 F	(337 − 342) = 5.0 U	(39.2 − 40) = 0.8 U
7	(385 − 379) = 6 F	(55 − 37) = 18 F	(374.2 − 379) = 4.8 U	(37.2 − 37) = 0.2 F
8	(440 − 412) = 28 F	(55 − 33) = 22 F	(409.6 − 412) = 2.4 U	(35.4 − 33) = 2.4 F

Now, if the standard were established based on an average-time 80 percent learning curve, the standard time would be as shown in the right column of table 22.8. Using the learning-curve standard, the labor-rate and labor-efficiency variances are as follows:

$$\text{Labor-rate variance} = (\$10.25 - \$10.00) \times 412 \text{ hours}$$
$$= \$103.00 \text{ unfavorable}$$

$$\text{Labor-efficiency variance} = (412 \text{ hours} - 409.6 \text{ hours}) \times \$10.00$$
$$= \$24.00 \text{ unfavorable}$$

Using the standard time based on the learning curve results in a $24 unfavorable labor-efficiency variance rather than the $280 favorable variance as determined when the constant standard was employed. Also, note in the columns on the right of table 22.8 that the standard hours based on the learning curve are much closer to the actual hours. This is certainly a better representation of what "should be under project conditions" rather than the results obtained using the constant standard.

Some important generalizations can be made from observing the variances in this example. If, indeed, learning is taking place and a constant standard is employed, then the labor-efficiency variance will tend to be favorable in the long run. The $280 favorable labor-efficiency variance reported using the constant standard indicates that 28 hours less than the standard were employed. This effort might be applauded while the learning-curve standard indicates an unfavorable variance of 2.4 hours. Thus, when learning is taken into consideration, unfavorable performance is detected.

If a firm has a policy of revising standards but does not consider the learning effect, its standards still could be inefficient. If at any time it takes the standard number of hours to complete a unit or lot of units when it should have taken less as predicted by the learning curve, then there will be no variance reported and again the problems and inefficiencies will go unnoticed. But the real danger here is that the standard may be set again at the same level as it was before. If learning is taking place, the next units should take even less time. Needless to say, any variance reported in a case such as this will be totally unreliable and severely distorted. Inefficiency could become a major problem in the system while favorable variances are being reported.

Incorporating learning into a labor standard increases the number of potential causes for the labor-efficiency variance. An unfavorable variance might indicate that the learning rate is specified incorrectly. However, if the standard is based on performance that took place in the prior period, previously cited evidence indicates that the rate of learning can be expected to continue at the same rate in the future. Therefore, it is unlikely that the rate is incorrectly specified. Probably, scheduling factors altered the rate.

For example, if workers are interrupted and do not work continuously on the eight units produced in the current period, then some of the learning realized will be lost. When learning is taking place, an interruption will result in a loss of learning. An interruption will have caused the work group to back up the learning curve. A complete loss of the learning effect would cause 100 hours to be needed to complete the ninth unit, which is the same time it took to complete the first unit.

If the task is a group project and the make-up of the work group is altered, a loss of learning or a change in the learning rate may result. Either one or both of these factors may contribute to the labor-efficiency variance. Under these conditions, a loss of learning will probably occur; but as the group continues to produce units, learning will continue at the same rate. However, if the composite skill level of the group is significantly changed, then the rate of learning will also change. From the above discussion, it is clear that turnover or shifts in the scheduling of work groups can contribute to the labor-efficiency variance.

There are certain situations in which learning should be considered in establishing labor standards. Whenever new or revised production operations are undertaken, learning will most likely be very dramatic, especially in the start-up phase. Whenever employees undertake an unfamiliar task, the learning effect will most likely be apparent. Production runs of short duration or production runs that are frequently interrupted for long periods are other situations in which the effects of learning are likely to be material.

In situations in which the impact of learning is expected, caution should be observed if overhead is applied as a function of standard direct-labor hours. Labor standards based on learning curves are not constant, and the variations in the standard hours may not be consistent with any variations in overhead costs. If a constant labor standard is employed and learning is present, this will affect any overhead-efficiency variance in the same manner as the labor-efficiency variance.

☐ EFFECTS OF
LEARNING ON NET INCOME

Assume the Sound Corporation has a contract to deliver two special radios each year for the next two years. The selling price is $3,500, and the estimated cost of materials is $2,000 for each radio. Labor hours are estimated to equal 100 hours for the first radio and are expected to follow an 80 percent learning curve using the average-time model. Recall that labor costs are assumed to be $10 per hour. Also assume that variable overhead is charged to production at the rate of $5 per direct-labor hour.

Table 22.10 contains the cost estimates for each radio and the expected contribution margin for each year. The expected contribution margin during the first year is $600, whereas for the second year the expected contribution margin is $1,560, or an increase of $960. The reason for the increase in the contribution margin is that the first two radios took 160 hours to assemble, while radios three and four took only 96 hours to assemble. (Refer to table 22.2 to confirm the numbers.) The 64-hour difference multiplied by $15 (the labor and variable-overhead rate) equals the $960 difference in the yearly contribution margins.

TABLE 22.10 Unit Cost Estimates

	Unit 1	Unit 2	Total year 1	Unit 3	Unit 4	Total year 2	Total/ years 1 and 2
Sales	$3,500	$3,500	$7,000	$3,500.00	$3,500.00	$7,000	$14,000
Materials	$2,000	$2,000	$4,000	$2,000.00	$2,000.00	$4,000	$ 8,000
Labor	1,000	600	1,600	506.30	453.70	960	2,560
Variable overhead	500	300	800	253.15	226.85	480	1,280
Total variable costs	$3,500	$2,900	$6,400	$2,759.45	$2,680.55	$5,440	$11,840
Contribution margin	$ 0	$ 600	$ 600	$ 740.55	$ 819.45	$1,560	$ 2,160

Reporting differences such as the one just cited that are caused by learning may be considered to be undesirable, especially for internal-reporting purposes. One means of altering this situation is to defer some of the initial learning costs. For example, assume it is desired to report average costs for each year over the life of the contract. Table 22.11 shows how the result would be reported when average labor costs are employed.

The following journal entry would be made at the end of the first year to defer the labor and overhead costs:

Deferred production costs	480	
Work-in-process—Labor		320
Work-in-process—Overhead		160

The $320 credited to work-in-process—labor is the difference between the actual labor cost incurred during the first year ($1,600) and the average yearly labor cost ($1,280). Because variable overhead is charged to production based on direct-labor hours, it is also necessary to defer part of the overhead charges. The $160 overhead entry is the difference between the overhead charged in the first year ($800) and the average yearly overhead ($640). At the end of the second year, the following entry is made:

Cost of goods sold	480	
Deferred production costs		480

The deferred production costs would appear on the balance sheet as an asset at the end of the first year. These costs might be referred to as start-up costs rather than deferred production costs for financial-reporting purposes.

TABLE 22.11 Contribution Margins Using Average Costs

	Year 1	Year 2	Total/ years 1 and 2
Sales	$7,000	$7,000	$14,000
Materials	$4,000	$4,000	$ 8,000
Labor	1,280	1,280	2,560
Variable overhead	640	640	1,280
Total variable costs	$5,920	$5,920	$11,840
Contribution margin	$1,080	$1,080	$ 2,160

□ SUMMARY

The learning effect has been widely documented and has a dramatic impact upon labor costs in the start-up phase of labor-intensive processes. Evidence has also been cited to suggest that learning does affect labor hours over extended production runs. The result is nonlinear cost functions that can be transformed into linear functions employing logs. In many cases, it is not necessary to employ logs in solving these problems if an electronic calculator is available. When appropriate, the learning effect should be considered in cost estimation, cost control, and income-based performance measures.

Marginal production time estimates can be determined using learning curves. The discrete approach involves subtracting the total time of the previous output from the total time to produce the units under consideration. The discrete approach is appropriate when determining marginal time for the first 200 units of output. When over 200 units are involved, the marginal time can be determined using a formula. In some cases, the rate of learning is not known. It is then necessary to determine the logs of the output and average time and use regression to estimate the learning rate.

The basic assumptions underlying all learning curves are that the rate of learning is sufficiently regular to be predictable and that learning will exist over the entire production cycle. There are numerous examples in the literature to support these assumptions. The majority of cases in the literature concerning learning are related to a work group.

KEY TERMS

Average-time model
Learning
Learning curve

Learning index
Marginal-time model

REVIEW PROBLEM

The Train Corporation is considering submitting a bid for the manufacture of four special valves for a high-pressure steam line. It is estimated that the first valve will require 200 direct-labor hours and that the direct labor will follow a 90 percent average-time learning curve. The standard direct-labor rate is $20 per hour, and variable overhead is charged to production at a rate of $10 per direct-labor hour.

Materials are estimated to cost $1,000 for each valve. The company's pricing policy is to determine the estimated variable cost and then to add a 50 percent markup.

Required □

1. Determine the unit selling price if all four valves are supplied.

2. Assume a contract is signed to supply the four valves at the selling price determined in requirement 1 and after supplying two valves the contract is canceled. Determine the total contribution margin on the two valves that were supplied.

3. Determine the contribution margin on the two valves that were not supplied.

4. After delivery of the first two valves at the price determined in requirement 1, the customer indicated that it only required one additional valve. What price would you charge for the third valve, considering that you want to receive the 50% markup on all three valves?

Solution ☐

1.

Unit	Total units	Average time	Total time	Marginal time
1	1	200	200.000	200.000
1	2	.9(200) = 180	360.000	160.000
1	3	169.242*	507.726	147.726
1	4	.9(180) = 162	648.000	140.274

$$*\frac{\text{Log }.9}{\text{Log }2} = -.152 \tag{22-4}$$

$$y = 200(3)^{-.152} = 169.242 \tag{22-1}$$

Materials	$ 4,000
Labor 648 × $20 =	12,960
Overhead 648 × $10 =	6,480
Total variable cost	$23,440
Markup—50%	11,720
Total	$35,160

$$\frac{\$35,160}{4} = \$8,790 \text{ unit selling price}$$

2.

Materials	$ 2,000
Labor 360 × $20 =	7,200
Overhead 360 × $10 =	3,600
Total variable cost	$12,800
Selling price 2 × $8,790 =	$17,580
Variable cost	12,800
Contribution margin—Valves 1 and 2	$ 4,780

3.

Materials	$ 2,000
Labor (648 − 360) × $20 =	5,760
Overhead (648 − 360) × $10 =	2,880
Total variable cost	$10,640
Selling price 2 × $8,790	$17,580
Variable cost	10,640
Contribution margin—Valves 3 and 4	$ 6,940

4.

Materials	$ 3,000.00
Labor 507.726 × $20	10,154.52
Overhead 507.726 × $10	5,077.26
Total variable cost	$18,231.78
Markup	9,115.89
Total sales valves −3	$27,347.67
Sales valves 1 and 2	17,580.00
Selling price valve 3	$ 9,767.67

APPENDIX: A Review of Logarithms

A log is an exponent. The subscript in the notation indicates the base. For example, the $\log_{10} 100 = 2$. Each log notation consists of two parts. In determining the $\log_{10}$ 125, it is not obvious as to the exponent. By observation, the exponent of 125 to the base 10 is between two and three.

It is the decimal part of the exponent that must be found. This decimal part of the log is found in standard tables. In appendix table 1, the decimal part of the exponent can be found. After finding the value for 125 in the table, the $\log_{10} 125$ = 2.0969. The integer 2 in the log notation is called the characteristic, and the decimal part found in the table is called the mantissa.

The following scientific notation relates to characteristics of the common log system:

Number		Scientific notation	Characteristic
10,000	....	10^4	4
1,000	....	10^3	3
100	....	10^2	2
10	....	10^1	1
1	....	10^0	0
0.1	....	10^{-1}	-1
0.01	....	10^{-2}	-2
0.001	....	10^{-3}	-3
0.0001	....	10^{-4}	-4

Now, consider the following list of numbers and their respective common logs:

12,500	....	$\log_{10}$ 12,500	=	4.0969
1,250	....	$\log_{10}$ 1,250	=	3.0969
125	....	$\log_{10}$ 125	=	2.0969
12.5	....	$\log_{10}$ 12.5	=	1.0969
1.25	....	$\log_{10}$ 1.25	=	0.0969
0.125	....	$\log_{10}$ 0.125	=	.0969 − 1
0.0125	....	$\log_{10}$ 0.0125	=	.0969 − 2
0.00125	....	$\log_{10}$ 0.00125	=	.0969 − 3

From the above, observe that the mantissa of the log is determined by the sequence of the digits. Therefore, numbers with the same sequence of digits have the same mantissa. The characteristic is determined by the location of the decimal point.

There is an alternative way of expressing the logs of 0.125, 0.0125, and 0.00125. Frequently, these logs are expressed respectively as 9.0969 − 10, 8.0969 − 10 and 7.0969 − 10.

Since appendix table 1 has only three-digit numbers, it is necessary to interpolate to find the mantissa. A linear-estimation procedure is employed to determine the mantissa. For example, the log of 1347 is found as follows:

$$
\begin{aligned}
\text{mantissa of 135} &= .1303 \\
\text{mantissa of 134} &= .1271 \\
\text{difference} &= .0032 \\
\text{interpolating } 7/10 \times .0032 &= .0022 \\
\text{mantissa of 134} &= .1271 \\
\text{mantissa of 1347} &= .1293 \\
\\
\log_{10} \text{1347} &= 3.1293
\end{aligned}
$$

APPENDIX TABLE 1 Common Logarithms of Numbers

Number	0	1	2	3	4	5	6	7	8	9	Average difference
1.0	0.0000	0043	0086	0128	0170	0212	0253	0294	0334	0374	
1.1	0414	0453	0492	0531	0569	0607	0645	0682	0719	0755	
1.2	0792	0828	0864	0899	0934	0969	1004	1038	1072	1106	
1.3	1139	1173	1206	1239	1271	1303	1335	1367	1399	1430	
1.4	1461	1492	1523	1553	1584	1614	1644	1673	1703	1732	
1.5	1761	1790	1818	1847	1875	1903	1931	1959	1987	2014	
1.6	2041	2068	2095	2122	2148	2175	2201	2227	2253	2279	
1.7	2304	2330	2355	2380	2405	2430	2455	2480	2504	2529	
1.8	2553	2577	2601	2625	2648	2672	2695	2718	2742	2765	
1.9	2788	2810	2833	2856	2878	2900	2923	2945	2967	2989	
2.0	0.3010	3032	3054	3075	3096	3118	3139	3160	3181	3201	21
2.1	3222	3243	3263	3284	3304	3324	3345	3365	3385	3404	20
2.2	3424	3444	3464	3483	3502	3522	3541	3560	3579	3598	19
2.3	3617	3636	3655	3674	3692	3711	3729	3747	3766	3784	18
2.4	3802	3820	3838	3856	3874	3892	3909	3927	3945	3962	17
2.5	3979	3997	4014	4031	4048	4065	4082	4099	4116	4133	17
2.6	4150	4166	4183	4200	4216	4232	4249	4265	4281	4298	16
2.7	4314	4330	4346	4362	4378	4393	4409	4425	4440	4456	16
2.8	4472	4487	4502	4518	4533	4548	4564	4579	4594	4609	15
2.9	4624	4639	4654	4669	4683	4698	4713	4728	4742	4757	15
3.0	0.4771	4786	4800	4814	4829	4843	4857	4871	4886	4900	14
3.1	4914	4928	4942	4955	4969	4983	4997	5011	5024	5038	14
3.2	5051	5065	5079	5092	5105	5119	5132	5145	5159	5172	13
3.3	5185	5198	5211	5224	5237	5250	5263	5276	5289	5302	13
3.4	5315	5328	5340	5353	5366	5378	5391	5403	5416	5428	13
3.5	5441	5453	5465	5478	5490	5502	5514	5527	5539	5551	12
3.6	5563	5575	5587	5599	5611	5623	5635	5647	5658	5670	12
3.7	5682	5694	5705	5717	5729	5740	5752	5763	5775	5786	12
3.8	5798	5809	5821	5832	5843	5855	5866	5877	5888	5899	11
3.9	5911	5922	5933	5944	5955	5966	5977	5988	5999	6010	11
4.0	0.6021	6031	6042	6053	6064	6075	6085	6096	6107	6117	11
4.1	6128	6138	6149	6160	6170	6180	6191	6201	6212	6222	10
4.2	6232	6243	6253	6263	6274	6284	6294	6304	6314	6325	10
4.3	6335	6345	6355	6365	6375	6385	6395	6405	6415	6425	10
4.4	6435	6444	6454	6464	6474	6484	6493	6503	6513	6522	10
4.5	6532	6542	6551	6561	6571	6580	6590	6599	6609	6618	10
4.6	6628	6637	6646	6656	6665	6675	6684	6693	6702	6712	10
4.7	6721	6730	6739	6749	6758	6767	6776	6785	6794	6803	9
4.8	6812	6821	6830	6839	6848	6857	6866	6875	6884	6893	9
4.9	6902	6911	6920	6928	6937	6946	6955	6964	6972	6981	9

$\log \pi = 0.4971$ $\log \pi/2 = 0.1961$ $\log \pi^2 = 0.9943$ $\log \sqrt{\pi} = 0.2486$.

$\log e = 0.4343$ $\log (0.4343) = 0.6378 - 1$

These two pages give the common logarithms of numbers between 1 and 10, correct to four places. Moving the decimal point n places to the right (or left) in the number is equivalent to adding n (or $-n$) to the logarithms. Thus, $\log 0.017453 = 0.2419 - 2$, which may also be written 2.2419 or $8.2419 - 10$.

$$\log (ab) = \log a + \log b \qquad \log (a^N) = N \log a$$

$$\log \frac{a}{b} = \log a - \log b \qquad \log (\sqrt[N]{a}) = \frac{1}{N} \log a$$

From Theodore Baumeister, ed., *Marks' Mechanical Engineer's Handbook* (New York: McGraw-Hill Book Company, 1958).

APPENDIX TABLE 1 —*Continued*

Number	0	1	2	3	4	5	6	7	8	9	Average difference
5.0	0.6990	6998	7007	7016	7024	7033	7042	7050	7059	7067	9
5.1	7076	7084	7093	7101	7110	7118	7126	7135	7143	7152	8
5.2	7160	7168	7177	7185	7193	7202	7210	7218	7226	7235	8
5.3	7243	7251	7259	7267	7275	7284	7292	7300	7308	7316	8
5.4	7324	7332	7340	7348	7356	7364	7372	7380	7388	7396	8
5.5	7404	7412	7419	7427	7435	7443	7451	7459	7466	7474	8
5.6	7482	7490	7497	7505	7513	7520	7528	7536	7543	7551	8
5.7	7559	7566	7574	7582	7589	7597	7604	7612	7619	7627	8
5.8	7634	7642	7649	7657	7664	7672	7679	7686	7694	7701	7
5.9	7709	7716	7723	7731	7738	7745	7752	7760	7767	7774	7
6.0	0.7782	7789	7796	7803	7810	7818	7825	7832	7839	7846	7
6.1	7853	7860	7868	7875	7882	7889	7896	7903	7910	7917	7
6.2	7924	7931	7938	7945	7952	7959	7966	7973	7980	7987	7
6.3	7993	8000	8007	8014	8021	8028	8035	8041	8048	8055	7
6.4	8062	8069	8075	8082	8089	8096	8102	8109	8116	8122	7
6.5	8129	8136	8142	8149	8156	8162	8169	8176	8182	8189	7
6.6	8195	8202	8209	8215	8222	8228	8135	8241	8248	8254	7
6.7	8261	8267	8274	8280	8287	8293	8299	8306	8312	8319	6
6.8	8325	8331	8338	8344	8351	8357	8363	8370	8376	8382	6
6.9	8388	8395	8401	8407	8414	8420	8426	8432	8439	8445	6
7.0	0.8451	8457	8463	8470	8476	8482	8488	8494	8500	8506	6
7.1	8513	8519	8525	8531	8537	8543	8549	8555	8561	8567	6
7.2	8573	8579	8585	8591	8597	8603	8609	8615	8621	8627	6
7.3	8633	8639	8645	8651	8657	8663	8669	8675	8681	8686	6
7.4	8692	8698	8704	8710	8716	8722	8727	8733	8739	8745	6
7.5	8751	8756	8762	8768	8774	8779	8785	8791	8797	8802	6
7.6	8808	8814	8820	8825	8831	8837	8842	8848	8854	8859	6
7.7	8865	8871	8876	8882	8887	8893	8899	8904	8910	8915	6
7.8	8921	8927	8932	8938	8943	8949	8954	8960	8965	8971	6
7.9	8976	8982	8987	8993	8998	9004	9009	9015	9020	9025	5
8.0	0.9031	9036	9042	9047	9053	9058	9063	9069	9074	9079	5
8.1	9085	9090	9096	9101	9106	9112	9117	9122	9128	9133	5
8.2	9138	9143	9149	9154	9159	9165	9170	9175	9180	9186	5
8.3	9191	9196	9201	9206	9212	9217	9222	9227	9232	9238	5
8.4	9243	9248	9253	9258	9263	9269	9274	9279	9284	9289	5
8.5	9294	9299	9304	9309	9315	9320	9325	9330	9335	9340	5
8.6	9345	9350	9355	9360	9365	9370	9375	9380	9385	9390	5
8.7	9395	9400	9405	9410	9415	9420	9425	9430	9435	9440	5
8.8	9445	9450	9455	9460	9465	9469	9474	9479	9484	9489	5
8.9	9494	9499	9504	9509	9513	9518	9523	9528	9533	9538	5
9.0	0.9542	9547	9552	9557	9562	9566	9571	9576	9581	9586	5
9.1	9590	9595	9600	9605	9609	9614	9619	9624	9628	9633	5
9.2	9638	9643	9647	9652	9657	9661	9666	9671	9675	9680	5
9.3	9685	9689	9694	9699	9703	9708	9713	9717	9722	9727	5
9.4	9731	9736	9741	9745	9750	9754	9759	9763	9768	9773	5
9.5	9777	9782	9786	9791	9795	9800	9805	9809	9814	9818	5
9.6	9823	9827	9832	9836	9841	9845	9850	9854	9859	9863	4
9.7	9868	9872	9877	9881	9886	9890	9894	9899	9903	9908	4
9.8	9912	9917	9921	9926	9930	9934	9939	9943	9948	9952	4
9.9	9956	9961	9965	9969	9974	9978	9983	9987	9991	9996	4

Another example will further clarify the procedure. Assume it is necessary to find the log of 13,475.

```
mantissa of 135  = .1303
mantissa of 134  = .1271
   difference     = .0032

interpolating 75/100 × .0032 = .0024
mantissa of 134              = .1271
mantissa of 13,475           = .1295

log₁₀ 13,475 = 4.1295
```

Multiplication and division are possible with logs. When multiplication is specified, the logs are added; for division, the logs are subtracted. Consider the following examples:

1. Multiply   125 by 25.

$$125 \times 25 = \log 125 + \log 25$$
$$= 2.0969 + 1.3979$$
$$= 3.4948$$

antilog(3.4948) = 3,125

2. Divide   125 by 25.

$$125 \div 25 = \log 125 - \log 25$$
$$= 2.0969 - 1.3979$$
$$= .06990$$

antilog(0.6990) = 5.0

Note that the antilogs are found by first finding the mantissa in the log table and then determining the number. The decimal point location is specified by the characteristic of the log.

QUESTIONS

Q22-1. What are the assumptions that underlie using learning curves in cost estimation?

Q22-2. In what kinds of manufacturing operations would you expect to encounter the learning-curve phenomenon?

Q22-3. Would you expect the learning phenomenon to be more prevalent in job-order or process-costing systems? Explain.

Q22-4. It is argued sometimes that the prices of newly introduced high-technology consumer items follow the learning phenomenon. Do you agree? If so, can you identify some examples?

Q22-5. Explain what is meant by a 75 percent learning curve using the marginal-time model?

Q22-6. Describe a situation in which you have observed the learning effect.

Q22-7. How does the ratio of machine to labor hours affect the learning rate?

Q22-8. Explain the relationship between the average-time and marginal-time learning models.

Q22-9. Identify some factors that will influence the learning rate.

Q22-10. Explain how the following could influence learning:

    a. Labor strike
    b. Excess absenteeism
    c. Hiring new employees
    d. Changing job assignments

Q22-11. How can the presence of learning influence standard-cost labor variances?

Q22-12. In a standard-costing system, why is it especially important to consider learning when setting standards?

Q22-13. Assume learning is present, what are some of the problems that would be encountered if overhead is charged to cost of goods sold as a percentage of direct-labor costs?

PROBLEMS

P22-1. Assume a constant rate of learning, and complete the following table:

Basic Learning-Curve Calculations

Cumulative output	Cumulative average time	Total time	Marginal units	Marginal time	Marginal cost
1	40	40	1	40	$ 200
2	32	___	___	___	___
3	28.1	___	___	___	___
4	___	___	1	___	___

P22-2. Assume a constant rate of learning, and complete the following table:

Basic Learning-Curve Calculations

Cumulative output	Cumulative average time	Total time	Marginal units	Marginal time	Marginal cost
1	40	40	1	40	$ 400
2	___	___	1	32	___
3	___	___	1	___	___
4	___	___	1	25.6	___

P22-3. Assume an 80 percent average-time learning curve, and complete the following table:

Basic Learning-Curve Calculations

Cumulative output	Cumulative average time	Total time	Marginal units	Marginal time	Marginal cost
1	___	___	1	___	$___
2	___	___	1	___	$___
4	51.2	204.8	2	76.8	$ 768

Basic Learning-   **P22-4.**   Assume an 80 percent marginal-time learning curve, and complete the
Curve   following table:
Calculations

Cumulative output	Cumulative average time	Total time	Marginal units	Marginal time	Marginal cost
1	_____	_____	1	_____	_____
2	_____	_____	1	_____	_____
4	78.55	314.21	2	64	$ 640

Multiple-Choice   **P22-5.**   The average number of minutes required to assemble trivets is predictable
Questions   based upon an 80 percent average-time learning curve. That is, whenever
                               cumulative production doubles, cumulative average time per unit be-
                               comes 80 percent of what it was at the previous doubling point. The trivets
                               are produced in lots of 300 units, and 60 minutes of labor are required
                               to assemble each first lot.

Using the concept of the learning curve and the letters listed, select the
best answer for each of requirements 1–5.

Let MT = Marginal time for the xth lot
   M = Marginal time for the first lot
   X = Lots produced
   b = Exponent expressing the improvement; b has the range
       $1 < b \leq 0$

Required ☐

1. A normal graph (i.e., not a log or log-log graph) of average minutes
per lot of production, where cumulative lots are represented by the x
axis and average minutes per lot are represented by the y axis, would
produce a

   a. Linear function sloping downward to the right
   b. Linear function sloping upward to the right
   c. Curvilinear function sloping upward to the right at an increasing
       rate
   d. Curvilinear function sloping downward to the right at a decreasing
       rate

2. A log-log graph of average minutes per lot of production, where cumulative lots are represented by the x axis and average minutes per
lot are represented by the y axis, would produce a

   a. Linear function sloping downward to the right
   b. Linear function sloping upward to the right
   c. Curvilinear function sloping upward to the right at a decreasing
       rate
   d. Curvilinear function sloping downward to the right at a decreasing
       rate

3. The average number of minutes required per lot to complete four lots
is approximately

   a. 60.0
   b. 48.5
   c. 38.4
   d. 30.7

4. Average time to produce X lots of trivets could be expressed

    a. MX^{b+1}

    b. MX^{b}

    c. MT^{b+1}

    d. MX^{b-1}

5. Assuming that $b = -.322$, the average number of minutes required to produce x lots of trivets could be expressed

    a. $40.08X^{.678}$

    b. $40.08X$

    c. $60X^{-.322}$

    d. $60X^{1.322}$

(CPA)

P22-6. Assume it took a firm 100 hours to assemble the first fork-lift truck. From past experience, the firm has determined that such activity generally follows an 80 percent average-time learning curve when output is doubled. Assume a labor rate of $5, construct a table showing the average time, total time, total cost, and marginal labor cost for assembling from one to eight trucks.

Basic Learning-Curve Calculations

P22-7. Assume it takes a firm forty hours to assemble the first electronic calculator. The firm has determined that such activity generally follows a 90 percent marginal-time learning curve when output is doubled, and the hourly rate is $5. Construct a table showing average time, total time, total cost, and marginal cost for assembling from one to eight calculators.

Determining Learning-Curve Parameters

P22-8. The Spangler Company manufactures process-control computers. They have just completed assembling sixty computers, and it took an average of 40.1 hours to assemble the units. For the first twenty units, the assembly time averaged 57.2 hours. From these two observations, we can imply an average-time learning-curve function of the form $y = ax^{b}$.

Determining Learning-Curve Parameters

Required ☐

1. Derive the values for a and b, and determine the percentage learning curve for the assembly operation.

2. Using the values from requirement 1, determine the average and total hours necessary to produce eighty units.

3. The labor rate averages $10 per hour. Determine the incremental labor cost in assembling the additional twenty units.

P22-9. The JWL Company manufactures electric gauges. They have just completed assembling seven gauges, and it took a total of 149.66 hours to assemble the units. For the first three units, the assembly time totaled 84.3 hours. From these two observations, we can imply an average-time learning-curve function of the form $y = ax^{b}$.

Determining Learning-Curve Parameters

Required ☐

1. Derive the values for a and b, and determine a percentage learning curve for the assembly operation.

2. Using the values from requirement 1, determine the average and total hours necessary to produce twenty units.

3. The labor rate averages $10 per hour. Determine the incremental labor cost in assembling the additional thirteen units.

Cost Estimation Using Learning Curves

P22-10. The Snowball Company is a subcontractor in the telecommunications industry. The company has just completed a display terminal for an aircraft control system. The following was taken from the cost sheet for the terminal:

Direct material	$1,000
Direct labor	
100 hours @ $6	600
200 hours @ $4	800
Variable overhead 300 hours @ $3	900
Total variable costs	$3,300

If an 80 percent average-time learning curve is assumed as a basis for cost estimation, prepare the required cost estimates.

Required □

1. Determine the total variable cost to make an additional display terminal.

2. Determine the total variable cost to make seven additional terminals. (This question is independent from the first question.)

3. Determine the total variable cost to make seven additional terminals if the effect of learning on the first terminal has been lost because of excessive delay between the jobs. (This question is independent of requirements 1 and 2.)

Learning Curves and Standard Costs

P22-11. Assume the first unit produced took 100 hours and it is estimated that labor will follow an 80 percent average-time learning curve. The standard time was set at 50 hours per unit, and the standard labor rate is $20 per hour. During the first month of production, 15 units were produced in 720 hours costing $15,810.

Required □

1. Determine the labor-rate and efficiency variances using the 50 hours standard.

2. Determine the labor-rate and efficiency variances using the 80 percent average-time learning curve in establishing the standard.

Learning Curves and Standard Costs

P22-12. Assume the first unit produced took 1,000 hours and it is estimated that the labor will follow an 80 percent average-time learning curve. The standard time was set at 600 hours per unit, and the standard labor rate is $15 per hour. During the first year, 10 units were produced in 4,970 hours costing $76,800.

Required ☐

1. Determine the labor-rate and efficiency variances using the 600 hours standard.

2. Determine the labor-rate and efficiency variances using the 80 percent average-time learning curve in establishing the standard.

3. What will the impact of learning be on the labor variances as the length of the production run increases?

P22-13. The Grace Hixson Corporation is building special radios for the space progam. Each of the radios is assembled by hand and then must be put through a series of tests. The assembly operation is expected to follow a 75 percent marginal-time learning curve, while the testing is expected to follow an 85 percent average-time learning curve. Materials for each radio are estimated to cost $2,000 each. Assembly labor is billed at $8 per hour; testing is billed at $10 per hour. Variable overhead is estimated at $5 per direct-labor hour for both assembly and testing.

Income Measurement and Learning Curves

The corporation's contract with the space agency calls for reimbursement for each radio equal to the total variable cost plus 25 percent. Assembly of the first radio took 2,000 hours, and the testing required 800 hours.

Required ☐

1. What is the estimated contribution margin for the second radio?

2. What is the estimated total contribution margin during the month of January if the first four radios are delivered during the month?

3. What is the estimated total contribution margin during the month of February if four additional radios are delivered during the month?

4. What is the estimated total contribution margin during the month of March if radios 9 through 12 are delivered?

5. Explain why the estimated contribution margins for each month are decreasing. What assumptions are made when a learning curve is employed?

P22-14. The Shelborn Company has found that, when output doubles, a 90 percent average-time learning curve results in very accurate estimates of the direct-labor hours required in the assembly of golf carts. A new model has been placed into production, and it took fifty hours to assemble the first cart. Direct-labor rates average $5 per hour.

Cost Estimation Using Learning Curves

Employing a learning curve of the form $y = ax^b$ where $b = -.152$, answer the following questions:

Required ☐

1. Determine the average time required to assemble 150 of the new golf carts.

2. Determine the estimated labor cost for assembling 150 of the new golf carts.

3. If 150 carts have already been assembled, what is the estimated incremental labor cost for assembling an additional 25 carts?

4. Explain the meaning of a 90 percent learning curve.

Determining **P22-15.** The SER Company manufactures electric typewriters. The factory has
Learning-Curve just completed assembling eight typewriters, and it took a total of 163.84
Parameters hours to assemble the units. For the first four units, the assembly time
totaled 102.4 hours. From these two observations, we can imply an average-time learning-curve function of the form $y = ax^b$.

Required □

1. Derive the values for a and b, and determine the percentage learning curve for the assembly operation.

2. Using the values from requirement 1, determine the average and total hours necessary to produce twelve units.

3. The labor rate averages $10 per hour. Determine the incremental labor cost in assembling the additional four units.

General **P22-16.** The Kelly Company plans to manufacture a product called Electrocal,
Learning-Curve which requires a substantial amount of direct labor on each unit. Based
Concepts on the company's experience with other products that required similar
amounts of direct labor, the management team believes that there is a
learning factor in the production process used to manufacture Electrocal.

Each unit of Electrocal requires 50 square feet of raw material at a cost
of $30 per square foot for a total material cost of $1,500. The standard
direct-labor rate is $25 per direct-labor hour. Variable manufacturing
overhead is assigned to products at a rate of $40 per direct-labor hour.
The company adds a markup of 30 percent on variable manufacturing
cost in determining an initial bid price for all products.

Data on the production of the first two lots (16 units) of Electrocal are as
follows:

1. The first lot of eight units required a total of 3,200 direct-labor hours.

2. The second lot of eight units required a total of 2,240 direct-labor hours.

Based on prior production experience, Kelly anticipates that there will
be no significant improvement in production time after the first 32 units.
Therefore, a standard for direct-labor hours will be established based on
the average hours per unit for units 17 through 32.

Required □

1. What is the basic premise of the learning curve?

2. Based upon the data presented for the first 16 units, what learning rate
appears to be applicable to the direct labor required to produce Electrocal? Support your answer with appropriate calculations.

3. Calculate the standard for direct-labor hours that Kelly Company should
establish for each unit of Electrocal.

4. After the first 32 units have been manufactured, Kelly Company was asked to submit a bid on an additional 96 units. What price should Kelly bid on this order of 96 units? Explain your answer.

5. Knowledge of the learning-curve phenomenon can be a valuable management tool. Explain how managers can apply the learning curve in the planning and controlling of business operations.

(CMA)

P22-17. You are considering submitting a bid for the manufacture of four special oil pumps. You estimate the first pump will take 100 direct-labor hours to produce and that the direct labor will follow a 90 percent marginal-time learning curve. The standard direct-labor rate is $10 per hour, and variable overhead is charged to production at a rate of $5 per direct-labor hour. Your pricing policy is to determine the estimated variable cost and then add a 50 percent markup. Materials cost $1,000 for each pump.

Impact of Learning on Income

Required □

1. Determine the unit selling price if you will supply all four pumps.

2. Assume you agree to supply the four pumps at the selling price determined in requirement 1, and after supplying two pumps, the contract is cancelled. Determine the total contribution margin on the two pumps supplied.

3. Determine the estimated contribution margin on the two pumps that were not supplied.

4. Explain any difference in your answers to requirements 2 and 3.

5. After delivering the first two pumps at the price determined in requirement 1, the firm indicated that it wanted only one additional pump. What price would you charge for the third pump, considering you want to receive the 50 percent markup on all three pumps?

P22-18. The LNK Corporation has a contract with the United States Air Force to construct four special research aircraft. Two planes are to be delivered each year for the next two years. Estimates indicate that 100,000 direct-labor hours at an average cost of $20 per hour will be required to produce the first aircraft. It is estimated that direct labor will follow a 75 percent marginal-time learning curve. Direct materials are estimated to cost $5 million for each aircraft.

Impact of Learning on Income

Required □

1. Determine the direct-labor cost that will be charged to cost of goods sold for each year of the contract.

2. Determine the total direct cost that will be charged to cost of goods sold for each year of the contract.

3. If the actual direct-labor costs followed an 80 percent marginal-time learning curve, determine the labor-cost overrun for the project.

4. If the actual hours followed a 75 percent learning curve and the United States Air Force terminated the contract after three aircraft were de-

livered, and paid LNK the direct cost incurred on the three aircraft plus 50 percent, how much will LNK receive from the Air Force?

Impact of Learning on Income

P22-19. The LNK Corporation has a contract to produce eight communication satellites for the United States Navy. Two satellites will be delivered each year for the four years of the contract. It is estimated that the first satellite will require 10,000 direct-labor hours at an average cost of $15 per hour. It is estimated that the direct-labor hours will follow a 90 percent average-time learning curve.

Direct-materials cost for each satellite is estimated to equal $10,000. Overhead cost per satellite is estimated to equal $25,000, plus $10 per direct-labor hour. The selling price of the satellites is $250,000 each.

Required □

1. Determine the estimated cost to produce the first satellite.

2. Determine the net margin from producing the first satellite.

3. Determine the estimated cost to produce the second satellite.

4. Determine the net margin from producing the second satellite.

5. Determine the estimated average cost if all eight satellites are produced.

6. Determine the average net margin if the cost-of-goods-sold account is charged with the expected average cost of a satellite.

7. Determine the balance of the deferred-cost account after producing the first satellite if average costs are used for the contract in determining cost of goods sold.

8. Determine the balance in the deferred-cost account after producing the second satellite if average costs are used for the contract in determining cost of goods sold.

9. If the Navy cancels the contract after four satellites are delivered, will the firm make or lose money? How much?

10. What is the balance in the deferred-cost account after eight satellites have been produced and the contract has been completed?

11. What are the assumptions made when a learning curve is used in estimating costs?

Learning Curve and Regression Analysis

P22-20. As an auditor, you are assigned the task of determining whether the direct-labor hours employed in manufacturing metal disks are following an 80 percent average-time learning curve. If it is not following an 80 percent average-time learning curve, what rate of learning better explains the behavior of the process?

Cumulative output	Total time
1	80.0
2	127.0
3	176.9
4	217.0
5	259.0

6	297.0
7	310.0
8	325.0

P22-21. As an auditor, you are assigned the task of determining whether the direct-labor hours employed in manufacturing C-B radios are following a learning curve. Determine which type of learning curve, if any, is appropriate for the manufacturing process. What is the appropriate rate of learning?

Learning Curves and Regression Analysis

Cumulative output	Total time
1	105
2	184
3	253
4	319
5	384
6	437
7	501
8	547

P22-22. The Xyon Company has purchased 80,000 pumps annually from Kobec, Inc. The price has increased each year and reached $68 per unit last year. Because the purchase price has increased significantly, Xyon management officials have asked that an estimate be made of the cost to manufacture it in its own facilities. Xyon's products consist of stamping and castings. The company has little experience with products requiring assembly.

General Learning-Curve Concepts

The Engineering, Manufacturing, and Accounting departments have prepared a report for the management team that includes the estimate shown for an assembly run of 10,000 units. Additional production employees would be hired to manufacture the subassembly. However, no additional equipment, space, or supervision would be needed.

The report states that total costs for 10,000 units are estimated at $957,000, or $95.70 a unit. The current purchase price is $68 a unit, so the report recommends a continued purchase of the product.

Components (outside purchases)	$120,000
Assembly labor[1]	300,000
Factory overhead[2]	450,000
General and administrative overhead[3]	87,000
Total costs	$957,000

1. Assembly labor consists of hourly production workers.

2. Factory overhead is applied to products on a direct-labor dollar basis. Variable overhead costs vary closely with direct-labor dollars.

Fixed overhead	50% of direct-labor dollars
Variable overhead	100% of direct-labor dollars
Factory overhead rate	150% of direct-labor dollars

3. General and administrative overhead is applied to 10 percent of the total cost of material (or components), assembly labor, and factory overhead.

Required □

1. Was the analysis prepared by the Engineering, Manufacturing, and Accounting departments of Xyon Company and the recommendation

to continue purchasing the pumps that followed from the analysis correct? Explain your answer and include any supportive calculations you consider necessary.

2. Assume Xyon Company could experience labor-cost improvements on the pump assembly consistent with an 80 percent learning curve. An assembly run of 10,000 units represents the initial lot or batch for measurement purposes. Should Xyon produce the 80,000 pumps in this situation? Explain your answer.

(CMA)

USE OF ELECTRONIC SPREADSHEETS

APPENDIX **A**

The advent of the microcomputer has resulted in significant changes to the practice of accounting. Many of these changes involve the use of electronic spreadsheets by accountants. Some authors have even gone so far as to attribute the success of the microcomputer to the availability of the electronic spreadsheet software packages. Regardless of what else may be said, it is unquestionable that use of electronic spreadsheets is required knowledge for today's accountants.

The widespread acceptance of electronic spreadsheets by accountants may be attributed to the following:

1. The electronic spreadsheet is organized just like the paper worksheet or columnar pad that accountants have used since the days of Luca Pacioli. Thus, its usefulness has been readily apparent to accountants.

2. Through the use of formulas and referencing of cells, the spreadsheet may be instantaneously recalculated for changes in the assumed facts, thus facilitating "what-if" type of analysis.

The design and development of an electronic spreadsheet closely parallels that of a manually prepared spreadsheet. Accordingly, the first applications of electronic spreadsheets consisted of entering manual spreadsheets as electronic spreadsheets. The design work had already been completed. The productivity gains were speed and improved appearance of the finished worksheet.

"What-if" analysis of accounting data is commonly performed by management accountants. Frequently, management will request an analysis of a pricing, production, financing or other decision under a given set of conditions. The management accountant completes the report, only to find that management now wants the analysis under a different set of conditions. Thus, the question "what if." With electronic spreadsheets, these what-if questions may be easily and efficiently answered.

Interestingly, the electronic spreadsheet has remained more the tool of the accountant as a business analyst than as a data processing manager. It is a decision-support software, not an information system software. Accordingly, although electronic spreadsheets are certainly the most important microcomputer software used by the management accountant, they are not the only software used. The standard packages used by management accountants will include data base management, word processing, graphics, communication, project management, and networking software. It is beyond the scope of this appendix to discuss these packages. Your approach to these packages, however, requires the same sense of excitement and willingness to ask questions that are necessary with electronic spreadsheets. The mind-set that you need to adopt is one of "There is no such thing as a dumb question." With these powerful computing tools, the accounting concepts found in this text may be applied to the problems of business in ways never before possible. As we approach the 1990s, computing power will become as available to the end user (the accountant) as it is to the data processing specialist in the 1980s. It is going to be exciting.

□ANATOMY OF AN ELECTRONIC SPREADSHEET

The electronic spreadsheet is organized into columns, referenced by alphabetic characters (A to Z, AA to AZ, BA to BZ, etc.), and rows, referenced by numbers, 1 to 2048 with Lotus 1-2-3, Release 1A. The spreadsheet is divided into "cells," each of which is one column wide by one row high. A cell is referenced by its column letter and row number, for example, A1, B45, Z876, IV2048. A rectangular group of cells is referred to as a "range" and is referenced by identifying the upper left-hand corner of the range, followed by the opposite corner cell address. For example, range A1.A5 refers to cells A1, A2, A3, A4, and A5. The range A1.B5 refers to the ten cells comprising the first five cells of both column A and column B. Many spreadsheets will also allow the user to assign a name, a string of characters, to a range in the spreadsheet. Afterwards, the range name may be used to refer to the range of cells.

The electronic spreadsheet is given life by defining the cells to be either labels or values. Refer to figure A.1 for an example of a worksheet displayed two ways: First, as the completed product would look; secondly, as the entries would be made by the user. Note the label, value, cell reference, formula, and format reference. Labels are entered by simply typing the desired alphabetic or other character. With most spreadsheet software, the input will be assumed to be a label if the first character is alphabetic. Values are either numbers, mathematical symbols ($+$ or $-$ for example), formulas, or functions (special formulas). All arithmetic operations may be performed on values. Labels may only communicate information; any arithmetic operation attempted will find the label defined as a zero.

The spreadsheet contains several frequently used functions that allow both more sophisticated analysis and significant time savings in the design of spreadsheets. For example, the sum of cells A1 to A10 may be obtained by defining a cell to be a formula as follows: $+A1+A2+A3+A4+A5+A6+A7+A8+A9+A10$. Significant time and typing may be saved by entering the function, @SUM(A1.A10) as the cell definition. Both definitions will result in the same value, the total of A1 to A10, in the cell. More significant functions, such as @Present Value, which determines the present value of a range of amounts, and @LOOKUP, which looks up a

number in a table of numbers or formulas, allow sophisticated computations with little typing.

Spreadsheet Commands

Spreadsheet "commands" are used to aid in the development of a spreadsheet application or "template," and to interact with peripheral equipment
such as a disk drive, printer, or sub-programs outside the basic spreadsheet
program. Spreadsheet commands also allow the user to "format," or improve the appearance of the spreadsheet, by adding decimals, dollar signs,
rounding off numbers to the nearest integer, adding additional rows or
columns, etc. Other commands allow the user to SAVE a spreadsheet on
a diskette, that is, to transfer the spreadsheet *from* the primary memory

FIGURE A.1
Electronic
Spreadsheet: As
Printed and as
Entered

```
                SCHEDULE OF DIVISIONAL RATE OF RETURN

                Divisional        Division         Rate of
Division        Net Income        Investment        Return
---------       ----------        ----------       ---------
Movie           $175,000          $1,000,000          17.5%
Corn             450,000           1,600,000          28.1%
Colas            250,000           1,800,000          28.1
                ----------        -----------
                $875,000          $4,400,000
                ==========        ===========
```

```
                A         B         C         D         E         F         G
        1
        2  LABELS   ------->       SCHEDULE OF DIVISIONAL RATE OF RETURN
        3    !
        4    !                Divisional          Division          Rate of
        5  Division           Net Income          Investment         Return
        6  \-                 \-                  \-                 \-
        7  Movie                 175000             1000000          +C9/E9
        8  Corn                  450000             1600000          +C10/E10
        9  Colas                 250000             1800000          +C11/E11
       10                      \-                  \-
       11  FORMULA  ------>    +C7+C8+C9           @SUM(E7..E9) <----  @FUNCTION
       12                      '========           '==========
       12
       13
       14
       15
```

(RAM) *to* a diskette; LOAD a spreadsheet *from* a diskette *to* the primary memory (RAM); or PRINT a spreadsheet with a printer.

One of the most useful commands in designing spreadsheets is the "COPY" or "REPLICATE" command. With this command the spreadsheet user is able to copy the definition of a cell, whether it is a label, value or formula, from the source cell to a target cell or target range. Accordingly, large spreadsheets may be designed with few key strokes by copying formulas and labels from cell to cell. Any formula (such as +A1 + B1) will automatically be adjusted when copied in a "relative sense." That is, it will be adjusted according to the position of the target address relative to the source cell. If the cell C1 is defined to be cell A1 + cell B1, when C1 is copied down one cell to cell C2 in a "relative sense," the resulting formula will be A2 + B2. Hence the formula is automatically adjusted. If no adjustment or change is desired, the formula may be copied in an "absolute" sense. If copied in the absolute sense, the copied formula will not change; it will be identical to the original, source formula. If cell C1 above is copied in an absolute sense, the resulting formula will still be A1 + B1. For more information on commands in general or the COPY or REPLICATE command in particular, refer to the software summary below.

Recalculation

One of the strengths of electronic spreadsheets, the automatic recalculation feature, is also an inconvenience when using a spreadsheet. As noted above, "what-if" questions are natural applications for electronic spreadsheets. Using "what-if" analysis means frequently changing one or more of the inputs to a spreadsheet and recomputing the output. If the automatic recalculation feature is turned on (or more appropriately, not turned off) each time a number is entered in a cell, every formula in the spreadsheet is recalculated. Although the recalculation of the formulas takes only seconds, 50 seconds seems a very long time when you become accustomed to a wait of less than a second between entering values or labels. While the spreadsheet is being calculated, the user may not interact with the spreadsheet in any other manner. Thus, the user cannot use any command or enter any values or labels; he or she may only sit and wait.

To reduce this inconvenience, spreadsheets provide the ability to "turn-off" the automatic recalculation feature, leaving the spreadsheet with "manual" calculation. Manual recalculation means that the spreadsheet will not be recalculated until the user enters the appropriate command (! with SuperCalc; F9, with Lotus 1-2-3). The seconds saved may add to hours if large amounts of data must be entered in the spreadsheet.

☐ MOVING AROUND IN THE SPREADSHEET

The primary method of moving around the spreadsheet is using the arrow keys. These keys serve two purposes: First, they act as enter keys, and secondly they move the cursor one cell in the direction of the arrow. If the keys are held down, they act similarly to repeating keys on a typewriter. Thus, a substantial area may be quickly covered with the arrow keys. For the beginner, the arrow keys will be the most convenient method of moving around the spreadsheet.

The GOTO key may be used to move to a specific cell. If the desired cell is off the screen, use of the GOTO key will place the desired cell in the upper left-hand corner of the screen. If the desired cell appears on the screen, use of GOTO will move the cursor within the screen to the desired cell. To use the GOTO command with SuperCalc, press the equal sign, the cell address, and the enter key. To use the GOTO command with Lotus 1-2-3, press function key F5, the cell address, and the enter key. In using the templates with this text, the GOTO command will be used frequently to move to the input and output screens.

☐ ELECTRONIC SPREADSHEET SOFTWARE

The explosion of the microcomputer age began about 1978 with the introduction of the preassembled Apple II and Tandy/Radio Shack's TRS-80 Model I. At the same time, Dan Bricklin, a Harvard Business School student who was frustrated with the hours of analysis required to solve the numerous cases assigned daily, and Robert Frankston, a programming friend, organized a company named Software Arts to develop what became VisiCalc. The electronic spreadsheet age had begun. For the next two years, Apple II and VisiCalc ". . . ruled the market for business microcomputers."*

The next major entrant to the spreadsheet software club was Sorcim (Micros spelled backwards—now Computer Associates) Corporation's SuperCalc. SuperCalc had all the power of VisiCalc plus additional features that made it much easier to design spreadsheets. Others followed these two, but none gained the importance of VisiCalc or SuperCalc at that time.

Second-Generation Spreadsheet

Integration of spreadsheet capabilities with data base management, graphics, and word processing capabilities marks the beginning of the second generation of spreadsheets. The most widely accepted of the second-generation spreadsheets is Lotus 1-2-3, developed by the Lotus Development Corporation. The people behind Lotus were unique among microcomputer software developers. They all had had previous experience in the microcomputer industry—in fact, the founding president had developed a well-respected graphics and statistical package (VisiPlot/VisiTrend) for VisiCorp. Thanks in part to a massive promotional campaign, Lotus 1-2-3 reached the top of the IBM PC and compatibles software best-seller list after only three months and remarkably stayed there for about three years.

In 1985, Lotus Development Corporation provided an upgrade to Lotus 1-2-3 by releasing a new version, Release 2. Although it is used in the same

*Thomas B. Henderson, Douglas Ford Cobb, Gena Berg Cobb, *Spreadsheet Software From VisiCalc to 1-2-3* (Indianapolis, Indiana: Que Corp., 1983), p. 17.

way as Release 1A, Release 2 does provide additional features. The market reaction to date has been to purchase Release 2 only when an additional copy of the software is needed. In general, corporations have not abandoned Release 1A to adopt Release 2. In effect, the market is saying that Release 1A is good enough for what we are doing, let's stick with it.

Third-Generation Spreadsheets

The third-generation spreadsheet is the fully integrated software with a spreadsheet, data base management, graphic capabilities, word processing, and communication—computer-to-computer data transmission. The first fully integrated packages were introduced with much fanfare. The primary integrated packages are Lotus Development Corporation's Symphony and Ashton-Tate's Framework. Symphony is based upon Lotus 1-2-3's Release 2, Lotus Corporation's extremely successful electronic spreadsheet, and uses its menu approach to commands. Framework introduced windows, a new approach to command selection. Later entrants have followed Symphony's menus. These include Ability, Enable, and Smart Software Systems. Of these, Symphony alone has the distinction of selling more copies in a month than Lotus 1-2-3.

Fourth-Generation Spreadsheets

Although the major software used by accountants continues to be the second-generation Lotus 1-2-3, the fourth-generation spreadsheet is now available—FOCUS, for example. The major advantage of this generation of spreadsheet software is its ability to run on both the mainframe computer and the personal computer. The advent of these software packages will bring the PC user and the mainframe user closer together, that is, the tasks being done on the PC will more closely resemble tasks done on the mainframe computer. At that point accountants will cease to be either personal computer users or mainframe users only and will become simply computer users.

What about the fifth-generation spreadsheet? It is under development and will in all probability soon be on the market. That is the way of electronic spreadsheets.

☐ COMPARISON OF SPREADSHEETS

As we leave the 1980s, the dominant electronic spreadsheet is the second-generation Lotus 1-2-3. Lotus 1-2-3 has proven so successful that others have copied it, producing clones, that is software that looks like Lotus 1-2-3, but is sufficiently different to avoid a lawsuit. Among the Lotus 1-2-3 clones, the most successful are The Twin, Farsight, and VP-Planner. The Lotus 1-2-3 clones' marketing strategy is to offer an equivalent product for a substantially lower price.

Among colleges and universities, the major electronic spreadsheets are Lotus 1-2-3 and SuperCalc. Of growing importance to the educational community is integrated software such as Ability, Enable, and Framework.

The tasks performed and the commands to perform such tasks are very similar in all of these spreadsheets. Figure A.2 lists the major tasks performed by spreadsheet commands and the actuals commands for Lotus 1-2-3, SuperCalc, and Educate-Ability.

The three primary sources for the purchase of spreadsheet software are retail computer stores, mail order software stores, and the software house that wrote the software. The software will be identical regardless of which vender is selected. However, the user should note that the mail order stores normally do not provide any services to their customers, but, of course, they do discount their prices. The computer stores not only sell the software, but they also provide important follow-up service. The usefulness of this additional service will depend upon the existing knowledge of the

DESCRIPTION OF COMMAND	Lotus 1-2-3	SuperCalc	EDUCATE-ABILITY
Blank or erase a cell or range of cells	/R E	/B	F2 B Y
Clear or erase the entire spreadsheet or worksheet	/W E	/Z	F2 O Q
Delete an entire row or column	/W D R or C	/D R or C	F2 R R or C
Edit the definition of any cell	F2, Function key two	/E	F4 E
Format the cell to integers, currency, and others	/R F	/F	F4 F
Adjust column widths	/W C	/F C	F4 W
Turn-off automatic recalculation feature, thereby setting to manual	/W R M	/G M	F2 O R
Insert an additional row or column	/W I R or C	/I R or C	F2 I R or C
Move cells around within the worksheet	/M	/M	F2 M
Print part or all of the worksheet to paper or disk storage	/P P or F	/O P or D	F2 P
Replicate or copy one cell to another cell either in an absolute sense (no change) or a relative sense (with change)	/C	/R	F2 C
To interface with disk storage to either load or save a file	/F R or S	/L or /S	Load-Library Save-F10
To lock or hold titles on the worksheet so they will not scroll (move) off the screen	/W T	/T	F2 T
To divide the screen into two windows, i.e. into two parts, either horizontally or vertically	/W W H or V	/W H or V	N /A

FIGURE A.2
Comparison of Commands

NOTE: There are many other features of these three electronic spreadsheet software packages. The above commands are the most common. The purpose in listing them is to emphasize the great amount of similarity among the major spreadsheets. Once you have mastered one, the others are easily conquered.

purchaser. Beginning users would be well advised to pay for additional support available from the computer stores. Frequently, software houses will offer site licenses to a company or an institution. A site license normally restricts the number of copies to be made, but offers very favorable per unit prices.

☐ DESIGN OF ELECTRONIC SPREADSHEETS

Electronic spreadsheets have four basic parts:

1. Menu range

2. Input range

3. Output range

4. Computations

The *menu range* may be the most important part of a spreadsheet. Spreadsheets may be very complicated with formulas entered in many cells throughout the spreadsheet. With any computer application, it is extremely important to provide adequate documentation of the application. The purpose of the menu range is to provide minimal documentation for the spreadsheet. The menu range should include the following:

1. A statement of the purpose of the spreadsheet and its filename.

2. Location (that is, the cell address) of the input range.

3. Location of the output range.

4. Location of the table of range names, that is, a table of all range names and their cell addresses.

5. Location of any macros or execute files used by the spreadsheet

6. Name and address of the creator of the spreadsheet and the date of its last revision.

   Any special instructions for the use of the spreadsheet.

The menu range should be located at the home screen, that is, the upper left-hand corner of the spreadsheet beginning at cell A1. If the menu range covers more than one screen, it should continue in the next screen, one page down beginning at cell A21. See figure A.3 for an example of a menu range as it would appear on the monitor's screen.

Input Range

A completed spreadsheet provides no information until data are entered. The *input range* is the range in which all data or variables are entered in the spreadsheet. It is these values that will vary from application to ap-

```
C2HILOW
The purpose of this application is to use the HIGH-LOW method to develop the
equation of a straight-line in the form y=a+bx, where a is the intercept of the y
axis (the fixed costs), and b is the slope of the line (the variable cost per unit.)
NOTE: Worksheet is protected.
- - - - - - - - - - - - - - - INDEX - - - - - - - - - - - - - - - - - - -
Cell address       Range Name address
 A1                Info                Information
 A21               Instru              Instructions
 A41               Input               Input, the data
 A61               Output              Output, the answer
 A81               Print               Instructions for printing file
```

plication of the spreadsheet. Accordingly, the input range should be at a convenient location in the spreadsheet, normally one page below the last page of the menu range. To aid in the entry process, the input range should be designed so that the data will be entered by moving down the rows in only one column. The worksheet should be protected, that is, no entry may be made to any cell (the **PROTECT** command is used) except the input range. A well-designed spreadsheet will require the input data to be entered only once, that is, cells in the input range are referenced when the input data are used later in spreadsheet formulas. Furthermore, values that are functions of other values should be computed, not entered directly by the user. For example, if a present value factor is needed, it should be computed by a spreadsheet formula rather than requiring the user to look up the value in a table and enter it into a spreadsheet. Refer to figure A.4 for an example of an input range. The input range is indicated by shading.

FIGURE A.3
Menu Range

Output Range

The *output range* is the location of the solution to your problem. It is the report that frequently will be printed for distribution to clients, bosses, or professors. Accordingly, the goal in designing an output range is to communicate the results of your analysis in the best possible manner. In such cases, appearance is very important, and extensive labels with ade-

```
- - - - - - - - -          INPUT          - - - - - - - - -
Input HIGH activity COLUMN C, cell C51; and the related total cost in cell C50.
Input LOW  activity COLUMN D, cell D51; and the related total cost in cell D50.
                    ***INPUT COLUMNS****
                    *   HIGH      LOW   *   VARIABLE
        TOTAL COST  *   25000    20500  *      Y
          ACTIVITY  *    3000     2100  *      X
                    *********************
```

FIGURE A.4
Input Range

quate spacing must be used. The format capabilities of the various spreadsheets are very powerful, allowing the use of dollar signs, commas, brackets, percent signs, and many others. Your work with the spreadsheet will be evaluated by the output presented. Thus, when the output range is printed, care should be taken to ensure that the printer is properly used. The beginning spreadsheet user must understand that using the printer involves interfacing the user, the software, the computer, and the printer. Errors may result from any source. See figure A.5 for an example of an output screen.

Computations

The last part of the spreadsheet is both unstructured and unlimited as to form and content. Designers of templates will vary greatly in the use of schedules within the worksheet. Perhaps the best way to think of the computation area is as a scratch pad where useful pieces of the worksheet are computed. The user may scroll (move) around in the worksheet to determine the location of ranges containing supporting schedules. To audit the computation area of the spreadsheet, begin in the output range and move backwards until you reach the input range. If all formulas along the way are correct, the results displayed in the output range will also be correct.

In designing worksheets, the designer must continuously keep in mind the amount of primary memory (random access memory or RAM) that is

```
                        Output Range
    - - - - - - - - -        OUTPUT       - - - - - - - - -

              SLOPE      - - - - - - ->      5    (b)
              INTERCEPT  - - - - - - ->  10000    (a)
    EQUATION OF THE LINE :

              Y  =      10000         +       5    X

    INTERPRETATION                          ESTIMATED TOTAL
         OF COSTS :        TOTAL            VARIABLE    FIXED
                         - - - - - - - -    - - - - - - - - - -
    HIGH VALUE OF Y $25,000                 $15,000   $10,000
    LOW VALUE  OF Y $20,500                 $10,500   $10,000
```

FIGURE A.5
Output Range

available. Some spreadsheets like Lotus 1-2-3, Release 1A, utilize memory in rectangular blocks. Thus, if an entry is made in a cell, that cell becomes the lower right-hand corner of a range that is now utilizing memory, regardless of whether any entry has been made in other cells in that range. As a minimum, spreadsheet users are advised to have 256k of primary memory available. Because of the diversity of form and structure of computation screens, none are illustrated.

□ SPREADSHEET TEMPLATES

The end product of designing a spreadsheet is a usable spreadsheet template. A template is a prepared spreadsheet, ready to be used to analyze information or prepare a report. All labels and formulas have been entered; the only missing part is the data. Spreadsheet errors are easy to make, but very difficult to discover. Before the template is considered usable, it should be thoroughly reviewed. One useful method of ensuring that the spreadsheet is correct is to compare the results with a similar report that has been prepared by hand and is known to be correct. A second way is to test the data with simple numbers, normally 1's or 10's. The accountant must never forget that if the results of the template are not logically consistent, if they do not make sense, the fact that the analysis was prepared with a computer is not enough to make the results correct. The acronym "garbage in, garbage out" applies equally to spreadsheets as to any computer program.

Using Templates

Many companies have invested heavily in the preparation or purchase of templates for use in analyzing financial information. In addition, for the new user of electronic spreadsheets, the simplest first step is to use a prepared template. Accordingly, the spreadsheet user must know how to use a prepared template. In the dynamic world of business, spreadsheet templates will continuously have to be updated or modified to reflect current conditions and policy. Thus, a second level of required knowledge for spreadsheet users is the ability to modify an existing template to solve a different problem or the same problem under different conditions. Lastly, someone will have to prepare these templates from scratch. Thus, the spreadsheet user must be able to take a blank spreadsheet and enter the necessary labels, values, and formulas to analyze the problem at hand.

Before a template may be designed, the user must understand the management accounting concepts that relate to the problem. From an educational point of view, these concepts may be reinforced by the process of entering formulas in partially completed spreadsheets. These partially completed spreadsheets will normally have all the necessary labels, but none of the formulas that do the computations. In these cases, the user has to enter the appropriate cell references to the input range and the formula necessary to apply the correct management accounting concepts.

Figure A.6 lists the templates that have been prepared for use with this text. The COMPLETE templates are ready to use. Simply enter the data and print the output. The PARTIAL templates have most or all necessary labels, but none of the necessary formulas. Complete the template and use it to solve the indicated problems. The following steps are necessary to use these templates. These steps assume that you are using an IBM PC or an IBM PC compatible computer. The commands for Lotus 1-2-3, SuperCalc, and Educate-Ability will be given. If you are using different software or different machines, you will have to adjust these steps accordingly.

STEP 1   Identify the problem to be solved. Generally, your professor will be of tremendous help at this point.

STEP 2   Refer to figure A.6, to identify the file name applicable to your problem, that is, the name of the template as it appears on your template disk. The file name may be a maximum of eight characters long. The templates are listed and cross-referenced to the appropriate problems in figure A.6.

STEP 3   Insert the system disk that comes with your electronic software package (Ability, SuperCalc, or LOTUS 1-2-3) in the default disk drive, Drive A, the left-hand drive on an IBM PC. When inserting the disk, be certain to have the label facing up and to insert the disk slowly.

STEP 4   Turn the machine on. The spreadsheet will be loaded into the primary memory (RAM). At this point, the spreadsheet disk could be removed—the program is in RAM. However, if the disk is removed, some help features may not be available; thus, it is advisable to leave the system disk in the default drive.

STEP 5   Insert the template disk in the second disk drive, Drive B, the right-hand drive on the IBM PC.

STEP 6   Load the appropriate file for the template as determined appropriate in step 2. Refer to the overview of the software at

FIGURE A.6
Listing of Templates, Templates Filenames, and Related Problems

Chap.	Template filename	Type of template	Related problems	Description of template
2	C2HILOWC	Complete	2-13, 2-16, 2-17, 2-20	C2HILOWC uses the High-Low method to de-
	C2HILOWP	Partial	2-14, 2-19	velope a cost formula in the form of $y = a + bx$.
3	C3JOBC	Complete	3-10, 3-11, 3-12	C3JOBC classifies costs according to Job Or-
		Partial	3-17, 3-18	der number and prepares a schedule of Cost
	C3JOBP			of Goods Manufactured.
3	C3GRAPHC	Complete	3-12	C3GRAPHC prepares a graph of the unit costs determined with the C3JOB template.
4	C4AVEC	Complete	4-1, 4-2, 4-3, 4-4, 4-9, 4-10, 4-12, 4-13	C4AVEC prepares a Cost-of-Production Report
	C4AVEP	Partial	4-6, 4-7	using the weighted average method of computing equivalent units.
4	C4FIFOC	Complete	4-8, 4-11, 4-14	C4FIFOC prepares a Cost-of-Production Report
	C4FIFOP	Partial	4-15, 4-16	using the FIFO method of computing equivalent units.
5	C5FIFOSC	Complete	5-2, 5-9, 5-11, 5-13, 5-14, 5-20	C5FIFOSC prepares a Cost-of-Production Re-
	C5FIFOSP	Partial	5-1, 5-3, 5-4, 5-5, 5-22	port using the FIFO method of computing equivalent units and considering the effects of spoilage.
6	C6JOINTC	Complete	6-2, 6-3	C6JOINTC sets up a worksheet to compute the impact of processing work-in-process further.
6	C6ALOCAC	Complete	6-17	C6ALOCAC will allocate costs of service departments to production departments using the step-down approach.
7	C7BUDGEC	Complete	7-3, 7-7	C7BUDGEC allows the user to prepare a master
	C7BUDGEP	Partial	7-13, 7-14, 7-15	budget from information provided by the user.
8	C8VARC	Complete	8-6, 8-7, 8-11, 8-14, 8-15, 8-19, 8-22	C8VARC computes the material, labor, and
	C8VARP	Partial	8-20, 8-21	overhead variances. Overhead variances are computed using a two, three, and four-way analysis.
9	C9MAVARC	Complete	9-1, 9-2, 9-4	C9MAVARC computes the material yield and
	C9MAVARP	Partial	9-8, 9-10	mix components of the material quantity variance.
10	C10DCOSC	Complete	10-5, 10-8, 10-18, 10-19, 10-20	C10DCOSC prepares income statements under
	C10DCOSP	Partial	10-11, 10-12, 10-13	both Absorption Costing and Direct Costing.
11	C11BEC	Complete	11-3, 11-5	C11BEC prepares a break even analysis.
	C11BEP	Partial	11-4, 11-6, 11-9, 11-10	
13	C13MAUC	Complete	13-5, 13-2, 13-8, 13-9, 13-10	C13MAUC compares the cost of making with
	C13MABUP	Partial	13-1, 13-3	the cost of purchasing the item.
14	C14CABUC	Complete	14-2, 14-7, 14-9, 14-10, 14-11, 14-12, 14-13	C14CABUC sets up an analysis of a capital
	C14CABUP	Partial	14-6, 14-8, 14-14	budgeting decision.
15	C15IRRC	Complete	15-1, 15-2, 15-3, 15-4, 15-5, 15-6	C15IRRC sets up a cash flow analysis to analyze capital expenditures or investment alternatives.
17	C17ROIC	Complete	17-10	C17ROIC sets up an analysis using Return on Investment for evaluating the success of a division.
19	C19PROC	Complete	19-4, 19-5, 19-6	C19PROC computes and graphically displays productivity indices for up to 4 periods.
20	C20EOQC	Complete	20-4, 20-5, 20-6, 20-8, 20-19, 20-20	C20EOQC determines the optimal strategy for an inventory problem.
21	C21REGRC	Complete	2-20, 2-21, 2-22, 21-9	C21REGRC computes the regression equation
	C21REGRP	Partial	21-4, 21-5	and graphs the data.
22	C22LCRVC	Complete	22-6, 22-7, 22-8	C22LCRVC utilizes learning curve techniques
	C22LCRVP	Partial	22-21, 22-22	to compute total and marginal costs.

the end of this appendix for instructions on loading a file. Recall that the template disk will normally be in the B or second disk drive, that is, not the default drive. Thus, to load the template using SuperCalc, a prefix, b:, must precede the filename. The template disk should be write-protected so that you will not accidentally invalidate or destroy the usefulness of the template. After you have more experience with spreadsheets, you may use the disk for other purposes.

STEP 7   Remove the template disk and insert a *formatted* disk in the B disk drive. This disk, dubbed "solutions disk," is the receptacle for your solutions to the problems. You are strongly urged and warned that you should save your work at frequent intervals—for example, every thirty minutes. Microcomputers do not have an automatic save capability as large mainframe computers do. Thus, if the power is turned off, even for a split second, your work will be lost. SAVE YOUR SOLUTIONS!

STEP 8   In order to reduce the time required to input the required items, the automatic recalculation feature may be "turn-off" with the appropriate command. However, with templates in this text the time saved will be very small.

STEP 9   Enter the data for the problem. If necessary, recalculate the spreadsheet by using the manual recalculate command, ! in SuperCalc, or F9 for LOTUS 1-2-3.

STEP 10   SAVE YOUR SOLUTION! You may wish to print or correct your solution at a later time. If you do not save your spreadsheet, it will be lost. Normally, your instructor will require a hard copy (paper copy) or print out of your solution to be handed in.

STEP 11   Use the PRINT or OUTPUT commands to print the output range to a printer.

STEP 12   Turn off the computer or clear your worksheet and repeat the process beginning at step 6, loading the template. Note that it is advisable to remove the disks from your computer *before* it is turned off. Otherwise, you may damage your diskettes.

Be an Explorer

After you have completed several problems, you are urged to modify the templates and use the modified template to solve additional problems. You will need to explore the many features of the spreadsheet software that you are using in order to modify the templates. Do not hesitate to do so. Remember, the templates are saved on disk storage; therefore you will always be able to recall the original template and start over. By modifying the templates, you gain proficiency in the use of your spreadsheet software. That knowledge is required of today's accountant.

☐ SPREADSHEET SOFTWARE PACKAGES

In the educational environment, the major spreadsheets currently in use are Lotus 1-2-3 and SuperCalc. In addition, the educational version of Ability, Educate-Ability, is becoming more available and is increasing in use. Students who use Educate-Ability will purchase a student manual with the software. Accordingly, the use of Educate-Ability is not included in this appendix.

Lotus 1-2-3 and SuperCalc are summarized below to give the user an introduction to these spreadsheet packages. We do not intend to re-create the manuals that accompany the software. Accordingly, you are encouraged to read the manual for a detailed discussion of the commands, formulas or functions, and other features of the software. After reading these overviews, you will be able to use the templates that accompany the text. Remember, you are encouraged to try, to explore, and to ask questions.

☐ GETTING STARTED

Before you may use spreadsheet software, the program disks must be installed by copying part of the operating system, normally DOS—Disk Operating System—onto the disks. While you are using the spreadsheet software, DOS operates in the background, that is, inside the computer. It is transparent to the user, or in other words, DOS is operating all the time, but the user does not see it. If you are not familiar with DOS, the template disk accompanying this text contains a short description of the most useful DOS commands. To use the file, insert a DOS disk in drive A, the left-hand drive; the template disk in drive B, the right-hand disk drive; and turn the computer on. You will be prompted to enter the date and time. Enter the date in the same form as the example that appears on the screen. For example,

> A>Date
> Current date is Tue 1-01-1980
> Enter new date: 2-11-87

In this example, you would have to enter the new date by typing 2 hyphen 11 hyphen 87, and pressing the enter key.

Next you will be prompted to enter the time. You may bypass this step by pressing the enter key. By doing so, you will be accepting the default time, the time that appears on the screen as the "current time." Using the correct time is not as important as using the correct date, but you may enter the new time, using a 24-hour clock (that is, 2:00 P.M. is 14:00), and using the same form as appears on the screen (for example, 14 colon 00 enters the time as 2:00 P.M.).

After you have entered the date and time, you will see the "DOS prompt" on the screen, that is, A> (the letter A followed by a greater than sign), with the version of DOS being used written above it. To review the materials on DOS, at the DOS prompt enter B:DOS, that is,

Press the letter b
Press the colon (:)
Press the letters D O S
Press the enter key

You will be able to read through the file, one screen at a time. At the bottom of the screen, you will see the prompt "--more--". To continue to the next screen, press any key—the space bar, for example. At the end of the file, you will be returned to DOS, that is, you will see the DOS prompt, A>. (Note, the DOS command "MORE" is used, thus *the DOS disk must be in the A drive* in order for the file to be read as stated.)

□ USING LOTUS 1-2-3

Lotus 1-2-3 is the most widely used electronic spreadsheet on the market today. The software combines the ability to prepare graphs and to sort and query data, common to a data base system, with a very easy-to-use electronic spreadsheet. Lotus 1-2-3 has become the standard, a standard that is being cloned by other software developers.

There are three releases or versions of Lotus 1-2-3. Release 1, the first version, was issued in 1982. Many accountants quickly adopted the software as their electronic spreadsheet. Release 1A was issued in 1983. Lotus Development Corporation provided for either free or low-cost upgrade from its Release 1 to Release 1A. Accordingly, most accountants switch to the new release. In 1985, Release 2 became Lotus Development Corporation's current version. Again a low-cost upgrade, from Release 1 or 1A to Release 2, was provided. However, many accountants have not adopted Release 2 as their standard. The additional features are important and very useful, but many accountants have decided to forgo the new features and have continued with Release 1A.

The two releases are not totally compatible. Release 2 will read files that are created with Release 1A, but it will not write a file that may be read by Release 1A. In addition, Release 1A will not read a Release 2 file. Accordingly, Release 2 will read a Release 1A file and convert it to a Release 2 file. But after conversion, Release 1A will no longer be able to read the file. In the educational environment, many schools have also decided to continue to use Release 1A. For this reason, we have decided to prepare the templates used in this text using Release 1A.

Getting Started

In using Lotus 1-2-3, you need to be aware of four disks: the system disk, the utilities disk, the print graph disk, and the tutorial disk. Each disk will have to be installed by copying part of DOS, the operating system on to the disk. After, the disks are installed, they will self-boot, that is, you put the disk in the default drive, drive A, and turn the machine on.

The *utilities disk* contains several files that may be used to perform housekeeping chores. For example, the utilities disk may be used to copy files, erase files, format disks, transfer files between other software and Lotus 1-2-3, and configure the Lotus 1-2-3 disks for a variety of machines. The *print graph disk* is only used to print a graph with a dot matrix graphics printer. The graph must be prepared with the GRAPH command in Lotus 1-2-3 before it may be printed with the print graph disk. The *tutorial disk* is an interactive tutorial on how to use Lotus 1-2-3. The tutorial is divided into lessons and covers all of the commands and many of the functions. It is well worth the time to review the tutorial. To use the tutorial, insert the tutorial disk into the A drive and type the word TUTOR. At this point, you will be prompted as to what keys to strike. Just follow the instructions.

The *system disk* contains the spreadsheet program and is the disk that you will use most of the time. Typically, when the system disk is installed, a DOS AUTOEXEC.BAT program will be written on to the disk. The purpose of this BAT program is to load Lotus 1-2-3 automatically, that is to read the program into RAM or internal memory.

There are two common ways of loading Lotus 1-2-3. One is to utilize the Lotus Access System (see figure A.7). From the Lotus Access System, you may select any of the features. If necessary, you will be prompted to insert the appropriate disk. To move into the Lotus 1-2-3 spreadsheet, you select "123" by pressing the enter key. You will be moved to the next step, the Lotus 1-2-3 copyright notice. The access system may be loaded directly from DOS by entering the word "lotus" at the DOS prompt.

The second way will bypass the Lotus Access System and move directly to the Lotus 1-2-3 copyright notice (see figure A.8). You will save some

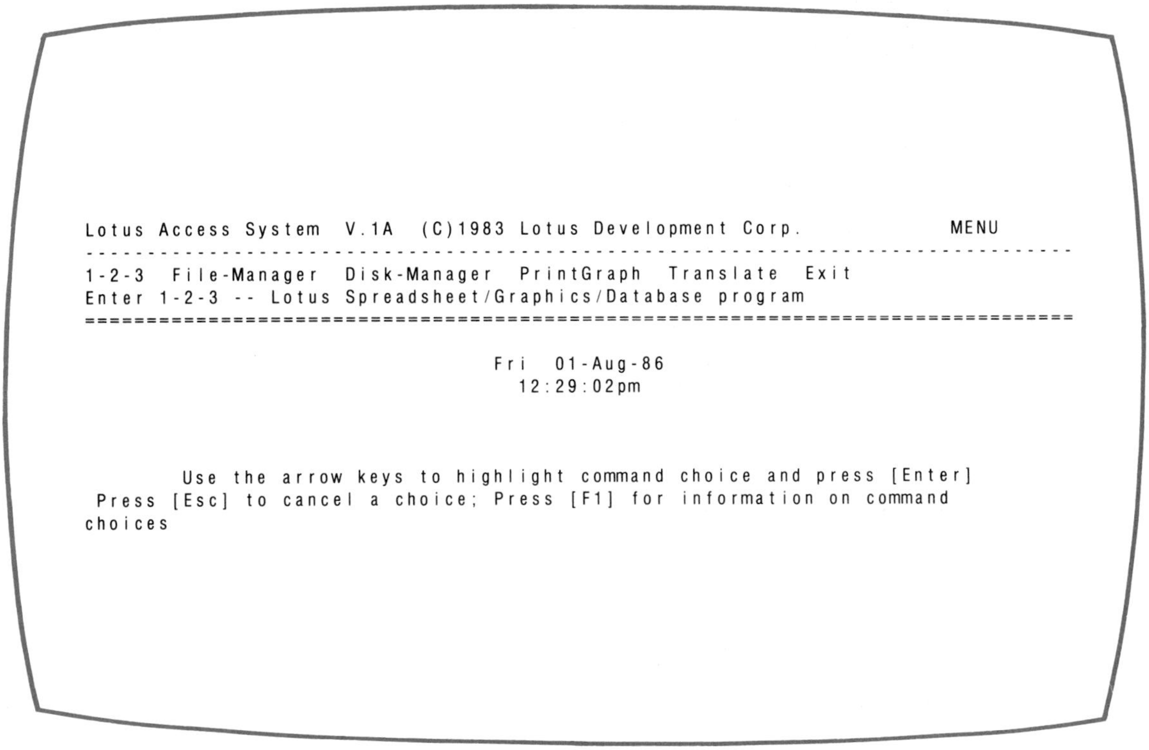

FIGURE A.7
Lotus 1-2-3
Access Screen

```
Lotus Access System  V.1A  (C)1983 Lotus Development Corp.              MENU
- - - - - - - - - - - - - - - - - - - - - - - - - - - - - - - - - - - - - - - -
1-2-3  File-Manager  Disk-Manager  PrintGraph  Translate  Exit
Enter 1-2-3 -- Lotus Spreadsheet/Graphics/Database program
================================================================================

                           Fri  01-Aug-86
                           12:29:02pm



         Use the arrow keys to highlight command choice and press [Enter]
    Press [Esc] to cancel a choice; Press [F1] for information on command
choices
```

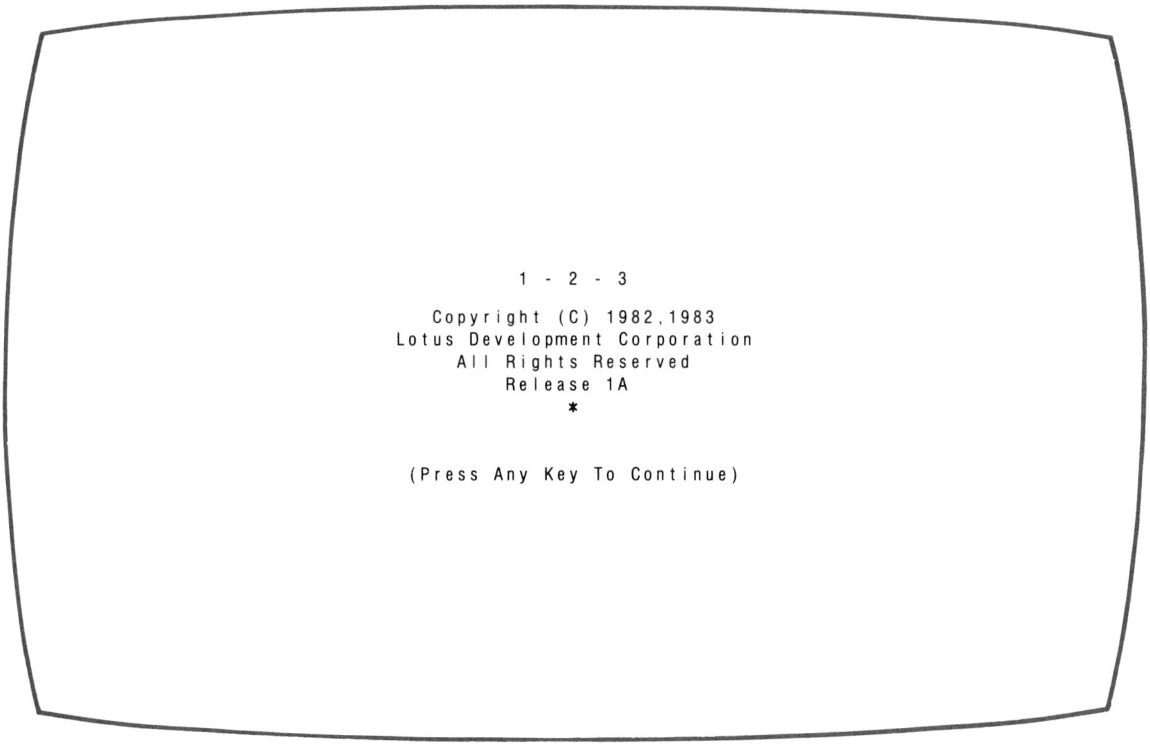

```
                    1 - 2 - 3

            Copyright (C) 1982,1983
         Lotus Development Corporation
            All Rights Reserved
                Release 1A
                    *


        (Press Any Key To Continue)
```

FIGURE A.8
Lotus 1-2-3
Copyright Notice

time if this method is used. To load the Lotus 1-2-3 spreadsheet directly into RAM, enter the word "123" at the DOS prompt. For example,

> A> 123

At the copyright notice, you will be prompted to "Press Any Key To Continue". The space bar is very convenient; it is frequently used. The result is an empty Lotus 1-2-3 spreadsheet (see figure A.9).

The Lotus 1-2-3 Worksheet

The Lotus 1-2-3 worksheet has 256 columns and 2,048 rows (8,192 in Release 2). The cells are identified by reference to a specific column and row. For example, cell A1 is the upper left-hand corner of the worksheet, at the intersection of column A and row 1. At the top of the screen is the Lotus 1-2-3 *control panel* (see figure A.10). It is important to focus your eyes on the control panel. Many mistakes may be eliminated by reviewing the control panel before pressing the enter key.

In the upper right-hand corner of the screen, you will note a "MODE" indicator. For many purposes the mode does not concern the user. However, you should be aware of the restrictions on the user that are indicated by the mode. For example, if the mode is **READY**, you may take any action

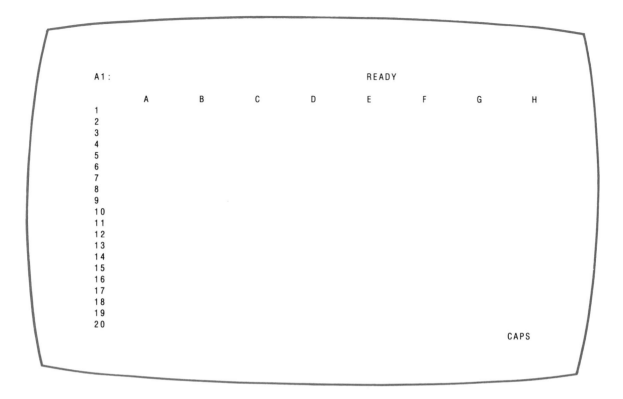

A1:   READY

	A	B	C	D	E	F	G	H
1								
2								
3								
4								
5								
6								
7								
8								
9								
10								
11								
12								
13								
14								
15								
16								
17								
18								
19								
20								

CAPS

FIGURE A.9
Empty Lotus 1-2-3
Worksheet

in Lotus 1-2-3. That is, the user is not limited. But, if you are in the MENU mode, you may only select from the menu. No data may be entered; no other action may be taken. If you are in the EDIT mode, you may only change the current cell. You may add or delete characters or numbers, but only to the current cell. At times you may find yourself attempting to take action without success. A quick look at the mode indicator may tell you what your problem is. Remember, if you are not in the READY mode, the actions you may take are limited.

Sources of Help Help in using the Lotus 1-2-3 worksheet is available from several sources. As mentioned above, the Lotus 1-2-3 tutorial is very useful even to the experienced 1-2-3 user. Spending the necessary time to review the tutorial is always time well spent. The Lotus 1-2-3 On-line Help Facility will give you pointers in using the worksheet and short descriptions of the various commands and functions (see figure A.11). You may access the Help facility by pressing function key 1, (F1) on the left side of the IBM PC keyboard. Other sources of help include asking a Lotus 1-2-3 user, reading this appendix, or reading one of the many books on Lotus 1-2-3. Another approach is to use one of the other on-line tutorials that are available. There are also, interactive, multi-media tutorials that involve the use of a video tape, disk tutorials, and written manuals. However, there is no replacement for actually using the software to solve a problem. To really appreciate the power of electronic spreadsheets, you have to use one.

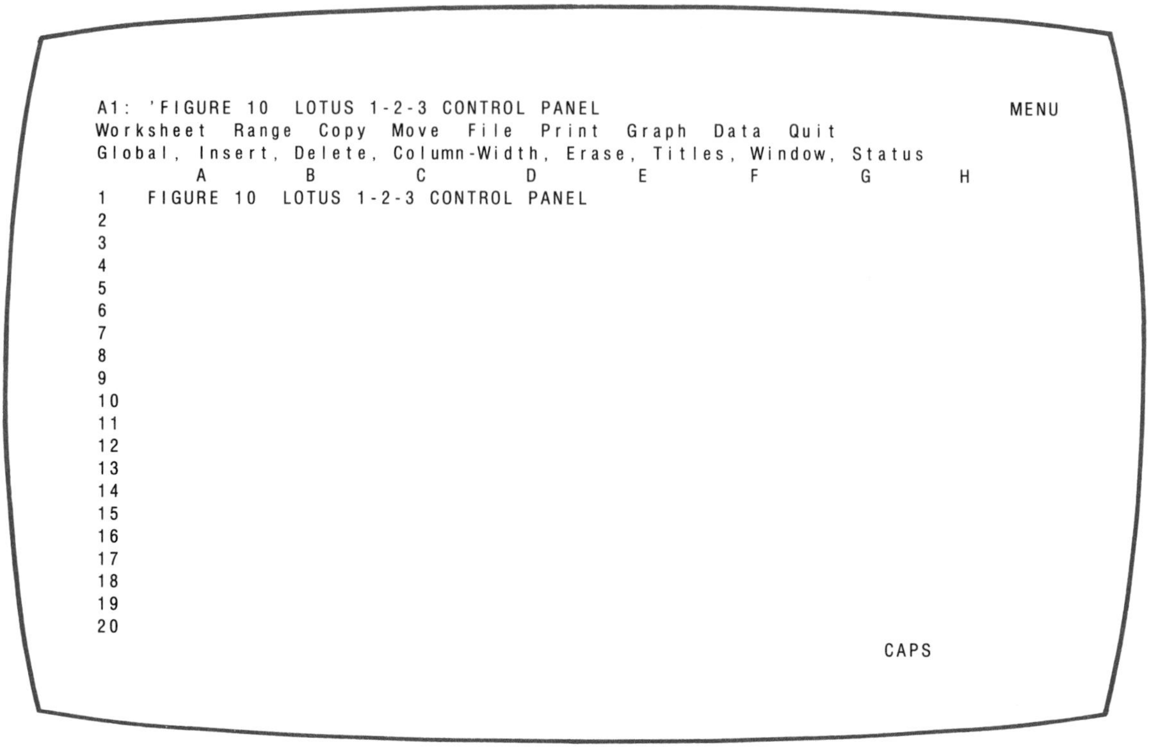

```
A1:  'FIGURE  10   LOTUS  1-2-3  CONTROL  PANEL                                    MENU
Worksheet   Range   Copy   Move   File   Print   Graph   Data   Quit
Global,  Insert,  Delete,  Column-Width,  Erase,  Titles,  Window,  Status
          A          B          C          D          E          F          G          H
 1      FIGURE  10   LOTUS  1-2-3  CONTROL  PANEL
 2
 3
 4
 5
 6
 7
 8
 9
10
11
12
13
14
15
16
17
18
19
20
                                                                                  CAPS
```

FIGURE A.10
Lotus 1-2-3
Control Panel

Moving Around in the Worksheet Lotus 1-2-3 makes use of most of the keyboard keys that are available with the **IBM PC** and other similar personal computers. The movement keys and how they are used in Lotus 1-2-3 are discussed below.

The arrow keys are the primary movement keys for moving short distances in the worksheet. It should be remembered that the arrow keys also act as "enter keys" whenever you are in the READY mode. Therefore when entering a long list of numbers, you will find it convenient to use the arrow key that points in the direction you are entering the numbers. It is possible to lock the numeric key pad in the ON position; however, this has the effect of shutting off the arrow keys. To move to another cell, you will have to press the shift key in order to toggle from "num lock" to the arrow keys. Even with this limitation you will still find it more convenient to use the Num Lock key for entering a long list of numbers. However, having the arrow keys available is very useful when entering numbers in formulas. Thus, the number keys at the top of the keyboard are normally used when designing spreadsheets.

Movement over greater distances in the worksheet is easily achieved by using the PgDn key, PgUp key, the tab key, the end key, the Home key, and the F5 function key, the "go to" key. The PgDn key or PgUp key moves the cursor the full length of the screen, 20 worksheet rows. The columnar position is not changed, thus the movement will be up and down the columns only. The tab key, the key with two arrows in opposite directions

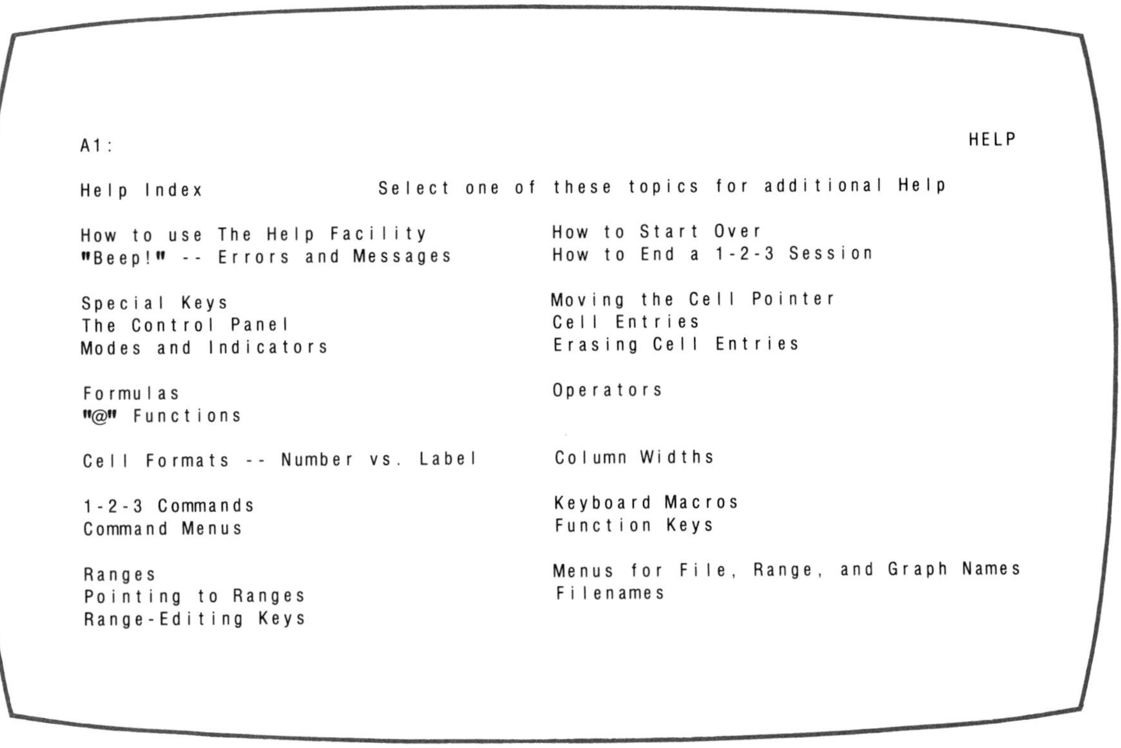

```
A1 :                                                              HELP

Help Index           Select one of these topics for additional Help

How to use The Help Facility      How to Start Over
"Beep!" -- Errors and Messages    How to End a 1-2-3 Session

Special Keys                      Moving the Cell Pointer
The Control Panel                 Cell Entries
Modes and Indicators              Erasing Cell Entries

Formulas                          Operators
"@" Functions

Cell Formats -- Number vs. Label  Column Widths

1-2-3 Commands                    Keyboard Macros
Command Menus                     Function Keys

Ranges                            Menus for File, Range, and Graph Names
Pointing to Ranges                Filenames
Range-Editing Keys
```

FIGURE A.11
Lotus 1-2-3
Help Facility

on the left side of the **IBM PC** keyboard, is used to move page by page left and right across the columns; the rows do not change. In terms of columns, one page is 8 standard 9-character columns, a total of 72 characters. The end key is used in conjunction with the arrow keys to go in the direction of the arrow to the last cell containing an entry. The order of entering the keys is "END" and then "ARROW" key. Use of the end key and the home key will move the cursor to the lower right-hand corner of the worksheet that you are currently using. Thus, you may use the END HOME combination to move to a vacant area of the worksheet.

The function key, F5, allows you to move to any single cell in the worksheet. The cell you move to will be in the upper left-hand corner of the screen if the target cell is off the screen. The home key will allow you to move the cursor to the A1 cell, the upper left-hand corner of the standard worksheet.

In the EDIT mode, the keys will perform differently. The left and right arrows keys will work as before, moving the cursor to the left or right, one character at a time. The up and down arrow keys and the PgDn and PgUp keys will take you out of the edit mode and to the ready mode. While in the edit mode, the HOME key will move the cursor to the beginning of the statement or formula that is to be edited; the END key, to the end of the edited entry. Also in the edit mode, the tab key will move the cursor five characters each time it is pressed. Use of these keys allows the user to move quickly to the part of the statement that he or she wishes to edit.

Data Entry A worksheet is made by entering either labels or values into the cells. A label may be any character or group (string) of characters. If an entry begins with an alphabetic character, Lotus 1-2-3 assumes that a label is being entered. Thus, A1 is assumed to be a label as in "A1 Sauce." Likewise, any entry that begins with a number is assumed to be a value. For example, 10 is assumed to be the number ten, not a label. To give you experience in making entries to cells, a template with the filename ENTRY has been prepared. To load or retrieve the file, follow the steps listed below.

STEP 1   Load the Lotus 1-2-3 software from the system disk into RAM.

STEP 2   With the worksheet on the screen, as in figure A.9, and the template disk in drive B, press the following keys.

/	The slash key on the right side of the keyboard. The command menu will appear in the control panel.
F	By pressing the letter F, you select the FILE command. The FILE command is used to interface with the disk storage.
R	By pressing the letter R, you have selected the Retrieve sub-command under the FILE command. Thus, the combination /FR, selects the command FILE RETRIEVE.
ENTRY	At this point you are requested to enter the filename. You may type the filename, ENTRY. Alternatively, you may move the menu cursor until it covers the filename, and then press the enter key.

STEP 3   Follow the instructions on the screen

Correcting Errors

Many accountants are terrible typists. If you press the wrong key, you may use the backspace key, to the right of the + = sign in the top row of the IBM PC keyboard, to correct an error *before* you press the enter key. If you have already entered the keystrokes, you may either reenter the data or edit the data. If you reenter, your new entry will simply replace the old. To edit, you press function key 2, (F2), on the left side of the IBM PC keyboard. Use the left and right arrow keys, tab key, HOME key or END key to move across the edit line. Corrections will automatically be inserted into the line. To delete the errors, use the DEL key, the delete key, at the lower right-hand corner of the IBM PC keyboard.

Using Lotus 1-2-3 Commands

The commands in Lotus 1-2-3 are used for a variety of purposes. The WORKSHEET, RANGE, COPY, and MOVE commands are used to design and configure the worksheet. The FILE command is used to interface with the disk drives; the PRINT command, the printer. Lastly, the GRAPH command is used to prepare graphs and the DATA command, to use the data base features of Lotus 1-2-3. To quit, the QUIT command is used to return to DOS to begin to use another software. If you are through for the day, simply remove the disks, and turn off the PC. Figure A.12 lists the commands and the related first-level sub-commands. Recall that the control panel will list the commands and give you a short description of their purpose.

The most frequently used commands and their purpose are discussed below. The discussion is not intended to be complete. You are referred to the manual for a more thorough discussion of each command. To select from the commands, the slash key (/) on the right side of the keyboard is used to call up the command menu. In the discussion below, the slash key is used only when listing the keystrokes required to use the command. These keystrokes will be shown in parentheses. For example, the command to retrieve a file is FILE RETRIEVE. The keystrokes are / F R, listed below as (/FR).

WORKSHEET Commands—The worksheet commands are concerned with the total worksheet, not with individual cells or ranges of cells.

WORKSHEET	FILE
Global	Retrieve
Insert	Save
Delete	Combine
Column-Width	Xtract
Erase	Erase
Titles	List
Window	Import
Status	Directory
RANGE	PRINT—Printer or File
Format	Range
Label-Prefix	Line
Erase	Page
Name	Options
Justify	Clear
Protect	Align
Unprotect	Go
Input	Quit
COPY	GRAPH
From	Type
To	X A – F Data Range
	Reset
MOVE	View
From	Save
To	Options
	Name
	Quit
DATA	QUIT
Fill	Yes
Table	No
Sort	
Query	
Distribution	

FIGURE A.12
Lotus 1-2-3
Commands

WORKSHEET COLUMN-WIDTH SET (/WCS)—Used to set the column width of the current column. It is entered, /WCS # enter key. The number entered indicates the number of characters per cell in the current column.

WORKSHEET INSERT OR DELETE (/WI or /WD)—Used to add or delete rows or columns above or to the left of the current location of the cursor. It must be remembered that the addition or deletion is throughout the entire worksheet. Thus, if you add a row above the cursor, that row will be added in all columns. The result may be that you will have to move or adjust your entries in some other part of the worksheet. Likewise WORK-SHEET DELETE will *delete* all cells in the row or column specified, even if you would prefer it did not.

WORKSHEET WINDOW (/WW)—Use of this command allows you to view two parts of the worksheet on the same screen. The command is useful in designing worksheets or reporting the results of your analysis. For example, if you prepare an analysis of a real estate investment under the assumption that the occupancy rate may be anywhere from 85 percent to 95 percent, you may use the window to view the final results as you move through the alternatives.

WORKSHEET GLOBAL RECALCULATION (/WGR)—Used to set the recalculation procedures to be followed in the worksheet. The most common use is to set the recalculation to MANUAL. When so set, the worksheet will not automatically recalculate each formula after each entry to the worksheet. If you are working with a large worksheet with many calculations, the use of manual recalculation can be a major time saver. The worksheet will be recalculated only upon your command by pressing function key (F9), the CALC key.

RANGE COMMANDS—The RANGE commands are used to design or adjust specific ranges of cells within the worksheet rather than throughout the entire worksheet, as is the case with the WORKSHEET command.

RANGE ERASE (/RE)—Unfortunately, some users of worksheet software find that errors are made. (By whom is another question!) The RANGE ERASE command provides for erasing one cell or a range of cells. The suggested range will be the cell where the cursor is currently located. The POINT mode will be available to aid in specifying the ranges that are to be erased. To use the point mode, position the cell pointer (cursor) at the upper left-hand corner of the range to be erased. When the command keystrokes, (/RE), are completed, the cell address suggested is the current cell. Use the arrow keys to point to the lower right-hand corner of the range to be erased. As you move the cursor, the cell range is entered on the action line of the control panel. When the enter key is pressed, the range to be erased is entered and the range is erased.

RANGE NAME (/RN)—Lotus 1-2-3 allows the user to refer to ranges or cells by name in addition to cell address. The RANGE NAME command is used to CREATE or DELETE the names of the cells or ranges. Thus, if you wanted to add the current balance of the accounts receivable ledger, you could specify the formula as @SUM(A1..A60) or as @SUM(balance). In order to refer to a range by name, you must first create the name in the worksheet by using the RANGE NAME CREATE command, identifying the range A1..A60 as "balance."

COPY COMMAND (/C)—The COPY command is one of the most used commands. The COPY command allows the user to copy or replicate formulas from one cell to any other single cell or to a range of cells. The useful feature of this command is that when copying from one cell to another, the formulas are automatically adjusted to reflect the change in the location of the formula. For example, if the formula in cell A34 adds the 33 previous cells, and is copied to cell B34, the formula will automatically be adjusted to add the previous 33 cells in column B, not column A. The adjustment is based upon the number of rows or columns that the original cell formula is moved. Thus, regardless of the number of times the formula is copied, the resulting formula will reflect the appropriate cell address. The keystrokes for the preceding example are as follows:

/	To move from the READY mode to the MENU mode.
C	To select the COPY command.
FROM:	At this point you are asked to enter the range that you wish to copy, that is the range to copy FROM. The suggested range is the current cell. Therefore, if you are trying to copy the formula in cell A34 to cell B34, the range you are copying FROM is A34..A34.
TO:	Next you are asked to indicate where in the worksheet you want to copy TO, the target range. In the example, you want to copy the formula from A34 to B34, thus the range to copy TO is B34..B34.

The result is that the formula that was in A34, @SUM(A1..A33), has been copied to cell B34 and adjusted to read @SUM(B1..B33). Thus, it is said that the formula was copied in a "relative sense," that is, all formulas were adjusted to reflect their new position.

The COPY command accounts for the number of rows and columns that the formula was moved, thus the formula may be affected by a subsequent addition or deletion of rows or columns. Lotus will display an error message if this happens. As always, there are cases where so many changes are made that all the formulas may be hopelessly modified and thus useless. Care should be taken when adding or deleting rows and columns to review essential formulas to determine that they are still effective.

Frequently, a formula will be written containing a value that is an absolute cell reference, that is, the reference is to only that one cell. For example, assume that the worksheet computes the dollars of sales commission. Assume that the commission rate is 20 percent and is entered in cell A10. The sales commission is computed by multiplying the dollars of sale times the sales commission (found in cell A10). Thus, it is desirable to be able to copy the formula without cell A10 changing. Lotus provides the user the option of restricting the amount of change in the formula by the use of the $ sign. Placing the $ sign in front of a column or row address will prevent that cell reference from being changed upon further copying of the formula. Any combination of row and column may be made absolute. For example $A10 will prevent the column from being changed, while allowing the row to be changed. A10 will prevent any changes in either part of the cell reference when it is copied, whereas A$10 will lock the row address, but allow the column to be changed.

MOVE COMMAND (/M)—The MOVE command operates similarly to the COPY command. The difference is that the MOVE command will move the contents of the cell to a new location instead of simply copying it. The usefulness of the MOVE command is in designing the worksheet for printing or ease of reading. Again, the relative positions of the cells address are maintained, that is, the formulas are adjusted.

FILE COMMAND (/F)—The File command is used for all actions relating to the worksheet file and the disk drive. Thus the command will retrieve a file from disk storage (/FR) or save a file to disk storage (/FS). FILE XTRACT (/FX) stores part of the current worksheet on disk, the part is specified by range address. FILE COMBINE (/FC) will add, copy, or subtract a named range or entire file from a worksheet file stored on the disk into the current worksheet. (Note that the range must be named through the use of RANGE NAME commands.) FILE IMPORT (/FI) may be used to add print files (PRN file type) from disk storage. The print file may have been created in an earlier worksheet and saved for future printing, perhaps as a part of a word processing file.

The question of when to save a file is a very important one. There is no automatic save command with Lotus 1-2-3 as there normally would be with a mainframe system. Thus, if the file is to be saved, the user (you are the user) must use the FILE SAVE (/FS) command. As a rule of thumb, the worksheet should be saved every thirty minutes while working on the worksheet. With FILE SAVE, the user may overwrite an existing worksheet (the REPLACE command) very conveniently. In addition, if the worksheet file represents either a substantial amount of time or a sensitive subject matter, and is therefore replaceable only at considerable cost, the disk storage should be backed up by making a copy of the disk and storing it offsite, that is, in a different location from the other disk. Each user should set a policy (and follow it) for handling disks. A rule of thumb would be to backup any disk that represents a week of work and store the disk offsite to protect it from fire or other casualty. It should be remembered that it is very simple to copy a disk, both for authorized use and for unauthorized use.

PRINT COMMAND (/P)—One of the strengths of the worksheet programs is the power to print out your results in reports that are in final form, that is, require no additional typing. Hardcopy reports are obtained with the PRINT command. The PRINT command governs all interaction between Lotus 1-2-3 and the printer. The user must simply specify a range to be printed and enter Go, the command to start printing. The Lotus default settings for the printer will be acceptable for most uses of the hardcopy worksheet. If special settings are required, the PRINT PRINTER OPTIONS SETUP command allows substantial control of the print quality and size to the user.

DATA COMMAND (/D)—DATA represents the data based management capability of Lotus 1-2-3. One useful sub-command is the SORT command. With SORT (/DS) any range in the worksheet may be sorted in either ascending or descending order, by either alphabetic or numeric character. With this capacity, significant re-ordering of the data is possible.

In using SORT, the user must specify a range to be sorted—which should not include the labels—and the column by which the sort is to be made. The column to be sorted is specified as the primary-key by reference to the cell address of the first entry in the column. The secondary-key is used to resolve ties in the primary-key column and is specified by reference to the cell address of the first entry in the secondary sort column.

By using the DATA QUERY (/DQ), the worksheet ranges may be searched for specific criteria as specified in a criterion range consisting of the columnar headings and one or more rows underneath. The column to be queried or the items to be searched for are specified in the row beneath the headings. Matching items may be extracted from the range and copied to the output range of the worksheet. The DATA TABLE (/DT) command allows the user to prepare a table of values that are computed on the basis of a user-specified formula where either one or two of the items in the formula is allowed to vary.

GRAPH COMMAND (/G)—GRAPH is the command that allows the user to use data that have been computed by the worksheet, to draw a graphical representation of the data. Lotus 1-2-3 Release 1A provides for five types of graphs: Line, Bar, Stacked-Bar, Pie, and XY (a graph of the relationship of a series of numbers to other numbers.) The graph is prepared from data that are contained in a defined range or a named range. Once the graph has been defined, it may be redrawn by use of the function key F10. Use of GRAPH allows the accountant to put to easy and practical use the phrase, "A picture is worth a thousand words."

Using Cell Format in Lotus 1-2-3

Lotus 1-2-3 worksheets are made up of labels and values. The values may be of three types of cell entries: numbers, formulas, or functions. Values will be right justified when they are entered in the worksheet, that is, they will be aligned with the right margin. Numbers are entered without any commas or format identification (that is, no dollar signs, percent signs, etc.) Thus, $1,200.34 is entered in the worksheet as 1200.34, and 34.3%, as .343. The FORMAT command is used to display the numbers with commas, dollar signs, etc. There are two format commands, RANGE FORMAT (/ RF) and WORKSHEET GLOBAL FORMAT (/WGF). Normally, the RANGE FORMAT command will be used because it allows the user to specify the specific cells that he or she wants to format. For example, to format the entry in cells, A34 and B34 to reflect dollars and cents, the command sequence would be as follows:

/	To move from the READY mode to the MENU mode.
R	To select the RANGE command.
F	To select the FORMAT sub-command. At this point all the format options will be shown in the menu.
C	To select the currency format. Note that the comma format, indicated on the menu by a , all by itself, is the same as the currency format except that there are no dollar signs.
2	To specify that we want two decimal places.
A34..B34	To identify the range of the worksheet that we want to display as dollars and cents.

Formulas

Formulas perform arithmetical operations on numbers in a cell. Because Lotus 1-2-3 assumes that any entry beginning with alphabetical characters will be a label, to enter a formula to add cell A34 to cell B34, the formula must begin with a leading + or other value indicator, that is, −, (, @, #, or $. Thus, the formula would be entered as +A34+B34. The basic arithmetic operands are

+	Addition
−	Subtraction
*	Multiplication
/	Division
^	Exponential

Functions

Lotus 1-2-3 has a large selection of preprogrammed formulas that are referred to as Lotus 1-2-3 @Functions. These functions have the common characteristics of beginning with the at sign, @, followed by a name and the area of the worksheet subject to the function. Figure A.13 lists the major functions that are used by accountants. In functions where a range is indicated, the beginning and ending cell address must be given. If a cell is listed, only the cell address is required.

One final characteristic of functions is that they all result in a single number. For example, the @SUM(A1..A33) function referred to above will result in the one number that is the sum of the previous 33 cells. Accordingly, the functions may themselves be used in formulas to produce what are called "nested formulas." Thus, it is acceptable to enter a formula @SUM(A1..A33) + @SUM(B1..B33). The Lotus 1-2-3 manual warns the user that the formulas may be as complex as your courage allows. However,

Financial Functions

@NPV (rate,range)   Computes the net present value using a discount rate of "rate" for the cash flows included in the "range."

@IRR(estimate,range)   Computes the internal rate of return for the amounts in the "range." You enter an estimated rate, or a guess.

@PMT(principle, interest, term)   Computes the amount required to amortize a mortgage with a principal, rate, and term as specified.

@FV(Payment, interest, term)   Computes the future value of an annuity of the amount "payment," with interest and term as specified.

@PV(payment, interest, term)   Computes the present value of an annuity of the amount "payment," with interest and term as specified.

Statistical functions

@COUNT(range)   Displays the number of occupied cells in the range.

@SUM(range)   Adds the values in the range.

@AVG(range)   Computes the average of the values in the range.

@MIN(range)   Determine the minimum value in the range.

@MAX(range)   Determine the maximum value in the range.

Mathematical functions

@RAND   Display a random number between 0 and 1.

@ROUND(value,places)   Rounds the value the number of places specified.

Other functions

@DSUM(input,column,criteria)   Sums the values in column specified of the input range that meet the criteria specified.

@DAVG(input,column,criteria)   Determines the average of the values in column specified of the input range that meet the criteria specified.

@IF(formula, true value, false value)   Evaluate the formula and displays the true value if the formula is true; false value, if not true.

@CHOOSE(indicator, value0, value1, etc)   If the indicator is a 0, displays the value0; if indicator is 1, displays the value1; etc.

@VLOOKUP(x value,table,column)   Displays the value that is found in the table in the column specified and on the row determined by the x value.

@FALSE   Displays the value 0.

@TRUE   Displays the value 1.

regardless of your courage, someone else may have to read your formulas. Thus, your goal should be to make the formulas as simple as possible.

FIGURE A.13
List of Lotus 1-2-3
@ Functions

The more commonly used functions are briefly discussed in the following paragraphs.

The @IF logical statement is very useful in classifying items. It may be used to define a cell to be either the value in another cell or zero, as would be the case if it is used in a check register application. The possibilities are very great in number and diverse in scope. One problem with the use of IF statements is that they require a large amount of memory. In one application to a check register with approximately 30 accounts, 256K of memory was completely used up with only about 100 checks. The application may still be very useful in the right situation, but for mass processing of checks, other methods would be preferable. The form of the IF statement is

@IF(A1 = D1,A2,0)

That is, if the value (not label, that is, the contents of the cell must be a number), in cell A1 is equal to the value in cell D1, then the current cell will be defined to the value in cell A2. If A1 is not equal to D1, the value in the current cell will be defined to be zero. The formula or cell being evaluated may itself be another @IF statement or any other formula.

Lookup tables are very useful to specify variables for computations that vary with some other number. For example, tax rates for income tax computations are specified as lookup tables. Lotus 1-2-3 has two forms of lookup functions: Horizontal and Vertical. The @VLOOKUP is the vertical lookup function where the value is looked up in the first column of the lookup range. The other columns in the lookup range will define the cell once the appropriate row is determined. The form of the function is

@VLOOKUP(A1,D1..F10,2)

Here, the value in the cell A1 is looked up in the first column of the range D1..F10. Once a value greater than A1 is found, the preceding row is considered to be the target row that defines the current cell. The third part of the formula specifies how many columns to go over in order to find the value defining the current cell. In this example, assume the value that is greater than cell A1 is found in cell D5. Then the row immediately preceding that row, row 4, is the row containing the desired value. That value is defined by the @VLOOKUP formula to be in the second column following the lookup column, that is, the third column in the range. In this example, the desired function would be found in cell F4. The end result—the value of the current cell—is defined by the value found in cell F4. Refer to figure A.14 for an example of a lookup function.

@HLOOKUP is similar to @VLOOKUP, except the value is looked up in a range of columns rather than a range of rows. The third part, therefore, specifies the number of rows to go down to find the desired value that defines the current cell.

Lotus 1-2-3 contains several very useful statistical functions. Among them are the @AVG(range), the average of the defined range; @SUM(range), the sum of the defined range; @MAX(range), the maximum value in the defined range; and @MIN(range), the minimum value in the defined range. All these functions perform as their names imply. Again the range may be a defined range (A1..A5, for example) or a named range ("Balance", for example).

The financial functions provided are as follows:

@IRR(guess, range)—the internal rate of return of a range of values;

@NPV(x, range)—the net present value of a range in the worksheet at x interest rate or discount rate;

@FV(payment, interest, term)—the future amount of an ordinary annuity compounding at a specified interest rate for a specified time period;

@PV(payment, interest, term)—the present value of an ordinary annuity with the interest rate and term specified; and

```
                 A          B          C          D          E          F          G
     1
     2     1,200        11%          0
     3     3,000        15%        132
     4     5,000        19%        450
     5     8,000        24%        950
     6    11,000        28%      1,920
     7
     8                                                            Results
     9  Taxable income      $5,500
    10
    11  Tax      rate      @VLOOKUP(C9,A2..C6,1)                        19%
    12
    13
    14  What will result from the following formula?
    15
    16
    17             @VLOOKUP(C9,A2..C6,2)                  450
    18
    19             @VLOOKUP(C9,A2..C6,0)                 5000
    20
```

@PMT(principal, interest, term)—the amount or payment necessary to amortize a mortgage over a stated term at a specified interest rate.

FIGURE A.14
The @VLOOKUP Function

The use of these financial functions should aid the accountant in preparing analysis of many types of capital budgeting and investment opportunities.

For practice in the use of Lotus 1-2-3's functions, use the FILE RETRIEVE (/FR) command to load the file named FUN. Follow the instructions on the screen.

How to Proceed

Like many useful acts of life, the use of Lotus 1-2-3 will become easier with practice. The more often you have the opportunity to use Lotus 1-2-3, the better you will be able to use its power. The time to begin is now.

☐ USING SUPERCALC

SuperCalc was developed after VisiCalc, the first popular spreadsheet, had been on the market for some time. Therefore, at the time it was first issued, it was more advanced than VisiCalc or any other spreadsheet. According to Computer Associates, the SuperCalc program paid special attention to clarity, simplicity, and common sense in writing the messages on the screen. The result is an easy-to-use electronic spreadsheet with sufficient formatting options to make the reports professional looking.

SuperCalc is a widely used electronic spreadsheet, second only to Lotus 1-2-3. The software combines the ability to prepare graphs and to arrange (sort) and query data, common to a data base system, with a very easy-to-use electronic spreadsheet. In addition, SuperCalc has consistently been sold for less than Lotus 1-2-3. The combination of a low price and a well-designed, full feature spreadsheet makes SuperCalc a very useful software product.

There are four releases of SuperCalc:SuperCalc, SuperCalc2, Super-Calc3 Release 1 and Release 2, and SuperCalc4. With each version, SuperCalc has improved both the features and the ease of use. SuperCalc4 departed from the previous versions by adding a full word command menu—the previous versions used a single letter menu. The promotional material for SuperCalc4, indicates that it has every feature that Lotus 1-2-3 has plus all those features unique to SuperCalc. With the price difference, SuperCalc4 is truly an excellent value.

Getting Started

In using SuperCalc, you need to be aware of two disks: the product or system disk, and the utilities disk. SuperCalc suggests that you prepare a working copy of the software that contains the necessary DOS files to boot the system and to configure the software to your printer and/or plotter. A batch file, STARTUP, is provided to help install your working copy. After the disks are installed, they will self-boot, that is, you put the disk in the default drive, drive A, and turn the machine on.

The UTILITIES disk contains several files that may be used to perform housekeeping chores. For example, the utilities disk may be used to copy files, erase files, format disks, transfer files between other software (including Lotus 1-2-3, that is, you may transfer data from a Lotus 1-2-3 file into SuperCalc) and SuperCalc, and configure the SuperCalc disks for a variety of machines. In addition to the disks, SuperCalc comes with a written tutorial "10 Minutes to SuperCalc" that is easy to follow and does a good job of introducing you to the software.

The PRODUCT disk contains the spreadsheet program and is the disk that you will copy on to your working copy. The STARTUP installation program will copy a DOS AUTOEXEC.BAT program on your working copy. Once you have prepared the working copy, you may make additional copies using the DOS copy commands (COPY or DISKCOPY). Thus, unlike Lotus 1-2-3, SuperCalc is not copy protected. Of course your license agreement prohibits using a working copy prepared from any one PRODUCT disk on more than one machine at a time. However, the convenience of being able to make working copies of your software is much appreciated by users. With the AUTOEXEC.BAT installed on the disk, SuperCalc will automatically load. To load the spreadsheet, enter SC# (that is, SC3 for SuperCalc3 and SC4 for SuperCalc4) at the DOS prompt. For example

A>SC3

At the copyright notice, you will be prompted to enter a question mark (?) for HELP, or to press the enter or return key to start, that is, to move into the spreadsheet. See figure A.15.

The SuperCalc Spreadsheet

The SuperCalc3 spreadsheet has 63 columns and 254 rows; SuperCalc4, 255 columns and 9,999 rows. The cells are identified by giving a cell reference to a specific column and row. For example, cell A1 is the upper left-hand corner of the spreadsheet. At the bottom of the screen is the SuperCalc CONTROL PANEL (see figure A.16). It is important to focus your eyes on the control panel. Many mistakes may be eliminated by reviewing the control panel before pressing the enter key.

The top line of the control panel, the STATUS LINE, indicates the active cell and the direction that the cursor will move in the spreadsheet. If there is an entry in the current cell, the nature and contents of that cell will also appear on the status line.

The second line, the PROMPT line, will give two types of information depending upon what operation is being performed. While entering data, the PROMPT line will display information about the width of the current column, the amount of internal memory remaining, the location of the lower right-hand corner of the spreadsheet (useful when you start to print the spreadsheet or if you are looking for empty space), and a reminder that HELP is available. When selecting from the SuperCalc commands, the PROMPT line will display the name or the first letter (depending on

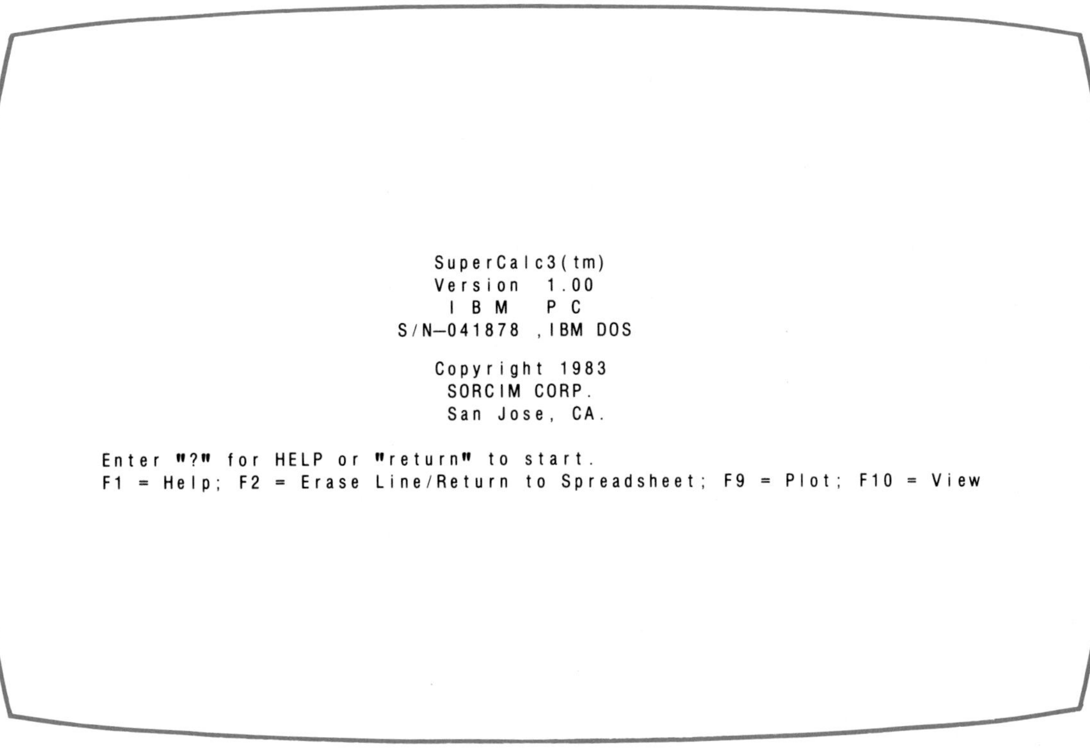

FIGURE A.15
SuperCalc3
Copyright Notice

```
                    SuperCalc3(tm)
                    Version  1.00
                     I B M   P C
               S/N—041878 , IBM DOS

                    Copyright 1983
                    SORCIM CORP.
                    San Jose, CA.

    Enter "?" for HELP or "return" to start.
    F1 = Help; F2 = Erase Line/Return to Spreadsheet; F9 = Plot; F10 = View
```

```
      !   A  !!  B  !!  C  !!  D  !!  E  !!  F  !!  G  !!  H  !
    1 | home
    2 |
    3 |
    4 |
    5 |
    6 |
    7 |
    8 |
    9 |
   10 |
   11 |
   12 |
   13 |
   14 |
   15 |
   16 |
   17 |
   18 |
   19 |
   20 |
   v  C13
   Width:   9  Memory:253 Last Col/Row:B7     ? for HELP
    23>This is the ENTRY line
   F1 = Help; F2 = Erase Line/Return to Spreadsheet; F9 = Plot; F10 = View
```

FIGURE A.16
SuperCalc3 Initial
Screen and
Control
Panel

the version) of the commands. After some practice the first letter will be sufficient information to help you recall the commands.

The third line of the control panel, the ENTRY line, is where all the aciton takes place. Before you have any impact on the SuperCalc spreadsheet, your entry will appear on the ENTRY line. Many mistakes may be identified before they are entered by reviewing the ENTRY line before you press the enter key. While on the ENTRY line, you may use either the backspace key or the left arrow key to erase the last character typed. After you have entered the information, you will have to use the EDIT command to change it. Figure A.16 is a copy of the initial screen of the SuperCalc3 spreadsheet with the control panel at the bottom of the screen. Note that the last row of the screen identifies the use of the active function keys.

Sources of Help Help in using the SuperCalc spreadsheet is available from several sources. As mentioned above, the SuperCalc manual contains a short tutorial that is very useful to obtain an introduction to SuperCalc. Spending the necessary time to review the tutorial is always time well spent. The SuperCalc Answer Screen will give you pointers in using the spreadsheet and short descriptions of the various commands and functions (see figure A.17). You may access the Help facility by pressing the function key 1, (F1) on the left side of the IBM PC keyboard, or by entering the question mark (?). Other sources of help are asking a SuperCalc user, reading this appendix, or reading one of the many books on SuperCalc. There is no replacement, however, for actually using the software to solve

```
    SuperCalc 3      AnswerScreen Entry/Edit Options:

    A quote mark (") or a letter begins a Text entry, unless the letter is the start of
    a Formula entry (such as the cell B7, or the function SUM).
    An apostrophe (') starts a Repeating Text entry.

    While entering data, the arrow keys (which normally move the cursor around the
    spreadsheet) become editing keys:
      Left arrow   -- Backspace one character.
      Right arrow  -- Move right one character.
      Up arrow     -- Insert one blank.
      Down arrow   -- Delete one character.

    Other keys also aid in editing the Entry Line:
      <TAB> -- Moves the Entry Cursor to the start or end of the entry.
      <ESC> -- Returns the location of the Spreadsheet Cursor to the Entry Line.
        After pressing <ESC>, the arrow keys can move the Spreadsheet Cursor to the
        desired cell, and any other key (such as +,-,*,/,:) fixes that current cell
        position in the entry. To leave this mode, press <ESC> again and edit the
        line, or press <DY> to send the entry to the current cell.
      <F2> or <CTRL Z> -- Erases the entry.

        Press any key to continue
    F1 = Help; F2 = Erase Line/Return to Spreadsheet; F9 = Plot; F10 = View
```

a problem. To really appreciate the power of electronic spreadsheets, you have to use one.

FIGURE A.17
SuperCalc3
Answer Screen

Moving around the Spreadsheet

SuperCalc3, Release 2 and SuperCalc4 make excellent use of the keyboard available with the IBM PC and other similar personal computers. The movement keys and the ways they are used in SuperCalc are discussed below.

The arrow keys are the primary movement keys for moving short distances in the spreadsheet. In addition, when you press the enter key, the cursor will move in the direction indicated by the first character on the STATUS line. If the first character is the less than sign, the cursor will move to the left one character when the enter key is pressed. Similarly, if the greater than sign is displayed, the cursor will move to the right; the v, down; and the caret ^, up. The usefulness of this automatic move is apparent when you have a column of numbers to enter. The NUM LOCK key may be used to turn on the number pad, giving you the ability to use the ten key touch method to enter the numbers. When the number is entered by pressing the enter key, the cursor will automatically move down the column. The direction of the movement is changed by using the arrow keys; the last arrow key pressed will set the direction the cursor will move when the enter key is pressed.

Movement over greater distances in the later versions of SuperCalc is easily achieved by using the PgDn key, the PgUp key, and the tab key. These keys will move the spreadsheet cursor by pages. The PgDn key or PgUp key moves the cursor the full length of the screen, twenty spreadsheet rows. The columnar position is not changed, thus the movement will be up and down the columns only. The tab key, the key with two arrows in opposite directions on the left side of the IBM PC keyboard, is used to move page by page left and right across the columns; the rows do not change. In terms of columns, one page is eight standard nine-character columns.

The Home key, the 7 key on the number pad, will always return the cursor to the home cell, normally cell A1. Being able to quickly move to cell A1 makes the home screen, from A1 to H20, a good candidate as a location for the menu screen. At times you will want to tell SuperCalc3 exactly where to go. The GO TO key, the equals sign (F5 in SuperCalc4), allows you to specify the exact cell address to go to. When the = key is pressed, the prompt line will ask you for the address to go to. You respond with the cell address of the cell you wish to move to. If the cell is off the screen, it will appear in the upper left-hand corner of the screen when you go to it. If the cell is on the screen, the cursor will simply move to the cell.

The movement keys act differently while you are entering (that is, before you press the enter key) or editing data. The left and right arrows keys will work as before, moving the cursor to the left or right one character at a time across the current entry. The up and down arrow keys will insert or delete spaces or characters while entering or editing a cell. The HOME key will move the cursor to the beginning of the cell contents that is being edited or entered. Similarly, the END key will move the cursor to the end of the row. Use of these keys allows the user to get quickly to the part of the statement that he or she wishes to edit.

Data Entry

A spreadsheet is brought to life by entering either labels or values into the cells. A label may be any character or group (string) of characters. If an entry begins with an alphabetic character and is not a cell reference, SuperCalc assumes that a label is being entered. Thus, Apple is assumed to be a label or text. Likewise, any entry that begins with a number is assumed to be a value. For example, 10 is assumed to be the number ten, not a label. To give you experience in making entries to cells, a template with the filename ENTRY has been prepared. To load or retrieve the file, follow the steps listed below.

STEP 1   Load the SuperCalc program from the system disk.

STEP 2   With the spreadsheet on the screen, as in figure A.16, and the TEMPLATE disk in the B drive, press the following keys.

       /   The slash key on the right side of the keyboard. The first command prompt (letter or word) will appear in the control panel.

       L   By pressing the letter L, you select the LOAD command. The LOAD command is used to interface with the disk storage.

> B:ENTRY At this point you are requested to enter the filename. You type the disk drive indicator, B:, followed by the filename ENTRY. Press the ENTER key.

STEP 3 Follow the instructions on the screen.

Correcting Errors

Many accountants are terrible typists. If you press the wrong key, you may use the backspace key, which is to the right of the + = sign in the top row of the **IBM PC** keyboard, or the left arrow key, which is on the number pad, to correct an error before you press the ENTER key. If you have already entered the keystrokes, you may either reenter the data or edit the data. If you reenter, your new entry will simply replace the old. To edit, you use the EDIT command. To use the EDIT command, press the slash key (/) followed by the letter E. While in the EDIT command, you may move left or right with the arrow keys to get to the error. To correct, either type over the erroneous character, or insert the correction and delete the error. To be able to INSERT corrections, the INS key, in the lower right corner of IBM keyboard, must be pressed. Errors may be deleted by using either the DEL key in the lower right corner of the IBM keyboard or the down arrow key. Use the left or right arrow keys, tab key, HOME key, or END key to move across the edit line.

Using SuperCalc Commands

SuperCalc commands are used to design the spreadsheet, interface with printers and disk drives, move data within the spreadsheet, format the spreadsheet, view graphs, use the data base management commands, and execute macros. The commands and their functions are summarized below.

SuperCalc Command	Task performend
COPY, REPLICATE, MOVE	Aids in entering data and formulas
EDIT, BLANK, ZAP, QUIT, INSERT, DELETE	Used for making corrections and inserting rows or columns
LOAD, SAVE, OUTPUT	Interface with peripherals, that is, allow use of the printer and diskdrives
FORMAT, TITLE	Design appearance of the spreadsheet, set the use of dollar signs, commas, width of columns, etc.
GLOBAL, WINDOW	Aid in the design of spreadsheet
ARRANGE, DATA	Data base management commands
VIEW	Prepare and view graphs
EXECUTE (/X)	Execute macros or programs

The commands are discussed below.

SuperCalc Commands

/ C COPY—The purpose of the COPY command is to copy one cell or a range of cells from one part of the spreadsheet to another. The user must state the source range and the destination range. The COPY command results in the same cell contents in two parts of the same spreadsheet. The COPY command does not copy one cell into more than one cell; that is the purpose of the REPLICATE command. For example, to copy the contents of cell A45 to the cell A60, you would enter the following key strokes:

User enters	SuperCalc prompts
/C	FROM?
A45	TO?
A60	

After entering the TO cell, the user may press the enter key and the COPY will be completed. If the FROM cell contains a formula, the formula would be adjusted (that is, the cell references would be modified). If the user wishes to copy the formula in an absolute sense (that is, no adjustments), he/she may press the comma (,) and select whether to copy the cell in an absolute sense or a relative sense.

/R REPLICATE   While /R is similar to COPY, the difference is that with REPLICATE you may copy one cell into many cells. For example, if you have a formula in cell D1 that you wish to copy into the 19 cells D2 to D20, REPLICATE will allow you to do so. The keystrokes are as follows:

User enters	SuperCalc3 prompts
/R	FROM?
D1	TO?
D2:D20	

As with COPY, you may select options by pressing the comma. The options allow you to copy in a relative sense (the formulas adjust) or in an absolute sense (no adjustment of formulas).

/M MOVE   The MOVE command is similar to COPY with the important difference that use of the MOVE command will result in the cell appearing in the spreadsheet only once; that is, the cell is moved from one part of the spreadsheet to another.

/E EDIT   The EDIT command allows a user to make corrections in cell definitions that have previously been entered. To correct the current cell (where the cursor currently is located), simply press /E and the ENTER key. To EDIT a different location, enter /E and the desired cell address.

/B BLANK   The purpose of the BLANK command is to erase either the current cell or a range of cells. The range is specified by stating the upper left-hand corner first, and the lower right-hand corner of the range secondly. The beginning and the end are separated with a colon; for example, /B A1:B5 would erase the ten cells found in the first five rows of columns A and B. (Note that SuperCalc helps you by inserting a colon if you press a period.)

/Z ZAP   SuperCalc word for clearing the entire spreadsheet. If the darn thing doesn't work, ZAP it.

/Q QUIT   Exits from SuperCalc to the operating system (DOS).

/D R or C DELETE ROW or COLUMN   The row number or column letter must be specified. The row or column will be deleted in its entirety; that is, all cells in the row or all cells in the column will be deleted—*all cells* including those off the screen.

/I R or C INSERT ROW or COLUMN   Inserts a row or a column throughout the spreadsheet. In effect, it is the reverse of DELETE.

/L LOAD   As discussed above, the LOAD command allows a file to be loaded from disk storage to RAM. Templates are loaded from the B disk drive (that is, the non-default disk drive.) For example, to load the file named C4FIFO, the command string is:

/LB:C4FIFO.

The LOAD command allows you to select to load *all* of the spreadsheet file or *part* of the file. The PART option is useful to combine two or more spreadsheets into one.

/S SAVE   It is most important to write your completed spreadsheets to the disk. The RAM storage is volatile; that is, if the power to the system unit is turned off, all data in RAM is lost. The solution is to use the SAVE command to write to the disk frequently. As a rule of thumb, the spreadsheet should be saved every thirty minutes while you are working on it. In addition, if the spreadsheet file represents either a substantial amount of time or a sensitive subject matter, and is therefore replaceable only at considerable cost, the disk storage should be backed up by making a copy of the disk and storing it offsite—that is, in a different location from the other disk. Each user should set a policy (and follow it) for handling disks.

The SAVE command allows you to save the spreadsheet on disk storage. If the B disk drive is to be used, it must be specified at the time the filename is entered unless you have previously changed the default disk drive. You may change the default disk drive by pressing the ENTER key to see the directory.

O/ OUTPUT   The OUTPUT command is used to print a spreadsheet in RAM to a printer or disk with options to print the contents (the formulas for each cell) or the display (what you see on the screen). The user must specify a range to be printed by specifying the beginning cell and the ending cell, separated by a colon, for example, A3:H25. If the entire spreadsheet is to be printed, you may specify ALL as the range.

/F FORMAT   Several useful formats are possible with SuperCalc. For example, /FG$ will enter numbers in dollar format, rounded to two places, throughout the entire spreadsheet. /FI will result in all numbers rounded to the nearest integer. /FTR will right justify all labels and other textual material. By selecting /FGU, you may select from eight user-defined formats. By using the user-defined format, you may display dollar signs, percent signs, embed commas, set decimal places, and others. The

FORMAT command may be used to format the entire spreadsheet (the G, GLOBAL, selection), a range (E, ENTRY), a ROW (R), or a COLUMN (C).

/T TITLE   The TITLE command locks specified rows or columns on the screen. For example, if you are entering a long series of numbers down column F, the columnar heading may be locked on the screen by using the /T command.

/G GLOBAL   The GLOBAL command is used to specify the graphic format, spreadsheet format, and calculation options. To set the recalculation option to manual, GLOBAL MANUAL, /GM is used. To return to automatic recalculation, /GA. The column letters and row numbers that border the spreadsheet may be removed or restored by use of the GLOBAL BORDERS command: for example, /GB takes off the borders; /GB restores the borders.

/W WINDOW   SuperCalc has 64 (or more) columns and 256 (or more) rows. On your monitor's screen, however, you can see only a small portion of that. The WINDOW command allows you to see two small portions of the spreadsheet at once. The two parts of the screen may move together (synchronous) or move independently of each other (unsynchronous). The window may be vertical or horizontal.

/A ARRANGE and //D DATA   The ARRANGE and DATA commands allow you to sort and query a range in the spreadsheet. These commands are data base management operations that are common to electronic spreadsheets. Refer to the manual for a complete description of these commands.

/V VIEW   The VIEW command is used to prepare a graph for display on the screen and to display the graph. Refer to the manual for a complete description of the graph features with SuperCalc. With spreadsheet graphs, there is no excuse for not using graphic representation of data in your reports.

/X EXECUTE   The EXECUTE command allows you to run a macro file that is on disk storage using the current spreadsheet. The macro will allow you to design automated spreadsheets. The steps are similar to programming. The use of EXECUTE files is left to a more advanced course.

Formulas

Formulas perform arithmetical operations on numbers and cells. SuperCalc has a set of predefined character strings or words that will perform predefined computations. These predefined words include all possible cell references. Thus, to enter a formula to add cell A34 to cell B34, all that is necessary is to enter A34 + B34. If you should desire to refer to the cell A34 in a label, you would have to add a label prefix, for example, the double quote ("). SuperCalc will perform all the basic arithmetical operations. The basic arithmetic operands are

+ Addition
− Subtraction

    *   Multiplication
    /   Division
    ^   Exponential

Functions

SuperCalc has a large selection of preprogrammed formulas that are known as SuperCalc Functions. These functions all have unique names that are recognized by SuperCalc as formulas to perform their defined task. For example, SuperCalc recognizes the function SUM(a23:a24) as meaning the same as A23 + A24. The major functions that are used by accountants are discussed below.

Some functions operate on a range, others on only one cell. If a range is indicated, the beginning and ending cell address must be given. If a cell is listed, only the cell address is required.

One final characteristic of functions is that they all result in a single number, or "textual label." For example, the SUM(A1:A33) function referred to above will result in the one number, the sum of the previous 33 cells. Accordingly, functions may themselves be used in formulas to produce what are referred to as "nested formulas." Thus, it is appropriate to enter a formula SUM(A1:A33) + SUM(B1:B33). Although SuperCalc formulas may be as complex as your courage allows, regardless of your courage, someone else may have to read your formulas. Thus, your goal should be to make the formulas as *simple* as possible.

The logical IF statement is very useful to classify items. It may be used to define a cell to be either the value in another cell or zero, as would be the case if used in a check register application. The possibilities are very great in number and diverse in scope. One problem with the use of IF statements is that they require a large amount of memory. In one application to a check register with approximately 30 accounts, 256K of memory was completely used up with only about 100 checks. The application may still be very useful in the right situation, but for mass processing of checks, other methods would be preferable. The form of the IF statement is

    IF(A1 = D1,A2,0).

Thus, if the value (not text, that is, the contents of the cell must be a number or "textual label") in cell A1 is equal to the value in cell D1, then the current cell will be defined as the value in cell A2. If A1 is not equal to D1, the value in the current cell will be defined to be zero. The formula or cell being evaluated may itself be another IF statement or any other formula or function.

Lookup tables are very useful to specify variables for computations that vary with some other number. For example, tax rates for income tax computations are specified as lookup tables. Lookup tables may be in columns or in rows. An example of a columnar lookup is

    Lookup(30000,e35:f40)

In this example, the value 30,000, is looked up in column E35 to E40. The current cell would be defined to be the value found in the column to the right. Thus, if 30,000 is found in cell E34, the value in cell F34 would appear in the current cell. A row lookup is similar; the difference is that the value is looked up in the first row down.

One useful function that overcomes the problem of the appearance of rounded numbers that are in fact not rounded is the ROUND function. The FORMAT command does not in fact round the numbers, rather they only appear rounded. The ROUND(value,places) function will round the value referenced the number of places specified. For example, ROUND(123.456,1) will result in 123.4; Round(123.456, −1) will result in 120.

SuperCalc contains several very useful statistical functions. Among these are the following.

AV(range) or AVERAGE(range)   Computes the average of the defined range; for example, AV(A3:A8) will average the values in cells A3 to A8.

SUM(range) or SUM(series of cells)   Computes the sum of the defined range, or sum of a series of cells. For example, sum(A4,B5:b8).

MAX(range)   Determines the maximum value in the defined range.

MIN(range)   Determines the minimum value in the defined range.

The financial functions provided are very useful to the accountant. SuperCalc provides the following:

IRR(guess, range)   Uses an iterative process to determine the internal rate of return of a range of values. The guess should be some value between 0 and 1; it does not have to be particularly close. The first cell in the range should be the investment and should be entered as a negative number. If there are multiple negative payments, there may be more than one acceptable answer. Normally, if the negative amounts begin in the first cell, a unique answer will result. For example, IRR(.3,F44:F60).

NPV(Discount,Range)   Computes the net present value of a range in the spreadsheet using the stated discount rate. For example, NPV(.1,V77:V101)

FV(payment, interest, term)   Computes the future amount of an ordinary annuity (an equal series of payments) compounded at a specified interest rate for a specified time period.

PV(payment, interest, term)   Computes the present value of an ordinary annuity with the interest rate and term specified.

PMT(principal, interest, term)   Computes the amount or payment necessary to amortize a mortgage, the principal, over a stated term at a specified interest rate.

The use of these financial functions should aid the accountant in preparing analysis of many types of capital budgeting and investment opportunities.

For practice in the use of SuperCalc's functions, use the LOAD command to load the filenamed FUN. Follow the instructions on the screen.

□ THE SUPERCALC MANUAL

The SuperCalc manual contains a detailed reference flow chart of all the commands and an abbreviated listing of the formulas and functions. These two aids are extremely useful when designing spreadsheets with SuperCalc. A careful reading of this overview and these detailed reference pages, plus about four hours at the computer working with SuperCalc will provide the user with a substantial understanding of what SuperCalc is all about. It should be remembered that the computer was designed to be used, even by the untrained user. It (the machine) will not break or blow up. A short time sitting at the keys and trying to use the machine will result in significant understanding and ability to use SuperCalc to do the dirty work for you.

Like many useful acts of life, the use of SuperCalc will become easier with practice. The time to begin is now.

MANAGEMENT ACCOUNTING TERMINOLOGY

APPENDIX **B**

ABC Method Inventory control technique that divides inventories into various subclassifications for control purposes.

Abnormal Spoilage Spoilage that is not expected from normal operating conditions and is usually considered controllable. As a result it should be treated as a loss in the period incurred.

Absorption Costing A product costing method in which all costs considered necessary to manufacture the product are included in the product cost. Fixed manufacturing overhead is included in the inventoriable costs.

Accelerated Cost Recovery System The Accelerated Cost Recovery System is to be used to depreciate most tangible depreciable property, for tax purposes, placed in service after 1980. It replaces all other depreciation methods formerly used for tax purposes.

Accounting Rate Of Return Represents the ratio of average annual after tax profits to the investment (or average investment) required. The method is also referred to as the average rate of return or accrual accounting rate of return.

Activity Base Production activity used to relate manufacturing overhead to the product manufactured. Typical activity bases are direct labor dollars, direct labor hours, and machine hours.

Actual Costing See actual job order costing.

Actual Costing System Method of product costing where actual direct materials, actual direct labor, and actual manufacturing overhead are charged to the cost of the product manufactured.

Allocation Assignment on some logical basis of cost or revenue items to organizational units or products.

Alternative Solutions In linear programming, the feasible region contains the alternative solutions. The optimal solution is one of the alternative solutions.

Applied Overhead Manufacturing overhead allocated to products or services on some predetermined basis.

Attainable Standards Standards that management expects to achieve with efficient manufacturing operations. Provides for normal spoilage and some down time.

Avoidable Cost Costs that will not be incurred if an existing operation is discontinued.

Basic Standards Often refers to a standard which is set only once and is used as a basis for comparing all subsequent expected and actual performance, or change in standards. They are useful only for updating performance trends.

Breakeven Point The volume of sales where total revenue is equal to total expense and profit is zero. Sales volume may be measured in units or dollars.

Breakeven Unit Volume See breakeven point.

Budgets Detailed written plans outlining management's expectations with respect to acquisition and use of resources for a specified period of time.

Byproducts Products of joint production processes whose sales value is not material when compared with that of the major or chief products. Contrast with joint products.

Capital Budgets These budgets reflect long-term planning for capital expenditures.

Capital Budgeting The process of determining how best to allocate a company's resources to long-term capital facility proposals, new products, and various other project proposals.

Capital Labor Ratio Ratio of capital to labor that is used in productivity measurement.

Capital Rationing A situation where companies find that there are more acceptable projects than they have funds to undertake because of limits placed on the amount of funds to be committed to capital investments in a given period. Available funds are then divided among various projects on some meaningful basis.

Carrying Costs Consist of the costs of storage space, breakage, obsolescence, deterioration, insurance, and personal property taxes. The desired rate of return or the investment in inventory is often included.

Cash Flow Budget A schedule of expected cash receipts and disbursements.

Cash Receipts/Disbursements System Subsystem of the accounting information system. Common subsystems are accounts receivable, accounts payable, and payroll.

Coefficient Of Determination The average percentage of the total variation in the dependent variable that is associated with the variation in the independent variable. Same as R^2.

Committed Costs Fixed costs that result from buying property, plant, equipment, and other long-term commitments.

Common Costs Costs of facilities and services shared by user departments. Also see fixed costs.

Communication The procedure by which one mechanism affects another mechanism, or the procedures by which one person may affect another.

Comprehensive Budget See master budget.

Constant Variance Uniform scatter of observations about a regression line. Also known as homoscedasticity.

Constraint Equations The set of equations in a linear program that specify the area of feasible solutions.

Continuous Budget A budget that continues to project twelve months by adding a new month in the future as a month completed is dropped.

Contribution Margin The difference between sales and all variable costs. It may be expressed as a total or unit cost and indicates amount available to cover fixed expenses and contribute to profits.

Contribution Margin Per Unit See contribution margin.

Contribution-Margin Ratio The ratio of contribution margin to sales.

Control Control represents the monitored state of a system. It involves the measurement of activities against a standard, performance evaluation, and taking corrective action whenever appropriate.

Control Charts Used in statistical quality control. Two types of charts are typically used. The $\overline{X}$ chart shows variations in the arithmetic mean of the characteristic being measured. The R chart shows the variations in ranges of the samples.

Control Limits The upper and lower bounds of a control chart that are used to indicate whether a process is in or out of control.

Controllable Cost A cost which can be significantly influenced by decisions of a manager.

Controller The controller has primary responsibility for the development and communication of financial information.

Conversion Cost The total of direct labor and manufacturing overhead costs.

Correlation Relationship between two variables.

Cost It represents some type of measured sacrifice evolving from an operational sequence of units and centering upon a particular activity or product. In effect it is a sacrifice made for goods or services.

Cost Accounting Techniques concerned with cost estimation, cost allocation, and product cost determination. Cost accounting plays a significant role in financial accounting because of the emphasis on product costing.

Cost Accounting System Procedures used to record, classify, summarize, and provide cost information.

Cost Allocation Assigning items of cost to various segments of an organization based on some logical measure of use.

Cost Behavior Pattern Indicates how costs react or respond to changes in levels of business activity.

Cost Center A responsibility center where the supervisor is responsible only for costs.

Cost of Capital See required rate of return.

Cost Estimation Measures by which predictable relationships between all activity component (independent variable) and overhead costs (dependent variable) are found so that overhead costs can be predicted.

Costs of Goods Manufactured Total cost of direct materials, direct labor and manufacturing overhead included in products completed during a specific period.

Cost-Volume-Profit Analysis The analysis of the relationships between selling price, variable cost, fixed cost, sales volume, and profits.

Current Cost Cost stated in terms of current market prices instead of historical cost.

Data Base A collection of data fundamental to an organization.

Decentralization Relative freedom to make decisions. The lower the level in the organization that decisions are made, the greater the decentralization.

Decision Table A summary of planned actions, events, probabilities, and outcomes.

Decision Variable Independent variable.

Defective Units Products which do not meet quality control standards but which can be reworked and sold as a finished product.

Differential Cost See incremental cost.

Differential Cost Analysis Cost analysis based on differential costs.

Dependent Variable A mathematical variable whose value is determined in a function by that of one or more independent variables.

Direct Analysis A technique where overhead costs are estimated by one or more people who simply rely on their knowledge of existing cost behavior.

Direct Cost A direct cost represents a cost incurred for a specific purpose which is uniquely traceable to that purpose.

Direct Costing A product costing method in which only the variable manufacturing costs are assigned to the product. Fixed manufacturing overhead is treated as a period cost.

Direct Labor Labor used directly in the process of transforming various components into a finished product.

Direct Labor Efficiency Variance Results from differences between actual direct labor hours incurred and standard hours allowed based on units produced. Also called a quantity and time variance.

Direct Labor Rate Variance The rate variance is caused because of differences between actual and standard weighted average of contract rates established for standard cost purposes. The total variance results from multiplying the difference by actual direct labor workers.

Direct Labor Variance Collected by comparing actual direct labor costs with standard direct labor costs charged to production.

Direct Materials All materials that are specifically identified with the finished product and in a practical sense can be traced to the finished product.

Direct Material Price Variance Results from differences between actual prices paid for materials purchased and price standards established. In some cases the variance is calculated at the time materials are put into production. In this case the variance represents the difference between actual unit price and standard unit price multiplied by quantity put into production.

Direct Material Quantity Variance The quantity variance results from differences between quantities of materials actually used and standard quantities allowed based on units produced. Also referred to as a usage or efficiency variance.

Direct Material Variance The direct material variance results from price differences and quantity differences. See material price variance and material quantity variance.

Disappearance Refers to direct material that evaporates or disappears as an expected part of the manufacturing process.

Discount Rate See required rate of return.

Discounted Cash Flow Method Means, recognizing time value of money, for valuing expected future cash inflows and outflows in terms of a common point in time.

Discretionary Costs See managed costs.

Divisionalization When a firm is organized around divisions—usually called profit or investment centers.

Dual The initial formulization of a linear programming problem is called the primal, the alternative problem is called the dual.

Economic Order Quantity (EOQ) Amount of inventory that should be ordered at one time so that the associated annual costs of the inventory can be minimized.

EOQ Model Mathematical method that determines the economic order quantity (EOQ).

Effectiveness Attainment of a predetermined goal.

Efficiency Relationship between inputs and outputs.

Employee Behavior Refers to the way employees react to various control methods. The goal is to evaluate employees so that goal congruence is achieved.

Equivalent Units The expression used where production is measured by converting units in production for a period from physical units to efforts expended, or the equivalent number of finished units which could have been produced based on manufacturing costs for the period. Equivalent, rather than physical units, are then used to express output and calculate unit costs in process costing systems.

Error Term See residuals.

Exception Reporting Usually employed in standard costing where only significant variances are reported to management.

Expected Value A weighted average using probabilities as weights.

Factory Overhead See manufacturing overhead.

Factory Overhead Applied See manufacturing overhead applied.

Feasible Region In linear programming the area bounded by the constraints that contains the optimal solution.

Feedback In control systems, it involves a comparison of the standard with the actual results.

FIFO Basis When used in process costing systems, the assumption is made that units in beginning inventories are completed before new units are started. In other situations it refers to the assumption that first goods completed or purchased are the first goods sold.

File A set of related records, e.g. in stock constraint, a file would consist of a set of invoices. A record is a set of related data words, treated as a unit. For example, in stock control each invoice could constitute a record.

Filtering In data processing, a process of screening unwanted elements as they are communicated from one point to another.

Financial Accounting Its purpose is to provide information on results of operations and financial position. Emphasis tends to be on external decision makers.

Financial Budget This part of the master budget that includes the pro forma income statement, pro forma balance sheet, cash flow budget, and capital budget.

Finished Goods When products are completed their costs are transferred from work in process to finished goods inventory.

Finished-Goods Inventory Products completed and ready for sale.

Fixed Cost A cost that does not vary as a total amount with changes in activity over a relevant range of activity.

Fixed Overhead Spending Variance Represents the difference between actual fixed overhead costs incurred and budgeted fixed costs.

Fixed Overhead Variance The difference between actual fixed overhead costs incurred and fixed overhead applied to production.

Flexible Budget A flexible budget is typically an overhead budget where overhead costs allowed are varied as activity varies. Actual overhead can then be compared with overhead allowed for a specific level of activity.

Full Costing See absorption costing.

General Ledger Systems Collects financial and statistical input from the entire accounting information system and maintains the reporting and allocation logic used by the system.

Goal Congruence Refers to the relationship between employees' goals and an organization's goals. It exists where goals of employees, to the extent possible, are consistent with overall company goals.

Goods In Process. Work-in-process.

Governmental Budgets In governmental entities expenditures are made based on appropriations authorized by a legislative body. In this sense the expenditure budget establishes a ceiling on expenditures by categories. The revenue portion of the budget indicates sources of funds for the authorized expenditures.

Gross Margin Excess of sales over the cost of goods sold; also referred to as gross profit.

Gross Profit See gross margin.

Heteroscedasticity Violation of the assumption of constant variance. In this text it is related to regression analysis.

Hierarchical System Any information system designed so that segregated data bases are divided among functional, departmental, or divisional lines.

High-Low Method A method of approximating a cost function by fitting a linear function to the high and low cost observations within a relevant range of activity.

Historical Standards See basic standards.

Homoscedasticity Normally distributed scatter of points about a regression line.

Hurdle Rate See required rate of return.

Ideal Standard This standard represents the lowest costs which could be attained under the best possible operating conditions.

Idle Time Represents wages paid for unproductive time caused by machine breakdowns or other problems.

In-Control State A situation where the process is operating in a planned manner.

Incremental Change in total results under one condition in comparison to some other condition.

Incremental Approach In capital budgeting, a method of determining which alternative is preferable by calculating the difference in net cash inflow between alternatives.

Incremental Cost Difference in total cost between two alternatives.

Independent Variable A measure of volume (activity component) subject to influence of a decision maker.

Indifference Probability The probability of being out of control where expected costs of not investigating are equal to the expected costs of investigating.

Indirect Cost All costs that are not considered direct costs. See manufacturing overhead.

Information Information is that which reduces uncertainty on the part of the decision maker.

Integrated Information System Characterized by a common data base and a separation of the data processing activity from the functional areas of the organization.

Internal Rate of Return The internal rate of return is the discount rate that sets the present value of expected future cash flows equal to the initial investment.

Inventoriable Cost Product cost.

Investment Base The denominator in the ROI calculation and the base for computing the capital charge with residual income.

Investment Center A responsibility center where the supervisor has responsibility for applicable revenue, expenses, and investments.

Investment Tax Credit Reductions of income taxes arising from the purchase of certain assets.

Iso-Contribution Margin Lines In a linear programming problem, lines that pass through the feasible region and have the same total contribution margin.

Job Cost Sheet The primary document used in a job order costing system to accumulate product costs.

Job Order Costing A product costing system that assigns manufacturing costs to specific jobs representing identifiable parts of product. It is used by companies that produce unique products or products to meet specifications.

Job Ticket A form used to record employees' specific activities (jobs worked or departments worked in) during a work period. When summarized they provide information on direct and indirect labor.

Joint Costs Cost of manufactured goods of relatively significant sales values that are simultaneously produced by a process or series of processes.

Joint Products Products produced from a manufacturing process that necessarily yield multiple outputs each of whose market value adds significantly to the total market value of all outputs at the split-off point.

Just-In-Time A system in which the final assembly line pulls only what is needed from the various work centers to produce a specific output. The goal is to produce and deliver goods just in time to be used or sold.

Kanban In manufacturing kanban means a marker to control the sequencing of job activities through sequential processes.

Lead Time Time interval between placing an order and receiving delivery.

Learning Curve Cost function such that average costs or marginal costs per unit of output decline systematically as cumulative production increases.

Learning Rate The rate of change in the cumulative average or marginal time per unit as the number of units produced doubles.

LIFO An inventory method which assumes last goods finished (or purchased) are the first goods sold.

Linear Programming (L.P.) A mathematical technique used to formulate and solve problems which have an objective and some constraints which can be expressed as linear equations.

Managed Costs These costs, also called discretionary costs, tend to be fixed for a rather short term period such as the budget period. They usually result from decisions made in the budgeting cycle for salaries, advertising and similar costs.

Management Accounting The primary focus of management accounting is on providing information for management planning and control. The National Association of Accountant's definition is as follows: Management Accounting is the process of identification, measurement, accumulation, analysis, preparation, interpretation of financial information used by management to plan, evaluate and control within the organization and to assure appropriate use of and accountability for its resources.

Management Control Encompasses all the activities involved in acquiring the various resources of a firm and insuring that they are used in an effective and efficient manner.

Manufacturing Overhead All costs other than direct materials and direct labor considered to be associated with the manufacturing process. These costs are, to some extent, subject to management's discretion.

Manufacturing Overhead Applied Manufacturing overhead allocated to production where an estimated rate and some activity component such as direct labor or machine hours are used at the basis for allocation. An account, manufacturing overhead applied, is often used to accumulated manufacturing overhead applied.

Margin of Safety Difference between budgeted sales volume and breakeven sales volume divided by the budgeted sales volume. It is used by managers as a measure of risk.

Marginal Cost The incremental cost incurred in producing an additional unit of output.

Marginal Income See Contribution Margin.

Marginal Revenue Incremental revenue received from the sale of an additional unit of output.

Market Based Transfer Price A transfer price based on the market price used in sales to customers outside of the firm.

Marketing Systems A subsystem of the accounting information system. Contains subsystems for marketing analysis, order processing, and finished goods inventory control.

Market Value Simply represents current value.

Master Budget The master budget reflects total plans and includes all the relevant operating schedules along with cash flow projections, expected income and financial position. It is also referred to as a comprehensive budget.

Material-Mix Variance See mix variance.

Material Requisition See stores requisition.

Materials Inventory Control System Subsystem of the production management system where inventory records are maintained for all parts and supplies.

Measurement A special language which represents real world phenomena by means of numbers and relations of numbers that are predetermined within the number system.

Method of Neglect A method of treating spoilage costs, whereby these costs are spread over good production by including only good units in equivalent unit calculations.

Minimum Desired Rate of Return See required rate of return.

Mixed Cost A cost that has both fixed and variable elements.

Mix Variance It results from mixing raw materials in a ratio different from the standard mix of materials. The variance is derived by determining the difference, by components, between the materials actually used by component and the total quantity used adjusted for components by the ratio established in the standards.

Motivation An individual's inner state that directs behavior.

Multicollinearity Existence of high correlation among the independent variables in a multiple regression problem.

Multiple Regression When more than two independent variables are included in a regression equation.

Negotiated Transfer Prices A transfer price resulting from negotiations between divisional management.

Net Present Values A method for evaluating projects where all expected future cash flows are discounted to the present, using some predetermined required rate of return. A proposal is considered acceptable if the present value of cash inflows exceeds the present value of the cash outflows.

Net Realizable Value A costing procedure that assigns the sales price less any separable costs to the by-product at the split-off point.

Noncontrollable cost A cost that cannot be significantly influenced by actions of the manager to whom it is charged.

Non-Negativity Constraints Constraints used in linear programming to eliminate negative values from the feasible region.

Normal Capacity Level of capacity expected to satisfy average demand over a reasonable period of time.

Normal Costing See normal job order costing. It means that estimated rather than actual overhead costs are charged to manufacturing.

Normal Costing System Method of product costing where actual direct materials, actual direct labor and estimated manufacturing overhead are charged to the cost of the product manufactured.

Normal Spoilage Spoilage that is expected to result from a particular process and is considered uncontrollable in the short run.

Null Hypothesis As used in regression analysis, the hypothesis that the true value of the regression coefficient is zero.

Objective Function Qualification of a goal to be maximized or minimized in a linear programming model.

Objectives Objectives represent specific targets that are to be achieved at some identifiable point in the future. Objectives are derived from goals and should lead to achievement of goals.

On Line Capabilities In a computer system where the input data enters the computer directly from the point of origin or in which output data is transmitted directly to where it is needed.

Operating Budget Various budgets and related schedules forming basis for pro forma income statement.

Operating Control Provides the mechanism needed to insure that individual jobs or projects are carried out within the framework of previously deferred criteria.

Operating Leverage A measure of how a firm can increase profits in relationship to increase in sales volume.

Opportunity Cost In a profit situation the opportunity cost is the difference between the profit that would have been earned had the optimal decision been made minus the profit earned. In a cost situation the opportunity cost is the difference between the cost incurred and the cost that would have been incurred if the optimal decision had been made.

Ordering Costs Consist of incremental clerical costs of preparing a purchase order or production order and special processing and receiving costs relating to the number of orders processed.

Organization Goals Goals specified by top management.

Organization Structure. Planned or formal relationships among individuals and segments within an organization.

Out-Of-Control State A situation where a process is operating in an unacceptable manner.

Over- or Underapplied Overhead The difference between the actual manufacturing overhead and the applied manufacturing overhead.

Overhead Efficiency Variance The efficiency variance represents the difference between the flexible budget at actual hours and the flexible budget at allowed hours. It identifies the effect on overhead costs of using more or less direct hours than the hours allowed for a given level of output.

Overhead Spending Variance The variance is calculated by subtracting from actual overhead costs the flexible budget. See also variable overhead spending variance and fixed overhead spending variance.

Overhead Volume Variance Volume difference resulting from (1) using a fixed overhead rate and (2) operating at a volume level other than the one used to establish the fixed overhead rate. It is calculated by subtracting from the flexible budget at allowed hours, the overhead applied.

Parameter A constant, such as a, or a coefficient, such as b, in a regression model.

Partial Productivity Ratio of total output to partial inputs.

Payback Provides a measure of the time required to recover the initial amount invested in a project. Cash inflows are usually stated in terms of after tax cash flows from operations.

Performance Measurement Measurement of actual results of the performance of a responsibility center.

Period Cost A cost recognized as an expense in an operating period without regard to the volume of activity. It is a noninventoriable cost.

Periodic System A system where physical inventory counts are used to update inventory balances and determine cost of goods sold.

Perpetual System Requires a subsidiary record which provides a continuous record of additions, reductions, and balances of a particular inventory item.

Planning The development of goals, and the establishment of operational guidelines and programs within restrictions imposed by technology and the environment. It involves the identification of alternatives and the selection of the best one for achieving goals.

Post Audit An audit made to provide feedback to management on results of actual performance versus projected performance of past capital expenditure decisions.

Practical Capacity Maximum level at which the plant or department can operate efficiently.

Predetermined Overhead Rate An overhead rate calculated from estimated overhead costs and estimated production activity.

Price Breaks Occur when unit purchase prices are decreased as the quantity purchased is increased.

Price Variance See material price variance.

Primal The initial formulation of a linear programming problem. See dual.

Prime Cost The total of direct material and direct labor costs.

Pro Forma Statements Estimated or budgeted financial statements.

Probability A value between zero and one indicating the likelihood of an event occurring.

Process Goal oriented operations.

Process Costing A product costing system that accumulates manufacturing costs by processes, operations or departments. Process costing is well-suited to situations where similar products are mass produced.

Product Cost The sacrifice made to obtain or produce a product for sale.

Product-Mix Problem When a firm has multiple products and is attempting to determine the product mix that will maximize total contribution margin. Linear programming is frequently used to solve this problem.

Production Management System A production management system consists of materials inventory control, work in process control, cost estimation, and production scheduling subsystems.

Production Scheduling A subsystem of the production management system. In this system all physical flows relating to production are monitored and materials, labor, and machines, are scheduled.

Productivity The ratio of some measure of output to some measure of input over various time periods. Common example is "output per man hour".

Profit as a percentage of sales The ratio of profit to sales.

Profit Center A responsibility center where the supervisor has responsibility for both applicable revenues and expenses.

Programs Specific activities set up to achieve objectives of the organization.

Programmed Transfer Prices When shadow prices (opportunity costs) from a linear programming solution are employed as the basis for establishing transfer prices.

Qualitative Factors Any factors in decision making that are relevant to the decision but cannot be quantified.

Quantity Variance See material quantity variance.

Raw Materials Inventory Purchases of direct materials and operating supplies which are still in inventory.

Reciprocal Service Allocation Method Method that allocates costs by explicitly recognizing the mutual services rendered among all departments.

Regression Analysis A method by which the average amount of change in a variable that is associated with changes in one or more other variables is measured. The method assures that the sum of the squared differences between observed and estimated points are minimized.

Relative-Sales-Value-Method Method used in determining the cost of joint products.

Relevant Cost Expected future costs that will vary among alternatives related to the decision.

Relevant Range This range of activity where the cost or revenue (dependent variable) and activity relationships (independent variable) are considered valid.

Relevant Revenue In decision making when revenue is associated with the alternative solutions, any revenue difference between the alternative solutions is relevant to the decision.

Reorder Point Quantity level of inventory at which a new order should be placed.

Required Rate of Return An expression indicating minimum return expectations regarding a particular capital expenditure proposal. Conceptually the required rate combines a risk free rate with a risk premium. Practically speaking the rate is developed by highly subjective means. Also referred to as cost of capital, hurdle rate and minimum desired rate of return.

Residual Income Net income of a profit center or investment center, less capital charge on the net assets used by the center.

Residuals (Error Terms) The vertical differences between the regression line and the actual historical data. A graphical analysis of the residuals can be used to evaluate the assumptions of regression analysis.

Responsibility Accounting Responsibility accounting is a system that views the organization as consisting of a group of responsibility centers. The centers are used as the basis for internal financial planning, reporting, control and performance measurement.

Responsibility Center A cost, profit or investment center that is responsible for certain activities. See also responsibility accounting.

Return On Investment A measure of performance calculated as the ratio of profit to investment.

Rework Defective units that can be repaired and sold as part of the major product line.

Risk Refer to degree of uncertainty about an outcome where there is exposure to possibility of loss. The standard deviation provides a measure of the risk.

Risk Analysis A form of analysis where probability estimates are made and used not only as an improved estimate of a variable, but also as input into information attempting to measure the amount of risk involved in a project.

ROI Abbreviation for return on investment.

Robinson-Patman Act Makes it unlawful for any person engaged in commerce to discriminate in price or terms of sale between purchases of commodities of like grades and quality.

R-Square See coefficient of determination.

Safety Stock Inventory retained as a cushion against unexpected demand during lead time.

Sales Mix The relative proportion from each product included in the total sales volume.

Scattergraph Method A method for estimating a cost function where all cost observations within a relevant range are plotted and a straight line is then visually fitted to the plotted lines.

Scrap Material The residual remaining at the conclusion of the manufacturing process that cannot be further used in the production cycle. Nevertheless it has a measurable but relatively minor value.

Segment An activity or part of an organization.

Semifixed Cost A semifixed cost, also called a step-fixed cost, remains constant as a total cost over a wide range of activity, but may change within the relevant range.

Semivariable Cost A semivariable (mixed) cost includes both fixed and variable components of cost.

Sensitivity Analysis A method of analysis that measures changes of expected values in decision models based on changes in key variables.

Separable Costs Costs incurred beyond the split-off point that are not part of the joint production process and can be exclusively identified with individual products.

Serial Correlation Refers to the relation of the error terms to each other. Also called autocorrelation.

Service Department Costs Costs incurred by departments that exist solely to aid production departments. These costs are generally allocated to production departments for the purpose of product costing.

Setup Time Time needed to prepare equipment on a production line for producing a specified number of finished units.

Shadow Prices Measures of the maximum contribution foregone by failing to have one more unit of scarce resources in a particular linear programming solution.

Simple Regression When only one independent variable is employed in regression analysis.

Simplex Algorithm General technique for solving any linear-programming problem.

Slack (padding) The difference between minimum required costs and budgeted costs proposed by a responsibility center manager.

Slack Variables Linear programming constraints are generally expressed as inequalities. Slack variable are introduced into the constraints so that they can be expressed as equalities.

Source Documents Original records of transactions.

Spending Variance See overhead spending variance, variable overhead spending variance, and fixed overhead spending variance.

Split-Off Point The point in a production process where the joint products become individually identifiable.

Spoilage Products which do not meet manufacturing standards and cannot be reworked. See normal and abnormal spoilage.

Spoilage Costs Includes the cost of production to the point of discovery, less any residual value attributable to the spoiled units.

Standard Absorption Costing An absorption costing system where standard, rather than actual or normal, costs are used. See absorption costing.

Standard Direct Costing A direct (variable) costing system where standard, rather than actual or normal, costs are used. See direct costing.

Standard Costs A standard cost can be defined in a number of ways. For instance, a standard cost is a predetermined cost. Often it refers to an estimate of the lowest cost that can be expected under current conditions with available management.

Standard Deviation A measure of the dispersion of the data around the mean.

Standard Error of Estimate Measure of the scatter of the actual observations around a regression line.

Standard Error of the Regression Coefficient Regression coefficients are estimates of a true value that specifies the relationship between the independent and dependent variable. A different set of observations will give a different regression coefficient. The standard error of the regression coefficient is an unbiased estimate of the standard error of the distribution from which the regression coefficients are being sampled.

Standard Hours Allowed The hours that should have been used, based on standards, to manufacture the actual units produced.

Standard Quantity Allowed Amount of direct materials or direct labor hours that should have been used to produce a given level of output. It is calculated by multiplying the quantity standard times the actual output achieved.

Standard Variable Costing See standard direct costing.

Statistical Quality Control Provides a systematic means for monitoring ongoing operations which distinguishes between random and nonrandom deviations from normal operations.

Step Allocation Method A method of allocating service department costs to production departments.

Step Cost See semifixed cost.

Stockout Costs Incremental costs incurred when an inventory stockout occurs.

Stockouts Occur when inventory supply is exhausted and there is demand for the items.

Stores Requisition Form used to record and control materials issued to production.

Strategic Planning Through strategic planning, basic objectives for an entity are established. This includes major decisions concerning products, processes and overall direction for the organization.

Substitution Coefficients In the simplex tableau containing the final solution of a linear programming problem, the substitution coefficients indicate the rate of change of variable in the solution if there are changes in the constraints.

Sunk Cost A cost that is already incurred and which is irrelevant to the decision process.

System A system represents a number of objects with an identifiable relationship between the objects and their properties. Management accounting systems are a component of overall management and information systems.

System Interfaces A shared boundary between two systems where outputs from one system become inputs for this system.

t-Value In regression the t-value is the ratio of a regression coefficient and the standard error of the regression coefficient. t-values of greater than two are generally considered necessary in determining if the regression coefficient is significantly different than zero.

Tax Shield Noncash items (e.g., depreciation) which when charged against revenue, provide some protection for revenue from taxation.

Theoretical Capacity A capacity level that assumes an ideal production level.

Time-Adjusted Rate of Return See internal rate of return.

Time Card A form used by employees to record their total hours worked. It provides the basis for the employer to determine the total payroll cost.

Time Ticket See job ticket.

Total Productivity Ratio The ratio of total outputs to total inputs.

Traceable Cost A fixed cost which can be directly identified with a particular segment. These costs should be separated into managed and committed cost categories.

Transfer Price Selling price charged by one segment of an organization for a production or service that it supplies to another segment of the same organization.

Transfer Pricing at Cost A transfer pricing system where some definition of cost (variable, full, or standard) is used in determining the transfer price.

Transfer Pricing at Cost Plus A transfer pricing system where some definition of cost (variable, full, or standard) plus a markup is used in determining the transfer price.

Transferred-In Costs In process costing, costs incurred in a previous department that have been transferred to a subsequent department.

Treasurer The treasurer is responsible for custody of fund flows. Responsibilities include investments, banking and credit policies, and insurance.

Type I Error Error which results from investigating a process when it is in control.

Type II Error Error which results from not investigating a process when it is out of control.

Variable Cost A cost that changes as a total amount directly in response to the activity measure being used. On a per unit basis the cost is constant within the relevant range.

Variable Costing See direct costing.

Variable Overhead Spending Variance Represents the difference between actual variable overhead costs incurred and the variable overhead rate multiplied by actual direct labor hours.

Variable Overhead Variance The difference between actual variable overhead costs incurred and variable overhead applied to production.

Variance The difference between an expected and actual result.

Volume Variance See overhead volume variance.

Weighted Average Method When used in process costing systems this method calls for beginning inventory to be treated as current period production. It assumes that all units are started in the current period, thus eliminating beginning inventories in calculating and assigning manufacturing costs.

Work in Process Control As the manufacturing process takes place the cost of direct materials used, direct labor costs incurred and the manufacturing overhead costs incurred are charged to the account. When products are finished their costs are credited to this account.

Work-In-Process Inventory Products being manufactured but not yet completed.

Yield A measure of the output obtained from a given amount of input.

Yield Variance Results when a quantity different from the quantity expected based on input is obtained. The yield variance can be calculated by multiplying the difference between actual quantity adjusted and the standard quantity by the standard price. See mix variance.

INDEX